"The range of issues, the depth of their treatment, and the collection of authors-top scholars in the field makes the *Routledge Handbook of Russian Security* a must read for all those seeking to understand Russia's perspective on global security."

Andrei P. Tsygankov, San Francisco State University, USA

"One of the doyens of Russia studies has pulled together a star-studded line up of outstanding writers who together have produced a truly impressive volume on Russian security policy. The term 'definitive' is sometimes used too liberally to describe only good books. But this is a truly outstanding work of scholarship to which the word 'definitive' can be attached without any hesitation at all."

Michael Cox, London School of Economics, UK

"Roger Kanet, a respected authority on the Soviet Union and post-communist Russia, has once again created an ensemble of top-flight scholars to explore many different aspects of Russian foreign policy. The essays in this superb book are both uniformly excellent and timely, and Kanet's introductions to each of its segments are invaluable in providing background and context."

M. Rajan Menon, City College of New York/City University of New York, USA

ROUTLEDGE HANDBOOK OF RUSSIAN SECURITY

The *Routledge Handbook of Russian Security* offers a comprehensive collection of essays on all aspects of Russian security and foreign policy by international scholars from across the world.

The volume identifies key contemporary topics of research and debate and takes into account the changes that have occurred in the study of Russian security strategy since the end of the Cold War. The handbook is organised into five sections:

- The theory and nature of Russian security policy
- The domestic and foreign policy nexus
- Instruments used by Russia in pursuing its security
- Global and regional aspects of Russian security and foreign policy
- Case studies of Russian involvement in a series of security conflicts.

The book concludes with case studies of the major examples of Russian involvement and operations in a series of security conflicts, including that in Georgia, the intervention in Ukraine and occupation of Crimea, and the ongoing Civil War in Syria.

This volume will be of great interest to students of Russian security, strategic studies, foreign policy, European politics, and International Relations in general.

Roger E. Kanet is a Professor of Political Science at the University of Miami, USA. His recent publications include *The Russian Challenge to the European Security Environment* (2017); with M. Sussex, *Power, Politics and Confrontation in Eurasia: Foreign Policy in a Contested Region* (2015); with M.R. Freire, *Russia and European Security* (2012); and *Resurgent Russia and the West: The European Union, NATO and Beyond* (2009).

ROUTLEDGE HANDBOOK OF RUSSIAN SECURITY

Edited by Roger E. Kanet

LONDON AND NEW YORK

First published 2019
by Routledge
2 Park Square, Milton Park, Abingdon, Oxon OX14 4RN

and by Routledge
52 Vanderbilt Avenue, New York, NY 10017

Routledge is an imprint of the Taylor & Francis Group, an informa business

© 2019 selection and editorial matter, Roger E. Kanet; individual chapters, the contributors

The right of Roger E. Kanet to be identified as the author of the editorial material, and of the authors for their individual chapters, has been asserted in accordance with sections 77 and 78 of the Copyright, Designs and Patents Act 1988.

All rights reserved. No part of this book may be reprinted or reproduced or utilised in any form or by any electronic, mechanical, or other means, now known or hereafter invented, including photocopying and recording, or in any information storage or retrieval system, without permission in writing from the publishers.

Trademark notice: Product or corporate names may be trademarks or registered trademarks, and are used only for identification and explanation without intent to infringe.

British Library Cataloguing-in-Publication Data
A catalogue record for this book is available from the British Library

Library of Congress Cataloging-in-Publication Data
Names: Kanet, Roger E., 1936– editor.
Title: Routledge handbook of Russian security /
edited by Roger E. Kanet.
Description: Routledge: Abingdon, Oxon; New York, NY, [2019] |
Includes bibliographical references and index.
Identifiers: LCCN 2018044649 (print) | LCCN 2018046733 (ebook) |
ISBN 9781351181235 (Web PDF) | ISBN 9781351181228 (ePub) |
ISBN 9781351181211 (Mobi) | ISBN 9780815396710 (hardback) |
ISBN 9781351181242 (e-book)
Subjects: LCSH: National security–Russia (Federation) |
Russia (Federation) -Military policy. | Russia (Federation)–
Foreign relations. | Geopolitics–Russia (Federation)
Classification: LCC UA770 (ebook) |
LCC UA770 .R6338 2019 (print) | DDC 355/.033047–dc23
LC record available at https://lccn.loc.gov/2018044649

ISBN: 978-0-8153-9671-0 (hbk)
ISBN: 978-1-351-18124-2 (ebk)

Typeset in Bembo
by codeMantra

Printed and bound in Great Britain by
TJ International Ltd, Padstow, Cornwall

This volume is dedicated to my wife of more than half a century, Joan Alice (nee Edwards), and to the generations of students, both graduate and undergraduate, who have challenged me and taught me over the course of the past 53 years!

Roger E. Kanet

CONTENTS

Lists of figures and tables — *xiii*
Contributors — *xiv*
Preface: Russian security policy — *xxiii*
Roger E. Kanet

PART I
The history and nature of Russian security strategy — **1**

1 Russia's pursuit of great-power status and security — 3
  Anne L. Clunan

2 Putin's operational code and strategic decision-making in Russia — 17
  Graeme P. Herd

3 The Soviet legacy in Russian security policy — 30
  Mark Kramer

4 Military might as a basis for Russian Great Power identity — 46
  Hanna Smith

5 The Russian challenge to the liberal world order — 58
  Suzanne Loftus and Roger E. Kanet

PART II
Domestic politics, threat perception and Russian security strategy   73

6 The domestic and foreign policy nexus: politics, threat perception and Russian security strategy   75
Stefan Meister

7 Understanding Russia's security strategy in a context of power   86
Tom Casier

8 Russia's economy and military expenditures   97
Susanne Oxenstierna

9 Russian strategic culture: the generational approach and the counter-intelligence state thesis   109
Mette Skak

10 The Security Council and security decision-making   119
Edwin Bacon

PART III
Instruments of Russian security strategy   131

11 Coercive diplomacy in Russian security strategy   133
Stanislav L. Tkachenko

12 The rebuilding of Russian military capabilities   144
Jennifer G. Mathers

13 Reflections on Russia's nuclear strategy   154
Stephen Blank

14 The economic tools of Russian security strategy   169
Nikita Lomagin

15 Russian security strategy and the geopolitics of energy in Eurasia   181
Mikhail A. Molchanov

16 The intelligence agencies and Putin: undermining Russia's security?   192
Kimberly Marten

17 Russian information security and warfare   203
Carolina Vendil Pallin

18 Information-psychological warfare in Russian security strategy 214
    Katri Pynnöniemi

19 Outer space in Russia's security strategy 227
    Nicole J. Jackson

PART IV
Global and regional aspects of Russian security strategy **239**

20 Russian security policy towards the United States 242
    Kathryn E. Stoner and Michael A. McFaul

21 NATO enlargement: a security dilemma for Russia? 257
    Alberto Priego

22 Russia's regional and global counterterrorism strategies: how
    Moscow's vision of the new global order affects its approach
    to terrorism 266
    Mariya Y. Omelicheva

23 Security challenges in Russia-European Union relations 277
    Maria Raquel Freire and Licínia Simão

24 Russian security strategy and the geopolitics of Eurasia 288
    John Berryman

25 The impacts of climate change on Russian Arctic security 299
    Stacy Closson

26 Caucasian chess or the greatest geopolitical tragedy of the
    twentieth century 309
    Lilia A. Arakelyan

27 Russian security strategy in Central Asia 321
    Graeme Gill and Yelena Nikolayevna Zabortseva

28 Russian-Chinese security cooperation: the Bear and the Dragon 332
    Marcel de Haas

29 The BRICs and Russian foreign and security policy: changing
    the narrative 342
    Rachel S. Salzman

PART V
Case studies of Russian security strategy   **353**

30 Instrumentalising the frozen conflicts of the greater
   Black Sea region   355
   Thomas Ambrosio

31 Russian security strategy in the Balkans   366
   Nadia Boyadjieva

32 The 2008 Russia-Georgia War   377
   Bertil Nygren

33 Russia's 'hybrid' aggression against Ukraine   388
   Yury E. Fedorov

34 Russia, the Middle East and the conflict in Syria   399
   Derek Averre

Index   *411*

FIGURES AND TABLES

Figures

8.1	Russia's defence budget and total military expenditure as share of GDP in comparison with selected countries, 2005–2020; *per cent*	101
20.1	Russian GDP annual growth rate, 1996–2014	247
20.2	Responses to monthly question: do you approve of the Job President (Prime Minister) Putin is doing? (Levada Center Data, August 1999 to April 2015, percentage approval rating)	248
26.1	Caucasus Mountains Map	310

Tables

7.1	Gross domestic product based on purchasing power parity (PPP) share of world total (%): the US, the EU and BRICS	88
7.2	Estimated numbers of nuclear weapons in 2017	89
7.3	Top ten countries with the highest share of global military expenditure, 2017 (%)	89
8.1	Russia's defence budget and total military expenditure, 2012–2020; *billion RUB, current prices; and billion (2016 prices) USD*	103
10.1	Membership of Russia's Security Council, May 2018	121
10.2	Secretaries of Russia's Security Council, 1992–2018	127
14.1	Russia's foreign policy priorities and main economic instruments	175
17.1	AGORA Internet freedom in Russia, 2011–2017	209
27.1	Immigration to Russia	324

CONTRIBUTORS

Thomas Ambrosio is a Professor of Political Science at North Dakota State University in Fargo. He has published three books, including Authoritarian *Backlash: Russian Resistance to Democratization in the Former Soviet Union* (Routledge, 2009) and edited two volumes, as well as numerous articles and book chapters. Dr Ambrosio's most recent articles have examined Russia-China relations, authoritarian learning, American perceptions of the Russian threat, Russia's perception management campaign over its annexation of Crimea, and Russian treaties with South Ossetia and Abkhazia.

Lilia A. Arakelyan is a Lecturer of Politics and International Relations at Florida International University. She holds a PhD in international studies from the University of Miami and has worked on numerous academic and policy-oriented projects and also taught at the University of Miami. Her published articles and book chapters focus on Russian foreign policy in the post-Soviet space, aspects of nationalism, ethno-national conflicts in the South Caucasus, and on international security more broadly. She is the author of *Russian Foreign Policy in Eurasia: National Interests and Regional Integration* (Routledge, 2017).

Derek Averre is Reader in Russian Foreign and Security Policy and former Director of the Centre for Russian, European and Eurasian Studies, Department of Politics and International Studies, University of Birmingham. Dr Averre's main research interests focus on Russian foreign/security policy, Russia-Europe relations and arms control/non-proliferation issues. He has co-edited a book and journal special issues, and written numerous journal articles and book chapters, as well as organising a series of policy and academic conferences and presenting widely in the United States and Europe on these topics. He is a member of the Editorial Board of the *Journal European Security*.

Edwin Bacon is Reader in International Politics at the University of Lincoln, UK. He has written seven books on Russian and Soviet affairs, including *Inside Russian Politics* (2017), *Contemporary Russia* (third edition 2014) and *Securitising Russia: The Domestic Politics of Putin* (with Bettina Renz and Julian Cooper, 2006). He has engaged with the policy world over many years, advising policymakers in several European countries, being a specialist adviser to the House of Commons Foreign Affairs Select Committee, and – briefly in the early 1990s – being a Senior Research Officer in the United Kingdom's Foreign and Commonwealth Office.

John Berryman teaches International Relations at Birkbeck College, University of London; is an Associate Professor of International Studies at Ithaca College, New York (London Division); and was formerly Head of the Division of European and International Studies at the University of Wolverhampton. His publications include 30 chapters/articles dealing with Russian foreign and security policy, including most recently "Russia and the European Security Order: Impact and Implications of the Ukraine Crisis" in Roger E. Kanet ed., *The Russian Challenge to the European Security Environment* (Palgrave, 2017). He is a member of the International Institute for Strategic Studies and The Royal Institute of International Affairs.

Stephen Blank is a Senior Fellow at the American Foreign Policy Council. He is a former MacArthur Fellow at the U.S. Army War College and was a professor there from 1989 to 2013. An internationally recognised expert on Russian foreign and defence policies and international relations across the former Soviet Union, he has consulted for the CIA, major think tanks and foundations, and chaired international conferences in the United States and abroad. He has published over 1100 articles and monographs on Soviet/Russian, U.S., Asian, and European military and foreign policies, including publishing or editing 15 books, specifically focused on the geopolitics and geostrategy of the former Soviet Union, Russia and Eurasia.

Nadia Boyadjieva obtained a PhD from Sofia University in 1999 with a dissertation on U.S. policy on Bosnia and Hercegovina, 1989–1995, later published as an award-winning book. She is a Full Professor in the Department of Contemporary Balkan Studies at the Institute for Balkan Studies of the Bulgarian Academy of Sciences in Sofia. She is also a Full Professor of International Law and International Relations at Plovdiv University as well as adjunct Professor at Sofia University. Since September 2015, she has been a Visiting Scholar at Harvard University. In 2017, she was awarded a Doctor of Sciences degree in International Law and International Relations. Her research and publications have dealt extensively with issues of international relations and diplomacy; USSR and U.S. foreign policy in the Balkans; NATO-Russia relations; and the evolution of various international security systems, human rights, minority issues and peacekeeping.

Tom Casier is Jean Monnet Chair and Reader in International Relations at the University of Kent's Brussels School of International Studies (BSIS). He is Director of the Global Europe Centre and Visiting Professor at the University of Leuven. Dr Casier's research focuses on Russian foreign policy and EU-Russia relations, with a particular interest in power and identity. His recent articles have appeared in *Cooperation and Conflict, Geopolitics and Contemporary Politics*. An edited volume (with Joan DeBardeleben), entitled *EU-Russia Relations in Crisis: Understanding Diverging Perceptions*, was published by Routledge in 2018.

Stacy Closson is a Global Fellow at the Kennan Institute, Wilson Center in Washington, D.C. During this time, Dr Closson was a Visiting Fellow at the University of Helsinki, Finland, where she conducted research on Russian foreign and security policy in the Arctic. She was previously an Assistant Professor at the Patterson School of Diplomacy and

International Commerce at the University of Kentucky. Her work on Russia, Eurasia, corruption and energy security appears in academic journals, edited books, think tanks and the media. Her most recent book with MIT Press (2015) is *Energy, Economics, and Geopolitical Futures: Eight Long-Range Scenarios*.

Anne L. Clunan is an Associate Professor of National Security Affairs at the Naval Postgraduate School in Monterey, CA. Her research focuses on Russian foreign and security policy, states' pursuit of international status, threat definition, and the implications of globalisation for state sovereignty and governance. She is the author of *The Social Construction of Russia's Resurgence: Aspirations, Identity and Security Interests* (Johns Hopkins University Press, 2009), two edited volumes, and publications on Russian security and foreign policy (most recently, "Russia and the Liberal Order" in *Ethics and International Affairs*), alternative governance and ungoverned spaces, and international status politics. She earned her PhD in political science at the University of California, Berkeley.

Yury E. Fedorov is an expert in Russian foreign and security policy. Until January 2006, Dr Fedorov was a Professor of the Moscow State Institute of International Relations (MGIMO), before that deputy director for research of the Center of Policy Studies in Russia (PIR-Centre), and the Institute for Applied International Research (a Yukos-funded institution). In 2006–2009, he was Principal Research Fellow and Associate Fellow of the Russia and Eurasia Program in The Royal Institute of International Affairs, London. Since 2008, Dr Fedorov is an Associate Fellow of the Czech Association for International Affairs. Dr Fedorov is the author and editor of several books and numerous articles and research papers published in Russia, the United States and Europe. His main research interests focus on Russia's strategic culture, foreign and security policy. His most recent books *Hybrid Warfare a la Russe* and *Russia between Fascism and Disintegration* were published in Kiev in 2016 and 2017, respectively.

Maria Raquel Freire is a researcher at the Centre for Social Studies (CES) and Associate Professor of International Relations at the School of Economics of the University of Coimbra (FEUC). Dr Freire holds a Jean Monnet Chair – EU External Relations towards the East. She is currently director of the PhD programme in international politics and conflict resolution, CES|FEUC. Her research interests focus on peace studies, particularly peacekeeping and peacebuilding; foreign policy; international security; Russia; and the post-Soviet space. Her most recent English-language book is *Managing Crises, Making Peace: Towards a Strategic EU Vision for Security and Defense*, co-edited with Maria Grazia Galantino (Palgrave, 2015).

Graeme Gill is a Professor Emeritus of Government and Public Administration in the University of Sydney. A Fellow of the Academy of Social Sciences in Australia and former President of the International Council for Central and East European Studies (ICCEES), Dr Gill is a long-time student of Soviet and Russian politics. His most recent books in this field are *Collective Leadership in Soviet Politics* (Palgrave Macmillan, 2018), *Building an Authoritarian Polity: Russia in Post-Soviet Times* (Cambridge University Press, 2016) and *Symbolism and Regime Change in Russia* (Cambridge, 2012).

Marcel de Haas is an Affiliated Professor as well as a Research Fellow on Russian security policy towards the Middle East, at the National Security Studies Centre, University of Haifa, Israel. He was a Full Professor of Public Policy at Nazarbayev University, Astana,

Kazakhstan. Dr de Haas' PhD thesis was on "Russia's security policy and airpower in the 1990s" (University of Amsterdam, 2004). His latest book was with Routledge (2010): *Russia's Foreign Security Policy in the 21st Century: Putin, Medvedev and Beyond*. As a Lieutenant-Colonel (Royal Netherlands Army, ret.), he was responsible for the drafting of the first edition of the Netherlands Defence Doctrine in 2005.

Graeme P. Herd is a Professor of Transnational Security Studies at the George C. Marshall European Center (GCMC) for Security Studies since January 2015. Before joining the GCMC, Dr Herd was a Professor of International Relations and founding Director of the School of Government, and Associate Dean, Faculty of Business, University of Plymouth, where he set up the "Centre for Seapower and Strategy" at the Britannia Royal Naval Academy, Dartmouth. He has a PhD in Russian history, University of Aberdeen (1995). He has published nine books, written over 70 academic papers and given over 100 academic and policy-related presentations in 46 countries. His major recent publications include *Understanding NATO in the 21st Century: Alliance Strategies, Security and Global Governance* (Routledge, 2013), co-edited with John Kriendler; *Critical Turning Points in the Middle East, 1915–2015* (Palgrave MacMillan, 2011), co-authored with Nayef Al-Rodhan and Lisa Watanabe; and *Great Powers and Strategic Stability in the 21st Century: Competing Visions of World Order* (Routledge, 2010).

Nicole J. Jackson is an Associate Professor of International Studies and Russian and Eurasian Politics at the School of International Studies, Simon Fraser University, Vancouver, Canada. She has authored multiple refereed articles and chapters on Russian and Central Asian security and foreign policy. She is the author of *Russian Foreign Policy and the CIS; Theories, Debates and Actions* (Routledge, 2003) and most recently "NATO's and Canada's Responses to Russia since the Crimea Annexation of 2014: A Critical Literature Review", *Simons Papers in Security and Development*, December 2017; and "Canada, NATO and Global Russia", *International Journal*, 2018 She is currently researching a manuscript that examines Russia's role in global security governance and the "global commons" and working on a project analysing NATO and Canada's approaches to hybrid warfare.

Roger E. Kanet is a Professor of Political Science at the University of Miami and Professor Emeritus of Political Science at the University of Illinois at Urbana-Champaign, where he was Head of that Department and later Associate Vice Chancellor for Academic Affairs and Director of International Programs and Studies; at Miami, he was Dean of the School of International Studies. Dr Kanet earned his PhD at Princeton University; he has authored more than 250S scholarly journal articles and book chapters, and edited or co-edited 34 books, including the most recent *The Russian Challenge to the European Security Environment* (Palgrave, 2017).

Mark Kramer is Director of Cold War Studies at Harvard University, Director of Harvard's Sakharov Program on Human Rights, and a Senior Fellow of Harvard's Davis Center for Russian and Eurasian Studies. He has taught at Harvard, Yale and Brown Universities and was formerly an Academy Scholar in Harvard's Academy of International and Area Studies and a Rhodes Scholar at Oxford University. Kramer is the author or editor of several books and has written nearly 200 articles on a variety of topics. He has worked extensively in newly opened archives in all the former Warsaw Pact countries and in several Western countries. He has been a consultant for numerous government agencies and international organizations.

Suzanne Loftus obtained her PhD at the University of Miami (in International Studies with a special focus on Russian affairs). She is Associate Professor of National Security at the George C. Marshall European Center Her publications include Insecurity and the Rise of Nationalism: The Case of Putin's Russia, Keeper of Traditional Values (2018), as well as co-authored articles such as "Whose Playground Is It Anyway? Power Rivalries in Post-Soviet Space," in Roger E. Kanet and Matthew Sussex, eds., Power, Politics and Confrontation in Eurasia: Foreign Policy in a Contested Region and "Growing Confrontation between Russia and the West: Russia's Challenge to the Post-Cold War Order," in Roger E. Kanet, ed., The Russian Challenge to the European Security Environment. Dr Loftus also received a Master's in Business from Webster University, Geneva, Switzerland. She has international work experience both in the private sector and at the United Nations.

Nikita Lomagin is academic director of the ENERPO program at European University in St. Petersburg and Professor in the World Economy Department at St. Petersburg State University. He was a postdoctoral fellow at the Davis Center for Russian Studies at Harvard and researcher at the Kennan Institute, University of Michigan Law School, Finnish Institute for international relations. He earned his doctorate at St. Petersburg Institute of History of the Russian Academy of Sciences and holds a diploma in law from St. Petersburg State University. He is the author of several monographs on the history of the Second World War and has contributed chapters to collective volumes on Russian foreign policy: *The Leningrad Blockade, 1941–1944: A New Documentary History from the Soviet Archives* (Yale University Press, 2012); "A Cold Peace between Russia and the West: Did Geo-economics Fail?" in *The Russian Challenge to the European Security Environment* (Palgrave, 2017); "Foreign Policy Preferences of Russia's Energy Sector: A Shift to Asia?" in *Russia, Eurasia and the New Geopolitics of Energy. Confrontation and Consolidation* (Palgrave, 2015); and "Interest Groups in Russian Foreign Policy: The Invisible Hand of the Russian Orthodox Church," *International Politics*, 2012. Vol. 49, № 4.

Kimberly Marten is Professor and Chair of the Political Science Department at Barnard College, and directs the Program on U.S.-Russia Relations at Columbia University's Harriman Institute. Dr Marten has written four books, including *Warlords: Strong-Arm Brokers in Weak States* (Cornell, 2012). Her first book, *Engaging the Enemy: Organization Theory and Soviet Military Innovation* (Princeton, 1993), won the Marshall Shulman Prize. Among numerous other writings is the monograph *Reducing Tensions between Russia and NATO* (Council on Foreign Relations, 2017). She is a frequent media commentator and a member of the Council on Foreign Relations. She earned her BA at Harvard University and PhD at Stanford University.

Jennifer G. Mathers is Reader and former Head of the Department of International Politics at Aberystwyth University. Her main research interests focus on Russian security, foreign policy and the armed forces as well as gender and conflict. Dr Mathers is the author of *The Russian Nuclear Shield from Stalin to Yeltsin* (Macmillan, 2000) and has co-edited, with Steve Webber, *Military and Society in Post-Soviet Russia* (Manchester University Press, 2005). She has published journal articles and book chapters on a range of topics related to Russia including military strategy, nuclear weapons, civil-military relations, women soldiers, the political protests in 2011–2012, and Russia's military interventions in Chechnya.

Contributors

Michael A. McFaul is a Professor of Political Science, Director and Senior Fellow at the Freeman Spogli Institute for International Studies, and the Peter and Helen Bing Senior Fellow at the Hoover Institution at Stanford University. Dr McFaul served for five years in the Obama administration, first as Special Assistant to the President and Senior Director for Russian and Eurasian Affairs at the National Security Council at the White House (2009–2012), and then as U.S. Ambassador to the Russian Federation (2012–2014). He has authored several books, including *Russia's Unfinished Revolution: Political Change from Gorbachev to Putin* (Cornell, 2001) and *Power and Purpose: U.S. Policy toward Russia after the Cold War* (Brookings, 2003), and co-edited with Kathryn Stoner, *Transitions to Democracy: A Comparative Perspective* (Johns Hopkins, 2013).

Stefan Meister is Head of the Robert Bosch Center for Central and Eastern Europe, Russia, and Central Asia at the German Council on Foreign relations (DGAP). Previously, he worked as a Senior Policy Fellow on the Wider Europe Team of the European Council on Foreign Relations and as a Senior Research Fellow at the DGAP (2008–2013). His areas of research include Russian domestic, foreign, and energy policy; EU's Eastern partnership; EU-Russia relations; and Russia's policy towards post-Soviet countries. He earned his doctorate at the University of Jena and holds an MA in political science and East European history. He has edited *Russia's Policy towards Post-Soviet Countries* (Nomos, 2013) and co-authored *The Eastern Question. Russia, the West and Europe's Grey Zone* (Brookings, 2016), *Eastern Voices: Europe's East Faces an Unsettled West* and *The Russia File. Russia and the West in and Unordered World* (both Routledge, 2016, 2017).

Mikhail A. Molchanov is a Visiting Professor at the American University of Sharjah, Sharjah, UAE. He has been senior policy analyst for the Government of Canada and served as professor of political science at several Canadian universities. In 2011, he was awarded the Japan Foundation's prestigious Japanese Studies Fellowship, and in 2012, he was elected Foreign Member of the National Academy of Educational Sciences of Ukraine. He received the inaugural Robert H. Donaldson prize of the International Studies Association (ISA) for the best paper written on the postcommunist region. Dr Molchanov has authored and co-authored nearly 120 articles and book chapters, and published 7 books, including the most recent *Eurasian Regionalisms and Russian Foreign Policy* (Routledge, 2015). He is Section Program Chair for the Postcommunist States Section of the ISA, leads the Working Group on International Political Sociology for the International Political Science Association, and sits on the Executive Council of the ISA's Interdisciplinary Studies Section and the Advisory Board of the University of Salamanca Global and International Studies Program's Think Tank.

Bertil Nygren is a retired Associate Professor of political science at the Swedish National Defence College and at the Department of Political Science, Stockholm University. Dr Nygren has written several monographs and edited anthologies, and published chapters primarily on Russian foreign policy and written several research reports for the Swedish Ministry of Defence. His most recent monograph is *The Rebuilding of Greater Russia: Putin's Foreign Policy towards the CIS Countries* (Routledge, 2008).

Mariya Y. Omelicheva is a Professor of Strategy at National War College, National Defense University. She holds a PhD (2007) in political science from Purdue University and a JD in international law (2000) from Moscow National Law Academy. Her research and teaching interests include Eurasian security, counterterrorism and human rights, democracy promotion, Russia's foreign policy, and terrorism/crime nexus. She is the author of Webs of Corruption: Trafficking and Terrorism in Central Asia (with L. Markowitz, Columbia University Press, 2019), Democracy in Central Asia: Competing Perspectives and Alternate Strategies (University Press of Kentucky, 2015) and Counterterrorism Policies in Central Asia (Routledge 2011), and the editor of Nationalism and Identity Construction in Central Asia: Dimensions, Dynamics, and Directions (Lexington, 2015).

Susanne Oxenstierna is a Deputy Research Director at the Swedish Defence Research Agency. She holds a doctorate in economics from Stockholm University, and her current research is focused on the institutional development of the Russian economy and Russia's military spending. During the 1990s, she worked in Moscow as a resident advisor to the Ministry of Finance and Ministry of Economic Development and Trade. Among her latest publications are "Russia's Military Expenditure and Declining Economic Growth", *Journal of Eurasian Studies*, 7, 2016 and the edited volume *The Challenges for Russia's Politicized Economy* (Routledge, 2015).

Alberto Priego holds a PhD from Complutense University (International Relations). He is currently a Senior Lecturer at the Universidad Pontificia de Comillas in Madrid, where he has been a faculty member since 2010. His research interests lie in the areas of Middle East studies, Islam, and diplomacy. He has collaborated actively with researchers in several other disciplines of history, economy, and political science. During 2007–2009, he was a postdoctoral fellow at SOAS (The University of London).

Katri Pynnöniemi is an Assistant Professor of Russian Security Policy at the University of Helsinki and National Defence University (Finland). Dr Pynnöniemi's research has focused on system change in Russia after the collapse of the Soviet Union and its implications, first for EU-Russia relations, and more recently, for Russia's foreign and military policy. She has published on Russia's policy on critical infrastructure, emergence of concept strategic planning as part of national security policymaking, and the adjustments made to the latest security strategies in Russia. Her most recent edited book is *Fog of Falsehood: Russian Strategy of Deception and the Conflict in Ukraine* (FIIA, 2016).

Rachel S. Salzman is a Visiting Scholar at the Johns Hopkins School of Advanced International Studies. She previously held a Postdoctoral Fellowship at the Center for Eurasian, Russian, and East European Studies at Georgetown University. Her research focuses on Russia, BRICS, and global governance, with emphasis on the role of BRICS in Russian foreign policy and the development of the BRICS group on the international stage. Her first book, *Russia, BRICS, and the Disruption of Global Order*, will be published by Georgetown University Press in 2019.

Licínia Simão is an Assistant Professor at the School of Economics, University of Coimbra (FEUC), where she is currently the Coordinator for the Master Programme in International Relations – Peace, Security and Development Studies. Dr Simão is also a researcher at the Centre for Social Studies, where she is involved in several research projects on the post-Soviet space. Her research interests include foreign policy analysis and security studies, with a focus on European foreign policy and the former-Soviet space. Her next publication is *The EU's Neighbourhood Policy towards the South Caucasus: Expanding the European Security Community*, forthcoming with Palgrave.

Mette Skak is an Associate Professor of political science at the University of Aarhus. Her primary research interest is Russia, notably Russian foreign and security policy. Dr Skak has also published on Baltic, East and Central European affairs, and served as principal investigator of a large research project on the five BRICS states. Her publications include the monograph *From Empire to Anarchy. Postcommunist Foreign Policy and International Relations* (Hurst & Co., 1996); "The Logic of Foreign and Security Policy Change in Russia" in Hedenskog, et al. (eds.) *Russia as a Great Power* (Routledge, 2005); the Danish-language anthology *Fremtidens stormagter. BRIK'erne i det globale spil. Brasilien, Rusland, Indien og Kina* (Aarhus Universitetsforlag, 2010); "Russia's New 'Monroe Doctrine'" in Kanet, Roger E. (ed.) *Russian Foreign Policy in the 21st Century* (Palgrave Macmillan, 2011); "The BRICS and Denmark – Economics and High Politics" in Hvidt and Mouritzen *Danish Foreign Policy Yearbook 2013*; and "Russian Strategic Culture: The Role of Today's Chekisty", *Contemporary Politics* Vol. 22, No. 3, pp. 324–341 – reprinted in Götz, Elias (ed.), *Russia, the West and the Ukraine Crisis* (Routledge, 2017).

Hanna Smith is Director of Strategic Planning and Responses at the European Centre of Excellence for Countering Hybrid Threats and Aleksanteri Fellow at the University of Helsinki. She is an expert on the foreign, security and domestic politics of Russia and the area of the former Soviet Union. She has published numerous articles in different books, academic journals and newspapers. She is a frequent lecturer at the Finnish land defence courses, organised by the Finnish Defence University, and has taught courses on different aspects of Russian foreign and security policy at the University of Helsinki and the University of Eastern Finland. Her PhD dealt with *Russian Greatpowerness: Foreign Policy, the Two Chechen Wars and International Organisations*, and she is the editor of Russia and Its Foreign Policy – Influences, Interests and Issues (Kikimora Publications, 2005) and The Two-Level Game: Russia's Relations with Great Britain, Finland and the European Union (Kikimora Publications, 2006).

Kathryn E. Stoner is the Deputy Director at the Freeman Spogli Institute for International Studies at Stanford University and a Senior Fellow at the Center on Democracy, Development and the Rule of Law, as well as the Deputy Director of the Ford Dorsey Program in International Policy Studies at Stanford University. She teaches in the Department of Political Science at Stanford, and in the Program on International Relations, as well as in the Ford Dorsey Program. Prior to 2004, she was on the faculty at Princeton University for nine years, jointly appointed to the Department of Politics and the Woodrow Wilson School for International and Public Affairs. In addition to many articles and book chapters on contemporary Russia, she is the author or co-editor of five books, including *Transitions to Democracy: A Comparative Perspective*, written and edited with Michael A. McFaul (Johns Hopkins, 2013); *Autocracy and Democracy in the Post-Communist World*, co-edited with Valerie Bunce and Michael A. McFaul (Cambridge, 2010). She is currently finishing a book entitled *Resurrected? The Domestic Determinants of Russia's Return as a Global Power*, Oxford University Press in 2018. She received a PhD in government from Harvard University. In 2016, she was awarded an honorary doctorate from Iliad State University, Tbilisi, Republic of Georgia.

Stanislav L. Tkachenko is a Professor of Russian Economy and Regional Policies at the University of Bologna (Italy) and Professor of International Political Economy at the Saint-Petersburg State University (Russia), where he is also the Director of Diplomatic Studies M.A. Programme and former Vice-Rector for International Relations. Dr Tkachenko has authored more than 140 scholarly articles and book chapters, including most recently: "Coercive Diplomacy of Vladimir Putin (2014–2016)," in Roger Kanet, ed., *The Russian Challenge to the European Security Environment.* Palgrave Macmillan, 2017; (with Anton Giulio de Robertis) "New Diplomacy of the Russian Federation: Coercion and Dialogue," *Rivista di Studi Politici Internazionali*, Ottobre–Dicembre 2017, Anno 83, Fasc. 332, pp. 553–566.

Carolina Vendil Pallin works at the Swedish Defence Research Agency (FOI), where she has headed the Russia Programme 2009–2012 and 2014–2016. Previous positions include Senior Research Fellow at the Swedish Institute for International Affairs, where she headed the Research Programme "Russia and Its Neighbours" (2006–2009), and as Expert Advisor for the Swedish Defence Commission (2012–2013). Dr Vendil Pallin is the author of *Russian Military Reform: A Failed Exercise in Defence Decision Making* (Routledge, 2009). She is a member of the Royal Swedish Academy of War Sciences.

Yelena Nikolayevna Zabortseva's last position was a lecturer at the Department of Government and International Relations at the University of Sydney, where she received her PhD. She worked as a researcher at the Center of Post-Soviet Studies at Moscow State University in International Relations (MGIMO), and an Associate Professor at Kazakh Economic University. Her professional experience has included work as Head of the Public Affairs and International Relations Department at Kazakhstan's Financial Superintendent, and international consultancy. She is the author of more than 40 articles and monographs on international relations, including peace and conflict studies, international competitiveness, international investment flows, and post-Soviet Studies. Dr Zabortseva's most recent book is *Russia's Relations with Kazakhstan: Re-thinking Ex-Soviet Transitions in the Emerging World System* (Routledge, 2016). *Ex-Soviet Transitions in the Emerging World System* (Routledge, 2016).

PREFACE
Russian security policy

Roger E. Kanet

Until approximately the final decade of the Cold War, the traditional academic and analytic study of security focused almost exclusively on military issues, sovereignty, territorial control and very closely related matters. It was at this time that an ever-growing group of analysts began the move to expand the study of security beyond 'the threat, use and control of military force', as Stephen Walt put it (1991, p. 212). The 'wideners' and 'deepeners' of the field of security studies, as Dunn Cavelty and Mauer (2010a, 2010b, p. 1) call them, are those who wished to expand the concept to include factors beyond only military and territorial factors. Although by no means the sole group contributing to this change, the so-called Copenhagen School of Security Analysis, represented initially by Barry Buzan, Ole Wæver, and Jaap de Wilde (1998), argued, in effect, that virtually any set of issues – political, economic, environmental or cultural – could become the focus of security concerns – or 'securitised' – simply by the fact that political elites or other political groups focused on it as a serious challenge to the safety and viability of a community. One important implication of this development was the fact that the concept 'security' is not stable, that it can and does change, and that it can have quite different meanings for different people and at different times.[1]

The relevance of these theoretical discussions in the general field of security can be seen most clearly in very recent developments in the Russian Federation. As the tone of Russian relations with the United States continued to become more hostile, President Putin, emphasising an aspect of 'traditional' security concern, noted that Russia had new missile technology in place that was able to penetrate all U.S. defences (MacFarquhar and Sanger, 2018). On the other hand, in recent years, the Russian leadership has mounted an extensive campaign basically aimed at 'securitising' the concept of Russian identity (Tsygankov, 2017). The argument, seemingly successfully accepted by most of the Russian people, is that Russian culture and identity is unique and is central to the very existence of the Russian people. This identity must be protected against the invasion of and erosion by any other set of norms and values, in particular the increasingly mongrel Western version. These two sets of arguments, so widespread in Russia in recent years, are clear examples of the two broad, general approaches to security mentioned earlier.

Our objective in the current handbook is to place the study of Russian security within this much-broadened conception of security that now characterises analysis, including aspects of the more traditional approach, and to introduce the reader to many, hopefully most, of the subareas of Russian security and security studies.

As we carry out this task, we will, of necessity, touch on topics that overlap with those dealt with so ably in the recently published *Routledge Handbook of Russian Foreign Policy* (Tsygankov, 2018) and in other volumes dealing with the foreign policy of the Russian Federation. But the contents of the current volume differ significantly from those in the foreign policy volume, as well as the other studies, despite the modest overlap. The contributors to those volumes are interested first and foremost in the strategies selected and carried out by state actors to protect their interests and to achieve their goals within the international system. While the contributors to this volume are also be concerned with state behaviour, their focus is much broader than that of the foreign policy analyst and includes challenges and threats to security regardless of their source – whether other state actors or non-state actors, environmental developments, or other non-human factors.

It is the goal of the current volume to introduce the reader to the broad array of approaches to the study of Russian security and to the vast involvement of the Russian Federation in issues directly focused on security.[2] The 34 substantive chapters that comprise this study of Russian security and security policy are organised around five major themes: (1) the history and nature of Russian security strategy; (2) domestic politics, threat perception and Russian security strategy; (3) the instruments of Russian security strategy; (4) global and regional aspects of Russian security strategy; and (5) case studies of Russian security strategy. Included in the discussions are issues as diverse as military security, cyberwarfare and information security, and economic security. The authors bring to the project quite different theoretical and political assumptions, and are at various stages in their careers. They come, as well, from a wide array of national backgrounds, including the United States, Russia, the United Kingdom, Canada, most of the Scandinavian countries, and elsewhere. The editor is especially appreciative of the contributions of these many colleagues.

Notes

1. For comprehensive discussions of the broadening and deepening of the concept of security and its multiple, and changing, meanings, see Kolodziej (2005) and Dunn Cavelty and Mauer (2010a).
2. In many respects, the theoretical frameworks employed in the analysis of foreign policy, including Russian foreign policy, overlap almost fully with those employed to study security policy. In the case of Russian security, see Kolodziej (2005), Kanet and Freire (2012) and Tsygankov (2018, pp. 1–11).

References

Buzan, Barry, Ole Wæver, and Jaap de Wilde (1998) *Security: A New Framework for Analysis*. Boulder, CO: Lynne Rienner Publishers.
Dunn Cavelty, Myriam, and Victor Mauer, eds. (2010a) *The Routledge Handbook of Security Studies*. London-New York: Routledge.
Dunn Cavelty, Myriam, and Victor Mauer (2010b) 'Introduction', in Myriam Dunn Cavelty and Victor Mauer, eds., *The Routledge Handbook of Security Studies*. London-New York: Routledge, pp. 1–6.
Kanet, Roger E., and Maria Raquel Freire, eds. (2012) 'Russia in the New International Order: Theories, Arguments, Debates', Special issue of *International Politics*, 49:4, pp. 393–544.
Kolodziej, Edward A. (2005) *Security and International Relations*. Cambridge: Cambridge University Press.
MacFarquhar, Neil, and David E. Sanger (2018) 'Putin's "Invincible" Missile Is Aimed at U.S. Vulnerabilities', *New York Times*, 1 March. Accessed at www.nytimes.com/2018/03/01/world/europe/russia-putin-speech.html
Tsygankov, Andrei P. (2017) 'In the Shadow of Nikolai Danilevskii: Universalism, Particularism, and Russian Geopolitical Theory', *Europe-Asia Studies*, 69:4, pp. 571–593.
Tsygankov, Andrei P., ed. (2018) *Routledge Handbook of Russian Foreign Policy*. London-New York: Routledge.
Walt, Stephen (1991) 'The Renaissance of Security Studies', *International Studies Quarterly*, 35, pp. 211–239.

PART I

The history and nature of Russian security strategy

Introduction

Roger E. Kanet

This first section of the *Handbook* examines the nature and historical roots of Russian security policy, including the carryover legacy of Soviet thinking and policy on the topic. We also relate the study of Russian security to the broader theoretical questions relevant to the field that have been the focus of scholarly and public debate in recent decades. In Chapter 1, entitled 'Russia's Pursuit of Great-Power Status and Security', Anne Clunan of the Naval Postgraduate School places Russian security policy in the context of Russia's elites' commitment to re-establishing Russia's status as both a totally independent sovereign power and a major global actor. In many ways, she provides the framework within which the remaining chapters of the volume are placed.

In Chapter 2, entitled 'Putin's Operational Code and Strategic Decision-Making in Russia', Graeme Herd of the George C. Marshall European Center for Security Studies examines the beliefs about the international system that underlie Russian security policy. He maintains that '[a]ccording to Russia's dominant national security narratives, Russia is encircled, besieged and threatened by enemies within and without…. That is why a significant amount of what occurs is considered in the context of "conspiracy theories" and virtually everyone is suspected of some form of villainy or "opposition to the regime"'. These beliefs are shared across political elites and society, and form the basis of Russian strategic thinking and foreign and security decision-making.

Chapter 3, by Mark Kramer of Harvard University, tracks 'The Soviet Legacy in Russian Security Policy'. He notes that 'Russian political leaders had to confront a wide range of foreign policy issues left over from the Soviet regime'; these included new territorial issues with neighbouring post-Soviet states, as well as those with other neighbours. It also involved economic problems, as well as the long-imbedded views of members of the foreign and security policy elites, many of whom were carryovers from the Soviet administration. Kramer concludes that '[u]nder Putin, continuity with the Soviet past has been increasingly conspicuous, despite the passage of time'.

In Chapter 4, Hanna Smith of the European Centre of Excellence for Countering Hybrid Threats and Aleksanteri Fellow at the University of Helsinki examines 'Military Might as a Basis for Russian Great Power Identity'. She notes the central importance for Russia historically of military might—and success—in its efforts to influence the international political system. She then examines in some detail the use that the Russian Federation has made of military capabilities over the past two and a half decades and the role that this has played in Russia's return to great-power status.

In the concluding chapter of this introductory section of the *Handbook*, Chapter 5, Suzanne Loftus of the George C. Marshall European Center for Security Studies and Roger E. Kanet of the University of Miami discuss the relationship of Russian security strategy to 'The Russian Challenge to the Liberal World Order'. After outlining the numerous challenges to the current Western-dominated order created over the past half century from within the system itself, they assess the efforts by Russia to undermine and replace that order. They conclude that, at a minimum, Russia will 'win' in terms of its desires to decrease Western influence in the world, including fewer democratisation projects and a dwindling American hegemony.

1
RUSSIA'S PURSUIT OF GREAT-POWER STATUS AND SECURITY

Anne L. Clunan[1]

Russian leaders have spent the early twenty-first century securing Russia's status as a sovereign state and great power. Both of these statuses were in question at the dawn of the Millennium, not least because the international understanding of these concepts had changed (Neumann, 2014). When the status attributes required for sovereign statehood and being a great power shift, the authority of states changes, with substantial potential for conflict over loss of or gain in rights and privileges. The end of the twentieth century saw significant changes in the standards for sovereign statehood and great-power status. Sovereignty became contingent upon the state's protection of its population's human rights and economic well-being and conformance with criteria of good governance (Clunan, 2009b; Neumann, 2014). Heads of state were put on trial in an International Criminal Court for crimes against their own people, while non-state actors gained increasing recognition in global and local economic and security governance (Clunan and Trinkunas, 2010).

These changes have led to substantial conflict between Russia and the West over their rightful roles and authority in the post–Cold War international system, conflict that will continue as Russia, China and Western countries vie to set the standards of international order in the twenty-first century. Russia much prefers an absolutist, nineteenth-century version of sovereignty and great-power status, rather than ones defined by good governance. The former ranks Russia as a great power in a sovereignty hierarchy. The latter challenges Russia's position as a full member of the sovereignty group.

The existence of an international status hierarchy, like any social structure, is part of the global hegemony that orders particular eras (Cox, 1981; Hopf, 2013). The architects of that hegemony and the arbiters of international status have long been European sovereigns, including Russia, and, since the early twentieth century, the United States. During the Cold War, the Western great powers fostered economic and political liberalism that diffused globally outside the Soviet bloc countries and eroded sovereignty, elevating non-state actors to the international political and legal stage. The collapse of the Soviet Union ushered in an era of global liberalism, one that demanded all states adhere to Western human rights, democracy and market standards.

Russia since 1996 has sought to strip the meaning of great-power status and sovereignty of liberal normative content. In their calls for recognition of a 'multipolar world' order and new 'Great Power Concert' (Krickovic and Weber, 2018, 297), Russia's post-Soviet leaders seek to limit the criteria associated with being a great power to military capabilities married with 'responsible' behaviour, by which they mean respect for absolute sovereignty and non-interference in great-power spheres of influence (Clunan, 2014a). They have sought to change the post–Cold War collective definitions of international status in such a way as to undo the softening of sovereignty brought about by the global spread of liberal humanism and market liberalism. 'Russian observers emphasise the destabilising effects of these changes, and they are especially concerned about the eroding power and authority of nation-states, which they still regard as the ultimate guarantor of stability and order, both domestically and internationally' (Krickovic and Weber, 2018, 296–297).

Internally, Russia has built a massive security and state-building apparatus (Bershidsky, 2017; Galeotti, 2017) to shore up sovereign-statehood and great-power status. Since 2000, Russia's leadership has actively cultivated statist patriotism, which focuses on the state, rather than the people, as the essence of Russia throughout its thousand-year history (Laruelle, 2014, 7–8). Recent ideological efforts to support Russia's great-power status and internal sovereignty emphasise Russia's 'old' European values, distinguished from the 'new' and 'radically' individualist values of Western Europe and the United States (Makarychev, 2018; Laruelle, 2017). This self-image places Russia on par with other great powers at the centre of distinct civilisations (Tsygankov, 2012, 2016).

Russian efforts to define the normative statuses of great power and sovereign statehood would, as often as not, place the United States beyond the pale, as an irresponsible state not worthy of being labelled a great power because of reckless ideological wars against sovereign nations and democracy promotion. In contrast, Russia's armed interventions are cast as the normal, responsible actions of a great power. Rather than the aggressive destruction of the post–Cold War security order that the West sees, Russia views its annexation of Crimea and armed intervention in Ukraine as upholding the norms of sovereign-statehood and great-power rights.

Russian officials associate 'security' with 'making Russia strong again—both domestically and internationally' (Snetkov, 2015, 2). At the root of this conception of security is an institutionally and economically strong and centralised state with the statuses of a sovereign, and great, power. Great-power and sovereign-statehood statuses are of such importance for Russian leaders and elites that they are called out as key security objectives in both Russia's 2009 and 2016 National Security Strategies (Schelin, 2016, 92).

Two core security questions will continue to occupy Russian elites in the twenty-first century: How to maintain Russia's status as a great power? And, can its status as a sovereign state be combined with the centripetal forces of globalisation in a century where its military, technological and economic capabilities are eclipsed by those of the United States and China? This chapter first explains why understanding status as a concept is necessary for explaining how Russian policymakers view security and act on those views. It next addresses what status and security mean for Russian security elites. It turns to the impact these meanings have had on Russia's use of force in the early twenty-first century, before drawing some conclusions for the security of Russia's status as a twenty-first-century great power.

Why status matters for understanding Russian security politics

Scholars of Russia agree that Russia's security behaviour stems from concerns about its status, both as a great power and as a sovereign state. Many view Russian security behaviour as resulting from the interaction of its search for a post-Soviet identity and domestic debates about its internal and external security (Snetkov, 2015). Authors in this vein variously stress status aspirations and conflicts (Clunan, 2014a; Neumann, 2008; Wohlforth, 2009), resentment of the West (Malinova, 2014), subaltern identity (Morozov, 2015), ontological security (Zarakol, 2011), disrespect from the West (Karaganov, 2016a, 2016b; Tsygankov, 2018) and different conceptions of the West (Leichtova, 2014). These all generate expectations of status recognition and respect from the West (Larson and Shevchenko, 2010, 2014; Sakwa, 2008; Tsygankov, 2012).

Great-power status is central to Russia's sense of security and is responsible for its approach to issues ranging from nuclear arms control, North Atlantic Treaty Organisation (NATO) expansion, wars in Ukraine and Syria to election interference to Chechnya (Clunan, 2009a; Krickovic and Weber, 2018; Snetkov, 2015). Great-power status remains the common unifying element in Russia's ongoing search for a national identity (Moshes, 2018). Russia's status, internally as a sovereign state and externally as a great power, is at the centre of Russian political debates about security. Understanding status is, therefore, critical to explaining Russian security conceptions and behaviour (Clunan, 2009a; Krickovic and Weber, 2018).

Status is about who is endowed with legitimate social power—authority. The struggle for sovereign and great-power statuses is over which political entities are legitimately seen to have rights and responsibilities on the international stage (Moldova but not Transdniestria, China but not Taiwan) and of those entities which ones have special responsibility over international peace and security (China, France, Russia, the United Kingdom and the United States) that 'ordinary' but powerful sovereigns lack (Brazil, Germany, India and Japan). Status is contingent on socially constructed standards of belonging to particular social groups and cannot be reduced to material attributes. States' status claims are judged not only by other states but also by their own societies.

The social standards of international and national society, therefore, are important in internal decisions about how to obtain or enact a particular status and thereby achieve a secure—a legitimate—identity. For this reason, status conflicts involve not only states but also leaders and their societies. The conveyance of authority makes status a power resource for the state and its leaders internally and externally, which has long made it of interest to realists (Gilpin, 1981; Renshon, 2016, 2017; Wohlforth, 2009). Such authority, however, is social (Wohlforth et al., 2018; Paul, Larson and Wohlforth, 2014)—it is intersubjectively agreed to exist when an entity is seen to have certain socially valued attributes (or status) and to act in accord with certain socially constructed procedures and standards required of the desired status (status enactment) (Clunan, 2014b).

For much of the post-Soviet period, Russia was viewed at best as a regional great power and at worst, a failing state (Willerton et al., 2005). It was an 'Upper Volta with missiles' in German Chancellor Kohl's depiction of the late Soviet Union, or an 'Upper Volta with gas' in Russian businessman and parliamentarian Aleksandr Lebedev's 2005 view (Simon, 2009). Russian and Soviet elites since the 1980s have challenged the international standards of status to give Russia a more favourable international place in the reigning status hierarchy (Clunan, 2009a; Larson and Shevchenko, 2003). For most in the West, Russia no longer had the authority to enact the status as a great-power guarantor of international security that was co-equal with the United States and superordinate to NATO (Clunan, 2014a; Pouliot, 2010). These external evaluations of Russia not only denied Russian claims that Russia was a great power, but they also raised questions about Russia's status as a sovereign state.

Holders of status may change the standards of belonging (Gong, 1984). Status claimants, such as post–Cold War Russia, will often contest these social standards or their lack of recognition in meeting them (Deng, 2008; Larson and Shevchenko, 2003, 2010). It is this revision and contestation of standards that connects status conflict with a state's level of satisfaction with the existing international order and its proclivity to accept or revise that order.

Changing its post–Cold War status has been central to the Russian leadership's agenda for the twenty-first century (Schelin, 2016; Snetkov, 2015). In so doing, Russia's international security elites put forward the world as they wish it to be. This perspective depicts,

> a stylised view of international politics that overstates the degree of international chaos in order to promote a vision of global order that advances Russia's status aspirations, justifying an enhanced status for Russia even as its material power continues to decline.
> *(Krickovic and Weber, 2018, 297)*

Pursuing status will somehow make this desired world materialise (Krickovic and Weber, 2018).

International status conflicts are fraught precisely because socially conferred status is what grants or denies a state the legitimacy, if not the material power, to enact that status and to set status standards. This means that states can be denied great-power status even when they defeat a recognised great power in war (Ward, 2017). This also allows states, such as post–Cold War Russia, to have a status that is higher than its material capabilities, and consequently to exercise more rights and privileges and carry more obligations in world politics than material capabilities alone merit (Duque, 2018; Jackson, 1990; Volgy et al., 2014).

It is the social and deontic[2] nature of status—the fact that it creates a sense of legitimacy—that makes it an emotional trigger that is associated with identity, honour, and feelings of anger, resentment and humiliation that shape behaviour (Clunan, 2014a; Forsberg, 2014; Lebow, 2008; Malinova, 2014; Smith, 2014; Tsygankov, 2012, 2014; Ward, 2017). Not recognising or denying these rights and privileges can lead to outbreaks of armed conflict and war (Murray, 2018; Wolf, 2011), as has been the case with post-Soviet Russia. In the mid-2000s, in a fundamental shift from its previous behaviour, Russia moved from rhetorically claiming it was a great power to enacting this status through lethal and non-lethal means while continuing to contest the West's moral authority to set international standards (Snetkov, 2015, 104).

Twenty-first-century Russia's understanding of security as status

Status and security are inseparable for the majority of Russian policy elite. Three fundamental elements are necessary for Russia to be secure in the twenty-first century, in its view: great-power status (*derzhavnost'*), sovereign statehood (*gosudarstvennost'*) (Hill and Gaddy, 2012) and economic advancement (Snetkov, 2015). This conception requires pursuing security through status-politics. This understanding is markedly different from post–Cold War Western understandings that view liberal international institutions, democracy, human rights and economic liberalism as necessary for international and national security and prosperity (Ikenberry, 2018). While Western leaders associate sovereignty with popular democracy, Russian leaders associate it with society's subordination to the state (Hill and Gaddy, 2012, 36). International security, on the Russian view, is also premised on sovereign states' domination of social forces (Krickovic and Weber, 2018).

In the conflict between Western and Russian views, 'sovereignty and democracy stand out as two of the most prominent keywords,… with both sides insisting that their understanding of these notions as being self-evident and universal, and dismissing the other's vision as ideological and distorted' (Morozov, 2008, 152–153). Western promotion of liberalism and civil society is seen in Russia as negating the basic precept of sovereign statehood, as it puts the individual above the state (Snetkov, 2015). Internationally, the global diffusion of liberalism has created an international status hierarchy based not purely on military and economic capabilities but on internal democracy (Pouliot, 2014, 2016). This is not a world order in which Russian leaders feel secure, as it challenges Russia's status as both a sovereign state and a great power. The third pillar of Russia's security is economic transformation into a post-industrial, high-tech economy.

Economic advancement

Russia's economic advancement is viewed as necessary for great-power and sovereign status across the policy elite. It was what newly named Prime Minister Putin, in his inaugural message to the country, wrote would determine Russia's fate in the twenty-first-century 'post-industrial society' (Clunan, 2009a). 'Russia must transform from a raw-materials exporter into a high-tech economy in order to become a global great power' (Arbatov, 2017). Successful engagement with the global economy and domestic modernisation are necessary both to develop the Russian state and to ensure great-power status (Hill and Gaddy, 2012; Snetkov, 2015).

Russia's leadership has a fundamentally statist view of the economy (Snetkov, 2015; Clunan, 2009a). Economic advancement is necessary to sustain and strengthen sovereign-statehood and great-power status. As such, it does not hew to any rigid set of ideological or theoretical principles. Rather, the imperatives of sovereign-statehood and great-power status guide it. So, while Putin has persisted in keeping economic liberals in prominent positions (Clunan, 2018; Laruelle, 2017; Hill and Gaddy, 2012), recent moves to support import substitution (Connolly and Hanson, 2016) reflect this non-ideological view of the economy.

Russia's leadership employs a 'sovereign globalisation' strategy (Gould-Davies, 2016), essentially neo-mercantilism or neo-imperialism under the guise of economic integration into European and post-Soviet markets (Losev, 2017). Russia has limited economic interdependence with the outside world while creating European dependence on Russian oil and gas and Central Asian dependence on Russia's continued growth (Stepanyan et al., 2015). The leadership has taken pains to signal Russia's economic strength through gestures such as repaying all of Russia's International Monetary Fund loans ahead of schedule. So long as it maintains its nineteenth-century view of sovereignty and global order, Russia will likely continue to pursue its sovereign globalisation approach in its efforts to become a post-industrial economy (Snetkov, 2015).

Aided by a rebound in domestic production after the 1998 devaluation of the rouble and by high oil prices, the Russian economy has grown rapidly, shoring up Putin's popularity and his efforts to restore the power of the state over Russia's regions and society (Hill and Gaddy, 2012). The World Bank reports that 'from the 1998–99 crisis until 2011, Russia experienced nearly uninterrupted strong growth and unprecedented gains in shared prosperity', making Russia the sixth largest economy in the world in terms of purchasing power parity, up four places since 1998 (World Bank, 2017a, 2017b, 2017c). This stretch of economic growth positively influenced Russians' perception of their country's international status, leading Russia's leaders in the late 2000s to declare Russia was the equal of the United States, one that no longer needed Western recognition of that fact (Snetkov, 2015). It also gave the Putin administration the confidence to exercise its great-power status with force, first in Georgia, then Ukraine and later Syria (Schelin, 2016).

Russian leaders also take advantage of opportunities to challenge the West's status in the international financial order.

> Elite-level discussions of the rouble's potential as a world currency and Moscow's future as an international financial centre symbolically underscore the domestic perception of Russia as a central pole and great power in the international system [and] … in what they see as their traditional regional backyard.
>
> *(Johnson, 2013)*

Replacing the U.S. dollar as the world's reserve currency and elevating trade in Russian roubles are part of the Putin administration's efforts to maintain its great-power status and retaliate for perceived slights, as seen in Russia's sell-off of U.S dollars in response to new U.S. economic sanctions (Rennison and Seddon, 2018). Russia and China have established a rouble-yuan payment system for bilateral trade, seeking to avoid reliance on dollar-denominated trade in oil, Russia's key export (Reuters, 2017; Russia Today, 2017, 2018).

This said, Russian policy elites recognise that their country is not an economic great power and that its status and security hinge upon economic upgrading (Arbatov, 2017; Karaganov, 2017; Kortunov, 2016; Losev, 2017; Snetkov, 2015). Putin and Medvedev started out in 1999 to rectify this situation. Their limited success in transforming the Russian economy to date reflects not only the difficulty the leadership has had in creating a high-tech economy but also the Russians' long-standing belief that military might and a strong state are the main prerequisites for great-power status (Clunan, 2014a; Krickovic and Weber, 2018; Larson and Shevchenko, 2010; Lukyanov, 2017; Makarychev and Morozov, 2011).

Great-power Status (*derzhavnost'*) and sovereign statehood (*gosudarstvennost'*)

Russian elites largely understand great-power status and sovereign statehood as mutually constitutive concepts (Snetkov, 2015), in that the lessons drawn from Russia's long history suggest that both internal discord and external great powers were the most potent threats to the Russian/Soviet state and its status as a great power. In this view, Russia is secure when its great-power status is respected and its state is internally strong and unified (Hill and Gaddy, 2012).

The intermingling of status and security means that Russia's leaders will never be willing simply to follow the West's lead on security. Great-power status matters 'both as a guarantee against "foreign support" for domestic protests, and as an ultimate means of gaining popular support for the government. Status is the recourse necessary to consolidate citizens and prevent domestic unrest' (Schelin, 2016, 100). Rebuilding statehood is central to the leadership's approach to security, as it is necessary to 'consolidate and expand the regime's power domestically and regain the prestige of a "great power" within the international system' (Snetkov, 2015, 2). Pursuing great-power status is also necessary to restore Russia's historical rights internationally and preserve the international state system (Krickovic and Weber, 2018).

This conception of sovereign statehood is not a twenty-first-century, but a largely nineteenth-century, Western one. In his 1999 Millennium address, Putin laid this out plainly:

> Statism. It will not happen soon, if it ever happens at all, that Russia will become the second edition of, say, the US or Britain in which liberal values have deep historic traditions. Our state and its institutions and structures have always played an exceptionally

important role in the life of the country and its people. For Russians a strong state is not an anomaly that should be got rid of. Quite the contrary, they see it as a source and guarantor of order and the initiator and main driving force of any change.

Putin has cultivated successfully state-centric nationalism based on 'sovereign democracy' at home over the past decade. This nationalism promotes Russia's distinctiveness as a great power built through centuries of centralised rule and loyalty to the state (Hill and Gaddy, 2012; Laruelle, 2015; Snetkov, 2015). More recently, Russia has sponsored populism, xenophobic nationalism and distrust of government in the West as part of its effort to replace the liberalising 'globalist elites' with ones that favour its absolutist view of sovereign statehood (Makarychev, 2017; Soldatov and Borogan, 2015).

From the Russian leadership's perspective, there has been an unceasing Western effort to erode sovereign statehood and Russia's great-power rights, beginning with NATO's 1998–1999 military campaign to end ethnic cleansing in Serbia and U.S. financial assistance to opposition groups who peacefully ousted Serbia's president in 2000. During 2003–2005, the 'coloured revolutions'—mass protests against fraudulent elections and corruption in Georgia, Ukraine and Kyrgyzstan—led to the fall of their presidents. Similar protests broke out in Azerbaijan, Belarus, Moldova, Mongolia and Uzbekistan in 2005–2006, without regime change. In 2009, opposition protesters clashed violently with Moldova's authorities; Putin denounced them as 'fascists intoxicated with hatred' (Barry, 2009). Then, the 2010 Arab Spring uprisings toppled authoritarian leaders in Tunisia, Egypt and Yemen. In 2011, sustained protests and violence rocked Bahrain and Syria, and the later fell into civil war. In Libya, NATO intervened against the Qaddifi regime, and his execution by rebels was broadcast worldwide. These events made Russia's leadership profoundly insecure.

Russia's post–Cold War pursuit of security through status

In the official Russian view, non-state actors, whether armed rebels, human rights democracy advocates, news organisations or businessmen, are potential threats to Russia's sovereign statehood at home, great-power status abroad and the sovereign-state system. Russia's security response has been to class them all as falling broadly under its counterterrorism operations (Baev, 2018; Snetkov, 2015). Its statist view of sovereign statehood extends this threat perception to democratic protests and activism worldwide, while its concerns for great-power status make anti-regime activism in the former Soviet republics of especial concern.

Russia's armed security operations in the twenty-first century have all been to uphold its conceptions of great-power status and sovereign statehood. Russia has and will continue to use force, lethal and non-lethal, to assert Russia's view that the international order is properly a multipolar great-power management system in which only sovereign states, not individuals, have rights (Bull, 1977; Krickovic and Weber, 2018). It has upgraded its military might, security agencies and operations in defence of both statuses (Bershidsky, 2017). Internal and external security requires external as much as internal security measures (Snetkov, 2015). This security conception will provide grounds for Russia's use of lethal and non-lethal force internally, in what Russia views as its sphere of influence, and occasionally in support of sovereign governments under threat from violent non-state actors or democracy promoters.

Russia first used armed force for reasons of great-power status in response to the West's intervention during the Kosovo crisis of 1998–1999. From Russia's perspective, NATO's war against Serbia denied Russia's historical role as a great power and protector of the Southern Slavs, ignored the United Nations Security Council great-power management system and violated sovereignty over an internal matter (Heller, 2014). When NATO's campaign began, Russian troops immediately moved from Bosnia to seize the Pristina airport ahead of NATO forces, surprising NATO commanders and delighting the Russian populace (Clunan, 2009a).

Russia first used force in the name of sovereign statehood in 1994 against secessionists seeking Chechnya's independence from Russia. The Yeltsin administration withdrew in defeat in 1996 to scathing criticism domestically and Western condemnation over gross human rights abuses. That defeat signified the precarious weakness of Russia's statehood. Restoring that status was Putin's first armed act (Baev, 2018; Smith, 2014; Snetkov, 2015). In 1999, Chechen rebels extended their operations into neighbouring Dagestan. Putin sent close to 100,000 troops to Chechnya to conduct what he called antiterrorist operations, and 'flattened Grozny' (Baev, 2018) its capital, in the process.

Counterterrorism became the *leitmotif* of Russia's security policy thereafter (Baev, 2018; Snetkov, 2015). The most important focus of Russia's use of armed force and military modernisation has been internal (Baev, 2018; Bershidsky, 2017; Snetkov, 2015). Putin announced his support for U.S. counterterrorism actions after the September 11, 2001 terrorist attacks on New York and Washington, D.C. The West muted its criticism of Russian actions in Chechnya, and the United States accepted Putin's definition of the second Chechen war as a counterterrorist operation. In 2003, however, the West increasingly criticised human rights violations in Chechnya, while Britain harboured a former Chechen leader wanted by Russian authorities as a terrorist. Over 1999–2004, a series of terrorist attacks in Russia perpetuated public support for Putin's brutal policies in Chechnya. After the September 2004 Beslan massacre, however, Russian elite and public support for the war in Chechnya began to wane. The West offered only lukewarm expressions of outrage over Beslan and called for political, rather than military, means be used to bring an end to the Chechen war. The fundamental conflict in worldviews between Russia and Western powers became much more serious with the anti-establishment 'coloured' revolutions that took place over 2003–2005. Whereas Kosovo challenged Russia's status as a global power, Western support for pro-Western movements in the former Soviet Union denied Russia the status of even being a regional great power. This marked a turning point in Russia's view of the West as a security partner.

After 2004, Putin blamed the West for deliberately channelling Muslim terrorists towards Russia. A presidential advisor stated that any efforts to 'rollback' Russia in the former Soviet republics would be met with force. Russian cooperation with the United States after 9/11 was replaced by rebukes of Western interference in the former Soviet Union. Russia moved to reduce U.S. influence in the former Soviet Union, establishing multilateral regional organisations with the Central Asian republics and China, and attempting to remove U.S. bases from Central Asia (Clunan, 2009a). The Putin administration increasingly claimed that the West put human rights and democracy ahead of the rights of sovereign states to achieve internal security.

Then, in 2008, at U.S. behest, NATO stated that Georgia and Ukraine would one day join the alliance, a declaration met with fury in Moscow. Russia responded with 'a combination of economic pressure, political intrigue, and limited use of military force' (Baev, 2018). A few months later, Russia invaded Georgia, the most overtly pro-U.S. ally in the former Soviet Union, nominally to protect the rights of Russian citizens and prevent ethnic cleansing. Russia's action was a war for status, a way to re-stake its claim as a great power with special rights and responsibilities in its sphere of influence and contest the West's liberal standard of sovereign statehood. Russia deliberately put the West on notice that if it could unilaterally invade sovereign states in the name of human rights, Russia could too (Makarychev and Morozov, 2011).

The Arab Spring and widespread anti-regime protests across Russia during 2011–2013 dramatically amplified the Russian leadership's sense of insecurity over sovereign statehood. Its counterterrorism strategy expanded to include opposition groups and democracy promoters. The prolonged Euromaidan protests in Ukraine pressured its pro-Russian president to suddenly flee the country on February 22, 2014. This 'turned out to be even more dangerous from the Kremlin's perspective when unexpected street protests in Moscow resonated with the victorious Euromaidan in Kyiv' (Baev, 2018). Moscow declared it a coup d'etat orchestrated by the United States and the European Union, and carried out by Ukrainian fascists. 'The main aim of the Kremlin's loosely defined struggle against terrorism has involved defeating armed separatist rebellions in Chechnya, suppressing extremist networks in the North Caucasus, and turning back the tide of colour revolutions' (Baev, 2018). On February 27, Russia invaded and annexed Crimea, and barely two months later invaded Eastern Ukraine, again ostensibly to protect the human rights of Russian nationals. 'The annexation of Crimea was, in Putin's strategy, a direct response to this eruption of Ukrainian "extremism", which is treated the same way as terrorism' (Baev, 2018).

Russia next intervened militarily in Syria in 2015 to support a brutally authoritarian regime in a civil war against armed anti-government actors, whether they were Islamic militants or rebels supported by the West. Russian officials stressed their intervention was to support the sovereignty of Syria and its legitimate government against terrorists. Russia, in its view, was acting as a '*status quo* power' (Karaganov, 2016b). It is through such lethal and non-lethal means that Russia has attempted to challenge the softened sovereignty of the post–Cold War order and reshape it as a multipolar great-power-management system in which only states have international status and attendant rights.

As the preceding suggests, the question of what is sacrosanct—sovereign statehood or popular sovereignty—will continue to produce the deepest and deadliest conflict between Russia and the West, particularly in the former Soviet republics (Sovet po vneshnei i oboronnoi politike, 2016). Russian leaders simply do not accept human rights or human security as an international concern. From the Russian perspective, the United States and its NATO allies are set on the 'further demolition of international law', evidenced by the 'barbaric bombing of Yugoslavia, the separation of Kosovo, and aggression against Iraq and Libya' (Karaganov, 2016a).

Eroding sovereignty, together with the perceived lack of respect for Russia's great-power status, has led Russia to use force repeatedly in the post–Cold War era. These issues are the reason Russia under Putin has reactivated what the Soviets called 'active measures' to destabilise Western democracies through disinformation campaigns and fifth column movements. Cyberspace has only made them that much easier and cheaper to undertake. Within Russian official circles, such acts are seen as overdue and legitimate resistance to 25 years of Western democracy promotion in the former USSR and globally, an ongoing assertion that Russia can and will defend its sovereignty and great-power rights at home and abroad (Krickovic and Weber, 2018, 296).

Implications for the security of Russia's great-power status in the twenty-first century

Outside the West and in Russia, the softening of sovereignty brought on by globalisation and neo-liberalism is often seen as a strategic grand plan of the United States to assimilate, undermine or contain its rivals and enrich itself—in other words, to perpetuate Western hegemony. Many in Russia believe this hegemony is declining. Russian security elites are divided, however, on what kind of twenty-first-century world will emerge as U.S. hegemony wanes, and many refuse to recognise Russia's own relative decline (Krickovic and Weber, 2018).

Russian optimists assume that U.S. decline will mean that sovereignty will automatically harden again as U.S.-style globalisation disappears and Russia's status as a global great power will be assured (Karaganov, 2017). Along these lines, many Russian policy elites seem to hope that a state-centric, multipolar security order akin to the early nineteenth-century Concert of Europe system can be built. Such an outcome relies on a grand partnership between Russia and China, where 'China will provide investment and resources, and Russia will contribute security and geopolitical stability' to balance the United States (Karaganov, 2016b). To this end, Russian leaders will continue to develop the military capabilities deemed essential for its great-power status (Bershidsky, 2017; Galeotti, 2017; Gorenburg, 2017).

In Russia, sceptics roundly criticise this view as anachronistic, as the current 'polycentric' order is much different in its asymmetric distribution of power and its economic interdependence (Arbatov, 2017). Millions of Russians, including Putin and his powerful supporters, have benefited mightily from Russia's engagement with the global liberal economy and its integration into European markets. Russia's economic advancement and, therefore, its sovereign and great-power statuses depend upon its ability to upgrade and diversify its exports (Sanghi, 2018). Russian liberals argue this necessitates a choice in favour of Western-style democratic societies (Arbatov, 2017; Kortunov, 2016). Turning inward or continuing neo-mercantilism will likely mean stagnation and decline economically, putting at risk Russia's great-power status and sovereign statehood (Losev, 2017).

Russian policy elites also express concern that Russia's pursuit of security through status will weaken Russia in the twenty-first century. Official assertion of great-power status through the use of force and rigid insistence on sovereign statehood over individualism at home may lead Russian leaders to overreach externally and resist necessary economic and political reforms internally. Such reforms are needed for Russia to thrive in the twenty-first century. As Alexei Arbatov states, Russia's status as a

> full-fledged global power requires vigorous efforts to break out of the emerging economic and political stagnation, which threatens decline.... it is impossible [to achieve via] the routes of great-power rhetoric, narcissism based on metaphysical spiritual traditions, economic autarky and building up military might beyond the limits of reasonable sufficiency.
> *(2017)*

Such sceptics argue that Russia will not come out the winner in a more sovereign, de-globalised world. Instead, Russia loses its political independence to China in the latter's bipolar standoff with an economically revived United States (Losev, 2017). They suggest that China is the greatest winner in the current standoff between Russia and the West. China, in their view, does not view Russia as an equal great power, but as its 'resource rear' (Arbatov, 2017). In the medium term, Russia's necessary (Sanghi, 2018) economic turn to Asia for its export markets may generate anti-Chinese and anti-Asian sentiment among the Russian elite and society. Such sentiment appeared immediately after the collapse of the Soviet Union, when conservative and nationalist media outlets warned of a 'yellow peril' invading the Russian Far East. It continues a subterranean existence in the form of daily violence against Asians in Russia's cities and more prominence of far-right nationalists in the state-controlled media. Russia's increasing reliance on China's market for its own growth raises the spectre of status conflicts with China, should Russian leaders come to feel they are treated as a 'junior partner' by their eastern neighbour.

Given all of the above, it is not at all clear that Russia can prosper in a more state-centric world, or in one that continues globalising without change in its understanding of security. Many in the West see the future as not multipolar, but non-polar, a 'no-one's world' (Kupchan, 2012) where there are overlapping spheres of authority (Cerny, 1995). The Russian leadership's early twenty-first-century search to secure Russia's statuses as a sovereign state and great power has failed to turn Russia into a 'post-industrial' powerhouse under conditions of global openness. Such efforts will become all the more difficult in a world dominated by economic and political nationalism. It is more likely that pursuing the current regime's concept of security-through-status will fracture Russia's relations with both Europe and China in ways that harm Russia's economy, statehood and great-power status more than it harms either Europe or China. That fracturing in turn could tip the world again into a great-power war, but one that begins in Eurasia.

Notes

1 The views expressed here are solely those of the author and not of the U.S. government or the U.S. Department of Defense or Navy.
2 Deontic pertains to ethical and moral standards in a society. Deontic logic in philosophy deals with the moral sense or feeling of 'obligation, permission, and prohibition … supererogation as well as any non-reductive logic for legal notions like claims, liberties, powers, and immunities' (McNamara, 2014). Social status is deontic, in that it generates these properties and gives them a moral grounding as what is just or right, and it establishes the 'proper' or 'normal' stratification of individuals in a society.

References

Arbatov, Alexey (2017) 'Khurshenie miroporyadka. Kuda povernet Rossiya?' *Russia in global affairs*, 8 December. Accessed 25 July 2018 at www.globalaffairs.ru/number/Krushenie-miroporyadka-19205.

Baev, Pavel (2018) 'Why Russia is failing the "Syria test" for counterterrorism cooperation with the West', *PONARS policy memo* no. 528. Accessed 27 June 2018 at www.ponarseurasia.org/node/9748.

Barry, Ellen (2009) 'Protests in Moldova explode, with help of twitter', *The New York Times*, 7 April. Accessed 25 July 2018 at www.nytimes.com/2009/04/08/world/europe/08moldova.html.

Bershidsky, Leonid (2017) 'Russia's military is leaner, but meaner', *Bloomberg news*, 14 December. Accessed 20 June 2018 at www.bloomberg.com/view/articles/2017-12-14/russia-s-military-is-leaner-but-meaner.

Bull, Hedley (1977) *The anarchical society*. New York: Columbia University Press.

Cerny, Philip (1995) 'Globalisation and the Changing Logic of Collective Action', *International Organisation*, Vol. 49, no. 4: pp. 595–625.

Clunan, Anne L. (2009a) *The social construction of Russia's resurgence: aspirations, identity and security interests*. Baltimore, MD: Johns Hopkins University Press.

Clunan, Anne L. (2009b) 'Redefining sovereignty: humanitarianism's challenge to sovereign immunity', in Noha Shawki and Michaelene Cox, eds., *Negotiating sovereignty and human rights: actors and issues in contemporary human rights politics*. London: Ashgate Publishing, pp. 7–26.

Clunan, Anne L. (2014a) 'Historical aspirations and the domestic politics of Russia's pursuit of international status', *Communist and Post-Communist Studies*, Vol. 47, no. 3–4, pp. 281–290.

Clunan, Anne L. (2014b) 'Why status matters in world politics', in Paul, Thazha V., Larson, Deborah and Wohlforth, William, eds., *Status in world politics*. Cambridge: Cambridge University Press, pp. 273–296.

Clunan, Anne L. (2018) 'Russia and the liberal international order', *Ethics & International Affairs*, Vol. 32, no. 1, pp. 45–49. doi:10.1017/S0892679418000096.

Clunan, Anne L. and Trinkunas, Harold A. (2010) 'Conceptualising ungoverned spaces: territorial statehood, contested authority, and softened sovereignty', in Clunan, Anne L. and Trinkunas, Harold A., eds., *Ungoverned spaces*. Stanford, CA: Stanford University Press, pp. 17–33.

Connolly, John and Hanson, Philip (2016) 'Import substitution and economic sovereignty in Russia', *Chatham House research papers*, 9 June. Accessed 30 May 2018 at www.chathamhouse.org/sites/default/files/publications/research/2016-06-09-import-substitution-russia-connolly-hanson.pdf.

Cox, Robert W. (1981) 'Social forces, states and world orders: beyond international relations theory', *Millennium*, Vol. 10, no. 2, pp. 126–155.

Deng, Yong (2008) *China's struggle for status: the realignment of international relations*. Cambridge: Cambridge University Press.

Duque, Marina G. (2018) 'Recognising international status: a relational approach', *International Studies Quarterly*, sqx001, doi:10.1093/isq/sqy001.

Forsberg, Tuomas (2014) 'Status conflicts between Russia and the West: perceptions and emotional biases', *Communist and Post-Communist Studies*, Vol. 47, no. 3–4, pp. 323–331.

Galeotti, Mark (2017) 'The truth about Russia's defence budget', *European council on foreign relations commentary*, 24 March. Accessed 1 July 2018 at www.ecfr.eu/article/commentary_the_truth_about_russias_defence_budget_7255.

Gilpin, Robert (1981) *War and change in world politics*. Cambridge: Cambridge University Press.

Gong, Gerrit W. (1984) *The standard of civilisation in international society*. Oxford: Clarendon Press.

Gorenburg, Dmitry (2017) 'Russia's military modernisation plans: 2018–2027,' *PONARS policy memo* no. 495. Accessed 27 June 2018 at www.ponarseurasia.org/memo/russias-military-modernisation-plans-2018-2027.

Gould-Davies, Nigel (2016) 'Russia's sovereign globalisation: rise, fall and future', *Chatham House research papers*, 6 January. Accessed 30 May 2018 at www.chathamhouse.org/publication/russias-sovereign-globalisation-rise-fall-and-future.

Heller, Regina (2014) 'Russia's quest for respect in the international conflict management in Kosovo', *Communist and Post-Communist Studies*, Vol. 47, no. 3–4, pp. 333–343.

Hill, Fiona and Gaddy, Clifford (2012) *Mr. Putin: operative in the Kremlin*. Washington, DC: Brookings Institution Press.

Hopf, Ted (2013) 'Commonsense constructivism and hegemony in world politics', *International Organisation*, Vol. 67, no. 2, pp. 317–354.

Ikenberry, G. John (2018) 'The end of liberal international order?' *International Affairs*, Vol. 94, no. 1, pp. 7–23.

Jackson, Robert (1990) *Quasi-states: sovereignty, international relations, and the Third World*. New York and Cambridge: Cambridge University Press.

Johnson, Juliet (2013) 'The rouble and the yuan: allies or competitors?' *PONARS policy memo* no. 255. Accessed 27 July 2018 at www.ponarseurasia.org/memo/ruble-and-yuan-allies-or-competitors.

Karaganov, Sergei (2016a) 'Global challenges and Russian foreign policy', *Russia in global affairs*, 20 November. Accessed 20 December 2017 at http://eng.globalaffairs.ru/pubcol/Global-Challenges-and-Russias-Foreign-Policy-18468.

Karaganov, Sergei (2016b) 'How the world looks from the Russian perspective', *Russia in global affairs*, 1 August 2016. Accessed 20 December 2017 at http://eng.globalaffairs.ru/pubcol/How-the-World-Looks-From-the-Russian-Perspective-18303.

Karaganov, Sergei (2017) '2016—A victory of conservative realism', *Russia in global affairs* no. 1, January–March. Accessed 20 December 2017 at http://eng.globalaffairs.ru/number/2016--A-Victory-of-Conservative-Realism-18585.

Kortunov, Andrey (2016) 'The inevitable, weird world', *Russia in global affairs* no. 4, October–December. Accessed 20 December 2017 at http://eng.globalaffairs.ru/number/The-Inevitable-Weird-World-18385.

Krickovic, Andrej and Weber, Yuval (2018) 'What can Russia teach us about change? Status-seeking as a catalyst for transformation in international politics', *International Studies Review*, Vol. 20, no. 2, pp. 292–300.

Kupchan, Charles A. (2012) *No one's world: the west, the rising rest, and the coming global turn*. Oxford: Oxford University Press.

Larson, Deborah W. and Shevchenko, Alexei (2003) 'Shortcut to greatness: the new thinking and the revolution in Soviet foreign policy', *International Organisation*, Vol. 57, no. 1, pp. 77–109.

Larson, Deborah W. and Shevchenko, Alexei (2010) 'Status seekers: Chinese and Russian responses to U.S. primacy', *International Security*, Vol. 34, no. 4, pp. 63–95.

Larson, Deborah W. and Shevchenko, Alexei (2014) 'Russia says no: power, status, and emotions in foreign policy', *Communist and Post-Communist Studies*, Vol. 47, no. 3–4, pp. 269–279.

Laruelle, Marlene, ed. (2014) *Russian nationalism, foreign policy and identity debates in Putin's Russia: new ideological patterns after the Orange Revolution*. Stuttgart: Ibidem Press.

Laruelle, Marlene (2015) 'Russia as a "Divided nation," from compatriots to Crimea: a contribution to the discussion on nationalism and foreign policy', *Problems of Post-Communism*, Vol. 62, no. 2, pp. 88–97.

Laruelle, Marlene (2017) 'The Kremlin's ideological ecosystems: equilibrium and competition', *PONARS policy memo* no. 493. Accessed 30 June 2018 at www.ponarseurasia.org/node/9483.

Lebow, Ned (2008) *A cultural theory of international politics*. Cambridge: Cambridge University Press.

Leichtova, Magda (2014) *Misunderstanding Russia: Russian foreign policy and the west*. London and New York: Routledge.

Losev, Alexander (2017) 'Neo-mercantilism, neo-modernism or neo-imperialism?' *Russia in global affairs* no. 3, July–September. Accessed 20 December 2017 at http://eng.globalaffairs.ru/number/Neo-Mercantilism-Neo-Modernism-or-Neo-Imperialism-19038.

Lukyanov, Fyodor (2017) 'In the moonlight', *Russia in global affairs* no. 3, July–September. Accessed 20 December 2017 at http://eng.globalaffairs.ru/number/In-the-Moonlight-19035.

Makarychev, Andrey (2017) 'The Russian world, post-truth, and Europe', *PONARS policy memo* no. 477. Accessed 30 June 2018 at www.ponarseurasia.org/node/9200.

Makarychev, Andrey (2018) 'Europe in crisis: "old," "new," or incomplete?' *PONARS policy memo* no. 515. Accessed 30 June 2018 at www.ponarseurasia.org/node/9640.

Makarychev, Andrey and Morozov, Viatcheslav (2011) 'Multilateralism, multipolarity, and beyond', *Global Governance*, Vol. 17, no. 3, pp. 353–373.

Malinova, Olga (2014) 'Obsession with status and ressentiment: historical backgrounds of the Russian discursive identity construction', *Communist and Post-Communist Studies*, Vol. 47, no. 3–4, pp. 291–303.

McNamara, Paul (2014) 'Supplement to deontic logic: challenges in defining deontic logic', in Zalta, Edward N., ed., *The Stanford encyclopedia of philosophy* (Winter 2014 Edition). Accessed 25 July 2018 at https://plato.stanford.edu/entries/logic-deontic/challenges.html.

Morozov, Viatcheslav (2008) 'Sovereignty and democracy in contemporary Russia: a modern subject faces the post-modern world', *Journal of International Relations and Development*, Vol. 11, no. 2, 152–180.

Morozov, Viatcheslav (2015) *Russia's postcolonial identity: a subaltern empire in a Eurocentric world*. Houndmills, Basingstoke, Hampshire: Palgrave Macmillan.

Moshes, Arkady (2018) 'What will replace Russia's dwindling Trump-euphoria? Russian foreign policy viewpoints today', *PONARS policy memo* no. 506. Accessed 30 May 2018 at www.ponarseurasia.org/node/9588.

Murray, Michelle (2018) *The struggle for recognition in international relations: status, revisionism, and rising powers*. Oxford: Oxford University Press.

Neumann, Iver B. (2008) 'Russia as a great power, 1815–2007', *Journal of International Relations and Development*, Vol. 11, no. 2, pp. 128–151.

Neumann, Iver B (2014) 'Status is cultural: Durkheimian Poles and Weberian Russians seek great-power status', in Paul, Thazha V., Larson, Deborah and Wohlforth, William, eds., *Status in world politics*. Cambridge: Cambridge University Press, pp. 85–112.

Paul, T. V., Larson, Deborah and Wohlforth, William, eds. (2014) *Status in world politics*. Cambridge: Cambridge University Press.

Pouliot, Vincent (2010) *International security in practice: the politics of NATO-Russia diplomacy*. Cambridge: Cambridge University Press.

Pouliot, Vincent (2014) 'Setting status in stone: the negotiation of international institutional privileges', in Paul, T. V., Larson, Deborah and Wohlforth, William, eds., *Status in world politics*. Cambridge: Cambridge University Press, pp. 192–216.

Pouliot, Vincent (2016) *International pecking orders: the politics and practice of multilateral diplomacy*. Cambridge: Cambridge University Press.

Rennison, Joe and Seddon, Max (2018) 'Russia sharply cuts its holdings of US Treasuries', *The Financial Times*, 18 July. Accessed 19 July at www.ft.com/content/24cd34b4-8a97-11e8-b18d-0181731a0340.

Renshon, Jonathan (2016) 'Status deficits and war', *International Organisation*, Vol. 70, no. 3, pp. 513–550.

Renshon, Jonathan (2017) *Fighting for status: hierarchy and conflict in world politics*. Princeton, NJ: Princeton University Press.

Reuters (2017) 'China establishes yuan-rouble payment system', 12 October. Accessed 20 July at www.reuters.com/article/us-china-yuan-rouble/china-establishes-yuan-ruble-payment-system-idUSKBN1CH0ML.

Russia Today (2017) 'Rouble-yuan trade between Russia & China makes dollar odd man out', 3 November. Accessed 20 July at www.rt.com/business/408670-russia-china-ruble-yuan-dollar/.

Russia Today (2018) 'Petro-yuan helps Russia & China dump US dollar in oil trade', 27 March. Accessed 20 July at www.rt.com/business/422472-russia-china-petro-yuan/.

Sakwa, Richard (2008) '"New cold war" or twenty years' crisis? Russia and international politics', *International Affairs*, Vol. 84, no. 2, pp. 241–267.

Sanghi, Apurva (2018) 'Russia's pivot to Asia: desirable, but possible?' *Forbes*, 25 May. Accessed at www.worldbank.org/en/news/opinion/2018/05/25/russias-pivot-to-asia-desirable-but-possible.

Schelin, Pavel (2016) 'Russian national security strategy: regime security and elite's struggle for "great power" status', *Slovo*, Vol. 28, no. 2, pp. 85–105. doi:10.14324/111. 0954–6839.047.

Simon, Rick (2009) '"Upper Volta with gas"? Russia as a semi-peripheral state', in Worth, Owen and Moore, Phoebe, eds., *Globalisation and the 'new' semi-peripheries*. Houndmills, Basingstoke: Palgrave-Macmillan, pp. 120–137.

Smith, Hanna (2014) 'Russia as a great power: status inconsistency and the two Chechen wars', *Communist and Post-Communist Studies*, Vol. 47, no. 3–4, pp. 355–363.

Snetkov, Aglaya (2015) *Russia's security policy under Putin: a critical perspective*. Abingdon: Routledge.

Soldatov, Andrei and Borogan, Irina (2015) *The red web*. Philadelphia, PA: Perseus Books Group.

Sovet po Vneshnei i Oboronnoi Politike (2016) 'Strategiia dlia Rossii. Rossiiskaia vneshnaia politika: konets 2010x-nachalo 2020x'. Accessed 30 May 2017 at http://svop.ru/wp-content/uploads/2016/05/тезисы_23мая_sm.pdf.

Stepanyan, Ara, Roitman, Agustin, Minasyan, Gohar, Ostojic, Dragana and Epstein, Natan (2015) 'The spillover effects of Russia's economic slowdown on neighboring countries', *International Monetary Fund Departmental Paper* no. 15/13.

Tsygankov, Andrei P. (2012) *Russia and the west from Alexander to Putin*. Cambridge and New York: Cambridge University Press.

Tsygankov, Andrei P. (2014) 'The frustrating partnership: honor, status, and emotions in Russia's discourses of the West', *Communist and Post-Communist Studies*, Vol. 47, no. 3–4, pp. 345–354.

Tsygankov, Andrei P. (2016) 'Crafting the state-civilisation: Vladimir Putin's turn to distinct values', *Problems of Post-Communism*, Vol. 63, no. 3, pp. 146–158.

Tsygankov, Andrei P. (2018) 'The sources of Russia's fear of NATO', *Communist and Post-Communist Studies*, Vol. 51, no. 2, pp. 101–111.

Volgy, Thomas J., Corbetta, Renato, Rhamey, J. Patrick, Baird, Ryan G. and Grant, Keith A. (2014) 'Status considerations in international politics and the rise of regional powers,' in Paul, T. V., Larson, Deborah and Wohlforth, William, eds., *Status in world politics*. Cambridge: Cambridge University Press, pp. 58–84.

Ward, Steven (2017) *Status and the challenge of rising powers*. Cambridge: Cambridge University Press.

Willerton, John, Beznosov, Mikhail and Carrier, Martin (2005) 'Addressing the challenges of Russia's "failing state": the legacy of Gorbachev and the promise of Putin', *Demokratisatsiya: The Journal of Post-Soviet Democratisation*, Vol. 13, no. 2, pp. 219–240.

Wohlforth, William (2009) 'Unipolarity, status competition and great power war', *World Politics*, Vol. 61, no. 1, pp. 28–57.

Wohlforth, William C., De Carvalho, Benjamin, Leira, Halvard and Neumann, Iver B. (2018) 'Moral authority and status in international relations: Good states and the social dimension of status seeking', *Review of International Studies*, Vol. 44, no. 3, pp. 526–546.

Wolf, Reinhard (2011) 'Respect and disrespect in international politics: the significance of status recognition', *International Theory*, Vol. 3, no. 1, pp. 105–142.

World Bank (2017a) 'From recession to recovery', *Russian economic report* no. 37, May. Accessed 2 December 2017 at www.worldbank.org/en/country/russia/publication/rer.

World Bank (2017b) 'GDP Ranking 2016', July. Accessed 22 December 2017 at https://data.worldbank.org/data-catalog/GDP-ranking-table.

World Bank (2017c) *World development indicators database*. Accessed 15 November 2017 at http://databank.worldbank.org/data/reports.aspx?source=world-development-indicators.

World Bank (2018) 'The Russian economy: modest growth ahead', *Russia economic report* no. 39, May. Accessed 23 June 2018 at http://pubdocs.worldbank.org/en/162681527086868170/RER-39-Eng.pdf.

Zarakol, Ayşe (2011) *After defeat: how the east learned to live with the west*. Cambridge University Press.

2
PUTIN'S OPERATIONAL CODE AND STRATEGIC DECISION-MAKING IN RUSSIA

Graeme P. Herd[1]

Introduction

Though we are not direct participants in strategic decision-making in Russia, by identifying the belief systems of Russian decision makers we are able to discern how they structure and weigh alternative courses of action, calculate risk and formulate strategies (Dyson and Parent, 2017, 2; George, 1969, 191). Nathan Leites, in his seminal *The Operational Code of the Politburo* (1951), argued that decision-making and negotiating behaviour within the 14-man Soviet Politburo was guided by an 'operational code' – the rules, causal relationships and fundamental assumptions which were believed to be necessary for effective political action and which guided Bolshevik interactions with the outside world (Dyson and Parent, 2017; Forsberg and Pursiainen, 2017; George, 1969; Leites, 1953). Such beliefs are usually internally consistent and logically coherent. Leites identified Soviet diagnostic and prescriptive beliefs – such as 'politics is a war', 'push to the limit', 'there are no neutrals', 'avoid adventures', 'resist from the start', 'retreat before superior force' and 'war by negotiation' – and explained this through three motivational images: (1) the question of *kto-kovo* ('who beats or destroys whom'), (2) the fear of annihilation and (3) the principle of the pursuit of power (Walker, 1983, 180). Black-and-white Manichean thinking is also a feature of post-Soviet politics: 'Whoever is not for Gaydar's reforms is for a return to communism', 'whoever is not for the dispersal of the Supreme Soviet is for the Red-Browns', 'whoever is not for Yeltsin for president is for Zyuganov', 'whoever is not for Putin is for the terrorists', and 'whoever is not for Navalny for mayor is for the Kremlin and Sobyanin' (Vishnevsky, 2017). In short, the classic zero-sum Bolshevik 'whoever is not with us is against us!' prevails. Building on the work of Leites – operationalizing it so to speak – George identified two sets of beliefs – philosophical and instrumental. Philosophical beliefs are attributional. They relate to the attributes we assign to people, events and situations, to how fundamentally hostile or benign we understand the world to be and how much control we perceive ourselves to have over our environment. Instrumental beliefs are prognostic in that they relate to what we understand needs to be done – in terms of cooperative or conflictual means – to achieve our preferred policy outcomes.

Can we discern a relationship between what Putin says and what Putin does? To address this question, Dyson and Parent adopted a computer-enabled content analysis approach to examine Putin's hostility/friendliness towards the political universe. They identified 13 foreign policy topics from May 2000 to December 2016, used a complete and verbatim record of Putin's public-speaking engagements, including set-piece speeches and interviews. This approach has three weaknesses. First, the Presidential website does not in fact reflect 'a complete and verbatim record'. Fabricated paragraphs, for example, were inserted demonstrating Putin's mastery of the detail of German political personalities in the late 1980s and early 1990s in the Presidential website transcript of a *Bild* interview, but did not appear in the original German *Bild*-online (Putin, 2016a, 2016b). Changing the record is especially prevalent in give-and-take press conferences with Putin. In the Kremlin's transcript of a briefing by German President Frank-Walter Steinmeier on Crimea in October 2017, Steinmeier noted that ties between Russia and Germany were 'far from normal' – 'There are still open wounds and unresolved issues, first and foremost when it comes to the annexation of Crimea and the conflict in eastern Ukraine, which are a burden and remain a burden on our relationship'. A transcript of the briefing on the Kremlin's website and a live translation on the Kremlin-funded RT television network's Ruptly service replaced the word 'annexation' with 'reunification' and instead cited the German President as saying, 'Crimea becoming part of Russia' ('Kremlin Blanks "Annexation"', 2017). Creative editing distorts the record.

Second, this approach appears to ignore Russian policy, practice and actions on the ground. It confuses the rhetoric of Russian foreign policy with the reality of Russian external relations and conflates what is said with what is done. Tatyana Stanovaya notes that President Putin expresses himself in terms of 'rhetorical camouflage' and 'ornamental proprieties' and so

> If we totally exclude the political context of what is happening – that is, disregard the events that are actually happening in Russia and the current conservative trends – and simply read the main points from Vladimir Putin's speeches, then his value system taken out of context is no different from the value system of the majority of leaders of developed democratic countries.

By contrast, in the 'real' world of decision-making,

> Russia lies at the center of hostile aspirations on the part of the outside world, an object of close interest from intelligence services, and the target of biological, genetic, nuclear, and chemical weapons. In Putin's a real world there is no equality between states, international norms are exploited within the logic of double standards on the principle that "might is right," and human rights activity is merely a cover for interference in sovereign states' affairs.
>
> *(2017)*

Third, President Putin's 'operational code' is driven by the personality of President Putin (a function of his education, training, life experiences and psychology-emotional state), as well as other variables, including a status quo political system predicated on the continuity of the current elite in power, and legitimacy stresses in the context of a deteriorating economy and high popularity of the president. These dynamics are not necessarily reflected in speeches, written by a roster of presidential speech writers.

An alternative but complementary approach is to synthesize the observations of analysts who look to the timing, manner in which decisions announced, check rhetoric against the reality and, on this basis, draw informed inferences as to the nature of decision-making.

While Putin's national security decisions and the decision-making process may appear erratic and confusing, when examining decision-making around the use of force with regard to Crimea and southeastern Ukraine and Syria, such study highlights five recurring decision-making characteristics. First, strategic calculation is based on poor threat analysis and understanding of the strategic environment. Second, Putin's understanding of risk, perception of costs/benefits and tipping points determine when decisions are made and define the intent of the decisions. Third, strategic decisions are tactical, improvised responses to changing circumstances, taking place in small groups operating outside formal structures, with few if any formal checks and balances. Fourth, a 'style of indirect interpretation' and ambiguity characterizes the communication of decisions. Fifth, decisions made appear to have more to do with affirmation, validation, acknowledgement and the need for respect, particularly from the US, as achieving the stated aim. Let us examine each in turn.

'Broken lens' syndrome and threat assessments informing decisions

First, Russian strategic calculation is rational but based on a poor or 'broken lens' threat analysis and understanding of the strategic environment. What are we to make of the January 2016 statement by Nikolai Patrushev, Secretary of the National Security Council, regarding regime change in Russia? Patrushev advances the argument that

> The US leadership has identified for itself the goal of dominating the world. In this connection it does not need a strong Russia. On the contrary, it needs to weaken our country as much as possible. The attainment of this goal through the disintegration of the Russian Federation is not ruled out either. That will open access for the United States to the very rich resources which in its opinion Russia does not deserve to own.
> *(Rostovskiy, 2016)*

Why would the US seek a disintegration the Russian Federation to gain Russia's 'very rich resources' when Russia sells hydrocarbons freely, in record post-Soviet volumes, at low prices, and the US is energy independent? Why would the US want to push regime change in Russia when this raises the risk of several thousand nuclear weapons falling into the hands of non-state actors, or becoming weapons in an intra-elite struggle for power, or used against the US itself? Vygaudas Usackas, head of the European Union (EU) Delegation in Moscow, in a farewell interview, noted that 'The Russian authorities, with the help of a media campaign, have convinced themselves and people living in the country that what happened on Maydan was a CIA operation under the EU flag' (2017).

How can we account for this broken lens? Igor Ivanov, before his departure from the presidential administration in 2016, and Nikolai Patrushev act as information gatekeepers, determining the flow of information and set the tone of the types of analysis President Putin receives: 'Putin is said to not to be using the internet but to be presented with three thick leather-bound folders every morning: one compiled by the FSB, another by the SVR and a third by the FSO' (Judah, 2014). A system of competitive intelligence exists between the Main Intelligence Directorate (GRU), Federal Security Service (FSB) and Foreign Intelligence Service (SVR). To gain Putin's attention – and so receive resources, promotion and demonstrate loyalty – results in worse-case scenarios marinated in extreme language being passed on to the President by the gatekeepers, with little information critique or feedback loops apparent. As a result, contradictory or dissonant information or evidence is filtered out, discredited, minimized or ignored (Galeotti, 2016; Wallander, 2015).

W. Bowman Cutter contends that 'Putin is neither a fool nor irrational, but he is playing the only game he knows in a world he no longer knows, and with a weak hand' ('How Dangerous is Vladimir Putin?' 2015). Danish Foreign Minister Kristian Jensen provides an explanation for what appears to be Russian irrational and unpredictable behaviour, arguing:

> Putin is not irrational, but his rationales are based on something different than ours. To Russia, it was completely rational to get involved on the side of al-Assad in Syria in the conflict against both ISIL and the rebel groups who want to have a revolution. In Putin's view, it was rational to reclaim Crimea for Russia. We do not want to risk civilian lives, Putin has no such considerations in Syria. We have the principle that only a ballot and pencil can move borders; Russia and Putin do not have that. It is just another rationale.
>
> *(2016)*

Vladimir Frolov, an independent Russian foreign policy analyst, commenting on the *Zapad-17* exercise, observed:

> Russia is acting on a faulty threat assessment and seeks to fashion a military response to largely imaginary threats and challenges that are not military in nature. It's all about strategic messaging of coercion and compellence directed at the U.S. and NATO, to prevent things the West has no intention of doing or the capability to accomplish.
>
> *(Birnbaum and Filipov, 2017)*

Vladislav Inozemtsev concurs, noting:

> more and more proof is emerging that the head of state takes his decisions on the basis of erroneous information and false conclusions, which, on the whole, are supplied to him by the surrounding officials and "people close to him".
>
> *(2017)*

According to Russia's dominant national security narratives, Russia is encircled, besieged and threatened by enemies within and without:

> During his career in the KGB, Vladimir Putin learnt to see the result of someone's machinations in everything and to divide the world only into friends and enemies (which is actually wrong: the overwhelming majority of the people on the planet, and even of politicians, simply could not care less about him and his country). So, he cannot assess the real degree of threat – both to Russia and his own regime – and his "strength" virtually always represents no more than an overreaction. That is why a significant amount of what occurs is considered in the context of "conspiracy theories" and virtually everyone is suspected of some form of villainy or "opposition to the regime".
>
> *(Inozemtsev, 2017)*

Such zero-sum thinking generates certain imperatives regarding the nature of a leader as a heroic 'sword and shield of the state', main stabilizer and the population's focus of symbolic reunion and solidarity. Russia must be under threat, and the threat must be existential following the logic: the greater the threat, the more indispensable the leader.

Every threat is evaluated in terms of its potential to trigger regime change in Russia. Worst-case scenarios predicated on the certainty of malign intent dominate any strategic analysis. Decisions reached reflect a paranoid and zero-sum worldview dominated by 'groupthink' – where national security decision makers look for the most consensual and harmonious decision and evidence-based 'objective analysis' understood to be a process in which President Putin fixes the objective and the analysts find evidence to support it. Gleb Pavlovsky, though, offers caution – the decision-making process is not necessarily utterly cynical, given: 'Moscow views world affairs as a system of special operations, and very sincerely believes that it itself is an object of Western special operations' (MacFarquar, 2016).

An overestimation of President Putin's ability to assess negotiating partners is in evidence. Following the financial crisis, President Putin believes that solidarity and shared responsibility in Europe are diminished. He believes that Western states prefer to act according to their own immediate interests and priorities, privileging this above the longer-term economic interests of the preservation of peace in the international system – whether it be Russian gas (Germany), arms sales (France) or banking and investments (UK). The US's perceived need to use Moscow's leverage in global strategic hotspots, to act with it in concert to contain the fallout in Syria, manage the Iran nuclear dossier, or the six-party talks on North Korea's nuclear programme, would, Putin calculates, limit a potential Western backlash against Russia. President Putin has underestimated the decision-making capacity of Western institutions and overestimated the power of his own personal diplomacy.

Defensive-reactive motivation as a strategic communication influence operation

Second, President Putin portrays his own motivation as 'defensive reactive', aiming to restore the status quo ante rather than revising existing norms and practice. Colonial theory offers a sound explanatory framework to understand decision-making motivation. According to Vyacheslav Morozov, Russia suffers from an 'imperial subaltern syndrome': Russia is part of the global imperial core (i.e. the 'political West') but constituting a semi-integrated periphery to Europe (2013, 2015). A feature of Russian historical development has been a Europeanized Russian elite sitting at the heart of empire, colonizing its periphery on behalf of a Westernization and Europeanization narrative, while itself being dependent in economic and normative terms on the West. Defensive-reactive captures the notion of Russia as victim and the West as an aggressor, and it constitutes a powerful tool in Russian strategic communication efforts, but, as we shall argue below, it cloaks the reality of Russian compellence and coercive diplomacy.

Putin makes decisions either when the benefits outweigh the costs or when the costs become acceptable, with order and stability counterpoised to paralysis, chaos and disintegration (Dyson and Parent, 2017). As a result, Putin's risk calculus, his perception of costs/benefits, is critical to understanding when and why strategic decisions are made. This characteristic can be amply evidenced: the decisions to use coercive force in South Ossetia and Abkhazia in 2008, as well as Russia's recognition of these breakaway republics as independent states; the formulation of the Gerasimov Doctrine in 2013; the 'preventative annexation' of Crimea in February 2014; nuclear signalling and the notion that tactical nuclear weapons can 'prevent a wider conflict'; subversion in Donbass; and the Syrian intervention (Winkler, 2017). Rostislav Ishchenko, the head of the Center for Systematic Analysis and Forecasting, a Russian think tank close to the Kremlin, published a report in April 2015 entitled 'On the Necessity of the Preventative Occupation of the Baltic Region', detailing how and why Russia and Belarus might be obliged to occupy Estonia, Latvia and Lithuania (Weiss, 2016). 'Preventative occupation' and 'preventative annexation' perfectly captures the notion of the 'defensive reactive' in Russian strategic thinking. Russian defence correspondent Pavel Felgengauer provides another example when he notes that 'If the Kremlin comes to realize that Ukraine is slipping away or that it is not going to fall apart, then its resorting to a military option will be quite likely' (2016). In the face of pushback, we see another aspect of decision-making: 'The system is effective, destructive and very simple. It works only by simplifying complicated issues. When it hits a strategic impasse, the Kremlin just raises the stakes and escalates the conflict, while also increasing the risks involved' (Pavlovskiy, 2015a, 2015b).

The corollary of this is that President Putin would avoid a solution if he benefited from a crisis. Putin appears to operate under the 'shadow of the future' – the expectation based on experience of possible future developments and how they might impact on the present. For President Putin, regime change is the greatest fear and avoiding this prospect the prime motivating factor explaining his analysis, intent and commitment to any given decision. Psychological factors, misperceptions and biases prevent states from learning the requirements of deterrence. Emotions precede choices, calculations differ, we learn differently from history, we have difficulty in accepting additional information that contradicts existing beliefs and credible threats can be distorted by motivated and unmotivated factors. Following this reasoning, the best guide to understanding Putin's policy choices is not ideology or conceptual frameworks but that he reacts to unacceptable provocations – a personal dimension to an insult is especially provocative for Putin given his impunity in Russia, where he is above the law and free to act without restraint – and understands himself to react defensively. Putin acts to demonstrate a capacity to act and a willingness to escalate but understands escalation as preventative. As President Putin himself stated, 'Fifty years ago the streets of Leningrad taught me a lesson: if a fight is inevitable, throw the first punch' (2015).

'Prospect theory' suggests that individuals are more cautious when they feel they have an advantageous position and winning hand in any given situation, but exhibit riskier behaviour when they think they are in the weaker position and hold the losing hand. Russia's rhetoric reflects the former in that Russia portrays itself as being a rising power on the right side of history. In reality, President Putin understands US actions after 1991 as having destroyed a stable Cold War regulatory structure and that Russia needs to restore the lost ground and be willing to take risks to that end. Putin appears much more prepared to accept risks and is prepared to suffer greater losses than opponents to prevent what he perceives to be a negative outcome than to secure a positive gain. With such a mindset, a higher tolerance for escalation and brinkmanship to compensate for weakness is part of President Putin's costs/benefits risk assessment analysis. It is also likely that over time Putin's nominal escalation ceiling is raised as his tolerance for risk increases.

Manual control and the process of decision-making

Third, 'manual control' (*ruchnaya control*) suggests that Putin is the key decision maker and personally makes the decisions not through institutional processes, but rather through a small trusted inner circle. Decisions are made outside formal structures, are subject to few, if any, formal checks and balances, and can be best understood as opportunistic, tactical and improvised responses to changing circumstances.

As with each identifiable decision-making characteristic, a number of explanations can be advanced as to why Putin relies on manual control. Soviet security agencies were largely autonomous, a tradition that continued and increased as successor KGB security services were not reformed in the post-Soviet period, restructuring and relabeling rather than lustration was the dominant approach (Walther, 2014). In the Soviet period, the First Chief Directorate of the KGB, which subsequently became the Foreign Intelligence Service (SVR), received the top 25% of graduates and was considered the most prestigious service. However, the SCD, today's FSB, was the most powerful, perhaps influenced by its ability to gather *kompromat* on sitting presidents and key members of the elite, not least in the case of Putin, the Prosecutor General of the Russian Federation (Marten, 2017; Skak, 2016; Waller, 1994). In the post-Soviet period, security service elites infiltrated the banking, media, heavy industry sectors and Russia's defence industrial complex. This gave and continues to give the *siloviki* an agenda-setting ability when it comes to domestic and foreign policy. The *siloviki*'s cohesion and unity has been questioned, with some analysts highlighting a mafia clan-type entity, in which unity is illusionary – a 'mixed pattern of bureaucratic infighting and personal rivalry' within and between the services predominates (Bateman, 2014; Galeotti, 2016). Institutions in Russia are weak. The State Duma Committee on Defense and Committee on Security have oversight over Russia's military budget, but 'The so-called representative branch has completely abandoned all attempts to control the siloviki through the state budget' (Golts, 2017).

In enumerating inferred explanations for manual control, one key explanation is centred on the requirements of palace politics. President Putin's information monopoly and last-minute decision-making maintains his decision-making autonomy and space, keeps his own elite (Putinocracy/the Kremlin Towers) off-balance, maintains their loyalty and acts to prevent and so suppress dissent (Solovey, 2017). From Putin's perspective, unpredictability in the making and announcement of his decisions may also act to pre-empt potential entrapment of the president by formally loyal subordinates. The fact that Putin is so clearly making the decision also signals or messages his inner circle and the wider elite that the answer to the classic question – *Kto Koziayn?* ('who is the boss?') – is Putin. Putin is at pains to emphasize that he and he alone is the decision maker, the final arbiter, albeit one increasingly hostile to questioning. In terms of personality-based explanations, narcissism and personal drama are said to characterize the end result decisions, if not the decision-making process itself.

Personal preferences mesh with professional experience, training and learning. As a counter-intelligence case officer working in Dresden in the 1980s, rather than, for example, a former military commander used to working in hierarchical structures and commanding troops, Putin has a penchant for secret and hybrid operations which can have a powerful asymmetric effects. The preference for covert and undetected action over diplomacy is clear. Secrecy denotes a mode of operation hardwired into the behaviour of President Putin and his national security team, which, for the first time in Russian history, is dominated by secret policemen:

> The group is opaque: secrecy is its stock in trade—and it's good at its trade. Putin and this "komanda" (team), in power since late in 1999, may well remain in power for another decade at least ... As Soviet intelligence services were militarized—with ranks, uniforms and a martial ethos—they all have a military background and are trained in the use of weapons.
>
> *(Wilson, 2015)*

Opportunism and improvisation are the hallmarks, suggesting a tactical rather than strategic mindset. As Sergey Alexashenko, a former deputy finance minister and first deputy chairman of the Russian Central Bank, has observed:

> Putin is extremely good at tactical moves, but fails in strategy. His favourite sport is judo. Here, all you need is a general vision in mind – victory – but you can hardly build any strategy and, instead, you hope tactical decisions will lead you to your goal. Putin's lack of strategy has meant it is impossible to predict moves and actions. The continuing economic slide will force Putin to dedicate more time and efforts to the economy in the coming years. At the same time, we can expect his decisions to be chaotic and they will hardly allow the economy to recover.
>
> *(2016)*

Manual control lends itself to secrecy and improvisation and allows for quick decisions, and this constitutes an 'equalizer' when compared to Western adversaries as it facilitates 'strategic surprise'. Galeotti argues that while there is no single command and control centre, the Presidential Administration is primus inter pares, acting as the command and control hub for active measure, influence and other destabilization operations. Although the Russian Security Council is tasked with coordinating all security-related issues, relative to the Presidential Administration with its 2000 staff, seven departments and Presidential Councils, it is a much smaller entity. Its 200 plus staff exercise a more limited secretariat-type function and provide threat assessments and other reports (Galeotti, 2017, 8–10). Within this framework, Galeotti identifies two occasions in which Putin becomes more directly involved in the implementation of active measure operations: first, when cross-agency coordination is required, as none of the ministries have the power to tell others what to do; and, second, when the scale and risk of operation carries strategic-level implications, should the operation backfire (11–13).

Ambiguity, deniability and no-lose scenarios

Fourth, ambiguity characterizes the communication of decisions. A search for the word 'promise' on the President of the Russian Federation website generates 688 hits. Of these presidential promises, only about 150 are direct and unambiguous commitments to action and results, about a third are ambivalent and cautiously worded ('I will consider', 'get acquainted', 'puzzle out', 'will think about it', 'will return to the question', 'pay attention') and the balance consist of promises to perform. Control is maintained through 'a technique of uncertainty' as orders are 'issued in the form of an indirect hint or, as they say, a "signal", and that launches a new series of deals' are core characteristics. Gleb Pavlovsky, in his book *The Russian Federation System. Sources of Russian Strategic Behavior*, characterizes Putin's 2012–2015 style of management model as 'the style of indirect interpretation' in which his entourage have 'an incomplete idea about what has been decided and trying to remember the words Putin uttered'. Pavlovsky observes that President Putin 'builds relations in such a way that he can always say: I did not know that, and I did not promise that' and he has 'constructed above the regime an unreachable floor where he alone resides. And although he still has contact with his entourage, he does not want to bear responsibility for decisions' (2015). Mark Galeotti argues that Putin not an originator or initiator of specific operations but rather identifies 'broad objectives and aspirations', 'sets the tone' and then 'arbitrates between rival approaches, picks from a menu of options, or gives people enough rope to hang or lift themselves' (2017, 8–10).

Ambiguity clearly has a utility when conducting *maskirovaka* operations and destabilizing neighbours with a combination of conventional and sub-conventional actors as it evades responsibility and attribution, and so compounds the distraction, destruction and dismay of Russia's perceived adversaries. However, less prosaic explanations can also be advanced. First, such ambiguity suggests that Putin does not fully trust his own wider elite, just the inner core group that exactly shares and reinforces his own worldview. Conflicting and contradictory messages to subordinates can be the result. Second, ambiguous direction may also be a result of Putin telling subordinates and so drawing a line precisely around what subordinates cannot do to achieve a goal, rather than what they can. Third, the instruction 'do as you think best' also allows for plausible deniability – at least from the president – and maintains his ability to evade blame for losses by moving goal posts after the fact. Ambiguity also allows for flexibility in interpretation, to redefine success and failure and to attribute responsibility for either accordingly, and allows for a gap between Putin's words and actions to exist. Fourth, it may also reflect the notion that foreign policy under President Putin is as much about symbolic acts that assert Russia's international presence and boost patriotism at home and thereby 'simulate sovereignty as achieving stated goals'. Lastly, President Putin may have a line-of-sight on where he wants to take Russia – 'the vision thing' – but he is increasingly unable to effectively communicate it, let alone provide a clear understanding of the ways and means to get there, as noted above. He has 'vision' and tactics but not strategy; as a result, a corrosive sense of drift fills the vacuum. A deficit of strategy and statecraft may also reflect his need to compensate through the surfeit of stagecraft and theatricality that accompanies each decision. Ambiguity can be constructive in the sense that it allows President Putin to play a great power game without great power resources. President Putin can 'fail fast, fail cheap' and use ambiguity to construct 'no-lose' scenarios.

We can posit a number of different types of 'escalation ceilings' that exist. In the case of Ukraine (Crimea and Donbass), Putin crossed the line between the use of sub-conventional non-kinetic and conventional kinetic, and by placing nuclear forces on alert threatened to move from conventional military to nuclear. In the case of the DNC and the actions of 'patriotic' Russian hackers, is President Putin now prepared to cross the line between the deniable use of sub-conventional actors to destabilize and admitting culpability? This was a line he was not prepared to cross on 17 July 2014 with the shoot-down of the Malaysian Airliner MH17 or 16 October 2016 with the exposure of a GRU-backed Montenegrin coup attempt. By 2018, the utility of 'plausible deniability' and defensive-reactive rhetoric was severely eroded, as evidenced by the annihilation of the detached 'Wagner' battalion on 7 February by the US military in Syria, the 'Skripal affair', with the UK's 'no other plausible explanation' regarding the 'means, motive and record' (attribution and intent) and the Dutch report on the MH17 shoot-down.

US as Russia's strategic benchmark

Fifth, the US is Russia's strategic benchmark, the yardstick against which Russia compares itself. Putin is driven by his vision of Russia as a great power operating according to the logic of *par in parem non habet imperium* ('an equal has no authority over an equal'). When we examine strategic decisions in Putin's Russia and the explanations offered to account for them, decisions made are always framed as much in terms of gaining US recognition (respect and validation), demonstrating Russia has parity and equality with the US or in terms of castigation of the US (blame) and then 'victory' over the US, as securing the stated aim.

This notion manifests itself in various ways. Putin uses both Russia's past and what other Great Powers, especially the US, are now perceived to be gaining to gauge losses. With regard to Syria, Russia feels it achieves direct deconfliction negotiations with the US on Russian terms and so can demonstrate parity with the US. President Putin's initial suggestion that US-Russian cooperation in Syria might constitute a viable 'risk management model' attests to this desire. Cooperation in Syria would ideally from a Russian perspective become the precursor for a Yalta-Potsdam-II-type 'Grand Bargain' with the US. A formally codified restoration of parity, the two would negotiate a new balance of power, agree to new spheres of influence and construct anew a rules-based, predictable, stable international system. According to this understanding – somewhat undiplomatically iterated by both President Putin and Foreign Minister Lavrov – the US and Russia, along with Brazil, China and India, are the only five truly sovereign states in the world able to express and achieve 'legitimate interests', while all other states enjoy 'vassals' status – Ukraine, Belarus and Kazakhstan are vassals of Russia just as Britain, France and Germany are US vassals.

At the same time, Russia seeks to outsmart the US and achieved a Russian 'victory' at US expense. Thus, a successful Russian policy would be one that is supported by the majority of states and opposed by a diplomatically isolated US, whatever its intrinsic merits as a policy. Nuclear signalling highlights the fact that Russia has a nuclear triad (three-quarters of Russia's military budget is spent on nuclear weapons) and in this dimension parity with the US. Putin believes Russia has the right to break international rules and, indeed, that to break rules without being punished is the hallmark of a Great Power. To put it simply, Russia believes the US breaks rules and lies, so Russia has right and duty to follow suit: rule-breaking does not prohibit action, rather it encourages it; rule-breaking allows Russia to exploit the predictability of interlocutors in the international system. Putin appears to almost fetishize his ability to take decisions without constraints and this may reflect his relationship with George W. Bush, and what Putin viewed as Bush's ability to launch an invasion of Iraq without any particular constraints. Rule-breaking does not prohibit action, rather it encourages as to break rules without being punished is the hallmark of a Great Power.

It follows that the corollary to this is that to follow the rules as set by the West is to be a marginal and irrelevant player – a 'Greater Kazakhstan with nuclear weapons' (to reprise the 'upper Volta with rockets' epithet). Irrelevance in the Russian mindset is a worse outcome than being a target of US's deliberate provocations as the US constitutes a 'dignified foe' and as such to be insulted is at least to register and matter. In addition, Russia believes the US seeks to destabilize Russia through colour revolution type technology. Its hybrid war against the West is thus simply a reciprocal Great Power response, a form of psychological revenge that restores parity. In reality, behavioural and structural differences inform the US-Russian relationship: President Trump speaks from a 'position of strength', President Putin does not agree under pressure; Russia is too weak for the US to recognize as an equal, but too strong to be willing or able to accept unequal tactical allay status.

Conclusions

The philosophical beliefs of Putin and his inner circle of decision makers are in line with Russian strategic culture. Such a culture, understood by and shared between elites and society in Russia alike, is overlaid and interwoven with myths and narratives, history and tradition. It sets national interest and broad foreign policy objectives and thus becomes the paradigm within which Putin and those shaping, making and implementing strategic decisions exist. The means chosen to achieve national interest and broad foreign policy goals are a product of the instrumental beliefs (how much cooperation or conflict is necessary to achieve desired ends) of Putin's leadership regime. While strategic culture changes slowly and aligns with the philosophical belief systems of Russian decision makers, the instrumental beliefs of decision makers, particularly when they are making many decisions, change much faster.

Over Putin's fourth presidential term, a more visible gap will emerge between elite interests and society, between Russia's strategic culture and the elite's operational code. Under conditions of increased sanctions, economic stagnation and no structural economic reform, subjective elite decisions aimed primarily at protecting their luxurious consumption habits, physical mobility and economic assets, will clash with objective Russian national interests – modernization, prosperity and stability. Putin will seek to preserve Russia's role in the global system through regulating Russia's elite economic global connectedness with the need to promote cultural-psychological isolation of Russian society. Putin's decisions will increasingly be explained by the need to prevent Russia's defence coalition (Vaiyno, Chemezov and Rotenbergs), fuel-energy complex (Kiriyenko, Sechin and Kovalchuks) and system liberals (Medvedev, Chubays, and small and medium private businesses) from uniting in order to preserve his mediation/arbiter role within the regime. Power in Russia is a measure of an individual's network connectedness to Putin (rather than his official position), and this reflects the individual's purpose-fulfilling value for the network. Thus, intra-regime competition and infighting for shrinking resources will continue to be managed by unwritten rules and norms enforced by whole group, but guaranteed by Putin. Putin will strive to rise above the battle and control flows between network nodes using tied and tested management tools, not least: personnel changes and rotation; manipulation of rent flows, budgets and property redistribution; surveillance, investigations and selective prosecutions; the use of 'active measures' and *kompromat*; and the complicity of elite corruption and *sistema*. Thus, President Putin's evolving operational code will prove to be a litmus test of governance in the late Putin period.

Notes

1 This chapter reflects my own views and not those of the George C. Marshall European Center for Security Studies, the US Department of Defense or German Ministry of Defence.
2 Unless otherwise referenced, all media sources were accessed through the Open Source Enterprise database (www.opensource.gov), available to all US federal government employees.

References[2]

Alexashenko, Sergey (2016) 'Storm Clouds Ahead: Putin Lacks Strategy to Save Russia's Economy.' *The Moscow Times*, August 11.
Bateman, A. (2014) 'The Political Influence of the Russian Security Services.' *The Journal of Slavic military Studies*, Vol. 27, no. 3: 380–403.
Birnbaum, Michael, and David Filipov (2017) 'Russia Held a Big Military Exercise This Week. Here's Why the U.S. is Paying Attention.' *The Washington Post*, September 23. www.washingtonpost.com/world/europe/russia-held-a-big-military-exercise-this-week-heres-why-the-us-is-paying-attention/2017/09/23/3a0d37ea-9a36-11e7-af6a-6555caaeb8dc_story.html?utm_term=.e3c0974212e0
Dyson, Benedict, and Matthew J. Parent (2017 April) 'The Operational Code Approach to Profiling Political Leaders: Understanding Vladimir Putin.' *Intelligence and International Security*, Vol. 33, no. 1: 1–17.
Felgengauer, Pavel (2016) Interview by Ihor Fedyk. *On Russia's Tremendous 'Patience' with Developments in Ukraine*, Defense-Express website, in Russian, March 11.
Forsberg, Tuomas, and Christer Pursiainen (2017) 'The Psychological Dimension of Russian Foreign Policy: Putin and the Annexation of Crimea.' *Global Society*, Vol. 31, no. 2: 220–244.

Galeotti, Mark (2016) 'Putin's Hydra: Inside Russia's Intelligence Services.' *European Council on Foreign Relations*, May 11. www.ecfr.eu/publications/summary/putins_hydra_inside_russias_intelligence_services

Galeotti, Mark (2017) 'Controlling Chaos: How Russia manages its political war in Europe.' *European Council on Foreign Relations*, September 1. www.ecfr.eu/publications/summary/controlling_chaos_how_russia_manages_its_political_war_in_europe

George, Alexander L. (1969) 'The 'Operational Code': A Neglected Approach to the Study of Political Leaders and Decision-Making.' *International Studies Quarterly*, Vol. 13: 190–222.

Golts, Aleksandr (2017) 'How to Tell Jokes in a Madhouse. The So-Called Representative Branch Has Completely Abandoned All Attempts to Control the Security Agencies Through the State Budget.' *The New Times Online*, in Russian, October 10.

Inozemtsev, Vladislav (2017) 'Strength and Weakness of Vladimir Putin.' Moscow, *Snob Online*, in Russian, August 31.

Jensen, Kristian (Danish Foreign Minister) (2016) Interview by Jacob Svendsen. *Denmark: We Would Like to Have A Dialogue with Putin*. Politiken website, in Danish, July 7.

Judah, Ben (2014) 'Behind the Scenes in Putin's Court: The Private Habits of a Latter-Day Dictator.' *Newsweek*, August 23. www.newsweek.com/2014/08/01/behind-scenes-putins-court-private-habits-latter-day-dictator-260640.html

'Kremlin Blanks "Annexation"' (2017) 'Kremlin Blanks "Annexation" From German President's Speech on Crimea.' *The Moscow Times*, October 26. https://themoscowtimes.com/new/kremlin-blanks-word-annexation-from-german-presidents-speech-on-crimea-59373

Leites, Nathan (1951) *The Operational Code of the Politburo*. New York: McGraw-Hill.

Leites, Nathan (1953) *The Study of Bolshevism*. Chicago, IL: The Free Press.

MacFarquar, Neil (2016) 'A Powerful Russian Weapon: The Spread of False Stories.' *The New York Times*, August 28. www.nytimes.com/2016/08/29/world/europe/russia-sweden-disinformation.html

Marten, Kimberly (2017) 'The 'KGB state' and Russian Political and Foreign Policy Culture.' *The Journal of Slavic Military Studies*, Vol. 30. no. 2: 131–151.

Morozov, Viatcheslav (2013) 'Subaltern Empire? Towards a Postcolonial Approach to Russian Foreign Policy.' *Problems of Post-Communism*, Vol. 60, no. 6: 16–28.

Morozov, Viatcheslav (2015) *Russia's Postcolonial Identity: A Subaltern Empire in a Eurocentric World*. London: Palgrave Macmillan.

Patrushev, Nikolay (Russian Federation Security Council Secretary) (2016) Interview by Mikhail Rostovskiy. *Nikolay Patrushev: 'The International Community Should Thank Us for Crimea'; Russian Federation Security Council Secretary Says Why Russia Will Not Disintegrate Like the Soviet Union*, MK (Moskovskiy Komsomolets) website, Moscow, in Russian, January 27.

Pavlovskiy, Gleb (Effective Policy Foundation head) (2015a) Interview by Natalya Galimova. *The Kremlin Is Living Without Sensing the Country Beneath It*, Gazeta.ru website, in Russian, December 26.

Pavlovskiy, Gleb (2015b) 'Russia's System of Managed Chaos.' *The Moscow Times*, in English, October 22.

Putin, Vladimir (2016a) *For Me, It Is Not Borders That Matter*. Interview by Nikolaus Blome, Kai Diekmann, and Daniel Biskop. Bild, in German, January 11.

Putin, Vladimir (2016b) *We Do Not Claim the Role of a Superpower*. Interview by Nikolaus Blome, Kai Diekmann, and Daniel Biskop. Bild, in German, January 12.

Rostovskiy, Mikhail (2016) 'Nikolay Patrushev: 'The International Community Should Thank Us For Crimea'; Russian Federation Security Council Secretary Says Why Russia Will Not Disintegrate Like the Soviet Union'; Moscow, *MK Online*, in Russian January 27.

Skak, Mette (2016) 'Russian Strategic Culture: The Role of Today's Chekisty.' *Contemporary Politics*, Vol. 22, no. 3: 324–341. doi:10.1080/13569775.2016.1201317

Solovey, Valeriy (political analyst) (2017) Interview by Aleksandr Grishin. *Political Analyst: Putin Has Postponed Nomination for New Term Until October to See How People in Power React*, Komsomolskaya Pravda Online, in Russian, August 29.

Stanovaya, Tatyana (2017) 'Despot and Liberal, or How Vladimir Putin's Secret World Is Becoming Manifest. Putin Lives in Two Worlds That Are Compatible but by No Means Identical: A World of "Proprieties" and a World of "Fighting the Enemy".' *Republic*, in Russian, November 1.

Usackas, Vygaudas (EU Ambassador to Russia) (2017) Interview by Yelena Chernenko. *Russia's Road to Europe Goes Through Kyiv*. Kommersant Online, in Russian, September 27.

Vishnevsky, Boris (2017) 'Same Old Songs About the Real Thing. If Navalny Aspires to Power He Must Get Used to Criticism. Boris Vishnevsky's Response to Yulia Latynina.' *Novaya Gazeta* website, in Russian, July 18.

Walker, Stephan G. (1983) 'The Motivational Foundation of Political Belief Systems: A Re-Analysis of the Operational Code Construct.' *International Studies Quarterly*, Vol. 27: 180.

Wallander, Celeste (one of Barack Obama's top advisors on Russia) (2015) Interview by 'Meduza' *Putin's Tactics May Be Brilliant*, MEDUZA, November 12.

Waller, Michael J. (1994) *Secret Empire: The KGB in Russia Today*. Boulder, CO: Westview Press, pp. 13–15.

Walther, Ulf (2014) 'Russia's Failed Transformation: The Power of the KGB/FSB from Gorbachev to Putin.' *International Journal of Intelligence and Counter-Intelligence*, Vol. 27: 666–686. See also: Interview with Valeriy Solovey by Ivan Davydov; date, place not given, 'Even the President's Friends Cannot Always Influence Decisionmaking.' Moscow, *The New Times*, in Russian, 24 April 2017.

Weiss, Michael (2016) 'The Baltic Elves Taking on Pro-Russian Trolls.' *The Daily Beast*, March 21. www.thedailybeast.com/articles/2016/03/20/the-baltic-elves-taking-on-pro-russian-trolls.html

Wilson, Kyle (2015) 'Putin the Chekist: A Sacred Calling.' *The Strategist*, in English, November 4.

Winkler, Thomas (Danish Ambassador to Russia) (2017) 'The Threat from Russia: Realities and Reactions.' Copenhagen, *Berlingske Online*, in Danish, August 21.

3

THE SOVIET LEGACY IN RUSSIAN SECURITY POLICY

Mark Kramer

> Today, Russia's Soviet-era institutions stamp out any idealism. It will take more than one generation to change that.
>
> —*Lev Gudkov (October 2017)*

After the Soviet Union broke apart in late December 1991 and the Russian Federation emerged as an independent country, Russian political leaders had to confront a wide range of foreign policy issues left over from the Soviet regime. The series of agreements codifying the dissolution of the Soviet Union, which led to the formation of the Commonwealth of Independent States (CIS) and broad international recognition of 15 new states by the end of 1991, designated Russia as the 'legal successor state' to the USSR, a status that, for many Russian leaders (both then and now), has blurred Soviet and Russian interests. As the official successor state, Russia was given sole possession of the vast Soviet nuclear arsenal and was also awarded the USSR's permanent seat on the United Nations (UN) Security Council.[1] In return, Russia took ultimate responsibility for the Soviet Union's foreign hard-currency debt to both private and government creditors. These and other formal aspects of the Soviet inheritance were bound to affect Russian foreign policy after 1991.

Equally important have been the informal dimensions of the Soviet legacy. The sense of a 'loss of empire' and of a continuity with the Soviet 'superpower' past have influenced the orientation, methods, and goals of Russian foreign policy over time, particularly after the mid- to late 1990s. As Lev Gudkov notes in the epigraph to this essay, the institutions and mindsets of the Soviet era were so deeply engrained that they could not be eradicated in a single generation or two. Indeed, far from diminishing, they have gained ever greater tenacity in the wake of Russian President Vladimir Putin's annexation of Crimea in 2014 and military intervention in Syria from 2015 on.

By now, nearly three decades after the Soviet Union disintegrated, some elements of the Soviet legacy have disappeared or abated, but others have endured. This essay briefly reviews the sundry aspects of the Soviet legacy, both formal and informal.[2] Russian foreign and security policy has departed from Soviet policy in numerous ways, but a good deal of continuity has also been evident.

The legacy of personnel and worldviews

One key reason for the relatively high degree of continuity with the Soviet past was the carryover of personnel. Many of the senior and mid-ranking Russian foreign policy officials, nearly all of the highest-ranking Russian military and intelligence officers, and a sizeable number of Russian political leaders got their start in public life during the Soviet era. Although all organs of the Communist Party of the Soviet Union (CPSU) ceased to exist after August 1991, most of the Soviet government bureaucracy, including the Ministry of Foreign Affairs (MID), the diplomatic corps, the Ministry of Defence, the State Security apparatus (the KGB, which was preserved largely unchanged but separated into what became the Federal Security Service, or FSB, and the Foreign Intelligence Service, or SVR), and other Soviet ministries and agencies handling foreign policy and national security were absorbed almost wholly intact by the Russian Federation after 1991 (Fedor, 2011).

The establishment of a presidential system in Russia, codified by the December 1993 constitution, meant that the highest policymaking organs in Russia were shaped and reshaped to conform to the post-Soviet era, but nearly all of the officials who served on these bodies got their start in the CPSU or the Soviet government (or both) (Gill, 1998). Although the passage of time has allowed for the emergence of younger elites who came of age after the breakup of the USSR, most of the officials on Russia's highest foreign policymaking and security bodies as of 2018 worked for the Soviet regime prior to 1991. In part for this reason, their outlook on foreign policy issues and on Russia's legitimate place in the world has tended to replicate some of the *Weltanschauung* of their Soviet past. Some, such as Vladimir Putin, Igor Sechin, Sergei Naryshkin, Nikolai Patrushev, Aleksandr Bortnikov, Viktor Zolotov, Andrei Belyaninov, Dmitrii Kochnev, Sergei Ivanov, and others who emerged from the KGB's ranks, have tended to embrace many of the concepts that characterised Soviet foreign policy in the years before it was transformed by the advent of Mikhail Gorbachev in 1985. The 'new thinking' in foreign policy under Gorbachev never took hold at the KGB.

During the first several years of the post-Soviet period, all of the mid-level and senior officials working in Russia's foreign policy and national security-related ministries had begun their careers under the Soviet regime. With time, some younger officials have joined these agencies in significant capacities, but the majority of the most influential foreign policy advisers are still holdovers from the Soviet period. To varying degrees, they have adapted to the post–Cold War era and to Russia's altered place in the world, but large bureaucracies are slow to change, and institutional outlooks tend to persist for years. Hence, it is not surprising that advice and inputs from the foreign policy and security agencies after 1991 have often reflected these bodies' Soviet pedigree.

The impact of the Soviet institutional outlook on Russian foreign policy has perhaps best been reflected in the perennial emphasis on Russia's status as a 'great power' and in the persistence of tensions with the West.[3] Even in the mid- to late 1990s, when Russian leaders were acutely aware that Russia did not carry the same weight in the world that the Soviet Union did, many of them were wont to fall back on the precepts that guided Soviet foreign policy. This was evident, for example, when Yeltsin and Russian military commanders sent an armoured column to Pristina airport in Kosovo in June 1999 in a direct challenge to the North Atlantic Treaty Organisation (NATO) that nearly led to a military clash.[4]

Under Putin, attempts to reassert great power status have become much more pronounced, especially in the years since he returned to the presidency in 2012 for his third and fourth terms. When Putin told the Russian parliament in April 2005 that 'the collapse of the Soviet Union was the greatest geopolitical catastrophe of the [20th] century', he was candidly summarizing his values and outlook, implying that his task as president is to undo that 'catastrophe' (Putin, 2005). The failure to make a complete break with the Soviet past helps to account for the difficulty that arose in the early to mid-1990s when some in Moscow hoped to integrate Russia more fully into the West (difficulty that was compounded by the durability of Cold War–era mindsets in some Western capitals and also by the deep concern in Poland and the Baltic states about potential threats from Russia, which spurred them to push relentlessly for NATO membership). Under Putin, officials in the key foreign policy and national security agencies have fallen back even more heavily on Soviet-era notions and principles, including an opportunistic reliance on anti-Westernism and xenophobia for internal control (Kramer, 2014b). These sorts of outlooks were present even before 2013–2014, but they have come to dominate Russian national security policy-making since the start of Russia's armed intervention in Ukraine and the deep tensions it caused with Western countries.

After Putin introduced Russian military forces into Syria in September 2015, he and other Russian officials repeatedly depicted the intervention as the type of action taken by great powers to manage international crises ('Rossiya pomogla Sirii', 2016; 'Rossiya – velikaya derzhava', 2016; 'Putin vernul Rossii', 2017). The emphasis on Russia's status as a great power in the wake of the annexation of Crimea and the intervention in Syria gave a strong fillip to Putin's favourability ratings. Public opinion surveys conducted by the Levada Centre (a widely respected polling firm) from 2014 through 2018 have shown that the main reason for the sharp increase in Putin's popularity from early 2014 was the Russian public's belief that he had succeeded in 'restoring Russia's status as a respected great power', an outcome most Russians viewed as Putin's 'greatest achievement' ('Velikaya derzhava', 2016).

Having become accustomed to the status of a global superpower during the Soviet era, many Russians in the 1990s had felt disoriented by the status to which Russia was relegated after 1991. Even though domestic upheavals and priorities dominated most Russians' attention in the 1990s, the loss of superpower status was frequently cited as a concern in opinion polls and focus groups (Analiticheskii Tsentr Yuriya Levady, 2006; Andreev, 2002; Bashkirova and Fedorov, 1999; Fedorov, Baskakova, and Zhirikova, 2017; Oslon et al., 2003; Popov, 2007). Hence, it is not surprising that Putin's efforts to 'return Russia to the position of a great power'—and thus to revive a key element of Soviet foreign policy—enjoyed widespread public backing.

The Soviet geographic legacy, Part 1: disputes inherited from the USSR

Another factor ensuring important strands of continuity with Soviet foreign policy is the impact of geography. Russia is one of only 15 countries that emerged from the Soviet Union, but it is vastly larger than any of the others and remains by far the world's largest country. The territory of the Soviet Union was around 22.4 million square kilometres, whereas the Russian Federation is only 17.13 million square kilometres, but Russia still accounts for more than one-eighth of all inhabited land in the world. The territory of Russia, spread over 11 time zones, is nearly double the size of Canada, the United States, and China, each of which is just over 9.5 million square kilometres. The external border of Russia extends for nearly 57,800 kilometres, by far the world's longest, including borders with 14 countries and lengthy borders on various seas and oceans.

Many of the geographic realities that helped to shape Soviet foreign policy are still present for Russia (Donaldson, Nogee, and Narkarni, 2014; Marshall, 2015, pp. 11–37). Russia, like the USSR, straddles both Europe and Asia, constituting a true Eurasian country. As in the Soviet Union, nearly 80 per cent of Russia's population lives in the western (European) part of the country, but the sparsely populated Asian part is more than three times larger—much larger than any other country on earth. The immense plains in western and eastern Russia and the steppe lands in southern Russia are not easily defensible against possible incursions. The vast stretches of Russia's boundaries cannot be protected in any ironclad way, especially in the Caucasus where formidable mountains severely complicate the tasks of border guards. Although Russia has lengthy borders with oceans and seas, the country possesses few outlets to open waters that are not frozen over for at least part of the year. These geographical circumstances are very similar to the ones that faced Soviet Communist Party leaders and helped to shape their decisions about foreign policy and national security. Geography does not determine everything, but the similar geographical constraints and endowments of the USSR and Russia are bound to cause Russian policymakers to approach many key issues in the same way Soviet leaders did.

For reasons of expediency, the Soviet Union dissolved along the borders of the 15 union-republics as they existed in 1991. This left Russia with borders that were challenged by some neighbouring countries, including former union-republics. In the Far East, Russia inherited the Southern Kurile Islands, which had been annexed by the Soviet Union at the end of World War II. Those islands, called the Northern Territories by Japan, have been an acute source of acrimony between Moscow and Tokyo ever since.[5] In 1992, after the Soviet Union broke apart, some observers in both Russia and Japan expected that President Boris Yeltsin might grant territorial concessions to entice the Japanese into making large investments in Russia. No such breakthrough ever occurred. In the face of domestic opposition, Yeltsin abruptly cancelled a planned visit to Japan in October 1992. When he did eventually travel to Japan a year later, the negotiations produced no results, and the same has been true of all other bilateral meetings in the years since. The territorial dispute has continued to forestall any major improvement of relations between the two countries. Even after Shinzo Abe became Japanese prime minister in 2012 and launched a vigorous effort to forge a solution with Putin, the Russian government did not alter its stance ('Putin Urges Patience', 2018). Laws adopted in Russia under both Yeltsin and Putin makes it all but impossible for the Russian government to consider reviving a compromise proposed by the Soviet government in October 1956 (the return of the two smallest islands, an offer rejected by Japan), much less agreeing to transfer back all four of the islands (Hara, 1991; Rozman, 2017). The deadlock seems likely to continue for years to come.

Russia also inherited 4,300 kilometres of boundaries with China that were originally established by treaties imposed on China in the mid-nineteenth century and then reaffirmed by the Soviet authorities in the 1920s and early 1950s. The Chinese Communist regime headed by Mao Zedong expressed a strong aversion to these 'unequal treaties' from an early stage, and after a bitter rift emerged between the Soviet Union and China at the end of the 1950s a series of territorial disputes between the two countries culminated in large-scale armed clashes on the disputed Damanskii (Zhenbao) Island on the Ussuri (Wūsūlǐ) River in March 1969 and an even bloodier confrontation in Xinjiang province in August 1969. Violence did not recur after 1969, but the borders remained in dispute for several more decades. Four years of negotiations in the late 1980s and early 1990s led to the signing of a border agreement in May 1991 that settled numerous important issues ('Soglashenie', 1993, pp. 5–12). The Soviet government had not yet ratified the agreement by the time the USSR broke apart, but Russia ratified it in 1992 and joined with China the next year to redefine the boundary line near Hunchun along the Hubutu River (Gu Liping, 2015, Item 14).[6] Even then, however, several issues remained in contention. Some were resolved in 1998, and the remainder were settled in October 2004 and May 2008, when Russia proved willing to accept China's position. Putin's concessions were spurred by his desire to strengthen ties with China as a counter against U.S. hegemony. The resolution of the border dispute gained scant notice in most of the world, but in Russia several political commentators focusing on the Far East expressed concern that Russia had yielded too much, possibly tempting China to push for concessions on other matters such as labour migration ('Kitaitsy privetstvuyut', 2015; 'Kitai zhdet ot Rossii peredachu Sahalina', 2015; Masyuk, 2015, pp. 8–9).

The Soviet geographic legacy, Part 2: disputes resulting from the breakup

The borders Russia inherited with former Soviet republics at the end of 1991 also have had far-reaching effects on Russian foreign policy. The Crimean peninsula was part of the Russian Soviet Federation of Socialist Republics until February 1954, when the Soviet government at Nikita Khrushchev's behest transferred Crimea to the Ukrainian Soviet Socialist Republic, ostensibly to mark the 300th anniversary of the Battle of Pereyaslav (Kramer, 2014a). At the time, the transfer seemed relatively insignificant because union-republic borders were of little importance in the highly centralised USSR. Only after the Soviet Union broke apart did the status of Crimea become a major source of friction between the two newly independent countries. During Leonid Kravchuk's presidency in Ukraine from 1991 to 1994, the Russian and Ukrainian governments repeatedly quarrelled and exchanged threats over Crimea and the division of the USSR's Black Sea Fleet (Kramer, 1998, pp. 253–333). The Russian government began actively helping the Crimean separatist movement headed by Yurii Meshkov, who wanted to return Crimea to its pre-1954 status, as part of Russia rather than Ukraine. The advent of Leonid Kuchma, who forged a much more amicable relationship with Russia after he won the Ukrainian presidency in July 1994, markedly reduced the degree of tension over Crimea.

Nonetheless, the issue continued to dog Russian-Ukrainian relations over the next two decades, particularly when the status of Russia's Black Sea Fleet came up for renegotiation in 2010. When Viktor Yushchenko was elected president of Ukraine in late 2004, he promised to end the Russian Navy's presence in Crimea once the existing lease for the Black Sea Fleet (signed in the early 1990s) expired in 2017. However, after Viktor Yanukovych was elected as Yushchenko's successor in February 2010, he agreed to extend the lease by 25 years—to 2042—ostensibly in return for concessions on pricing of Russian natural gas (though the purported concessions on gas pricing seemed ethereal). The extension was denounced in many quarters of Ukraine, setting the stage for Putin's actions in the wake of the Euromaidan Revolution of 2013–2014, an event that caught him off-guard (Kramer, 2014b, pp. 1–7). After the violent overthrow of Yanukovych in February 2014, Putin dispatched heavily armed troops to occupy and seize control of Crimea, which he then formally annexed to the Russian Federation at a Kremlin ceremony in mid-March 2014.

Russia's borders with Estonia, Georgia, Azerbaijan, and even Kazakhstan have also influenced Russian foreign policy. The border issue with Estonia has been at an impasse for almost the entire post-Soviet era. Because NATO had stipulated that prospective new members of the alliance would have to resolve border disputes with their neighbours before applying to join, the Russian authorities from the mid-1990s on deliberately refrained from trying to resolve the conflict with Estonia, hoping to derail the country's chances of gaining membership in NATO. The United States and other allied member-states, upon realising what was going on, pledged that deliberate obstruction of border negotiations by another party would not affect the possible entry of the Baltic countries into NATO (Kramer, 2002, pp. 731–756). Yet, even after Estonia along with Latvia and Lithuania was invited to join the alliance in November 2002 (and was then formally admitted in 2004), talks on the Russian-Estonian border dispute remained stalled until May 2005, when the two countries signed a border treaty along with a separate bilateral agreement demarcating their maritime boundaries ('Dogovor', 2005). Soon thereafter, Russia abruptly rescinded its signature of both treaties and kept them in abeyance until February 2014, when Russian Foreign Minister Sergei Lavrov signed a slightly modified version with his Estonian counterpart ('Dogovor', 2014). Nevertheless, neither country ultimately ratified the treaties, and the Russian government continued to exploit the border dispute as a source of pressure vis-à-vis Estonia and NATO.

Because NATO began secret planning in 2009 to expand the alliance's Eagle Guardian 'defence plan' for Poland to cover the whole 'Baltic region' against an unspecified enemy, the problematic status of the Russian-Estonian border potentially could affect NATO's relations with Russia. In 2010, after the alliance's expanded defence planning for the 'Baltic region' came to light in documents released through Wikileaks (allusions to the planning had already surfaced in 2009, but the documents confirmed the new efforts), Russian officials declared that 'hostile actions' by NATO member-states would not deter Russia from defending its 'legitimate territorial claims' (Kramer, 2013, 2015).[7]

The borders Russia inherited with Georgia have affected bilateral ties from the moment the Soviet Union broke apart. The Russian government backed separatist forces in two regions of Georgia adjoining Russia, South Ossetia and Abkhazia. With military support from Russia, both regions established de facto independence from Georgia in 1992–1993 (Birch, 1996, pp. 150–189; Hewitt, 1996, pp. 190–225; Baev, Zürcher, and Koehler, 2005, pp. 259–298; George, 2009). Russian 'peacekeeping' forces remained deployed in the two regions long after the Georgian government demanded that they leave and long after 1999 amendments to the Conventional Forces in Europe (CFE) Treaty—to which Russia was a party until its withdrawal from the treaty in March 2015—required the Russian army to pull out all its forces. In August 2008, Russia finished the process that had begun in 1992–1993. Russian military forces were able to overwhelm the much smaller Georgian army after war broke out over South Ossetia (Cornell and Starr, 2009, pp. 143–185; Independent International Fact-Finding Mission, 2009; Allison, 2013, pp. 150–169). The war gave Russian authorities the opportunity to carve both South Ossetia and Abkhazia off from Georgia and to recognise them as independent states.

Although Moldova does not border on Russia, it has encountered similar problems involving Russian support for separatist forces in Transnistria, a region that was a legacy of the Soviet era. Russian forces intervened in Transnistria and Moldova in 1992 to protect the separatist government of Igor Smirnov, who aspired to sever Transnistria from Moldova and have it become part of the USSR again (King, 2000; Bomeshko, 2017; Coyle, 2018, pp. 157–178). Russian troops have remained deployed there ever since, despite repeated requests by the Moldovan government for them to leave and despite the 1999 amendments to the CFE Treaty (now renounced by Russia) requiring that they pull out. Although negotiations organised by the Organisation for Security and Co-operation in Europe (OSCE) in 2016 and 2017 achieved some results, the net impact on the conflict was evanescent at best. The deadlocked status of Transnistria is not as acute an irritant in Russian-Moldovan relations as the occupation of South Ossetia and Abkhazia is in Russian-Georgian relations, but until the issue is resolved (which seems unlikely anytime soon), the dispute hinders an improvement of bilateral relations between Russia and Moldova and induces Moldova to look more to the European Union (EU) (Calus and Kosienkowski, 2018, pp. 111–148; Flenley and Mannin, 2018).

The Soviet geographic legacy, Part 3: other key aspects

Beyond the conflicts Russia has experienced with individual countries as a result of the borders left over from the Soviet Union, the sprawling expanse of Russia, with long borders stretching from the Kaliningrad exclave in the west to Sakhalin in the Far East, has had far-reaching effects on Russian foreign policy since 1992. As noted earlier, Russian territory includes huge areas that are difficult to defend, whether from China, from a spillover of Islamic extremism in Central Asia, or from NATO. To the extent that Russian political leaders and military commanders have seen their country as potentially vulnerable to attack from outside, they have sought to maintain a large army, a task that has imposed a considerable economic burden. Even in the 1990s, when precipitous cuts were made in military spending, the Russian armed forces were kept artificially large to defend Russia's borders (Miller and Trenin, 2004). Under Putin, military spending has sharply increased, and both conventional and nuclear forces have been expanded and modernised (Cooper, 2016; U.S. Defense Intelligence Agency, 2017; Renz, 2018). Some economic officials, such as Aleksei Kudrin, have advocated cuts in military expenditures, but proposals for lower spending along with reductions in troop levels have been firmly rejected in recent years by senior figures who argue that Russia's enormous land mass must be adequately defended against 'hostile forces'.

Whether this is truly feasible is, of course, a different matter. The vast transportation and communications difficulties that would arise when deploying large contingents of troops from one remote part of the country to another would make it hard to defend against all potential adversaries no matter how large the armed forces are. Regardless, most Russian political leaders have come to believe that Russia, as the world's largest country, must possess military forces of a commensurate size.

One final geographic circumstance of Russia that is redolent of the Soviet (and Tsarist) era is the question of whether the country should look more to Europe or to Asia. As the largest single entity on both continents, Russia, like the Soviet Union before it, has had to decide on the geographic orientation of its foreign policy. During the Cold War, the primary focus of Soviet foreign policy was always the United States, but within that context Soviet foreign policy shifted between Europe and Asia. From 1949 to 1959, the emergence of a Communist regime in the People's Republic of China (PRC), the establishment of a close Sino-Soviet alliance, the three-year war on the Korean peninsula (in which large numbers of Soviet military pilots were secretly involved), and the advent of a friendly government in India caused Soviet foreign policy to be oriented toward Asia. However, after a bitter Sino-Soviet split erupted at the end of the 1950s, Soviet foreign policy gravitated back toward Europe, in part because Soviet leaders wanted to ensure that the Warsaw Pact countries would side firmly with the USSR against the PRC. One Warsaw Pact country, Albania, did side with China and eventually left the Warsaw Pact, but all the others (with the partial exception of Romania from the mid-1960s on) remained staunchly loyal to Moscow. After the Soviet invasion of Czechoslovakia in 1968 solidified the East-West divide in Europe, Soviet leaders shifted even more of their focus to Europe, spurred on by the advent of West Germany's Ostpolitik. The Soviet-West European détente that gathered pace in the 1970s survived the breakdown of the U.S.-Soviet détente in the late 1970s and early 1980s, reinforcing the Soviet Union's orientation toward Europe. Although Soviet leaders preserved close ties with Communist governments in Mongolia and Vietnam (and to a lesser extent North Korea) and made conciliatory overtures toward China starting in 1982, the primary orientation of Soviet foreign policy throughout the 1970s and 1980s, including the momentous six-and-a-half years under Mikhail Gorbachev (1985–1991), was still mainly toward Europe along with North America.

The Russian government under both Yeltsin and especially Putin has fluctuated between Europe and Asia. On the one hand, EU countries are still the dominant customers for Russian natural gas (a supply relationship that began in the 1980s and is reflected in the westward orientation of Russia's gas export pipeline network), and Russia's place in the Council of Europe makes European norms hard to ignore entirely (Neumann, 2017).[8] On the other hand, Russia's disaffection with NATO and especially with the United States have caused Russian leaders to emphasise, at least rhetorically, entities that link Russia with Asian countries such as the Shanghai Cooperation Organisation and the Collective Security Treaty Organisation (Allison, 2004, pp. 463–483; Kramer, 2008; Lukin, 2018). More generally, efforts to forge links with China and India as counterweights to U.S. power ensure that Russia, like the Soviet Union in earlier decades, will adhere to an orientation that best suits its interests at a given time.

Perquisites of the 'legal successor state'

As noted above, Russia was designated the 'legal successor state' to the USSR via the international agreements that codified the dissolution of the Soviet Union and the creation of new countries. One of the perquisites of this status was Russia's inheritance of the permanent seat on the UN Security Council that had been held by the USSR from the mid-1940s on (Blum, 1992, pp. 354–361). That position lent visibility to the USSR's claim of being a dominant power in the world and a vantage point from which to try to obstruct U.S. and West European actions. Even though the East-West split on the UN Security Council (and the paralysis that often ensued) meant that both superpowers routinely bypassed the Security Council on key national security issues, the USSR's permanent seat gave Soviet policymakers greater ability to try to affect important issues such as the Middle East.

Russia's inheritance of the Soviet Union's permanent seat on the UN Security Council has afforded Russian leaders many of the same levers at a time of greater opportunity to make use of them. With the end of the Cold War, the UN Security Council came to be a more prominent and functional body (especially in the early to mid-1990s), a body often depicted as the 'legitimate' forum for international discussions and decision-making. That factor alone ensured that Russia, by inheriting a permanent seat, would gain a key vantage point from which to try to influence and, when necessary, obstruct U.S. foreign policy. Because Russia still has fewer alternatives than the Soviet Union did to hinder and thwart U.S. actions, Russia's permanent seat on the UN Security Council is considerably more important, in relative terms, for Russia than it was for the Soviet Union.

Russia's veto within the UN Security Council did not prevent the United States from going to war against Serbia in 1999 and against Iraq in 2003, nor did it prevent most Western governments from recognising Kosovo as an independent country in 2008, a step vehemently opposed by Russia. But on many other key issues (the ongoing crisis in Syria, Iran's nuclear weapons program, etc.), Russia has been adept at using the UN Security Council to stymie effective action and to ensure that any measures approved by the Security Council will be conducive to Russia's interests (Grishaeva, 2007; Belenkova, 2012, pp. 147–150). Hence, it is not surprising that Russian officials have vigorously promoted the UN Security Council as the only appropriate forum for deciding matters of war and peace (though Russia itself has used military force many times since 1991 without UN Security Council authorization).

The other major perquisite inherited by Russia as the successor state to the Soviet Union is control over the huge array of strategic and tactical nuclear forces, including land- and sea-based missiles and heavy bombers, as well as the nuclear armaments production complex that built all the weaponry (Blank, 2011). Although reductions in ex-Soviet strategic nuclear weapons were carried out after 1991 in accordance with U.S.-Soviet and U.S.-Russian bilateral agreements, Russia has retained a vast nuclear arsenal capable of wreaking catastrophic destruction on the United States and its allies. Putin, in his March 2018 annual address to the Russian parliament, boasted about the 'remarkable advances' in Russian nuclear forces under his leadership that drew on but went beyond the Soviet legacy:

> [Russia's] newly developed strategic arms—in fact, new types of strategic weapons—are not the result of something left over from the Soviet Union. Of course, we relied on some ideas from our ingenious predecessors. But everything I have described today is the result of the last several years, the product of dozens of research organizations, design bureaus, and institutes.
>
> *('Poslanie Prezidenta Federal'nomu Sobraniyu', 2018, pp. 1–3)*

Although it is certainly true that Russia's nuclear weaponry has been significantly modernised over the past 15 years, the very fact that Russia is a nuclear weapons state and possesses a nuclear arms production complex that oversaw the modernisation is entirely a legacy of the Soviet era.

The preservation of the Soviet nuclear weapons legacy ensured that Russia remained high on the U.S. security agenda and a key global actor throughout the post-Soviet era, but the impact of the legacy did not always benefit Russian foreign policy. The carryover of the Soviet nuclear arsenal was part of the reason that Russian political and military leaders made only erratic progress with proposals for military reform for nearly two decades after the demise of the USSR (Gol'ts, 2014). Russia's strategic nuclear power acted as a crutch or a cushion for Russian leaders to fall back on, giving them little incentive to stick with arduous reforms that were politically and bureaucratically costly.

To the extent that the cushioning effect of the ex-Soviet nuclear arsenal detracted from Russia's non-nuclear capabilities, it limited some of Russia's foreign policy options during Putin's first two terms. Even against a very small country like Georgia in August 2008, Russian military performance was marred by crucial shortcomings (Bukkvoll, 2009, pp. 57–63; McDermott, 2009, pp. 65–80; Vendil Pallin and Westerlund, 2009, pp. 400–424). But that event proved to be a turning point for the Russian military. The defence minister at the time, Anatoly Serdyukov, was able to point to the Russian army's lacklustre performance against Georgia to make the case for wide-ranging military reforms. These reforms were accompanied by significant increases in Russian military spending, which rose still further after Putin returned to the presidency in 2012. Although Serdyukov was forced out amid scandals in November 2012, the Russian armed forces continued to improve under his successor, Sergei Shoigu, who has enjoyed Putin's full support. The major improvements in Russia's conventional forces were very much evident during Russia's seizure of Crimea and military operations in and near eastern Ukraine as well as the Russian air operations in Syria.

Even though Russia now has far more non-nuclear military options than it did during the 1990s, the nuclear inheritance from the Soviet Union will remain a dominant part of

Russian national security policy. For Putin, as for Yeltsin, Russia's nuclear forces are the key equaliser, guaranteeing not only Russian security against external threats but also the country's great-power standing.

Conceptions of global and regional alignments

In part because of Russia's own ambivalence and in part because of certain actions by NATO, many Russian officials and most high-ranking Russian military commanders after 1991 continued to see—or came to see—Russia as still being fundamentally at odds with NATO and even at odds with the EU. Even though most of them did not perceive NATO as a dire threat (the sort of image that prevailed during the Cold War), they did sense that Russia's and NATO's interests were incompatible and they continued to view the relationship between the two mainly in zero-sum terms.

This sense of an enduring conflict with NATO has spurred the Russian government's frequent pronouncements under both Yeltsin and Putin about the desirability of a 'multipolar world' (Haynes, 2009). Such appeals are reminiscent of the Soviet Union's efforts in the 1930s to fashion a 'collective security' arrangement that would constrain German power. The post-1991 rhetorical emphasis on the need for a multipolar world has been crafted with a similar goal—in this case, to limit and impede U.S. and NATO power. Even officials who do not perceive a military threat from the United States and its allies have assented to security arrangements that impede NATO's actions.

The Russian government's espousal of a multipolar world is designed to preserve a hierarchical global order based on spheres of influence, with Russia enjoying complete freedom of action in its own sphere, the CIS (Kramer, 2008). This conception is similar to the scheme the Soviet Union pursued in Europe during the Cold War. In much the same way that the Soviet Union maintained hegemony over Eastern Europe as codified in the Brezhnev Doctrine, so too has Russia sought freedom of action within the CIS. The hegemonic Warsaw Pact regional system of the Soviet era was at times explicitly cited by Russian officials in the 1990s when they thought about the sort of arrangement they wanted in the CIS, and this legacy of the past has been equally salient under Putin. After the Russian army defeated Georgian forces in the August 2008 war and facilitated the separation of South Ossetia and Abkhazia from Georgia's jurisdiction, Russian leaders proclaimed that 'Russia, like other [great powers] in the world, has regions in which it enjoys privileged interests' and can act with impunity (Kuzar, 2008, p. 1). Putin expanded on this notion in March 2014, declaring that Russia 'must consistently defend [its] national interests' in its sphere of influence and thwart 'external interference' there, or else 'we will forever give in and retreat to who knows where' ('Obrashchenie Prezidenta Rossiiskoi Federatsii', 2014, pp. 1, 3).

Although Russian hegemonic power in the CIS does not have the same sort of ideological overlay that Soviet power did in the Warsaw Pact, Russian leaders have embraced their own version of the Brezhnev Doctrine. The notion of a regional hierarchy headed by Moscow—whether to protect orthodox Communist regimes or to safeguard the interests of ethnic Russian communities in neighbouring countries—is quintessentially the same. In both cases, it envisages a hegemonic state that enjoys an unfettered right to exercise dominance over its smaller neighbouring states.

Russian weapons supplies to the Third World

The Russian government inherited some 70–80 per cent of the huge Soviet military-industrial base. Although most of Russia's military industries fell on hard times in the 1990s amid steep reductions in military spending that sharply curtailed the quantity of new weapons procured by the Russian army, Russian weapons plants tried to make up part of the gap by selling more armaments abroad, albeit with mixed success. The Soviet Union from the late 1970s until the late 1980s had been by far the world's largest supplier of weaponry to the Third World, but by 1989 the United States surpassed the USSR and became the dominant supplier to the Third World throughout the 1990s.

The decline in Russia's arms exports to the Third World in the early 1990s stemmed in part from unfavourable conditions in the global arms market and in part from turbulence in the former Soviet weapons industry, but it also reflected a transactional shift that began in the late Soviet period (Kramer, 2011). By 1990, the Soviet government was no longer interested in providing armaments to developing countries via grants or highly concessionary loans and was seeking instead to be paid in hard currency. This emphasis on arms exports as a source of hard currency was continued by the Russian government. Russian arms supplies to the developing world fell during a period of adjustment in the first half of the 1990s, but by the latter half of the 1990s Russia had regained a firm footing as the world's second largest supplier of weapons to the Third World. Under Putin, Russia has alternated with the United States as the leading exporter of armaments to developing countries ('U.S., Russia Remain World's Top Exporters of Weapons', 2018; Theohary, 2016; Grimmett, 2010).

Russia's continuation of the Soviet Union's emphasis on selling arms to Third World countries in order to earn hard currency stems partly from the lack of other options. Although Russia's energy exports are a lucrative source of hard currency (as they were for the Soviet Union), weaponry is Russia's only manufactured export that generates hard currency revenues in appreciable quantities. Thus, Russia's export structure, like the USSR's, is based mainly on arms and energy (Rivlin, 2005; Blank and Levitzky, 2015; Broadshaw and Connolly, 2016). In 1990 and 1991, the Soviet Union made a vigorous (albeit unsuccessful) push to increase military exports to Third World states and energy exports to Western Europe in order to earn hard currency. The drive to sell more weapons and natural gas abroad continued all through the 1990s and into the Putin era, with varying success. The pressure to earn hard currency thus ensures that arms transfers will remain a salient instrument in Russian foreign policy in the years ahead.

Although the customer base for Russia's weapons exports is more diversified than the Soviet Union's was, an important carryover from the Soviet era is the willingness—even eagerness—of Russian leaders to supply weapons to countries hostile to the United States. Among the largest recipients of Russian-made arms throughout, the Putin era has been Venezuela under its stridently anti-American president Hugo Chavez and his successor, Nicolás Maduro (Beehner, 2006; Theohary, 2016; Connolly and Sendstad, 2017). Until Venezuela descended into a catastrophic socio-economic crisis in the 2010s because of Chavez's and Maduro's economic mismanagement and authoritarian abuses, the Venezuelan government was able to pay for its weapons imports promptly in hard currency, which made it an attractive customer for Russian armaments factories. However, even after the economic breakdown, mass unrest, and political instability in Venezuela deprived the country of its ability to pay in hard currency (or even via offsets) in a timely manner, the Russian government was still willing to supply large quantities of weapons. The ongoing shipments demonstrate that, for Putin, the main appeal of selling weapons to Venezuela is that Chavez and Maduro have flamboyantly defied U.S. power. Russian arms transfers to Venezuela have thus been reminiscent of Soviet weapons exports to far-left governments in Angola, Mozambique, and Ethiopia in the 1970s and 1980s, to Iraq under Saddam Hussein, to Iran under the ayatollahs, to Nicaragua under the Sandinistas, to North Korea, and to Cuba.

Conclusion: weighing the Soviet legacy

The durability of the Soviet imprint on Russian foreign policy after 1991 is not surprising. After the Bolsheviks seized power in Russia in 1917, they vowed they would make a fundamental rupture with Tsarist-era foreign policy. Crucial changes were indeed adopted, but Bolshevik leaders soon found that personnel and practices from the Tsarist era could not be discarded overnight. For post-Soviet Russia, departures from the Soviet era have been more gradual and less sweeping in most cases, and the legacy has thus been more evident. Apart from abandoning Soviet Marxist-Leninist ideology (which had already severely eroded in Gorbachev's final years), Russian leaders moved more cautiously in rejecting the Soviet past. Large numbers of personnel and many specific policies were carried over from the Soviet period, and institutional outlooks persisted. On the whole, these circumstances resulted in greater continuity after 1991 than after 1917.

Geography also produced a considerable degree of continuity between Soviet and Russian foreign policy. The Russian Federation inherited more than three-quarters of the Soviet Union's landmass and therefore also inherited both the advantages and the disadvantages of the USSR's geographical configuration. Territorial disputes between the Soviet Union and Northeast Asian countries had to be dealt with by the Russian government, which almost always adopted the same positions the Soviet government had. Additional territorial disputes resulted from the way the Soviet Union broke apart, particularly along Russia's western flank. The sheer immensity of Russia's landmass and the extraordinary length of its external boundaries also had far-reaching effects on foreign policy, just as they did in the Soviet Union. Russian leaders, like Soviet leaders before them, have seen their country as a great power that must possess a large army suitable for its size.

Russia's designation at the end of 1991 as the 'legal successor state' to the Soviet Union was another obvious contributor to the durability of the Soviet legacy. Russia's inheritance of the USSR's permanent seat on the UN Security Council, the Russian government's acquisition of sole control over the former Soviet nuclear arsenal and nuclear weapons production complex, and Russia's commitment to assume all of the Soviet Union's obligations and responsibilities under a wide range of international treaties guaranteed a significant degree of continuity. The external circumstances of the USSR's disintegration thus accentuated the Soviet legacy in Russia's foreign policy.

Under Putin, continuity with the Soviet past has been increasingly conspicuous, despite the passage of time. Not only has he expressed deep regret at the demise of the USSR and spoken proudly about his years in the KGB, but he has also revived some of the sinister language of the Soviet era, launching a vigorous campaign in 2012 against 'foreign agents' (a designation he has applied mostly to non-governmental organisations working to promote democracy, free elections, and human rights) and denouncing a 'fifth column of national-traitors' in his March 2014 address ('Obrashchenie Prezidenta Rossiiskoi Federatsii', 2014, p. 3). Putin's pronouncements about foreign policy have also taken on some of the phrasing of the Soviet era, as in his March 2018 address to the Russian Federal Assembly:

> Russia's growing military power provides a solid guarantee of global peace. This [military] power has preserved and will continue to preserve strategic parity and the balance of forces in the world, which, as is known, have been and remain a key factor of international security after World War II and up to the present day.
>
> *(Putin, 2005)*

This statement, with 'Russia's' replaced by 'the USSR's', could easily have been uttered by a Soviet leader like Leonid Brezhnev or Yurii Andropov. In that same speech, Putin went on to warn that Russia would undertake full-scale nuclear retaliation against any 'act of aggression' that 'threatened the very existence of the [Russian] state'. These sorts of warnings, too, are in line with Soviet-era statements. Putin's prolonged hold on power has been another key facilitator of continuity.

On the other hand, some aspects of the Soviet legacy have gradually abated by now and will eventually disappear altogether, if only because of actuary tables. By 2031, four decades after the demise of the USSR, almost no personnel from the Soviet era will be left in high positions of political authority. Most likely, by then the major institutions dealing with foreign policy and national security will have less of the Soviet residue. The magnitude of Russia's departure from Soviet foreign policy will ultimately depend in part on international events and trends that are not fully within Russia's control. Of particular importance will be steps taken by the United States and its NATO allies and by the EU to accept Russia as a full-fledged partner or, alternatively, to counter it or, alternatively, to do neither. But to the extent that internal factors continue to drive Russian foreign policy, the Soviet legacy will be waning in the years ahead even if it never fully disappears.

Notes

1 The transfer of all Soviet tactical nuclear weapons from other former republics to Russian territory occurred quickly (within a few months), but the transfer of all strategic nuclear missiles took much longer, in part because of cunctation by Ukraine before agreeing in 1994 to sign the Non-Proliferation Treaty as a non-nuclear weapons state. All strategic nuclear warheads (which were never under Ukrainian operational control) were transferred from Ukraine to Russia by June 1996. The dismantling of SS-24, SS-19, and SS-18 delivery vehicles in Ukraine and Kazakhstan took considerably longer but was eventually completed with U.S. funding.
2 Two recent comparative studies of 'legacies' in the former Communist world cover political, bureaucratic, economic, industrial, legal, social, ethnic, intellectual, religious, attitudinal, cultural, and artistic legacies but do not deal at all with legacies in foreign policy. See Beissinger and Kotkin (2014) and Pop-Eleches and Tucker (2017).
3 Kanet and Sussex (2015), esp. the chapters by Graeme Gill and Peter Shearman.
4 For a vivid account of this incident by one of the main participants, see Jackson (2007), pp. 216–275.
5 The literature on this issue is immense. For a small sample, see Kimura (2008, 2000a, 2000b), Hasegawa (1998a, 1998b), and Glaubitz (1995).
6 Three of the newly independent Central Asian countries adjoining China (Kazakhstan, Tajikistan, and Kyrgyzstan) ratified the 1991 agreement separately.
7 On the Russian government's retraction of its signature in 2005, see 'Rossiya otozvala podpisi' (2005).
8 EU sanctions against Russia have not led to any diminution of Russian natural gas exports to the EU, which account for roughly 40 per cent of the EU's total gas consumption ('Russia's Gas Exports to Europe', 2018, p. 4).

References

Allison, Roy (2004) 'Regionalism, Regional Structures, and Security Management in Central Asia,' *International Affairs* (London), Vol. 80, No. 3 (July), pp. 463–483.
Allison, Roy (2013) *Russia, the West, and Military Intervention*. New York: Oxford University Press, pp. 150–169.
Analiticheskii Tsentr Yuriya Levady (2006) *Obshchestvennoe mnenie – 2005: Ezhegodnik*. Moscow: ATsYuL, pp. 219–236.
Andreev, A. L. (2002) '"My" i "oni": K kharakteristike vneshnepoliticheskoi orientatsii rossiiskogo obshchestva,' in Stepan Sulakshin, ed., *Rossiya v usloviyakh transformatsii: Istoriko-politologicheskii seminar*. Moscow: FRPTs, pp. 54–69.

Baev, Pavel K., Christoph Zürcher, and Jan Koehler (2005), 'Civil Wars in the Caucasus,' in Paul Collier and Nicholas Sambanis, eds., *Understanding Civil War: Evidence and Analysis*. Washington, DC: The World Bank, pp. 259–298.

Bashkirova, E., and Yu. Fedorov (1999) 'Labirinty posttotalitarnogo soznaniya,' *Pro et contra* (Moscow), Vol. 4, No. 2, pp. 120–143.

Beehner, Lionel (2006) *'Russia-Iran Arms Trade,' Background Brief*. New York: Council on Foreign Relations, November.

Beissinger, Mark R., and Stephen Kotkin, eds. (2014) *Historical Legacies of Communism in Russia and Eastern Europe*. New York: Cambridge University Press.

Belenkova, Elena (2012) 'Rol' OON v sovremennom mire: Osnovnye kontseptii rossiiskikh uchenykh,' *Vlast'* (Moscow), No. 7 (July 2002), pp. 147–150.

Birch, Julian (1996) 'The Georgian/South Ossetian Territorial and Boundary Dispute,' in John F. R. Wright, Suzanne Goldenberg, and Richard Schofield, eds., *Transcaucasian Boundaries*. London: UCL Press, pp. 50–89.

Blank, Stephen J., ed. (2011) *Russian Nuclear Weapons: Past, Present, and Future*. Carlisle Barracks, PA: U.S. Army War College.

Blank, Stephen J., and Edward Levitzky (2015) 'Geostrategic Aims of the Russian Arms Trade in the Middle East and East Asia,' *Defence Studies*, Vol. 15, No. 1 (February), pp. 63–80.

Blum, Yehuda Z. (1992) 'Russia Takes Over the Soviet Union's Seat at the United Nations,' *European Journal of International Law*, Vol. 3, No. 2 (August), pp. 354–361.

Bomeshko, Boris (2017) *Istoriya Pridnestrovskoi voiny 1992 goda*. Tiraspol: RIO PGU.

Broadshaw, Michael, and Richard Connolly (2016) 'Barrels and Bullets: The Geostrategic Significance of Russia's Oil and Gas Exports,' *Bulletin of the Atomic Scientists*, Vol. 72, No. 3 (May–June), pp. 156–164.

Bukkvoll, Tor (2009) 'Russia's Military Performance in Georgia,' *Military Review*, Vol. 89, No. 6 (November–December), pp. 57–63.

Calus, Kamil, and Marcin Kosienkowski (2018) 'Relations between Moldova and the European Union,' in Paul Flenley and Michael Mannin, eds., *The EU and Its Eastern Neighbourhood: The Contradictions of Europeanisation and European Identities*. Manchester: Manchester University Press, pp. 111–148.

Connolly, Richard, and Cecilie Sendstad (2017) *Russia's Role as an Arms Exporter: The Strategic and Economic Importance of Arms Exports for Russia*, Chatham House Research Paper. London: Royal Institute for International Affairs, March.

Cooper, Julian (2016) *Russia's State Armament Programme to 2020: A Quantitative Assessment of Implementation, 2010–2015*, FOI-R-4239-SE. Stockholm: Swedish Defense Research Agency, March.

Cornell, Svante E., and Frederick S. Starr (2009) *The Guns of August: Russia's War in Georgia*. Armonk, NY: M. E. Sharpe, pp. 143–185.

Coyle, James L. (2018) *Russia's Border Wars and Frozen Conflicts*. New York: Palgrave Macmillan, pp. 157–178.

'Dogovor', (2005) 'Dogovor mezhdu Rossiiskoi Federatsiei i Estonskoi Respublikoi o rossiisko-estonskoi gosudarstvennoi granitse,' 18 May, transcribed in *Rossiiskaya gazeta* (Moscow), 1 June, p. 4.

'Dogovor' (2014) 'Dogovor mezhdu Rossiiskoi Federatsiei i Estonskoi Respublikoi o rossiisko-estonskoi gosudarstvennoi granitse,' RIA-Novosti, 18 February, Item 2.

Donaldson, Robert H., Joseph L. Nogee, and Vidya Narkarni (2014) *The Foreign Policy of Russia: Changing Systems, Enduring Interests*, 5th ed. New York: Taylor & Francis.

Fedor, Julie (2011) *Russia and the Cult of State Security: The Chekist Tradition, from Lenin to Putin*. New York: Routledge.

Fedorov, Valerii, Yuliya Baskakova, and Anna Zhirikova (2017) *Rossiya udivlyaet: Pyat' epokh v rossiiskom obshchestvennom mnenii (1987–2017)*. Moscow: VTsIOM, March.

George, Julie (2009) *The Politics of Ethnic Separatism in Russia and Georgia*. Medford, MA: Springer.

Gill, Graeme (1998) 'Elites and the Russian Transition,' in Graeme Gill, ed., *Elites and Leadership in Russian Politics*. New York: Palgrave Macmillan, pp. 134–157.

Glaubitz, Joachim (1995) *Between Tokyo and Moscow: The History of an Uneasy Relationship, 1972 to the 1990s*. Honolulu: University of Hawaii Press.

Gol'ts, Aleksandr (2004) *Armiya Rossii: 11 poteryannykh let*. Moscow: Zakharov.

Grimmett, Richard F. (2010) *Conventional Arms Transfers to Developing Nations, 2002–2009*. Washington, DC: U.S. Congressional Research Service, September.

Grishaeva, L. E. (2007) *Rossiya i OON: Istoriya i sovremennost'*. Moscow: Kampaniya Sputnik.
Gu Liping (2015) 'Boundary Drawn for Territory Returned by Russia,' *ECNS Newswire*, 5 November, Item 14.
Gudkov, Lev (2017) 'The Evolution of Homo Sovieticus to Putin's Man,' *The Moscow Times*, 9 October, p. 11.
Hara, Kimie (2001) '50 Years from San Francisco: Re-Examining the Peace Treaty and Japan's Territorial Problems,' *Pacific Affairs*, Vol. 74, No. 3 (Autumn), pp. 361–382.
Hasegawa, Tsuyoshi (1998a) *The Northern Territories Dispute and Russo-Japanese Relations*, Vol. 1: *Between War and Peace, 1697–1985*. Berkeley: University of California Press.
Hasegawa, Tsuyoshi (1998b) *The Northern Territories Dispute and Russo-Japanese Relations*, Vol. 2: *Neither War nor Peace, 1985–1998*. Berkeley: University of California Press.
Haynes, Susan (2009) 'Russia, China, and a Multipolar World Order: The Danger in the Undefined,' *Asian Perspective*, Vol. 33, No. 1 (January), pp. 159–184.
Hewitt, R. G. (1996) 'Abkhazia: A Problem of Identity and Ownership,' in John F. R. Wright, Suzanne Goldenberg, and Richard Schofield, eds., *Transcaucasian Boundaries*. London: UCL Press, pp. 190–225.
Independent International Fact-Finding Mission on the Conflict in Georgia (2009) *Report*, 3 vols. Brussels: Council of the European Union, September.
Jackson, General Mike (2007) *Soldier: The Autobiography*. London: Bantam Books, pp. 216–275.
Kanet, Roger E., and Matthew Sussex, eds., (2015) *Power, Politics and Confrontation in Eurasia: Foreign Policy in a Contested Region*. New York: Palgrave Macmillan.
Kimura, Hiroshi (2000a) *Distant Neighbors*, Vol. 1: *Japanese-Russian Relations under Brezhnev and Andropov*. Armonk, NY: M. E. Sharpe.
Kimura, Hiroshi (2000b) *Distant Neighbors*, Vol. 2: *Japanese-Russian Relations under Gorbachev and Yeltsin*. Armonk, NY: M. E. Sharpe.
Kimura, Hiroshi (2008) *The Kurillian Knot: A History of Japanese-Russian Border Negotiations*. Stanford, CA: Stanford University Press.
King, Charles (2000) *The Moldovans – Romania, Russia, and the Politics of Culture*. Stanford, CA: Hoover Institution Press.
'Kitaitsy privetstvuyut' (2015) 'Kitaitsy privetstvuyut peredachu Rossiej ocherednogo kuska zemli i zhdut ocheredi Sahalina, Vladivostoka i Tuvy,' *Newsru.ru* (www.newsru.ru), 6 November.
'Kitai zhdet ot Rossi' (2015) 'Kitai zhdet ot Rossii peredachu Sahalina, Vladivostoka i Tuvy – SMI,' *PrimaMedia* (www.primamedia.ru), 6 November.
Kramer, Mark (1998) 'Neo-Realism, Nuclear Proliferation, and East-Central European State Strategies,' *International Politics*, Vol. 35, No. 2 (September), pp. 253–333, republished in Michael Mastanduno and Ethan B. Kapstein, eds., Unipolar Politics: Realism and State Strategies after the Cold War. New York: Columbia University Press, pp. 385–465.
Kramer, Mark (2002) 'NATO, the Baltic States, and Russia: A Framework for Sustainable Enlargement,' *International Affairs* (London), Vol. 78, No. 4 (October), pp. 731–756.
Kramer, Mark (2008) 'Russian Policy toward the Commonwealth of Independent States: Recent Trends and Future Prospects,' *Problems of Post-Communism*, Vol. 55, No. 6 (November–December), pp. 1–19.
Kramer, Mark (2011) 'The Decline in Soviet Arms Transfers to the Third World, 1986–1991: Political, Economic, and Military Dimensions,' in Artemy M. Kalinovsky and Sergey Radchenko, eds., *The End of the Cold War and the Third World: New Perspectives on Regional Conflict*. New York: Routledge, pp. 46–100.
Kramer, Mark (2013) 'Russia, the Baltic Region, and the Challenge for NATO,' *PONARS Eurasian Policy Memo*. No. 267, Washington, DC, July.
Kramer, Mark (2014a) 'Why Did Russia Give Away Crimea Sixty Years Ago?' *CWIHP e-Dossier*. No. 47, 19 March, Cold War International History Project website (www.cwihp.org).
Kramer, Mark (2014b) 'Russia's Great-Power Ukraine Strategy,' *The National Interest* (nationalinterest.org), 25 August.
Kramer, Mark (2015) 'The New Russian Chill in the Baltic,' *Current History*, Vol. 114, No. 3 (March), pp. 8–15.
Kuzar, Vladimir (2008) 'Pyat' printsipov vneshnei politiki,' *Krasnaya zvezda* (Moscow), 2 September, p. 1
Lukin, Alexander (2018) *Russia and China: The New Rapprochement*. Cambridge: Polity.

Marshall, Tim (2015) *Prisoners of Geography: Ten Maps That Explain Everything about the World*. New York: Scribner, pp. 11–37.

Masyuk, Elena (2015) 'Lyubit' drakona,' *Novaya gazeta* (Moscow), No. 70 (6 July), pp. 8–9. Masyuk's lengthy commentary was republished by *Argument* under the more colorful title 'Kak Kitai s'edaet Rossiyu' (How China Will Swallow Russia).

McDermott, Roger N. (2009) 'Russia's Conventional Armed Forces and the Georgian War,' *Parameters*, Vol. 39, No. 1 (Spring), pp. 65–80.

Miller, Steven E., and Dmitri Trenin, eds., (2004) *The Russian Military: Power and Policy*. Cambridge, MA: MIT Press.

Neumann, Iver B. (2017) *Russia and the Idea of Europe: A Study in Identity and International Relations*. New York: Routledge.

'Obrashchenie Prezidenta Rossiiskoi Federatsii' (2014) *Rossiiskaya gazeta* (Moscow), 19 March, pp. 1, 3.

Oslon, Aleksandr Anatol'evich et al., (2003) *Mir glazami rossiyan: Mify i vneshnyaya politika*. Moscow: Institut geografii RAN.

Pop-Eleches, Grigore, and Joshua A. Tucker (2017) *Communism's Shadow: Historical Legacies and Contemporary Political Attitudes*. Princeton, NJ: Princeton University Press.

Popov, N. N. (2007) 'Nostalgiya po velichiyu: Rossiya v postsovetskom prostranstve,' *Monitoring obschestvennogo mneniya* (Moscow), No. 1 (January–February), pp. 50–54.

'Poslanie Prezidenta Federal'nomu Sobraniyu' (2018) *Rossiiskaya gazeta* (Moscow), 2 March, pp. 1–3.

Putin, Vladimir (2005) 'Poslanie Federal'nomu Sobraniyu Rossiiskoi Federatsii,' *Rossiiskaya gazeta* (Moscow), 26 April, p. 1.

'Putin Urges Patience', (2018) 'Putin Urges Patience on Island Row with Japan, in Setback for Shinzo Abe,' *South China Morning Post* (Hong Kong), 27 May, p. 1.

Putin vernul Rossii' (2017) 'Putin vernul Rossii status velikoi derzhavy, zayavil Tuleev,' *RIA Novosti*, 7 December, Item 1748.

Renz, Bettina (2018) *Russia's Military Revival*. Cambridge: Polity.

Rivlin, Paul (2005) *The Russian Economy and Arms Exports to the Middle East*, Memorandum No. 79. Tel Aviv: Jaffee Center for Strategic Studies, University of Tel Aviv, November.

'Rossiya otozvala podpisi' (2005) 'Rossiya otozvala podpisi pod dogovorami o granitse s Estoniei,' *Rossiiskaya gazeta* (Moscow), 1 September, p. 3.

'Rossiya pomogla Sirii' (2016) 'Rossiya pomogla Sirii dostich' rezul'tatov v bor'be s terroristami,' *Rossiiskaya gazeta* (Moscow), 3 November, p. 2.

'Rossiya – velikaya derzhava' (2018) 'Rossiya – velikaya derzhava. No gde zhe spravedlivost'?' *Pravda* (Moscow), 7 May, p. 4.

Rozman, Gilbert (2017) 'Unanswered Questions about Japan-Russia Relations in 2017,' *Asia-Pacific Review*, Vol. 24, No. 1, pp. 74–94.

'Russia's Gas Exports (2018) 'Russia's Gas Exports to Europe Rise to Record High,' *Financial Times* (London), 3 January, p. 4.

'Soglashenie' (1993) 'Soglashenie mezhdu Soyuzom Sovetskikh Sotsialisticheskikh Respublik i Kitaiskoi Narodnoi Respublikoi o sovetsko-kitaiskoi gosudarstvennoi granitse na ee vostochnoi chasti,' 16 May 1991, in *Byulleten' mezhdunarodnykh dogovorov* (Moscow), No. 1 (January), pp. 5–12.

Theohary, Catherine A. (2016) *Conventional Arms Transfers to Developing Nations, 2008–2015*. Washington, DC: U.S. Congressional Research Service, December.

U.S. Defense Intelligence Agency (2017) *Russia Military Power: Building a Military to Support Great Power Aspirations*, DIA-11-1704-161, Washington, DC.

'U.S., Russia Remain World's Top Exporters of Weapons' (2018) Agence France-Presse, 12 March, Newswire No.

'Velikaya derzhava' (2016) '"Velikaya derzhava": Rossiyane nazvali glavnyi uspekh Putina,' *Ekonomicheskie novosti* (Moscow), 7 May, p. 3.

Vendil Pallin, Carolina, and Fredrik Westerlund (2009) 'Russia's War in Georgia: Lessons and Consequences,' *Small Wars & Insurgencies*, Vol. 20, No. 2 (June), pp. 400–424.

4

MILITARY MIGHT AS A BASIS FOR RUSSIAN GREAT POWER IDENTITY

Hanna Smith

Introduction

In order to be a Great Power that has the status of a leader in international affairs, a country needs to hold the respect of other countries as well as the resources of power. In Russia's case, the main resource of power has been its military. Through successful military operations (victories in wars), Russia has managed to gain and increase its Great Power status. The military has also been used in order to maintain already established status quos. These maintaining operations have not always been so successful, and declining military capabilities have also decreased Russia's Great Power status. Therefore, the military's role is significant in Russian Great Power identity – greatpowerness.

While Great Power status needs resources and recognition, an important part of *greatpowerness* is a country's self-image. The self-image of Russia as a Great Power exerts a decisive influence on how Russians interpret any particular situation they find themselves in and how they define interests. Furthermore, the self-image also defines the *means* by which perceived Great Power status will be maintained, or through which desired Great Power status will be achieved.

During the Cold War, there was no question regarding the Soviet Union's status in the international system. The Soviet Union was recognised as the undoubted second superpower in the bipolar world order. This status was based largely on two things: ideological leadership and military might. After the fall of the Soviet Union, Russia's quest to maintain its Great Power status based on its historical self-perception was not a major topic of analysis in the Western literature of the 1990s. Ideological confrontation ceased to exist, and the Soviet Union's military might weakened significantly. Therefore, most discussions of Great Power status concentrated on the question of whether the Russian claim to Great Power status was valid, and if so on what grounds (Wallander and Prokop, 1993; Adomeit, 1995; Neumann, 1996; Skak, 1996; Hedenskog et al., 2005), rather than looking at the implications of the Russian self-image and particularly how Russia perceived the sources of its greatpowerness. There was a lot of emphasis on the economic side and the source of traditional Great Power status – military might – was sidelined. Since 2009, questions of status, state identity and self-perceptions in general as well as in the specific Russian context have received more attention from researchers (Clunan, 2009; Larson and Shevchenko, 2010; Light, 2010;

Feklyunina, 2012; Forsberg et al., 2014; Smith, 2016). It is in this context that Russian Great Power identity – greatpowerness – is examined in this chapter.

This chapter looks into the role of the military in Russian Great Power identity. It first examines the importance of Great Power identity in the Russian context. Then, it analyses the role of historical military modernisations in terms of increasing Russia's Great Power status. And finally, the chapter moves on to look at post-Soviet times and how Russia has used its military to maintain, secure and develop its post-Soviet Great Power identity.

The conclusion reached is that the Russian military has always played an important part in Russian state- and nation-building, where greatpowerness has become an essential part of both state- and nation-building as well as an integral part of Russian policymaking.

Great Power identity

General Alexander Lebed declared in the mid-1990s that 'People without roots, do not form great powers' (Allensworth, 1998, 53). The Russian Federation inherited a Great Power status and identity from the Soviet Union and, looking further back, from Imperial Russia. Russia's past, and in particular its standing as a Great Power, continued to influence popular opinion after the collapse of the USSR (Kivelson and Suny, 2016, 382). This continuation was important precisely from the point of view that the Russian Federation, which was born out of the Soviet Union, needed a past upon which to build its national and state identity. Moments in history which were seen as important milestones in Russian Great Power status, as well as unifying factors for the nation, had to be maintained in public memory. For example, the Soviet victory in the Great Patriotic War was an important part of this discourse, which then directly involved Russia's military as a core element of its Great Power status. As Russian Foreign Minister Sergey Lavrov has stated, 'It has long been noticed that a well thought-out policy cannot be detached from history' (2016). Lavrov himself, when making a point in 2016 that Russia has played a special role in European and world history, referred to Russian military history and several important landmarks from the Russian perspective: the 70th anniversary of the victory in World War II (1945); the centenary of World War I (1914); the 200th anniversary of the Battle of Borodino (1812) and the 400th anniversary of the liberation of Moscow from the Polish invaders (1612) (Lavrov, 2016). In this way, as Bettina Renz has argued, 'a strong military has always been central in Russia's self-perception as a Great Power and military has played various roles and functions in the country's foreign and defence policy throughout history' (2018, 51).

In official Russian discussions of the early 1990s, this 'influence of the past' was largely sidelined, and therefore the role of the military in Russia's self-image was seen as less prominent both in the official policy and in outside analysis. If the debates in the Western literature showed what might have been the grounds for Russian Great Power status, the debates of the 1990s inside Russia reflected Russian visions of what kind of a state Russia *should be* (Boobbyer, 1996). The most pressing tasks concerned Russia's economic transformation, and debates were therefore more forward looking rather than based on understandings of the past. These debates were also influenced by the analysis of Western observers relating to the economy as the key element for Great Power status. Thus, discussions of security were more on the margins early on, while state identity in relation to economic directions dominated.

However, this did not mean that historical aspects relating to Russian greatpowerness and security concerns relating to it were somehow forgotten or that the military did not play an important role in Russian politics. More importantly, even if in many ways Russian society is divided and different opinions are floating around, both society and political elites agree that Russia is a Great Power (Smith, 2014). Denis Volkov, an analyst at the Russian public opinion centre Levada, has given one of the main reasons for Putin's high-approval rating as people's feeling that he has restored the status that belongs to Russia – Russia as a Great Power (Levada Center, 2015a).

How this status is gained and maintained is, however, a matter around which there is still no consensus, with views diverging along the lines of economic versus military and security factors. Interestingly, it seems that Russian society, just as with its foreign and security policy elite, is divided by opinions as to what exactly would be the right way of Russia being a Great Power. The Levada Centre asked respondents what kind of country they would like to see Russia be. On the one hand, 49 per cent answered that they would like to see Russia as a country with high living standards but not necessarily as powerful militarily, and on the other hand, 47 per cent replied that they want to see Russia as a traditional Great Power that is respected and feared by other countries (Levada Center, 2015b).

Alexey Arbatov has listed four theses about what changed in Russian foreign and security policy thinking in 2007: Russia was seeking equal Great Power status with the US, the European Union and China; it was ready to challenge the US' hegemonic position in the world order and to create a real multipolar world, where Russia is one of the power poles; Russia was to secure the non-interference of the West in the post-Soviet space; and finally, it sought to push the West to react and interact with Russia and to have a real Russia policy (Arbatov, 2007). Behind all of those changes is a perceived self-image of greatpowerness. In 2007, when Arbatov wrote about the changes, it was not clear how Russia was going to fulfil them. In 2018, one can make an argument that the military modernisation programme and use of military force have made a difference.

Military modernisation behind gaining Great Power status

Even if Russia is a large country with rich natural resources and history of strong involvement in European and global politics, it has always had to, arguably, make choices of where to reform and develop. Economic reforms require the inclusion of much more political reform in order to secure success. Military reforms can be carried out without reforming anything from the political system. Therefore, one could argue that Russian military modernisation projects have been very significant factors in Russian Great Power identity building, and at the same time military might has remained constant for Russia as an important resource for gaining influence in international affairs (Renz, 2018).

There have been several significant military modernisations during the time of the Russian Empire. In Peter the Great's reign in the late seventeenth and early eighteenth centuries, Russia became a military power to be reckoned with. In the early nineteenth century, the military reforms of Alexander I led to Russia's achieving military victory in the Napoleonic wars. This resulted to the fact that Russia was an undoubted Great Power in European politics with an army of 800,000 men superior to any other on the European continent (Donaldson and Nogee, 2009, 21). In the late nineteenth century, Alexander III focused on economic modernisation as well as on military reforms.

After the October 1917 revolution, the Soviet Union needed to modernise and build up its military strength in order to be taken seriously in international politics. With the help of rapid industrialisation of the 1930s, the Red Army and the Soviet Union came out of World War II as one of the victors. After victory in World War II, the Soviet Union achieved superpower status through its victor status as well as by joining the US as the second nuclear power in the world.

After the fall of the Soviet Union, the image of the Russian army declined. As Russia's conventional military disintegrated throughout the 1990s, so did the country's international image as a powerful global actor. '… 1990s and much of the 2000s, troop readiness, training, morale, and discipline suffered, and most arms industries became antiquated' (Nichol, 2014). It was not until Vladimir Putin became president that the urgency of military modernisation in Russia gained serious attention. In a televised address broadcast on the eve of the presidential elections in March 2000, Putin said that two factors would be important for him, if he would be elected as a president: to restore Russia's international standing and that the military would play an important role in this process:

> On 26th March we are electing not only the head of state but also appointing the Supreme Commander because the President, by virtue of his office, is simultaneously the Supreme Commander of the Armed Forces. Russia is one of the biggest countries in the world and a strong nuclear power. This is something that not only our friends remember. Let me repeat that we are electing the President, whose duty is to ensure economic recovery, restore the country's prestige and leading role in the world, make Russia governable again, and deliver stability and prosperity to everyone.
>
> *(Putin, 2000)*

Putin also connected economic recovery to Great Power status. It took until 2008 for real military reforms to start. By 2018, the Russian military had experienced a revival, and it would be safe to say that the process is still ongoing and, by no means, complete (Renz, 2018, 85).

This brief historical account shows that Russian Great Power status has been connected to military victories and that the victories have been possible due to military modernisation processes. The historical military victories that are associated with successful military modernisation have left a mark on Russian historical memory. Each victory is also connected to Russian status as a leading European power.

Russian use of military to maintain Great Power status

Russian military modernisations have in most cases resulted in military victories and gaining more Great Power status. However, the Russian military has also been used in efforts to maintain Russian Great Power status and not always successfully. In the post-Soviet era, three different contexts can be identified where Russia has been using its military. Naturally, there are also other reasons and more nuanced explanations for the Russian use of military (see Renz, 2018), but one of the underlining factors is Russia's Great Power identity.

The three contexts for Russia's use of the military since the fall of the Soviet Union are as follows: internally, in the post-Soviet space and internationally. Internally, Russia has used military force twice, in the First and Second Chechen Wars. The reasons for going to war in Chechnya are many and it is still often disputed, why the decision was made in 1994 and in 1999 to use military force. In the post-Soviet space, there have been six military interventions – in Moldova-Transnistria, in the breakaway Georgian regions of South Ossetia and Abkhazia, in Tajikistan's Civil War, in Georgia in 2008 and in Ukraine since 2014. Also in the post-Soviet context, many security concerns can be stated as reasons behind Russia's use of military force. In the international context, there are three cases: Russian involvement in peacekeeping operations in the 1990s, Kosovo in 1999 and Syria since 2015. Both in the internal context and in the post-Soviet context, one can see multiple and complex reasons and motivations behind the use of military force. However, an argument can be made that Russian Great Power identity has had a significant impact in all of the cases. That has perhaps come to the surface more clearly in the aftermath of military operations than at their beginning.

Internal context

One of the first tasks of the newly independent Russian state was to establish control over its constituent republics. From a position of weakness in early 1992, the Russian Federation managed to negotiate Federal Treaties with 18 regions. The follow-up to the Federal Treaties was a long process of negotiation between early 1994 and 1998. This process resulted in 46 asymmetric bilateral 'power-sharing treaties' between the central authorities and the regions (Filippov and Shvetsova, 1999, 61–62). Yeltsin's success in getting from the initial Federal Treaties to bilateral treaties and in pushing through the 1993 Constitution had a military element to it. In autumn 1993, Yeltsin used the army to defeat opponents in the Russian duma, to demonstrate the power of the central authorities and to ensure that the regions would accept the constitution. This appeared to remove the risk that the Russian Federation would itself disintegrate. Two and a half years after the fall of the Soviet Union, Yeltsin was able to declare in August 1994 that the danger of Russia falling apart had passed (Colton, 2008, 287). However, not all of the regions had acquiesced. Two were particularly resistant: Tatarstan and Chechen-Ingushetiya. Each of these republics stood up to the central authorities, but in very different ways and only in the case of Chechnya, central authorities had to use military power.

The territory of Chechnya itself provided little of value to the Russian Federation. Some oil could be found underground, and pipelines from the richer reserves of Azerbaijan passed across its territory. But these could easily be done without. However, the small republic presented the greatest threat after the fall of the Soviet Union to the Russian Federation's statehood. While the regions of Russia had each been encouraged to declare their sovereignty by Yeltsin in the last Soviet years, the process now presented a challenge to Russia's own new sovereignty. This took the form of a challenge to central power. The way Great Power identity works in the context of state identity is that the state needs to have total control over its constituent entities in foreign and security policy. At the time this was difficult anywhere, but Chechnya's declarations of independence went further than anywhere else in Russia and therefore it became in the perception of Moscow a serious threat to the state identity of greatpowerness.

By the time of the Second Chechen War, Chechen rebels were portrayed as part of a broader global radical Islamic and terrorist movement, which clearly was a threat to Russia. In this way, the association with a broader Islamic movement rather than just the demand for Chechen independence made Chechnya a case where decisive action would be needed. No country can accept such an outside challenge, but in the case of a Great Power, the response needs to be an act of strength. At the same time, very strong Great Power rhetoric was adopted by the Kremlin to 'rally the nation around the flag'.

The act of strength did not work in the First Chechen War, and even in the case of the Second Chechen War some doubts remained about Russian capabilities. The result was that the First Chechen War turned out to be a humiliation for the Russian armed forces as well as for the Russian state and undermined Russian Great Power status both in Europe and globally. The natural conclusion to be drawn was summed up by Epperson: 'as events in Chechnya have shown, the Russian military has ceased to be an effective fighting force' (Epperson, 1997, 93). It was the military humiliation that effected the status factor more than the weak Russian economy.

Post-Soviet space context

The fall of the Soviet state presented the Russian Federation with numerous challenges, not only internally but also externally, especially in the security field. Many of its strategically important subjects were now located beyond its borders. The situation divided political elites in Moscow, including military and security elites. Several important military bases from Soviet time were now in different countries, of which Sevastopol in Ukraine is the most well-known. As for many actors, the situation during the years 1991–1994 was confusing and chaotic for the Soviet/Russian military. For a while, Soviet military units based outside Russia's borders were not under any clear command. At this point, Moscow floated the idea that the Commonwealth of Independent States (CIS) could facilitate its military structure in the post-Soviet space. This idea also showed how difficult the idea of independence of the post-Soviet countries was for Moscow. The idea was eventually rejected by all of the Newly Independent States (NIS) countries apart from Russia. The security vacuum that existed in the other NIS exaggerated the tendency for Russia to assume the role of the leading provider of security for the whole post-Soviet space, excluding the Baltic states. The situation only strengthened the hand of those in Moscow arguing for Russia to resume the Soviet Great Power identity based on military strength.

It was clear that Russia took the Great Power legacy of the Soviet Union and Imperial Russia onto its shoulders. Most Russians also continued to believe that Russia, uniquely compared to other NIS, was a Great Power and that greatpowerness should be recognised as an integral part of its foreign and security policy even before it was formulated in official documents. One implication of this legacy was clearly seen in Moscow's policy towards the other NIS. Moscow saw itself as the natural guarantor of peace in the post-Soviet space. In Sergei Ivanov's words, Russia had an obligation in regard to 'the strengthening of regional stability, conflict prevention and resolution of local conflicts, especially near the Russian borders' (cited in Davies, 2015, 84).

This viewpoint heavily influenced Moscow as it worked out its doctrines on paper. The Russian foreign policy concept of 1993 determined that a long-term mission was to prevent new conflicts emerging within the borders of the former Soviet Union. By contrast, the military doctrine emphasised the threat of internal armed conflict. At a 1993 press conference, Foreign Minister Andrei Kozyrev made it clear that it was unthinkable for Russia to pull out completely from the zones of Russian traditional interests (Allison, 2013, 123). Statements such as these made it clear that, even if the Russian state was weak and struggling to deal with its own internal challenges, it would view the post-Soviet space through the lenses of its imperial legacy and greatpowerness. As Alexander Vladislavlev, an influential and long-serving Russian politician, and Sergey Karaganov, nowadays Dean of the School of World Economics and International Relations at the Higher School of Economics in Moscow, put it early in the 1990s: 'Russia must bear its cross and fulfil its duty by playing an enlightened post-imperial role throughout the ex-Soviet Union' (cited in Sergunin, 2007, 57).

As Mikhail Tsypkin observed, 'the military, in effect, runs Moscow's security policy in the "hot spot" of the near abroad without much control by the civilian authorities' (cited in Mörike, 1998, 101). This allowed for an uncomfortable dual situation in those cases where the Russian military was active outside Russia's borders. On the one hand, Russia was only at the stage of planning its own policy towards the other NIS at the level of doctrine. But meanwhile, in the field the military was taking its own initiatives according to the situation on the ground, which then had implications for the development of doctrine, since the realities had to be taken into account.

Three factors have played a prominent role in Russia's use of military power in the post-Soviet space since 1991: the potential for conflicts beyond Russia's borders affecting the security of Russia and its military bases; the Russian notion of a sphere of interest, closely tied to a sense of responsibility for a region which had historically been dominated by Russia for centuries; and concern for the position of Russians and Russian speakers in the near abroad. This was formulated in the foreign policy doctrine as follows:

> The objective reality is this: reciprocal interests are involved here, and – while agreeing to compromises to resolve emerging problems – Russia will not make unilateral concessions in order to develop relations; it will not accept damage to its national interests, or encroachment on the rights of ethnic Russians abroad.
>
> *(RF FP, 1993, 35)*

Such concerns are not unique in post-Imperial situations: most obviously, the British Commonwealth preserves in an institutional form the continuing responsibilities and interests of Great Britain in the territory of its former empire. Recent French military intervention in Mali is just the latest in a pattern of actions in its former colonies. But the particular nature of Russia's Imperial legacy, the strength of attachment to the notion of Russia as a continuing Great Power, and the vocal concern for Russians stranded abroad as the result of earlier colonising policies are more marked in the Russian case. Coupled with the fact that Russia's former subjects are its near neighbours rather than distant overseas former colonies, this makes the potential for military intervention higher (Renz and Smith, 2016).

Global context

In the early 1990s, it seemed that Russian foreign policy was fully focused on integration with the West, even at the expense of other perceived priorities. For example, Foreign Minister Kozyrev declared, 'securing Russia's influence in the Balkans had been subordinated to the larger aim of establishing cooperative relations with the Western democracies' (Averre, 2009, 577). By 2015, however, relations between Russia and the West were at an all-time low, and Russia was conducting military operations in defiance of the West, not only in the former Soviet space (Ukraine) but further afield in Syria. The military interventions beyond the former Soviet borders – in Kosovo in 1999 and in Syria starting in 2015 – have brought Russia into a direct competition with the West, but that it is a type of competition that has in fact enhanced Russia's Great Power standing and status. Bobo Lo has observed that it is recognised in Russia how their actions are unpopular in Russia but 'for them this matters less than the restoration of national self-respect and strategic independence' (2015, 203).

What both Kosovo and Syria show is that, for Russia, pursuit of multilateral cooperation could be backed up by ostentatious displays of military force. In both cases, Russia started out in cooperation with the US and North Atlantic Treaty Organisation (NATO), but initiated its own military actions once it felt that it was not being treated as an equal partner. Greatpowerness and multilateralism, therefore, combined in unpredictable and unexpected ways. The Russian interventions in Kosovo and Syria took place in very different circumstances and had very different outcomes. But there was a good deal in common in the underlying logic behind Russia's actions. In the case of Kosovo, Regina Heller has pointed out that the risks of falling out with the West were lower than the resulting gains for Russia's prestige (2014, 340).

The Kosovo case significantly redefined Russia-West relations. The reasons the Kosovo case and the bombing of Serbia were so important for Russia rested on two factors. One was that 'The real issue is that Serbia is an ally of Russia, and the Russians did not want Kosovo independence to happen' (Gorenburg and Gaffney, 2006; Friedman, 2007; Mendeloff, 2008). The other was that 'the main threat was political and concerned Russia's status in international affairs' (Averre, 2009, 580; Heller, 2014). Roy Allison drew similar conclusions. In his words, 'the intention therefore was to avoid Russia being frozen out by NATO'. Using the situation as leverage in negotiations about Russian involvement in the Kosovo Force NATO-led peacekeeping mission was also important (Allison, 2013, 53). This shows that the use of the military as a bargaining tool, as Samuel Charap has argued, was also an important factor (2016).

As in the case of Kosovo, also in the case of Syria several factors coincided in the case of Russia's military intervention into the Syrian Civil War. Russia has long been seen as a strategic partner for Syria for a number of reasons: Russia has enjoyed access to the strategically important naval base in Tartus, Russia sells arms to Syria and had also been building up economic ties including joint infrastructure projects with Syria since 2005. Syria was central to Russia's Middle East policy. 'Russia has its own strategic interests in the Middle East, which include the security of its Southern neighbourhood, good relations with Islam, and access to the Mediterranean' (Kreutz, 2010, 8). Analysis of Russia's aims in the Middle East since Russia began its military campaign in Syria in 2015 has followed similar lines to those back in 1999 relating to Russia's intervention into the Kosovo conflict. However, there is also one significant difference, in that combatting the threat of Islamic State and radical Islam is an additional factor in Syria's case:

> Russia fears the total collapse of the Syrian state, which would end a decades-old alliance and threaten its strategic position in the Middle East and it views Islamic insurgents as not only a threat to Assad, but also a potential threat at home.
> *(Knight, 2015; see also Allison, 2013, 810)*

Following on from this, the use of military force can also be seen as a tool of bargaining when seeking an international role. As Arbatova and Dynkin have argued, Russian involvement could play a crucial role in the settlement of major issues, while recognising a common threat (such as that posed by Islamic State in Iraq and Syria, ISIL) could make Russia and the West cooperate on a basis where Russia is treated equally to the US (Arbatova and Dynkin, 2016). The multilateral approach could therefore restore something of Russia's Great Power prestige and status.

Relating to intervention in Syria, Russia also tested the success of its military modernisation programme. The successful coordination between air force and navy, and with foreign forces, demonstrated in several respects that Russia continues to be a Great Power and should be taken seriously as such. 'Apart from its geopolitical objectives, it [the Russian intervention in Syria] was designed to test improvements in Russian military capabilities resulting from military reforms carried out over the last seven years and to highlight these improvements to potential adversaries' (Gorenburg, 2016). Putin also justified the Russian incursion in Syria as a fight against global terrorism (Knight, 2015). The US, Turkey and other powers were also involved in this fight, but the complexity of the situation on the ground led Russia to take its own path, leading to tensions with other military powers.

Alexander Baunov, editor-in-chief of the Carnegie Moscow Centre, said shortly after the Russian military operation started in Syria that the operation's diplomatic task was to overcome the isolation Russia had suffered as a result of Crimea, Donbas and the shooting down of a Malaysian airplane. He also stated 'Russia desires to reconcile with the West. Not by falling on its knees, but by showing its influence and irreplaceability' (Hatsaturov, 2015). Thus, as with earlier conflicts, a central aim for Russia was to gain recognition of its Great Power status. In this regard, Russia has been successful to the extent that 'for the first time since the 1980s, Moscow's military and diplomatic backing is something truly worth having' (Matthews, 2016).

In 1999, the Russian intervention in Kosovo was an operation aimed at maintaining Russian Great Power status, while in 2015 the Syria intervention was to assert Russian global Great Power status. On both occasions, use of military force was needed. Furthermore, in both cases, Russian actions came, to a certain extent, as a surprise to Western countries and the Russian intervention increased tensions with the West, especially with the US and NATO. Interestingly, Russian actions on both occasions, whether trying to maintain its status or increase it, can be viewed as successful from the perspective of status. The global dimension of greatpowerness was only achieved through military intervention is Syria. The Kosovo case, even if reflecting Russia's Great Power ambitions, left many doubting Russian military capabilities and, therefore, the Russian ability to be a global Great Power.

Conclusion

For Russia and Russians, Great Power identity is an integral part of policymaking and state identity. There continues to be a rift inside Russia, over what kind of Great Power Russia should be: modern, based on high living standards and economic performance, or a strong military power able to project military might also in global terms. Nuclear weapons naturally continue to be the basic guarantee of that status. They maintained Russian Great Power status even at times of serious weakness during the 1990s.

However, it has been clear, looking also at historical experiences, that in Russia's case, Great Power status requires a capable military and show of power. Russian military modernisations have provided Russia with military victories which have added to Russian Great Power status. The military modernisation programmes have been much easier to fulfil than economic reforms since economic reforms require also political changes to be fully successful.

Since 1991, Russia has engaged in sustained military action within its own borders in the two protracted Chechen Wars; in a number of cases in the former Soviet space; and on two occasions outside the post-Soviet borders, in Kosovo in 1999 and Syria from 2015. On each of these occasions, the circumstances were very different and there were specific causes for each intervention. In each case, the time when they occurred also has to be considered. And yet many of the conflicts shared the same underlying causes.

In the two Chechen wars, Russia's use of military force was to try to maintain its status. These attempts were not as successful as hoped. They did, however, enhance the central power's position in the end, even if the military humiliations were endured. The First Chechen War resulted from the chaos surrounding the breakup of the Soviet Union. Russia's greatpowerness was threatened by the potential loss of territory and the defiance shown by a small region on its border. For this reason, Russia was even ready to risk using an unprepared military. In the Second Chechen War, the war that could not be lost, a type of multilateralism emerged as, especially after 9/11, Putin presented the war as part of the international war on terror in which the US and NATO were also engaged. This connection diverted some of the attention away from military shortcomings. The wars defined Russian statehood where Great Power rhetoric was reinstated during the Second Chechen War. The wars showed that even with shortcomings, the military is an integral part of Russian sovereignty and greatpowerness.

In the interventions in the post-Soviet space, there were three underlying factors behind the Russian military interventions: first, the ethnic tensions that the Soviet Union and in some cases Imperial Russia had contained re-emerged in the power vacuum that accompanied the breakup of the Soviet Union. The conflicts that this gave rise to were viewed by Russia in terms of regional security and the threat posed by instability on Russia's borders. Second, Russia's Imperial legacy led to it treating the post-Soviet space as its sphere of influence. This included a sense of responsibility for regional affairs that was evident, for example, in Tajikistan. The sphere of influence thinking is directly linked with Great Power identity. Third, Russia pursued the notion of the protection of the rights of ethnic Russians and Russian speakers beyond Russia's borders. This extension was in part down to a history of Russian identification with something broader than its own citizenship. Greatpowerness also dictated that Russia could not be seen to abandon populations which had their origins in playing a key role in Russian Imperial and Soviet expansion.

Russia's engagements beyond its own borders in Kosovo and in Syria have involved attempts to assert Russia's status as one of the Great Powers of the world. In Kosovo, the Russian action at Pristina was a response to being treated with a lower status by the other major powers. In Syria, the aerial campaigns provided the opportunity for Russia to demonstrate the fruits of its military renewal. Unlike in the post-Soviet space or in the Russian Federation itself, in these cases greatpowerness was not to be satisfied by establishing domination over former or current subordinate territories. It dictated, rather, that Russia should be treated at least as an equal by the other Great Powers, and so relates to the traditions of multilateralism as understood by Russia.

The revival of the Russian military has brought back the image of Russia as a Great Power. That image is, however, based only on Russian capabilities to project power and so it has not solved the Russian dilemma of aspiring to become a modern Great Power with high living standards, but remaining as a traditional Great Power relying on the military.

References

Adomeit, H. (1995), "Russia as a 'great power' in world affairs: Images and reality", *International Affairs*, 71(1), 35–68.
Allensworth, W. (1998), "'Derzhavnost': Alexander Lebed's vision for Russia", *Problems of Post-Communism*, 45(2), 51–58.
Allison, R. (2013), *Russia, the West, and Military Intervention*. Oxford: Oxford University Press.
Arbatov, A. G. (2007), "Is a New Cold War Imminent", *Russia in Global Affairs*, 03/2007, http://eng.globalaffairs.ru/number/n_9127
Arbatova, N. and A. Dynkin (2016), "World Order after Ukraine", *Survival: Global Politics and Strategy*, February–March.
Averre, D. (2009), "From Pristina to Tskhinvali: The legacy of operation allied force in Russia's relations with the west", *International Affairs*, 85(3), 571–591.
Boobbyer, P. (1996), "The turbelent decade: Soviet and Russian politics 1985–1995", in B. Brivati, L. Buxton, and J. Seldon (eds.), *The Contemporary History Handbook*. Manchester: Manchester University Press, 161–169.
Charap, S. (2016), "Russia's use of military force as a foreign policy tool: Key issues in light of recent developments", in B. Renz and H. Smith (eds.), *After 'hybrid warfare', what next? Understanding and responding to contemporary Russia*. Valtioneuvoston selvitys- ja tutkimustoiminnan julkaisusarja 44/2016, https://tietokayttoon.fi/documents/10616/1266558/Understanding+and+responding+to+contemporary+Russia/49bdb37f-11da-4b4a-8b0d-0e297af39abd?version=1.0

Clunan, A. (2009), *The Social Construction of Russia's Resurgence; Aspirations, Identity and Security Interests*. New York: John Hopkins University Press.

Colton, T. J. (2008), *Yeltsin: A Political Life*. New York: Basic Books.

Davies, L. (2015), "Russian institutional learning and regional peace operations: The case of Georgia and Moldova", *Comilas Journal of International Relations*, 3, 81–99.

Donaldson, R. H. and J. L. Nogee (2009), *The Foreign Policy of Russia: Changing Systems, Enduring Interests*, 4th edn. London: Routledge.

Epperson, R. (1997), "Russian Military Intervention in Politics 1991–96", *The Journal Of Slavic Military Studies*, 10(3), 90–108.

Feklyunina, V. (2012), "Image and reality: Russia's relations with the West", in R. Kanet and R. Freire (eds.), *Russia and European Security*. Dordrecht: Republic of Letters Publishing, pp. 29–103.

Filippov, M. and Shvetsova, O. (1999), "Asymmetric bilateral bargaining in the new Russian Federation", *Communist and Post-Communist Studies*, 32(1), 61–76.

Forsberg, T., Heller, R. and Wolf, R. (2014), "Special issue: Status and emotions in Russian foreign policy", *Communist and Post-Communist Studies*, 47(3), 261–268.

Friedman, G. (2007), "Russia: Kosovo and the asymmetry of Perceptions", Stratford, Geopolitical Intelligence Report, December 8, https://worldview.stratfor.com/article/russia-kosovo-and-asymmetry-perceptions

Gorenburg, D. (2016), "What Russia's military operation in Syria can tell us about advances in its capabilities", *PONARS Policy Memo*, no. 424, http://www.ponarseurasia.org/sites/default/files/policy-memos-pdf/Pepm424_Gorenburg2_March2016_2.pdf

Gorenburg, D. and Gaffney, H. H. (2006), "Great promise unfulfilled: How Russia lost its way after independence", *Insight Turkey*, 8(1).

Kivelson, V. and R. Suny (2016), *Russia's Empires*. Oxford: Oxford University Press.

Knight, A. (2015), "Why Russia needs Syria", The New York review of books, October 8, www.nybooks.com/daily/2015/10/08/why-russia-syria/

Kreutz, A. (2015), "Syria: Russia's best asset in Middle East", Russie.Nei.Visions nr.55, October, www.ifri.org/sites/default/files/atoms/files/kreutzengrussiasyrianov2010.pdf

Larson, D. W. and A. Shevchenko (2010), "Status seekers: Chinese and Russian responses to U.S. primacy", *International Security*, 34(4), 63–95.

Lavrov, S. (2016), "Russia's foreign policy in a historical perspective", *Russia in Global Affairs*, 30 March, http://eng.globalaffairs.ru/number/Russias-Foreign-Policy-in-a-Historical-Perspective-18067

Levada Center (2015a), 8 July, www.levada.ru/08-07-2015/analitik-levady-u-poloviny-naseleniya-net-politicheskikh-predpochtenii

Levada Center (2015b), 24 March, www-levada.ru/24-03-2015/bolshinstvo-grazhdan-schitatyut-rossiyu-velikoi-derzhavoi

Light, M. (2010), "Russian foreign policy", in S. White, R. Sakwa, and H. E. Hale (eds.), *Developments in Russian Politics*. Basingstoke: Palgrave, 225–244.

Lo, B. (2015), *Russia and the New World Disorder*. Baltimore, MD: Brookings Institution Press.

Hatsaturov, A. (2015), "Kogo my bombim v Sirii i komu voobshse verit, colta.ru", 5 October, www.colta.ru/articles/society/8744

Hedenskog, J., Konnander, V., Nygren, B., Oldberg, I., and Pursiainen, C. (eds.), (2005), *Russia as a Great Power: Dimensions of Security under Putin*. London: Routledge.

Matthews, O. (2016), "Putin's winning in Syria – but making a powerful new enemy", The Spectator, 20 February, www.spectator.co.uk/2016/02/putins-winning-in syria-but making-a-powerful-new-enemy/#

Mendeloff, D. (2008), "'Pernicious History' as a Cause of National Misperceptions Russia and the 1999 Kosovo War", *Conflict and Cooperation*, 43(1), 31–56.

Mörike, A. (1998), "The Military as a political actor in Russia: The cases pf Moldova and Georgia", *The International Spectator*, 33(3), 119–131.

Neumann, I. (1996), *Russia and the Idea of Europe: A Study in Identity and International Relations*, 2nd edn, London: Routledge.

Nichol, J. (2014), "Russian Political, Economic, and Security Issues and U.S. Interests", March 31, Congressional Research Service Report, https://fas.org/sgp/crs/row/RL33407.pdf

Putin, V. (2000), "Open letter to Russian voters", www.nns.ru/Elect-2000/info_war/st/113.html

Renz, B. (2018), *Russia's Military Revival*. Cambridge: Polity Press.

Renz, B. and Smith, H. (2016), *Russia and the hybrid warfare: Going beyond the label*. Aleksanteri Papers, University of Helsinki: Kikimora Publications, Helsinki

RF FP (1993), "Foreign Policy Concept of the Russian Federation (1993)," in A. Melville and T. Shakleina (eds.), (2005), *Russian Foreign Policy in Transitions, Concepts and Reality*. Budapest: Central European University Press, 27–64.

Sergunin, A. (2007), *International Relations in the Post-Soviet Russia: Trends and Problems*. Nizhny Novgorod: Nizhny Novgorod Linguistic University Press.

Skak, M. (1996), *From Empire to Anarchy: Postcommunist Foreign Policy and International Relations*. London: Hurst and Company.

Smith, H. (2014), *Russian Greatpowerness: Foreign policy, the two Chechen wars and international organisations*. Helsinki: Helsinki University.

Smith, H. (2016), "Putin's third term and Russia as a Great Power", in M. Suslov and M. Bassin (eds.), *Eurasia 2.0: Russian Geopolitics in the Age of New Media*. London: Rowman and Littlefield.

Wallander, C. A. and Prokop, J. E. (1993), "Soviet security strategies towards Europe: After the wall, with their backs up against it", in R. Keohane, J. Nye, and S. Hoffmann (eds.), *After the Cold War: International Institutions and State Strategies in Europe, 1989–1991*. Cambridge, MA: Harvard University Press.

5

THE RUSSIAN CHALLENGE TO THE LIBERAL WORLD ORDER

Suzanne Loftus and Roger E. Kanet

Introduction: Erosion of the liberal world order

Vladimir Putin was elected President of Russia for the fourth time on March 18, 2018. Putin has been 'on a roll' lately, gaining influence among European populist parties, whose aims to weaken the established liberal democratic order parallel his own. In Italy, the winners of the 2018 parliamentary elections are highly sympathetic to Putin. These include the anti-immigrant Northern League and the populist Five Star Movement. In Austria, Chancellor Sebastian Kurz rules alongside the far-right Freedom Party, which has strong ties to United Russia. In Germany, gains were made in September 2017 for the far-left Left Party and the far-right Alternative for Germany, parties that are popular with pro-Putin voters. In Greece, the Russia-friendly left-wing government of Alexis Tsipras has been in power since 2015. In Hungary, the Russia-friendly right-wing government of Viktor Orban has ruled since 2010. Marine Le Pen finished second in the 2017 French elections and Donald Trump won the 2016 US elections; both are proponents of increased nationalism and reduced multilateralism. In Britain, Putin benefitted in 2015 from the election as leader of the Labour Party of Jeremy Corbyn, who in 2011 called the North Atlantic Treaty Organisation (NATO) 'a danger to world peace' (Milne, 2014). Then there was Brexit – a victory for Putin, as it symbolised an accelerating trend towards European disintegration (Stephens, 2018).

The world is experiencing a significant resistance to the established liberal democratic order and a resurgence of nationalist tendencies. In this essay, we first outline the numerous challenges to that order from within the system itself before turning to an assessment of the efforts by Russia to undermine and replace that order.

As history has shown, countries begin to look inward when experiencing economic, political or existential threats. After the 2008 financial crisis, the negative effects of globalisation became apparent, as inequality increased sharply within societies. In the US, for example, the top 1 per cent of households by income seized 95 per cent of total income gains between 2009 and 2012, compared with 68 per cent of gains between 1993 and 2012. Contrastingly, income of the bottom 90 per cent of households fell by an amount equivalent to 16 per cent of all the income gains between 2009 and 2012. By comparison, between 1993 and 2012, the bottom 90 per cent lost income equivalent to 5 per cent of gains (Saez, 2017).

In the aftermath of the global financial crisis, policymakers warned against protectionist and inward-looking measures and pushed for more free movement of goods, services, capital, labour and technology. As a result of the loosening of restrictions, these measures led to an increase in global mass migration and inequality which have triggered a sense of nostalgia for past stable and supposedly homogeneous nation-states. As one nation begins to express such nostalgic feelings, others begin to emulate them. The new nationalism that is observed has taken on the forms of trade barriers, asset protection, reactions against foreign direct investment, policies favouring domestic workers and firms, anti-immigration measures, state capitalism and resource nationalism. In the political realm, the rise of populist parties that oppose globalisation and immigration is evident. These anti-globalist forces oppose supra-national governance institutions, such as the European Union (EU), the UN, the World Trade Organisation and the International Monetary Fund, and pro-globalist movements (Rachman, 2017).

These trends are caused by uneven and weak economic recovery that has allowed populist parties to promote protectionist policies and to blame foreign trade and immigrants for the lack of recovery. Wealth inequality has also made clear that globalisation creates winners and losers, a reality on which populist parties have capitalised. The elite rule in both advanced economies, where large-scale financing of elected officials by powerful interest groups has a corrupting effect on politics, and in emerging markets where oligarchs dominate the economy and the political system. For the rest of society, stagnation of employment and wages results in economic insecurity for the working and middle class. Since the 1960s, populist parties of the right and left have doubled and quintupled their share of the vote in European countries. Moreover, since 2010, the share of seats for right-wing and left-wing populist parties has risen to 13.7 per cent and 11.5 per cent, respectively (Inglehart and Norris, 2016).

The slow growth the world is experiencing is tightly correlated with changes in demographics, as well. The West has experienced a decline in fertility rates, which, therefore, results in fewer labourers to support the ageing population. This has a fundamental negative impact on economic growth (Sharma, 2016). While the overall effect of increased global trade is positive, the drawback is that specific sectors are negatively affected and that many unskilled and semi-skilled workers have become unemployed. Another important trend is the information revolution that has reinforced the effects of globalisation and rendered specific job types obsolete to an even greater extent than trade has. The limited distinction between the centrist parties and the lack of change has led to a growing frustration among many voters who seek dramatic solutions and a bold decisive leader willing to decree them. This may help to explain the election of President Donald Trump in the US or the praising of Vladimir Putin's anti-establishment and anti-Western rhetoric by many Western politicians (Zakaria, 2016).

Migration is a serious consequence of globalisation, and Trump exploits immigration in his rhetoric, as do most populist politicians. The world is experiencing an age of mass migration and has already been transformed by the globalisation of goods, services and information, but is now witnessing the 'globalisation of people', which ignites a more emotional reaction among the public. Populist parties tend to exploit the public's feelings of fear, racism and xenophobia as a political tool (Zakaria, 2016). Putin has periodically met or shown support for populist leaders in the West. Russia is working to empower Europe's far-right and Eurosceptic parties through cooperation, loans, political cover and propaganda in return for praise from these parties for its foreign policy and strongman leadership. He does this to undermine Western liberal democratic values and institutions, as a divide and conquer strategy. Putin represents a patriotic hero who prioritises national traditions and realpolitik, which leaders of these parties want to imitate, over the globalisation that characterises Western liberal democratic values (Wesslau, 2016). Similar to Putin, these parties tend to be anti-immigration and tough on terrorism. As Donald Trump has done, many of Europe's far-right leaders have praised Putin – for example, Nigel Farage, one of the main proponents of Brexit, was among the first to praise Putin and the annexation of Crimea (Coynash, 2016). The European Centre on Foreign Relations conducted a survey of these parties, which they term 'insurgent' parties, and found that a majority of them are positively inclined towards Putin's Russia (Dennison and Parijs, 2016). This can be explained through the parties' ideological affinity with socially conservative values, defence of national sovereignty and rejection of liberal internationalism and interventionism. The more left-leaning populist parties have an affinity towards Putin's criticism of globalisation and his challenging of the US-dominated international capitalist order. In these ways, Russia is seen as a counter to the US' global domination of Western liberal values.

The Syrian refugee crisis also contributed to xenophobic sentiment in Europe. The European countries did not reach a consensus about how many refugees to accept. While Germany and Sweden were welcoming, others, especially the post-communist states of Central Europe, refused to accept refugees on their soil. The lack of coordination on the Syrian refugee crisis among European nations, coupled with the continued economic challenges after the economic crisis, left many disenchanted with the European liberal project. Populist parties claim that mainstream politics are globalist and anti-patriotic, which resounds with the beliefs of many concerned citizens (Mortimer, 2015; Stanley, 2016).

Based on these issues, one can conclude that the liberal democratic order is experiencing challenges – challenges on which Russia is gladly capitalising and have only supported Putin in his quest for increased international power and prestige. The remainder of this chapter discusses the Russian-Western relationship after the fall of the USSR up to its current security challenges after Russia's annexation of Crimea and de facto invasion of eastern and southern Ukraine. An argument is made that Putin is accumulating important gains in his objective to weaken the liberal international order. The security environment in Europe is experiencing difficulty as a result of a lack of a united stance in the West. An increasingly multipolar world order is on the rise, one which realist thinkers have predicted will cause widespread instability. Part of the future of this order will lie in the hands of the West and its long-term strategy towards Russia.

Russian-Western affairs and narratives

Russia and the West had very different expectations of how the new world order would unfold after the Cold War. Two competing narratives evolved, and no consensus has been reached about the differences. While the US and the EU viewed the end of the Cold War as a triumph of liberal democratic values and a defeat of the USSR and its values, Russia saw the end as a victory for all and a stepping stone to a new world order where both Russia and the West would be the founding members. The West expected Russia to join the expanded Atlantic Community and abide by its pre-established norms and values. Russia, on the other hand, aimed at 'transcending' the liberal order and installing a more pluralistic community through the idea of a 'Greater West' (Sakwa, 2017). The concept of 'transcendence' refers to the act of forming a new order in conjunction with Russia which sought a shared approach to politics – a process of engagement that would ultimately transform both subjects involved. By denying the process of 'transcendence', the West precipitated exactly what it sought to avert, which is a revived and aggressive Russia. Although Russia's heightened assertiveness in international relations has geopolitical consequences, namely, that Ukraine is now a divided nation and Crimea belongs to Russia, the motivation behind its actions were inspired by its commitment to a transcendence of international relations (Sakwa, 2017).

As the 1990s unfolded, Russia perceived the West to be using a value-based ideology in an expansionist manner in its promotion of liberal democracy. This triggered the current Russian policy of resistance to the Western hegemonic order. Russia's main issue was not so much the values themselves, but rather the political order in which they were framed. Russia perceived Western expansion of its value-based system as one that undermined the traditional Westphalian state-centric model of international relations and saw it as a threat to Russia's great power status, security and status as an independent subject of international politics. Over time, the West continued with its victory narrative and Russia continued to believe that it deserved great power status, leaving it to feel left aside on many pertinent issues and decisions in international relations.

Former US President Bill Clinton's miscalculation that great power politics was a thing of the past led to his NATO expansion policies, which ended up having disastrous consequences in terms of alienating the Russians.[1] Offensive realists predicted that the US would promote liberalism while applying classical methods of containment to Russia to prevent it from challenging the US' hegemonic position. Through NATO, the US ensured that the North Atlantic system remained preeminent on the continent. Conversely, should the West have been able to include Russia in the greater West, it would have satisfied their status concerns and enhanced security across the continent. Nevertheless, this was not the case, and Russia's resentment grew stronger as it began resisting democratic governance and regime change ever more fervently.

The fundamental Russian argument is that the values that characterised the West would be Russian values too after the Cold War ended – but the act of the West assuming ownership over liberal democratic values is illegitimate. The end of the Cold War did not signify the triumph of the Western power system in Russia's view. This 'decoupling' argument became the foundation of Russian neo-revisionist behaviour (Sakwa, 2017).

Yeltsin's pro-Western approach to international relations was based on Gorbachev's vision of a 'Common European Home'. This would only have been feasible had Russia committed to liberal democracy, capitalism and alignment with the West. For these reasons, Yeltsin and Gorbachev repeatedly warned of the effects that NATO expansion would have by marginalising Russia and denying the logic of 'Greater Europe'. The March 1999 NATO expansion exemplified that the West was exploiting and perpetuating Russian weakness as opposed to embracing Russia and incorporating it into the West.

Moreover, NATO's decision to bomb Serbia without a UN mandate made clear that it was no longer a defensive alliance. Thus, it marked the end of the Yeltsin vision for Russian-Western relations and paved the way for a new solution under the leadership of Vladimir Putin. Putin emphasised negotiating from a position of strength, while continuing the pro-Western approach. Instead of conceding to the demands of the West, Russia would assert its equality. Nevertheless, this strategy was short-lived, as sometime between the US war in Iraq, the expansion of NATO and the EU into Central Europe and the Baltics, the EU's eastern neighbourhood policy announcement, and after the West's support for colour revolutions, Russia concluded that the West did not accept Russian interests as equal (Casier, 2012; Stent, 2014, 101–106). While a breakthrough was reached with the EU-Russia 'Common Spaces Agreement' in 2005 when both sides committed to creating a Greater Europe, Moscow proposed an inclusive pan-European security architecture and an EU-Russian Union with free trade and free movement of people from Lisbon to Vladivostok.

This was rejected as 'anti-European' and undermining the primacy of the EU and NATO as the representatives of 'Europe' (Diesen, 2016). After this period, European integration became a zero-sum game, where the shared neighbourhood would have to choose between the West and Russia. The EU's proposed Association Agreement with Ukraine expected Kiev to decouple from Moscow and pivot towards Brussels economically, politically and militarily. The EU even rejected a proposal by Kiev and Moscow to preserve Ukrainian neutrality and replace the Association Agreement with a trilateral EU-Ukraine-Russia Agreement (Diesen, 2016). Since Putin's reformed pro-Western policy failed, the argument that Russia must prepare its military to counter NATO became the dominant policy in Russia. Evidence of growing confrontation arose with the gas wars with Ukraine in 2006 and 2009, the invasion of Georgia in 2008, the annexation of Crimea in 2014, Russian involvement in Syria and increasing evidence of Russian military presence in Europe. In addition, Russia has continued to expand its challenge to the West and the existing international order with the use of rhetoric, cyberattacks on national elections and support for right-wing political groups in the West.

At the Munich Security Conference in 2007, Putin announced that Russia was back as a major international actor and would not simply follow the lead of the West in terms of security and foreign policy issues. He also stated that Russia was trying to establish a 'sovereign democracy' that would be independent from external influence (Petrov and McFaul, 2005; Herd, 2009). This system represents a challenge to the promotion of Western values and norms implemented through NATO and EU cooperation agreements with the former Soviet states, demonstrating Russian soft power projection of its influence and legitimacy (Stent, 2014, 142–143).

On December 31, 2015, Putin approved a new national security strategy that presents a Russia focused on increasing its influence and prestige in the world and remaining more unified nationally (Olicker, 2016). It emphasises Russia's status as one of the world's great powers and aims to raise its gross domestic product (GDP) to one of the largest in the world. The national security policy is mostly inward focused and emphasises national defence, state and social security, quality of life of Russian citizens, economic growth, science, technology, education, health, culture, ecology and the environment. It is also highly focused on what Russia believes its values to be, including Russian traditional and moral values. The Security Strategy describes these values as being under threat from foreign values and in need of protection and reinforcement. The document simultaneously promotes plurality of faith and tolerance, as well as the importance of the Orthodox Church in Russian society. Internationally, the document describes Western efforts at overthrowing legitimate regimes, provoking domestic instability and conflict abroad as security threats that challenge Russian national interests. The threats range from the US and its allies seeking to contain Russia, in order to maintain their dominance of world affairs to various groups trying to destabilise Russia, including foreign and domestic non-governmental organisations, financial structures and individuals. The document suggests that the world is becoming more dangerous due to US desires to limit Russian power. Ultimately, Russia believes in cooperation with the West on common interests such as terrorism, instability and proliferation but insists that cooperation is only possible if the West accepts Russia's leadership role (Olicker, 2016).

In the case of Russian-Western relations, NATO expansion has always been perceived as a threat to Russia's security and power. Russia's invasion of Ukraine and annexation of Crimea served to assert Russian dominance over Ukraine by capturing its base in Sebastopol, worried that it would fall into the hands of NATO should Ukraine ever join the alliance. By doing so, it also attempted to ensure that Ukraine would no longer be appealing to join any EU agreements and institutions. Mearsheimer argues that the crisis in Ukraine is the West's fault and that Russian leaders have repeatedly opposed NATO enlargement (2014). Neo-liberal institutionalism failed to predict Russia's realist reaction in international politics. In the quest to spread liberal democracy and peace, the West overlooked the possibility that regional powers were going to resist any Western encroachment in their surrounding area. Constructivists, on the other hand, argue that the historical relationship among Russia, Ukraine and the EU has defined their identity and in turn their behaviour towards one another. Putin states that Crimea has always been an inseparable part of Russia, a conviction that was passed on from generation to generation (Putin, 2014). Ukraine has always been seen as a fraternal country for Russia and the Russian people. When applied to the Crimean case, constructivism helps to shed some perspective on Moscow's behaviour towards Ukraine that realist explanations do not quite cover. Russia wants to re-establish itself as a great power on the world stage and recapture the prestige and status that it had during the time of the USSR. The question after the USSR collapsed was whether Russia was going to become Westernised and Europeanised, or become its own unique Eurasian nation. Due to a complicated Russian-Western trajectory, the response to this question now lies with Putin's consolidation of a unique Russian civilisation and identity belonging to both European and Asian civilisations, while possessing its own values and norms. Putin wants to protect this identity and limit Western influence in the near abroad and especially in Russia itself. Putin wants to protect his regime and the Russian objectives of achieving great power status as a unique civilisation. The Russians want respect and status in the world and believe that they have been treated as a less important power over the years. Its reassertion into global international affairs, including but not limited to its actions in Ukraine, has gained Russia an important place in world affairs (Evans, 2008; Sakwa, 2015).

The NATO-Russian relationship and the strained European security environment

The Russia-NATO relationship is a contentious one. By signing the NATO-Russia Founding Act, Russia agreed to respect states' 'inherent right to choose the means to ensure their own security' (NATO, 2018). Twenty-nine countries have chosen freely to join NATO. In the years after the Ukraine crisis, Russia accused the West of violating an important part of the 1997 NATO-Russian Founding Act relating to new permanent stationing of forces. The 'Substantial Combat Forces' pledge states that NATO would not station additional permanent substantial combat forces. According to NATO, the recent deployment of its four multinational battle groups to the east is rotational and defensive, therefore below any reasonable definition of substantial combat forces (NATO, 2018). As a result, Russia pledged it would act similarly and has increased the numbers of its troops along allied borders and has breached transparency agreements on military exercises. But Russia has also broken the principle of the Founding Act that stated it would not use force against NATO allies or any other state by annexing Crimea and invading Ukraine. Nevertheless, Russia denies that such rule-breaking did occur, since the annexation of Crimea was done through a 'legal referendum' and the Kremlin still denies the presence of the Russian military in the rest of Ukraine.

Until today, NATO members have not felt the need to invest in modernising their military. However, as of 2015 and 2016, they have increased their defence budgets and have received US support in so doing, a move initiated by the Obama Administration. In addition, Lithuania has reintroduced compulsory military service and Poland has recently decided to create a paramilitary 'Territorial Defense Force' of tens of thousands of units

(Bitondo, Marrone, and Sartori, 2017). After the Russian invasion of Ukraine, NATO responded by reinforcing its commitment to its member-states, including the creation of a 5000-member joint task force that is deployable within 72 hours, sending four multinational combat battalions to Poland and the Baltics, and establishing command and control headquarters in all eastern member-states and multinational headquarters in Poland and Romania. It has also increased the number of exercises it conducts in Central and Eastern Europe, made infrastructure investments and ramped up its naval and air presence in the Baltic Sea and the Black Sea (Sokolsky, 2017). As Moscow firmly believes in its rightful sphere of influence, Poland and the Baltic states now fear Russia will engage in similar behaviours in their countries, as it did in Ukraine under the guise of protecting ethnic Russians (Hill and Gaddy, 2013, 312–314). The NATO budget has now increased from 1 billion dollars two years ago, to a request of 5 billion this year. This is the largest reinforcement effort since the Cold War (Daalder, 2017).

Naturally, Russia has built up its military presence, too. In the north, it has reopened former military bases near the Arctic Ocean (Craw, 2017). It has also been caught regularly invading other countries' airspace such as Norway, which intercepted 74 Russian warplanes conducting air patrols along its coast in 2014 – up from 58 in 2013 (Mortimer, 2017). Russia has also increased its presence from the Norwegian border south to the Ukrainian border and in the Kaliningrad enclave. More than 300,000 troops are deployed there and are fully equipped with modern military equipment, including a nuclear capable short-range missile system ('Russia Kicks Off', 2017). Russia has sent additional brigades and announced the creation of three new divisions that will face Ukraine. Along with its 30,000 new troops in Crimea, it has also placed 30 combat ships, 5 submarines, 100 combat aircraft and 50 combat helicopters there along with long-range anti-ship and anti-aircraft missiles and radar systems. Russia now has total domination of the Black Sea region. It has also deployed thousands of troops to occupied areas in Ukraine, Georgia, Moldova and Armenia (South, 2017). Moreover, Russia has enlarged its air and naval presence in Syria, ending previously unchallenged NATO control of the eastern Mediterranean, a strategic region for the West. Russia's navy in the Mediterranean now has missiles that can threaten most of Europe. To help Assad in Syria, Russia has fired long-range missiles from naval vessels in the Caspian and Mediterranean Seas. Russia has engaged in provocative behaviour, such as flying fighter and bomber missions close to NATO airspace, deploying nuclear submarines containing ballistic missiles to the Atlantic, conducting military exercises and modernising its nuclear capabilities by building new long-range missiles, submarines and bombers ('Russia Reinforcing Mediterranean', 2017).

The tension between Moscow and the West has brought back dangerous NATO-Russia confrontations that need to be addressed. Dialogue with Russia is necessary in order to reduce tensions in Europe and the world at large. After two years of frozen relations between NATO and Russia, the NATO-Russia Council met three times in 2016. Although no convergence on views occurred, this was a first step to supporting mutual understanding. Germany showed no firm position on Russia at the NATO summit in Warsaw nor its presence in the Baltics and Poland. This is because Germany is very cautious with its stance on Russia. According to a survey by the Körber Foundation, 81 per cent of Germans favour closer ties with Russia and see Russia as an equal power and a country with a rich history and culture (Körber Stiftung, 2016). Moreover, Germany is increasingly dependent on Russia for its energy supplies and wants to maintain its economic interests in relation to gas pipelines. Fifty-seven per cent of Germans replied 'no' to the question by a German public opinion poll on whether German soldiers should stand in defence of Poland and the Baltic states if they are attacked by Russia. Moreover, 49 per cent of respondents do not believe that a permanent NATO military presence will increase their sense of security and that NATO should not create permanent bases in Eastern Europe and the Baltic states (Bertelsman Stiftung, 2016). This view differs sharply from those in Poland and the Baltic states, as they have expressed their wish for NATO to increase its defence efforts for them. NATO allies are divided on Russia – France, Germany and Italy insist on a strategic partnership with Moscow, while Poland and the Baltics warn that Russia poses a threat. In order to have a successful strategy, NATO members need to be aligned in their views on how to move forward. In this regard, the West is not only experiencing external challenges, but internal ones as well, which only strengthen Vladimir Putin and his desire to weaken the Western establishment.

The challenges to the liberal democratic order

The world is changing, and the liberal democratic order is facing existential threats, as we noted earlier. Security threats in Europe, such as refugee flows and terrorist attacks, are creating a sense of insecurity among citizens. These new realities have created public order issues of racism and intolerance, exacerbating nationalist sentiments. People in Europe feel less secure and demand more protection from their leaders. A recent Eurobarometer survey showed that approximately two-thirds of EU citizens would like to see greater EU engagement in matters of security and defence policy. In 2016, European politicians finally responded to the deteriorating security situation around Europe's borders and made EU defence a priority (Pawlak, Grosek, and Dobreva, 2016). Defining a clear and unified strategy and action plan to overcome these issues has proven to be very challenging to the EU. Faced with these multiple challenges, along with the UK's exit from the EU, some EU countries have increased their budget in the field of defence. The EU Global Strategy, presented on June 28, 2016, by the High Representative and Vice President Federica Mogherini, has further boosted this acceleration. The EU and NATO have expressed their will to relaunch cooperation and develop a strategic partnership (Mogherini, 2016). Since the illegal Russian annexation of Crimea, the two actors have recognised the necessity to come together in the face of common threats and promote joint actions (Dempsey, 2016). As stated by the President of the European Commission Jean-Claude Junker, 'a stronger European Union means a stronger NATO, and a stronger NATO means a stronger European Union' (Juncker, 2016). However, a few challenges have presented themselves to NATO. European nations are divided on their approach to Russia and immigration issues, and Donald Trump's approach towards NATO and the EU is a more nationalist approach, which considers multilateralism and alliances as mere instruments to pursue immediate US national interest.

Divided Europe: Poland and Hungary

Poland feels threatened by increased Russian aggression and demands more defence efforts from NATO. Additionally, Poland's internal situation has seen an important policy shift away from the status quo which alienates it from Brussels. The Party of Law and Justice and Civic Platform won the parliamentary elections, shifting the country towards more conservative, even authoritarian, domestic policies. Polish official rhetoric has since become anti-Western and anti-European. Polish President Jaroslaw Kaczynski claims that Poland should dismiss the weight of liberal democracy and pave its own way (Buras and Balcer, 2016). Since its democratic transition, Poland positioned itself as a leader of the anti-Russian coalition in Eastern Europe. Because of its current fears of a Russian invasion, Poland has modernised and reformed its army. It also borders Ukraine and is subsequently also affected by that conflict. Until 2014, Poland and Ukraine were stable economic partners. Due to its particular circumstances, Poland believes that its security concerns are taking a second place to the Mediterranean refugee crisis and the Syrian conflict (Vukadinović, Begović, and Jušić, 2017).

Another Eastern European country that worries NATO is Hungary. Hungary and Russia maintain excellent political relations and economic ties. Hungary began its Russian turn in 2010 with the election Viktor Orban as Prime Minister. One of Orban's first official visits to a foreign country was a visit to Russia in November of that same year. Before the sanctions against the Russian Federation were imposed, imports from Russia amounted to 6.89 per cent of total imports to Hungary (Hegedus, 2016). This percentage included most Hungarian gas, oil and other fuel imports. Hungary and Gazprom signed a deal that guarantees Hungary a low price for about 22 billion cubic metres of gas. NATO leaders were worried that this price could be the result of an agreement which would protect Russian interests within the alliance. Nevertheless, Hungary did not veto the decision to impose sanctions on Russia. Hegedus calls Hungarian foreign policy a 'peacock dance' in which Hungary takes two steps forward and then one back. An example of this occurred when Hungary introduced sanctions against the Russian Federation, but also stopped the return of gas to Ukraine. The political party 'Jobbik' has become another political option in Hungary in the past few years and, unlike Orban's 'Fidesz', which is financially connected to Moscow through organised crime deals, 'Jobbik' is directly funded by the Kremlin. In addition, the Jobbik representative in the European Parliament, Bela Kovacs, was accused of espionage for the Russian Federation by the Hungarian high state prosecutor in 2014, but never went to trial due to his immunity status as a Member of the European Parliament (Hegedus, 2016).

Donald Trump

The election of Donald Trump poses another important challenge to the liberal order as the US has always been its leader and has now elected a President that prioritises nationalism and realism in international relations. Trump is less a proponent of international institutions and alliances than his predecessors. National interest is Trump's priority, and in this sense, globalisation and the liberal world order are only beneficial if they are valuable to US interests (Friedman, 2016). Former US President Barrack Obama prioritised multilateralism, alliances and institutions, maintaining a Wilsonian liberal international order which Trump believes is no longer serving US economic and security interests (Gove and Diekmann, 2017). For Trump, foreign policy decisions are made on a case-by-case basis. Since the US has retreated from leadership of the liberal world order (Haas, 2018), there is now more room for other powers to act more independently and aggressively in their regions through conventional or hybrid warfare, demonstrating the accuracy of Waltz's predictions of the instability that arises from a multipolar world order. International institutions may be rendered useless compared to the will of the nation-state in such a system (Waltz, 1979).

Russian hybrid warfare against democracy

Russia today has launched hybrid warfare on Western democracy. This type of warfare takes place throughout many domains, such as the military, politics, the economy and information systems. It was not until the confrontation with Georgia in 2008 and more recent concerns about Ukraine that Moscow developed the use of force to achieve policy objectives (Tkachenko, 2017). Russia has rebuilt its military, but limits its use in order not to challenge the security order directly. Rather, its goal is to assure its own security and regional power, which in itself already poses a threat to that order. Between 2007 and 2016, Russia's annual military spending nearly doubled, reaching 70 billion dollars, the third highest military spending in the world behind the US and China. In 2011, Russia announced a ten-year modernisation plan which includes 360 billion dollars in new military procurement (Biden and Carpenter, 2018). Russia's strategies are changing and becoming more sophisticated. Special forces were deployed in Ukraine, took over important spaces, and cyber operations spread disinformation to hide what was really happening. The 'little green men' were said to have been local opposition forces, reflecting the popular will to reject political changes in Kiev and be reunited with Russia. Moscow justified this invasion, saying Russian-speaking people in Ukraine were being attacked by violent nationalists, neo-Nazis, Russophobes and anti-Semites who carried out a coup in Kiev. Less overtly, Russia has also tried to weaken Western democracy through information warfare, energy policies and corrupt business dealings. By attacking the West, attention shifts away from the corruption and economic troubles inside Russia and activates national sentiment while keeping Western democracies focused on their own internal divisions. Russian power at home and abroad has increased as a result of these hybrid tactics, but the current US Administration has no interest in protecting Western democracy.

In addition, the Kremlin has been using social media tactics to undermine democracy in Europe and the US by spreading disinformation through fake accounts. Through proxies in the 'Dark Web', the Kremlin has managed to discourage voter turnout and boost attendance at political rallies for Russian preferred candidates. During the 2016 US presidential race, a troll farm in St. Petersburg purchased thousands of ads on Facebook, and in the US and French presidential elections, emails were hacked and distributed through WikiLeaks. Russia also tried to sway campaigns in the Netherlands on referendums for Ukraine's integration with Europe, in Italy on governance reforms and in Spain on Catalonia's secession. Russian support for Alternative for Germany, a far-right party, aimed to increase the group's vote totals in last fall's parliamentary elections by amplifying its messaging on social media. A similar Russian effort supported the nationalist Northern League and the populist Five Star Movement in Italy's parliamentary elections (Biden and Carpenter, 2018).

Another important strategy the Kremlin uses to gain leverage and power in its near abroad is the use of energy manipulation tactics. Until the time of the colour revolutions, Russia was willing to negotiate its economic and political differences and accept any disadvantaged economic relationship. However, after democratisation efforts in these regions occurred and they moved closer to Europe and NATO, pragmatic relationships were more difficult for Moscow and hence resulted in conflicts such as the 'gas wars' with Ukraine (Moulioukova and Kanet, 2015, 2017). Russia threatened to cut off gas to Ukraine several times and in 2006 and 2009 actually stopped the flow in the middle of winter. The Kremlin also uses energy to pressure European governments, particularly in the Baltics, the Balkans and Central Europe. It also uses energy to gain influence with European political and business leaders. The Kremlin also has corrupt business dealings in luxury real estate markets in London, Miami and New York, which grant it access to Western political and business elites. These dealings have also served to support anti-establishment candidates or movements in Europe that support closer partnership with Russia or question the values of NATO and the EU (Biden and Carpenter, 2018).

Future prospects and conclusions

If the West wants to stop Moscow's influence in dividing Western democracies, it needs to address its own vulnerabilities. Disinformation and propaganda must be exposed, and social media platforms need to increase advertisement funding transparency. Most importantly, however, dialogue with Russia is vital to try to reach certain compromises in matters of international relations. Russia is not responding to sanctions nor to assertive Western actions, but rather responds similarly and escalates the situation. The West, however, does not want to give Russia the impression that it can act with impunity either. As the two largest nuclear powers in the world, Russia and the US have an obligation to maintain strategic stability. If Russia were granted more influence in a more pluralist international system, it would not have the need to behave so aggressively. However, given the thrust of Russian policy under President Putin, that would result in dismantling much of the existing Western-dominated liberal international system. Preserving NATO is important for the member-states, but reaching an agreement with Russia would ease tensions in Europe. Yet, attempting to create a regional security framework structured in ways that Russia would accept would have many negative implications that those committed to more democratic governance would not accept.

Although the liberal democratic world order is being challenged significantly, it is far from collapse. The liberal order is, however, less able to function and no longer has the leadership it once had. Nevertheless, Western power and the liberal discourse are still the dominant order of the day. No country in the world, not even China, has the ability or the willingness to replace the US role of ultimate guarantor of international security (Alcaro, 2015).

This chapter has argued that although the liberal order may be in trouble, it will not be replaced by another order. Rather, the order will be slightly modified as nations take a more pragmatic approach to multilateralism. The Putin regime is less threatened than it was under stronger liberal leadership, but due to its own structural problems, it will not emerge as a world superpower that threatens the existence of the liberal order, but will however retain and strengthen its regional dominance. Russia wants a louder voice – which it is gaining and will continue to gain in today's changing climate. Russia will 'win' in terms of its desires to decrease Western interference in the world, fewer democratisation projects and a dwindling American hegemony. However, it does not appear that NATO is backing down – in this sense, military escalation on both sides will continue and reach a standstill. There will be no all-out war between Russia and the West, as it is simply not in anyone's interest to do so.

Cooperation and dialogue are needed to come to a consensus on the NATO, EU and Russia issues. NATO must realise that further expansion will result in balance of power responses by Russia. Russia is not an expansionist country – it is not seeking world domination – it is seeking to increase its power relative to the other world powers, so as to be included as one of the great powers. Although Russia is not a liberal democracy, its leader has the consent of the governed, demonstrating that the majority of the population has no qualms with the way Russia is run (Loftus, 2018). Perhaps a more pluralistic Euro-Atlantic security architecture, could it be crafted, would be the most practical solution to ensure security and stability.

This chapter reflects the author's own views and not those of the George C. Marshall European Center for Security Studies, the US Department of Defense or German Ministry of Defence. Moreover, it was written before the author was associated with the Center.

Note

1 These negative consequences were predicted by analysts such as George F. Kennan (cited in Friedman, 1998) and Stephen F. Cohen (2001).

References

Alcaro, Riccardo (2015) 'The West, Multipolarity and the Challenge of Global Governance', *Transworld*, 27 January. www.transworld-fp7.eu/?p=1738

Bertelsmann Stiftung (2016) 'Frayed Partnership: German Public Opinion on Russia', *Gutersloh & Institute for Public Affairs*, Warsaw. www.bertelsmann-stiftung.de/fileadmin/files/ user upload/ EZ_Frayed_Partnership_2016_ENG.pdf

Biden, Joseph R. Jr. and Michael Carpenter (2018) 'How to Stand Up to the Kremlin: Defending Democracy against Its Enemies', *Foreign Affairs*, January/February. www.foreignaffairs.com/articles/2017-12-05/how-stand-kremlin

Bitondo, Francesca, Alessandro Marrone and Paola Sartori (2017) 'Challenges to NATO and Italy's Role: Trump, Brexit, Collective Defence and Neighborhood Stability', *Instituto Affair Internazionale*. January. www.iai.it/sites/default/files/iai1618e.pdf

Buras, Piotr and Balcer, Adam (2016) 'An Unpredictable Russia: The Impact on Poland', *European Council on Foreign Relations*, 15 July. www.ecfr.eu/article/commentary_an_ unpredictable_russia_the_impact_on_poland

Casier, Tom (2012) 'Are the Policies of Russia and the EU in Their Shared Neighborhood Doomed to Clash?' in Roger E. Kanet and Maria Raquel Freire, eds., *Competing for Influence: The EU and Russia in Post-Soviet Eurasia*. Dordrecht: Republic of Letters Publishing, 31–54.

Cohen, Stephen F. (2001) *Failed Crusade: America and the Tragedy of Post-Communist Russia*. New York: W. W. Norton.

Coynash, Halya (2016) 'A British Foreign Secretary Who Excuses Russia's Invasion of Crimea?' *Human Rights in Ukraine*, 14 July. http://khpg.org/en/index.php?id=1468447666

Craw, Victoria (2017) 'Arctic Outpost Becomes Hotbed of Russian Military Activity News', June 26. www.news.com.au/world/europe/arctic-outpost-becomes-hotbed-of-russian-military-activity/news-story/25108f508fd511205cac25f6d6371e70\

Daalder, Ivo H. (2017) 'Responding to Russia's Resurgence: Not Quiet on the Eastern Front', *Foreign Affairs*, November/December.

Dempsey, Judy (2016) 'NATO and the EU Agree to End Their Rivalry', *Strategic Europe*, 8 July. http://carnegieeurope.eu/strategiceurope/?fa=64045

Dennison, Susi and Dina Parijs (2016) 'The World According to Europe's Insurgent Parties: Putin, Migration and People Power', *European Council on Foreign Relations*, 27 June. www.ecfr.eu/publications/summary/the_world_according_to_europes_insurgent_parties

Diesen, Glenn (2016) 'Putin: Russia's Last "Pro-Western" Alternative', *The Interpreter*, 7 June. www.lowyinstitute.org/the-interpreter/putin-russias-last-pro-western-alternative

Evans, Alfred B. Jr. (2008) 'Power and Ideology: Vladimir Putin and the Russian Political System', *The Carl Beck Papers in Russian & East European Studies*, 1902: 43.

Friedman, Thomas (1998) Interview with George F. Kennan, *New York Times*, 2 May. www.scribd.com/document/272588202/George-Kennan-on-Russia

Friedman, Uri (2016) 'How Donald Trump Could Change the World,' *The Atlantic*, 7 November. www. theatlantic.com/international/archive/2016/11/trump-election-foreign-policy/505934

Gove, Michael and Kai Diekmann (2017) 'Full Transcript of the Interview with Donald Trump', *The Times*, 16 January.

Haas, Richard N. (2018) 'Liberal World Order, R.I.P.', *Project Syndicate: The World's Opinion Page*, 21 March. www.project-syndicate.org/commentary/end-of-liberal-world-order-by-richard-n--haass-2018-03

Hegedus, D. (2016) 'The Kremlin's Influence in Hungary: Are Russian Vested Interests Wearing Hungarian National Colors?' *DGAP Kompakt*, 8(1): 1–11.

Herd, Graeme P. (2009) 'Russia's Sovereign Democracy: Instrumentalization, Interests, and Identity', in Roger E. Kanet, ed., *A Resurgent Russia and the West: The European Union, NATO, and Beyond*. Dordrecht: Republic of Letters Publishing, 3–18.

Hill, Fiona and Clifford G. Gaddy (2013) *Mr. Putin. Operative in the Kremlin*. Washington, DC: Brookings Institution Press, February 1.

Inglehart, Ronald F. and Pippa Norris (2016) 'Trump, Brexit, and the Rise of Populism: Economic Have-Nots and Cultural Backlash', https://www.hks.harvard.edu/publications/trump-brexit-and-rise-populism-economic-have-nots-and-cultural-backlash

Juncker, Jean-Claude (2016) 'European Commission, Remarks by President Jean-Claude Juncker at the Joint Press Conference with Donald Tusk, President of the European Council and Jens Stoltenberg, Secretary General of NATO,' Warsaw, 8 July. http://europa.eu/rapid/press-release_SPEECH-16-2460_en.htm

Körber Stiftung (2016) *Russia in Europe: Rapprochement or Isolation*? www.koerber-stiftung.de/fileadmin/user_upload/koerber-stiftung/mediathek/pdf/2016/Survey_Russia-in-Europe.pdf

Loftus, Suzanne (2018) *Insecurity and the Rise of Nationalism: The Case of Putin's Russia: Keeper of Traditional Values*. Cham, Switzerland: Palgrave Macmillan.

Mearsheimer, John (2014) 'Why the Ukraine Crisis Is the West's Fault', *Foreign Affairs*, September/October.

Milne, Seumas (2014) 'Far from Keeping the Peace, Nato Is a Threat to It', *The Guardian*, 3 September. www.theguardian.com/commentisfree/2014/sep/03/nato-peace-threat-ukraine-military-conflict

Mogherini, Frederica (2016) 'NATO, Joint Declaration by the President of the European Council, the President of the European Commission, and the Secretary General of the North Atlantic Treaty Organisation', Warsaw, 8 July. www.nato.int/cps/en/natohq/official_texts_133163.htm

Mortimer, Caroline (2015) 'Hungarian PM Viktor Orbán Says "All the Terrorists Are Basically Migrants" in Response to Paris attacks', *Independent*, 24 November. www.independent.co.uk/news/world/europe/hungarian-pm-viktor-orb-n-says-all-the-terrorists-are-basically-migrants-in-response-to-paris-a6746356.html

Mortimer, Caroline (2017) 'Russia Is Building Up Its Arctic Military Presence and Nato Should Be Worried, Says New Report', *The Independent*. Caroline Mortimer @cjmortimer Thursday 7 September. www.independent.co.uk/news/world/europe/russia-arctic-military-presence-nato-worried-us-report-tensions-north-america-a7934741.html

Moulioukova, Dina and Roger E. Kanet (2015) 'Russian Energy Policy: Implications for Global Energy Security', in Bruce R. Bagley, Dina Moulioukova and Hanna Kassab, eds., *The Impact of Emerging Economies on Global Energy and Environment: Challenges Ahead*. Lanham, MD: Lexington Books, 81–100.

Moulioukova, Dina and Roger E. Kanet (2017) 'Decoding Russia's Energy Security. Perceptions Matter', in Rémi Piet, Bruce Bagley and Marcello R. S. Zorovich, eds., *Energy Security and Environmental Policy in the Western Hemisphere*. New York: Lexington Books, 275–298.

NATO (2018) 'North Atlantic Treaty Organization: NATO-Russia Relations: The Facts', Last updated: 28 February. 15:44 www.nato.int/cps/en/natohq/topics_111767.htm

Olicker, Olga (2016) 'Unpacking Russia's New National Security Strategy', *Center for Strategic and International Studies*. 7 January. www.csis.org/analysis/unpacking-russias-new-national-security-strategy

Pawlak, Patryk, Kristina Grosek and Alina Dobreva (2016) 'Briefing Public Expectations and EU Policies', July 2016.| European Parliamentary Research Service. Graphics by Eulalia Claros, based on data from the Public Opinion Monitoring Unit, DG COMM Members' Research Service PE 586.583 EN Security and defence policy. www.europarl.europa.eu/RegData/etudes/BRIE/2016/586583/EPRS_BRI(2016)586583_EN.pdf

Petrov, Nikolay and Michael McFaul (2005) 'The Essence of Putin's Managed Democracy', *Carnegie Center for International Peace*. 18 October. www.carnegieendowment.org/2005/10/18/essence-of-putin-s-managed-democracy/2a3

Putin, Vladimir (2014) 'Address by President of the Russian Federation', *Kremlin*, 18 March. http://eng.kremlin.ru/transcripts/6889

Rachman, Gideon (2017) 'Trump, Putin, Xi and the Rise of Nostalgic Nationalism', *Financial Times*, 2 January. www.ft.com/content/198efe76-ce8b-11e6-b8ce-b9c03770f8b1

'Russia Kicks off' (2017) 'Russia Kicks Off Huge War Games on Europe's Borders', *Cbs news*. 14 September. www.cbsnews.com/news/russia-zapad-2017-military-exercise-belarus-nato-europe-crimea-ukraine-putin/f

'Russia Reinforcing Mediterranean Formation' (2017) Posted on June 12, 2017. Russian defense policy blog. https://russiandefpolicy.blog/2017/06/12/russia-reinforcing-mediterranean-formation/

Saez, Emmanual (2017) 'Income Inequality: Evidence and Policy Implications', UC Berkeley Arrow Lecture, Stanford, January 2013: *'The Demographics of Stagnation Why People Matter for Economic Growth,' Foreign Affairs*, http://eml.berkeley.edu/~saez/lecture_saez_arrow.pdf

Sakwa, Richard (2015) *Frontline Ukraine: Crisis in the Borderlands*. London: IB Taurus and Co. LTD.

Sakwa, Richard (2017) *Russia against the Rest: The Post-Cold War Crisis of World Order*. Cambridge: Cambridge University Press.

Sharma, Ruchir (2016) 'The Demographics of Stagnation: Why People Matter for Economic Growth', *Foreign Affairs*, March/April Issue. www.foreignaffairs.com/articles/world/2016-02-15/demographics-stagnation

Sokolsky, Richard (2017). *The New NATO-Russia Military Balance: Implications for European Security*, Task Force White Paper, Carnegie Endowment for International Peace, 13 March. https://carnegieendowment.org/2017/03/13/new-nato-russia-military-balance-implications-for-european-security-pub-68222

South, Todd (2017) 'What's Putin Up to? The Russian Military Buildup in Europe Raises Tension', 13 September. www.militarytimes.com/news/2017/09/13/whats-putin-up-to-the-russian-military-buildup-on-europes-border-raises-tension/

Stanley, Sarah (2016) 'A Decade of Decline for Global Freedom', *Acton Institute Powerblog*, 29 January. http://blog.acton.org/archives/84738-a-decade-of-decline-for-global-freedom.html

Stent, Angela (2014) *The Limits of Partnership: Us-Russian Relations in the Twenty-First Century*. Princeton, NJ and Oxford: Princeton University Press.

Stephens, Bret (2018) 'The Rise of Euro- Putinism', *New York Times*, 16 March. www.nytimes.com/2018/03/16/opinion/vladimir-putin-russia-elections.html

Tkachenko, Stanislav L. (2017) 'The Coercive Diplomacy of Vladimir Putin (2014–2016)', in Roger E. Kanet, ed., *The Russian Security Challenge to the European Security Environment*. Chapter 5. UK-New York: Palgrave Macmillan.

Vukadinović, Lidija Čehulić, Monika Begović and Luka Jušić (2017). 'NATO in Europe: Between Weak European Allies and Strong Influence of Russian Federation'. *Croatian International Relations Review*, XXIII (80 Special Issue). Zagreb, Croatia: CIRR, Institute for Development and International Relations. http://cirr.irmo.hr/wp-content/uploads/2017/11/CIRR-80.pdf

Waltz, K. N. (1979) *Theory of International Politics*. Reading, MA: Addison Wesley.

Wesslau, Fredrik (2016) 'Putin's Friends in Europe', *European Council on Foreign Relations*. 19 October. www.ecfr.eu/article/commentary_putins_friends_in_europe7153

Zakaria, Fareed (2016) 'Why the West is in Trouble', *Foreign Affairs*. November/December Issue. www.foreignaffairs.com/articles/united-states/2016-10-17/populism-march

PART II

Domestic politics, threat perception and Russian security strategy

Introduction

Roger E. Kanet

In this second section of the *Handbook*, the authors focus on the relationship of domestic politics and threat perception to both Russian foreign and security policy. In Chapter 6, entitled 'Domestic and Foreign Policy Nexus: Domestic Politics, Threat Perception and Russian Security Strategy', Stefan Meister of the Robert Bosch Centre for Central and Eastern Europe, Russia and Central Asia at the German Council on Foreign Relations, tracks the interrelationship of domestic and foreign factors in influencing Russian security policy. He argues that 'the interlink between domestic and foreign policy is crucial to the understanding of Vladimir Putin's Russia'. In fact, confrontation with the outside world has become an essential component of the security elites' ability to consolidate power since Putin's return to the presidency in 2012.

In Chapter 7, entitled 'Understanding Russia's Security Strategy in a Context of Power', Tom Casier of the University of Kent's Brussels School of International Relations describes the role of power in Russia's foreign policy and security strategy. He takes a pluralist approach and examines power as a complex phenomenon operating along diverging dimensions and in different contexts. The goal is to understand Russia's current security strategy within the context of its relative power position: how does Russia seek to regain great power status; how powerful is it effectively; and how should we understand Moscow's use and showcasing of a wide array of power means?

In Chapter 8, Susanne Oxenstierna of the Swedish Defence Research Agency (FOI) provides a detailed examination of 'Russia's Economy and Military Expenditures'. She notes that, as part of his commitment to upgrading Russian military forces, 'Russia gave priority to high defence spending and building military strength despite a considerable weakening of economic growth' during Putin's third presidential term. Not until 2017 did this trend change. The author concludes that until Russia overcomes problems with economic development – including problems with the rule of law and top-down management – military spending cannot increase substantially without cutting into the economic objectives that the Putin administration has set for itself.

In Chapter 9, entitled 'Russian Strategic Culture: The Generational Approach and the Counter-Intelligence State Thesis', Mette Skak of the University of Aarhus argues that research on Russian strategic culture must abandon geographic and macro-historical determinism ('geopolitics') for the benefit of a dynamic generation-sociological approach akin to that of Karl Mannheim, who proposed that people are influenced by dramatic personal or societal events in their youth. The effect carries over and re-emerges in future generations, as we can currently observe in the offensive turn in Russian political culture, the driving force in Russian foreign and security policy.

The final chapter in this second section of the *Handbook*, Chapter 10 by Edwin Bacon of the University of Lincoln, concerns 'The Security Council and Security Decision-Making'. After describing the institution and the importance of its major member, the discussion tracks the role of the Council over the quarter century of its existence and shows that its importance has increased and decreased largely according to the will of the president who heads it.

6

THE DOMESTIC AND FOREIGN POLICY NEXUS

Politics, threat perception and Russian security strategy

Stefan Meister

Defining the socio-political landscape through the lens of security perception

In the aftermath of the 2004 Beslan terror attack, President Vladimir Putin criticised the Russian leadership's inability to assess and react adequately to external and internal threats with the words: 'We displayed weakness. And the weak are beaten' (Putin, 2004). This sentence gives the best understanding of his policy afterwards, which emphasises doing everything possible to ensure that the Russian state is strong enough to face any external or internal threat.

As the historian Igor Torbakov argues, 'Russian history is best understood as the process of adaptation to (relative) backwardness and perceived external threats' (Torbakov, 2011, 5). Out of a sense of insecurity and vulnerability, the elite mobilises all natural and human resources for the purpose of combatting real and imagined foreign and domestic threats. The need to be ready and to mobilise structures Russia's society and elite into a militarised and securitised state. As Alexander Golts argues, the framework of Putin's foreign and security policy is based on realpolitik of the nineteenth and first half of twentieth centuries. It is also based on a militarism that takes any conflict situation in international and domestic politics as a threat requiring a military response. This way of thinking of the (current) Russian elite contributed to the creation of a vertical of power, to the concentration of decision-making in the hands of the president and to the lack of civil and public control in Russian politics (Golts, 2018).

The current regime operates from a strong culture of secrecy and informal networking. There are two policy milieus in Putin's Russia: the real and the virtual. The irony is that public statements and official documents present broader trends and visions, but limited understanding, about how policy is made or what the real policy is about. The real policy is exclusive and almost invisible. It is the president who makes the decisions; the vast majority of the political elite plays a small role and the public's input is negligible (Lo, 2015, 5). Even if the existence of an inner circle is always discussed, and the role of security actors and system liberals must be borne in mind, it is uncertain who influences whom. The very nature of the current elite, which mostly comes from the intelligence and security institutions, fuels the paranoia and sense of insecurity of the regime, and it influences how decisions are made and how problems are solved.

In Putin's Russia, foreign and security policy plays a crucial role in achieving domestic consensus and mobilisation. While the annexation of Crimea and the conflict with the West have helped Putin regain legitimacy, military interventions and foreign policy have also helped to distract the public's attention away from the country's modernisation deficits and from the postponement of domestic reforms. Since Putin came to power, state security with the regime as its sole guarantor has been at the heart of the government policy. In combination with the renationalisation of the energy sector and the redistribution of cash flows by the leadership, the result is an extreme concentration of power at the highest level (Kastueva-Jean, 2015, 6–7).

The growing role of people from the security services in politics since 2000 has impacted on the perception in decision-making circles and the public that Russia is under threat and needs to invest more in its security. This is also the result of the breaking up of the Soviet Union and the uncontrolled privatisation of the economy and politics during the 1990s. With the appearance of Putin on the scene, there was a demand in society for order and stability. Russia ranked in the 1990s and 2000s among the top ten countries in the world with a high risk of terrorist attacks (Maplecroft, 2010). According to the Global Terrorism Index, in 2016, it ranked 30th of the riskiest countries, behind France, showing that the situation has improved, but is still fragile (Global Terrorism Index 2016, 2016, 10). Despite the relative quiet in Chechnya under its current President Ramzan Kadyrov, the North Caucasus has exported the terrorism risk to other regions of Russia and the world at large. Furthermore, the risk has increased with Russia's involvement in the Syrian conflict (Mazurova, 2016).

This chapter argues that the interlink between domestic and foreign policy is crucial to the understanding of Vladimir Putin's Russia. Foreign and security policy serves as a key source for the domestic legitimisation of the regime. At the same time, the way security threats are instrumentalised, how they are 'solved' in a military and brutal way, and the complete disregard for human rights and the idea of reconciliation, foster exactly the insecurity and vulnerability Russia's leadership wants to prevent.

The insecurity of the regime

With the return of Putin to the presidency in 2012, there were fundamental changes in domestic and foreign policy. The main trigger was the global financial crisis of 2008–2009, which was followed by the mass demonstrations in the big cities in 2011–2012. With this, the social contract between society and the ruling elite – political inactivity in return for growing income and consumption – that developed during Putin's first two terms (2000–2008) with the help of steadily rising oil and gas prices was de facto cancelled by the regime because of the lack of resources.

The attempt to open up the social and political discourse, to begin small steps of modernisation and to pursue an economic and security rapprochement with the West during the presidency of Dmitry Medvedev (2008–2012) has since been stopped by key parts of the ruling elite. Substantial economic modernisation linked with the rule of law, real competition and transparency appeared too dangerous because this would lead to a loss of power by the elite. While the so-called economic liberals in the regime were attempting to reach through Medvedev a further economic opening towards the West, the security elite (the so-called Siloviki) wanted to prevent exactly this. Putin had to return to the presidency in 2012 also because important parts of the ruling elites felt they could lose control over the state and their rent-seeking options. Thus, he had to return as the guarantor of the system for his own security as well as for his circle.

In the context of the Duma election at the end of 2011 and the presidential election in early 2012, the mass demonstrations in the big cities, especially those in Moscow and St. Petersburg, triggered fears in the leadership of a Russian Maidan. Putin and some of the security players have described these demonstrations as an attempted colour revolution initiated by the United States' leadership, which had in mind the worst-case scenario for Russia (Herszenhorn and Barry, 2011). In their perception, Russia was under attack by the West, which was using the media, non-governmental organisations (NGOs), social media and other instruments of soft power to weaken Russia's leadership at home and abroad (Ivanov, 2015). In this understanding, the ultimate goal of the West is regime change in Russia, similar to that in Ukraine in 2013–2014. The demonstrations increased the alienation from the West, led to more influence by the security elite in politics and to fundamental changes in the domestic as well as foreign and security policy of the Kremlin.

In fact, the 2011–2012 demonstrations showed a loss of legitimacy of the Putin system in important parts of the population, which was reflected in polls showing the United Russia Party as the party of the ruling elites with a little over 30 per cent approval and Putin with 40 per cent at the end of 2011 and the beginning of 2012 (Levada, 2013). Especially in the eyes of the growing middle class, Putin had no ideas for the modernisation of the country and their future. It was the urban middle class that went into the streets to demonstrate for a Russia without Putin and a state with fair elections and rule of law as well as without corruption (Meister, 2018a).

Control of civil society

Putin's goal with his return to the presidency in 2012 was to retain control and to prevent regime change. In line with his previous policy, the Parliament adopted numerous laws against NGOs, and especially their foreign funding, and the independent media to control the opposition and the Internet. The laws passed since 2012 have limited freedom of assembly and freedom of speech on the Internet as well as discredited elections through a campaign against NGOs and increased state control over media (Chikov, 2014, 15). All the major media, including television, Internet outlets and newspapers, have become the voice of the leadership, with very few exceptions such as *Novaya Gazeta* and Rain TV as niche products. The media are used as instruments to mobilise patriotic support and to give society the impression of a de facto war situation with enemies inside and outside Russia. At the same time, political and administrative pressure on the media and their owners has led to self-censorship by journalists and to the sale of independent outlets to state companies or to business people loyal to the Kremlin (Human Rights Watch, 2017, 29–35).

In 2016, the Parliament passed a law requiring telecommunications and Internet companies to retain the contents of all communications for six months and the data about communications for three years (Human Rights Watch, 2017, 2). This law is part of a series of reactions to the 2011–2012 demonstrations, which helped to identify those people who support protests. It makes it easier for the authorities to identify social media users and collect personal data without judicial control.

The laws on foreign agents (2012) are first of all additions or amendments to existing NGO laws. These are the third step by the government under Putin to bring NGOs under direct state control after laws in 2001 and 2005–2006 that led first of all to a bureaucratisation of the work of NGOs (Siegert, 2014, 17). The new regulations discredit those NGOs that take foreign funding. All NGOs that receive funding from foreign states and their organs, from international and foreign organisations, or from citizens of foreign states have to register with the Ministry of Justice and apply to themselves and their activities the 'foreign agent' label (Law on Foreign Agents, 2012). In 2012, the Duma introduced monetary penalties for failing to register as a 'foreign agent' (Penal Law, 2012). Since June 2014, the Ministry of Justice can enter NGOs into the register without their agreement (Siegert, 2014, 17). An additional part of this policy is rhetoric to discredit these groups through statements by key officials who publicly refer to specific organisations as unpatriotic or tools of foreign governments. Studies show how the government has successfully marginalised and discredited in the public eye those groups that are critical of the leadership (Gilbert, 2016, 1556, 1565).

Regime transformation with impact on security policy

The return of Putin to the presidency was accompanied by a shift in the equilibrium between different elite groups. He tilted the balance of power between the so-called economic liberals and the Siloviki in favour of the latter. If the liberals continue to hold key positions in economic policy (at the Central Bank, the Ministry of Economy and Sberbank), they have gradually been replaced in other areas, such as in state companies or as heads of regions or republics.[1] They have become useful instruments of the regime to stabilise the economy and minimise macroeconomic risks, but they have no impact on any relevant decision outside economic policy anymore. The circle around Putin has tightened, and the opportunities for trying to apply correctives to his policy decisions have been reduced. At the same time, the security apparatus has gained influence on domestic, economic and foreign policy, and it has been favoured with growing budgets despite the ongoing economic crisis. The modernisation of the armed forces and their equipment has become a top priority. Military spending grew from 3.8 per cent to 5.5 per cent of gross domestic product (GDP) between 2012 and 2016, though it fell to 4.3 per cent in 2017 (SIPRI, 2018, 13). Simultaneously, the government has spent less in key areas such as health, education and science (Zhavoronkov, 2017).

Since 2014, however, stability and the prevention of change is not the ultimate aim of the regime anymore (Stanovaya, 2018, 1). There has been a change in the elite and a reshuffle at the middle and top levels of the administration. Young technocrats have replaced old associates of Putin from his time in the mayor's office St. Petersburg in the 1990s and have professionalised it (Petrov, 2017, 4). With the annexation of Crimea and the conflict in Ukraine, the role of the Siloviki in decision-making has increased at the expense of civilian elites. There is also a trend of more security actors being placed in executive positions in the federal and regional administrations as well as in state enterprises. That means, not only a generation change at the working level but also at the top level. As a result, the main competition is no longer between liberals and Siloviki, as until 2012, but between technocrats and security actors. The technocrats are able to undertake reforms in less politicised areas, including improving investment conditions, which has been reflected in the improvement of Russia's rating in the World Bank's Doing Business Index from 124th in 2012 to 35th in 2018 (The World Bank, 2018). As a reaction to the ongoing economic stagnation, the domestic economic agenda has also been given greater political importance and the government started a pension and tax reform (Petrov, 2018).

At the same time, the role of Putin as the national and military leader has become more important for the legitimacy of the political system since 2012. The dependence of the different elites on Putin has increased while his dependence on them is declining (Petrov, 2017, 2). The personalisation of the regime goes with the weakening of civil society and of important institutions like the judiciary, local government and elections. The young technocrats have no power resources of their own and are dependent on Putin. It will be much easier to replace them than was the case with the former friends of the president.

According to a key economic advisor of the government, the aim of the Ministry of Economy is to make Russia less dependent on foreign investment and on the price of oil and gas, because this dependence limits economic sovereignty. In the coming years, massive investment is planned in infrastructure, real estate and services in order to boost domestic demand and to achieve more growth independent from the global economy (Dmitriev, 2018). How promising this is given the persistently high levels of corruption, low growth and a shrunken National Welfare Fund, is an open question. Furthermore, higher debt is planned, which may be possible because of the low foreign debt compared to many Western countries. Russia still has a very low external debt of 3.5 per cent of GDP in 2017, compared to 1.7 per cent in 2011 (BOFIT, 2018). All this is also a reaction to the Western sanctions that were imposed after the annexation of Crimea and the start of the war in eastern Ukraine.

This shift in power and priorities has had an impact on Russian foreign policy. There has been a securitisation of politics and the public. The population is constantly shown the threats Russia is facing and that only Putin is able to provide stability and order. The economic crisis, the decline in GDP and the limited spending in future areas like research, education, health and infrastructure seem to be less important in that light. Russia is constantly overstretching with its focus on military modernisation, massive investment in the military industrial complex and operations abroad, especially in Syria and, to a lesser extent, in Ukraine.

Changes in the domestic security forces

It is in this context that a comprehensive reshuffle of the internal security forces took place with the creation of a National Guard in 2016. While the Siloviki have been strengthened since 2012, with this reform some have lost power again. The Interior Troops, the special forces of the police (including the riot police OMON) and the special forces for fighting terrorism, all from the Ministry of Interior, were incorporated into the National Guard, as well as the federal state security company Ochrana (Galeotti, 2017). This new elite organ is directly under the president and is headed by a close and loyal ally of Putin, Viktor Zolotov, who like him served before in the KGB (Committee for state security - Soviet intelligence service) and headed this security service in 2000–2013 (Klein, 2016, 3).

The main tasks of the National Guard are to protect public order and security, to fight extremism and terrorism, and to support border and territorial defence. While it lacks the infrastructure to be more than a support for the police and the Federal Security Service (FSB) in anti-terror operations, its main task is to protect the regime from mass demonstrations like those in 2011–2012 and a possible colour revolution (Galeotti, 2017).

Even if the protest mood in Russian society is low at the moment,[2] in the National Guard the leadership has built up an effective instrument to deter and supress mass protests in times of economic crisis (Klein, 2016, 3). While the NGO and media laws should help to prevent any mass protests or opposition before they start, the National Guard with its 400,000 troops is able to protect the regime against any public threat. A second aim of the new structure is to discipline the elites and particularly the competing security organs (Baunov, 2017, 28). With Putin having successfully marginalised the liberal elites and increased the dependence of oligarchs on the state, the only relevant power players in the system are the Siloviki. The creation of the National Guard gives Putin direct access to a loyal paramilitary organisation with more troops than that of the FSB.

With this reform, Putin has reshuffled the security structures and fuelled institutional competition and insecurity (Klein, 2016, 4). Parts of the existing institutions like the federal migration service have been abolished; in others, like the FSB, the prosecution office and the Investigative Committee, a cleansing took place at the deputy level, while the Ministry of Interior lost two key special forces and de facto its role as a power ministry (Petrov, 2017, 6). In times when the resources for distribution among the elites decline, intra-elite conflicts will grow. According to Putin, one task of the National Guard is to control people who own weapons and to control arms circulation (Kremlin, 2016). That underlines the argument that he does not trust the different power ministries and actors and that he sees them as a potential threat to his personal security.

Furthermore, the security forces of Chechnya's president, Ramzan Kadyrov (the *Kadyrovtsy*), are now directly subordinated under the National Guard. In August 2017, the head of the National Guard, Zolotov, became also the head of counterterrorism in the North Caucasus. While Kadyrov has become an increasingly independent player in Russian domestic and (partly) foreign policy, this subordination limits the independence of his powerful army. In the past, the security and power structure Kadyrov has built up were not controlled by Russia's law enforcement and security structures (Halbach, 2018, 13–15). Furthermore, he played an active role towards the international Muslim world and with his security forces in Syria (Aliyev, 2018). Only his personal loyalty to Putin was the base for the control of the Kremlin over the Chechnyan leader. These changes, besides giving Moscow more control over the *Kadyrovtsy*, mean that as a part of the National Guard, they could become also a last resort in the case of a mass upheaval (Shlapentokh, 2017, 1).

Securitisation of all policy areas and the inner abroad

Russia's foreign and security policy is strongly interest oriented, tactically and strategically, and it can react quickly to crises and challenges with short decision-making processes and without being encumbered by a critical public. Putin is the central decision maker and an experienced tactician. Military intervention is explicitly a means for its foreign and security policy. Except for the UN Security Council, international institutions play only a limited role for a leadership that does not see values and norms as guidelines for international relations. Instead everything is permissible as long as it leads to success and serves the interests of Russia's elite. There is no win-win, only win-lose; and there are no red lines, unless the price for action is seen as too high based on a cost–benefit calculation. The goal is always to improve Russia's bargaining position, so that the best possible result can be achieved with Russia being treated on an equal footing. The United States is the pivotal point of all Russian action; in this perception, everything it does is to weaken Russia (Liik, 2017).

The Western sanctions have increased the view in Russia that interdependence is a source of vulnerability. Therefore, the 'Russian government has developed ... a set of economic policies that emphasised self-sufficiency and a reassessment of Russia's pattern of integration with the global economy' (Connolly, 2016, 766). The alienation from the West strengthens those groups that argue for more autonomy and want to replace Western technologies and build Russian autonomous systems that are completely controlled by the Russian state, such the GLONASS navigation system or Internet search engines like Yandex. As next steps, a Russian payment system and more independence from currency reserves like the US dollar have been discussed (Kastueva-Jean, 2015, 15). This securitisation of the economic and financial sector is not just the result of the sanctions; it also matches the trend of seeing any economic and political dependence as something that can undermine the state and as a security risk.

State security is linked to the security of Putin's regime. He came to power in the context of the Second Chechnya War, and since this his public image has been linked with the ability to impose peace and guarantee security (Kastueva-Jean, 2015, 10). While Putin may have failed in his communication strategy with the Beslan crisis, and before that in the Kursk incident in 2000, state security has been linked from the beginning to the president personally. Counterterrorism and the need to stabilise the borders have become important in Russian political rhetoric.

The North Caucasus, where the majority of Russia's Muslim population is concentrated, is viewed as a problem region by the regime. It is seen as an inner abroad, a region which is not completely under the control of the Russian state and its security forces. Islamic terrorism is discussed as a major threat to the security of Russia and also to the Syrian intervention. At the same time, critics argue, Russia's harsh domestic policy in the North Caucasus and its ruthless military operation in Syria are escalating the domestic and global terrorist threat more than they serves to solve the problem (Mazurova, 2016, 1). Russia's violations of human rights in Chechnya and Syria, as well as the murder of journalists and human rights activists dealing with the situation in the North Caucasus, underline the lack of any civilian strategy to get the problems under control. Even in the case of the murder of the opposition politician Boris Nemtsov in 2015, the clues lead into the North Caucasus (Human Rights Watch, 2016).

Conflict with the West as a key source of legitimisation

After the 2012 presidential election, Putin had to regain his legitimacy; given the ongoing economic crisis, for this he needed new sources. Since the power elites have decided against the modernisation of the state and the economy, the conflict with the West has become a crucial source of legitimisation for the Putin system. This includes paradigmatic friend–enemy thinking: the idea of the West (meaning the United States, North Atlantic Treaty Organisation and the European Union) as an enemy of Russia was reactivated in society from Soviet times and supported by emphasising Russia's unique identity (Meister, 2018b, 5).

The regime also tries to base its legitimacy on moral and legal foundations (Baunov, 2017, 29). The elites have developed a discourse in which Russia is the main patron of conservative values in Europe and the world at large. Russian values include the traditional family system, patriotism, centralisation and the superiority of fairness over formal rules. In international relations, this values-oriented thinking includes the support for the sovereignty of the state and for pluralism as opposed to Western universalism (Busygina, 2018, 3). All this aims to draw a difference between the West and Russia, to promote among society the country's uniqueness and to show that there is no (liberal) alternative to the Putin system.

Dmitri Trenin argues that, since February 2014, the Kremlin has been de facto operating in war mode and that Putin has been acting as a wartime leader (Trenin, 2017). The media play a crucial role in focusing society's attention to foreign policy issues as well as to Russia's role and success as a global player. Russia's external behaviour is now built on the idea of global opposition to the West and its conspiracy against Russia (Busygina, 2018, 2). The paradigm of Western-organised regime change in Ukraine, and the taking over of power by 'Ukrainian fascists' was for a period of time a successful narrative with the Russian public (Shekhovtsov, 2015).

With regard to the war in eastern Ukraine and the creation of two de facto states in the Donbas region, in the beginning the media gave a lot of attention to the Russian volunteers fighting there. But their growing popularity could have posed problems for the bureaucrats if they had become players in domestic politics. Therefore, since the summer of 2015, the media and politicians have generally stopped talking about the volunteers (Baunov, 2017, 23–24). Russia's leadership has an interest in not letting the role and the influence of nationalistic and patriotic groups in domestic politics become too important, even if they were useful in the first part of the Ukrainian campaign.

With the annexation of Crimea in 2014, Putin got back his legitimacy in the eyes of the Russian population. The feeling of strength, through the impression that Russia could integrate part of a neighbouring country without the West being able to do anything about it, temporarily brought Putin the support of more than 80 per cent of the population (Levada, 2018). The feeling since the end of the Soviet Union of being secondary in international politics has been a fundamental driver of Putin's foreign policy that resonates in the society. Taking over Crimea served above all to secure the Black Sea Fleet, but Russia's leadership quickly recognised how much support it could generate, if it propagandised the victory. With the annexation of Crimea, the successful military campaign in Syria and the self-perception of Russia's return as a great power, the public's perspective changed and domestic problems became secondary.

However, since 2017, the Crimea effect has been declining and the economic crisis in the face of the modernisation deficits and the massive self-enrichment of the elites is the target of criticism from different parts of the population. Putin was re-elected with high support in March 2018 and has become the ultimate leader who has decoupled from everyday political business. More and more Russians ask what comes next and how to improve the situation, which makes the regime vulnerable. But they do not blame Putin personally, but the government, the administration and the regional leadership. A key challenge for a system of leader- and security-based legitimacy is the constant perception of an external threat and the necessity of unity around the leader (Petrov, 2017, 3). As a result, the regime has no interest in solving the conflict with the West; it needs an external enemy to prop up domestic support.

Conclusion

With the return of Vladimir Putin as president in 2012, there has been a shift in foreign and security policy towards growing conflict with the West, destroying the balance among different elite groups and increasing repression against the opposition, the independent media and NGOs. This is due to the insecurity the regime feels since the global financial crisis of 2008–2009 and the mass demonstrations in 2011–2012. The influence of security and intelligence actors has grown in all sectors of the state and fuels the regime's paranoia about external and internal enemies. Fighting terrorism and protecting the state against the West are simultaneously the top priority of the regime and are instrumentalised to distract the public's attention from failures of domestic policy. The insecurity of all parts of the elites and society is a growing trend and has become an instrument of control for Putin.

Though it has been updated since, Russia's National Security Strategy of 2015 still provides an honest assessment of the domestic challenges for the country (Russian National Security Strategy, 2015). It provides a long list of internal problems that remain unsolved, including corruption, organised crime, shadow economy, citizens' lack of confidence in institutions, the deficit in the quality of life, risks of terror attacks, technological backwardness, rising economic inequality, low quality of food and services, demographic problems, lack of protection of individual rights and freedoms, dependence of the economy on the export of raw material and so on. All remain unsolved, but the securitisation of domestic and foreign policy based on the conflict with the West has successfully diverted public attention.

What appears initially as a foreign and security problem might be rooted in the area of domestic policy. What the Kremlin argues to be first of all a security issue is rather a problem from Russia's inability to complete the construction of a modern state, which is law governed and based on political and economic pluralism (Torbakov, 2011, 11). As long as the definition of national interests and (the ruling elites') group interest are congruent, it is always insecurity that drives Russian elites' action.

Notes

1 In 2016, the reshuffle in two key positions seemed to point in a different direction, but in fact they show above all the rise of the technocrats and the interest of Putin in professionalisation. Silovik Sergey Ivanov was replaced by the young technocrat Anton Vaino as the new head of the presidential administration and former Rosatom boss Sergey Kiriyenko (as part of the liberal camp but also a technocrat) replaced Silovik Vyacheslav Volodin as head of the domestic politics department at the presidential administration (Burkhardt, 2017, 128).
2 According to Levada Centre, 82 per cent of Russians said they were not willing to participate in protests at the end of 2017 (Levada, 2017). This might have changed a little bit with the protest mood against the pension reform in the summer of 2018 but not substantially.

References

Aliyev, Huseyn (2018) 'The Year of a strongman: Ramzan Kadyrov in 2017', *Russian Analytical Digest*, no. 222, pp. 5–9. Accessed on (9 August 2018) at www.css.ethz.ch/content/dam/ethz/special-interest/gess/cis/center-for-securities-studies/pdfs/RAD222.pdf

Baunov, Alexander (2017) 'Going to the people-and back again: The changing shape of the Russian regime', Carnegie Moscow Center. Accessed on (9 August 2018) at https://carnegieendowment.org/files/CP_292_Baunov_Russian_Regime_Web.pdf

BOFIT (2018) 'Russia statistics', Bank of Finland Institute for Economies in Transition. Accessed on (10 August 2018) at https://app.powerbi.com/view?r=eyJrIjoiOWQwM2VjNTUtZTdmZC00N2IyLTkyNTMtY2MwYjMxYjdhYzc0IiwidCI6ImVkODlkNDlhLTJiOTQtNGFkZi05MzY0LWMyN2ZlMWFiZWY4YyIsImMiOjh9&pageName=ReportSection0670cd3fe87e80037c8d

Burkhardt, Fabian (2017) 'Presidential power in Putin's third term: Was Crimea a critical juncture in domestic politics?', in Barabashin, Anton, Fabian Burkhardt, Olga Irisova, Ernest Wysiszkiewicz, eds., *A successful failure. Russia after Crime(a)*, Warsaw: The Centre for Polish-Russian Dialogue and Understanding, pp. 119–141.

Busygina, Irina (2018) 'Russian foreign policy as an instrument for domestic mobilisation', Norwegian Institute of International Affairs, Policy brief, 1. Accessed on (9 August 2018) at https://brage.bibsys.no/xmlui/bitstream/handle/11250/2493768/NUPI_Policy_Brief_2_18_Busygina.pdf?sequence=2&isAllowed=y

Chikov, Pavel (2014) 'Zivilgesellschaft und Staat in Russland', *Russlandanalysen*, no. 284. Accessed on (9 August 2018) at www.laender-analysen.de/russland/pdf/RusslandAnalysen284.pdf

Connolly, Richard (2016) 'The empire strikes back: Economic statecraft and the securitisation of political economy in Russia', *Europe-Asia Studies*, Vol. 68, no. 4, pp. 750–773.

Dmitriev, Mikhail (2018) Unpublished manuscript of a presentation at the German Council on Foreign relations, Berlin, 15.03.2018, German Bundestag (a copy is available by the author of this text).

Galeotti, Mark (2017) 'National Guard: The watchdog that could break the leash', *Raamoprusland*, August 14. Accessed on (9 August 2018) at https://raamoprusland.nl/dossiers/militair-beleid/677-national-guard-the-watchdog-that-could-break-the-leash

Gilbert, Leah (2016) 'Managing society in Putin's Russia', *Europe-Asia Studies*, Vol. 68, no. 9, pp. 1553–1578.

Global Terrorism Index 2016 (2016) 'Measuring and understanding the impact of terrorism', Institute for Economics & Peace. Accessed on (9 August 2018) at http://economicsandpeace.org/wp-content/uploads/2016/11/Global-Terrorism-Index-2016.2.pdf

Golts, Alexander (2018) 'Determinants of Russian foreign policy: Realpolitik, militarism and the vertical of power', in Meister, Stefan, ed., *Between old and new world order. Russia's foreign and security rationale*, Berlin: DGAP, pp. 9–12. Access on (10 November 2018) at https://dgap.org/en/article/getFullPDF/31356

Halbach, Uwe (2018) 'Tschetscheniens Stellung in der Russischen Föderation. Ramsan Kadyrows Privatstaat und Wladimir Putin's föderale Machtvertikale', *SWP-Studie*, no. 1. Accessed on (9 August 2018) at www.swp-berlin.org/fileadmin/contents/products/studien/2018S01_hlb.pdf

Herszenhorn, David M. and Ellen Barry (2011) 'Putin contends Clinton incited unrest over vote', New York Times, December 8. Accessed on (9 August 2018) at www.nytimes.com/2011/12/09/world/europe/putin-accuses-clinton-of-instigating-russian-protests.html

Human Rights Watch (2016) "Like walking a minefield'. Vicious crackdown on critics in Russia's Chechen Republic'. Accessed on (10 August 2018) at www.hrw.org/report/2016/08/31/walking-minefield/vicious-crackdown-critics-russias-chechen-republic

Human Rights Watch (2017) 'Online and on all fronts. Russia's assault and freedom of expression' Accessed on (10 November 2018) at www.hrw.org/report/2017/07/18/online-and-all-fronts/russias-assault-freedom-expression

Ivanov, Maksim (2015) 'Vladimir Putin razgljadel 'zvetnye technologii' na ulicach i v socsetjach' [Vladimir Putin notices 'Color Technologies' in the streets and social networks], Kommersant, March 4. Accessed on (10 August 2018) at www.kommersant.ru/doc/2679694

Kastueva-Jean, Tatiana (2015) 'Russia's domestic evolution. What impact on its foreign policy?', IFRI, *Russie.Nei.Visions*, no. 84. Accessed on (9 August 2018) at www.ifri.org/sites/default/files/atoms/files/ifri_rnv_84_eng_tatiana_jean_russie_april_2015.pdf

Klein, Margarethe (2016) 'Russlands neue Nationalgarde', *SWP-Aktuell*, no. 55. Accessed on (9 August 2018) at www.swp-berlin.org/fileadmin/contents/products/aktuell/2016A55_kle.pdf

Kremlin (2016) 'Tseremoniya predstavleniya ofitserov, naznachennykh na komandnye dolzhnosti' [The ceremony of presenting the officers, assigned to the highest command positions], President of Russia. Accessed on (9 August 2018) at http://kremlin.ru/events/president/news/51764

Law on Foreign Agents (2012) 'Federal'ny zakon Rossiyskoy Federatsii ot 20 iyuliya 2002 g', no. 121. Accessed on (9 August 2018) at https://rg.ru/2012/07/23/nko-dok.html

Levada (2013) 'Elektoralnye reytingi partii i onf' ['Electroal rating of parties and ONF'], Levada-Center. Accessed on (9 August 2018) at www.levada.ru/2013/07/25/elektoralnye-rejtingi-partij-i-onf/

Levada (2017) 'Rossjanie nje verjat v protesty' ['Russian's don't trust in protests'], Levada-Center. Accessed on (9 August 2018) at www.levada.ru/2017/09/28/rossiyane-ne-veryat-v-protesty/

Levada (2018) 'Putin's approval rating', Levada-Center. Accessed on (9 August 2018) at www.levada.ru/en/ratings/

Liik, Kadri (2017) 'What does Russia want?', *ECFR commentary*, May 26. Accessed on (9 August 2018) at www.ecfr.eu/article/commentary_what_does_russia_want_7297

Lo, Bobo (2015), *Russia and the new world disorder*, London, Washington, DC: Brookings Institution Press.

Maplecroft (2010) 'Terrorism Risk Index'. Accessed on (9 August 2018) at www.maplecroft.com/about/news/terrorism.html

Mazurova, Nicole (2016) 'Russia's response to terrorism. History and implications for U.S. policy', *American Security Project*. Accessed on (9 August 2018) at www.americansecurityproject.org/wp-content/uploads/2016/10/Ref-0200-Russias-Response-to-Terrorism.pdf

Meister, Stefan (2018a) 'Stably instable. Putin's reelection will not stop social change in Russia', *DGAPstandpunkt*, no. 9. Accessed on (9 August 2018) at https://dgap.org/en/article/getFullPDF/30649

Meister, Stefan (2018b) 'In der Eskalationsspirale. Russland und der Westen nach der Wahl', *DGAPkompakt*, no. 7, pp. 3–5. https://dgap.org/de/article/getFullPDF/30694

Penal Law (2012) 'Federal'nyi zakon "O vnesenii izmeneniy v Kodeks Rossi'skoy Federacii ob administrativnyck pravonarushenijach"' [Federal law 'On introduction of changes in the Code of the Russian Federation about administrative statutory violation']. Accessed on (9 August 2018) at https://rg.ru/2012/11/14/koap-dok.html

Petrov, Nikolay (2017) 'Russland im Vorfeld der Präsidentschaftswahlen 2018', *Russland-Analysen*, no. 339. Accessed on (9 August 2018) at www.laender-analysen.de/russland/pdf/RusslandAnalysen339.pdf

Petrov, Nikolay (2018) 'Skomkannoe prezidentstvo: sto dney nogogo sroka' ['Crumbly presidency: 100 days of the new term'], Republic.ru. Accessed on (9 August 2018) at https://republic.ru/posts/91607

Putin, Vladimir V. (2004) 'Putin tells the Russians: 'We shall be stronger'', New York Times, September 5. Accessed on (10 August 2018) at www.nytimes.com/2004/09/05/world/europe/putin-tells-the-russians-we-shall-be-stronger.html

Russian National Security Strategy (2015) Accessed on (10 August 2018) at www.ieee.es/Galerias/fichero/OtrasPublicaciones/Internacional/2016/Russian-National-Security-Strategy-31Dec2015.pdf

Shekhovtsov, Anton (2015) 'The uneasy reality of anti-fascism in Ukraine', *Ukrainian policy*. Accessed on (9 August 2018) at http://ukrainianpolicy.com/the-uneasy-reality-of-antifascism-in-ukraine/

Shlapentokh, Dmitri (2017) 'The Kremlin's last ressort: Kadyrovtsi in Russia's National Guard', *Central Asia-Caucasus Analyst*, March 3. Accessed on (9 August 2018) at www.cacianalyst.org/publications/analytical-articles/item/13430-the-kremlin-last-resort-kadyrovtsi-in-russias-national-guard.html

Siegert, Jens (2014) 'NGOs in Russland', *Russland-Analysen*, no. 284, October 24. Accessed on (9 August 2018) at www.laender-analysen.de/russland/pdf/RusslandAnalysen284.pdf

SIPRI (2018) 'Military expenditure by country as percentage of gross domestic product', 2003–2017, Stockholm International Peace Research Institute. Accessed on (10 August 2018) at www.sipri.org/sites/default/files/3_Data%20for%20all%20countries%20from%201988%E2%80%932017%20as%20a%20share%20of%20GDP.pdf

Stanovaya, Tatyana (2018) 'Illusory stability: Putin's regime is readier than ever for change', Carnegie Moscow Center. Accessed on (10 August 2018) at https://carnegie.ru/commentary/76729

Torbakov, Igor (2011) 'What does Russia want? Investigating the interrelationship between Moscow's domestic and foreign policy', Deutsche Gesellschaft für Auswärtige Politik. Access on (10 November 2018) at www.google.de/url?sa=t&rct=j&q=&esrc=s&source=web&cd=1&ved=-2ahUKEwjbnaD0jsreAhVH4YUKHf1VDtgQFjAAegQICBAC&url=https%3A%2F%2Fdgap.org%2Fde%2Farticle%2FgetFullPDF%2F17753&usg=AOvVaw2RRICt1mJLcscu5W4OTbuE

Trenin, Dmitri (2017) 'Demands on Russian foreign policy and its drivers: Looking out five years', Moscow Carnegie Center. Accessed on (9 August 2018) at https://carnegie.ru/commentary/72799

The World Bank (2018) 'Doing business, Economic ranking'. Accessed on (9 August 2018) at www.doingbusiness.org/rankings

Zhavoronkov, Sergey (2017) 'Two lean years: Russian budget 2018–2020', The Russia File, Kennan Institute. Accessed on (10 August 2018) at www.wilsoncenter.org/blog-post/two-lean-years-russias-budget-for-2018-2020

7
UNDERSTANDING RUSSIA'S SECURITY STRATEGY IN A CONTEXT OF POWER

Tom Casier

Introduction

When leafing through media reports of the past years, Russia often appears as an omnipotent player, with tentacles all over the world. It is seen as capable of influencing elections in the US, hacking well-protected databases, tipping domestic debates, reversing Assad's chances of winning the war in Syria, holding European countries in an energy stranglehold and so on. The image of Russia as a threat has become widespread again. It is presented as re-emerging power, challenging Western hegemony. But is Russia indeed so powerful? And what is the role of perception?

This chapter looks at the role of power in Russia's foreign policy and security strategy. It takes a pluralist approach, looking at power as a complex phenomenon operating simultaneously along diverging dimensions and in different contexts. The aim is to understand Russia's current security strategy against the background of its relative power position. The three sections of this chapter seek to answer the following questions. First, how does Russia seek to regain great power status? Second, how powerful is it effectively? Third, how should we understand Moscow's use and showcasing of a wide array of power means?

A constant ambition but changing strategies

As a successor state to the Soviet Union, Russia was facing in the early 1990s a dramatic loss of power. The USSR disintegrated in what President Putin has called 'the greatest geopolitical catastrophe of the 20th century' (Putin, 2005). In the bipolar system of the Cold War, the Soviet Union was a superpower, leader of one of the world's two dominant military and economic blocs. In this context, it is understandable that the first and foremost strategic objective of Russia's post-communist foreign policy became one of regaining status (Freire, 2011; Larson and Shevchenko, 2014). This great power ambition has been there from the beginning, this means also under the presidency of Boris Yeltsin.

So, the ambition to regain the status of great power has been a constant strategic objective. What has changed is the Russian strategy to reach this objective.[1] It could be argued that it changed in three fundamental ways. First, the perception of threat has changed. If one revisits security and foreign policy documents from the first decade of post-communist Russia, it is striking how much emphasis was put on Russia's internal problems. In other words, if the country was to become a great power, it would need to create order in its own house. This meant dealing with the disastrous economic and financial situation (which culminated in the financial crisis of 1998), overcoming political instability and creating internal security, in particular in Chechnya. Today, we are facing an 'externalisation' of threats (Snetkov, 2012). The main threats for Russia are coming from the West and radical Islamist terrorism.

A second change is Russia's attitude towards the international system and its structures of governance. In the 1990s, young post-communist Russia was predominantly following a strategy of 'social mobility' (Larson and Shevchenko, 2014). It sought to be accepted as 'a normal great power' (Tsygankov, 2005), largely following in the slipstream of the West and even accepting an inferior position, in which the West is the master, Russia the pupil – full of good will, though not always performing well. In these years, Russia joined the Council of Europe (1996), was admitted to the G7 (1997),[2] signed the North Atlantic Treaty Organisation (NATO)-Russia Founding Act (1997) and, after a couple of years of America-first policy, ultimately declared the European Union (EU) to be its priority partner. During this year, Russia could be considered a status quo state. It largely accepted the existing structures and dominance of the Euro-Atlantic community and hoped to gain status through close cooperation. This changed fundamentally with a Russia growing critical about an 'unrepresentative' international system. In an increasingly vocal and assertive way, Russia refused to accept any longer 'the unilateral Diktat' of the West (Putin, 2014). As Richard Sakwa has argued, Russia placed itself on a neo-revisionist stance (Sakwa, 2012), not envisaging the overhaul of the international structures, but making them more representative.

Finally, a major change has occurred in the capabilities that Russia uses to achieve great power status. Initially, in the early 1990s, Russia largely withdrew from its global military role, closing most military bases outside former Soviet territory, though it constantly maintained its nuclear deterrence capacity at parity with the US. It is exactly Putin (in his early years as president) and his Foreign Minister Igor Ivanov who became the embodiment of an 'economisation' of foreign policy. Russia had to regain status by making strategic use of its natural resources, gas and oil in the first place. Putin's timing was lucky: oil prices rose drastically in his first years as president. Today, Russia has taken up its global military role again. Nowhere has this become clearer than in the war in Syria, where Russia was a game changer. It is clear that more was at stake than simply defending Russian strategic interests (such as its naval base in Tartus). The military operation was clearly also symbolic. It was a message to the world that Russia was ready to play a military role outside the former Soviet space, that it was willing to use military force to obtain not only a place at the negotiation table, but even to make itself inevitable in any settlement of the conflict. More broadly, the renewed emphasis on military force went hand in hand with an assertive rhetoric and showcasing of the country's nuclear capabilities.

The complexity of power

Russia, thus, clearly seeks to present itself as a powerful player, a re-emerging great power. But to what extent is this effectively the case? Many analysts have answered this question by looking at Russia's material capabilities. Yet, we need to take a broader view on power, trying to understand power in its multiple, complex dimensions.

Barnett and Duvall (2005) have tried to integrate diverging theoretical perspectives on power into one taxonomy. They define power as 'the production in and through social relations, of effects that shape the capacities of actors to determine their circumstances and fate'

(Barnett and Duvall, 2005, 42). They distinguished power along two crucial dimensions: power as interaction versus power as social constitution; power as direct versus indirect or diffuse control. The matrix on this basis reveals four major types of power. In a somewhat simplified form, they can be defined as follows (Barnett and Duvall, 2005). *Compulsory power* refers to direct control over the action and circumstances of another actor. *Institutional power* is indirect control over conditions in which actors operate. Institutions and the rules they are composed of imply unevenly distributed rewards and capacities, but do not seek to directly control a specific actor. Through *structural power*, actors produce identities and structures of subordination that determine their social capacities. Finally, *productive power* refers to socially diffuse production of subjectivity in 'systems of signification and meaning' (Barnett and Duvall, 2005, 55).

Against the background of this taxonomy of power, the following issues stand out as particularly important and are analysed in more detail below. First, the potential of compulsory power created by material capabilities: economic, military and through energy dependence. Second, Russia's role in institutional arrangements. Third, its capacity to determine identities and hierarchies.

Comparing economic capabilities

Economically, the Russian economy is about the same size as the economies of the Benelux countries combined.[3] With 144 million inhabitants and huge reserves of natural resources, this is modest, at best. Russia has been struggling to recover from the collapse of the Soviet Union in 1991. Its production collapsed, and negative growth reached depths close to −13 per cent (IMF, 2018). It took Russia until 2007 before it had recovered from the economic implosion that followed the collapse of the Soviet Union (Sakwa, 2008, 246). Structurally, it continues to be overly dependent on the export of oil and gas, making its economy and state revenues vulnerable to fluctuating energy prices.

In terms of the country's great power ambitions, the evolution of its relative share of the world economy is a more significant measure (see Table 7.1). Russia and China represented similar shares (5.18 per cent and 4.49 per cent, respectively) of the world economy in 1992, the first year after the disappearance of the USSR. In 2017, this has changed dramatically; China stands for over 18 per cent, while Russia's has fallen back to a share of a good 3 per cent. Russia finds itself well behind the three major economic players – the US, the EU and China – but also increasingly behind India, with 7.44 per cent.

Table 7.1 Gross domestic product based on purchasing power parity (PPP) share of world total (%): the US, the EU and BRICS

	1992	2017
United States	19.89	15.26
European Union	24.71	16.51
China	4.49	18.22
Russia	5.18	3.15
India	3.38	7.44
Brazil	3.21	2.55

Source: IMF (2018).

Compared to former Soviet states, Russia is economically much stronger. The size of its gross domestic product (GDP) exceeds that of the runner-up, Kazakhstan, almost by factor ten (IMF, 2018). Moreover, many post-Soviet states are strongly dependent on Russia for trade.

Comparing military capabilities

When we look at military capabilities, the picture is substantially different. Through the START agreements, Russia and the US have maintained strategic parity, with both having a similar number of nuclear weapons around 7,000 (see Table 7.2).

When it comes to military expenditure, however, the gap with the US is big. Of the 100 USD spent on military affairs globally in 2017, Russia spent 3.8 USD, against 35 for the US (see Table 7.3). This is almost a 1:10 ratio. When considering the military expenses of NATO countries jointly, the ratio is closer to 1:15. Clearly, Russia is very far from the old Soviet status of rivalling superpower.

In terms of troops, Russia has an estimated 800,000 (half of which are conscripts) versus 1,400,000 for the US (Renz, 2017, 10). It has gone through a modernisation programme of its army in 2008, but overall has more limited out of area operations capacity than the US.

Of course, the perspective changes radically if we look at Russia's relations with its direct neighbours. Vis-à-vis all former Soviet states, Russia is a superior economic and military power. Several former Soviet states find themselves in a situation of dependency on Russian energy but in

Table 7.2 Estimated numbers of nuclear weapons in 2017

Russia	7,000
United States	6,800
France	300
China	270
United Kingdom	215
Pakistan	130–140
India	120–130
Israel	80
North Korea	10–20

Source: Kile and Kristensen (2017).

Table 7.3 Top ten countries with the highest share of global military expenditure, 2017 (%)

United States	35
China	13
Saudi Arabia	4
Russia	3.8
India	3.7
France	3.3
United Kingdom	2.7
Japan	2.6
Germany	2.5
South Korea	2.3

Source: SIPRI (2018).

several cases also security (Armenia, Tajikistan). The wars with Georgia and particularly Ukraine have dramatically increased the perception of Russia's willingness to use military force. Yet, several countries have made clear anti-Russian choices, undermining Russia's potential of influence.

Control over resources and asymmetrical energy interdependence

Energy has often been regarded as a major source of Russian power. This is particularly the case for natural gas, which is transported by pipelines and subject to longer term contracts. In an extreme scenario where supplies are shut down, immediate alternatives to purchase gas may not be available. Oil, in contrast, could be purchased on international markets. As Keohane and Nye (1989, 10–11) have argued, asymmetrical interdependence generates uneven costs and thus potential control over outcomes. It may thus form a source of power. Several post-Soviet states are fully dependent on the import of Russian gas and have often few or no alternatives available.

The image of EU dependence on Russian gas, on the other hand, needs some nuance. First, the dependence is highly diverse among EU member-states, with some of them importing all their gas from Russia, while others consume no Russian gas at all. Second, a distinction should be made between the dependence on Russian gas imports and what this represents in the total energy mix. Around 37 per cent of all gas imports into the EU in 2015 was of Russian origin, a new peak; for oil, this was 30 per cent (European Commission, 2017, 26). Yet, within the mix of EU total energy consumption, Russian gas represents a much lower figure, which has been stable around 6.5 per cent over the past decades (Casier, 2011). This is still considerable but sounds different from the more often quoted figures referring to Russia's share in EU gas imports. Finally, Russia itself remains until today strongly dependent on demand from the rest of Europe. 61.8 per cent of Gazprom gas exports go to the EU-28; 96.5 per cent go towards geographic Europe and Turkey (Sharples, 2016, 885).

Institutional arrangements

Institutional power results from the uneven effects generated by certain institutional arrangements or the capacity to set rules and norms. These arrangements may not be aimed at direct control, but the costs and the benefits will be distributed unevenly over different countries (Barnett and Duvall, 2005, 48). For example, when a country engages in a free trade agreement with other countries, this generates diffuse benefits. Some countries will benefit from lower trade tariffs, while third countries will find their products to be less competitive and trade flows diverted. The same holds for regulations for products. A country that gets its regulations (for example, technical, environmental, hygienic standards) accepted by other countries will gain competitive advantages over others.

At the global level, Russia is a member of the UN Security Council, where its veto right gives it blocking power. Yet, overall, Russia deplores the lack of representativeness of the international system, which it regards as dominated by a small 'liberal club' seeking to impose its will on the rest of the world and not giving a voice to emerging powers. Lavrov, for example, stated:

> We categorically reject the allegations of those who accuse Russia and the new centres of global influence of attempting to undermine the so-called "liberal world order". This global model was pre-programmed for crisis right from the time when this vision of economic and political globalisation was conceived primarily as an instrument for ensuring the growth of an elite club of countries and its domination over everyone else.
> *(2017)*

As mentioned above, Moscow has taken a neo-revisionist stance, pledging a better representation without rejecting the international structures of governance. Russia has also tried to foster alternative institutional arrangements at global level. It is the major promoter of the BRICS consultations, in itself a rather fragile form of cooperation between countries with diverging interests.

At the regional level, Russia and the EU got entangled in a competition over rivalling institutional arrangements. The EU first enlarged eastwards in 2004 and 2007. Its European Neighbourhood Policy and later the Eastern Partnership (launched in 2009) were aimed at setting up privileged relations with countries that once belonged to the Soviet Union and Russia continued to consider as an area where it had 'privileged interests' (in the words of Medvedev). Three Association Agreements have been signed between the EU and Georgia, Moldova and Ukraine in 2014. They provide for the so-called Deep and Comprehensive Free Trade Area (DCFTA), including approximation of relevant legislation and the alignment of the foreign policy of the associated countries. De facto this meant an extension of the EU's legal and economic sphere towards countries in the common neighbourhood and thus an increase in the EU's institutional power. Russia, from its side, changed its regional strategy away from the Commonwealth of Independent States (CIS) to closer forms of cooperation with willing partners. It set up the Eurasian Customs Union (ECU) in 2010, renamed the Eurasian Economic Union (EEU) in 2015. Currently, it counts five members: Armenia, Belarus, Kazakhstan, Kirgizstan and Russia. DeBardeleben argues that Brussels and Moscow moved from a 'common Europe' paradigm to one of 'competing regionalisms'. The latter is based on mutually exclusive integration projects, competing regulatory norms and a securitisation of the relationship with the EU (DeBardeleben, 2018, 129). Rivalry over the neighbourhood became a determining factor of the relations between Brussels and Moscow. It led to an escalating spiral of tensions, eventually culminating in the Ukraine crisis of 2014.

When it comes to alliances, Russia saw NATO enlarge eastwards in different waves, increasing a shared border. Even if this may not imply 'direct control' over Russia, it has important indirect effects. NATO enlargement was probably the most important factor fostering a national consensus in Russia that the West was disrespecting its key geostrategic interests. From its side, Russia is the leading power in the Collective Security Treaty Organisation (CSTO).[4] Yet, this is not an alliance similar to NATO, with its much larger membership, three nuclear powers and central command structure.

The capacity to determine identities and hierarchies

The final category of power refers to forms of constitutive power. Of particular relevance here is the capacity of actors to produce identities and categories of subordination. Barnett and Duvall (2005, 52–53) refer to this as structural power. It refers to the capacity of Russia to get recognition of the identity it claims for itself and to produce identities for others. Two elements in particular deserve attention: the recognition of Russia as great (global or regional) power and its in-/exclusion from Europe.

As argued in the first section of this chapter, Russia has never abandoned its key ambition to regain the status of great power. Ultimately, this requires recognition by those who have the social capacity to grant status and create categories of dominance and subordination. Many times, Russia got frustrated for not getting this recognition. According to DeBardeleben, the establishment of the ECU was precisely meant to create a better balance to replace the asymmetrical relations between the EU and Russia at the heart of their Strategic Partnership (DeBardeleben, 2018). Moscow's demand at the June 2012 EU-Russia summit that the EU would discuss trade matters with the then ECU rather than bilaterally with Russia could be seen as an attempt to get implicit recognition as the leader of a regional economic bloc. The refusal by the EU was read as a refusal to grant Russia this status. Also at global level, Russia has been struggling to obtain recognition of its much-desired status.

In the aftermath of the collapse of communism, the EU disposed of an unrivalled and unquestioned 'normative hegemony' (Haukkala, 2010). Not only did a broad consensus underpin the norms it promoted in former communist countries (from democracy and the rule of law to neo-liberal principles), but its capacity to export these norms was strengthened by the strongly asymmetrical economic and political relations between the EU and its post-communist neighbours. This dominant position gave the EU the capacity to determine the Europeanness of its neighbours. In the 1990s, this identity was granted to both Russia and Ukraine: both were labelled members of a European civilisation, sharing European values. As relations with Russia deteriorated and the country's policies changed, this European identity was withheld from Russia (in contrast to Ukraine whose European identity was framed in stronger words). In the new pragmatic approach of 'constructive engagement' that the EU adopted in 2000, Russia was considered a key partner because of its importance, not because it was a member of the European family. More recently, Moscow started to reject this imposition of a certain European identity, claiming Russia itself was the protector of genuine European values. The latter were understood in a 'paleo-conservative' way (Morozov, 2018).[5]

In sum, Russia has been involved in a sustained competition with the EU – and by extension the West – about institutional arrangements in the neighbourhood and the capacity to determine identity. It could be argued that the change of regime in Ukraine after the Euromaidan protests and its pro-Western orientation were seen in the Kremlin as a major defeat within this struggle for institutional and structural power. This may have prompted Moscow to a new strategy in which forms of compulsory power got the upper hand. Having lost its own ability to control Ukraine, it opted to undermine Western control over Ukraine. This could be seen as a 'negative' form of compulsory power, whereby Russia's strategy focused on making Ukraine a liability for the West, rather than a useful ally (see Casier, 2018).

Russia's counter-hegemonic offensive: acting on all fronts

As mentioned above, Russia's foreign policy externalised the main threats, whereby the West was increasingly held responsible for its weak position and for distorted international relations in general. As tensions grew sharper and policies radicalised, Russia began to invest in a counter-hegemonic offensive of some sort, seeking to make maximal use of the minimal means at its disposal. The strategy can be defined as counter-hegemonic as it openly challenges Western hegemony. Major strategic decisions went hand in hand with small activist steps on many different fronts. The former included institutional repositioning, such as the establishment of the EEU or collaboration within the Shanghai Cooperation Organisation or BRICS. They also consisted of increased military expenditure and attempts to produce technologically advanced weapons. Finally, also Russia's wars and its plan for the diversification of energy export indicate strategic change. The small steps complementing this strategic reorientation are a multitude of often secretive actions on different fronts: military, diplomatic, economic, intelligence, cyber and ideology. In a misleading way, this 'full-spectrum approach' (Monaghan, 2017, 3) has been referred to as Russia-invented hybrid warfare. It has also been labelled as the Gerasimov doctrine, referring to an article by the Russian General and Chief of Staff published in 2013. Yet, as the inventor of the term, Mark Galeotti, indicated himself, it is neither a doctrine nor can it be attributed to Gerasimov (Galeotti, 2018).

It is worth noting Gerasimov's point of departure. His article is written on the basis that the US has changed its strategy of forced regime change. According to the General, the US has resorted to more subtle, secretive and indirect means, rather than immediate open warfare. Washington makes use of media and non-governmental organisations (NGOs) to destabilise a government. As this happens, Special Forces or private military companies may be used to increase the pressure. When the government reacts with repression, sanctions may be introduced. When it collapses, peacekeepers can be sent and help to install a US-friendly regime (Bartles, 2016). In other words, Gerasimov's article was exactly a reply to what was perceived as American hybrid warfare. What he advocates is that Russia makes use of similar diverse and asymmetrical instruments to counter these threats. These means have later on appeared as troops without insignia (the 'little green men' in Crimea), making use of peacekeeping troops (like in South-Ossetia and Abkhazia), promoting Russian interests via its own NGOs and media (Russia Today), restrictive trade measures (as used against Moldova, Georgia and Ukraine when negotiating the Association Agreement with the EU) hacking (as in the US elections), support to opposition groups and Internet trolls (from the referendum on Brexit to that on Catalonia). On the latter, Valentina Feklyunina argues that Russian propaganda focuses on 'communities of grievance' within the West (2017, 35). These anti-establishment groups are not created by Russian propaganda, but the latter helps to amplify their grievances.

Of particular importance is the fact that Gerasimov defines war in a much broader way than just military conflict, referring to a 4:1 ratio of non-military versus military measures (Bartles, 2016, 34). This does not automatically imply a coherent approach. Rather, the diverse military and non-military means form a basket of different instruments to be used in different combinations in function of the nature of a conflict. This appears from the different approaches followed over the past years. In the case of Crimea and Eastern Ukraine, Moscow followed the tactics of what Roy Allison called a 'deniable intervention' (Allison, 2014). In the case of the Syria War, on the contrary, Russia's intervention was open and mediatised. It clearly served symbolic purposes as well, making a claim to great power status.

Thus, despite its relative weakness, Russia seeks to regain power and status through tactical steps. An analysis of power would not be complete without looking into the significance of these tactics. Yet, from a research perspective, it is difficult to assess the scale and impact of these diverse and asymmetrical means. Because of the secretive nature of these operations and the exceptional media attention, there is a real risk of overestimating Russia's capacity. Of course, power is also a matter of perception: the perception of not only capabilities but also the willingness to use them. Even if the Russian impact is much smaller than often assumed, the sheer perception of it may enhance the country's de facto leverage. Russia's assertive and vocal foreign policy rhetoric serve as an amplifier of these effects. Bettina Renz (2017) uses Robert Art's term of 'swaggering' to grasp the essence of this approach. Art defined 'swaggering' as the display of military might 'to look and feel more powerful or important, to be taken seriously by others in the councils of international decision-making, to enhance the nation's image in the eyes of others' (Art quoted in Renz, 2017, 11).

A crucial question is whether these mixed (non-)military instruments serve a long-term strategic objective or are ad hoc reactive steps. Andrew Monaghan dismisses the idea of a Russian master plan and of the '"seamless coordination" of activities against the Euro-Atlantic Community' (2017, 4). The real change is that security concerns have come to dominate the agenda, in response to the looming threats the Kremlin detected. The real strategy is more about the internal consolidation of the state apparatus and the enhancement of military capabilities. Monaghan speaks in this respect of 'a missed diagnosis of Russian state mobilisation' (2017, 5).[6]

While we are unable to know the intention of Russia's leadership, we can ask the question whether the new approach has paid off. In the case of Syria, Russia was clearly a game changer in the conflict. It has made itself an inevitable party for any settlement and has taken partial leadership in the negotiations. In the case of Crimea, the annexation is a fait accompli. Combined with Lugansk and Donetsk, a large area of Ukraine's official territory is not under Kyiv's control. But there is a flip side to the coin. Ukraine has decisively abandoned its ambiguous position between the West and Russia. The conflict with Russia has led to a spectacular reinforcement of a redefined Ukrainian identity, positioned against Russia as major Other. Chances for a reconciliation over the next – possibly – decades have dwindled. Moreover, the annexation of Crimea has created concerns among Russia's partners. Belarusian President Lukashenka called it 'a bad precedent' (Lukashenko, 2014). Kazakh President Nazarbayev has emphasised that the EEU 'should remain a purely economic alliance not reducing the sovereignty of the country' (Libman, 2017, 90). At the same time, Western sanctions have been in place since March 2014. As a result, Russia's isolation is bigger than ever and with that its most important foreign policy problem is bigger than ever. Vladislav Surkov, former Deputy Chief of Staff in the Kremlin and key advisor to Putin, wrote an article in the journal *Rossiya v global'noy politike*, in which he states that the rift with the West over Ukraine in 2014 is the beginning of a new era of 'one hundred years (two hundred? three hundred?) of geopolitical solitude' for Russia (Surkov, 2018).

A seemingly obvious alternative for close relations with Europe after the suspension of the EU-Russia Strategic Partnership would be a closer partnership with China. It has been heralded in Moscow's foreign policy rhetoric as a major shift and at times even labelled an alliance. No doubt the two countries share some common concerns, not least about US dominance. They do collaborate through the BRICS consultations and the Shanghai Cooperation Organisation (SCO). Yet, the relationship is a highly asymmetrical one. Bobo Lo has argued that collaboration between both neighbours is based on a fragile balance. Beijing recognises Russia's military primacy, while Moscow recognises China's economic primacy (Lo, 2016). But this is a very precarious balance, as China's military power increases rapidly. Already now the country spends more than three times as much on military affairs than Russia (see Table 7.3). Moreover, there is considerable suspicion about China's growing influence in Central Asia. Moreover, the partnership has not resulted yet in a major shift in trade or energy flows.[7]

Conclusion

Assessments of Russia's current power have far too often been distorted by speculations over its intentions. Rather than following this murky path, it is essential to understand the complexity of power and its different faces. Drawing on Barnett's and Duvall's taxonomy of power, this chapter has tried to give a nuanced, complex answer to the question of Russia's power. It considered Russia's military and economic capabilities, control over institutional arrangements and capacity to define identities. Moscow's global military strength draws to a large extent on its strategic nuclear capacity, at par with the US. But nuclear deterrence does not necessarily generate power in daily diplomatic dealings. In terms of military expenditure, Russia is far behind the US and increasingly China. Economically, it is a very weak player. It has a limited impact on the creation of institutions and international rules. Nor is it in a strong position to determine identities and the hierarchies they imply. It was argued that the developments over Ukraine were read in Moscow as a major defeat in the competition with the Euro-Atlantic community over institutional and structural power in the common neighbourhood. This prompted Russia to a policy of 'negative' compulsory power, seeking to prevent the West of obtaining useful control over Ukraine.

The goal to regain great power status has remained static since the birth of post-communist Russia. The strategies to reach this goal, however, have changed over time. Three main trends were identified: the externalisation of threats, neo-revisionism and a return to global military engagement. Russia has embarked on a counter-hegemonic strategy through which it seeks to challenge US and Western dominance on many different fronts and in a vocal way. This has led to an increased use of a mixed bag of military and non-military means, which has often been misunderstood as a Russia-invented new type of warfare, hybrid war. These instruments have been applied and combined in different ways in different conflicts. Often they appear as ad hoc reactive measures, rather than a new strategic master plan. Some of these actions seem to have paid off in the short term and to have allowed Russia to punch above its weight. The many allegations of successful Russian hacking or meddling in elections have for sure increased the perception of the country's power. Yet, the longer-term effects of all these remain to be seen. Actions such as the annexation of Crimea have increased suspicion among some of Russia's partners and burned bridges with Ukraine for many years to come. Combined with the deep confrontation with the West, this may have pushed Russia further into isolation, making one of its key foreign policy problems bigger rather than smaller.

Notes

1. The term strategy is used here in the broad sense of the term, not suggesting per se that there is a consistent and coherent master plan.
2. Russia's membership was suspended in 2014 after the annexation of Crimea.
3. When GDP is measured in purchasing power parity, it is closer to the size of the German economy (IMF, 2018).
4. The Treaty on Collective Security was signed in 1992 in Tashkent. It was renamed the CSTO in 2002.
5. As Russia combines this claim to true Europeanness with the promotion of a Eurasian identity concept, its approach is rather ambiguous.
6. The Russian government defines mobilisation as 'a complex of state measures for activating the resources, strengths and capabilities for the achievement of military-political aims' (quoted in Monaghan, 2017, 9).
7. Volumes of trade and energy with the EU have remained roughly constant since the Ukraine crisis, despite sanctions and countermeasures being in place.

References

Allison, Roy (2014) 'Russian "Deniable" intervention in Ukraine: How and why Russia broke the rules', *International Affairs*, Vol. 90, no. 6, pp. 1255–1297.
Barnett, Michael and Duvall, Raymond (2005) 'Power in international politics', *International Organization*, Vol. 59, no. 1, pp. 39–75.
Bartles, Charles (2016) 'Getting Gerasimov right', *Military Review*, Vol. 96, no. 1, January–February 2016, pp. 30–38.
Casier, Tom (2011) 'Russia's energy leverage over the EU. Myth or Reality?', *Perspectives on European Politics and Societies*. Vol. 12, no. 4, pp. 493–508.
Casier, Tom (2018) 'The different faces of power in European Union – Russia relations', *Cooperation and Conflict*. Vol. 53, no. 1, pp. 101–117.
DeBardeleben, Joan (2018) 'Alternative paradigms for EU-Russian neighbourhood relations'. In: Casier, Tom and DeBardeleben, Joan, eds., *EU-Russia Relations in Crisis. Understanding Diverging Perceptions*. London: Routledge, pp. 115–136.
European Commission (2017) *EU Energy in Figures. Statistical Pocketbook 2017*. Accessed on 23 May 2018 at https://publications.europa.eu/en/publication-detail/-/publication/2e046bd0-b542-11e7-837e-01aa75ed71a1/language-en/format-PDF/source-search

Feklyunina, Valentina (2017) 'Russia's soft power beyond the post-Soviet space'. In: Kuhrt, Natasha and Feklyunina, Valentina, eds., *Assessing Russia's Power. A Report.* pp. 34–38. Accessed on 25 May 2018 at www.bisa.ac.uk/files/working%20groups/Assessing_Russias_Power_Report_2017.pdf

Freire, Maria Raquel (2011) 'USSR/Russian Federation's major power status inconsistencies'. In: Volgy, Thomas et al., eds., *Major Powers and the Quest for Status in International Politics. Global and Regional Perspectives.* Basingstoke: Palgrave, pp. 55–75.

Galeotti, Mark (2018) 'I'm sorry for creating the 'Gerasimov doctrine', *Foreign Policy*. Accessed on 25 May 2018 at http://foreignpolicy.com/2018/03/05/im-sorry-for-creating-the-gerasimov-doctrine/

Haukkala, Hiski (2010) *The EU-Russia Strategic Partnership: The Limits of Post-Sovereignty in International Relations.* London: Routledge.

IMF (2018) *World Economic Outlook Database.* Accessed on 23 May 2018 at www.imf.org/external/pubs/ft/weo/2018/01/weodata/index.aspx

Keohane, Robert and Nye, Joseph (1989) *Power and Interdependence.* New York: Harper Collins.

Kile, Shannon and Kristensen, Hans (2017) 'Trends in world nuclear forces, 2017', *SIPRI Fact Sheet.* July 2017. Accessed on 23 May 2018 at www.sipri.org/sites/default/files/2017-06/fs_1707_wnf.pdf

Larson, Deborah and Shevchenko, Alexei (2014) 'Russia says no: Power, status and emotions in foreign policy' *Communist and Post-Communist Studies*, Vol. 47, no. 3–4, pp. 269–279.

Lavrov, Sergey (2017) 'Foreign Minister Lavrov's address and answers to questions at the 53rd Munich Security Conference', Munich, February 18, 2017. Accessed on 1 February 2017 at www.mid.ru/en/press_service/minister_speeches/-/asset_publisher/7OvQR5KJWVmR/content/id/2648249/pop_up?_101_INSTANCE_7OvQR5KJWVmR_viewMode=print&_101_INSTANCE_7OvQR5KJWVmR_qrIndex=1

Libman, Alexander (2017) 'Russian power politics and the Eurasian Economic Union. The real and the imagined', *Rising Powers Quarterly*, Vol. 2, no. 1, pp. 81–103.

Lo, Bobo (2016) 'The illusion of convergence – Russia, China and the BRICS', *Russie.Nei.Visions*, 92 (March). Accessed on 1 February 2017 at www.ifri.org/sites/default/files/atoms/files/ifri_rnv_92_bobo_lo_brics-eng_march_2016_0.pdf

Lukashenko, Aleksander (2014) 'Belarus sees Russia's Crimea incursion as "bad precedent", *Reuters*, https://uk.reuters.com/article/uk-ukraine-crisis-belarus/belarus-sees-russias-crimea-incursion-as-bad-precedent-idUKBREA2M04Z20140323

Monaghan, Andrew (2017) *Power in Modern Russia. Strategy and Mobilisation.* Manchester: Manchester University Press.

Morozov, Viacheslav (2018) 'Identity and hegemony in EU-Russia relations: Making sense of the asymmetrical entanglement'. In: Casier, Tom and Joan DeBardeleben, eds., *EU-Russia Relations in Crisis: Understanding Diverging Perceptions.* London: Routledge, pp. 30–49.

Putin Vladimir (2005) *Annual Address to the Federal Assembly of the Russian Federation* (25 April 2005). Accessed on 1 February 2017 at www.kremlin.ru

Putin, Vladimir (2014) '[Speech at the] Meeting of the Valdai International Discussion Club'. 24 October 2014. Accessed on 1 February 2017 at http://en.kremlin.ru/events/president/news/46860

Renz, Bettina (2017) 'Russia's conventional military power', In: Kuhrt, Natasha and Feklyunina, Valentina, eds., *Assessing Russia's Power. A Report.* pp. 9–12. Accessed on 25 May 2018 at www.bisa.ac.uk/files/working%20groups/Assessing_Russias_Power_Report_2017.pdf

Sakwa, Richard (2008) 'New Cold War' or twenty years' crisis? Russia and international politics', *International Affairs*, Vol. 84, no. 2, pp. 241–267.

Sakwa, Richard (2012) 'The problem of 'the international' in Russian identity formation', *International Politics*, Vol. 49, no. 4, pp. 449–465.

Sharples, Jack (2016) 'The shifting geopolitics of Russia's natural gas exports and their impact on EU-Russia gas relations', *Geopolitics*. Vol. 21, no. 4, pp. 880–912.

SIPRI (2018) *SIPRI Military Expenditure Database.* Accessed on 23 May 2018 at www.sipri.org/databases/milex

Snetkov, Aglaya (2012) 'When the internal and external collide: A social constructivist reading of Russia's security policy', *Europe-Asia Studies*, Vol. 64, no. 3, pp. 521–542.

Surkov, Vladislav (2018) 'Odinochestvo polikrovki (14+)', *Rossiya v global'noy politike.* Accessed on 23 May 2018 at www.globalaffairs.ru/global-processes/Odinochestvo-polikrovki-14-19477

Tsygankov, Andrei (2005). 'Vladimir Putin's vision of Russia as a normal great power', *Post-Soviet Affairs*, Vol. 21, no. 2, pp. 132–158.

8
RUSSIA'S ECONOMY AND MILITARY EXPENDITURES

Susanne Oxenstierna

During the 1990s, Russia's military sector underwent a transformation from being the most prioritised part of the Soviet economy to becoming a sector lacking resources and trying to survive the winds of market reform. During Soviet times, military expenditure had amounted to 14–15 per cent of the economy or more, and Soviet society was in a constant state of mobilisation where military needs always had priority over people's living standard and the civilian sector in general. When the Cold War was over, the Armed Forces found themselves in a new situation that required economising on scare resources. Low oil prices and the newly created tax service could not generate sufficient income to the federal budget to sustain either a high defence budget or the large armament acquisitions to which the defence industry had been accustomed. The situation for the Russian defence sector improved in the 2000s, when oil prices rose and the economic reforms started to generate growth. Military expenditure began to increase, but more money is not the sole precondition for building military strength. The war in Georgia 2008 revealed many deficiencies in Russia's military capabilities, and it became obvious that the Armed Forces needed to be reorganised and modernised. In 2008, the then Defence Minister Anatoly Serdjukov launched a military reform that was supposed to give the Armed Forces a 'new look' (*novyj oblik*).

Since then, Russian military expenditure has risen substantially. Between the mid-2000s and 2018, expenditures more than doubled and reached over 5 per cent of gross domestic product (GDP). Economic conditions have worsened, however, and instead of 6–7 per cent growth, the economy is now lingering around 1–1.5 per cent growth at best. Despite contraction of the economy after 2014, the political leadership maintained high military spending up to 2016, but in 2017 spending declined and the government plans to keep the growth of the defence budget at a more moderate level during 2018–2020. President Vladimir Putin's public statements on the economy after the presidential election in March 2018 indicate that reviving the economy and increasing the population's living standard are prioritised goals during his fourth presidential term.

This chapter analyses the tendencies in the Russian economy and military expenditure in the 2000s. Economic growth is an important factor explaining growth in a country's military expenditure, but it is not the only one. In the Russian case, it is obvious that the political priority attributed to defence has played a major role in how much of GDP is spent on the military sector. During periods of weakening growth, the defence budget has not been adjusted, which points at the political leadership prioritising increasing military capability over other public needs. The chapter also highlights the new trend of lower military expenditure in 2018–2020 and its implications.

The outline of the chapter is as follows. First, the development of the Russian economy under Putin is reviewed. Second, Russia's military expenditures are analysed with focus on the period after 2011. Third, Putin's plans for the economic development during his fourth presidency are discussed. The conclusions are presented in the final section.

Economic development

Russia's economic development took off in 1999 after the Russian state had defaulted on its debt in 1998. During the 1990s, economic reforms had been undertaken to turn the Soviet command economy into a market economy. The reform process developed in a situation of low oil prices, which put a lot of pressure on the federal budget. The government eventually abandoned the practice of monetary financing of the budget deficit, which fuelled hyper-inflation, and created a modern system of debt management with the Ministry of Finance issuing debt in the form of T-bills (GKO) and T-bonds (OFZ). Ultimately, the interest rate on these instruments became very high, and on 17 August 1998, the government defaulted on its domestic debt of $70 billion (Åslund, 2018). International bank payments were frozen and soon the rouble was devalued to one-quarter of its dollar value. As a consequence, half of Russia's commercial banks went under.

Already in 1999, however, the price of oil rose and the economy recovered and started to grow. During the period 2000–2008, the economy grew by an average of 7 per cent per year thanks to the undertaken reforms in the 1990s, the high oil incomes, free capacity in the economy, and the devalued exchange rate that gave domestic producers an advantage over imported goods and services. This development coincided with Putin's becoming president in 2000, and thanks to the restored growth, his first term was assessed rather positively by economists. Putin had several liberal advisors when he came to power, and central market reforms were consolidated in legislation and implementation, a flat income tax of 13 per cent was introduced, as well as measures to promote business development. But after a couple of years, the high oil prices obstructed the will to reform. The *siloviki* fraction[1] got more influence, the state's role in the economy increased, corruption flourished, and oligarchs were targeted and suspected of various crimes, which in many cases led to their leaving the country. In 2003, Mikhail Khodorkovsky, the owner of one of Russia's most successful companies, Yukos, was arrested and the Russian state confiscated his oil company (Åslund, 2018). At this point, it became clear that Putin and his loyal collaborators were more interested in enriching themselves than in developing the rule of law or other market-supporting institutions. In 2008, the Russian economy stood at its peak, but in 2009, the global financial crisis hit the economy and the Russian GDP contracted by 7.8 per cent (IMF, 2018).

The Russian government managed the financial crisis with fiscal support programmes, but the exchange rate was fixed to protect big companies, loyal to Putin, that had huge loans in foreign currency. Eventually, the exchange rate was reduced, but in the meantime, the Central Bank had lost $200 billion of its foreign reserves. Growth recovered in 2010 to 4.5 per cent, but after that, the economic performance worsened. Despite oil prices staying at around $100 per barrel ($/bbl), growth fell from 4.3 to 0.7 per cent between 2011 and 2014 (IMF, 2018). This was due to weak productivity development and the structural problems in the economy that are largely caused by Russia's hydrocarbon growth model and the high dependence on commodity rents. In addition, the weak institutions and in particular the increasing lack of rule of law aggravated the poor performance of the economy. Resource allocation became increasingly political, as market institutions and competition were set aside in favour of state control and preferential treatment of sectors and actors deemed important for the political leadership (Oxenstierna, 2015).

Finally, the breakdown of relations between Russia and the West following Russia's aggression against Ukraine in 2014 further deteriorated Russia's economic performance because of sanctions and counter-sanctions. On top of this, the oil price fell from $98/bbl in 2014 to $53/bbl in 2015, which seriously diminished growth and the incomes to the federal budget (World Bank, 2015, 24).

Investors lost confidence in Russia, and capital flight more than doubled, in 2014 to $152 billion, from $61 billion in 2013 (Businessinsider, 2015). In 2015, GDP contracted by 2.5 per cent mainly due to the sharp drop in the oil price, but the Western economic sanctions added to this weakening (see estimates of effects below). This time the government decided not to protect big economic actors with foreign debt, and already in November 2014 the Central Bank introduced a floating exchange rate regime, which resulted in the rouble devaluating from 20RUB/$ to 60RUB/$. Growth contracted by 0.2 per cent in 2016, when the price of oil periodically fell to under $40/bbl (Oxenstierna and Olsson, 2015, 34–35). In response to these external shocks, the Russian government introduced counter-sanctions, primarily a ban on food imports from the European Union (EU) and other Western countries (Oxenstierna and Olsson, 2015, 43–46). Later, sanctions were introduced against Turkey in connection with the downing of the Russian fighter jet in November 2015.[2]

To fight the negative economic tendencies, the government introduced 'import substitution' as a national policy. Import substitution is a protectionist measure by which domestic producers are protected from competition from abroad, by import bans or tariffs, and are subsidised to produce what was previously imported. Liberal economists criticise this policy because it is not geared at producing goods for export but primarily protects domestic producers from competition, which generates lower quality and rising prices. Furthermore, it is another way of transferring money to the non-profitable rent-addicted sector and draining the rest of the economy of scarce resources.

Effects of sanctions on Russia's GDP

The president was initially most reluctant to officially admit the negative effects of sanctions, but already in 2014 the Russian Minister of Finance, Anton Siluanov, stated that the estimated the annual cost of sanctions to the Russian economy at $40 billion (2 per cent of GDP) compared to the loss of $90–$100 billion (4–5 per cent of GDP) owing to the lower oil prices (*Reuters*, 2014). The IMF estimated in 2015 that US and EU Ukraine-related sanctions together with Russia's retaliatory ban on agricultural imports reduced output in the short term by 1–1.5 per cent. In the medium term, the loss would be 9 per cent (Nelson, 2017, 8). Gurvich and Prilepskiy (2015) of the Economic Expert Group in Moscow estimate the effect of sanctions at 2.4 per cent for 2014–2017.[3]

They look at both direct effects, i.e. restrictions on the foreign borrowings of sanctioned entities, and indirect effects. The latter mainly have to do with higher uncertainty and country risk, e.g. due to fears of imposition of more wide-ranging sanctions, or retaliation by Russian authorities in the form of freezing the assets of non-residents. In terms of the balance of payments, these effects impact a wide range of its components: foreign borrowings of non-sanctioned entities, inflow of direct and portfolio investment, and the outflow of Russian capital.

The financial sanctions are those that have had the most negative impact on the Russian economy. Russian financial markets are not developed, and banks and big companies have been used to raise capital for investment and financing debt on international capital markets. The sanctions imply that Russian state banks and sanctioned companies in the energy and defence sector cannot not raise loans with longer duration on EU and US capital markets. Therefore, there has been strong pressure on government reserves. Private actors usually turning to international capital markets now turn to the government, which has resulted in that large parts of planned infrastructural investments and other long-term government programmes have been put on hold in favour of more immediate needs. As early as August 2014, Rosneft, the big state oil company, applied for state support of over $40 billion to refinance its debt (Kragh, 2014, 60). The Russian aluminium giant *Rusal*, owned by Oleg Deripaska, turned to the government for help with state orders for the company and loans after being targeted by the new wave of American sanctions in 2018 (*Reuters*, 2018).

In response to the capital flight and the difficulties of accessing Western financial markets, Putin announced an amnesty for capital voluntarily declared to the Russian Tax Service in his annual statement to the Federation Council in December 2014 (Poslanie, 2014). In 2018, amendments to the legislation were made, and a second round of capital amnesty was announced for the period from 1 March 2018 to 28 February 2019 (*Tass*, 2018).[4] The Reserve Fund was depleted in 2017 (Ministry of Finance, 2018), and it has become urgent to identify all sources capital available and to build up new reserves.

Thus, the sanctions bite and have created severe obstacles, but when it comes to the magnitude of the fall of the growth rate, it is due to the failure to cast off Russia's dependence on the export of hydrocarbons and promote diversification. With the commodity-export growth model, any fall in the oil price inevitably produces lower growth and less revenue to the state budget. Putin's authoritarian domestic policies and the increased role of the state in the economy further inhibit a shift towards diversification, any thriving entrepreneurial initiative, growth of small and medium enterprises (SMEs) or necessary technical innovation. The need for diversification and modernisation has been discussed for years, but nothing happens. The reason is that such changes would challenge Putin and his rent-addicted, rent-collecting elite. Western sanctions have contributed to the weakening of the Russian economy and made it harder to cooperate with the West in core areas such as international finance. This puts pressure on the political leadership, but it is not strong enough to generate reform; instead, Russia has opted for becoming more self-sufficient, protectionist and isolated.

Defence spending

During the 2000s, up to the financial crisis in 2009, the defence budget grew on average by almost 7 per cent per year, at the same rate as GDP. At that time, when it was affordable and did not limit other public spending, the defence budget's share of GDP was

Russia's economy and military expenditures

around 2.5 per cent of GDP (Oxenstierna and Bergstrand, 2012, 45, 49). However, in 2011, economic growth started to decline, while military spending continued at a high level (Oxenstierna, 2016, 135–136). In 2016, the GDP share of the defence budget had risen to 4.4 per cent of GDP. In terms of Russia's total military expenditure, according to SIPRI's definition, military spending amounted to $40.2 billion in 2008, which corresponded to 3.3 per cent of GDP (SIPRI, 2018). Eight years later, in 2016, the level of total military expenditure had risen by a factor of 1.7, to $69 billion and 5.5 per cent of GDP (Oxenstierna and Bergstrand, 2012, 45, 49; Figure 8.1).

There are two main reasons behind this increase in the share of defence in GDP. The first is that defence has been given increased political priority, which is linked to Russia's amplified security policy ambitions and the wish to be perceived as a military superpower. The present political leadership no longer accepts the European security order established after the Cold War. To improve military capabilities, in 2008 Russia launched a military reform to bring the Armed Forces' capability into the twenty-first century. The second reason behind the increase is the substantial armaments programme for the period 2011–2020, hereafter GPV-2020, which impacts the defence budget through the yearly state defence order, GOZ.[5] The part of the GPV-2020 assigned to the Ministry of Defence (MOD) amounted to RUB19 trillion. The goal of the GPV-2020 is that, by 2020, 70 per cent of the armaments of the Armed Forces should be modern (Oxenstierna, 2016, 143).

The emphasis on defence is reflected in strategies and doctrines. The new National Security Strategy adopted in 2015 says that the main national interest is 'to strengthen

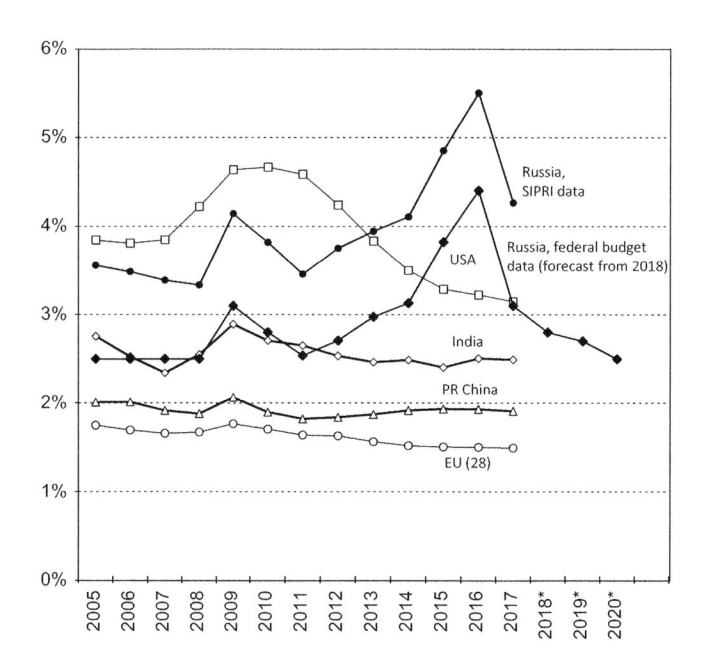

Figure 8.1 Russia's defence budget and total military expenditure as share of GDP in comparison with selected countries, 2005–2020; *per cent*

Sources: Accounts Chamber (2017; 2018); Oxenstierna (2016, 203); SIPRI (2018).

Note: SIPRI's definition of military expenditure is broader than the one based on only the Russian defence budget. Cooper (2013, 23–24) provides a full account of how to calculate total military spending, according to SIPRI's definition of military expenditure, from the Russian national defence budget.

the country's defence', while economic security is in only in fourth place (Security Strategy, 2015, §30). This stands in sharp contrast to how the main national interests were presented in the 2009 Security Strategy: 'to develop democracy and strengthen the civil society' (Hedenskog et al. 2016, 4). The changes in wording indicate that, in the eyes of the political leadership, economic development and other civil concerns are secondary to national defence. Despite the economic downturn after 2011, defence has been given priority in resource allocation to build capability at the expense of other economic sectors.

Figure 8.1 shows Russian total military expenditure, according to the SIPRI definition, in terms of share of GDP, compared to the US, China, and India, and the average for the 28 EU countries. The figure also shows a line for the Russian defence budget's share of GDP in 2011–2017 and the federal budget forecast for it in 2018–2020. It may be noted that Russia's trend of dramatically increasing the share of military spending in GDP up to 2016 is quite opposite to that of the US, which has decreased its share, after the war in Iraq, to 3.2 per cent, and that of the average EU share which now lies around 1.5 per cent. China's expenditure has a positive development, but the GDP share is only around 1.9 per cent. In 2017 the Russian defence budget was decreased which has resulted in a share of GDP of 3.1 per cent. According to the three year budget the share of defence in GDP should fall to 2.5 per cent in 2020.

State arms procurement

Besides the political will to prioritise defence spending, arms procurement under the GPV-2020 is a main factor behind the significant increase in the defence budget during the past decade. In 2000, arms procurement corresponded to 0.7 per cent of GDP, but in 2015 the share had increased to 2.6 per cent. As a result, the GOZ that amounted to 35 per cent of the defence budget in 2006, increased to 60 per cent of the defence budget in 2015, and 54 per cent in 2016. Procurement of armaments corresponded to over 80 per cent of the GOZ, which means that the shares of R&D and of maintenance and repairs in the GOZ have declined (Oxenstierna, 2016, 143). Russia is not integrated in international R&D defence cooperation in a way comparable to Western countries, which pool resources together to accomplish big R&D projects. During a short period under former Minister of Defence Anatoly Serdjukov, there were purchases of Western equipment that were partly motivated by the idea of obtaining access to more advanced technologies.[6] Moreover, this was an attempt to introduce some competition for domestic producers, but because of this and other measures geared at controlling prices and raise efficiency, Serdjukov became unpopular with the defence industry and was soon discharged on allegations of corruption. Under the present Minister of Defence, Sergej Shojgu, the trend of buying abroad was discontinued. After 2014, Western sanctions on the export of defence and dual-use goods to Russia rule out any defence industrial cooperation with the West. More importantly, the Ukrainian embargo on defence industrial cooperation with Russia has caused disruptions in the Russian production because this cooperation was substantial. Thus, sanctions from different actors have resulted in the defence industry's becoming even more isolated from competition and technology transfer. Instead, it is engaged in Putin's strategy of 'import substitution', i.e. replacement of foreign components with domestic substitutes.

The procurement system has changed numerous times since the beginning of the 2000s. Transparency International (TI, 2018) places Russia in group D in its Defence Anti-Corruption Index, one of the lowest-ranked among G20 nations, which means that the process is opaque and cannot be followed. The MOD has attempted to address these challenges by introducing organisational changes, such as creating separate agencies under different jurisdictions, to manage the orders and audit of deliveries (Oxenstierna, 2013, 113–115). This has not produced the expected results, and it now seems that procurement is again handled directly by the MOD. A measure that is claimed to have had positive results is that the GOZ advance payments to producers are paid into special accounts in state banks that MOD can control and audit (RG, 2016).

Yet, the basic problems – the monopolistic structure of the defence industry and the lack of competition – have not been addressed. In addition, many companies are located in remote areas, and whole cities (*monogoroda*) and regions are dependent on single companies, which means that there are social and regional policy arguments for subsidies instead of shutdowns. In other words, soft budget constraints still prevail (Oxenstierna and Westerlund, 2013). The bargaining position of the producers remains strong, and the large GPV-2020, with its high political profile and demands for timely deliveries, has enhanced this strength.

Future military expenditures

Is Russia entering a period of less military expenditures? That defence spending is to decrease in real terms was first signalled in the three-year federal budget for 2017–2019. This trend was confirmed by the fall of actual defence spending in 2017, and by the three-year budget 2018–2020. The defence budget's share of GDP in 2017 dropped to 3.1 per cent, and the preliminary three-year federal budget for 2018–2020 indicates that the nominal yearly defence budget to be kept at about the same level over the three years, which implies a decrease in real terms. The defence budget's share of GDP is planned to fall to 2.5 per cent in 2020 (Figure 8.1; Table 8.1).

Table 8.1 Russia's defence budget and total military expenditure, 2012–2020; *billion RUB, current prices; and billion (2016 prices) USD*

	2012	2013	2014	2015	2016	2017	2018	2019	2020
							\multicolumn{3}{c}{*Budget figures*}		
National defence budget, federal budget execution, billion RUB, current prices	1,812	2,104	2,476	3,181	3,775	2,853	2,772	2,799	2,808
Total military expenditure, SIPRI, billion (2016) USD	53	56	60	65	69	55	NA	NA	NA

Sources: Oxenstierna (2016, 204): Accounts Chamber (2017, 2018); SIPRI (2018).
Notes: The 2016 figures includes a repayment of state guaranteed loans taken by the industry to implement the GPV-2020 of RUB 792 billion. Also the 2017 figure contains repayments but at a lower level. For information on how the national defence budget is related to SIPRI's definition of total military expenditure, see Cooper (2013). NA is not applicable.

One reason for the lower growth of defence spending is that the new state armament programme for the period 2018–2027 is smaller than the previous one. The GPV-2027 was finally signed by the president in February 2018 (*Tass*, 2018). The part of GPV-2027 assigned to the MOD is worth RUB19 trillion, which means that the GPV-2027's nominal rouble value is the same as that of GPV-2020, but the rouble exchange rate against the dollar has fallen and its dollar value is, therefore, only about $295 billion (compared to $690 billion of the GPV-2020 in 2011).

The defence industry has benefitted from the GPV-2020 and the federal target programmes accompanying it to improve its technological base. The industry's situation has improved considerably compared to the beginning of the 2000s, when it was still starved of funding owing to small state orders. Now, during Putin's fourth presidency, the defence industry is faced with a new challenge. It is supposed to increase the manufacture of civilian goods, especially competitive, high-technology products with export potential. This is becoming a key priority of the government. The overall goal is to increase the civilian share of the defence sector's total output from 17 per cent in 2017 to 30 per cent in 2025 and 50 per cent in 2030 (Malmlöf, 2017b). In addition, less domestic arms procurement implies that incomes from international arms sales will become more important. Russia is second only to the US as arms supplier to the global market, where Russia's share in 2012–2016 was 23 per cent, compared to 33 per cent for the US. Several Russian producers are well established on the world market, but export is hardly an option for all Russian defence companies. Furthermore, increased competition from other actors limits the industry's possibilities to fully substitute the anticipated shortfall of domestic demand with foreign customers (Malmlöf, 2017a).

Economic outlook

A growth rate of around 1–2 per cent is what most economic observers forecast for Russia in the coming years. To investigate how this prediction could be improved, Putin assigned the Centre for Strategic Research (CSR) and the Stolypin Club to develop strategies for Russian development up to 2024, besides the Ministry of Economic Development's (MED) strategy for 2018–2024 (see Idrisov et al., 2017). These strategies address the serious challenges that stand before the Russian economy, which are, in my summary: continuing dependence on hydrocarbon export, negative demography, low social mobility, low capitalisation of human capital, technological backwardness, structural limitations to growth (e.g. lack of rule of law, high state involvement in the economy, weak governance, weak property rights, rent addiction), deficient business climate, and lack of competitiveness.

The strategies differ in that they stress different challenges and suggest different approaches to remedy the problems. The MED emphasises the negative demographics, structural problems, the need for closer integration in the Eurasian Economic Union (EAEU), creation of a stable business environment, and policies to increase labour and capital input, and productivity. The CSR highlights the technical backwardness and the weak quality of state regulation. Reconstruction of the economy and the state is recommended as well as more focus on increasing productivity and human capital. For the CRS, it is essential that measures are introduced under macroeconomic balance, i.e. the budget deficit must be kept under control within the bounds of the budget rule. Finally, the Stolypin Club focuses on the problems of low return to investment and low profitability. They recommend that entrepreneurship and competition should be stimulated as well as investments in import substitution. Unlike the other two strategies, they also recommend going back to control of the exchange rate (an advantage for big businesses), to increase of hydrocarbon export, and to allow macroeconomic imbalance to create conditions for accelerated growth (*uskorenie*) (see Idrisov et al., 2017, 6).

Putin appears to have been inspired by parts of these strategies, but the official documents describing Putin's views on the economy for the coming six years do not reflect their respective overall concepts of how to make different drivers in the economy work. Already in the statement to the Federation Council in March 2018, Putin said that by 2030 the GDP per capita should have risen 1.5 times and the average life expectancy of the population should increase from 72 to over 80 years (Poslanie, 2018). In the decree on the strategic goals and tasks for the development of Russia up to 2024 from 7 May (Ukaz, 2018), the president presents a large number of goals that the government must achieve during this presidential term. For example, Russia should be among the five largest economies in 2024. Living standard should be improved and the level of poverty should be halved. Addressing the demographic problem, Putin stipulates that the number of births should increase to 1.7 per women and the number of infant deaths should be reduced to 4.5 per 1,000 children. The health of the population should improve, for instance, by getting 55 per cent of the population to systematically engage in physical activities and sports. The share of public health funding should increase to 4–5 per cent of GDP, which represents a doubling of health costs over six years. Improvements of the environments should be prioritised, and the role of SMEs should get closer to 40 per cent of the GDP. Exports of non-commodities should be doubled (Ukaz, 2018).

It is positive that Putin focuses more on the population's well-being than previously, but there are no proposals for changes of the economic system that would facilitate these developments. Instead, the quantitative results cited in the document resemble plan targets and the president appears to envisage a top-down approach, where the government should manage these changes and make them happen by administrative means. Many goals will be hard to reach. Presently, Russia has about 2 per cent of the world economy (IMF, 2018) and ranks between 11th and 13th, depending on which ranking system is used. To be among the top five, as Putin wishes, demands that Russia expand its international trade cooperation and remove all its internal and external impediments to growth. Increasing the per capita income by 50 per cent would imply that it should rise from almost $12,000 today to $18,000 by 2030; also this requires higher growth than what is foreseen. On decreasing the poverty rate, Russia had 19.3 million people (poverty rate of 13.2 per cent) living under the official poverty line (RUB10,088 per month) in 2017. Halving this number means they should decrease to about 9–10 million in 2024, and achieve a poverty rate of 6–7 per cent, which would be a record low level for Russia. In 2017, the average life expectancy was 72 years of age. Only Rosstat's most positive population scenario makes an average life expectancy of 80 years attainable by 2030 (Rosstat, 2018).

These are only a few examples of the challenges the government will encounter attempting to fulfil Putin's plan and, despite these efforts, Russia's economic growth will most probably stay at the present level. Radical reforms of the economic model are required if the economy should deliver and there is no sign of such steps on Putin's agenda.

Conclusion

During Putin's third presidency, Russia gave priority to high defence spending and building military strength despite a considerable weakening of economic growth. This reflects the shift of Russia's security policy and a harder line against the West. Russia finds that the West took advantage of the collapse of the Soviet Union and advanced its positions by welcoming the Baltic states and Eastern Europe into the EU and North Atlantic Treaty Organisation (NATO). For Russia, it is paramount that this expansion of Western interests does not continue further into countries that Russia still unilaterally regards as its 'sphere of influence'. Furthermore, Russia fears the spreading of 'colour revolutions' into Russia, and the vast demonstrations of 2011 in Russia against Putin made the government respond with an array of measures restricting civil society. The popular protests in Ukraine in 2013–2014 could eventually have ignited similar protests in Russia and the chance that Ukraine would get closer to the EU, which Russia sees as a highway to NATO membership, had to be stopped. This security thinking made Russia intervene by military means on Crimea in 2014, which led to sanctions and a general rupture of Russia's relations to the West.

The military reform launched in 2008 was intended to reform the Armed Forces to restore their strength and reputation. Thanks to high growth at the time the government could pledge strong financial support to the reform and the huge armament programme 2011–2020 accompanying the reform. However, already in 2009, the global financial crisis hit Russia and after that the economy has not recovered to the exceptionally high growth rates of the 2000s. Instead a new economic crisis emerged in 2014, when economic sanctions were adopted against Russia because of its aggression against Ukraine and, on top of that, the oil price fell to half of its previous level. Military expenditure was not adapted to these dramatic changes in economic circumstances. The political leadership kept its commitment to the military sector and instead, other items in the federal budget were cut to accommodate the high defence budget. During the period 2013–2016, there is no correlation between economic growth and growth of the defence budget. The resulting level of defence spending and its share of GDP must be seen as results of purely political considerations.

In 2017, Russia's defence spending fell substantially, and the three-year federal budget for 2018–2020 says that the defence budget should be kept at this new lower level, which implies a much lower defence share in GDP. At last, after a long pause, Putin seems to have listened to his more liberal economic advisors and understood that the economic recession is structural and long term and that military build-up cannot be further accelerated until other basic economic challenges are addressed. So far the indications of the policies to come are that measures improving the population's living standard should be prioritised. Serious considerations are given to developing human capital and healthcare that are crucial for productivity development and growth, as well as to infrastructure and measures to support technological innovations. Yet, this is hardly enough to dramatically improve the performance of the economy. The suggested economic policies represent a top-down approach where the government should administer change in certain areas, it is not a programme that addresses the core mechanisms of growth and income distribution in Putin's Russia. Economic reforms that could radically improve the performance of the economy are not on the table, and growth of 1–2 per cent or stagnation is what may be awaited. Nevertheless, the military sector is not forgotten and it will continue developing military capability, although the defence budget will grow at a more moderate pace than earlier.

Notes

1 Label referring to the group of politicians and state officials who come from or sympathise with the *security* and *military* services.
2 Russia partly lifted these sanctions in June 2017 after an apology for the incident by Turkish President Recep Erdoğan.
3 In an updated later version of this research, Gurvich and Prilepskiy (2018) adjust this estimate to −1.9 per cent, which is explained by the reallocation of resources from non-tradable to tradable sectors that occurred because of the rouble depreciation.
4 The capital amnesty implies that Russian citizens will have an opportunity within the amnesty framework to file on a voluntary basis returns on their property and assets along with overseas accounts and controlled foreign companies in exchange for exemption from tax, administrative

and criminal liability for tax and customs duties payment evasion, and failure to comply with laws on currency regulation and currency control. The amnesty covers all revenues, operations, and transactions related to overseas assets and accounts (TASS, 2018).

5 GPV – *Gosudarstevennaja programma vooruženija* – state aramament programme. GOZ – *Gosudarstvennyj oboronnyj zakas* – state defence order.
6 The most spectacular was the purchase of four French Mistral class amphibious assault ships (Oxenstierna and Bergstrand, 2012, 54). The €1.2 billion order had to be cancelled in 2015 because of the sanctions.

References

Accounts Chamber (2017) *Zakljuchenie Shchetnoj Palaty Rossikoj Federatsij na proekt federal'nogo zakona 'O federal'nom byudžete na 2018 god in a planovyj period 2019'*, 11 October. Accessed (14 February 2018) at http://audit.gov.ru/activities/audit-of-the-federal-budget/31622.

Accounts Chamber (2018) *Operativnaja informatsija o khode ispolenija federal'nogo budžeta, konsolidirovannykh byudžetov i byudžetov vnebyudžetnykh fondov za janvar-dekabr 2017 god*, 13 February. Accessed (19 February 2018) at http://audit.gov.ru/activities/audit-of-the-federal-budget/32539.

Åslund, Anders (2018) 'Russia's economy: Macroeconomic stability but minimal growth', *Russian Analytical Digest*, no. 220, 16 May.

Businessinsider (2015) 'Russian capital flight more than doubled', 19 January. Accessed (20 June 2018) at www.businessinsider.com/afp-russia-capital-flight-more-than-doubled-in-2014-to-151-bn-2015-1?r=US&IR=T&IR=T.

Cooper, Julian (2013) *Russian Military Expenditure: Data, Analysis and Issues*, FOI-R-3688-SE, September.

Gurvich, Evsey and Prilepskiy, Ilya (2015) 'The impact of financial sanctions on the Russian economy', *Russian Journal of Economics*, Vol. 1, pp. 1–27.

Gurvich, Evsey and Prilepskiy, Ilya (2018) 'Western sanctions and Russian responses: Effects after three years', in Becker, Torbjörn and Oxenstierna, Susanne (eds.), *The Russian economy under Putin*. Abington, New York: Routledge.

Hedenskog, Jakob, Oxenstierna, Susanne, Persson, Gudrun, and Vendil Pallin, Carolina (2016) 'Den ryska nationella säkerhetsstrategin', *FOI Memo*, no. 5624.

Idrisov, Georgy, Mau, Vladimir, and Božechkova, Alexandra (2017) 'V poiskakh novoj modeli rosta', *Voprosy ekonomiki*, no.12, pp. 5–23.

IMF (2018) *World Economic Outlook Database*, April. Accessed (13 June 2018) at www.imf.org/en/Data#data.

Kragh, Martin (2014) 'Ryssland efter Krim – en ekonomisk konsekvensanalys', *Ekonomisk debatt*, Vol. 42, no. 8, pp. 51–62.

Malmlöf, Tomas (2017a) 'Russia's arms exports: Successes and challenges', in Facon, Isabelle and Marangé, Céline (eds.), *L'ambivalence de la puissance Russe, Revues Défence Nationale*, Summer, pp. 64–71.

Malmlöf, Tomas (2017b) *Rysk materielförsörjning fram till 2035*, FOI-D-0795-SE, October.

Ministry of Finance (2018) *Obem sredstv Rezervnogo Fonda*. Accessed (9 June 2018) at www.minfin.ru/ru/perfomance/reservefund/statistics/volume/.

Nelson, Rebecca (2017) 'U.S. sanctions and Russia's economy', *CRS Report* 7-570. Washington, DC: Congressional Research Service, 17 February.

Oxenstierna, Susanne (2013) 'Defence spending', in Hedenskog, Jakob and Carolina Vendil Pallin (eds.), *Russia's Military Capability in a Ten-Year Perspective – 2013*. Stockholm: FOI, FOI-R-3734-SE, December, pp. 103–120.

Oxenstierna, Susanne (2015) 'The decline of the Russian economy. Effects of the non-reform agenda', *Baltic Worlds*, Vol. 8, no. 3–4, pp. 87–95.

Oxenstierna, Susanne (2016) 'Russian military expenditure', in Persson, Gudrun (ed.), *Russian Military Capability in a Ten-Year Perspective – 2016*. Stockholm: FOI. FOI-R-4326-SE, December, pp. 133–150 & 200–203.

Oxenstierna, Susanne and Bergstrand, B.-G. (2012) 'Defence economics', in Vendil Pallin, Carolina (ed.) *Russian Military Capability in a Ten-Year Perspective – 2011*. Stockholm: FOI, FOI-R-3474-SE, August, pp. 43–63.

Oxenstierna, Susanne and Westerlund, Fredrik (2013) 'Arms procurement and the Russian defense industry', *Journal of Slavic Military Studies*, Vol. 26, no.1, pp. 1–24, February.

Oxenstierna, Susanne and Olsson, Per (2015) *The Economic Sanctions Against Russia. Impact and Prospects of Success*. Stockholm: FOI, FOI-R-4097-SE, September.

Poslanie (2014) *Poslanie Prezidenta RF ot 04.12.2014 (O položenij v strane i osnovnykh napravlenijakh vnutrennej i vneshnej politi gosudarstva)*, 4 December. Accessed (4 April 2018) at http://kremlin.ru/acts/bank/39443.

Poslanie (2018) *Poslanie Prezidenta Federal'nomu Sobraniju*, 1 March. Accessed (9 June 2018) at http://kremlin.ru/events/president/news/56957.

Reuters (2014) 'Russia puts losses from sanctions, cheaper oil at up to $140 billion per year', 24 November. Accessed (16 June 2018) at www.reuters.com/article/us-russia-siluanov/russia-puts-losses-from-sanctions-cheaper-oil-at-up-to-140-billion-per-year-idUSKCN0J80GC20141124.

Reuters (2018) 'Oleg Deripaska asks Russian state to buy aluminium from Rusal – government source'. Accessed (21 June 2018) at https://uk.reuters.com/article/uk-usa-russia-sanctions-deripaska/oleg-deripaska-asks-russian-state-to-buy-aluminium-from-rusal-government-source-idUKK.

RG (2016) 'Rubl ushel v oboronu', *Rossiiskaja gazeta*, 3 April. Accessed (21 June 2018) at https://rg.ru/2016/04/03/tatiana-shevcova-socvyplaty-v-armii-ne-sokratiat.html.

Rosstat (2018) *Federal'naja služba gosudarstvennaja statistika/Naselenie*. Accessed (17 June) at www.gks.ru/wps/wcm/connect/rosstat_main/rosstat/ru/statistics/population/demography/#.

Security Strategy (2015) 'Ukaz Prezidenta RF "O Strategij natsional'noj bezopasnosti"', no. 683, 31 December. Accessed (17 February 2018) at http://kremlin.ru/acts/bank/40391.

SIPRI (2018) *Military Expenditure Database*. Accessed (21 May 2018) at www.sipri.org/databases/milex.

Tass (2018) 'Putin signs laws on extension of capital amnesty', 20 February. Accessed (4 June 2018) at http://tass.com/economy/990802.

TI (2018) Government *Defence Anti-Corruption Index*, Transparency International. Accessed 21 February 2018) at http://government.defenceindex.org/countries/russian-federation/.

Ukaz (2018) 'Prezident podpisal Ukaz "O natsional'nykh tselijakh i strategicheskikh zadachas razvitija Rossijskoj Federattsii na period do 2024 goda"', 7 May. Accessed (22 May 2018) at http://kremlin.ru/events/president/news/57425.

World Bank (2015) 'The dawn of a new economic era?', *Russia Economic Report*, no. 33, April. Accessed (19 June 2018) at www-wds.worldbank.org/external/default/WDSContentServer/WDSP/IB/2015/04/12/000333037_20150413141814/Rendered/PDF/956970NWP00PUB0B0WB0RER0No0330FINAL.pdf.

9
RUSSIAN STRATEGIC CULTURE
The generational approach and the counter-intelligence state thesis

Mette Skak

> Artificial intelligence is the future, not only for Russia, but for all humankind. It comes with colossal opportunities, but also threats that are difficult to predict. Whoever becomes the leader in this sphere will become the ruler of the world.
>
> *(Russian President Vladimir V. Putin, 2017)*

Old habits die hard. This saying captures well why strategic culture matters. Culture, as viewed by the Danish cultural historian Hartvig Frisch, may be defined simply as habits. The qualifier 'strategic' refers to issues of security policy, notably to norms about the use of force, and to the noun 'strategy' in the sense of a plan or vision often inspiring security policy. Take, for instance, the grand strategy of containment pursued by the United States during the Cold War. One purpose behind strategic culture analysis is, therefore, to specify the grand strategy of a given actor (Kitchen, 2010). Some scholars understand 'grand strategy' in the generic sense of offensive vs. accomodationist strategy (Johnston, 1995) or as the preferred means of an actor, not ends (Gray, 1999). In the analysis below, I shall discuss both ends and means characterising Russian strategic culture today. Although the latter understanding of grand strategy sounds trivial, assessing Russia's preference for military vs. non-military means or overt vs. covert methods is critical for assessing Russian strategic culture. The opening quotation of Putin's strategic embrace of artificial intelligence technology should bring home this point.

What I argue here is that research on Russian strategic culture must abandon geographic and macro-historical determinism ('geopolitics') for the benefit of a dynamic generation-sociological approach akin to that of Karl Mannheim (1923). In his seminal essay, Karl Mannheim proposed that people are influenced by dramatic personal or societal events in their youth. This logic of age cohort certainly applies to security policy decision makers, the focus of most empirical studies of strategic culture beginning with Jack Snyder (1977), who coined the term strategic culture. My research review below presents works employing this common-sense method that turns contemporary history into relevant context. Of particular importance, I further argue that strategic cultural research on Russia must integrate findings about Russia's political degeneration towards a counter-intelligence state made within intelligence studies.

Below I base my analysis on the aforementioned definition of strategic culture of Snyder, the concept of keepers (Lantis and Howlett, 2013) and insights from Colin S. Gray (1999, 2009). I then present major findings on Russian strategic culture beginning with those of Stephen Blank (1993) who suggested Soviet atavisms within contemporary Russian strategic culture. Studying Russian strategic culture is much about identifying Soviet atavisms among contemporary Kremlin decision makers as the way to operationalise culture as old habits dying hard. Hereby, I broaden my earlier work on today's Russian *chekisty* as keepers of Russian strategic culture rather than their military cousins among the so-called *siloviki* (Skak, 2016). Features of the Putin generation, Soviet role models for Putin and likely formative events for him are cited. From this, I infer the grand strategy in terms of ends and means. I further comment on the official Russian threat perception in various doctrines and strategies. The conclusion reflects on the strategic culture of Putin's post-Soviet Russia and the added value of strategic culture as a method for studying security.

On strategic cultural studies

Strategic culture analysis has been reinvented by constructivists, but the field was pioneered by the Russo-American Sovietologist Nathan Leites as hermeneutic research on the 'operational code' of the Kremlin (see Chapter 3). The first formal definition aimed at Soviet nuclear strategy; since this is not the focus here, this phrase should be ignored for the benefit of the stress on habits as the gist of culture in Jack Snyder's pioneering definition of strategic culture:

> Strategic culture can be defined as the sum total of ideas, conditioned emotional responses, and patterns of habitual behavior that members of a national strategic community have acquired through instruction or imitation and share with each other with regard to nuclear strategy.
>
> *(1977, 8)*

While offering this holistic approach to strategic culture, Snyder adds that strategy is mainly about cognitive behaviour. Accordingly, the analysis below goes into the habitual thinking of Putin and his *chekist* fellow decision makers in terms of both sources and contents and later into the grand strategic behaviour of Putin's Russia. Snyder's empirical study pointed to the Soviet Great Fatherland War (1941–1945) as the formative experience for the post–World War II generation of Soviet decision makers and identified the Soviet military as actual decision maker on doctrine and nuclear force posture. Using the terminology of Jeffrey Lantis and Darryl Howlett (2013), Snyder turned this bureaucracy into keeper of Soviet strategic culture – i.e. custodian of the legacy from 1941 to 1945. As I shall show later, some scholars still hold the military to be the keeper of post-Soviet Russian strategic culture.

Unfortunately, Lantis and Howlett (2013) seem blind to the possibility of strong intelligence bureaucracies as keepers, so this will be my analytical twist to their contribution. Otherwise, their advice of identifying keepers of strategic culture is a great methodological help that serves to demystify the field. The concept builds upon Berger's constructivist insight that strategic culture is a negotiated reality among elites (Lantis, 2009). Leaders select the cultural canons – Lenin in the Soviet case – and decide when to move beyond them, as did Russia's post-Soviet decision makers following the collapse of the Soviet Union. The unique powers vested in the office of the Russian President in the country's constitution, including oversight over foreign policy, points to the President as decisive keeper of Russian strategic culture. Putin's energetic personality as foreign and security policy decision maker makes it all the more expedient to reconstruct his operational code (cf. Chapter 3) and the broader Kremlin-level strategic culture.

Lantis and Howlett (2013) offer a comprehensive analytical typology for sources of strategic culture. They consider the historical evolution of states and their security policy experience to influence strategic culture by creating a differentiated universe of state identities held by decision makers (e.g. great powers vs. small states). Of particular interest for updating the study of strategic culture is their perception of interplay between generational change and technology as seen in the opening quotation of Putin who perceives strategic empowerment from artificial intelligence. They state that

> ... information and communications technology can have important ramifications for issues of empowerment and strategic reach. While information technology has transformed societies, it has also allowed individuals and groups to [...] cause disruption at a distance.
>
> *(Lantis and Howlett, 2013, 81)*

Accordingly, strategic cultures cannot be considered static, although inertia to change is implied in the term culture. Strategic cultures do undergo incremental generational and technological change. Traumatic events like revolutions and defeat in war may cause paradigmatic change.

Another insight stems from Gray (1999) who holds that some societies display low context, i.e. pragmatic strategic cultures, whereas Russia exemplifies a high-context strategic culture prone to seeing subtexts, subplots and subtle interconnections. In other words, a propensity towards conspiracy theorising as a legacy from Russia's truly traumatic twentieth century, but also a strategic culture energetically cultivated from above in the shape of recurring war scares, etc. (Velikanova, 2002). Citing the rather self-destructive case of Russia, Gray allows for dysfunctional strategic cultures. He rejects geopolitical analysis by insisting that culture is destiny in the sense that geography and security policy history are subject to authoritative interpretation by humans (Gray, 2009). This master narrative or plot in his terminology must be the focus when studying strategic culture. Concerning Russia, the plot arguably consists of a great power identity, a perception of being a besieged fortress and a zero-sum mentality regarding the use of force dubbed *kto-kogo* (cf. Velikanova, 2002; Lo, 2015, xviii and *passim*; see also Chapters 1 and 4).

Research on Soviet and post-Soviet Russian strategic culture

The work on post-Soviet Russian strategic culture was initiated by Blank (1993). He described the revolution in strategic culture brought about by Lenin in 1917 – a turn towards relentless political and military warfare termed class struggle for the sake of overthrowing the bourgeois world order. Any means the party had sanctioned were legitimate (Blank, 1993, 8). Although terror declined after Stalin's death in 1953, the Soviet Union expanded its covert, intelligence and ideological-organisational means of warfare abroad and upheld the arms race (Blank, 1993, 24). This led Blank to question the depth of Gorbachev's presumable revolution in strategic culture – also in view of the technological espionage of the Soviet secret police, the *Komitet Gosudarstvennoi Bezopasnosti* or KGB (Blank, 1993, 46). Blank dismissed New Political Thinking as mainly disinformation or pretence – paying lip service to Western buzzwords like interdependence. He acknowledged retrenchment, retreat and restraint but doubted the lasting nature of the new trends.

Here Blank comes across as more pertinent than Henrikki Heikka (2000), otherwise an incisive analyst of the Soviet cultural legacy – the cult of the offensive. This outcome is an utter irony in that the true lesson drawn from the stunning Russian and Soviet success in defeating invaders from the West ought to have been a cult of the defensive. Heikka portrays a hypermilitaristic Soviet strategic culture corresponding to the permanent war footing of the Soviet economy as observed by Oskar Lange and Blank (1993). While acknowledging the influence of post-Soviet Russia's intelligence services and the coming into power of Putin whom he calls a creation of the security apparatus, Heikka concludes in terms of a miracle – Russia's turn towards defensive realism (Heikka, 2000, 90).

Fritz Ermarth (2009) updates research on Russian strategic culture by pointing to Putin's geo-economics as grand strategy, oil and gas being Russia's only allies in the twenty-first century, whereas in the past the army and fleet were the only allies, as the aphorism goes. Nowadays, however, scholars hold geopolitics to be the clue to the Russo-Ukrainian drama. Ermarth powerfully exposes the contradictory approach of Russian national security elites: defensiveness bordering on paranoia, on the one hand, and assertiveness bordering on pugnacity, on the other (Ermarth, 2009, 88). Russia is a tricky counterparty excelling in hard diplomacy and soft coercion (Sherr, 2013) – or plain coercion.

Then there is the research into the national identities of Russian and China by Gilbert Rozman (2014), who contributes significantly to research on their strategic cultures by pointing to substantial overlaps. Both Russia and China were alerted by North Atlantic Treaty Organisation's (NATO) humanitarian war over the Kosovo issue and driven into strategic partnership through their common aversion to the American-led war in Iraq and to colour revolutions like the Orange Revolution in Ukraine in 2004. The Arab Spring of 2011–2013 further mobilised their illiberal instincts inspiring them to civilisational arguments against the West (ibid., 274). Yet, Rozman deems the Sino-Russian entente less solid than the Transatlantic alliance and concludes in terms of an identity gap.

As for cyber technology, James J. Wirtz (2015) argues that Russia more than any other actor is integrating cyberwarfare into a grand strategy of achieving political objectives. The Russian mix of hybrid and cyberwar in Ukraine in 2014 succeeded in defeating the NATO strategy of collective defence – here Wirtz builds upon the faulty assumption of an article 5 NATO commitment to defend Ukraine. Notwithstanding this, he writes convincingly about the Russian strategic culture of carefully considering uses and abuses of technological breakthroughs along with innovative warfare as enabling Russia to orchestrate surprises. He quotes a 2012 publication about the holistic Russian concept of information warfare as spanning intelligence, counter-intelligence, deceit, disinformation, electronic warfare, debilitation of communications, psychological pressure, DDoS (i.e. distributed denial of service) and Russia Today combined – thus anticipating the whole gamut of Russian disruptive tactics we are witnessing now (cf. below).

In a similar vein, Stephen R. Covington (2016) insists on the holistic, non-Western Russian approach to military warfare – what he calls Russia's Homeland Hybrid Strategic Offense. Russian doctrine considers the initial phase of war decisive because of Russia's economic inferiority vis-á-vis NATO and insists on avoiding war on Russian soil. Hereby Russia is 'securing herself at the expense of the security of others' (Covington, 2016, 41). The significance of the Putin era lies in the symbiosis between him and the military brass. Covington speaks of the unrealities of Putin's worldview, so it is of little comfort that his operational code, as reconstructed by Herd (see Chapter 3), is defensive and reactive in his own perception. The bottom line, according to Covington, is a pre-emptive Russian approach to warfare upgraded to the twenty-first-century speed of light technology that puts a premium on surprise and offensive initiative. An outcome harking back to the Soviet cult of the offensive.

Analytically, Covington (2016) reiterates Snyder (1977) by turning the Russian military and its General Staff into keepers of Russian strategic culture. This matches the perception of the Russian military analyst Pavel Felgenhauer (2018) who offers an equally chilling interpretation of the Russian grand strategy as one of Finlandising Europe. He holds that the General Staff and the military intelligence GRU are in the driver's seat. They distort their intelligence deliveries to Putin into Western decapitation strategies targeted at his person and a planned onset of resource wars against Russia from 2025, meaning that the years 2025–2030 will be dangerous. Following Felgenhauer, the underlying problem about Russian security is the lack of civilian control over the military.

Conversely, I have argued that it is rather the non-military *siloviki*, known as *chekisty* (they do cherish the legacy from Lenin's counter-intelligence[1] called Cheka), who deserve attention as keepers and entrepreneurs of contemporary Russian strategic culture (Skak, 2016). They represent an all-encompassing approach to security and a professional focus on regime security, resulting in a spiral of securitisation of Russian politics (see also Chapter 6). This is not to deny the merits of Covington, Felgenhauer and others, but so as to complement insights on contemporary Russian strategic culture and security policy. My specific argument in Skak (2016) is that it was the overblown Soviet counter-intelligence instincts of Putin, his close companion Nikolai Patrushev and other *chekisty* that triggered the annexation of Crimea and the Russian instigation of armed rebellion in Donbas in 2014. Their socialisation into KGB active measures (*aktivnye meropriyatia* – the Soviet equivalent to covert action) offers a clue to the surprising execution of the intervention. Hence, the Russian secret services must be considered autonomous actors behind the arguably dysfunctional, high-context strategic cultural outcome characterising Russia (see also Chapter 16). I shall elaborate on this below via the counter-intelligence state thesis beginning with an excursus into generation sociology on the Putin generation and present turning points shaping Putin's acute fear of regime change at home and deep aversion to it abroad (Gel'man, 2016; Shchelin, 2016).

Russia – a counter-intelligence state: chekisty as keepers of strategic culture

As stated earlier, generation sociology was invented by Mannheim (1923) and reinvented by Lantis and Howlett (2013) as a welcome methodological twist to strategic culture analysis. What matters here is that Putin and his fellow Kremlin decision makers belong to the post-Stalin generation that experienced a return to normalcy on Soviet premises. Their childhood was not one of wars, forced collectivisation and terror like that of their parents and grandparents. One Russian friend of mine insists that she had a happy Soviet childhood except for the war scare at the time of the U-2 incident in 1960; similarly, Gel'man (2016, 34) cites the 'long 1970s' as a normative ideal for the current generation of Russian rulers. Underneath the surface of normalcy, however, there was an internal, long-lasting Soviet Cold War against Khrushchev and the legacy from his secret speech on de-Stalinisation as reconstructed by Yitzhak Brudny (1998). Likewise, Blank (1993), Gel'man (2016) and Robert W. Pringle (2015, 23–24) consider Yuri Andropov's time as KGB boss (1967–1982) anything but benign due to his use of active measures. Andropov is a key role model for Putin; the former's hawkish approach to counter-intelligence was shaped by a political near-death experience akin to Putin's (Skak, 2016).

I have in mind Andropov's trauma from the Budapest rising in 1956 and, regarding Putin, his recollections about the drama in Dresden during the fall of the Berlin Wall in 1989. What is more, Putin misperceives causes and effects in the liquidation of the Libyan dictator

Gaddafi and the entire Arab Spring as another formative event for him. In an article whose title translates into "Russia and the changing world", Putin (2012) attacks 'the exaggerated use of force by the United States and NATO', referring to the intervention in Libya. He interprets the Arab Spring as one of

> [...] interference from abroad in support of one of the parties to the conflict and the violent nature of this interference. Things went so far that several states under the pretext of humanitarian slogans with the help of the air force took action (*razdelalis'*) against the Libyan regime. And as apotheosis – the grim, not even medieval scenery, but quite barbarian (*pervobytnoi*) showdown with M. Gaddafi.
>
> *(Putin, 2012)*

The problem with Putin's account and the Kremlin account of the Maidan rising is the disregard for local agency (cf. Bryanski, 2011). The fact that the Secretary General of the United Nations officially declared NATO not to have violated its mandate during the Libyan intervention is never mentioned (Charbonneau, 2011). Instead, Putin speaks of Arab 'pseudo-NGOs' as 'influence agents of the great powers' and delivers a flawed definition of soft power: 'Soft power is the complex of instruments and methods for the achievement of foreign policy goals without using weapons'. Putin here postulates micro-management by the United States whenever people rise in protest no matter the local circumstances and warns that he will not allow anyone to orchestrate a 'Libyan scenario' in Syria (Charbonneau, 2011).

Russia's own wave of protest demonstrations in September 2011 against Putin's overt manipulation of the planned presidential elections in 2012 through his mouthpiece, interim President Dmitry Medvedev, represents an even more clear-cut case of a political near-death experience for Putin – one for which he pointedly blamed U.S. Secretary of State Hillary Clinton (Herszenhorn and Barry, 2011). Seen in retrospect, this may be what motivated the presumably Russian hacking of the U.S. presidential elections in 2016. The tragic bias in all this is the projection of the near-almighty power of Andropov's KGB – something the *chekisty* know all about – onto foreign actors and intelligence services like the CIA which happen to be subject to checks and balances leading to ominous Kremlin groupthink.

This is where the concept of counter-intelligence state comes in handy to capture the political degeneration in Russia that pushes Russian foreign and security policy in bizarre directions (Bateman, 2014). It was modelled on totalitarian secret police systems like the KGB and coined by an intelligence analyst, Professor J. Michael Waller, who wrote, 'the counter-intelligence state is characterised by a large elite force acting as watchdog of security. This apparatus is not accountable to the public and enjoys immense police powers' (Waller, 1994 quoted from Bateman, 2014, 383). The analytical criterion is the autonomy of the secret services, something that does characterise the Russian successor to the KGB, the FSB, as concluded by another expert on the KGB: '[...] the FSB unlike the KGB operates without political supervision and has detained political opponents with little regard for the law' (Pringle, 2015, 108). A rich scholarly literature underpins this observation, namely works on Putin's recruitment policy for the benefit of the *siloviki* including the *chekisty* (for further references, see Skak, 2016). Aaron Bateman (2014) is certainly not alone when concluding that *siloviki* nowadays not only influence policy but make it – take, for instance, the unique agenda-setting role of another *chekist* mentor for Putin, the late Evgeni Primakov (Skak, 2016).

Moreover, several scholars have documented the Mark Twain-like death of the KGB (e.g. Waller, 2006; Walthers, 2014). It is no coincidence that the Russian investigative journalists Andrei Soldatov and Irina Borogan use Patrushev's term new nobility about the FSB as the title for their inquiry into this bastion of power. Certainly, one must be wary about jumping to conclusions about Russia's intelligence community as a monolith. Its multiple specialised organs and their particular groupthink about world affairs make them dangerous for Russia's neighbours. Intelligence agencies – FSB vs. GRU vs. the foreign espionage agency SVR, etc. – are often mired in mutual rivalry and constitute a not too efficient hydra (Galeotti, 2016). But their greed and appetite for power along with their misperceptions with respect to, say, counterterrorism may jeopardise the security of the Russian rank and file.

The Kremlin grand strategy today – ends vs. means

The counter-intelligence thesis about the *chekist* distortion of Russian security policy turns the Kremlin quest for regime security into the grand strategy, meaning the essence of Russian security policymaking. *Mutatis mutandis*, this is being argued by the Russian scholars Vladimir Gel'man (2016) and Pavel Shchelin (2016). The latter holds Russian foreign policy to be driven exclusively by domestic needs of regime survival, a logic which he finds permeates the Russian National Security Strategy of 31 December 2015. Whereas the 2009 strategy stressed global competitive conditions, the new version is myopic and acutely fearful of colour revolutions in continuation of Putin's statements about the Maidan Revolution. The game changer cited by Shchelin is once again the Arab Spring and the coinciding Russian near-colour revolution in the winter of 2011–2012. In short, a post-2011 change in grand strategy from a preoccupation with restoring Russia as a great power through energy geoeconomics to a counter-colour revolutionary obsession with regime security, meaning that the pursuit of Russian great powerhood is now merely instrumental (ibid.).

Even so, the Kremlin may partly be earnest and defensive in its mobilisation of Russians around the message of Russia as a great power and patriotism. As pointed out by some Russian experts and Western think tanks, centre-periphery zero-sum conflicts over budgets and regional identities represent substantial issues (Goble, 2015). Climate change causing a gradual melting of the permafrost in Russia's vast permafrost regions adds to the complex, perhaps disruptive nature of regionalism inside Russia. On the other hand, there is a striking change of tenor from Putin's original matter-of-fact ways to the mythology surrounding the current grand strategy – 'Andropov 2.0' as it were. The shelving of Medvedev's modernisation strategy along with the founding of *Rosgvardia*, a National Guard of presidential loyalists, that enjoys ever-widening powers is also telling for actual Kremlin priorities.

As for Putin's grand strategy concerning means employed, another logical implication from the counter-intelligence state thesis is the all-too willing resort to active KGB measures – a reinvention of the Soviet holistic and offensive approach to legitimate means. The novelty lies in the embrace of the unique digital options of the twenty-first century – IT, social media and cyberwarfare – out of the belief that they represent force multipliers (Splidsboel Hansen, 2017). Much has been written about this not so new hybrid warfare that includes a critical dimension of information warfare – warfare targeted at the cognitive sphere (Galeotti, 2017). Suffice it to illustrate the holism of the Kremlin through the likely dual use of the commercial energy project Nord Stream 2. Danish defence and intelligence analysts expect their Russian colleagues to install electronic surveillance gear on this new Baltic Sea gas pipeline if it becomes operational (Beim and Arnfred, 2018). The offensive Kremlin information warfare against liberal Western democracies is matched by a defensively motivated domestic information war targeted at Russian audiences (Splidsboel Hansen, 2017). Furthermore, the Russian interventions in Georgia and Ukraine displayed coordinated military and cyber action (Windrem, 2016).

Doctrines and strategies expressing the Russian threat perception

Given this turn towards information warfare, the Russian Information Security Doctrine of 2016 represents a critical sequel to the alarmist National Security Strategy of December 2015. Its article 12 holds that the 'intelligence services of certain States' are 'increasingly using information and psychological tools with a view to destabilizing the internal and political and social situation in various regions across the world' (Doctrine of Information Security …, 2016). An ominous threat perception mirroring the disruptive practices of Russia herself. The Finnish security experts Katri Pynnöniemi and Martti Kari (2016) consider the outcome 'a besieged cyber fortress' doctrine, citing its almost bellicose tone. The document articulates the Orwellian *Chekist* conviction that the information sphere is 'a tool to change the fabric of society'. Pynnöniemi and Kari perceive an IT inferiority complex, but oddly enough, the new information security doctrine fails to mention the BRICS project of creating an alternative Internet as an option.

The additional Economic Security Strategy of May 2017 (Ukaz …, 2017) underscores the Kremlin holism via verbal securitisation. Its provisions mark the securitisation of the Western resort to economic sanctions as a reprisal for Russia's annexation of Crimea and sponsoring of Donbas separatism. The buzzword here is economic sovereignty. Climate change is mentioned as threatening global food production, and among its benchmarks it lists (the notoriously low) productivity in Russia, but the document specifies no reform strategy. Although the Arctic is the region that receives mention in both the National Security Strategy and the military doctrine, there is no separate Arctic strategy of recent origin, only a militarised Kremlin policy there (see also Chapter 25). A 2025 Environmental Security Strategy was issued in 2016, a document that lacks guidance on the struggle against air pollution, something that caused angry demonstrations against toxic dump fumes in Volokolamsk earlier in 2018.

So, what is striking about the official Kremlin threat perception and pursuit of security is often what is not being addressed, just as much as what is being articulated and how that occurs. A case in point is the silence surrounding the economic rise of China – maybe out of a fear that dare not speak its name, as quipped by Natasha Kuhrt. Yet – to repeat, – regime security as operational grand strategy is what unites governments in Moscow and Beijing (Rozman, 2014; cf. Chapter 28).

Conclusion

The analysis above documents an offensive turn in post-Soviet Russian strategic culture albeit for defensive reasons. The core observation is a post-2011 turn towards a grand strategy of pursuing regime security in the vein of Andropov and a return to his disruptive active measures updated to the digital twenty-first-century options – including artificial intelligence, as made clear by Putin himself. Collectively, I dwelled on the *chekisty* and Putin in particular as keepers of Russian strategic culture in the sense of key security policy agenda setters (along with the General Staff). The concept counter-intelligence state implies autonomy of the intelligence services, meaning state capture concerning security policymaking. This outcome signifies a dysfunctional, myopic security policy – a syndrome of besieged cyber fortress (Pynnöniemi and Kari, 2016) as the plot that haunts Russia today (Gray, 2009). Hereby, the Kremlin ignores vital issues like Russia's economic modernisation or how to really cope with a rising China and Asia.

As for the added value inherent in analysing security issues through strategic culture, it is an indispensable, inductive way of grasping actual state-level security dynamics. The approach is hermeneutic and goes into the mental universe of decision makers and stresses the overarching, maybe not too rational 'plot' of a national security community in contrast to, e.g. the neorealist abstractions (Gray, 2009). Although not everything boils down to strategic culture, the approach guarantees an adequately up-to-date security analysis once it is based on a healthy mixture of generation sociology and awareness of contemporary digital options.

Note

1 Counter-intelligence is the antonym to intelligence or espionage and refers in general to prevention against foreign espionage or attempts to undermine a state's political system. But the Soviet secret services committed terror, massacres and miscarriages of justice on a mass scale in the name of counter-intelligence as established, e.g. in a recent two-volume history of Russia (Zubov, 2011).

References

Bateman, Aaron (2014) 'The Political Influence of the Russian Security Services', *The Journal of Slavic Military Studies,* Vol. 27, No. 3, pp. 380–403.
Beim, Jakob Hvide and Carl Emil Arnfred (2018) 'Advarsel om overvågning i Østersøen', *Politiken* (A Danish Daily), 19. February.
Blank, Stephen J. (1993) 'Class War on a Global Scale. The Leninist Culture of Political Conflict', in idem et al. eds. *Conflict, Culture, and History. Regional Dimensions.* Alabama: Air University Press, Maxwell Air Force Base, pp. 1–55.
Brudny, Yitzhak M. (1998) *Reinventing Russia. Russian Nationalism and the Soviet State, 1953–1991.* Cambridge, MA; London: Harvard University Press.
Bryanski, Gleb (2011) 'Putin: Libya Coalition Has No Right to Kill Gaddafi', *Reuters,* April 26. http://reuters.com/assets/print?aid=USTRE73P4L920110426
Charbonneau, Louis (2011) 'U.N. Chief Defends NATO from Critics of Libyan War', *Reuters,* December 14. https://reuters.com/article/worldNews/idAFTRE7BD1XF20111214
Covington, Stephen R. (2016) 'The Culture of Strategic Thought Behind Russia's Modern Approaches to Warfare', *Defense and Intelligence Projects. Paper.* Belfer Center for Science and International Affairs. Harvard Kennedy School, 53 pp.
Doctrine of Information Security of the Russian Federation (2016) Unofficial translation, MFA Russia, 5 December. Accessed on 24 April 2018 at www.mid.ru/en/foreign_policy/official_documents/-/asset_publisher/CptICkB6
Ermarth, Fritz W. (2009) 'Russian Strategic Culture in Flux: Back to the Future?', in Johnson, Jeannie L. et al. eds. *Strategic Culture and Weapons of Mass destruction. Culturally Based Insights into Comparative National Security Policy Making.* New York: Palgrave Macmillan, pp. 84–96.
Felgenhauer, Pavel (2018) 'Rusland ønsker 'finlandisering' af hele Europa', in *Ny Kold Krig. Marie Krarup taler med 17 eksperter fra øst og vest,* Sydslesvig: Hovedland, pp. 158–171.
Galeotti, Mark (2016) 'Putin's Hydra: Inside Russia's Intelligence Services', *European Council on Foreign Relations,* 11 May. www.ecfr.eu/publications/summary/ putins_hydra_inside_russias_intelligence_services#
Galeotti, Mark (2017) 'Controlling Chaos: How Russia Manages Its Political War in Europe', *European Council on Foreign Relations,* August. www.ecfr.eu/publications/summary/controlling_chaos_how_russia_manages_its_political_war_in_europe
Gel'man, Vladimir (2016) 'The Politics of Fear: How Russia's Rulers Counter their Rivals', *Russian Politics,* Vol. 1, pp. 27–45.
Goble, Paul (2015) 'Regional Identities Strengthening Faster than All-Russian One, Petrozavodsk Historian Says', *Window on Eurasia – New Series,* December 4. Accessed on 29 August 2016 at http://windowoneurasia2.blogspot.dk/2015/regional-identities-strengthening.html
Gray, Colin S. (1999) 'Strategic Culture as Context: The First Generation of Theory Strikes Back', *Review of International Studies,* Vol. 25, No. 1, pp. 49–69.
Gray, Colin S. (2009) 'Out of the Wilderness: Prime Time for Strategic Culture' in Johnson, Jeannie L. et al. eds. *Strategic Culture and Weapons of Mass Destruction. Culturally Based Insights into Comparative National Security Policy Making.* New York: Palgrave Macmillan, pp. 221–241.
Heikka, Henrikki (2000) *Beyond the Cult of the Offensive. The Evolution of Soviet/Russian Strategic Culture and Its Implications for the Nordic-Baltic Region.* Helsinki: Ulkopoliittinen Instituutti & Institut für Europäische Politik.

Herszenhorn, David M. and Ellen Barry (2011) 'Putin Contends Clinton Incited Unrest Over Vote', *The New York Times,* December 8. www.nytimes.com/2011/12/09/world/europe/putin-accuses-clinton-of-instigating-russian-protests.html

Johnston, Alastair I. (1995) 'Thinking about Strategic Culture', *International Security,* Vol. 19, No. 4, pp. 32–64.

Kitchen, Nicholas (2010) 'Systemic Pressures and Domestic Ideas: A Neoclassical Realist Model of Grand Strategy Formation', *Review of International Studies,* Vol. 36, No. 1, pp. 117–143.

Lantis, Jeffrey S. (2009) 'Strategic Culture: From Clausewitz to Constructivism', in Johnson, Jeanni L. et al. eds. *Strategic Culture and Weapons of Mass Destruction. Culturally Based Insights into Comparative National Security Policy Making.* New York: Palgrave Macmillan, pp. 33–52.

Lantis, Jeffrey S. and Darryl Howlett (2013) 'Strategic Culture', in Baylis, John et al. eds. *Strategy in the Contemporary World. An Introduction to Strategic Studies. Fourth Edition.* Oxford: Oxford University Press, pp. 76–95.

Lo, Bobo (2015). *Russia and the New World Disorder.* London: Chatham House; Washington, D.C.: Brookings.

Mannheim, Karl (1923) 'The Problem of Generations', reprinted in Kecskemeti, Paul. *Essays on the Sociology of Knowledge. Collected Works.* Vol. 5, New York: Routledge, pp. 276–322.

Pringle, Robert W. (2015) *Historical Dictionary of Russian and Soviet Intelligence Services. Second Edition.* Lanham, etc.: Rowman and Littlefield.

Putin, Vladimir V. (2012) 'Rossia i meniaiushchiisia mir', *Moskovskie Novosti,* 27 fevralia. www.mn.ru/politics/78738

Putin, Vladimir V. (2017) 'Putin Says the Nation that Leads in AI 'Will Be the Ruler of the World', by James Vincent, *The Verge,* September 4. Accessed on 29 December 2017 at www.theverge.com/2017/9/4/16251226/russia-ai-putin-rule-the-world

Pynnöniemi, Katri and Martti J. Kari (2016) 'Russia's New Information Security Doctrine', *FIIA Comment,* No. 26, December. Helsinki: Ulkopoliittinen Instituutti/Utrikespolitiska Institutet/The Finnish Institute of International Affairs

Rozman, Gilbert (2014) *The Sino-Russian Challenge to the World Order. National Identities, Bilateral Relations, and East versus the West in the 2010s.* Stanford: Stanford University Press.

Shchelin, Pavel (2016) 'Russian National Security Strategy: Regime Security and Elite's Struggle for 'Great Power' Status', *Slovo,* Vol. 28, No. 2 (Spring), pp. 85–105.

Sherr, James (2013) *Hard Diplomacy and Soft Coercion. Russia's Influence Abroad.* London: Chatham House.

Skak, Mette (2016) 'Russian Strategic Culture: The Role of Today's Chekisty', *Contemporary Politics,* Vol. 22, No. 3, pp. 324–341.

Snyder, Jack L. (1977) *The Soviet Strategic Culture: Implications for Limited Nuclear Options.* Santa Monica: Rand R-2154-AF.

Splidsboel Hansen, Flemming (2017) 'Russian Hybrid Warfare. A Study of Disinformation', *DIIS Report* 06. Copenhagen: Danish Institue for International Studies.

Ukaz prezidenta Rossiiskoi Federatsii O Strategii ekonomicheskoi bezopasnosti Rossiiskoi Federatsii na period do 2030 goda (2017) 13 maia 2017 goda No. 208.

Velikanova, Ol'ga V. (2002) 'The Myth of the Besieged Fortress. Soviet Mass Perception in the 1920s–1930s', *Working Paper* No. 7, The Stalin-Era Research and Archive Project. Centre for Russian and east European Studies, University of Toronto.

Waller, J. Michael (2006) 'Russia: Death and Resurrection of the KGB', in Berman, Ilan and J. Michael Waller eds. *Dismantling Tyranny. Transitioning Beyond Totalitarian Regimes.* Rowman & Littlefield, pp. 1–28.

Walthers, Ulf (2014) 'Russia's Failed Tranformation: The Power of the KGB/FSB from Gorbachev to Putin', *International Journal of Intelligence and Counterintelligence,* Vol. 27, pp. 666–686.

Windrem, Robert (2016) 'Timeline: Ten Years of Russian Cyber Attacks on Other Nations', *NBC News,* December 18. Accessed on 14 February 2018 at www.nbcnews.com/storyline/hacking-in-america/timeline-ten-years-russian-cyber-attacks-other-nations-n697111

Wirtz, James J. (2015) 'Cyber War and Strategic Culture: The Russian Integration of Cyber Power into Grand Strategy', in Geers, Kenneth ed. *Cyber War in Perspective: Russian Aggression against Ukraine.* Tallinn: NATO CCD COE Publications, pp. 29–37 (freely available from the internet).

Zubov, Andrei Borisovich (otv. red.) (2011) *Istoria Rossii. XX vek. Tom I: 1894–1939; Tom II: 1939–2007.* Moscow: AST – Astrel.

10
THE SECURITY COUNCIL AND SECURITY DECISION-MAKING

Edwin Bacon

Russia's Security Council sits at the centre of security decision-making in the Russian Federation. If there is any body in Russian politics that represents an 'inner circle' or could be seen as—in functional terms at least—the equivalent of the Soviet Politburo, then the Security Council of the Russian Federation is that body.

Chaired by Russia's President, Russia's Security Council brings together a top table of the most significant figures in those organisations that hold political, military, and judicial power in the Russian Federation. Foremost amongst its members are the prime minister, key government ministers (foreign affairs, internal affairs, justice, defence, and finance), the speakers of both chambers of the Russian Parliament, the head of the presidential administration, the presidential representatives in each of the federal districts covering Russia's vast territory, the mayor of Moscow, the governor of St. Petersburg, the chief prosecutor, the heads of Russia's internal and external security services, the chief of general staff, and—of course—the powerful Secretary of the Security Council itself (for a full list of members, see Table 10.1).

The Security Council meets in full session about once a quarter, when its permanent and ordinary members gather together in the Kremlin, with usually around 25–30 of them around a long table at the head of which sits the President. Such formal gatherings, however, have less day-to-day policy significance than do the weekly meetings of the Permanent Members of the Security Council. These usually take place in the Kremlin or in the President's residence (Novo-Ogarevo during the Putin presidencies, Gorky-9 during the presidency of Dmitry Medvedev). It is in these meetings, attended by around a dozen Permanent Members, that the political and security elite of the Russian Federation, led by the President, discuss the pressing issues of the moment.

In this overview of the Security Council of the Russian Federation, we consider its formal status and membership, the apparatus that serves the Security Council, the role of Secretary of the Security Council, the history of the Security Council, and the Council's assessment of threats to Russian security. Beyond formal and empirical assessment, we essay too a more behaviourist analysis of the influence of Russia's Security Council, and its Secretary, in Russia's political and security affairs today.

The role of Russia's Security Council

Russia's Security Council is an organ of the Russian state whose existence is set out in Russia's Constitution. Given the institutional framework of the Russian state as it currently functions, having formal status as a constitutional body represents a degree of permanence and importance that not all institutions possess. Whilst—at the federal level—the presidency, the government, and both chambers of parliament are, along with the Security Council, formally established by the extant constitution that came into force by popular referendum in 1993, there are a number of other state institutions functioning in today's Russia that have no such constitutional mandate. The federal districts, with their presidential plenipotentiaries, the State Council, the Public Chamber, and the two dozen or so Presidential Commissions and Presidential Councils, all lack such constitutional status. These have been established by the President and can be abolished in the same way without contravening the constitution; not so the Security Council.

Whilst the Security Council has a constitutional mandate for its existence, the body thus established is markedly, indeed purposefully, hollow when it comes to the constitutionally defined detail of its role. Article 83.7 of the Russian Constitution simply states that the President shall 'form and head the Security Council of the Russian Federation, the status of which is determined by the federal law'. So vague a formulation does no more than say that Russia must have a Security Council headed by the President. It is within the prerogative of the President and of federal law to decide all the important questions of what the Security Council does, who is on it, how well resourced it is, and so on. As our overview of the Security Council's history sets out below, the significance of the Security Council waxed and waned during its early years as power struggles were waged in the newly established post-Soviet system. The current, and seemingly enduring, position of the Security Council is the key arena in which the important political, judicial, intelligence, and military branches of Russian state power come together to discuss and formulate policy in a wide range of areas. Undermining formal democratic notions of a separation of power between the executive, legislature, and judiciary, the vast majority of Security Council members hold positions in one or other of these branches of the state. The few that do not are at the head of either the armed forces or the security services of the Russian Federation.

Table 10.1 sets out the membership of the Russian Security Council at the end of President Putin's third term in office, May 2018. Of course, individuals change as personnel move from or into those positions that merit a place on the Security Council. The only legal constant in the make-up of the Security Council is that it must be headed by the President. The President then appoints a Secretary of the Security Council, Permanent Members, and ordinary members. In an echo of the old Soviet Politburo, with its full members and candidate members, it is only Permanent Members of the Security Council who have a binding vote, in the rare event that a divided Security Council should have to make a decision by voting. Ordinary members participate fully in the meetings, but their voice and their votes are advisory. Furthermore, it is the Permanent Members who gather with the President on an almost weekly basis, whereas the other members—unless specifically invited to a weekly meeting because of their expertise in or responsibility for the issue under discussion—only attend the full meetings of the Security Council. Formally, the Permanent Members of the Security Council all have equal rights in terms of decision-making. Details of the formal role, procedures, and personnel of Russia's Security Council are all openly available on its website (www.scrf.gov.ru/), which contains too a list of its meetings and a limited amount of information about the content of the same.

Table 10.1 Membership of Russia's Security Council, May 2018

Name	Position	Status within the Security Council
Vladimir Putin	• President of the Russian Federation	• Chairman
Aleksandr Bortnikov	• Director of the Federal Security Service (FSB)	• Permanent Member
Sergei Ivanov	• Presidential Special Representative on questions of the environment, ecology, and transport	• Permanent Member
Vladimir Kolokol'tsev	• Minister of Internal Affairs	• Permanent Member
Sergei Lavrov	• Minister of External Affairs	• Permanent Member
Valentina Matvienko	• Chairman of the Federation Council	• Permanent Member
Dmitry Medvedev	• Prime Minister	• Permanent Member
Sergei Naryshkin	• Director of the Foreign Intelligence Service (SVR)	• Permanent Member
Nikolai Patrushev	• Secretary of the Security Council	• Permanent Member
Sergei Shoigu	• Minister of Defence	• Permanent Member
Anton Vaino	• Head of the Presidential Administration	• Permanent Member
Vyacheslav Volodin	• Chairman of the State Duma	• Permanent Member
Mikhail Babich	• Presidential Representative in the Volga Federal District	• Member
Aleksandr Beglov	• Presidential Representative in the North-West Federal District	• Member
Oleg Belaventsev	• Presidential Representative in the North Caucasus Federal District	• Member
Vladimir Bulavin	• Head of the Federal Tax Service	• Member
Yurii Chaika	• General Prosecutor	• Member
Valerii Gerasimov	• Head of the General Staff of the Armed Forces	• Member
Aleksei Gordeev	• Presidential Representative in the Central Federal District	• Member
Igor Kholmanskikh	• Presidential Representative in the Urals Federal District	• Member
Aleksandr Konovalov	• Minister of Justice	• Member
Sergei Menyailo	• Presidential Representative in the Siberian Federal District	• Member
Rashid Nurgaliev	• Deputy Secretary of the Security Council	• Member
Georgii Poltavchenko	• Governor of St. Petersburg	• Member
Vladimir Puchkov	• Minister for Emergency Situations	• Member
Anton Siluanov	• Minister of Finance	• Member
Sergei Sobyanin	• Mayor of Moscow	• Member
Yurii Trutnev	• Presidential Representative in the Far Eastern Federal District	• Member
Vladimir Ustinov	• Presidential Representative in the Southern Federal District	• Member
Viktor Zolotov	• Director of the Federal Guard Service	• Member

As constituted in 2018, and indeed throughout the Putin era since 2000, about two-thirds of the Permanent Members of the Security Council come from the executive or the legislature. In terms of the latter, the chairs (speakers) of the two chambers of Russia's Parliament retain permanent membership, thereby strengthening the link between the President and the parliament. In practice, such a link can serve as a mechanism for facilitating presidential oversight of parliamentary matters. On the executive side of the Security Council's permanent membership, the government is represented by the prime minister and the three key security-related ministers (for foreign affairs, internal affairs, and defence); and, in addition to the President himself, the presidency is represented by the Head of the Presidential Administration and the Secretary of the Security Council. The more operational side of security affairs has a significant voice on the Security Council in the form of the heads of both the internal and the external security services of Russia, the FSB, and the SVR, respectively. Sergei Ivanov remains as a presidential pick as Permanent Member of the Security Council, for reasons that arise from a combination of factors, such as his long experience on the Security Council dating back to when he was appointed Secretary in 1999, his closeness to Vladimir Putin dating back to service in the KGB in the 1970s, and a measure of compensation for his removal from the position of Head of the Presidential Administration in 2016. Ivanov's continuing Permanent Member status on the Security Council, despite not filling any of the usual offices associated with that position, serves to emphasise that the make-up of this body sits in the gift of the President.

With regard to the duties and functions of Russia's Security Council, the formal constitutional position and close presidential oversight already noted come together in determining these. According to the Constitution, as set out above, the Security Council of the Russian Federation must exist and be headed by the President, but beyond that its status is a matter for enabling legislation to clarify. The latest relevant enabling legislation, as of 2018, stems from presidential rather than parliamentary initiative and is contained in the presidential decree 'The Status of the Security Council of the Russian Federation' signed off by President Medvedev in May 2011 (Sovet Bezopasnosti, 2011). According to this decree, the tasks of the Security Council are to:

- safeguard the conditions that enable the President to exercise his powers in the area of national security;
- formulate state policies in the area of national security;
- analyse potential threats to national security, including military threats, and develop countermeasures;
- prepare on behalf of the President proposals for dealing with crises, for (re)structuring the institutions of national security, and for clarifying issues of national security and defence in various conceptual and doctrinal documents;
- set out the basic direction of Russia's foreign and military policy;
- coordinate the organs of federal and regional executive power in the area of national security;
- evaluate the effectiveness of the federal organs of executive power in relation to ensuring national security.

As well as setting out these responsibilities, the presidential decree on the Security Council's status is explicit that 'the President of the Russian Federation may assign to the Security Council other tasks and functions in keeping with the laws of the Russian Federation'.

Having set out the duties of the Security Council, the 2011 decree proceeds to outline its functions, in a lengthy section that develops and amplifies the broad themes set out in the tasks outlined above. Much of this section of the decree is taken up by designating particular policy areas as within the remit of the Security Council where national security is deemed to be at stake, and charging the Security Council with providing strategic analysis and plans in relation to these concerns. Some of the areas so designated are self-evidently security matters, others are less obviously matters of national security.

The policy areas that come within the ambit of the Security Council's input include:

- the armed forces
- arms production
- military mobilisation plans
- military cooperation with other states
- international security cooperation
- the socio-political and economic situation
- rights and freedoms of citizens
- law and order
- combatting terrorism and extremism
- tackling illegal drugs
- information security
- oversight and coordination of regional security bodies within Russia.

Across all of these areas, Russia's Security Council functions as the strategic planning and oversight body. It is in the Security Council, and more specifically within its extensive apparat that is described below, that reports and recommendations are drawn up, laws are drafted, the expenditure of allocated defence and security budgets is monitored, research on questions within the Security Council's remit is commissioned, and the Annual Report by the Secretary of the Security Council is prepared and scrutinised. To engage across the field of security issues in this manner, Russia's Security Council requires a substantial apparatus, housed in its Old Square offices near to the Kremlin.

Russia as a target of security threats

The central analytical question, when considering the functions of Russia's Security Council, is what constitutes a threat to national security? In scholarly analysis, the securitisation approach, first set out in the field of International Relations in the 1990s (Buzan et al., 1998), has been developed in relation to domestic politics since the first decade of the twenty-first century (Bacon and Renz, 2006; Østbø, 2016). Central to this concept is the idea that a ruling regime seeks to assert the right to act outside the accepted norms in relation to a particular issue by convincing a relevant audience—perhaps the political elite, or the population at large—that the issue in question is a matter of national security and so requires urgent, or emergency, measures to address it. For example, those in power may assert that abuse of the Internet or social media represents an existential threat to the state or the nation and therefore is a matter of national security. Once such a discourse of threat is accepted, then any associated political debate takes on a more axiological tenor, where—to continue to use our example of information technology—to oppose tighter state control over the Internet and social media usage is to side with those who would threaten security.

The designation of an area of policy as a security issue emboldens political actors to arrogate to themselves the right to act outside democratic norms when dealing with it. Without engaging with questions of wider applicability in the development of the securitisation approach as it has been formulated by its initiators in the Copenhagen School of International Relations (Buzan et al., 1998; Buzan and Wæver, 2009), in the specific case of the Russian polity, for a policy area to be overseen by the Security Council alongside—or, more precisely, above—the appropriate government ministry represents an example of securitisation. When Russia's Security Council takes a matter into its area of competence, it is designating it as an area of security threat to Russia. Issues such as communications technology, the economy, or the environment have all been the subject of Security Council sessions, with the expectation that the government ministries responsible for these areas of policy will follow the Security Council's lead.

This is more than Russia's Security Council acting as a governmental cabinet or inner council; after all, such a body already exists, and meets regularly under the chairmanship of the prime minister. When the Security Council arrogates to itself a particular policy area, it is taking it to a level above the government, and declaring the nature of that policy area to be of a higher order and urgency in that it affects the very security of Russia. Russia's Security Council, with its constitutional mandate, presidential leadership, and ill-defined area of oversight, provides an institutional setting where any area of policy can be designated a security issue and brought under direct presidential management, and where the key officials of all branches of the Russian national and regional polity and judiciary likewise sit under direct presidential management. Such a process undermines the democratic principle of the separation of powers and allows policy areas to be taken out of 'normal' politics to be decided on in this exceptional constitutional and institutional space.

In the settled state of the Putin regime, the exceptional status of Russia's Security Council—stemming, as we have seen, from its constitutional mandate, presidential control, and ill-defined area of activity—serves to bolster presidential control over key policy areas and key political actors alike. During the 1990s, the exact same institutional setting served as a locus for power grabs on the part of ambitious politicians who served as Secretary of the Russian Security Council in the immediate post-Soviet years. In this period, a mixture of state collapse, newly formed political institutions, and a comparatively weak president—Boris Yeltsin, 1991–1999—meant that the Security Council's combination of constitutional mandate and vague but potentially all-encompassing remit served to create an institutional space rich with potential for those who sought to strengthen their political position. That the Security Council's essential institutional framework remains relatively unchanged since those years demonstrates that it still retains the potential to be re-shaped and serve as an institutional base in any future power struggle.

Russia's Security Council Secretary—the 1990s

Two figures in particular fit the description of ambitious politicians who tried, during the 1990s, to use their position as Secretary of Russia's Security Council to enhance their own, and the Security Council's, power—namely, Yurii Skokov, Secretary of the Security Council, April 1992 to May 1993; and Aleksandr Lebed, Secretary of the Security Council, June to October 1996. These two political figures also campaigned together in Russia's 1995 general election, heading up the nationalist party, the Congress of Russian Communities, along with Sergei Glaz'ev, who was later to be a key figure in Lebed's attempt to bring Russian economic policy under the Security Council. Both Skokov and Lebed served as Secretary of the Russian Security Council during a time of instability in Russia's political leadership.

Yurii Skokov was appointed as the first ever Secretary of Russia's Security Council on its formation in April 1992, shortly after the Soviet collapse and before Russia's new constitution came into force in December 1993. The position of the Security Council in the institutional architecture of the newly formed Russian state was even more unclear than that of the Russian presidency and the Russian Parliament, both of which had last been elected, in 1991 and 1990 respectively, when Russia's political institutions remained formally subordinate to the Soviet Union. After the collapse of the Soviet Union at the end of 1991, the period 1992–1993 saw a power struggle between Russia's Parliament and president as to the division of powers in the new constitution that both sides saw as necessary. This power struggle was eventually resolved in favour of the President unconstitutionally and by military force in October 1993, and the formation of Russia's Security Council represented an early move on behalf of President Yeltsin in the post-Soviet presidential-parliamentary power struggle.

Russia's Security Council was formally established by the Law on Security of March 1992, with the intention of creating an organ of executive power, chaired by the President, where quick decisions could be made on national security questions and longer terms security plans laid. In creating this body, Yeltsin appears to have taken his lead from his political rival and last Soviet President, Mikhail Gorbachev, who had instituted a Security Council of the USSR led by the President in 1990 as part of his last ditch attempt to hold onto central power during the Soviet Union's final crises. Ironically, despite having been appointed to a position designed to bolster the President's political power, Yurii Skokov's removal from the Secretaryship of the Security Council in May 1993, a little more than a year after being appointed to the role, stemmed from his refusal to get fully on board with President Yeltsin's attempt to establish direct presidential rule by decree in March 1993.

Skokov's short-lived tenure as Secretary saw him adopt a three-pronged approach to building up the Security Council's, and his own, power. Skokov sought to consolidate federal power in the Security Council, to build coalition with potential participants in a power struggle, and to enhance links with regional authorities (an essential element of 1990s politics in a Russia that many feared would break up into constituent parts). In terms of consolidating power in the Security Council, Skokov built on its potentially wide remit to fill the vacuum of power created by the struggle between the president and the parliament, and by the collapse of the Communist Party of the Soviet Union, which had functioned as the transmission mechanism of political power for decades. He wasted little time—and showed his political naivety—by making his ambitions clear in his first broadcast interview as Secretary of the Security Council, when he compared this new body to the all-powerful Soviet Politburo (Bacon, 1997, 767). This move signalled overtly and prematurely Skokov's power grab. He followed it up with further maladroit manoeuvring when it came to coalition building, in that, despite being clearly appointed to be the President's man in the developing power struggle, Skokov became ever more closely identified with Vice President Aleksandr Rutskoi, who was also moving over to the parliamentary side. In terms of regional links, Skokov began an attempt to establish local commissions of the Security Council. Such political plotting as Skokov engaged in ignored the central institutional fact required to understand how Russia's Security Council works; namely, the President is the head of the Security Council. Skokov would not be the only Secretary of the Security Council to apparently confuse running the body on a day-to-day basis with being in charge of it. President Yeltsin sacked Skokov in May 1993.

Similar attempts to use Russia's Security Council as a springboard to political power were made by General Aleksandr Lebed in 1996. As had been the case during Skokov's tenure in 1992–1993, Lebed was made Secretary of the Security Council at a time of political upheaval and with something of a power vacuum opening up at the apex of Russian politics. His appointment came on 18 June 1996, between the first and second rounds of Russia's presidential election. Lebed had come third in the first round, behind the two candidates who went forward to the second round, Boris Yeltsin and the Communist Gennady Zyuganov.

His appointment to the Secretaryship of the Security Council was a politically motivated move by Yeltsin, who sought to swing behind his own candidacy the 15 per cent of voters who had supported Lebed in the first round. Once Yeltsin was re-elected for a second term, however, he became seriously ill and was largely absent from the political stage for months as he eventually underwent and convalesced from quintuple heart bypass surgery. With the President all too absent, the three main organs of Russia's executive structure—the government, the presidential administration, and the Security Council—vied to exert their pre-eminence. As Skokov had done before, so Aleksandr Lebed likewise sought to centralise authority in the Security Council, build up a coalition, and strengthen regional links.

Lebed's major achievement as Secretary of the Security Council was to negotiate an end to the First Chechen War. Such a task stood firmly within the security remit. At the same time, though, Lebed sought to gain control over policy areas that are less obviously matters of security. In particular, he appointed Sergei Glaz'ev to head up an Economic Security Commission that sought to have government spending decisions subsumed under the security rubric (Byzhutovich, 1996; Nevezhin, 1996). Only a few days before his dismissal from the Secretaryship of the Security Council, Lebed was talking publicly of the need for the Security Council to coordinate policy with the government and the presidential administration. As well as adopting the tactic of widening the Security Council's remit, Lebed also sought to build coalition and to strengthen ties with the regions not only through the appointment of Glaz'ev but also through backing the military in its call for resources and—in what was reported to be the final trigger for his sacking—proposing the establishment of a 'Russian Legion' under the operational control of the Secretary of the Security Council (Izvestiya, 1996). President Yeltsin's initial appointment of Lebed between the two rounds of 1996's presidential election stemmed from political expediency, and he had acceded to Lebed's wish to widen the Security Council's remit in a presidential decree of 10 July 1996. In a typical piece of Yeltsin politicking, however, within a couple of weeks of appearing to strengthen the Security Council, the President undermined it by creating the Russian Defence Council. This short-lived body (1996–1998) had no constitutional mandate; as with a number of institutions within the Russian polity, it was a-constitutional, rather than unconstitutional. Its remit overlapped starkly with that of the Security Council and there was a strong element of 'divide and rule' in Yeltin's move, crowding and confusing the political space in which the Security Council could operate.

Russia's Security Council Secretary—the twenty-first century

These two examples—during the Secretaryship of Yurii Skokov and Aleksandr Lebed—represent those periods in the 1990s when Russia's Security Council came to the fore in the political life of the country. Set against the period as a whole, however, they were untypical and transitory. For much of the 1990s, and indeed lengthy periods in the 2000s, the Security Council retreated more into the background under the Secretaryship, indeed in one case the Acting Secretaryship, of less prominent individuals. Table 10.2 lists the Secretaries of Russia's Security Council.

Nikolai Patrushev became Secretary of Russia's Security Council in May 2008, in what at first seemed like a demotion of Patrushev from his previous position as Head of the FSB, Russia's internal security service, on the part of incoming president, Dmitry Medvedev. Some observers explained this move as resulting from an illness afflicting Patrushev that meant he needed a less burdensome role than heading up the FSB; an indicator of the relative prominence of the Security Council at that time. Alternatively, Patrushev's appointment to

Table 10.2 Secretaries of Russia's Security Council, 1992–2018

Secretary of the Security Council	Date of Tenure
Yurii Skokov	• April 1992 to May 1993
Yevgenii Shaposhnikov	• Appointed June 1993, never formally confirmed
Oleg Lobov	• September 1993 to June 1996
Aleksandr Lebed	• June 1996 to October 1996
Ivan Rybkin	• October 1996 to March 1998
Andrei Kokoshin	• March 1998 to September 1998
Nikolai Bordyuzha	• September 1998 to March 1999
Vladimir Putin	• March 1999 to August 1999
Sergei Ivanov	• November 1999 to March 2001
Vladimir Rushailo	• March 2001 to March 2004
Igor Ivanov	• March 2004 to July 2007
Nikolai Patrushev	• May 2008–

Note: Between July 2007 and May 2008, Valentin Sobolev served as Acting Secretary of the Security Council.

the Secretaryship of the Security Council may have been designed to boost by proxy Putin's position during his four years away from the presidency (2008–2012). Patrushev certainly goes a long way back with Vladimir Putin. Both of them were born in Leningrad in the 1950s and joined the KGB in the 1970s. When Putin rose to the presidency in 2000, he identified those figures in his working life to whom he was particularly close, naming Nikolai Patrushev, Sergei Ivanov, and Dmitry Medvedev; two of whom have served as Secretary of the Security Council and one as both President and Prime Minister of Russia (Gevorkyan et al., 2000, 201).

The fact that Nikolai Patrushev has spent more than a decade as Secretary of the Security Council, under both President Medvedev and President Putin and spanning three presidential terms, means that he has been able to stamp something of his own authority and thinking on the institution. What sort of a man is Nikolai Patrushev? How does he conceptualise Russian security and the role of the Security Council? According to the best-selling Russian political journalist Mikhail Zygar,

> People from Putin's inner circle say that Nikolai Patrushev is the most underestimated figure in the Russian leadership. In fact Patrushev has been the nerve centre of most of Putin's special operations … After the unification with Crimea he began to comment on matters of Russian security and foreign policy. Until then only President Putin and Foreign Minister Lavrov had dealt with these themes. In this way, Nikolai Patrushev became Russia's chief hawk and the go-to man for anti-Westernism and anti-Americanism inside the Russian leadership.
>
> *(2016, 445–446, translation by the author)*

As head of the FSB between 1999 and 2008, Patrushev was open about his admiration for former KGB chief and Soviet leader, Yurii Andropov, penning a laudatory article about him to mark the 90th anniversary of his birth in 2004 (Patrushev, 2004). In the same newspaper a decade later, an interview with Patrushev—by now firmly established as Secretary of the Security Council and writing in the wake of Russia's 2014 annexation of Crimea—revealed his strong anti-Westernism in a sweeping account of Soviet and Russian history over the past several decades. The collapse of the Soviet Union was set out as a long-standing and deliberate policy of the West, and particularly the United States, which was then followed by strategies aimed at breaking up Russia. According to Patrushev, the Chechen Wars saw the special services of the United States and Great Britain, along with allies in Europe and the Islamic world, attempting to realise these strategies on the ground. In the end, according to Patrushev, it was only 'the strong political will of the President of Russia, Vladimir Putin' that held the Russian Federation together (Egorov, 2014). A further interview with the same journalist in 2017 saw no toning down of Patrushev's anti-Americanism, for example, in noting the Security Council's contribution to Russia's Information Security Doctrine as stemming from the United States use of the Internet 'for intelligence and other purposes, aimed at preserving of their dominance in the world' (Egorov, 2017a).

The significance of Russia's Security Council

Russia's Security Council, having waxed and waned in significance over more than quarter of a century in existence, now stands in the first rank of Russia's institutions. By bringing together the top officials from across the executive, legislature, judiciary, regions, and security services, under the leadership of the President, it occupies a uniquely influential political space for the consolidation of decision-making. Under the day-to-day direction of its Secretary, it provides analysis and policy guidance across a broad range of policy areas, bounded only by questions of what is defined as a security threat. The Security Council's apparatus includes a scientific council, made up of academic and business specialists, as well as interdepartmental commissions on:

- the Commonwealth of Independent States
- military security
- societal security
- security in the economic and social sphere
- information security
- ecological security
- strategic planning.

On the 25th anniversary of the Security Council's establishment, its Secretary, Nikolai Patrushev, was asked to name its most important decisions over these years (Egorov, 2017b). At the top of Patrushev's list were 'the restoration of constitutional order on the territory of the Chechen Republic' and the assertion that it was the Security Council—whilst headed by President Medvedev in August 2008—that took the decision to send the Russian army into Georgia. It was noteworthy that Patrushev did not mention the annexation of Crimea in his answer; perhaps President Medvedev's authority for military action in Georgia required the imprimatur of the Security Council, whereas President Putin's personal authority sufficed when it came to Crimea. Beyond these specific events, Patrushev emphasised the many doctrines, concepts, and strategies that have come from—and continue to come from—the Security Council, and to set out Russian security policy in important areas. Such policy areas as the development of the armed forces, the Economic Security Strategy (2017), industrial security policy, ecological security, the protection of the population during emergency situations, counteracting terrorism, and cooperating with the Commonwealth of Independent States.

Beyond the question of what the Security Council does and in what policy areas it operates lies a deeper question around the nature of its contribution to Russian security. Russia's Security Council sits in so prominent a position, with a purview over many policy areas, that the substance of its positioning and advice matters. Its long-standing Secretary, Nikolai Patrushev, appointed in 2008, has few qualms about openly declaring to the world that he sees the West, and the United States in particular, as a malevolent force out to undermine, and even break-up, Russia in the second version of the Cold War; just as it did the Soviet Union in the first. The Security Council sets the tone and the policy line across much of Russia's polity—economic security, societal security, information space, foreign affairs, industrial production, and so on—from this perspective of intentional strategised threats to Russia from outside that require countering.

Such a position leads policy advice in a particular direction, and not one that all members of the Russian elite are happy with. A critical article in the Russian press in 2016 talked of the Security Council as a body that tackles the world of the twenty-first century with concepts and doctrines whose answers come from the Soviet past, from the 1970s, 'when the idea of a besieged fortress was considered to approximate to the real world' (Nezavisimaya gazeta, 2016). The pre-eminent position of the Security Council in Russia's security-related politics makes it a highly significant body. However, it is not the only source of advice and information for Russia's president, nor do its reports and doctrines automatically have hegemonic force.

As the history of the Security Council has shown, its importance has increased and decreased largely according to the will of the president who heads it. During President Putin's third term, which saw—amongst other security issues—the annexation of Crimea, war in south-eastern Ukraine, and Russian engagement in Syria, the significant position and hardline tone of the Security Council appeared to represent a settled state. Such is not necessarily the case. As economic concerns come to the fore, or international relations take on a less antagonistic tone, or personnel shifts occur, so the stance or significance of the Security Council may change. As well as having almost weekly meetings with the permanent membership of the Security Council, Russia's President meets too on a similarly regular basis with economic advisers, whose advice lacks such a security focus. Nonetheless, despite the caveat that any observer of a particular political institution is always well advised to gain perspective by seeing that institution in its wider context, there is no denying the pre-eminent position of Russia's Security Council and its apparatus in the coordination and direction of Russian security policy.

References

Bacon, Edwin (1997) 'The politics of defence in post-Soviet Russia: Russia's Security Council, Institutional Continuity During Transition', in Stanyer Jeffrey and Stoker Gerry (eds.) *Contemporary Political Studies 1997, Proceedings of the Political Studies Association of the UK Annual Conference 1997, University of Ulster 8–10 April 1997*. Oxford: Blackwell, pp. 761–771.

Bacon, Edwin and Bettina Renz (2006) *Securitising Russia: The Domestic Politics of Putin*. Manchester: Manchester University Press.

Buzan, Barry and Ole Wæver (2009) 'Macrosecuritisation and security constellaions: reconsidering scale in securitisation theory', *Review of International Studies*, Vol. 35, pp. 253–276.

Buzan, Barry, Ole Wæver, and Jaap de Wilde (1998) *Security: A New Framework for Analysis*. Boulder, London: Lynne Rienner.

Byzhutovich, Valerii (1996) 'General poshel v ataku na byudzhet', *Izvestiya*, 13 September, Moscow.

Egorov, Ivan, (2014) 'Vtoraya "kholodnaya"', *Rossiiskaya gazeta*, 15 October, Moscow, p. 1.

Egorov, Ivan, (2017a) 'Mir bez illiuzii i mifov', *Rossiiskaya gazeta*, 16 January, Moscow, p. 1.

Egorov, Ivan, (2017b) 'Voiny i miry', *Rossiiskaya gazeta*, 19 May, Moscow, p. 1.

Gevorkyan, Nataliya, Nataliya Timakova, and Andrei Kolesnikov (2000) *First Person: An Astonishingly Frank Self Portrait by Russia's President*. London: Hutchinson.

Izvestiya (1996) 'Rossiiskii legion po obrazu franzuskogo inostrannogo', 19 October, Moscow.

Nevezhin, Yurii (1996) 'Otvetstvennyi za ekonomicheskuyu bezopasnost' nedovolen ekonomicheskoi politikoi Chernomyrdina', *Izvestiya*, 21 August, Moscow.
Nezavisimaya gazeta (2016) 'Sovet bezopasnosti kak mozgovoi tsentr', 8 December, Moscow, p. 2.
Østbø, Jardar (2016) 'Securitizing "spiritual-moral values" in Russia', *Post Soviet Affairs,* Vol. 33, no. 3, pp. 200–216.
Patrushev, Nikolai (15 June 2004) 'Taina Andropova', *Rossiiskaya gazeta*, Moscow.
Sovet Bezopasnosti Rossiiskoi Federatsii (2011) *Polozhenie o Sovete Bezopasnosti Rossiiskii Federatsii,* 6 May. Accessed at www.scrf.gov.ru/about/regulations/
Zygar', Mikhail (2016) *Vsya kremlevskaya rat': kratkaya istoriya sovremennoi Rossii*. Moscow: Intellektual'naya literatura.

PART III

Instruments of Russian security strategy

Introduction

Roger E. Kanet

The nine chapters that comprise this third section of the *Handbook* treat instruments employed by the Russians in their efforts to implement their security and foreign policy objectives. These range from military and economic capabilities used, either positively or negatively, to achieve those goals traditionally viewed as central to national security to propaganda, information technology and control over outer space.

'Coercive Diplomacy in Russian Security Strategy', by Stanislav Tkachenko of St. Petersburg State University, is the topic of Chapter 11. For the author, the year 1999 was a turning point for the national security of Russia for, thereafter, Moscow adopted a range of coercive instruments for its return to the centre of world. Instrumental in that shift was the end of the economic crisis that has wracked Russia during the prior decade and the rise of Vladimir Putin and his appointment of senior officials at the 'power ministries'. Although coercive diplomacy has been successful in Moscow's achieving some of its objectives, Russia's relative economic weakness is a drawback in influencing developments when military actions cease and the time for post-conflict reconstruction starts.

In Chapter 12, entitled 'The Rebuilding of Russian Military Capabilities', Jennifer Mathers of Aberystwyth University examines the rebuilding of the Russian armed forces, especially since the war with Georgia in August 2005. She notes the initial resistance to structural changes that eventually were implemented and the importance of moving towards volunteer forces and the dramatic increase in military expenditures and the replacement or equipment in the revitalisation of the Russian military. The author concludes that

> The Russian armed forces of today are almost unrecognisable in comparison with the 2008 version, especially in the streamlining of its structure and the significant improvement in its ability to deploy forces quickly and carry out its assigned missions . . . .

In Chapter 13, entitled 'Reflections on Russia's Nuclear Strategy', Stephen Blank, Senior Fellow at the American Foreign Policy Council, maintains that 'Nuclear weapons represent priority, even critical, parts of Putin's so called asymmetric or indirect strategy. And their continued procurement is unceasing'. They are part of an arsenal that includes psychological and cyberwarfare employed by the Russians, along with other tools, to challenge opponents and achieve foreign and security policy objectives.

Chapter 14, by Nikita Lomagin of the European University at St. Petersburg, concerns 'Economic tools in Russian security Strategy'. It 'argues that, although Russia's economy is rather modest, Russia surpasses its main competitors in post-Soviet space, the EU and US, in its ability to deliver economic benefits to its loyal neighbours'. Markets for their goods, but even more important, employment and remittances for their citizens are essential to the economies of a number or neighbouring counties. But this economic dependence also provides Russia with the opportunity to pressure neighbours whose policies they oppose.

In Chapter 15, entitled 'Russian Security Strategy and the Geopolitics of Energy in Eurasia', by Mikhail Molchanov, Visiting Professor at the American University of Sharjah, central to Russian concerns in this area are secure access to markets, given the Russian economy's heavy dependence on energy exports. Thus, control over pipelines to those markets has been an important part of Russian security policy. Subsidising energy and withholding it from neighbouring states dependent on Russian supplies have been ways in which Russia has used its dominant position to further its objectives. Molchanov concludes that '[t]he politics-to-economics balance in Moscow's approach to energy security has moved toward politics,' as Western economic sanctions began to impact the Russian economy.

Chapter 16, entitled 'The Intelligence Agencies and Putin: Undermining Russia's Security Strategy?', Kimberly Marten of Barnard College of Columbia University, is concerned, among other matters, with the degree to which Russian intelligence agencies are able to act independently. She notes that '[t]he Kremlin . . . finds itself with a classic principal-agent problem, where individual officers and even whole units have both the motive and the economic means to act beyond centralised monitoring and control'. She tracks the rivalries among Russian intelligence agencies and discusses ways in which this complicates efforts to assure both domestic and international security. She concludes by questioning the degree to which these agencies 'are truly serving a coherent Russian security strategy. Instead they are securing Putin's personalistic and autocratic regime, while enriching themselves in the process'.

Chapter 17, entitled 'Russian Information Security and Warfare', by Carolina Vendil-Pallin of the Swedish Defence Research Agency (FOI), examines official Russian documents concerning Russian attempts to protect itself from attacks on its information sphere. It has even gone so far as considering developing its own Internet and withdrawing from the global Internet as a measure to protect information.

In Chapter 18, entitled 'Information-Psychological Warfare in Russian Security Strategy', Katri Pynnöniemi of the University of Helsinki and the National Defence University expands the discussion of information warfare to place it more fully in the context of propaganda and psychological warfare – an integral part of what the Russians now term 'hybrid warfare' – and of historical Soviet conceptions of its place in global class war. For Moscow, the 'colour revolutions' that occurred in neighbouring states in the 2000s were examples of the Western use of information-psychological warfare. 'The deep-rooted image of Russia as a "besieged fortress" is an important part of the argumentation on information security' and seemingly justifies the Russian use of such weapons against the West.

In Chapter 19, Nicole Jackson of Simon Fraser University examines 'Outer Space in Russia's Security Strategy', an emerging part of Russian security concern. She examines why outer space is so important for Russia and tracks the way in which Russia's outer space strategy and capacities have developed in the quarter century since Russian independence. She concludes her analysis with the assessment that, since Russia can with great difficulty compete economically in the competition for control of outer space, it has adopted several strategies to stay in the game – especially working diplomatically to multilateralise the approach to outer space.

11
COERCIVE DIPLOMACY IN RUSSIAN SECURITY STRATEGY

Stanislav L. Tkachenko

The historical context for the emergence of Russia's coercive diplomacy

The image of the Russian Federation as a sovereign state, which is able to ensure its security by using all means, including military ones, has been crystallised rather recently. Mikhail Gorbachev's foreign policy was driven by a willingness to avoid international conflicts and manage them via negotiations and compromises. President Boris Yeltsin was a strong advocate of rapprochement with Europe, and initially with the USA. The years of his Presidency (1991–1999) coincided with a deep socio-economic crisis, whose scale could be compared with the disastrous consequences of World War II for Russia as one of USSR's republics. The foreign and security policy of the Russia Federation in the 1990s was reactive, and its role in the international security system was gradually declining.

The year 1999 was a turning point for the national security of Russia. Subsequently, the Kremlin adopted a range of coercive instruments for its return to the centre of world politics. There were two factors, which have played a remarkable role in that transformation:

- *The end of the severe crisis and the beginning of rapid economic growth (1999–2008)*, which later was called the 'golden decade' for the Russian national economy. During that decade, the average annual growth of gross domestic product (GDP) was about 7 per cent. The Kremlin received resources, which were beyond the reach of the first generation of post-Soviet Russian leaders.
- *The rise of Vladimir Putin to power.* On March 29, 1999, the then Director of the Federal Security Service Vladimir Putin was appointed simultaneously as Secretary of the Security Council (SC) of Russian Federation. President Yeltsin's power had been declining since his re-election in 1996, and the central seat at the SC gave to Vladimir Putin an opportunity to coordinate activities of all security-related public institutions, as well as to work hand in hand with senior officials at the 'power ministries' (Ministry of the Interior; Ministry of Civil Defence, Emergencies and Disaster Relief; Ministry of Foreign Affairs; Ministry of Defence; Ministry of Justice) and intelligence services of Russia.

It was in 1999 that the qualitative transformation of Russian foreign and security policy began. Two separate events have signified that.

First, overnight from June 11 to 12, a composite battalion of Airborne Forces of the Russian Federation, stationed in Bosnia and Herzegovina as a component of international peacekeeping contingent under North Atlantic Treaty Organisation (NATO) command, carried out an accelerated 600-kilometre march through the territory of Bosnia, Serbia and Kosovo. Early in the morning of June 12, the Russian military unit occupied the International Airport 'Slatina' in Kosovo's capital Pristina. For several hours, 200 Russian paratroopers were stood against British units, which were attempting to squeeze the Russian military out of the airport. Only after NATO commander, US General Wesley Clark, ordered his troops to seize the airport by force, and British General Michael Jackson, who was in charge of all the NATO ground forces in Pristina, questioned that order, not wanting to start World War III, USA-Russia negotiations started. They ended up with a compromise, which allowed the NATO countries to utilise Pristina Airport for the transit of their troops and munitions.

Second, in August to September 1999, several Russian cities, including Moscow, suffered villainous terrorist attacks, which left 300 civilians dead. Simultaneously, military units of de facto independent Chechnya invaded neighbouring Dagestan, in order to occupy its territory and gain direct access to the Caspian Sea. Russian troops in 1994–1996 had suffered military defeat in Chechnya, which was formalised in the Khasavyurt agreement of 1996 that ended the First Chechen War. In autumn 1999, Russian authorities responded by executing a broad operation in which almost all combat-ready units of the Russian military forces participated. Simultaneously, negotiations of Kremlin envoys with Chechen elders started, despite severe criticism from the Western nations for multiple brutal acts on the ground. The Russian Army in the period between October 1999 and March 2000 crushed Chechen troops and established control over all the territory of the breakaway republic. A group of former Chechen leaders, headed by Akhmad Kadyrov, the Chief Mufti of the Chechnya in the 1990s during and after the First Chechen War, took the Kremlin's side in the conflict and guaranteed an end to the conflict that was favourable for Moscow.

The events of 1999 convinced a new generation of Kremlin leaders that careful use of military power may become a valuable asset in foreign policy. Since then, there has been a firm belief in Moscow that, if used properly, coercive diplomacy may assist in the revision of Russia's position in international politics, which has been considered as unfair. Since then, the Russian Federation has utilised some elements of coercion for conflict management, which followed Georgia's attack on South Ossetia in August 2008; during Russia's annexation of Crimea in February to March 2014, as well as at the acute phase of the Civil War in Eastern Ukraine in summer 2014 to winter 2015, when the Russian Federation came down on the side of the separatist regions; and during the Russia-Turkey crisis, which followed the downing of Russia's SU-24M attack aircraft in November 2015.

The contemporary model of Russia's coercive diplomacy has been introduced by Vladimir Putin personally in a documentary film of Andrey Kondrashev *Crimea: The Way Back Home* (2015). This film has been translated into 30 languages and widely promoted by Russian embassies to generate a global audience. In the documentary, President Putin with remarkable openness presented his own version of a story, which proceeded to annexation of the Crimean peninsula from Ukraine and its inclusion into the Russian Federation as one of its regions. For research on Russia's coercive diplomacy, it was important to learn Putin's description of instruments for coercion, which were at his disposal and have been used one after the other, depending on the fluctuating situation on the ground in 2014–2015. His key command to four unnamed members of his inner circle, which he gave in the early morning of February 23, 2014, was the following: 'The situation in Ukraine has turned out in such a way that we are forced to begin work on returning Crimea back to Russia' (Kondrashev, 2015).

Coercive diplomacy: theoretical perspective

Coercive diplomacy, or forceful persuasion, is the attempt to get a target – a state, a group within a state or a non-state actor – to change its objectionable behaviour through either the threat to use force or the actual use of limited force (Art and Cronin, 2003, 6). According to Alexander George, coercive diplomacy offers an alternative to reliance on military action. It is based on the threat of force rather than the use of force, in order to get other actors to comply with one's wishes (George, 1994, 2).

While addressing an issue of coercion as a diplomatic asset in contemporary global politics, we should mention that it is not available for all states, but just for a few great powers. They are able to benefit from the status of genuine sovereign states, whose politics are not subordinated to the interests of other, more powerful, states. The origin of the concept goes back to the Cold War period with its severe rivalry between the USA and the USSR for domination in different regions of the world.

In his book *Arms and Influence*, Thomas Schelling identifies five necessary conditions for the success of coercive diplomacy, which are still valid for analysis of USA-Russia relations, as well as behaviour of a few other genuinely sovereign states in world politics:

1. The threat conveyed should be sufficient to convince the adversary that the costs of non-compliance with demands will be unbearable;
2. The threat must be credible for the adversary;
3. The adversary should have some time to comply with the demands of the coercer;
4. Both sides should have a minimal level of trust to believe that compliance will not lead to more demands at future rounds of their communication;
5. The conflict should not be seen by both sides as just zero-sum (Schelling, 1966, 3–4, 69–76).

The notion that the strategic purpose of coercive diplomacy is to change the policies of other states, and the major instrument for that is the threat of the immediate use of military force, has become widespread in academic literature (George, 1991). In 1998, Hermann and Kegley observed that, since the early 1980s, the norm of international law on non-intervention had eroded, opening the way for the protection of human rights and peace enforcement (1998). No doubt the main victim of that shift in world politics was sovereignty as one of the cornerstones of contemporary world politics. Another victim is the right of nations for self-determination.

Meanwhile, the popularity of the concept of coercive diplomacy could be explained by the fact that it may become an attractive alternative to military conflicts. Coercive diplomacy measures (diplomatic threats, war games in one's own territory near borders of the target country, sweeping economic sanctions) still keep hopes alive that an interstate conflict may be limited to mutual threats, diplomatic demarches and sooner or later political compromise in establishing a new peaceful status quo (Jakobsen, 2016, 477).

Since the end of the Cold War, US coercive diplomacy has required an ideological justification and, when possible, its legalisation by the UN SC. The economic crisis in Russia and Russia's reduced role in international politics in the immediate post–Cold War period offered a unique opportunity for aggressive US actions without providing sound justification (Trenin, 2015). Violations of human rights in Bosnia and Herzegovina, East Timor, Iraq, Kosovo, Liberia, Rwanda, Somali and Sierra Leone opened for the USA a possibility to utilise its military forces and/or UN peacekeepers for the construction of an international security model that fits the strategic plans of Washington. Progressively, a situation was created in which any threat of using US armed forces oversees was considered acceptable, while the military superiority of the US Army and Navy guaranteed that any opponent could be defeated.

Moscow looked cautiously in the 1990s on US operations overseas, trying to determine when their diffusion posed a grave danger to its national security. NATO's eastwards enlargement and the bombardment of Yugoslavia in spring 1999 sent to Russia a clear signal that the real target of US-led democratisation of Eurasia was Russia itself. Awakening to that fact and willing to send its global partners a warning that the period of Moscow's powerlessness was gone were key drivers of Putin's speech in Munich in February 2007 (Putin, 2007).

Game theory, which is at the heart of the coercive diplomacy studies, requires the establishment of a channel of communication between opponents. It could be used for exchange of threats and for the search for an exit from a conflict, which should be seen by all parties involved as a non–zero-sum game (Brams, 1985). Contemporary Russian diplomats have inherited from their Soviet predecessors a pragmatic attitude to dialogue. *Rejection of conducting negotiations* is not an instrument in the toolkit of Russian diplomacy.

Priority in activation of this instrument of diplomatic coercion belongs to the State Department. Two diplomatic cultures (the US and the Soviet/Russian) collide here (Tsygankov, 2009, 10). Moscow considers the refusal to negotiate as potentially dangerous, especially in those occasions when the Kremlin was sure that its proposals to Washington were attractive and mutually beneficial. The practice of renouncing negotiations, when they have already begun, is seen by Russian diplomacy as an unseemly innovation to ages-old diplomatic tradition. It is hardly a coincidence that Washington decided to use it since summer 2013[1] simultaneously with Moscow's activation of its innovative coercive diplomacy.

Studies of coercion were too often concentrated around a clear-cut dichotomy between success and failure (Allen, 2011). Deeper analysis of the original intentions and the results of coercive actions shows that it is a very rare situation when any side of the conflict obtains what was originally expected (Baldwin, 1985). Academic debates that address coercion in global politics, and coercive diplomacy as its main tool, have rarely moved beyond the realist/idealist debate with its overwhelming attention to national security goals. Unlike military instruments of state power, diplomatic tools should be differentiated by their efficiency of persuasion, as well as by the groups to be influenced by diplomatic demarches. But very often diplomatic concessions emerge as a 'lesser evil' than full-scale war.

Coercive diplomacy is a privilege enjoyed by genuinely sovereign states, their distinguishing marker in contemporary politics. Historically, coercion has been a crucial element for enforcement of norms in international society. Today, two permanent members of the SC (the UK and France) are subordinating their security interests to those of the USA. Their ability and willingness to use coercion without US permission seems illusive. India and Japan openly reject using coercion internationally. That is why only the USA, China and Russia are subjects of coercive diplomacy in global scale nowadays.

Russia's coercive diplomacy in action: resources and traditions

The genesis of Russia's coercive diplomacy reflects the evolution of the worldview of Russia's Foreign Service. For many centuries, it was highly reactive, entering a proactive mode only at the periphery of its areas of strategic interests.[2] But it was not the same in the Russian Empire's policy towards European states during the whole period between the French Revolution and World War I. Transit towards practical implementation of coercive diplomacy measures was emphasised in 1999. It was presented in its full-fledged form for the first time during the Five Days' War in Georgia. Since then, its actions no longer have reactive and ad hoc nature. It is now the totally new diplomacy of a resurging Russia.

For the Kremlin, coercive diplomacy is based on the beliefs that hard power matters only if it is used for practical purpose. It also rests on the ability of public servants to utilise carefully military resources for interventions into conflicts, which are of strategic importance for Russia. Traditional coercive diplomacy, which has been studied by Thomas Schelling and his successors since the late 1950s, was applied by the USA in their standoff with Moscow mostly for defensive purposes. Russia's coercive diplomacy today is different. It should be seen as a new type of international behaviour, which reflects the realities of an emerging multipolar world.

Russia's coercive diplomacy rests upon its nuclear arsenal, as well as on the newest conventional weapons, and is used for both defensive and offensive purposes. The fundamental distinction of the new Russian version of coercion from the Soviet one is in the conviction that relative power in International Relations prevails over absolute power. It means in practice that contemporary international politics is rather a chain of small clashes between confronting states rather than there being a single major battle.

This phenomenon is frequently presented as 'hybrid war' (McDermott, 2016, 97). We believe that term 'war' in our analysis of Russia-Western relations could be misleading. A process of making changes in regional security arrangements via a combination of negotiations and military actions designed to put pressure on an opponent, is a form of 'diplomacy' rather than 'war'. We apply methods, typical for studies of diplomatic traditions and practices. Because of that, in contemporary interstate conflicts, it is more productive 'to do harm' to an opponent by instruments of diplomacy rather than 'to defeat' by military resources. To a great extent, Western economic and other sanctions against Russia since March 2014 are based on the intention 'to do harm'. The same logic is typical for the Kremlin's coercive diplomacy. Russian diplomatic and military authorities are trying to harm an opponent's interests, changing the balance of forces in conflicts for Russia's own benefit.

Almost all cases of UN-approved coercive diplomacy since the end of the Cold War (towards Iraq in August 1990 to early 1991, Serbia during war in Bosnia and Herzegovina in 1992–1995, as well as towards generals, who organised a coup *d'état* in Haiti in September 1991) could be evaluated as inefficient and even destructive in their long-term consequences. Russia was unable to utilise economic sanctions, which were crucial instruments of US coercive diplomacy in the UN since the early 1990s. The underlying rationale behind UN SC decisions to apply coercion was the willingness of the five permanent members to keep the door open for peaceful resolution of conflicts, even if the UN strategy in each case entailed limited use of military force. Furthermore, the level of conventional weapons' employment was designedly minimal. In each of the above-mentioned cases, a small authoritarian state confronted the broad international community, and public opinion has always been on the side of the UN and its institutions. Confrontation of a small authoritarian state with the large democracies could not go for a long time, at least theoretically (Schultz, 2001, 121–122).

Being involved in a number of conflicts along its national borders since 1999, Russian diplomacy has never faced the same kind of situation – confrontation with a weak authoritarian regime whose domestic policies have been openly condemned by the UN SC. Still, in deciding to get involved in a conflict and to utilise coercive diplomacy, Russian civilian and military authorities do believe that the conflict itself could be located within existing norms of international law. Russia's economic and military resources would allow a standoff against any opponent along Russian borders for a limited period of time, while its nuclear weapons prevent the conversion of a conflict into full-fledged war.

The US decision to withdraw from the ABM Treaty in June 2002 became the final argument for Russia's decision to apply coercive diplomacy. In the process of years-long USA-Russia negotiations, including summits and multiple ministerial rounds, Moscow made a number of attractive propositions to save the ABM Treaty, assured that its initiatives were beneficial for the USA and served the highest interests of global security. Unfortunately, they never led to full-fledged negotiations. US tactics of avoiding negotiations with Russia on the most important topics of global security did bring essential changes to Russia's coercive diplomacy. It has also deprived Russia and its Western partners useful mechanisms of interplay, in such negotiations, which in previous stages of their relationship provided them with consistency and prevented escalation to open military conflicts.

The impact on international security of Russia's cross-border military operations since 1999, as part of its coercive diplomacy, has been rather limited. The main reason is Russia's strategic preference: the Kremlin looks to change the previous status quo into a new one, which is slightly better than the previous situation, but still keeps conflicts 'frozen'. There would be no 'victory' in the ongoing conflict, but rather some changes, favourable for Russia. Moscow believes that it would be easier for the USA and Western Europe to accept Russia's coercion as a 'done deal'. Even the targeted and defeated country has something to discuss as well. Its presence at a negotiation table may provide a future settlement with highly needed legitimacy. That is why Georgia since 2008 has been taking part in the 'Geneva format' (with Russia, Abkhazia and South Ossetia, the USA, the European Union [EU], the UN and Organisation for Security and Co-operation [OSCE]), as well as Ukraine since August 2014 participating in the 'Normandy format' (with France, Germany and Russia).

Key element of coercive diplomacy in the contemporary multipolar world is readiness to use military force, even if on a limited scale. Belief in its military power is the key characteristic of Russian foreign policy towards zones of 'privileged interests'. The Kremlin's coercive diplomacy is diplomacy at the brink of military conflict. On the one hand, it says something about the assertive and even aggressive nature of Russian foreign policy. Nevertheless, it is also an invitation for the opponent to discuss a conflict through negotiations instead of using military force. Taking unexpected and bearish international actions, such as sending troops from Bosnia to Pristina, occupation of Gori in Georgia and holding a referendum on the annexation of Crimea, the Kremlin has eliminated many disadvantageous options for bargaining with opponents and created a new reality. Since Russia did these actions, a chain of events has occurred with a glance to the new reality on the ground, making useless all preparations of Russia's opponents for managing a crisis according to their own original scenario. That is why we may see Russian foreign policy as a competition with the West in risk-taking, a test of nerves for the parties involved.

Coercive diplomacy of the Russian Federation: peculiarities

The Russian Federation sees itself as a great power rising after a decade of military and economic decline. Moscow's principal goal is to consolidate its great power potential inherited from the USSR. Boris Yeltsin's strategy of rapprochement with the USA, designed to establish collaboration with the only superpower, failed dramatically. Growing Kremlin irritation with the George W. Bush administration's unilateralism reached its peak in November to December 2004 during the Ukrainian Orange Revolution. Since then, Russian leaders have intensively opposed the West's export of democracy to post-Soviet countries, considering it as a threat to regional security. In addition, the War in Iraq demonstrated the growing crisis of existing Euro-Atlantic structures: in spring 2003, Moscow found itself in a group of strong opponents to US unilateralism together with Berlin and Paris (Tkachenko, 2017, 127).

Russia concedes the possibility of limited military conflicts as an instrument of coercive diplomacy. From a political perspective, losing a military conflict may have dangerous ramifications for a leader, who insisted on the transformation of a diplomatic conflict into a military one (de Mesquita, 1995). Only a few risk-taking politicians are likely to make that choice. However, there are two requirements for successful 'coercive diplomacy' – the vast majority of the population should support it and the risk of failure should be moderate. These two conditions were met in August 2008 in South Ossetia and Abkhazia (Asmus, 2010) and later, in 2014–2016, in Crimea and Syria (Charap and Shapiro, 2015).

An earlier example of coercive diplomacy can be found in the Kremlin's response to the conflict in Chechnya in 1999–2001. In the late 1990s, the majority of experts considered the Chechen conflict as unresolvable, threatening the territorial integrity of Russia and even its existence as a sovereign state. But Russian leaders discovered a combination of diplomatic and military practices for settlement of the conflict. We argue that Russia repeated the same pattern later, in Georgia, Crimea, Donbass and Turkey. There are five key elements in this model.

First: demonstration of superior military power and limited military victory

In the above-mentioned cases, Russia demonstrated its ability to use military force at some stage of a conflict's genesis. That action was named by some experts as 'military persuasion' (Cimbala, 2010) or as 'military coercion' (Wijk, 2005). For the Kremlin, the key verifier that conflict is over on favourable terms is the re-establishment of territorial control and partial military defeat of an adversary. 'Territorial control' and 'military defeat' sound like terms from the nineteenth century, but the Chechen conflict took these patterns back to day-to-day realties. 'Control' and 'defeat' are key elements of coercive diplomacy and conflict management. The model also includes finding at the beginning of a conflict's 'military' stage a politician in the enemy's camp, who is ready to start negotiations with the Kremlin. This role was performed in autumn 1999 by Akhmat Kadyrov, the Mufti of Chechnya and one of the leaders of the anti-Russia opposition. His motivation was obvious for the local public: to avoid further casualties among the military and civilian population, even if Chechen radicals called him a 'traitor'. The Chechen example shows that it is possible to present military defeat not as 'total' but just as 'partial', as the failure of a small group of 'radicals' to find common ground with legitimate authorities.

At the initial stage of conflicts, Russia employs a new strategy for nuclear powers. We could call it 'careless pedestrian behaviour', which involves a person entering a road and forcing drivers to stop their cars. In several cases, Russian leaders have utilised military means in a mass, holistically and in a risky manner. Russian leaders today consider military standoffs with political opponents in neighbouring states as comprehensive operations of its Army, acting under authority of a single commander, while all needed resources are mobilised for the sake of immediate breakthrough. Usually, there is no preliminary political (not to say, diplomatic) statements before decision is made and the order to troops is delivered. Russia's coercive diplomacy does not utilise graduated pressure tactics, i.e. movement from using of light weapons towards heavy weaponry at later stages of conflicts.

Second: refusal of celebration of 'victory' over the defeated enemy

According to traditions of the twentieth century, total war demands total victory (Hobsbaum, 2002, 31). Contemporary Russian coercive diplomacy rejects that view. In cases under analysis, there were no 'unconditional surrender declarations', 'victory celebrations' and 'victory parades'. That has been Russia's political innovation. There were no doubts that Russian Army defeated international terrorists and local radicals in Chechnya. However, neither army nor society celebrated that victory. Military and political deprivations of Ukrainian army's units in Crimea (February to March 2014) were broadcast live by international TV channels all around the world. But Russia did not celebrate military victory in Ukraine. Russia's public propaganda made enormous efforts to shift the attention of its citizens and the international community from military aspects of annexation of Crimea to the results of the popular referendum on March 16, 2014, as well as to mostly peaceful nature of Crimea's transfer from Ukraine to Russia. Such a policy of concealing military aspects of interstate struggle preserves the relationship between the conflicting parties, leads to de-escalation of conflict and opens the way for its peaceful settlement in the far future.

Probably this element of Russia's coercive diplomacy reflects the personality of President Vladimir Putin. Until now, he is the only leader in Russia's recent history who did not decorate himself with the highest national awards. Obviously, it was his personal choice – to avoid the negative experience of Leonid Brezhnev, who was five times named as 'the Hero of the Soviet Union', provoking just jeering and anger. National awards in contemporary Russia are a rather unusual occurrence, and the only exception has been made for the military, for whom awards are crucial elements of career advancement. That is why a medal 'For taking back Crimea' has a low profile of 'professional award' and many people, involved in the 'return of Crimea back to Russia' were awarded via secret or at least 'non-public' decoration orders. In the cease of the Five Days' War against Georgia, there was no governmental award. The only medal 'For Peace-Enforcement, August 2008' got 'non-governmental' status and was fabricated by extra budgetary resources. For Russia's coercive diplomacy, it was more important not to irritate citizens of Georgia or Ukraine when decorating its own military.

Third: the readiness to consider 'transitional deals' as inherently valued and, in some cases, as optimal for keeping a favourable status quo

Experts like to ask the rhetorical question: 'How can Vladimir Putin, with a sinking economy and a second-rate military, continually dictate the course of geopolitical events?' (Rice and Gates, 2015, 4). For a proper answer, we should study how the Russian leadership has been able to concentrate diplomatic efforts and military resources in one place and at one time. This is a 'risky' policy, according to Vladimir Putin. But if everything is done professionally, it could bring some positive results. That is why Russian leaders prefer 'transitional deals' and, in almost all of the cases, President Vladimir Putin was personally involved in negotiations: the Minsk negotiations concerning Ukraine in August 26, 2014, and February 12, 2015; talks on Syria with US President Barack Obama in New York on September 29, 2015; negotiations with Turkish President Recep Erdogan in Saint Petersburg on August 9, 2016. Agreements at these negotiations could be considered as 'transitional,' but they have been done with the personal involvement of the Russian President and are considered by Russian diplomats, military and civil servants as expression of the political will of the Kremlin. At the moment of signing, it was the maximum that Russia could get from defeated opponents and influential international mediators. So the key leitmotiv of Russian coercive diplomacy was 'A bird in the hand is worth two in the bush'.

Russia's interest in coercive diplomacy has been driven by the changing nature of security threats, originating from NATO enlargement, several 'colour revolutions' in post-Soviet states and the Arab Spring revolutions since late 2010. The Kremlin made no bones about US attempts to use the rhetoric of 'promoting democracy' for intervening in the domestic affairs of sovereign states by backing the pro-democratic opposition. 'Colour revolutions' in Georgia, Ukraine and Kyrgyzstan in 2003–2005 were seen by Moscow as direct threats to national security and a challenge to the fragile status quo in the post-Soviet area (Kanet, 2017, 180). Any action, which may guarantee a return to the status quo ante, is welcomed by Moscow, even if it is considered as a 'transitional deal' and does not look like a final settlement of the conflicts.

Fourth: the personal involvement of President Vladimir Putin in decision-making and management of coercive diplomacy

In a recent documentary film *Crimea: The Way Back Home*, which was based on a long interview by Vladimir Putin about the Crimean crisis in February to March 2014, he explained in detail why his personal involvement in all stages of the conflict was a crucial precondition for the mobilisation of all required public resources and why it was so important for Russia's civil servants and military to know that the President personally involved in a crisis and take responsibility for its consequences. From Putin's point of view, involvement of the highest official (the First Person) was very powerful signal to everybody engaged in the operations that it was not his or her personal risk, but the political will of Russia and all available resources would be employed. With the 'blessing' from the President, ministers have not been afraid to act decisively, and ordinary performers of these giant operations knew that Russian authorities would not change their mind in the process and not cheat.

Fifth, and the most important: already at the initial stage of a conflict Russian leaders can formulate explicitly and rationally what they want as its final result

In using coercive diplomacy, Russian leaders have learnt how to formulate its aim in a realistic way. Achievement and preservation of the most essential goal was key objective for Russia's involvement into conflicts. In Chechnya, the aim was to re-establish the territorial integrity of the country. In Georgia, Moscow has tried to block prospects for Tbilisi's membership in NATO. In Ukraine, Russia nowadays is aspiring for formal establishment of its neutral status, as well as for those legitimate leaders in Kyiv, who would be tolerant to the strategic interests of Russia in the region. As soon as the simple aims of the Kremlin are achieved, Russia will activate additional resources to develop the political and security dialogue with Kiev and to restart economic and trade relations. This position is based, from the Kremlin's perspective, on 'statist' logic: Ukraine's membership in NATO would bring its military infrastructure to Russia's borders. In pure military terms, Moscow prefers to face NATO tanks at a frontline along the Dnieper River rather than on the flat topography around Belgorod and Bryansk. Nowadays, NATO under US command is the only organisation in the world which may annihilate Russia. The Kremlin knows perfectly well that

Washington has no vision how Russia could be integrated into the existing unipolar model of international relations as both an equal US partner and a fearful, but powerful, opponent.

Conclusion

Does Russia have inspirations to restore the USSR, to reunite the Russian-speaking territories in other Commonwealth of Independent States (CIS) countries and establish control over its neighbours? At this moment, answers to all three questions are negative. Putting the interests of economic integration in the Eurasian Economic Union (EAEU) in front of geopolitics, deleting any aspect of political integration from debates on the future of the CIS and the EAEU, Russia is trying to guarantee the peaceful image of its current foreign policy. In recent years, this strategy brought positive results (growing interstate trade, new member-states at the EAEU, etc.), even in the situation of growing Western sanctions. But the real intentions of Russia's diplomacy concentrated on control of neighbours' foreign and security policy. The main targets are six states between Russia and the EU: Belarus, Ukraine, Moldova, Azerbaijan, Armenia and Georgia. Russian diplomacy has 'finlandisation' model as an example to follow,[3] and instruments of coercive diplomacy to promote that model. This policy could be peaceful or aggressive, but it is definitely assertive and contains the threat of interstate conflicts. That is why the ability of Russia to formulate aims of foreign policy rationally and explicitly is declining as time passes.

The distinctive features of Russia's coercive diplomacy today include its *complex nature*, i.e. concentration not just on threats and occasional military operations (Kosovo, Georgia, Crimea, Syria), but on a broader set of action, including sales of the most advanced weaponry to opponents of Washington (Iran, Venezuela), financial assistance (member-states of the EAEU), the opening of domestic markets for friends (Serbia, Vietnam) and their closing for opponents (the EU, USA).

The crucial distinction between the current Syrian conflict and earlier examples of Russia's coercive diplomacy is that Moscow sees the Syrian War as a global one. It differs from cases of Chechnya, Georgia and Ukraine, which have only a regional dimension. That is why Russian advances there do not pose a strategic threat to the reputation of the USA and their allies. Moscow demands from the US recognition of an apparent fact – Washington is not able to win all conflicts around Russia's borders. That is why the best solution for the USA is to keep a low profile, leave Ukraine and Georgia alone and never cross Russia's 'red lines' in the former USSR area in future.

A problem, which cannot be solved by Russian coercive diplomacy today and most probably, will not be solved in the mid-term future – its lack of economic resources to continue coercive diplomacy measures by wide-range post-conflict reconstruction of an area under conflict. Russia's relative economic weakness in recent years did not have a direct impact on its possibility to carry out short- and rather large-scale military operations, as well as the ability of its diplomats to make unexpected and well-calculated moves. Even without significant resources Russian authorities are able to use remarkable information resources to convince the broader international community of the historical fairness and legal coherence of their actions.

Russian coercive diplomacy starts to face hurdles at that moment, when guns become silent and the time for post-conflict reconstruction starts. There were enough resources for total reconstruction of the city of Grozny, capital of Chechnya, as well as major elements of the infrastructure in this republic. But in the case of Crimea since spring 2014, Russia's budget could not afford the same scale of expenses for reconstruction of crumbling infrastructure and its enhancement up to the level of the most developed Russian regions. If anti-Russian sanctions of the Western states will be able to put constrains on its overall socio-economic development, positive evolution of Russia could be stalled for a long period.

Notes

1 Reacting on the Edward Snowden case, US President Barack Obama cancelled his summit with Vladimir Putin, which was scheduled for September 3–4, 2013, in Moscow.
2 For example, Russia's policy towards the South Caucasus and Central Asia in the nineteenth century was proactive.
3 'Finlandisation', according to Robert Kaplan, is the process by which one powerful country makes a smaller neighbouring country abides by the former's foreign policy rules while allowing it to keep its nominal independence and its own political system (Kaplan, 2015, 26).

References

Allen, Susan H. (2011) 'Bombing to Bargain? The Air War for Kosovo', *Foreign Policy Analysis*, vol. 7, no. 1, pp. 1–26.
Art, Robert J., and Patrick M. Cronin (2003) *The United States and Coercive Diplomacy*. Washington, DC: U.S. Institute of Peace Press, p. 6.
Asmus, Ronald D. (2010) *A Little War That Shook the World*. New York: Palgrave Macmillan.
Baldwin, David A. (1985) *Economic Statecraft*. Princeton: Princeton University Press.
Brams, Steven (1985) *Superpower Games: Applying Game Theory to Superpower Conflict*. New Haven, CT and London: Yale University Press.
Charap, Samuel, and Jeremy Shapiro (2015) 'Consequences of a New Cold War', *Survival*, vol. 75, no. 2, pp. 37–46.
Cimbala, Stephen J. (2010) *Military Persuasion: Deterrence and Provocation in Crisis and War*. University Park, PA: Penn State Press.
de Mesquita, B., and Siverson, R. (1995). 'War and the Survival of Political Leaders: A Comparative Study of Regime Types and Political Accountability', *American Political Science Review*, vol. 89, no. 4, pp. 841–855.
George, Alexander L. and William Simons (1994) *The Limits of Coercive Diplomacy*. San Francisco and Oxford: Westview Press, p. 2.
Hermann, Margaret G., and Kegley, Charles W., Jr. (1998) 'The U.S. use of military intervention to promote democracy: Evaluating the record', *International Interactions*, vol. 24, no. 2, pp. 91–114.
Hobsbaum, Eric (2002) *The Age of Extremes. The Short Twentieth Century: 1914–1991*. London: Abacus.
Jakobsen, Peer Viggo (2016) 'Coercive Diplomacy', in Costas M. Constantinou, Pauline Kerr, and Paul Sharp, eds., *The SAGE Handbook of Diplomacy*. Thousand Oak, CA: SAGE Publishing, pp. 476–486.
Kanet, Roger E. (2017) 'Russia and Global Governance: The Challenge to the Existing Liberal Order', *International Politics*, vol. 55, no. 2, pp. 177–188.
Kaplan, Robert D. (2015) *Asia's Cauldron*. USA: Random House Trade Paperbacks.
Kondrashev, Andrey (2015) Documentary Film 'Crimea: The Way Back Home'. https://vimeo.com/123319119.
McDermott, Roger N. (2016) 'Does Russia have a Gerasimov Doctrine'? *Parameters*, vol. 46, no. 1, pp. 97–105.
Putin, Vladimir (2007) 'Speech and the Following Discussion at the Munich Conference on Security Policy'. February 10. http://en.kremlin.ru/events/president/transcripts/24034.
Rice, Condoleezza, and Robert M. Gates (2015) 'How America Can Counter Putin's Moves in Syria'. *The Washington Post*, October 8, 2015.
Schelling, Thomas C. (1966) *Arms and Influence*. New Haven, CT: Yale University Press, pp. 3–4, 69–76.
Schultz, Kenneth (2001) *Democracy and Coercive Diplomacy*. Cambridge: Cambridge University Press.
Tkachenko, Stanislav (2017) 'Coercive Diplomacy of Vladimir Putin (2014–2016)', in Roger Kanet, ed., *The Russian Challenge to the European Security Environment*. Cham, Switzerland: Palgrave Macmillan Publishers, pp. 115–136.
Trenin, Dmitry (2015) *From Greater Europe to Greater Asia? The Sino-Russian Entente*. Washington, DC: The Carnegie Endowment for International Peace. http://carnegie.ru/publications/?fa=59728, accessed August 5, 2016.
Tsygankov, Andrei (2009) *Russophobia: Anti-Russian Lobby and American Foreign Policy*. London: Palgrave.
Wijk, Rob de (2005) *The Art of Military Coercion. Why the West's Military Superiority Scarcely Matters*. Amsterdam: Amsterdam University Press.

12
THE REBUILDING OF RUSSIAN MILITARY CAPABILITIES

Jennifer G. Mathers

Comparing Russia's current military capabilities to those that Moscow was able to command in 2008, it is clear that a great deal of progress has been made in rebuilding them and, more than that, in transforming Russia's military into something resembling the efficient, mobile, well-equipped and highly professional force that has been the declared aim of Russia's most senior military and political leaders since the formation of its armed forces in 1992. The catalyst was the armed forces' performance in the 2008 war with Georgia, which was fought for control over the separatist regions South Ossetia and Abkhazia. In many respects, this was a successful operation for Russia: it was carefully planned in advance and carried out by troops from a large number of different units and services who had trained together, and included the rapid deployment of nearly 20,000 soldiers to the conflict zone (Vendil Pallin and Westerlund, 2009, 400–401). But, while Russia managed to achieve its military aims in just five days, its victory can largely be attributed to its vastly superior numbers and firepower, and its conduct of the operations revealed many weaknesses. Coordination of forces was hampered by communications equipment that was incompatible between services, limiting the ability of the Air Force to provide effective support for ground units and forcing some military commanders to use their personal mobile phones for relaying orders (Vendil Pallin and Westerlund, 2010, 157, 159). Commanders keenly felt their limited access to equipment that is taken for granted by North Atlantic Treaty Organisation (NATO) armed forces, including precision-guided weapons, thermal imaging equipment, night vision goggles and satellite navigation (Klein, 2012, 29). Such gaps in equipment significantly reduced the efficiency of Russia's military operations, while exposing its troops to greater risk. Faulty intelligence about the location of Georgian forces meant the loss of Russian aircraft to enemy air defences, while the ageing vehicles used by the Ground Forces were prone to breaking down at crucial moments (Vendil Pallin and Westerlund, 2010, 158, 160).

The catalogue of failures revealed by the Georgian War provided the new Minister of Defence, Anatoly Serdyukov, with the excuse – and the high-level political backing – that he needed to carry out extensive changes. With no experience of military service beyond his period as a conscript, Serdyukov was an unconventional choice to lead the Ministry of Defence. His lack of military credentials, together with a stint in the retail sector, led many officers who were disgruntled with his reforms to refer to him disdainfully as 'that furniture salesman', but it was his more recent experience as the head of Russia's tax police that brought Serdyukov to the attention of Vladimir Putin. Appointed in 2007 to address corruption in the Ministry of Defence – which, according to a 2008 report by Russia's Audit Chamber, was responsible for the loss of over 164 million rubles allocated to the armed forces (Herspring and McDermott, 2010, 284–285) – Serdyukov's lack of close ties to the armed forces made him the ideal candidate to push through radical change in the military. Together with his adviser and former GRU officer Vitalii Shlykov, Serdyukov developed a programme, known as the New Look (or *Noviy Oblik* in Russian), to transform Russia's military that focussed on changing its structure and organisation, modernising its weapons and equipment, and reducing the size and changing the composition of its staffing. The overarching aim of New Look reforms was to reshape the armed forces from a mass mobilisation army based on a Second World War model to a much smaller but better-trained and -equipped force able to respond swiftly and effectively to the regional security threats facing Russia in the twenty-first century. In this effort, both Shlykov and Serdyukov were keen to borrow from successful practice in other countries' armed forces, especially the United States (Bukkvoll, 2011, 697–698).

The process of military reform launched by Serdyukov was well underway but still incomplete by the time he was removed from office in 2012 accused of corruption – ironically, given the original reason for his appointment – but with widespread speculation that Serdyukov had finally offended too many people in powerful positions. His replacement, Sergei Shoigu, has enjoyed a much better relationship with senior figures in the Ministry of Defence. Shoigu came to the Defence Ministry with a strong reputation for professionalism based on his performance in his previous role as head of the Ministry of Emergency Situations and has shown himself willing to listen to senior officers and adapt the New Look military reform. While Shoigu is committed to the overarching goals of military reform, he is far less interested in reproducing structures and practices found in Western militaries. Perhaps as a result of this change in leadership, Russia's military is not easily pigeonholed; it no longer adheres strictly to Soviet-era traditions nor is it clearly moving towards a Western model.

Structure and organisation

On 14 October 2008, Serdyukov announced the main elements of his military reforms and set an ambitious timetable for carrying them out over the next four years. Along with changes to staffing that will be addressed later in this chapter, the announcement focussed chiefly on the goal of transforming all military units into 'permanent readiness units' and to improving the effectiveness and coordination of military operations by streamlining the command structure (creating a smaller, three-tiered structure and making the brigade rather than the division the basic unit), reducing the size of the Main Intelligence Directorate (GRU) and bringing it fully under the control of the Defence Minister rather than the Chief of the General Staff, and rationalising the number of military facilities for education and training and for medical care (Gorenburg, 2012, 224–225). These reforms were intended to create an armed force that was smaller but much more tightly organised, more closely under the control of the Defence Minister himself, and able to respond more swiftly to Moscow's instructions.

The possession of an armed force composed entirely of units that were fully staffed, fully equipped and prepared for immediate or near-immediate deployment had been an aspiration articulated for post-Soviet Russia since it formed its own, independent military in 1992.

Russia's first Minister of Defence, General Pavel Grachev, expressed this aim in a speech delivered to the Royal United Services Institute in London in July 1992, in which he stressed the importance of developing a small but highly effective armed force characterised by the use of 'action readiness forces' and 'mobile forces' (inspired by Western rapid deployment forces) to deal with local and regional conflicts, especially those within the borders of the former USSR (Grachev, 1992). The reality of the Russian armed forces in the 1990s was very far from the picture painted by Grachev. The Russian armed forces were created out of the remnants of the Soviet military and, despite Mikhail Gorbachev's efforts in the late 1980s to scale it down and reorient it towards a defensive posture, it continued to be organised to meet the needs of a large-scale ground war, and based on the assumption that any future war would be signalled sufficiently far in advance (and last long enough) to call up reserves and unite weapons and equipment with the right soldiers in the right places. As a result, Russia's army was organised into a large number of units, the vast majority of which were routinely kept at skeleton rates of staffing and equipment. By the time of the 2008 war with Georgia, only 17 per cent of Russia's units were fully staffed and equipped and ready to be deployed quickly to a conflict zone (Renz, 2018, 63–64).

Only very limited steps were taken towards reshaping the structure and organisation of Russia's military before the Serdyukov reforms. Grachev announced a three-stage reform process that was intended to reduce the size and streamline the structure of the armed forces, transform it into an all-volunteer force and be completed by 2000 (Arbatov, 1998, 112). Little progress had been made in implementing this plan by the time Grachev was replaced as Minister of Defence in 1996, and each of the subsequent holders of that post launched military reform anew. Far from being reformed and revitalised, during Boris Yeltsin's two terms as president (1990–1999), Russia's armed forces experienced a downward spiral which, at times, seemed irreversible (Arbatov, 1998), as they struggled to cope with the practical demands of preparing for post–Cold War security threats that were poorly understood and defined, with rapidly diminishing budgets and a political leadership headed by a man who had little interest in the military beyond its willingness and ability to support him in his internal power struggles.

Vladimir Putin's presidency marked the beginning of a sustained period in which the armed forces – along with the other security forces controlled by the Russian state – have enjoyed a higher priority as well as significantly greater levels of funding. Under Putin, the defence budget rose from a low point of about US$19 billion in 1998 to approximately US$58 billion a decade later (Renz, 2018, 62). Since he was first appointed acting president by Yeltsin in 1999, Putin has spoken consistently about the importance to Russia of having a strong military, while the sinking of the *Kursk* submarine with the loss of all the men on board in August 2000 demonstrated to Putin that Russia's military capabilities had deteriorated significantly and that the armed forces were in need of effective reform (Vendil Pallin, 2009, 121–122). Military reform was, nevertheless, initially approached gradually, with commissions set up to study the problem and produce reports for Russia's Security Council to consider before major changes were introduced (Herspring, 2005, 141). Important ground was cleared by Putin's willingness to intervene in power struggles within the Ministry of Defence on the side of the Minister and to establish clear lines of accountability. General Staff headquarters underwent a series of further personnel changes in 2008, when a number of commanders, including the Chief of the General Staff, were replaced with men who were more supportive of serious reform (Gorenburg, 2012, 224).

By the time that the Ministry of Defence was reviewing its performance in the 2008 war in Georgia, key elements were in place to enable radical and rapid change in the Russian military. In Anatoly Serdyukov, Russia had a new Minister of Defence who was both committed to serious reform and able to view the military dispassionately. Serdyukov's efforts to push through change were strongly supported by his recently appointed Chief of the General Staff General Nikolai Makarov and by political leaders at the highest levels – newly elected President Dmitry Medvedev as well as Putin, who had just begun a term as Prime Minister. Serdyukov had a clear set of ideas about the nature of change he wanted to introduce, informed by many years' worth of internal investigations, reports and studies as well as by examples drawn from the experiences of Western militaries.

Serdyukov set a deadline of 1 December 2009 for implementation of the first stage: reducing the number of units and reshaping them into permanent readiness brigades that were fully staffed and fully equipped. In sharp contrast to virtually all previous reform efforts, this step was carried out more or less within the timescale originally announced (Giles, 2012, 12). The elimination of skeleton units was a clear indication that Russia was moving away from the old model of the mass army. As well as the assumptions that went along with it of the need to prepare for large-scale land war. The intention was to designate brigades as heavy, medium or light formation to enable them to respond effectively to the needs of different types of operation. In order to improve combat readiness and to address the failures of communication and coordination that were so heavily criticised in reports of the 2008 war with Georgia, the New Look structural reforms included the creation of joint strategic commands or *Obedinonnye Strategicheskoe Komandovanie* in Russian (OSKs), which brought under a unified command all the military – and paramilitary – formations located in the same geographical area (Giles, 2012, 12). Navy fleets were subordinated to OSKs, and the Navy high command was absorbed into the General Staff (Giles, 2012, 19). The air base was to be the main structural element for Russia's air capabilities, dividing it into three categories according to size and capacity and using squadrons rather than the traditional regimental structure (IISS, 2015, 54).

There have been some amendments to the New Look reforms since Sergei Shoigu became Defence Minister. Brigades continue to be the main structural unit in the Ground Forces, but the idea of light, medium and heavy formations seems to have been abandoned while two divisions have been reintroduced. The Air Force has similarly moved away from the idea of large air bases housing mixed air groups (IISS, 2017, 184). A separate command for Cyber Security was announced in 2012, reflecting Moscow's recognition of the importance of this type of activity for defence and national security (Giles, 2014, 157), and in 2013 a new Special Operations Force was established (Renz, 2016, 291). The introduction of regular, large-scale military exercises by Serdyukov in 2009 provides evidence that readiness is being improved and that new structures are being put to the test (Giles, 2012, 20–21). Shoigu has not only increased the size and scale of these military exercises but also introduced snap inspections that closely simulate the conditions troops would face at the outbreak of a conflict and give him the opportunity to discover cases of mismanagement and corruption (IISS, 2017, 187). While they are not irreversible, the major changes to the structure and organisation of the Russian military introduced since 2008 appear to have been implemented successfully and are now in the process of being refined and consolidated.

Modernisation of weapons and equipment

Changes to the structure and organisation of Russia's armed forces have been crucial to the rebuilding of the country's military capabilities since 2008, but in many respects, these were the most straightforward elements of military reform to implement. Equally important but far more complex is the task of modernising the Russian military's stock of weapons and equipment. Indeed, Dmitry Gorenburg (2012, 229) has referred to providing the army with new equipment as the big missing component of military reform. For while there has been a significant improvement in the modernisation of military hardware over the past decade, Moscow has no reason for complacency in this area.

The Russian military inherited from its Soviet predecessor a supply of outdated weapons and equipment and a large but inefficient defence industry that had specialised in incremental improvements on existing designs. The defence sector withered throughout the 1990s; in the first half of the decade alone, the state defence budget dropped by an estimated 45 per cent (IISS, 1996, 107). Moreover, only a small proportion of the funds that were allocated to defence in the state budget ever found their way to their intended recipients; there was always a shortfall of revenue as the Russian state struggled throughout the 1990s to carry out the basic function of taxation, while significant portions of the allocated funds were routinely withheld by the Finance Ministry, and widespread corruption allowed state resources earmarked for defence to end up in the pockets of individuals (Barany, 2007, 53). This combination of factors meant that the Ministry of Defence placed few orders for new weapons and equipment and the defence industry made little capital investment in production facilities, while the demand for the intellectual work of research and development also all but dried up; the average age of both machine tools and industry employees rose significantly (Shlykov, 2004, 160–161). The decline of the defence industry meant that the introduction of new military technology to units and bases slowed to a trickle or halted entirely, and efforts at modernisation were focussed on modifying existing equipment (Vendil Pallin, 2009, 100). Less than 10 per cent of the Air Force's procurement projects were funded throughout the 1990s (Lefebvre, 2003, 155), while 90 per cent of the Navy's ships were in need of repair by 2001, and some ships that had been in service for only a decade or so were decommissioned because there was no prospect of money to fund the repairs that were needed (Tsypkin, 2003, 163).

Russian defence spending has risen dramatically since Vladimir Putin first became president in 1999, facilitated by high economic growth (especially in the first two terms of his presidency) and the clear priority that Putin set for security and defence in the state budget. Russia's defence spending doubled in the decade between 2003 and 2013, and by 2013 Russia was judged to have the third highest level of military spending in the world, equivalent to approximately US$88 billion or 4.4 per cent of its gross domestic product (Oxenstierna, 2016, 61). But while investment is clearly underway, the lost decade of the 1990s casts a long shadow on Russia's ability to equip its military with modern weapons; even with the dramatic rise in defence spending, the extent of remedial work to be done meant that it has taken a considerable time to see results in terms of the production, testing and delivery of new equipment and weapons systems. Russia's defence industry continues to face obstacles, and it struggles to meet orders placed by the government on time and within the allocated budget. There is still a heavy reliance on incremental developments and the use of decades-old designs and limited progress on developing and delivering high-tech conventional weapons. Economic sanctions imposed on Russia after its annexation of Crimea in 2014 mean that it can no longer rely on plugging its technological gaps by importing systems from the West (e.g. France's cancellation of its planned sale of Mistral ships to Moscow). Russia's intervention in Ukraine has also cut it off from the source of key components produced in that country, such as maritime gas-turbine engines (IISS, 2015, 56). Finally, corruption continues to siphon off substantial portions of the funds allocated to defence each year.

Despite these problems, the State Armament Programme for 2011–2010 (SAP 2020) has delivered an improvement in the quality of weapons and equipment reaching units. Unlike the structural elements of the post-2008 reform that have focussed primarily on conventional forces, the modernisation effort has sought to upgrade Russia's nuclear weapons capability also, and this is an area which has seen some of the most significant advances. Three new ICBM programmes are underway: the Yars or SS-27, which is now in series production, and the new heavy-liquid fuelled Sarmat (SS-X-30) and the rail-based Barguzin, which are both under development (IISS, 2017, 193). The Air Force has taken delivery of a range of fixed-wing aircraft and helicopters, although the new fifth-generation T-50 combat aircraft has yet to reach series production (IISS, 2017, 193). The Ground Troops have seen their armoured vehicles upgraded and have taken delivery of several hundred upgraded and modernised battle tanks, allowing the disposal of outdated models, and a range of unmanned aerial vehicles (UAVs) are being developed (Giles, 2014, 151; Renz, 2018, 79). The new generation of Armata battle tanks, promised for mass production during SAP 2020, were still in testing and only a handful of prototypes delivered to units by the time the armament programme was overtaken by its successor (Renz, 2018, 79). The main advances in equipping the Navy have been in upgraded versions of existing models of submarines and smaller surface vessels. In spite of receiving the largest share of the funding in SAP 2020, the Navy has made the least progress of any of the services, reflecting its historic under-funding, ongoing struggles with corruption and its dependence on production facilities in Ukraine for crucial components (Renz, 2018, 79, 81). The problems affecting the production of naval systems extends to the sea-based leg of the nuclear triad, with delays continuing to plague the testing and production of the new Borey-A class strategic submarines and indications that the Bulava ballistic missiles that these submarines are designed to carry are also not completely trouble-free, despite having been in testing since 2007 (IISS, 2017, 193).

While the SAP 2020 did not meet its very ambitious target of modernising between 70 per cent and 100 per cent of Russia's weapons and equipment, Defence Minister Shoigu announced in December 2017 that modernisation overall had reached the level of 59.5 per cent (Russian Defence Policy, 2018). The successor to SAP 2020, the State Rearmament Programme for 2018–2027 (SAP 2027), is expected to have a budget at roughly the same level as SAP 2020, indicating a levelling off of the resources devoted to defence after a period of significant increases (Gorenburg, 2017). The real test of Russia's ability to rebuild its military capabilities will be to make the transition from improving on existing systems based on old designs and provide its troops with truly new weapons and equipment.

Staffing

Of all the aspects of military reform, staffing is the area where Russia has struggled most. The task of recruiting and retaining sufficient personnel of an appropriate quality is yet to be fully addressed, largely due to the persistence of Soviet attitudes and practices towards military service. Although steps have been taken to make improvements in those areas and there are signs of positive change, it is unlikely that Russia will be able to solve its military staffing problems in the foreseeable future.

Conscription has historically been the basis for the Russian armed forces, and present-day Russia continues to rely upon compulsory male military service to a large extent. Russia has several reasons for maintaining a conscript army. Conscription provides the basis for a mass force in arms, together with a large reserve of trained citizens who can be called up at the outbreak of war. Conscription also gives the state the opportunity to cultivate patriotism and promote other desired attitudes and behaviours in a substantial portion of society. But a universal male draft has proven increasingly difficult for Russia to sustain, while the moves towards voluntary or contract service have not been entirely successful either.

Problems with implementing conscription started in the late Soviet period. One of the many revelations of Gorbachev's policy of *glasnost'* (publicity or openness) was the extent of brutality experienced by conscripts; the result was a spectacular loss of faith by society in the ability and willingness of the state to look after young men performing their military service. The system of *dedovshchina* (the bullying of junior conscripts by the senior ones), which often resulted in severe beatings and sometimes in suicide or in death at the hands of fellow soldiers, motivated many parents of teenaged boys to seek the advice of their local Committee of Soldiers' Mothers (CSM) about ways to avoid conscription. CSM is not only one of Russia's most enduring and successful civil society groups, but its practical support for those seeking to evade military service was so successful that it has raised serious questions about the viability conscription in Russia (Eichler, 2012, 88–107). In 1992, only 20–25 per cent of young Russian men of conscription age performed their compulsory military service (Dawisha and Parrott, 1994, 243).

In an attempt to fill some of the gaps that draft dodging created, voluntary military service (known as contract service) was introduced by the Ministry of Defence in the early 1990s. Defence Ministry officials had hoped that contract service would attract young men who had recently finished or were about to complete their periods of conscription, thus reducing the additional training required of the new recruits. Instead, contract service mainly attracted those who had difficulty in finding employment in the civilian economy: the poorly educated, those with criminal records, those addicted to drugs and alcohol, and women. The appeal of contract service to women was a completely unexpected development for Russian military officials. Although there was a precedent for women soldiers during the Second World War when more than a million had served in a wide variety of capacities (Krylova, 2010; Pennington, 2001), as soon as the war ended they were swiftly demobilised. While military service had been open to women on a voluntary basis after 1945, very few were interested. By the early to mid-1990s, however, joining the military had become an attractive option for many women, especially those who already had some connection to the armed forces. With the decline in the pay and living standards of Russian officers, contract service offered the chance for many of their wives and daughters to gain additional income for the household, while women who were already employed by the Ministry of Defence as civilians found that they could earn more money as contract soldiers. During the 1990s, approximately 100,000 women took up contract service, comprising about 10 per cent of Russia's armed forces (Mathers, 2006, 210).

While the Russian military was struggling to fill the rank and file through some combination of conscription and voluntary service, it had far more senior officers than it needed. Serdyukov's reforms addressed the staffing crisis by starting at the top and imposing drastic cuts on the senior ranks of the officer corps. By 2012, more than half of all officer posts were eliminated, including 75 per cent of majors, 64.5 per cent of colonels and 20.8 per cent of generals (Klein, 2012, 35). A new, extended course of training was introduced for non-commissioned officers (NCOs) with the aim of professionalising them; previously, NCOs had been recruited from contract soldiers or senior conscripts with very little preparation for their new roles. Efforts were devoted to make conscription more tolerable, both to the young men serving and to society, by improving their pay, food, accommodation and medical care, and also by reducing the term of service to just 12 months. Similar efforts were made to increase the appeal of contract service by improving the pay and conditions for volunteers.

By 2016, the Russian military appeared to have turned a corner: more than half of its rank and file were serving on a voluntary basis (427,000 out of 760,000) (Galeotti, 2017). Reaping the public relations benefits of the smooth military operation in Crimea and the well-disciplined behaviour of the Russian soldiers dubbed 'polite people', there were signs that society was viewing the armed forces and military service in a much more positive light. An opinion poll in 2017 indicated that the army was the second most trusted institution in Russia after the president, with 69 per cent saying it was completely trustworthy (Levada Centre, 2017), while in another poll conducted in 2018, 71 per cent said they would like to see a close relative serving in the armed forces (Russian Public Opinion Research Centre, 2018). These are important indications that the rift between the military and society in Russia may be closing, which would be a crucial step in solving the long-term staffing problems facing the armed forces. There are, however, a number of contradictions and issues yet to be resolved.

Russia's political leadership insist on the aim of a million man army, which is impossible to achieve in the near future, whether through conscription or voluntary service; the sharp decline in the birth rate starting in the early 1990s means the number of young men reaching conscription age is likely to stay around 600,000–700,000 per year well into the 2020s (Vendil Pallin, 2009, 157). And while women have proven to be a demographic which can be attracted to military service, the Ministry of Defence has shown little interest in recruiting and retaining them. In fact, the reduction in the number of officers has also reduced the largest source of potential women soldiers (the female family members of officers), with the result that the number of women in Russia's military is in decline (Mathers, 2014, 236). Reducing the period of conscription to 12 months may have made compulsory service more acceptable to society, but it also means that conscripts spend more time being trained than actually putting their training into practice. One of the justifications for keeping conscription – that it provides a pool of trained reserves – is undermined by the Defence Ministry's haphazard approach to training demobilised soldiers; fewer than one in ten are receiving refresher training within five years of leaving the military (Galeotti, 2017). A significant proportion of Russia's senior officers remain opposed to voluntary service, even though, in its current form, conscription is clearly not providing the military with meaningful resources. Golts (2012, 213) argues that this attitude reflects the mindset of a generation of generals whose only idea of fighting a war relies on being able to overwhelm the enemy with sheer numbers of troops. The conduct of voluntary service is also not without its problems. There are indications that some commanders fraudulently inflate the number of contract soldiers in their units and pocket the extra salaries, as well as persistent claims that young men have been tricked or coerced into signing contracts, especially those who have been sent to fight in the Donbas since 2014 (Golts, 2012, 210).

Conclusions

Russia has made very considerable progress in rebuilding its military capabilities since the start of the Serdyukov reforms. The Russian armed forces of today are almost unrecognisable in comparison with the 2008 version, especially in the streamlining of its structure and the significant improvement in its ability to deploy forces quickly and carry out its assigned missions, as we have seen in Crimea in 2014 and in Russia's intervention in the war in Syria since 2015. While there continue to be limits to the ability of the defence industry to perform at the level that the Russian state demands, there is nevertheless a stream of new weapons and equipment being delivered each year, and a clear determination to develop the technological basis for new generations of weapons.

As Bettina Renz (2014) points out, we should not assume that Russia must transform its armed forces into a Western-style military in order for it to be effective in meeting the security challenges facing the country in the twenty-first century. A combination of more traditional and high-tech conventional forces, together with the maintenance of its nuclear deterrent, could be a mixture that is entirely suitable for Russia. The question of staffing, however, is the outstanding, pressing issue with the potential to undermine this scenario. While some militaries successfully combine compulsory and voluntary service, Russia's problem is that it has not managed to make either of these systems work very well.

References

Arbatov, Alexei (1998) 'Military Reform in Russia: Dilemmas, Obstacles, and Prospects', *International Security*, Vol. 22, No. 4, pp. 83–134.

Barany, Zoltan (2007) *Democratic Breakdown and the Decline of the Russian Military*. Princeton, NJ and Oxford: Princeton University Press.

Bukkvoll, Tor (2011) 'Iron Cannot Fight – The Role of Technology in Current Russian Military Theory', *Journal of Strategic Studies*, Vol. 34, No. 5, pp. 681–706.

Dawisha, Karen and Bruce Parrott (1994) *Russia and the New States of Eurasia: The Politics of Upheaval*. Cambridge and New York: Cambridge University Press.

Eichler, Maya (2012) *Militarizing Men: Gender, Conscription and War in Post-Soviet Russia*. Stanford, CA: Stanford University Press.

Galeotti, Mark (2017) *The Modern Russian Army: 1992–2017*. Oxford: Osprey.

Giles, Keir (2012) 'Russian Operations in Georgia: Lessons Identified versus Lessons Learned', in Roger N. McDermott, Bertil Nygren and Carolina Vendil Pallin, eds., *The Russian Armed Forces in Transition: Economic, Geopolitical and Institutional Uncertainties*. London and New York: Routledge, pp. 9–28.

Giles, Keir (2014) 'A New Phase in Russian Military Transformation', *The Journal of Slavic Military Studies*, Vol. 27, No. 1, pp. 147–162.

Golts, Alexander (2012) 'Conscription: A Basic Question of Civil-Military Relations in Russia', in Roger N. McDermott, Bertil Nygren, and Carolina Vendil Pallin, eds., *The Russian Armed Forces in Transition: Economic, Geopolitical and Institutional Uncertainties*. London and New York: Routledge, pp. 209–221.

Gorenburg, Dmitry (2012) 'The Military', in Graeme Gill and James Young, eds., *Routledge Handbook of Russian Politics and Society*. Abingdon and New York: Routledge, pp. 220–231.

Gorenburg, Dmitry (2017) 'Russia's Military Modernization Plans: 2018–2027', *PONARS Eurasia Policy Memo*, No. 495, November. Accessed on 4 June 2018 at www.ponarseurasia.org/memo/russias-military-modernization-plans-2018-2027.

Grachev, Army General Pavel S. (1992) 'The Defence Policy of the Russian Federation', *Royal United Services Institute Journal*, Vol. 137, No. 5, pp. 5–7.

Herspring, Dale R. (2005) 'Vladimir Putin and Military Reform in Russia', *European Security*, Vol. 14, No. 1, pp. 137–155.

Herspring, Dale R. and Roger N. McDermott (2010, Spring) 'Serdyukov Promotes Systemic Russian Military Reform', *Orbis*, Vol. 54, No. 2, pp. 284–301.

IISS (1996) *The Military Balance 1996–97*. Oxford: Oxford University Press for the International Institute for Strategic Studies.

IISS (2015) *Strategic Survey: The Annual Review of World Affairs*. London and New York: Routledge for the International Institute for Strategic Studies.

IISS (2017) *The Military Balance 2017: The Annual Assessment of Global Military Capabilities and Defence Economics*. London and New York: Routledge for the International Institute for Strategic Studies.

Klein, Margarete (2012) 'Towards a "new look" of the Russian Armed Forces?', in Roger N. McDermott, Bertil Nygren, and Carolina Vendil Pallin, eds., *The Russian Armed Forces in Transition: Economic, Geopolitical and Institutional Uncertainties*. London and New York: Routledge, pp. 29–48.

Krylova, Anna (2010) *Soviet Women in Combat: A History of Violence on the Eastern Front*. Cambridge: Cambridge University Press.

Lefebvre, Stephane (2003) 'The Reform of the Russian Air Force', in Roger N. McDermott, Bertil Nygren, and Carolina Vendil Pallin, eds., *The Russian Armed Forces in Transition: Economic, Geopolitical and Institutional Uncertainties*. London and New York: Routledge, pp. 141–161.

Levada Centre (2017) 'Institutional Trust' Accessed on 4 June 2018 at www.levada.ru/en/2017/11/10/institutional-trust-3/.

Mathers, Jennifer G. (2006) 'Women, Society and the Military: Women Soldiers in Post-Soviet Russia', in Stephen L. Webber and Jennifer G. Mathers, eds., *Military and Society in Post-Soviet Russia*. Manchester and New York: Manchester University Press, pp. 207–227.

Mathers, Jennifer G. (2014) 'The Military, Security and Politics', in Stephen White, Richard Sakwa, and Henry E. Hale, eds., *Developments in Russian Politics Eight*. Houndmills: Palgrave Macmillan, pp. 231–246.

Oxenstierna, Susanne (2016) 'Russia's Defence Spending and the Economic Decline', *Journal of Eurasian Studies*, Vol. 7, No. 1, pp. 60–70.

Pennington, Reina (2001) *Wings, Women, and War: Soviet Airwomen in World War II Combat*. Lawrence: University Press of Kansas.

Renz, Bettina (2014) 'Russian Military Capabilities after 20 Years of Reform', *Survival*, Vol. 56, No. 3, pp. 61–84.

Renz, Bettina (2016) 'Russia and "Hybrid Warfare"', *Contemporary Politics*, Vol. 22, No. 3, pp. 283–300.

Renz, Bettina (2018) *Russia's Military Revival*. Cambridge and Medford, MA: Polity Press.

Russian Defence Policy (2018) 'The Annual Report', *Blog Entry*, 13 January. Accessed on 4 June 2018 at https://russiandefpolicy.blog/2018/01/13/the-annual-report/.

Russian Public Opinion Research Center (2018) 'February 23 Holiday and The Views of Russian Army' Accessed on 4 June 2018 at https://wciom.com/index.php?id=61&uid=1510.

Shlykov, Vitaly V. (2004) 'The Economics of Defense in Russia and the Legacy of Structural Militarization', in Steven E. Miller and Dmitri Trenin, eds., *The Russian Military: Power and Policy*. Cambridge and London: The MIT Press, pp. 157–182.

Tsypkin, Mikhail (2003) 'Rudderless in a Storm: The Russian Navy, 1992–2002', in Roger N. McDermott, Bertil Nygren, and Carolina Vendil Pallin, eds., *The Russian Armed Forces in Transition: Economic, Geopolitical and Institutional Uncertainties*. London and New York: Routledge, pp. 162–186.

Vendil Pallin, Carolina (2009) *Russian Military Reform: A Failed Exercise in Defence Decision Making*. Abingdon and New York: Routledge.

Vendil Pallin, Carolina and Fredrick Westerlund (2009) 'Russia's War in Georgia: Lessons and Consequences', *Small Wars and Insurgencies*, Vol. 20, No. 2, pp. 400–424.

Vendil Pallin, Carolina and Fredrik Westerlund (2010) 'Russia's War in Georgia: Lessons and Consequences', in Paul B. Rich, ed., *Crisis in the Caucasus: Russia, Georgia and the West*. London and New York: Routledge, pp. 150–174.

13

REFLECTIONS ON RUSSIA'S NUCLEAR STRATEGY

Stephen Blank

Introduction

Russia's invasion of Ukraine in 2014, continuing military buildup, and ongoing information attacks on Western governments have forced Western experts to awake from their dogmatic slumbers and take Russian defense policy and thinking seriously. Therefore, one of the most critical questions we must answer concerns the role of nuclear weapons in Russian strategy. Nuclear weapons remain the priority in Russian procurement for the new defense plan through 2025, as in the previous plan through 2020 (Gorenburg, 2017). And this occurs even though doctrinally and in practice the government and military proclaim their emphasis on non-nuclear deterrence in current and future military planning.[1] Neither can we hide behind the old cliché that Russia values nuclear weapons because they endow it with great power status and because it cannot compete with North Atlantic Treaty Organisation's (NATO) superior conventional technologies. While both these points are true, Moscow actually retains a comfortable margin of superiority along all of its borders vis-à-vis NATO. Moreover, NATO clearly is reluctant to rearm and certainly cannot mount anti-Russian offensives, as Moscow knows. Nowhere does Russia predict that combat operations are in sight or imminent (*Voyennaya Doktrina Rossiiskoi Federatsii*, 2014). Moreover, its strictures against U.S. missile defenses in Europe that supposedly are the greatest military issue dividing East and West and a threat to strategic stability are a canard, as Russian writers freely admit (Arbatov and Dvorkin, 2013, p. 8).

Nuclear weapons represent priority, even critical, parts of Putin's so-called asymmetric or indirect strategy. And their continued procurement is unceasing. Chief of the General Staff, General Valery Gerasimov, has recently admitted that Russia has violated the INF Treaty and his description of Russia's enhanced nuclear and aerospace strike capability attests to these weapons' priority ('Army,' 2017; Lisitcin, 2017).[2] In addition, the video that accompanied Putin's annual speech to the Federal Assembly on March 1, 2018, showed missile systems that also clearly violated the INF Treaty (Putin, 2018).

These sectors are critical not only because they are procurement priorities but also because Russia has clearly envisaged fighting a limited nuclear war and may still think in terms of doing so. Admittedly, Russia's most recent military doctrines proclaim greater reliance on non-nuclear or conventional deterrence (Text of Russian Defense Doctrine, 2010; 'Military

Doctrine of the Russian Federation,' 2010; *Voyennaia Doktrina Rossiiskoi Federatsii*, 2014; *Natsional'naya Strategiya Bezopasnosti Rossii, do 2020 Goda*, 2009). But procurements and exercises, such as the recent Zapad 2017 exercise, point to an entirely different conclusion, namely anticipation of actual nuclear warfighting. Therefore, controversies over the role of nuclear weapons in Russian strategy and the question whether or not Russia has a high or low threshold for nuclear use remain unresolved (Ven Bruusgaard, 2017).

This evidence could explain Russia's nuclear priority and programs. Therefore, we must first grasp that Russia is at war with the West and sees the West as an inveterate adversary (Shalal, 2017). Indeed, Putin is intensifying Russia's militarization. In November 2017, he demanded that Russian business prepare for wartime production and mobilization while unveiling a $321 billion defense program through 2025 (Golts, 2014, 2016; Carroll, 2017). Recent reports suggest further joint Russo-Belarusian development of military infrastructure in Belarus and that the Zapad 2017 exercise were at least partly about seizing command of Belarusian forces, launching offensives to connect Russia by land with Kaliningrad, forcing Baltic neutrality by occupying those states, and preparing then for further offensives toward Warsaw ('Belarus, Russia to Develop Military Infrastructure,' 2017; Fedyk, 2017). Putin is even pondering having the defense industrial complex develop natural gas liquefaction plants, clearly a Soviet-type move ('Russia's Putin Says Defence Industry Could Aid LNG Sector,' 2017). Finally, the influence of the military in Russian foreign policy also appears to be growing (Osborn and Stubbs, 2017). Nevertheless, except for Ukraine and possibly Syria, this is not yet a kinetic anti-Western war.

Vladimir Putin has been at war with the U.S. and the West for over a decade ('Putin's Revenge,' 2017). Already on January 18, 2005, Defense Minister Sergei Ivanov told the Academy of Military Sciences that

> Let us face it, there is a war against Russia under way, and it has been going on for quite a few years. No one declared war on us. There is not one country that would be in a state of war with Russia. But there are people and organizations in various countries, who take part in hostilities against the Russian Federation.
>
> *(Gareyev, 2010, p. 729)*

More recently, Dmitri Trenin, Director of the Moscow Office of the Carnegie Endowment, observed that, for some time, 'the Kremlin has been de facto operating in a war mode' (2017). For example, by 2007–2008 – i.e. a decade ago – European Security services were reporting an enormous across-the-board expansion in Russian espionage, both traditional and economic (Open Source Center Report, 2008). This alleged war against Russia appears in current military thought as the promotion of 'color revolutions,' which the Russian military now defines as any insurgency against authoritarian regimes (Bunce and Hozic, 2016, p. 444). Moreover, the U.S. Defense Intelligence Agency argues that Moscow is building and modernizing its military forces to prepare for virtually any contingency to 'conduct the range of conflicts from local war through regional conflict to a strategic conflict that could result in massive nuclear exchange.' Consequently, we apparently do not face the threat of an imminent kinetic war, although the threat of such operations against our interests, our allies, and us has grown by several orders of magnitude since 2014 and the invasion of Ukraine.

This background helps clarify the reasons for the enduring nuclear priority. To be sure, many Russian analysts now argue that the defense sector, much like the Soviet sector, is virtually autonomous (Podvig and Sokov, 2016). Therefore, this sector is essentially producing, at least with regard to nuclear weapons, systems for which no real mission is indicated. Rather, they are only producing what they can do. Producers subsequently rationalize the mission, often couched in offensive and very threatening terms, to suit existing production instead of matching production to strategy (Podvig and Sokov, 2016).[3] If this analysis is correct, then the Russian defense industry, much like its Soviet predecessor, can supply many reasonably high-tech weapons to the Ministry of Defense and the military. But, also like its predecessor, the defense industry is regressing by imposing unfocused capabilities upon the state. This also comports with the dominance of the military and military rhetoric in policymaking and creates a powerful stimulus for a policy stressing military answers and threats of force first, rather than last (Osborn and Stubbs, 2017).

The nuclear program

Russian nuclear modernization programs encompass all three legs of its triad of air, sea, and land-based nuclear weapons along with short-, intermediate-, and long-range nuclear weapons. According to General Paul Selva (USAF), Vice Chairman of the Joint Chiefs of Staff, Russia is also developing new tactical nuclear weapons to tailor its forces to virtually any contingency (Schneider, 2017a, p. 132). And that is only one of over 20 Russian programs currently underway to manufacture and deploy nuclear weapons – e.g. a heavy intercontinental ballistic missile (ICBM), new bombers, new sea-launched ballistic missiles (SLBMs), and missile submarines (Schneider, 2017a, p. 135). Moreover, given current procurement plans and counting rules under the New START Treaty, Russia could actually increase its nuclear weapons and still comply with that treaty (Schneider, 2017a, p. 135). Finally, all conventional plans and exercises have an accompanying nuclear component, integrating nuclear options into operational plans and rehearsing them beforehand. Submarine-based nuclear strikes from the Arctic accompanied the recent Zapad 2017 exercises as did much less heralded nuclear exercises in Novosibirsk involving some of Moscow's newest nuclear weapons (Andriukaitis, 2017; Baev, 2017; Kofman, 2017; McDermott, 2017; 'Recent Russian,' 2017). This followed a pattern of coinciding nuclear and conventional exercises for Zapad 2009 and 2013 (Blank, 2015).

Thus, it appears that Russia's concept and program for nuclear weapons presents it with an apparent advantage over the U.S. As Mark Schneider writes,

> Contrary to popular belief, the United States does not enjoy nuclear parity with Russia. In fact, Russia has nuclear superiority. The illusion of nuclear parity is created by: 1) comparing the Russian active stockpile with the U.S. active and inactive stockpiles, 2) ignoring the 10-1Russian advantage in tactical nuclear weapons, 3) dismissing the modernization asymmetry, 4) disregarding the massive Russian advantage in nuclear weapons production capability, and 5) ignoring operating practices that keep relatively more Russian warheads on alert than American.
>
> *(2017a, p. 123)*

Russian political and military figures not only invoke nuclear responses to conventional attacks, but they also raise the prospect of preemptive and/or preventive nuclear strikes and freely make nuclear threats against any state 'rash enough' to join NATO if it is neutral like Sweden or that increases its defense effort like Denmark (Schneider, 2017a, pp. 121–140).

Moscow is also developing low-yield, high-precision nuclear weapons. When it refers to high-precision weapons, it does not specify whether they are conventional or nuclear because many systems such as the Iskander missile and all fighter-bomber units are dual-capable (Schneider, 2017a, pp. 121–140). Its tactical nuclear weapons are apparently intended both to compensate for conventional capabilities that may be lacking and to respond to conventional strikes (Schneider, 2017a, p. 126). In other words, tactical, if not other, nuclear weapons will be used in a first-strike mode. Exercises in Europe, Asia, and the Indian Ocean confirm this first-strike use of Russian nuclear weapons (Schneider, 2017a, p. 134).

Preparing for nuclear war scenarios Moscow also has deployed the new Sarmat heavy ICBM that possesses 10 metric tons of throw-weight and will reportedly carry 10 heavy and 15 medium warheads. Its launch weight is about 170 tons, and its destructive potential is 8 megatons and will clearly be Moscow's main counterforce weapon (Schneider, 2017a, p. 137). Similarly, Moscow is also building the 'Maritime Multifunctional System Status-6' a nuclear armed, high-speed 10,000 kilometer range weapon that could operate at a depth of 1,000 meters and reportedly carries a 10-megaton weapon. Its only conceivable purpose is massive countervalue slaughter (Schneider, 2017a, p. 137).

More recently, Pentagon sources and experts such as Schneider and James Howe estimated that at current rates by 2026, Russia will deploy 8,000 warheads while also modernizing deep nuclear bunkers. This total reflects certain trends beyond what we have noted above. First, at current procurement rates, Russia will reach the New START Treaty limits during 2018 and will probably break the treaty, as it has broken every other arms control treaty in the last generation. This 8,000-weapon arsenal includes larger, low-, and very low-yield strategic warheads. This assessment also contends that Russia plans to blend conventional forces with nuclear ones in future conflicts. The smaller yield warheads will be deployed on new short- and medium- or intermediate-range missiles like the SSC-8 cruise missile (the prime suspect in the violation of the INF Treaty) and the SSN-27 Kalibr' anti-ship land attack cruise missile. These new very low-yield weapons include clean weapons with little fallout, pure fusion weapons that do not require a nuclear blast to trigger them and, tailored effects weapons, e.g. neutron bombs, electromagnetic pulse blasts, and x-ray and gamma ray weapons (Gertz, 2017).

Meanwhile, Russia has systematically violated every arms control treaty except the New START Treaty: the INF and CFE Treaties, the Vienna Note on conventional exercises and deployments, and the treaty prohibiting emplacement of nuclear weapons on the ocean floor. Indeed, according to Schneider, 'we now have *four* different Russian ground-launched cruise missiles, two revealed in U.S. government sources and two reported in both the Russian and Western press, which have reported ranges that violate the INF Treaty' (Schneider, 2017c). These systematic violations of arms control treaties clearly aim to give Russia nuclear advantages vis-à-vis the U.S. But if the strategy is one of escalation dominance, it is also clear that based on its procurements Moscow intends to reach a state where it can threaten nuclear strikes tailored to the occasion to retain escalation dominance, intimidate potential adversaries, and be able to wage what it thinks are limited conventional or limited nuclear wars with impunity.

Nuclear strategy

Moscow's deployment of nuclear and conventional weapons indicates that it believes nuclear weapons deter both nuclear and conventional attacks. Such thinking directly rebuts the complacent and groundless notion that nuclear weapons only deter other nuclear weapons. For Russia both sets of weapons aim to deter the U.S. and/or NATO aerospace attacks (as Russia calls it), allowing Russia to operate offensively within the umbrella of its potent integrated air defense system (IADS). Consequently, Russian defense policy emphasizes medium to large-scale conventional and even nuclear warfighting at the expense of insurgency, counter-insurgency, stability operations, etc., even though those smaller-scale wars are the most likely threat its troops will face either in the North Caucasus or potentially in Central Asia once NATO leaves Afghanistan. Therefore, nuclear weapons are at the core of Putin's so-called asymmetric strategy to forestall NATO's conventional superiority. In May 2016, complaining about U.S. placement of missile defenses in Romania, Putin told the leadership of the Defense Ministry,

> As we have discussed already, we are not going to be drawn into this race. We will go our own way. We will work very carefully, without exceeding the planned spending on the rearmament of the army and navy, plans we have had for years, but we will adjust them in order to curb the threat to Russia's security.
>
> *('Meeting on Defense Industry Development,' 2016)*

Thus, the impetus toward asymmetry vis-à-vis the West is a principled, long-term Russian military strategy for waging high-tech conventional war with substantial and usable nuclear weapons on standby and on display. Even in Moscow's wars of a new type where information warfare (IW), cyber-strikes, media penetration, subversion, etc. play large roles, nuclear weapons are integral to this 'asymmetric' strategy and Russia believes this strategy could not succeed without those weapons.

Nuclear weapons serve a much broader strategic need than deterring real or potential conventional or nuclear strikes. As Dmitry Adamsky observes, 'The nuclear component is an inseparable part of Russian operational art that cannot be analyzed as a stand-alone issue.' This is because it abets Russian conventional threats and aggression through the deterrence of adversaries' counteraction to that aggression (Adamsky, 2015, p. 9). Similarly, Major Amos C. Fox (USA) writes that the strategic defense provided by Russian nuclear weapons and its IADS facilitate attainment of all of Russia's conventional warfare objectives: deterring NATO expansion into Russia's historic sphere of influence, retaining regional hegemony in Eurasia, and demonstrating improvements to Russian military capabilities (Fox, 2017, pp. 18–19). Beyond that

> The presence of nuclear weapons is perhaps the first critical component for modern hybrid warfare. Nuclear weapons provide insurance against a massive ground response to an incremental limited war. The offensive nation that possesses nuclear weapons knows that the adversary or its allies will not likely commit large ground forces to a conflict for fear of the aggressor employing those weapons against ground [or naval-SB] forces. This dynamic emboldens the aggressor nation. In the case of Russia, its possession of nuclear weapons emboldens leaders to take offensive action because they know that even the threat of nuclear employment forces potential adversaries to a standstill.
>
> *(Fox, 2017, p. 56)*

Moscow's behavior and apparent nuclear strategy validate these points because the document detailing that strategy and conditions for nuclear use is classified while open doctrinal statements are hardly revealing. To say that nuclear weapons might be used in a first strike if there is a vital threat to the state's survival is hardly revelatory for any nuclear power, especially one haunted by the real specter of state disintegration, cannot afford to lose any war. But Russia's 'nuclear behavior' is sufficient grounds for real anxiety. As Colin Gray observes, even though there is no sign of Russian discourse coming true concerning use of a nuclear weapon to defeat NATO in limited nuclear scenarios, Moscow talks as if it can achieve this outcome.

> In a manner that is ominously reminiscent of Adolf Hitler, Putin and others have chosen to introduce explicitly ruthless threats, including nuclear threats, into Russian reasoning about acute international crises. They hypothesize about the high political value that would accrue as a result of nuclear use on a limited scale. The hope, apparently, is that the NATO enemy, certainly the less robust members, at least, would be out-gunned either by the actuality, or more likely only by the credible threat of nuclear use (especially in a first-strike mode-SB).
>
> *(Gray, 2017)*

Not surprisingly, and as we argue here, Gray's inescapable conclusion is that escalation dominance is Russia's strategic goal.

> In the language of now-classic strategic theory from a past generation of theorists, the Russians currently are talking with apparent seriousness about *nuclear escalation dominance*. Russian theorists claim, perhaps expect, they could win a war wherein Russia employs nuclear weapons only a very modest scale. This expectation follows from a Russian belief that Moscow's employment of a few nuclear weapons would give them a decisive coercive edge in the diplomacy that should follow. Russian authors have advised us ironically that the use of these weapons would prove to be a decisive de-escalatory move – de-escalatory because NATO would be expected to capitulate. The high determination shown unmistakably by the fact of Russian nuclear use would surprise, even shock, audiences politically around the world. Thus with unmatched boldness Russia should achieve a considerable political, perhaps even military, victory.
>
> *(Gray, 2017)*

While no such scenario has yet occurred nor is it immediately likely, this does show just how nuclear scenarios are intertwined with conventional wars. Arguably a seamless web leads from conventional scenarios to and including these supposedly limited nuclear war scenarios perhaps using tactical nuclear weapons for which the West as yet has found no response (Giles, 2017, p. 3). Or as Finnish LTC Pertti Forsstrom argues,

> In this way the content of the concept of traditional strategic deterrence is broadened to cover both Russian nuclear and conventional assets. On the other hand, the abolishment of the restrictions for the use of nuclear weapons means that the dividing line between waging war with conventional or with nuclear weapons is vanishing. When the principle of surprise is connected to this idea, it seems that Russia wants to indicate that non-strategic nuclear weapons could be regarded as "normal" assets on a conventional battlefield. This is the basis upon which Russia regulates the level of deterrence for example in the Kaliningrad exclave. By introducing the concept of pre-emptive strike to its military means, Russia is trying to enhance its non-nuclear deterrence even further.
>
> *(Cited in Blank, 2018)*

And when one looks at today's and tomorrow's Russian nuclear procurement, this inextricability of nuclear weapons with Russia's war strategy becomes even sharper.

Nevertheless, the worst aspect of these deployments and plans is that they highlight the General Staff's and government's strategy as still being one of (supposedly limited) nuclear war. Previously key officials confirmed limited nuclear war as Russia's officially acknowledged strategy against many diverse contingencies (Franchetti, 2008; O'Mahony, 2008). The correspondent Ilya Kedrov, in his 2010 discussion of armored vehicles, ratified his understanding that Russian doctrine affirms this strategy (Kedrov, 2010). Likewise, Colonel-General Nikolai Solovtsov, Commander in Chief of the Strategic Missile (Rocket) Forces, stated in 2008 that new military uses for nuclear weapons are coming into being. Thus,

> The radical changes that have occurred since the end of the Cold War in international relations and the considerable reduction of the threat that a large-scale war, even more so a nuclear one, could be unleashed, have contributed to the fact that in the system of views on the role of nuclear arms both in Russia and the US, a political rather than military function has begun to prevail. In relation to this, besides the traditional forms and methods in the combat use of the RVSN, a new notion "special actions" by the groupings of strategic offensive arms has emerged. – Such actions mean the RVSN's containment actions, their aim to prevent the escalation of a high-intensity non-nuclear military conflict against the Russian Federation and its allies.
>
> *(Solovtsov, 2008b)*

At a September 2008 roundtable on nuclear deterrence, Solovtsov noted that Russia was explicitly considering the concept of 'special actions' or 'deterring actions of the RVSN aimed at the prevention of escalation of a non-nuclear high-intensity military conflict against Russia.' Solovtsov further stated that

> These actions may be taken with a view to convincingly demonstrating to the aggressor [the] high combat potential of Russian nuclear missile weapons, [the] determination of the military-political leadership of Russia to apply them in order to make the aggressor stop combat actions – In view of its unique properties, the striking power of the Strategic Missile Forces is most efficient and convincing in the de-escalation actions.
>
> *(2008a)*

Whatever changes have subsequently occurred in actual operational planning, nuclear weapons remain Russia's priority procurement program item and new models are being developed with hypersonic capabilities even as Russia modernizes older systems. And the extent of these programs far outstrips current U.S. modernization (Adamsky, 2018; Howe, 2018; Schneider, 2018a). Indeed, Russian officials – e.g. Viktor Bondarev, head of the Federation Council Defense and Security Committee – not only see no threat from recent U.S. nuclear exercises but actually claim that 'Russia's nuclear potential is significantly superior to America's' (Bondarev, 2017).

Since the late 1990s, Russia has developed and deployed: two new types of ICBMs, including a new road-mobile missile and a silo-based variant (Topol-M Variant 2 and Yars); a new type of SLBM, the Bulava-30, and two upgraded versions of an existing SLBM (Sineva and Liner); a new class of ballistic missile submarine (Borey); modernized heavy bombers, including the Tu-160 (Blackjack) and Tu-95 (Bear); and a new long-range strategic cruise missile (Raduga). Russia is also developing additional strategic nuclear weapons systems, including: a new road-mobile ICBM (Rubezh) and a new rail-mobile ICBM (Barguzin); a new heavy ICBM (Sarmat) with multiple independently targetable reentry vehicles (MIRVs); a new 'fifth-generation' missile submarine to carry ballistic and cruise missiles; and a new stealthy heavy bomber to carry cruise missiles and reportedly hypersonic missiles.

Despite Moscow's professed interest in new arms control treaties, this program hardly espouses disarmament. Furthermore, Moscow has long sought and is continuing to test weapons whose explicit purpose is to evade U.S. missile defenses which it continues to regard, in defiance of all science and innumerable American and Western briefings, as a major threat to its second-strike capability. In September 2017, Moscow tested both the road-mobile and silo-based versions of the RS-24 Yars solid-fuel ICBM in conjunction with the Zapad 2017 exercises, using 'experimental warheads' (Majumdar, 2017). In addition, Russia has recently announced that it will soon test a new generation of ICBMs that 'can beat US defense systems' and hold the US and Europe at risk. The new Sarmat, or Satan-2, RS-28 ICBM can allegedly destroy an area the size of Texas or France, evade missile defenses, and do so using hypersonic MIRVs that are permitted under the New START treaty. The hypersonic missiles that allegedly can be fitted to this system are currently in development under the title Project 4202, a label that evidently refers to the hypersonic glide vehicle (HGV) the Yu-71 (Gady, 2017). Russian sources claim an 11,000 kilometer range and up to 15 warheads for this weapon, a yield of up to 760 kilotons and the building of launch silos that could withstand seven nuclear strikes (Gady, 2017; Sharman, 2017).

Today, as Putin deliberately stimulates a domestic and foreign war psychosis, the prominent display of Russian nuclear capability aims to reassure Russian audiences, while intimidating Western ones (Van Herpen, 2016). As Paul Schulte suggests, they are also used for domestic political and psychological-informational purposes (Schulte, 2013, pp. 195–220). As he argues, devaluing nuclear weapons not only reduces Russia's domestic and global status, it also leaves Russia, seen through its leaders' eyes, vulnerable to Western probes and attacks on both its foreign and domestic interests since they see us as using military power to threaten domestic change (Schulte, 2013, p. 205). We cannot overlook the overall importance in Russian political culture of displaying Russia's capacity to intimidate others. Just as Russia desperately needs to see itself as a great power, it equally needs to be feared abroad. But since intimidation expresses a psychological relationship between the parties involved, prominently displaying nuclear weapons carries with it a powerful informational-psychological charge that also fully comports with Russian strategic thinking.

Russian writers since 2005 have increasingly delineated IW and the manipulation of targeted adversaries' psychological states as the most crucial element in modern war (Thomas, 2011). The intimidation effect carried by prominent displays of nuclear weapons aims to convince foreign observers that defying Russia means war and potentially nuclear war. Accordingly, since nuclear war is unthinkable, we must yield, or so the logic of Russia's position goes, at least in part, to Russian demands. Consequently, efforts at intimidation continue as regular probes – e.g. in the Baltic – that serve among many objectives keeping those states and NATO psychologically off balance. And those probes regularly include nuclear threats, as do probes against the UK, Sweden, Denmark, etc.

This thinking is discussed in a paper by Jacob Kipp and Matthew Kroenig. In the past decade and a half, Russia has come to rely more on nuclear weapons as a means of deterrence and for warfighting to manage local wars. The possibility of a local war against NATO remains Moscow's highest priority security threat. Russia relies on the early resort to nuclear use in part to offset its aggregate conventional inferiority vis-à-vis NATO. Moscow's concept of 'de-escalatory' nuclear strikes envisions limited nuclear strikes on NATO targets early in a conflict in a bid to frighten Western leaders into suing for peace on terms favorable to Moscow. Even if such strikes are never employed, the possibility enhances Russia's coercive leverage in a crisis and to blackmail threats in peacetime (Kipp and Kroenig, 2017).

Given steadily deteriorating perceptions of the external security order, growing apprehensions about the threat, and given Russia's continuing conventional inferiority to a fully mobilized NATO and the US, this perception and strategy for nuclear weapons creates strong pressures for first-strike use. As Kipp and Kroenig observe,

> Russia's nuclear forces and strategy also present a number of weaknesses, however, that could be subject to Western exploitation. Russia does not prefer dependence on nuclear weapons, but is forced to rely on them largely in order to offset conventional disadvantages. This creates a number of problems, including imposing demands for rapid escalation in the case of successful initial operations by opposing forces. In addition, leaders in Moscow must confront the prospect that limited nuclear warfare might be conducted across the depths of Russia's homeland if NATO honors commitments to the Baltic States and the conflict escalates to the nuclear level.
>
> *(2017)*

But while nuclear use in a first-strike mode to retrieve a losing conventional war and force NATO to de-escalate may be part of the strategy (escalate to de-escalate), that arguably is merely a part of a much broader nuclear strategy that relies heavily upon the psychological and intimidating or informational component of nuclear weapons (Schneider, 2017b). Thus, we see a broader nuclear strategy that aims to use these weapons to control the entire process of escalation throughout the crisis from start to finish. If the crisis becomes kinetic, then escalating to de-escalate may well become an operative possibility.

In a meeting in March 2015, Russian generals told Western delegates that any NATO effort to retake Crimea and return it to Ukraine would lead them to consider 'a spectrum of responses from nuclear to non-military' (Kalb, 2015, p. 233). Apart from the obvious physical threat and its intimidation 'quotient,' the information conveyed here clearly partakes of IW understood in Russian terms as manipulating opponents' psychological reactions and hence their ensuing policies. Putin too, undoubtedly with similar ends in mind, has frequently threatened nuclear strikes. Regular dispatches of bomber and submarine probes to all members of NATO clearly aim to intimidate and deter as that is the peacetime mission par excellence of bombers and submarines (Kirkham, 2018; Neff and Cimbala, 2018). But obviously for Russian leaders and commanders, nuclear weapons are also to be used for warfighting missions and operations. Indeed, as Sir Richard Shirreff, NATO's Deputy SACEUR from 2011 to 2014, has stated that 'Russia hardwires nuclear thinking and capability to every aspect of their defense capability' (Cooper, 2016).

Conclusions

Russia, since NATO's Kosovo operation in 1999, has gradually developed a nuclear capability and strategy that Western elites either cannot or will not understand. That strategy far transcends the catch phrase escalate to de-escalate (Schneider, 2017b). That formulation unfortunately exemplifies the increasing U.S. tendency to mirror image countries like Russia and depict their strategies and goals as if they were Americans. In fact, the nuclear strategy far transcends what Western leaders believe Russian strategy to be.

We must view Russia's nuclear strategy in the context of its thinking about and conduct of contemporary war in general. We now face an innovative kind of asymmetric warfare that constitutes a comprehensive challenge that simultaneously and constantly comprises conflicts that need not have any discernible starting point or phases as in U.S. literature. To use the U.S. military terminology, it is always phase zero and there is no discernible gap between war and peace. Or, as Lenin might have said, and certainly acted, politics is the continuation of war by other means. Ceasefires, actual conventional warfare, and incessant IW – defined as attempts to alter mass political consciousness in targeted countries – occur together or separately as needed and are in constant flux. Regular forces can be used conventionally or as proxies, irregular, or even covert forces allegedly for 'peacekeeping' or other operations. The actual use of military force depends on the effectiveness of nonmilitary instruments of power, organized crime, ethnic or other irregular paramilitary groups, espionage, political subversion and penetration of institutions in the targeted country, economic warfare, IW, and special operations forces. Outright victory need not be the intended outcome. It may suffice to secure constant leverage and influence on the military-strategic, political, and social situation in a state of no war no peace. Therefore, prosecution of such a war and resistance against it demand 'quick decision-making processes, effective inter-agency coordination, and well trained and rapidly deployable special forces' (Klein, 2016). It also demands a strategy of escalation dominance, even from a position of inferiority, in order to secure quick victories and inhibit a NATO response. Unfortunately, those are all areas where NATO is particularly deficient.

Therefore, we greatly err if we fail to realize that Putin and his regime have a strategy that they are following. Putin, despite the widespread view to this effect, is not a mere tactician or an uncannily gifted one. Instead, he possesses a strategy that we must grasp and illuminate (Hill and Gaddy, 2015). Putin is no strategic genius, but Washington's strategic insolvency and incompetence in crafting grand strategy over the last generation has allowed him to succeed as much as he has. Meanwhile, his reign is prone to major strategic failures – e.g. in Ukraine. In strategy as elsewhere, in the kingdom of the blind, the one-eyed man is king, and we are still blind.

Russia is still adding nuclear weapons at a rapid rate (Gady, 2017; Howe, 2018; Schneider, 2018a). At current rates of production, Russia will reach the New START limits in 2018 and past performance points to it violating the treaty. And the Pentagon evidently believes that within a decade, it could have as many as 8,000 nuclear warheads and modernized bunkers (Gertz, 2017). Moscow might well prefer non-nuclear deterrence, but its procurement, behavior, and overall psychology clearly betray an inclination toward nuclear warfighting and a strategy of escalation dominance.

Russian leaders, like their Soviet forbears, compensating for military and economic weakness relative to the other great powers, have innovated what they call a new-generation war or new type of war much as Lenin and Stalin used the international Communist movement and mass propaganda, and a gradually developing Red Army to lay the foundation for a permanent state of siege in world politics that only ended with the collapse of the Soviet Union in 1991. Not surprisingly, a leadership composed of KGB alumni under Putin has resurrected Leninist thinking and warfare, shorn of its Marxist ideology, but with its mentality and tactics fortified by new technologies and new tactics deriving from them. Consequently, the Russian strategy, for all its innovation, derives from profound Russian and Soviet historical roots and must be understood in the light of Russo-Soviet categories of thought and action, to be countered (Blank, 2017). Mirror imaging or complacent self-regard will misread the current war and result in severe losses. Therefore, we must grasp the nature of our situation and innovate in both thought and action to meet these new challenges.

Although Russia more often than not utilizes non-kinetic tools like active measures, cyberwarfare and IW, and the energy weapon, among others, this war features a profound militarization of Russian policy and an aggressive threatening posture toward the outside world. For example, in October 2017, Putin unusually publicly announced his personal participation in a nuclear exercise using all three elements of Russia's nuclear triad – air-, land-, and sea-launched nuclear weapons ('Vladimir Putin Took,' 2017). He also publicly displayed the use of the TU-22 Backfire bomber as a weapon carrying ICBMs directed against the continental US (Schneider, 2018b). Putin also confirmed the ongoing militarization of Russian policy by announcing that to date over 2,500 military exercises had taken place in 2017 ('Presentation of Officers,' 2017).

This posture derives from a long-standing threat assessment, like that offered above by Ivanov and the Public Broadcasting Service on its Frontline program on October 25 and November 1, 2017 ('Putin's Revenge,' 2017). It is hardly surprising that this has occurred, as Russia long ago abandoned any effort to impose democratic controls over its security services and has assigned its military intelligence service, the GRU, to formulate that threat assessment. In fact, Putin in 2007 stated that if the military determines something is a threat, then it is a threat (Felgenhauer, 2005; 'Putin Interviewed,' 2007; Tsypkin, 2012; 'Putin's Revenge,' 2017). Thus, this hostile posture, and the pervasive state message of Russia being a 'besieged fortress,' is an essential and long-standing component of Putin's domestic and foreign policy (Stoyanova, 2011).

Even more crucial is the need to realize that this state of war and threat assessment preceded Russia's invasion of Crimea and subsequent new defense and national security doctrines of 2014–2016 by several years (*Voyennaya Doktrina Rossiiskoi Federatsii*, 2014). Indeed, given production schedules, the nuclear weapons that have come on line in the past few years were ordered in 2005–2007, exactly when Ivanov first said that Russia was at war with the West. Thus, the strategy transcends wartime escalation to compel NATO or the US to de-escalate. Rather, nuclear weapons are part of a broader strategy of escalation control throughout any crisis and thus have the purpose of constant intimidation. As Dmitri Adamsky indicates, they are an essential component of a cross-domain strategy. Thus, cross-domain coercion actually represents a form of warfare targeted on societies and states' resilience and ability to comprehend and act upon reality. As Adamsky writes,

> The current Russian cross-domain coercion campaign is an integrated whole of non-, informational, and non-nuclear types of deterrence and compellence. Finally, the campaign contains a holistic informational (cyber) operation, waged simultaneously on the digital-technological and on the cognitive-psychological fronts, which skillfully merges military and non-military capabilities across nuclear, conventional, and non-conventional domains.
>
> *(2018, pp. 1–2)*

Indeed, nuclear weapons fit right into this perspective on contemporary war. Deliberately reckless rhetoric, nuclear overflights, and submarine probes all comprise this aspect of contemporary wars and none of these phenomena would be unfamiliar to the fathers of deterrence theory, Schelling, Brodie, Kissinger, Wohlstetter, Kahn, etc. But these tactics do highlight the fact that the psychology and character of the regime are essentially those of an intimidation culture. As Andrei Soldatov and Irina Borogan observe, 'The Putin system is all about intimidation, more often than actual coercion, as an instrument of control' (2015, p. 314). Accordingly, the emphasis on nuclear weapons not only relates to this system or culture of intimidation, it also fully comports with the long-standing element of Russian political culture that relies on the external projection of fear in order to augment the regime's domestic support (Durkalec, 2016; Nalbandov, 2016; O'Mahony, 2008). Consequently, Putin's strategy has been to amass instruments comparable to what he and his entourage believe the West is deploying against them and deploy them preemptively and uninterruptedly against the West. Moreover, while the West devalues nuclear weapons in rhetoric and policy Russia must elevate their utility because it lacks other means of suasion that can be deployed instead of nuclear weapons and intimidating threats (Schulte, 2013, p. 204). This effort at nuclear intimidation continues. Therefore, we can expect that Russia's reliance upon nuclear weapons will grow even if it procures more advanced conventional deterrence systems and nuclear weapons duly remain the procurement priority through 2025 (Schulte, 2013, p. 204).

We can say much more about Russian nuclear policy and strategy, but what is crucial here is that we see this strategy not through Western eyes and/or categories and premises that Moscow has never accepted, i.e. mirror imaging. Rather, we should see it through Russian perceptions and categories. Then, the bureaucratic factors of potential defense sector autonomy and the policy factors deriving from Putin and the military's understandings and perceptions become clear. There are many reasons why Moscow sees nuclear weapons and nuclear war differently than we do. And if we fail to grasp that, then our renewed effort to make sense of Russian military thinking and policy will founder on the rocks of our own myopia.

Notes

1 For the latest such example, see 'Russian Navy to Focus on Strategic Non-nuclear Deterrence' (2018); for doctrinal information, see *Voyennaya Doktrina Rossiiskoi Federatsii* (2014).
2 Both items were made available to the author by Dr. Mark Schneider.
3 For the Soviet period, see Almquist (1992).

References

Almquist, Peter (1992) *Red Forge: Soviet Military Industry Since 1965*, New York: Columbia University Press.
Andriukaitis, Lukas (2017) 'Military Matters: Russia's Big Guns on the Move: Analyzing Russia's Strategic Missile Forces,' *Novosibirsk Oblast*. www.medium.com, October 24, 2017.
Arbatov, Alexei and Vladimir Dvorkin (2013) *The Great Strategic Triangle*, Carnegie Endowment for International Peace, The Carnegie Papers. http://carnegieendowment.org/files/strategic_triangle.pdf
'Army; Russia Sets Up Delivery Vehicles that Can Carry Precision-Guided Missiles Up to 4,000 km – General Staff,' (2017) *Interfax*, November 7.
Baev, Pavel K. (2017) 'Militarization and Nuclearization: The Key Features of the Russian Arctic,' *Real Clear Defense*, November 1. www.realcleardefense.com/articles/2017/11/01/militarization_and_nuclearizaFtion_the_key_features_of_the_russian_arctic_112562.html
'Belarus, Russia to Develop Military Infrastructure,' (2017) *Tass*, December 8, 2017. Retrieved from BBC Monitoring.
Blank, Stephen (2015) 'What Do the Zapad-2013 Exercises Reveal?' in Liudas Zdanavicius and Matthew Cezkaj, Eds., *Russia's 2013 Zapad Military Exercise: Lessons for Baltic Regional Security*, Washington, D.C.: Jamestown Foundation, pp. 8–13.
Blank, Stephen (2017) 'The Flight of the Red Phoenix: The Historical Basis of Russian Non-Linear Warfare,' in Mahendra Gaur, Ed., *Area Studies Europe*, New Delhi: Foreign Policy Research Centre, pp. 69–100.
Blank, Stephen (2018) *The Russian Military in Contemporary Perspective*, Carlisle Barracks, PA: Strategic Studies Institute, US Army War College.

Bondarev, Viktor (2017) 'Corridors of Power; Head of Federation Council Defense Committee Sees No Threat in U.S. Nuclear Exercise,' *Interfax-America*, October 30, 2017 as made available to the author by Mark Schneider.

Bunce, Valerie and Aida Hozic (2016) 'Diffusion-Proofing and the Russian Invasion of Ukraine,' *Demokratizatsiya*, XXIV, No. 4, Fall, p. 444.

Carroll, Oliver (2017) 'Vladimir Putin Says All Big Russian Businesses Should Be Ready for War Production,' November 22. www.independent.com.uk

Cooper, Charlie (2016) 'NATO Risks Nuclear War with Russia "Within a Year," Warns Senior General,' *The Morning Bulletin*, May 18. www.themorningbulletin.com.au/news/nato-risks-nuclear-war-russia-within-year-general/3029027/

Durkalec, Jacek (2016) 'Russia's Evolving Nuclear Strategy and What It Means for Europe,' *European council on Foreign Relations*, July 5, 2016. www.ecfr.eu

Fedyk, Igor (2017) 'Zapad 2017: A Test for the West,' *Eurasia Daily Monitor*, October 3, 2017. www.jamestwon.org

Felgenhauer, Pavel (2005) 'Russia's Imperial General Staff,' *Perspective*, XVI, No. 1, October–November. www.bu.ed./iscip/vol16/felgenhauer

Fox, Amos C. (2017) 'Hybrid Warfare: The 21st Century Russian Way of Warfare,' School of Advanced Military Studies United States Army Command and General Staff College, Fort Leavenworth.

Franchetti, Mark (2008) 'Russia's New Nuclear Challenge to Europe,' *www.Timesonline*, August 17.

Gady, Franz-Stefan (2017) 'Russia to Test Deadliest Nuke Twice before Year's End,' *The Diplomat*, October 24. https://thediplomat.com/2017/10/russia-to-test-deadliest-nuke-twice-before-years-end/

Gareyev, Mahmut Akhmetovich (2010) *Srazheniya na Voenno-Istoricheskom Fronte*, Moscow: ISAN Press, p. 729, cited in MG I.N. Vorob'ev (RET) and Col. V.A. Kisel'ev (Ret), 'Strategies of Destruction and Attrition,' Moscow, *Military Thought*, in English, NO. 1, 2014, January 1, 2014–March 31, 2014, accessed, June 2, 2014.

Gertz, Bill (2017) 'Russia Sharply Expanding Nuclear Arsenal, Upgrading Underground Facilities,' *Washington Free Beacon*, December 13. http://freebeacon.com/national-security/russia-sharply-expanding-nuclear-arsenal-upgrading-underground-facilities/

Giles, Keir (2017) 'Assessing Russia's Reorganized and Rearmed Military,' Carnegie Endowment for International Peace, May 3. http://carnegieendowment.org/2017/05/03/assessing-russia-s-reorganized-and-rearmed-military-pub-69853

Golts, Aleksandr (2014) 'Russia Is Preparing for a New Arms Race,' *Moscow times*, December 15, 2014. www.moscowtimes.com

Golts, Aleksandr (2016) 'Modernization Vs. Mobilization,' Paper Presented to the Conference, the Russian Military in Contemporary Perspective, Washington, D.C. May 9–10, 2016, in Stephen J. Blank, Ed., *The Russian Military in Contemporary Perspective*, Carlisle Barracks, PA: Strategic Studies Institute, US Army War College, 2018.

Gorenburg, Dmitry (2017) 'Russia's Military Modernization Plans: 2018–2027,' *Ponars Eurasia, Program on New Approaches to Security and Research in Eurasia,* Policy Memo 496, November. www.ponarseurasia.org/memo/russias-military-modernization-plans-2018-2027

Gray, Colin S. (2017) 'Strategic Sense and Nuclear Weapons Today,' *National Institute for Public Policy*, Information Series No. 425, December 11. www.nipp.org

Hill, Fiona, and Clifford G. Gaddy (2015) *Mr. Putin: Operative in the Kremlin*, Washington, D.C.: Brookings Institution Press, Revised Edition, pp. 339–340.

Howe, James R. (2018) 'Future Russian Strategic Nuclear and Non-Nuclear Forces: 2022,' in Stephen J. Blank, Ed., *The Russian Military in Contemporary Perspective*, Carlisle Barracks, PA: Strategic Studies Institute, US Army War College.

Kalb, Marvin (2015) *Imperial Gamble: Putin, Ukraine, and the New Cold War*, Washington, DC: Brookings Institution Press.

Kedrov, Ilya (2010) 'An Expert Evaluation: A Universal Armored Vehicle; The Infantry Needs a Fundamentally New Combat Vehicle and Not a Taxi to the Forward Edge of the Battle Area,' Moscow, *Voyenno-Promyshlennyi Kuryer Online*, in Russian, May 26, 2010, *FBIS SOV*, June 4, 2010.

Kipp, Jacob and Matthew Kroenig (2017) 'Russian Nuclear Weapons Programs: Strengths and Weaknesses,' Paper Prepared for the Lexington Institute, July 24, 2017.

Kirkham, Thomas C. (2018) 'Modernizing the Nuclear Bomber Force: A National Security Imperative,' in Stephen J. Cimbala and Adam Lowther, Eds., *Defending the Arsenal: Why the Nuclear Triad Still Matters*, Forthcoming, Aldershot: Ashgate Publishing Company, pp. 79–90.

Klein, Margarete (2016) *Russia's Military; on the Rise?* Transatlantic Academy, 2015–2016 Paper Series, pp. 8–9. www.gmfus.org

Kofman, Michael (2017) 'Zapad 2017: Beyond the Hype, Important Lessons for the US and NATO,' *European Leadership Network*, October 27. www.europeanleadershipnetwork.org/commentary/zapad-2017-beyond-the-hype-important-lessons-for-the-us-and-nato/

Lisitcin, Pavel (2017) 'Russia's Nuclear Forces Can Inflict "Unacceptable Damage" on Any Aggressor – MoD,' *Sputnik.com*, November 7.

Majumdar, Dave (2017) 'Russia's Just Tested Its New ICBM Armed with "Experimental Warheads",' *Yahoo*, September 23. www.nationalinterest.org

McDermott, Roger (2017) 'Zapad 2017 and the Initial Period of War,' *Eurasia Daily Monitor*, September 20. www.jamestown.org

'Meeting on Defense Industry Development,' (2016) May 13. http://en.kremlin.ru/events/president/news/51911

'Military Doctrine of the Russian Federation,' (2010) February 5. *Open Source Center, Foreign Broadcast Information Service, Central Eurasia, (FBIS SOV)*, February 9, 2010. www.kremlin.ru

Natsional'naya Strategiya Bezopasnosti Rossii, do 2020 Goda (2009). Moscow, Security Council of the Russian Federation, May 12. www.scrf.gov.ru; available in English from *FBIS SOV*, May 15, 2009, in a translation from the Security Council website (NSS); *Natsional'naya Strategiya Bezopasnosti Rossii*, December 31, 2015. www.kremlin.ru

Neff, Donald M. and Stephen J. Cimbala (2018) 'Nuclear Arms Reductions after *NEW START*: Obstacles and Options,' in Stephen J. Cimbala and Adam Lowther, Eds., *Defending the Arsenal: Why the Nuclear Triad Still Matters*, Forthcoming, Aldershot: Ashgate Publishing Company.

Nalbandov, Robert (2016) *Not By Bread Alone: Russian Foreign Policy Under Putin*, Washington, DC: Potomac Books, pp. 19–116.

O'Mahony, Paul (2008) 'Bildt Plays Down Russian Nuclear Threat,' *The Local*, August 18, 2008. www.thelocal.se/13780/20080818

Open Source Center Report (2008) *Europe –Economic Espionage a Growing Concern for Intelligence Services, Business*, May 12.

Osborn, Andrew and Jack Stubbs (2017) 'Backed By Putin, Russian Military Pushes into Foreign Policy,' December 13. www.reuters.comn

Podvig, Pavel and Nikolai Sokov (2016) Remarks during the Program, 'Russian Nuclear Strategy,' Center for Strategic and International Studies, Washington, D.C., June 27, 2016. www.csis.org/events/russian-nuclear-strategy

'Presentation of Officers Appointed to Senior Command Posts,' (2017) October 27. http://en.kremlin.ru/events/president/news/55923

Putin, Vladimir (2018) 'Presidential Address to the Federal Assembly,' March 1, 2018. http://en.kremlin.ru/events/president/news/56957

'Putin Interviewed by Journalists from G8 Countries – Text,' (2007) June 4, 2007. Retrieved from Nexis-Lexis. www.kremlin.ru

'Putin's Revenge,' (2017) November 25–December 1. www.pbs.org/wgbh/frontline/film/putins-revenge

'Recent Russian Nuclear Forces Exercises Larger than First Believed,' (2017) *Forward Observer*, Oct. https://forwardobserver.com/2017/10/recent-russian-nuclear-forces-exercises-larger-than-first-believed/

Russian Defense Doctrine (2010) www.carnegieendowment.org/files/2010russia_militarydoctrine.pdf

'Russian Navy to Focus on Strategic Non-nuclear Deterrence – Commander-in-Chief,' (2018) TASS Russian News Agency, January 1. http://tass.com/defense/983872

'Russia's Putin Says Defence Industry Could Aid LNG Sector,' (2017) *Interfax*, December 8, 2017. Retrieved from BBC Monitoring.

Schneider, Mark B. (2017a) 'Russian Nuclear Strategy,' *Journal of Strategy and Politics*, II, No. 1.

Schneider, Mark B. (2017b) 'Escalate to Deescalate,' *Proceedings of the US Naval Institute,* February 2017. www.usni.org/magazines/proceedings/2017-02/escalate-de-escalate

Schneider, Mark B. (2017c) 'Additional Russian Violations of Arms Control Agreements,' *Real Clear Defense*, December 18. ww.readlcleardefense.com

Schneider, Mark B. (2018a) 'Russian Nuclear Weapons Policy and Programs, the European Security Crisis, and the Threat to NATO,' in Stephen J. Blank, Ed., *The Russian Military in Contemporary Perspective*, Carlisle Barracks, PA: Strategic Studies Institute, US Army War College.

Schneider, Mark B. (2018b) 'Putin Nukes Trump,' *Real Clear Defense*, November 28, 207, www.realclear defense.com/articles/2017/11/28/putin_nukes_trump_112689.haml

Schulte, Paul (2013) 'The Strategic Risks of Devaluing Nuclear Weapons," *Contemporary Security Policy*, XXXIV, No. 1, pp. 195–220.

Shalal, Andrea (2017) 'NATO Sees Growing Russia, China Challenge: Higher Risk of War,' *Reuters*, November 28. www.businessinsider.com/r-nato-sees-growing-russia-china-challenge-higher-risk-of-war-2017-11

Sharman, Jon (2017) 'Russia to Test New Generation of Intercontinental Missile that Can' Beat US Defense Systems,' *Independent*, October 24. www.independent.co.uk

Soldatov, Andrei and Irina Bogoran (2015) *The Red Web: The Struggle between Russia's Digital Dictators and the New Online Revolutionaries*, New York: Public Affairs.

Solovtsov, Nikoaie (2008a) 'Russia RVSN Military Academy Discussing Strategic Deterrence,' *ITAR-TASS*, Johnson's Russia List, No. 173, September 22, 2008, ww.worldsecurityinstitute.org

Solovtsov, Nikolai (2008b) *Foreing Broadcast Information Service. Soviet Union*, October 19.

Stoyanova, Tatiana (2011) 'Are 'They' the Main Threat to Russia?' Moscow, *politkom.ru*, in Russian, *FBIS SOV*, February 25.

Thomas, Timothy L. (2011) *Recasting the Red Star: Russia Forges Tradition and Technology through Toughness*, Ft. Leavenworth, KS: Foreign Military Studies office, US Army.

Trenin, Dimitri (2017) cited in Ivo H. Daalder, 'Responding to Russia's Resurgence: Not Quiet on the Eastern Front,' *Foreign Affairs*, November–December 2017. www.foreignaffairs.com/articles/russia-fsu/2017-10-16/responding-russias-resurgence

Tsypkin, Mikhail (2012) 'Russia, America, and Missile Defense,' *Defense & Security Analysis*, XXVIII, No. 1, p. 57.

Van Herpen, Marcel H. (2016) *Russia's Nuclear Threats and the Security of the Baltic States*, Cicero Foundation Great Debate Paper, No. 16/05, 2016, pp. 3–6.

Ven Bruusgaard, Kristin (2017) 'The Myth of Russia's Lowered Nuclear Threshold,' *War on the Rocks*, September 22. https://warontherocks.com/2017/09/the-myth-of-russias-lowered-nuclear-threshold/

'Vladimir Putin Took Part in Strategic Nuclear Forces' Training,' (2017) October 27. http://en.kremlin.ru/events/president/news/55929

Voyennaya Doktrina Rossiiskoi Federatsii (2014). December 31. www.kremlin.ru

14

THE ECONOMIC TOOLS OF RUSSIAN SECURITY STRATEGY

Nikita Lomagin

As Paul Stronski and Richard Sokolsky recently observed, since Vladimir Putin returned to the Kremlin in 2012,

> Russia has engaged in a broad, sophisticated, well-resourced, and – to many observers – surprisingly effective campaign to expand its global reach. Russia's objectives include, first and foremost, building a multipolar world order, demonstrating its status as a global superpower, and promoting specific Russian commercial, military, and energy interests. By doing so, Moscow has relied on a wide array of diplomatic, military, intelligence, cyber, trade, energy, and financial tools to influence political systems, public attitudes, and elite decision-makers not only in post-Soviet states, but also in Europe, the Middle East, Africa, Asia, and Latin America.... Finding examples of Russian global activism is easy. Assessing its motivations, consequences, and effectiveness is not.
>
> *(2017, pp. 3–4)*

The paradox of Russian power seems to be in the substantial gap between what is traditionally viewed as economic power and the Kremlin's foreign policy results. Indeed, as World Economic Forum data show, the Russian Federation's economic power is rather modest. But, despite declines in commodity prices, the effects of economic sanctions imposed by the US and other nations, a high rate of capital flight and brain drain from Russia, and for all of Russia's domestic problems – it has projected a surprising amount of power, not only in its neighbourhood but also beyond (Stent, 2016, p. 106).

How could a state with a rather weak economy[1] have achieved so much – managed to build its own integration grouping in post-Soviet space, went well beyond the ambitions of a regional power, and even challenged US predominance on the world stage, being called a 'revisionist' state alongside China (see National Defense Strategy, 2018)? Is it a matter of luck or the incompetence of other players, or maybe Russia is not as weak as it is presented in mainstream reports and media? What role do economic tools play in Russia's foreign and security policy? What are the limits of Russia's economic power?

This chapter aims at the analysis of economic power as one of the key instruments of Russian foreign policy. It argues that although Russia's economy is rather modest, Russia surpasses its main competitors in post-Soviet space, the European Union (EU) and the US, in its ability to deliver economic benefits to its loyal neighbours. Since the collapse of the Soviet Union, general market access, a free visa regime, and access to its labour market, as well as energy subsidies and rapid financial assistance on easy terms are all available at a level that surpasses those offered by the US, the EU, the International Monetary Fund (IMF), the World Bank or European Bank for Reconstruction and Development (EBRD).

Harvard University Professor Joseph S. Nye correctly observed that the material dimensions of any kind of power are as important as strategy and the will to act and, in the case of economic power, should be assessed in the context of each market and its asymmetries of vulnerability (Nye, 2011, pp. 4, 51–80). If a state can utilize its most important comparative advantages and is capable of hedging its weaknesses, it is on the safe side. We will argue that the so-called 'strong' states (see Krasner, 1989, pp. 293–296) with medium-sized economies, which control the commanding heights of the economy via the predominant role of 'national champion' enterprises, can gain at least in the short run quite a lot in comparison with bigger economies operating within traditional liberal models.

Russia's advantages include the rather large size of its economy in comparison with those of other post-Soviet states, macroeconomic stability including substantial hard currency reserves and, hence, appropriate capability to provide financial help. Also, extremely favourable location between the two biggest global markets (Europe and Asia) might become vital for the shipment of goods in the future via the Northern sea route controlled by Russia. Yet, another geographic strength is the fact that Russia serves as the gateway between Central Asia and the EU. Possession of huge deposits of various mineral resources (first of all hydrocarbons, and metals) gives Russia some leverage in relations with resource-poor countries. And last, but not least, Russia enjoys some technological achievements which can be viewed as foreign policy tools for those who want to increase their energy security (capacity to build nuclear power stations, as well as various types of energy infrastructure, including pipelines) or to enhance the military capability of its partners (Russia is the second biggest exporter of weapons and is able to produce almost all kinds of sophisticated arms).

In *Geo-economics in the post-Cold War period*, Edward Luttwak asserted before the collapse of the Soviet Union that the waning of the Cold War has reduced the significance of military power in international affairs. Summarizing a supposed consensus within the Western foreign policy community in 1990, he posited a transition from geopolitics to geo-economics:

> Everyone, it appears, now agrees that the methods of commerce are displacing military methods – with disposable capital in lieu of firepower, civilian innovation in lieu of military-technical advancement, and market penetration in lieu of garrisons and bases.' Thus, the coming geo-economic age will not be one of harmonious global interdependence, but rather an age of continued state rivalry where 'the logic of conflict' will be expressed in 'the grammar of commerce'.
>
> *(Luttwak, 1990)*

This observation is not a new idea in International Relations. Economic strength has always been an instrument of political power, although the association between military and economic power is increasingly intimate. Marx compared the use of the economic weapon as an instrument of political power with the replacement of cannons by capital ('the dollar diplomacy' of the US). Attempts to solve international problems by the application of economic principles divorced from politics are doomed to sterility.[2]

For President Putin, the management of the economic agenda became a central component of Moscow's relations with the international community and its outlook on the world. The Kremlin sees nothing incompatible in using economic instruments to achieve long-standing political and strategic objectives. The former economic advisor to Vladimir Putin, Andrei Illarionov, even argued that since the mid of 2000s, the world had to deal with 'Russia, Inc.', where geo-economics and geopolitics are interrelated entities.[3] The fact that a lion's share of Russia's gross domestic product (GDP) is produced by the so-called 'national champions', where the state directly or indirectly occupies the dominant position, making this proposition quite convincing. Of course, it would be an oversimplification to state that such a 'Russia, Inc.' controls all the foreign economic activity of Russian companies.[4]

All of Russia's foreign policy concepts since 2008 stipulate economic instruments as one of the key factors in contemporary world politics. FPC (2008) reads, 'Together with the military power of states, economic, scientific and technological, environmental, demographic and informational factors are coming to the fore as major factors of influence of a state on international affairs.' FPCs (2013, 2016) put economic instruments in the centre of power relations.[5] Russia believes that the economic interdependence of states is a key factor of international stability and goes further in trying to legitimize its ambitions in post-Soviet space by arguing that

> new centers of economic growth and political power increasingly take responsibility for their respective regions. Regional integration becomes an effective means to increase competitiveness of the participating states. Networks and associations, trade pacts and other economic agreements, as well as regional reserve currencies serve as instruments to enhance security and financial and economic stability.
>
> *(FPC, 2013, 2016)*

There is no lack of literature on Russia's foreign and security policy tools and on Russia's strategy (see Pynnöniemi, 2018). As far as economic instruments are concerned, the bulk of publications are devoted to energy, in general, and to Russian oil and gas in particular.[6] Gas and oil diplomacy is presented as the main 'weapon' of Moscow in its relations with Europe and many post-Soviet states. Only a few research papers are devoted to other economic instruments (Nye, 2011; Stronski and Sokolsky, 2017). Indeed, energy, as such, and access to the vast Russian resources are the key for all Russia's neighbours, whether the former Soviet republics or the EU or Asian states (first of all, China and Japan).

Recalibration of energy tools: stabilizing oil prices, building pipelines, and focusing on the export of nuclear technology

Much academic work, as well as political and media coverage in the West, views the Russian energy sector from the perspective of European energy security, understood as security of supply. Concern is expressed about Europe's level of dependence on Russian gas, and the lack of readily available alternatives. Little academic research, however, aims at discussing the overall role of the energy sector in Russia's foreign policy. By and large, researchers study either the oil or gas sector, and a few experts try to provide an overview of the whole oil and gas industry, but no one looks at national energy companies (NECs) as a whole. As a result, a very important relationship between the Russian government and the NECs is missed, for the government has the authority to instruct and control the NECs in terms of their crucial decisions such as price policy, ownership, asset swaps and building joint ventures with foreign partners (Putin, 2012). As Georgetown University Professor Harley Balzer (2005) observed, even before becoming Yeltsin's heir, Vladimir Putin had argued in favour of the state's controlling all the commanding heights in Russia's energy sector.

Russia remains the key supplier of natural gas to the EU with about one-third of its market and will hold this position for quite a long time as other traditional suppliers such the Netherlands and Norway cannot meet growing demand in the EU while liquefied natural gas producers opt for higher profits in Asian markets. Obviously, part of Russian gas diplomacy is about relations with transit states, especially with Ukraine and Poland. New pipeline projects such as Nord Stream 2 under the Baltic Sea will allow Russia to bypass both states and, hence, will diminish bargaining power of those states based on their ability to stop gas flowing through pipelines that crossed their territory. If Nord Stream 2 and Turk Stream projects are implemented, transit of Russian gas through Ukraine will not only decline almost fourfold (up to 20–25 billion cubic metres per year) but also it might become much cheaper, which means a big loss of transit fee revenues by Ukraine and, thus, a further decline of the economic power of Kiev.

Still, building multibillion dollar pipelines to Europe and Turkey amidst low economic growth is an uneasy task for the Russian government. Non-trivial decisions were needed in order to finance those projects, and those decisions were made. In order to stabilize oil prices at a 'fair' level and increase oil revenues Russia made a deal with Organization of the Petroleum Exporting Countries (OPEC) in 2016 on output cuts.[7] The reduction in Russia's oil production was in marked contrast to its only previous collaboration with the group in 2001, when it agreed to cut supply, but actually delivered very little (Lee, 2018). In May 2018 with oil at about $80 per barrel, Russia and OPEC not only reached their goal but also established a high level of trust to ensure that this deal would be long-lasting through new forms of cooperation including, inter alia, 'measuring market stability', consultations, etc. The impending return of US sanctions aimed at Iran's oil exports along with the radical decline of oil production in Venezuela offer the opportunity for Russia and other producers to raise output while the group as a whole remains within its overall target. Thus, being a price-taker on the global oil market, Russia has substantially changed her oil diplomacy and achieved some tangible results in negotiations with the key OPEC member-state, Saudi Arabia. Contrary to the Cold War era, when OPEC led by the Saudis substantially contributed to the demise of Soviet power, especially after invasion of Afghanistan, it seems that Russia's deep involvement in the Syrian crisis did not prevent OPEC states from finding a common denominator with Russia. Oil (or interest in keeping oil prices stable and high) now closely binds former foes. This recalibration of the 'oil' factor might have substantial impact on other dimensions of Russia's economic tools, including gas and nuclear power diplomacy financed to a large extent from oil revenues.

Cooperation within the OPEC+ group went in parallel with big energy deals with new centres of energy demand, such as China, Japan and India, which have been looking for diversification in their energy supplies. Russia, with its vast natural resources, is an indispensable partner. For China, dealing with Russia means a secure flow of both oil and gas. In order to counter Western sanctions aimed at Russia's energy sector and to boost energy cooperation with its Asian partners, Russia provided access to its oil and gas fields of 'strategic significance'.[8] The government made it clear that exceptions for the subsoil law can be made, if foreign companies invest in Russia's energy sector. In 2016, the Russian government stated that Russia is willing to let Chinese and Japanese investors take majority stakes in large-scale oil and natural gas projects. Before the crisis over Ukraine, Russia rarely allowed significant foreign ownership of major onshore oil and gas fields, which it deems strategically important assets. As a result, several Chinese companies have since acquired Russian energy concessions. In 2016, Japan was also invited to invest and accepted the offer ('Russia opens', 2016).

Another important area of economic activity in the energy sector aims at creating long-term dependences via building nuclear power plants, first of all, in Europe (Belarus, Hungary, the Czech Republic, Finland) and Asia (China, India, Vietnam, Iran, Turkey, Jordan, etc.) (Stronski and Sokolsky, 2017). Almost all of these projects are financed by Russia and envisage storage of nuclear waste in Russia. While Russian national oil and gas giants – Rosneft and Gazprom – make the bulk of Russia's export profits, Rosatom projects Russian power to a number of states almost for century. In 2018, the portfolio of Rosatom's export orders envisages the construction of 33 nuclear power units valued at US$133 billion (Rosatom, 2018), while at the beginning of 2012 export orders were half as large, US$66.5 billion (Russia in Review, 2013).

Thus, Russia continues to diversify its income by exporting nuclear power stations to as large a market as possible ('Ten-year Russia nuclear export', 2014). The state has supported heavily Rosatom's export activities not only by building strategic long-term relations with importers of Russian high-tech but also by supporting the most important pillar of Russian security – its nuclear component. Moreover, by putting petrodollars into the nuclear sector, the state also creates a number of jobs in the most sophisticated sector of the economy and makes an important step towards its diversification. As Rod Adams observed,

> Nuclear power plants are long term, valuable assets that provide reliable, emission free electricity for many decades. The rub is that they also require a substantial amount of capital investment before there is any product to sell…. Russia's decision to invest in nuclear energy capabilities is a brilliant strategic move befitting a nation of chess players. It recycles an unexpectedly large revenue stream provided by selling oil and gas into assets that will provide long lasting power.
>
> *(2014)*

The migration regime – one of the key economic instruments of Russia in post-Soviet space

Migration policy in Russia under President Putin has evolved from a restrictive one at the beginning of his term in office, when the country faced severe security risks related to the Second Chechen War and international terrorism, to one of the most liberal in the territory of the former Soviet Union (FSU). Uncertainty in the late 1990s and the war on international terrorism fuelled feelings in the Kremlin that Russia was a sort of 'besieged' state where illegal migration was one of the most pressing 'soft' security threats. While the 2000 National Security Concept of the Russian Federation emphasized migration as a challenge, rather than as a chance to solve the urgent demographic issues in Russia, a more active approach to solving the demographic and labour market concerns has appeared since 2004.

The authorities decided both to stimulate the country's birth rate (e.g. the 'National Project' which grants a 'maternity capital' of US$10,000 to a family with two or more children) and to change the stance towards immigration by opening the doors for labour migration and the settlement of ethnic Russians residing in the territory of the FSU. A special national programme was started in 2006 for the accommodation of ethnic Russians who had immigrated. Labour migration has been more substantial, as it compensated for about half of Russia's loss in population in 2007 (contrary to just 13 per cent in 2006). According to the 2007 UN Report, Russia was the second biggest importer of labour after the US with 12.9 million immigrants who work mostly in construction in big cities such as Moscow and St. Petersburg.

Following the new 2007 migration laws, 2.1 million foreigners received work permits in Russia. This was viewed in the West as an important symptom that Russian was regaining its soft power (Hill, 2006). The old quota system for immigration existed until 2013, when the Federal Migration Service of Russia introduced an even more liberal law allowing foreigners to buy work permits for a very modest 1,000 RUR a month ($14), which makes the Russian migration law one of the most liberal not only in the region but also in the world. As a result, over the past several years, Russia has become a migration magnet for Eurasia (Lomagin, 2007). Since 2000, Russia's greatest contribution to the security and stability of its vulnerable neighbours has been through absorbing the surplus labour of these states, providing markets for their goods and transferring funds in the form of remittances (rather than foreign aid). Central Asian states, in particular, are fearful of the social consequences of large numbers of labour migrants returning to the region from Russia, if there were to be a political backlash against migrants or a Russian economic downturn. This migration to Russia has become a safety valve for the whole region.

The inclination to a migration model of development (contrary to service, industrial or resource-based models) became remarkable not only with regard to the Central Asian states of the Commonwealth of Independent States (CIS) but also for western and central regions of Ukraine, Moldova, Belarus, Azerbaijan and Georgia. According to some expert estimates (World Bank, 2016), annual money transfers from Russia to these CIS member-states before 2014 reached $10–$12 billion. In this respect, Russia plays the same role for the CIS member-states as the US does for Latin America, Germany for the Balkans, Turkey for refugees from Libya, Iraq and Syria since 2013, and France for North Africa, Saudi Arabia and other oil-rich states of the Gulf, as well as for Egypt, Pakistan and Palestine.

The bulk of revenues in most post-Soviet states come from migrants.[9] According to the World Bank data, in 2017 worldwide remittance flows were estimated to have exceeded US$615 billion and Russia was the third biggest remittance-sending state only after the US and Saudi Arabia with $16,590 billion – almost double the amount in 2015 ($32.6 billion). As a share of GDP, the small developing economies of post-Soviet space represent extremely high remittance dependency and can easily fall victim of external turbulence. The importance of remittances from Russia in GDP for post-Soviet states is quite high – Tajikistan (42 per cent), the Kyrgyz Republic (30 per cent), Moldova (26 per cent), Armenia (17.9 per cent) and Georgia (12.0 per cent) (OECD, 2016). It is worth noting that Ukraine is also highly dependent on remittances with $6.2 billion in 2015, which is exactly twice as much as the World Bank's current investment project portfolio in Ukraine (World Bank, 2016). Figures for 2017 did not change substantially as Annual Remittances Data show. In absolute terms, remittances to Ukraine, for instance, even increased to $7,895 billion. As for members of the Eurasian Economic Union – Belarus, the Kyrgyz Republic and Armenia which now enjoy free access to Russian labour market – remittances flows are quite stable (World Bank, 2018). Table 14.1 highlights Russia's foreign policy priorities and main economic instruments in order to achieve its key objectives in post-Soviet space. The focus is placed on both integration projects, as well as on the non-North Atlantic Treaty Organisation (NATO) status of former Soviet republics. Economic tools vary from country to country, and sometimes Russia has opted for simultaneous usage of several instruments from a box

Table 14.1 Russia's foreign policy priorities and main economic instruments

State	Interests			Instruments			
	Hard security (fighting terrorism; CSTO, military bases)	Eurasian Economic Union and soft security (drugs, illegal migration, etc.)	Status of compatriots (dual citizenship) and of Russian language	Energy subsidies	Market access	Liberal migration regime/visa regime	Loans/aid/debt relief
Kyrgyz republic	x	x	x		x	x	x
Ukraine before 2014	Black Sea Fleet, non-NATO status	CIS; transit of gas and oil	x	x[a]	x	x	x
Belarus	CSTO, military bases	Transit	x	X	x	x	x
Kazakhstan	CSTO	Status of Caspian Sea[b]	x	None	x	x	None
Armenia	CSTO, military bases	x	X	X	x	x	x
Tajikistan	CSTO, military bases	x	X	X	x	x	x
Turkmenistan		Status of Caspian Sea* gas and projects with China	None	None	None	None	None
Azerbaijan	Non-NATO status, missile defence	Status of Caspian Sea with Armenia	X	None	x	x	x
Moldova	Non-NATO status	Transnistria	x		x	x	x
Uzbekistan	Terrorism	X	x		x	x	x
Georgia	Non-NATO status	None	x	x	x	x	

a By 2004, energy subsidies to Ukraine reached $5.5 billion per annum.
b Including Trans-Caspian projects.

of sticks and a box of carrots. The common interest of all post-Soviet states is access to the Russian labour market. Comparatively high salaries in Russia along with visa-free regime made Russia a main magnet for migrants not only in post-Soviet space but also in Eurasia.

A time for muscle-flexing: cases of Russia's market rejection

Following the 1991 Soviet collapse, tensions increased after the election as president of Georgia in 2004 of Mikheil Saakashvili, who campaigned to bring the country into NATO – a red line for Russia – and made noises about reigning in two rebel regions backed by Moscow. Around the time that bans on water and wine from Georgia were imposed in 2006, a Russian tabloid printed full-page ads advising Russians to stay away from Georgian wine, mineral water and food. Then, Russia's chief sanitary doctor Gennady Onishchenko said the decision to ban Borjomi mineral water had been prompted by lab tests of the water on sale and checks that had exposed 191 Borjomi bottles without documents needed to reflect the quality and safety of the product. 'Checks that uncovered batches of the mineral water Borjomi without proper documents gave me grounds for ordering the customs service to ban imports of this mineral water into Russia,' Onishchenko said (Sputnik International, 2006). The damage to the Georgian economy was huge, for Russia was the biggest market for Borjomi, where the company controlled about 10 per cent of the Russian mineral water market. 'I had hoped the situation with [Georgian] wine would not be repeated, as it is a more civilized market, but the producers' inertia forced me to give up these hopes,' Onishchenko said (Sputnik International, 2006). 'It was purely political,' former Russian minister and top economist Yevgeny Yasin said. 'They were looking for a way to punish Saakashvili.'

The effects of the bans were severe, although robust foreign investment and state spending helped keep the country's economy growing. Georgia's wine exports plunged from $81.4 million in 2005 to $29.2 million in 2007 and have not fully recovered, reaching $64.9 million in 2012, according to government statistics. Mineral water exports suffered less and rebounded robustly, dropping a bit from $32.5 million in 2005 but reaching $59.3 million in 2012, as Borjomi looked further abroad for buyers. Winemakers did the same, with some success, but they are thirstily eyeing a chance to once again tap the market in Russia, with its population of 144 million. The failure of Mikhail Saakashvili to gain re-election after the August War of 2008 and following rapprochement between Tbilisi and Moscow paved the way for reopening the market for Georgian wine and mineral water, although there is still no visa-free travel regime for citizens of Georgia to come to Russia (Gutterman, 2013).

'Milk war' with Belarus

The factors that led to Russia's muscle-flexing with Minsk were different from those with Tbilisi. Minsk was and is in the orbit of Russia and has never seriously tried to escape. The reason for conflict was the unwillingness of the Belarusian leadership to allow Russian business to privatize some of Belarus's major milk producers. Milk in Belarus plays a significant role in the economy, as the country ranks fifth in the world milk market, and the President's Property Administration owns several dairy plants. Milk and dairy products are important exports for Belarus' agricultural sector, which employs 1 out of 10 people in the nation of 10 million.

Despite the large scale of production, Belarus exports milk mainly to Russia, thus rendering Belarus's position vulnerable to pressure. The response to this by the Belarusian government was to start talks with the EU on certification of Belarusian milk standards according to EU norms. But the chances of getting a significant market share in the EU are doubtful. According to Michael Griffin from Food and Agriculture Organization (FAO), the EU itself increased its milk production by 1.3 per cent to 165.7 million tonnes in 2016 and significantly reduced farmgate prices in many member countries ('Milk and milk products', 2016).

The reaction of Russia was to send its health inspectors, headed again by Gennady Onishchenko who had previously banned the import of several food products of Polish, Moldovan, Latvian and Georgian origin. Onishchenko advised Moscow to ban all imports of Belarusian dairy products, claiming they fell short of proper certification. The Russian authorities banned Belarusian milk and dairy imports and sales on June 6, 2009. These developments deepened a politically charged dispute between the two ex-Soviet neighbours, which are linked through a special treaty of alliance. Onishchenko's announcement came a day after Belarusian President Alexander Lukashenko claimed that Russia made a $500 million loan contingent on its recognition of the independence of Abkhazia and South Ossetia from Georgia. In late May 2006, Russia's finance minister, Alexei Kudrin, withheld the $500 million, the last instalment of a $2 billion loan, warning that the country could face default by the end of this year unless it overhauled its economic policy. Mr. Lukashenko reacted angrily. 'If it's not working out with Russia, let's not bow down, let's not whine and weep,' he told a gathering of economic officials the next day, BelTA reported. 'Let's look for our happiness in a different part of the planet' (Barry, 2009). According to Reuters, the relations between Belarus and Russia had been at a low since 2007, with Minsk being upset at rising prices for Russian gas and Moscow by Lukashenko's rapprochement with the EU. In response, Lukashenko accused Russia of trying to take control of Belarus' industries and destroy its sovereignty, adding that a long-discussed confederation of Russia and Belarus would create 'another Chechnya'. The Belarus Foreign Ministry said the ban was 'discriminatory trade restrictions violating international agreements'. Lukashenko and his delegation refused to travel to Moscow for the summit of the Collective Security Treaty Organisation (CSTO) of seven ex-Soviet states at which a plan for a joint rapid-reaction force was approved on April 14, 2009 (Barry, 2009). The Russian Foreign Minister Sergey Lavrov described the Russian ban as purely an economic problem, criticizing Lukashenko for linking it with 'issues of military and political security that answer to the interest of all CSTO members'.

Later in 2010, the Kremlin once again, for a short time, imposed restrictions on the import of Belarusian dairy products. In 2014, Russian Prime Minister Dmitry Medvedev threatened Belarus with an anti-dumping investigation of potential subsidies in the dairy industry. So milk always remains the focus of elites in Russia and Belarus. Most Belarusian milk products end up on Russian shelves. In the first half of 2013, Belarus exported more than $1 billion in dairy products to Russia, about 95 per cent of total dairy exports. The situation of extremely high dependence of Belarusian milk producers on access to the Russian market has not changed until now. Milk production remains one of the biggest priorities for agriculture. Over a 10-year period, Belarus increased its milk production from 4 to 6.5 million tonnes, and now it ranks fifth in the global trade of milk with 4 per cent of the market. However, the export of milk has almost only one direction, which is to Russia.

But it seems that this tool of Russia's policy towards Belarus is losing its power. As the member of the Eurasian Economic Union, Belarus can invoke article 58 of chapter 11 of Eurasian Economic Union (EAEU) Treaty which severely restricts the use of sanitary measures by member-states. Such measures can be imposed only in case of threat to the epizootic wellbeing of member-state. Obviously, milk and milk products do not fall under this category. Hence, the most recent decision of Russia to impose restrictions on milk products from Belarus from June 6, 2018, was successfully challenged by Belarus in the Committee for Technical regulation of the Eurasian Economic Commission ('Rossiju objazali poshadit' Belorussiju', 2018).

Concluding remarks

Since it is closely integrated into the world economy, Russia has paid a substantial price since 2014 for the overdependence of its financial and energy sectors on the West. Sanctions hit Russia's economy hard – direct losses reached more than $100 billion, while overall costs can be substantially higher. Still, Russia remains the biggest economy in post-Soviet space with practically the same economic instruments in its toolbox, thereby allowing it to maintain at a minimum the status quo. Having effectively recalibrated its energy tools, Russia has managed to overcome the economic slowdown and regain economic power vis-à-vis the EU, Turkey, and some transit states – Ukraine and Poland. Pipeline diplomacy not only enhances the energy security of exporters and importers but also creates jobs, fosters investments and paves the way for the normalization of the relationship with Europe. Closer engagement of Asian partners in the Russian energy sector gives flexibility to the Kremlin, in order to convey balanced global and regional politics. Rosatom's proactive strategy abroad provides for long-lasting interdependencies with a number of key states across the globe.

As for the future, Russia's liberal migration regime and easy access to the Russian labour market will remain one of the main trump cards in the Kremlin's game for dominance in Central Asia, where social and political stability depends heavily on remittances from Russia. This factor will be important in the near future, although remittances from Russia to the CIS declined as a result of the economic slowdown in Russia and the depreciation of the ruble. Finally, in order to dominate by economic means in certain regions, it is not necessary to be the biggest global economy. As structural realists have pointed out, in politics *what matters is first and foremost the relative power of states*. Thus, well-tailored economic policies to every particular actor might be enough to achieve the expected outcome, whether it is just one tool (access to the labour market) or a set of tools (general access to the market, subsidies, loans and credits).

Notes

1 Russia is the 12th largest economy in the world and about one-tenth the size of the US or the EU economies (World Economic Forum, 2017).
2 See the work of Marx, Lenin, Carr, Nye and other top analysts on the issue of power. Of special relevance here is Carr (1984).
3 For a detailed analysis of Putin's economic policy and the role of state, see Miller (2018).
4 The most vivid example of the contrary is the successful international business of Russian TMK group, which is one of the world's leading producers of tubular products for the oil and gas industry. Ironically, this Russian company's American division called TMK IPSCO, with almost 25 per cent of market share of welded and seamless pipe and premium connections, significantly contributed to the success of the so-called 'shale revolution' in the US. Since 2008, IPSCO has invested $437 million in manufacturing facilities in the US. IPSCO pipe is used under the most challenging conditions of hydraulic fracturing, horizontal-directional drilling and offshore production in all major oil and gas producing regions, including the Marcellus Shale, Eagle Ford, Permian Basin, Canadian Oil Sands and the Gulf of Mexico. – https://ipsco.com/wp-content/uploads/2018/02/IPSCO_Corporate_Factsheet.pdf – Accessed on May 25, 2018. As this gas began to be shipped to European markets, it reduced the power that Russia could develop through its pipeline diplomacy (Bordoff and Houser, 2014).
5 The terms 'economy' and 'economic' were used 66 times in various contexts in the 2016 Russian Foreign Policy Concept.
6 See, for instance, the studies by Stulberg (2007), Nye (2011), Åslund (2010) and Sussex and Kanet (2015).
7 Russia agreed to gradually cut 300,000 barrels per day. The deal, in place since January 2017, has 24 OPEC and non-OPEC countries jointly cutting a combined 1.8 million barrels per day. – www.platts.ru/latest-news/oil/stpetersburg/novak-says-opec-pact-favors-days-not-barrels-10447935. Accessed on May 26, 2018.
8 According to the Russian Federation Law on Subsoil Resources, to the category of 'strategic' plots belong recoverable oil reserves equal to or exceeding 70 million tons, and gas reserves equal to or exceeding 50 billion cubic meters.
9 For a comparison between Russian and EU migration policy, see OECD (2015).

References

Adams, Rod (2014). 'Russia Using Oil Wealth to Finance Nuclear Exports', Accessed on May 25, 2018 at http://atomicinsights.com/russia-using-oil-wealth-finance-nuclear-exports/

Balzer, Harley (2005). 'The Putin Thesis and Russian Energy Policy', *Post-Soviet Affairs*, 21(3), pp. 210–225.

Barry, Ellen (2009). '"Milk War" Strains Russia-Belarus Ties', *The New York Times*, 14 June. www.nytimes.com/2009/06/15/world/europe/15belarus.html?_r=0

Bordoff, Jason and Trevor Houser (2014). 'American Gas to the Rescue? The Impact of US LNG Export on European Security and Russian Foreign Policy', September 2014. Center on Global Energy Policy. Columbia University. New York, p. 34.

Carr, Edward H. (1984). *The Twenty Years' Crisis 1919–1939. An Introduction to the Study of International Relations*. Second ed. reprinted. New York: Macmillan.

The Foreign Policy Concept of the Russian Federation (2008). July 12. Accessed on May 24, 2018 at http://archive.kremlin.ru/eng/text/docs/2008/07/204750.shtml

The Foreign Policy Concept of the Russian Federation (2013). Approved by President of the Russian Federation V. Putin on February 12. http://archive.mid.ru//brp_4.nsf/0/76389FEC168189ED44257B2E0039B16D

The Foreign Policy Concept of the Russian Federation (2016). Approved by President of the Russian Federation Vladimir Putin on November 30. Accessed on May 20, 2018 at www.mid.ru/en/foreign_policy/official_documents/-/asset_publisher/CptICkB6BZ29/content/id/2542248

Gutterman, Steve (2013). 'Russia Set to Resume Imports of Georgian Wine and Water', February 4. Accessed on September 1, 2016 at www.reuters.com/article/us-russia-georgia-idUSBRE91402R20130205.

Hill, Fiona (2006). 'Moscow Discovers Soft Power', *CURRENT HISTORY*, October.

Krasner, Stephen D. (1989). 'Policy Making in a Weak State', in Ikenberry G. John ed. *American Foreign Policy. Theoretical Essays*. Princeton, NJ: HarperCollins Publishers, pp. 293–317.

Lee, Julian (2018). 'Russia Flexes Its Soft Power Muscles Extending Output Cuts Deepens Its Role in Global Affairs', Accessed on May 20, 2018 at www.bloomberg.com/view/articles/2018-05-20/russia-flexes-its-soft-power-muscles

Lomagin, Nikita (2007). *An Annual Overview of International Migration in Central and Eastern Europe – 2007*. Accessed on May 24, 2018 at www.migrationonline.cz/centraleasterneurope/2007/

Luttwak, Edward (1990). 'From Geopolitics to Geo-Economics: Logic of Conflict, Grammar of Commerce,' *National Interest*, Summer, pp. 17, 19.

'Milk and milk products' (2016). Accessed on May 25, 2018 at www.fao.org/fileadmin/templates/est/COMM_MARKETS_MONITORING/Dairy/Documents/FO_Dairy_June_2016.pdf

Miller, Chris (2018). *Putinomics. Power and Money in Resurgent Russia*. Chapel Hill: The University of North Carolina Press.

National Defense Strategy (2018). 'Sharpening the American Military's Competitive Edge', Accessed on May 23, 2018 at www.defense.gov/Portals/1/Documents/pubs/2018-National-Defense-Strategy-Summary.pdf

Nye, Joseph S. (2011). *The Future of Power*. New York: Public Affairs.

OECD (2015). 'International Migration Outlook', Accessed on May 24, 2018 at www.keepeek.com/Digital-Asset-Management/oecd/social-issues-migration-health/international-migration-outlook-2015_migr_outlook-2015-en#page12

OECD (2016). 'Non-ODA Flows to Developing Countries: Remittances'. Accessed on May 24, 2018 at www.oecd.org/dac/stats/beyond-oda-remittances.htm

Pynnöniemi, Katri (2018). 'Russia's National Security Strategy: Analysis of Conceptual Evolution', *The Journal of Slavic Military Studies*, 31(2). Accessed on May 20, 2018 at doi:10.1080/13518046.2018.1451091

Rosatom (2018). Accessed on May 27, 2018 at www.rosatom.ru/en/global-presence/

'Rossiju objazali poshadit' Belorussiju' (2018). Rossiju objazali poshadit' Belorussiju' June 6. Accessed on June 7, 2018 at https://m.lenta.ru/news/2018/06/06/bela_rus/

Russia in Review (2013). Accessed on May 27, 2018 at www.belfercenter.org/publication/russia-review-141

Russia open (2016). 'Russia Open to Japanese Ownership of Siberian Energy Ventures. Interview with Russian Deputy Prime Minister', February 22. Accessed on May 24, 2018 at http://asia.nikkei.com/Politics-Economy/International-Relations/Russia-open-to-Japanese-ownership-of-Siberian-energy-ventures. Accessed on September 1, 2016.

World Economic Forum (2017). 'Russian Federation', Accessed on May 21, 2018 at http://toplink.weforum.org/knowledge/insight/a1Gb0000000M77BEAS/explore/summary

Sputnik International (2006). 'Russian Borjomi Mineral Water Ban a Trade War – Georgia', RUSSIA. *Sputnik International*. May. https://sputniknews.com/russia/20060505/47350086.html

Stent, Angela (2016). 'Putin's Power Play in Syria. How to Respond to Russia's Intervention', *Foreign Affairs*, January/February, pp. 106–113.

Stronski, Paul and Sokolsky, Richard (2017). 'The Return of Global Russia: An Analytical Framework', *Carnegie Endowment for International Peace*. Accessed on May 20, 2018 at https://carnegieendowment.org/2017/12/14/return-of-global-russia-analytical-framework-pub-75003

Stulberg, Andam N. (2007). *Well-Oiled Diplomacy. Strategic Manipulation and Russia's Energy Statecraft in Eurasia*. New York: State University of New York Press.

Sussex, Matthew, and Roger E. Kanet, eds. (2015). *Russia, Eurasia and the New Geopolitics of Energy. Confrontation and Consolidation*. Houndmills: Palgrave Macmillan.

World Bank (2016). *Migration and Remittances Factbook 2016*. Third Edition. Washington, DC. Accessed on May 25, 2018 at http://siteresources.worldbank.org/INTPROSPECTS/Resources/334934-1199807908806/4549025-1450455807487/Factbookpart1.pdf

World Bank (2018). 'Annual Remittances Data (updated as of April 2018)', Accessed on May 27, 2018 at www.worldbank.org/en/topic/migrationremittancesdiasporaissues/brief/migration-remittances-data

15
RUSSIAN SECURITY STRATEGY AND THE GEOPOLITICS OF ENERGY IN EURASIA

Mikhail A. Molchanov

A key role that energy security plays in Russia's national security strategy has been determined by a combination of factors of structural, positional and relational nature. Starting with its global position, Russia is the biggest producer and the world's top exporter of natural gas, the third biggest producer and the second largest exporter of oil, and the sixth biggest producer and the third biggest exporter of coal. It is the third largest nuclear power producer and the fourth largest producer of electricity in the world. Russia's natural gas reserves are one-fourth of the planet's total, which is more than the combined endowment of six out of the top ten holders of natural gas reserves in the world. Russia is also the third largest consumer of energy in the world. Clearly, it is interested in securing national sovereignty over its energy resources and maintaining effective control over their use and development.

Talking of structure, Russia's key problem is the sheer size of the country, its vastness, diversity and the poor integration of its constituent parts. The National Security Strategy (2015) specifically mentions the completion of the formation of the basic transportation, energy, information and military infrastructures, particularly in the Arctic, East Siberia and the Far East, as a strategic imperative in the development of the economy. This is no less important for considerations of national security. Integration through the construction of new oil and gas pipelines, highways and railroads is one of the principal tasks of the intended infrastructural development.

Relational factors have to do with international trade and foreign and security policies of Russia and its partners. As one of the world's top exporters of energy, Russia is quite vulnerable to the external fluctuations in demand. This vulnerability gets even more pronounced because of the share of energy exports in the overall structure of foreign trade and the role energy exports play for the country's economy. Consequently, energy security is understood to include the state's fostering of the competitiveness of Russian energy companies, the safeguarding of the 'country's sovereignty in the world energy market' and the 'prevention of discrimination' against Russian energy exporters and extraction companies working outside the Russian Federation, the countering of the 'attempts to regulate markets in energy resources on the basis of political rather than economic expediency' (The National Security Strategy, 2015).

The country's security is always a function of its position and capabilities, relations with other states and the overall structure of the international system at the time. As geopolitics ties position, structure and relations together, any talk of international security implicitly involves geopolitical considerations. Energy security is no different.

Geopolitics and energy security

Conceptualizations of energy security have long been informed by geopolitical thinking. Just as national security broadly understood, energy security implies an ability to exercise a form of control over some physical space (geographic territory), which is subject to intentional (political) influences from outside. The political importance of the space can be assessed in terms of its natural endowments (resources feeding into material capabilities), structural properties (integrity, vulnerability, centrality and connectedness) and strategic value (i.e., position in relation to other areas of importance and an ability to serve as a conduit of influence). Energy is key to all these aspects.

Geopolitics forms an essential background in examinations of energy security for two main reasons: first, because both address the problem of resource determination of political agency, and second, because both assess power distribution in the world system of states. Considerations of energy security are those that relate to the state's ability to ensure that it has enough energy at its disposal to discharge its military and civilian functions effectively. Effective discharge of the state defence functions is demonstrated by its success in repelling aggressors and cultivating allies. Domestic effectiveness is gauged by economic development and comparative prosperity of the people. Both domestic stability and international security are assessed in comparison to other nations. Thus, energy security, while clearly related to resource endowments, geographic location and physical environment of a nation, should always be approached as a relational quality that reflects the inherently political nature of international relations: whether one nation is 'secure' or not is determined by a concrete configuration of forces in the international arena.

The central precept of geopolitics is the idea of political control and domination of physically defined space. Geopolitical analysis focuses on spatial aspects of power distribution in the world and on geography as a resource in, or an impediment to, power accumulation and dispensation in international relations. Since power is largely a function of the state's material capabilities – its economic and technological reach, the size and prowess of its armed forces and the extent of its command of the material world generally speaking – studies of the nation's relative standing in the world cannot skirt the question of the nation's material endowments. People and resources, energy first and foremost, form the foundation of the latter.

From its first appearance in Rudolph Kjellen's writings, geopolitics was concerned with the idea of national self-sufficiency (autarky) in natural resources. Karl Haushofer borrowed the idea of self-sufficiency from Kjellen and advocated ready access to energy carriers and steady supply of energy as important strategic goals. Haushofer's idea of a Lebensraum ('living space') was applied to validate imperialist conquests of resource-rich areas.

For Halford Mackinder, the world's centre of power was to be found in the Eurasian Heartland – the core area of what he called the World Island. The Heartland's self-sufficiency in natural resources, in addition to its sheer size and strategic location, informed the famous dictum: 'Who rules the Heartland commands the World-Island: Who rules the World-Island commands the World' (Mackinder, 1919: 194). This has some parallels to Friedrich List, who, in his National System of Political Economy (1841), maintained that economic growth of a nation must be premised on a robust combination of political and spatial controls over its territory, trade and industry.

James Fairgrieve, another early geopolitician, argued that the centre of power and influence in international relations was to be determined by the location of the world's strategic sources of energy. Fairgrieve suggested that states' ability to control energy was subject to geographic determinants and limitations, specifically those of a place and naturally given distribution of energy carriers. Fairgrieve predicted that, with the exhaustion of coal and oil production in the North, the energy-rich areas of the global South were bound to 'gain an importance at the expense of others not so fortunate' (1915: 334).

Modern Russian geopoliticians are continuing in this line of thinking. Thus, Alexander Dugin (2012) writes,

> In our world, energy resources are the direct instrument of a struggle for world domination. Americans are building the unipolar world. We are fighting for the multipolar [world]. This is why Russian energy politics is the most important, decisive domain in the upholding of our national interests.

Authors of a collective monograph entitled *Global Energy and Geopolitics (Russia and the World)* (Shafranik, 2015: 28) argue that because of its resource and energy potential, Russia 'not only can, but must formulate new geopolitical challenges herself, write her own "scenarios" for the development of the world's energy'. An idea of Russia's special, 'civilizational' role in the world acquires a new ring through an emphasis on the country's centrality for the development of energy transportation infrastructure in Eurasia: 'Energy increasingly becomes one of the key elements of geopolitics, while defining the character and configuration of international relations' (Bushuyev and Mastepanov, 2015).

Historical antecedents

In playing out energy geopolitics as a tool of its security strategy, Putin's Russia repeats what has already been firmly established by the former Soviet Union: that the control of energy resources not only helps international trade but adds to the negotiating power of the state on practically any other issue of international significance.

The principal objective of Russia's foreign policy has always been creation of a powerful state (McDonald, 2007). Energy sufficiency was seen as a necessary attribute of such a state. Characteristically, in one of his post-revolution speeches, Lenin (1920) chose to define communism as 'Soviet power plus the electrification of the whole country'. The growth in energy production was considered a prime objective of the state industrial policy and a key part of national security. Simultaneously, energy trade was used as a tool of Soviet foreign policy. In 1921, the Politburo approved the idea of oil concessions to foreign investors. At the Genoa Conference in 1922, Soviet negotiators succeeded in breaking the united front of Western firms and governments by dangling the prospects of oil concessions in the Caspian in front of the Italian government and Royal Dutch Shell. Soon thereafter, the Soviet policy of playing the USA-based Standard Oil against the Royal Dutch Shell precipitated the collapse of the oil blockade imposed by the West (Alekperov, 2011: 108–112).

By the early 1940s, Soviet specialists were prospecting for oil in Mongolia. In 1960, the Soviet government concluded its first 'oil for pipes' agreement with the Italian oil major Ente Nazionale Idrocarburi (ENI). In turn, ENI's head Enrico Mattei was instrumental in facilitating a visit to Moscow by the President of the Italian Republic Giovanni Gronchi, which caused much chagrin to those in the West who were bent on international isolation of the USSR.

Leonid Brezhnev and Alexei Kosygin made gas trade with Western Europe into a prominent tool of Soviet diplomacy that, among other things, pushed Willy Brandt's *Ostpolitik*. The February 1970 'gas for pipes' deal between the USSR and West Germany ensured modernization of the Soviet gas industry and fomented a 'gold rush mentality' (Lippert, 2011: 175) on the part of German businesses seeking to explore new opportunities in the East. Moreover, Russians demanded, and received, a number of political and economic concessions. The Soviets even managed temporarily to drive a wedge between Western Europe and the USA, which sought to block all sales of the advanced energy equipment and technologies to its Cold War adversary. The purchases of the Western-made pipes and compressor stations not only won Russians new friends in the European North Atlantic Treaty Organisation (NATO) countries, but helped bring Siberian gas to the countries of the Eastern bloc, thus cementing their loyalty to the USSR.

A successful formula of using Western money and technology to bring energy resources to the market essentially for free – repaying debts with oil and gas exports – was tried again and again. The construction of the Urengoi-Pomary-Uzhgorod pipeline for Soviet gas exports to Western Europe, called a 'deal of the century' by its promoters, was also dubbed 'Europe's new road to serfdom' by its critics. The detractors feared that, upon the project's implementation, Western Europe would be satisfying near 40 per cent of its gas needs with Soviet gas. Although this amounted to less than 10 per cent of the West European total energy demand, the USA went hysterical, claiming that 'the pipeline was meant to develop a dependency effect' and would assuredly become 'a handle of political manipulation through periodic withdrawals of the flow of gas' (Elek, 1982: 170). Soon thereafter, the American government was blacklisting European firms for doing business with the Soviets:

> Paradoxically enough, the US tried to blackmail Europe by imposing a ban on technology exports while contending that its main goal was to protect European countries from potential Soviet blackmail through a future ban on gas exports.
>
> *(Bonin, 2007: 248)*

The tactics did not work, however, and the embargo was soon lifted. The Soviet Union had never attempted to disrupt its gas flow to Europe for political reasons and was, in fact, deemed a more reliable supplier than, for example, Norway (Högselius, 2013: 201, 204). Russia's reliability as a gas supplier was brought in question only after the USSR republics became newly independent states and got themselves embroiled in conflicts over resource control and rents distribution. Even so, the share of Russian gas in Europe's natural gas consumption remained stable at around 25–30 per cent, and even grew to one-third of the total in spite of the Ukraine-related sanctions (Reuters, 2018).

Energy subsidies

The energy subsidies that the USSR had provided to its clients cemented what used to be called the world socialist camp and oiled the gears of its Council for Mutual Economic Assistance (CMEA). After the USSR ceased to exist, the Russian Federation continued providing oil and gas at preferential prices to Armenia, Belarus and Ukraine. The subsidies to Ukraine were fully eliminated only after the collapse of the Russia-friendly regime of Viktor

Yanukovych in 2014. The unified electric grid of the former USSR survived in the form of the Integrated Power System (IPS) of the region, which included Azerbaijan, Belarus, Georgia, Kazakhstan, Kyrgyzstan, Moldova, Russia and Ukraine.

Throughout the post-war period, preferential pricing in Soviet energy trade with members of the CMEA and friendly regimes worldwide amounted to indirect financial supports. Cuba and Vietnam were among the primary recipients of Soviet largesse, which helped them survive the USA-imposed trade embargoes. Cheap Russian petroleum propelled the economies of the Warsaw Pact states. The total value of the Soviet trade subsidies to its six East European clients during 1960–1978 was about $57.7 billion in 1980 dollars. Between 1974 and 1984, trade subsidies to these states varied from $10.7 billion to $29.8 billion a year (Marrese and Vanous, 1983, 1988). The USSR exported oil to other CMEA members at a price that was, on average, 1.8–2.7 times lower than the world market prices (Crane, 1988: 49; Jackson, 1986: 103, 105).

After the end of socialism, Russia kept providing substantial energy discounts to the Commonwealth of Independent States (CIS) member-states. Economists have estimated that energy subsidies to Belarus amounted to 10–15 per cent of the republic's gross domestic product (GDP) annually, or between US$1.2 and $2.0 billion a year in the 1990s and US$4.0 and $6.0 billion a year in the 2000s. The ten years' value of various supports that Moscow provided to Minsk reached $106 billion by 2015, or nearly $9.7 billion each year since 2005. The bulk of these supports were energy subsidies. Preferential prices on Russia's energy exports to Ukraine financed more than one-fifth of Ukraine's GDP through the 1990s. By the end of the 2000s, the sum total of Russia's energy subsidies to Ukraine reached $75–$100 billion (Molchanov, 2015; Tkachev and Feinberg, 2017).

An obvious question is, why would Russia show such magnanimity? One answer has to do with Russia's own dependence on energy export routes through Belarus and Ukraine – the dependence that kept subsidies to the transit countries in place for as long as Russia's own revenues remained conditional on good relations with these very same transit countries. Another popular explanation ties subsidies to Russia's quest for international security – a naval or military base here or there, a supportive vote in the United Nations, accommodation of Russia's defence interests and the like (Orttung and Overland, 2011).

It is also possible that, with oil and gas prices relatively low through the mid-2000s, there was a 'certain degree of inertia from the Soviet period' per 'business as usual' model (Closson, 2011: 350). Thus, the Baltic states, in spite of their tenuous relations with Moscow, continued getting gas at a price below the average European mark for almost 17 years after proclaiming independence, even after joining the European Union (EU) (Grigas, 2012: 10). The search for commercial benefits cannot be ruled out either, as Russia sought, and acquired, important energy infrastructure in Belarus and made similar, albeit unsuccessful, passes on gas pipelines and reservoirs in Ukraine. Finally, we cannot exclude ulterior personal motives in top officials' support of practices that made little sense economically: these energy subsidies enabled corruption and kickbacks on a scale never seen before.[1]

Securitization of energy trade

Most Western studies of Eurasian energy security are written, unabashedly, from the perspective of limiting Russia's ability to derive political and economic benefits from its natural endowments, while ensuring unimpeded Western access to these riches (Mankoff, 2009: 5). The security of interest to the writer is solely the security of the Western consumer of energy and the protection of the Western entrepreneurs' right to exploit this planet's resources wherever they might be located. The security of energy-exporting countries, which can be further subdivided into producer security, supplier security and security of demand, has been a much less popular item to discuss and is debated mostly on the pages of obscure academic periodicals (Dike, 2013; Jonsson et al., 2015).

Exceptions do appear. As Daniel Yergin (2006) observed, energy exporters have no choice but to focus on maintaining the security of demand for their exports, which generate a large, if not predominant, share of their government revenues. Ever since the end of the Soviet Union, Russia has been struggling to reassert national control over its strategic energy resources and get a secure grip on the main pipelines through which it ships its oil and gas abroad. Its behaviour has been no different in this regard from that of other petroleum-exporting nations, all of which have vested interests in the availability of energy resources subject to some form of domestic control, reliability of energy outflows abroad (distributional security), and availability and diversity of customers (Jonsson et al., 2015).

There are also post-Soviet sensibilities. The history of the 'dashing nineties' serves as a constant reminder of dangers of the open market. When Soviet energy resources were put up for sale with few controls from the Kremlin, many Russians saw it as a strategic defeat. The transfer of oil development rights in Western hands became a sign of Russia's international marginalization.

As the USSR was still breathing its last breaths, businesspeople from far away wasted no time jostling for the best position in a fast-growing line of those trying to buy Russian oil wealth on the cheap. The sell-off of national resources had caused a global scramble for their control. Privatization of the energy sector had changed economics and transformed the security calculus of the state. Western oil majors had all showed up in Moscow and established themselves as not only economic but also political players. Privatizing governments all over the post-Soviet Eurasia had soon found themselves hostage to business interests (Molchanov, 2016: 22–24).

Some of the Russian oligarchs, like Mikhail Khodorkovsky, got emboldened enough seemingly to pursue their own foreign economic policy:

> He negotiated directly with China on building a pipeline, bypassing the Kremlin on something of great strategic importance, and on which Putin had very different views. He was moving fast to acquire Sibneft… which would make Yukos possibly the largest oil company in the world. And he was in talks with both Chevron and ExxonMobil about selling controlling interest in Yukos. That would have moved control over a substantial part of the country's most important strategic asset, oil, out of Russia….
>
> *(Yergin, 2012: 39)*

Khodorkovsky's plans were applauded in America, even as American statesmen reinvented themselves as oilmen. The USA-Azerbaijan Chamber of Commerce featured such names as James A. Baker III, Zbigniew Brzezinski, Henry Kissinger, Brent Scowcroft, John Sununu, Richard Perle, Graham Allison, Richard Armitage and Dick Cheney. Cheney was also a member of Kazakhstan's Oil Advisory Board, and helped broker an oil deal with Chevron, where the future Secretary of State Condoleezza Rice served on the Board. Ms. Rice had personally travelled to Kazakhstan to make sure that the deal would go through.

Strategic interest in Caspian oil was acknowledged in Washington, London and Brussels. Western governments gave strong backing to the Baku-Tbilisi-Ceyhan (BTC) pipeline whose main purpose was 'to keep vast quantities of oil out of Russian hands' (Evans and Hencke, 2003). The war in Afghanistan had flooded the whole Transcaspian region with

NATO military personnel and lent muscle to the Western oil majors negotiating productions deals with weak post-Soviet governments (Johnson, 2004: 172–173).

As the USA moved in, Russia was squeezed out of the region. The American policy of 'opening an oil and natural gas Southern Corridor from Central Asia and the Caucasus to European and global energy markets' continued with the construction of the South Caucasus Gas Pipeline (SCP) from Azerbaijan to Turkey and the Trans-Anatolian Natural Gas Pipeline (TANAP) through Turkey to Europe (Committee on Foreign Relations, 2012: v). In all of these instances, Western governments worked hard to ensure the interests of the transnational corporations headquartered in their own countries, yet Russia's attempts of a similar nature were perceived – and described – as a threat.

As a fairly standard formulation of the U.S. position goes, '[e]nergy is the economic lifeblood of many NATO allies and partners in the Europe and Eurasia region, and dependence on Russia and Iran for energy imports or exports remains a central detriment to those nations' sovereign independence' (Committee on Foreign Relations, 2012: 2). By actively working to undermine Russia's market position and accusing Moscow of some sort of a hidden agenda detrimental to the national interests of its partners, the USA was the first to push securitization of energy trade in the region. Russia had no choice but to respond.

The pipeline diplomacy helped Russia improve its position vis-à-vis not only energy importers but also transit and producer countries. Ukraine and Belarus feared potential cut-offs of supply, while Turkmenistan and Kazakhstan were dependent on the Russia-controlled pipelines for their own energy exports. More than one author has noted that Russia seemed to be using its energy resources as a tool of foreign and security policies towards neighbouring states (Nygren, 2008; Sotiriou, 2014). Disruptions of gas supply to Ukraine's 'orange' government in 2006 and 2009 have become favourite illustrations of the alleged 'energy weapon' being used as an instrument of political diktat (Newnham, 2011; Wigell and Vihma, 2016).

Other studies are more sceptical concerning Russia's ability to extract political concessions from the EU member-states (Judge, Maltby and Sharples, 2016; Smith Stegen, 2011). Documenting the EU's energy vulnerabilities is easy; explaining why Russia might want to withhold energy supply in spite of a devastating effect on the country's reputation and domestic economy is much more difficult. Even if European dependence on external sources of fuel supply is expected to grow, seeing Russia's market position as a security threat seems to be a stretch.

Politics or economics?

Since it is hard to provide much evidence of Moscow's twisting European powers' hands through the use of energy blackmail, the threat of Russia's 'gas weapon' must be exaggerated. While Gazprom may not always follow spot market prices, it is a utility maximizer nonetheless. Therefore, it should not be expected to engage in self-destructive practices, such as, for example, blackmailing its largest customer for reasons that have nothing to do with their commercial relationship and extend well beyond the negotiated deal. The same is true for the country's leadership, which is a utility maximizer in its own right. Admittedly, the Kremlin's understanding of utility and the best ways to maximize it may differ from perceptions common in Russia's business circles.

What, exactly, is the balance of power between tycoons and strongmen remains an open question. Undoubtedly, the Kremlin is very much in control. But what is the role of the energy companies? While some scholars insist on a symbiotic relationship between the state and the energy companies (Bilgin, 2011), a more cautious position recognizes a certain symmetry but not a full coincidence of their interests (Jirušek and Vlček, 2015). Stern (2006), Goldthau and Boersma (2014) and Casier (2016) all dispute reductionist assumptions of the use of energy trade as a foreign policy weapon and argue that Russian companies are motivated by a plethora of motifs which do not mirror the state's position.

The idea that the Kremlin always calls the shots simplifies a complex picture of interactions between business interests and politicians. While Gazprom's very origins, out of the Ministry of Gas Industry of the USSR, betray its political dependencies, the profit motif was arguably a decisive cause of its coming into existence. Soon after the former Minister of the Gas Industry Viktor Chernomyrdin had created Gazprom as a money-making machine, he was called to sit as Prime Minister in Boris Yeltsin's government. He then led his former company to fill the gaps in the state budget during the 1990s. As Russian monopoly gas exporter, Gazprom has remained the working horse of the Russian economy under Chernomyrdin's successors Rem Vyakhirev and Alexey Miller. The state holds a majority stake in the company and extracts significant revenues through taxation. It is no surprise then that Moscow is not shying away from applying political leverage to secure Gazprom's business interests and shore its position in international markets, specifically by trying to expand its control of gas export routes in the region (Heinrich and Pleines, 2014).

The use of Gazprom as an instrument of Russia's security policy came second and almost by chance. In the fall of 1992, amidst Lithuanian demands that Russia would speed up withdrawal of its forces from the newly sovereign country, Gazprom reduced the supply of gas to Lithuania by 45 per cent, cutting it off completely for two days. In June 1993, Russia reacted to Estonia's Law on Aliens, which denied citizenship to the majority of the Russian-speaking population there, by halting gas deliveries (RIA Novosti, 2008). Later in the year, Boris Yeltsin called out Ukraine's gas debt and authorized cutting of gas supply by one-fourth to prop up Russia's position on division of the Black Sea Fleet and full transfer of Soviet nuclear weapons under the Russian control (Molchanov, 2002: 254).

By the end of the nineties, the idea that energy politics must play a key part in Russia's security policy was every man's wisdom. Vladimir Putin's dissertation in 1997 advocated reassertion of the state's control over the raw materials sector and the use of national champions to extend Russia's influence abroad. When Putin came to power, securing access to energy infrastructure abroad became one of his government's strategic objectives. At a time when all other instruments of power were either abandoned or severely diminished, resources remained the last hope for Russia's resurrection. Considerations of energy security branched out into such areas as pipeline politics, security of demand and security of control over the national energy resources.

Russia's predominance as Eurasia's main petroleum exporter has been diluted with the construction of the Kazakhstan-China oil pipeline in 2006. Three years later, the Central Asia-China gas pipeline (CAGP) started functioning. By March 2017, Kazakhstan pumped 100 million tonnes of crude to China (Xinhua, 2017), while the CAGP network expanded to three functioning lines. By the early 2018, it had transported 203.2 billion cubic metres of natural gas from Central Asia to China's customers (Xinhua, 2018).

In the current climate of worsening Russian relations with Europe, the attraction of China's market grows – to the extent that Russian producers are now vying for the right to use Kazakhstan's transit networks to China, while taking away from Russia's own Transneft system. The Russia-China oil pipeline (Skovorodino-Daqing), inaugurated in late 2010, had its capacity doubled to 600,000 barrels a day with the completion of the second trunk in January 2018. Parallel to that, Russia and China have also agreed on the natural gas supplies in the amount of 38 billion cubic metres a year via the spur of the "Power of Siberia" pipeline, to go online by the end of 2019. Even so, Russia's competition with its former Soviet satellites in Central Asia is bound to intensify.

Conclusion

The politics-to-economics balance in Moscow's approach to energy security has moved towards politics when the Western sanctions' bite had started threatening public confidence in the government. Parallel to that, oil had lost over half of its value in less than a year (from $97.6 per barrel in 2014 to $41.8 per barrel average in 2016). Russia's economy contracted 2.8 per cent in 2015 and 0.2 per cent in 2016, before returning to a modest growth of 1.7 per cent in 2017–2018. The poverty rate, which stood at 10.7 per cent in 2012, grew to 16 per cent in early 2016, while the share of vulnerable population increased from 33.5 per cent in 2014 to near 40 per cent in 2016 (World Bank, 2017: 12, 14). A few months before the presidential election in 2018, only 52 per cent of Russians believed that their country's leadership was headed in the right direction, with 22 per cent claiming the opposite (Ray and Esipova, 2017).

The April 2018 Russia sanctions expansion by the USA serves as a stark reminder of the realities of the global age and the intimate links between energy and security. This time, several oil executives and the chief executive officer of Gazprom, Alexei Miller, were added to the list. The immediate results of Russia's punishment by the USA and its allies, however, run counter to the Western expectations.

Not only have the Russian people shown the unprecedented levels of support to the embattled President Putin, entrusting him with the post for yet another six years until the 2024 presidential election (Meyer et al., 2018), but the Russian international behaviour hardened as a result of the sanctions and ostracism that the vast majority of the Russian people perceive as undeserved.

As the Cold War 2.0 mentality settles in, the search for proper tools to counter Western pressure cannot but subordinate economic considerations to international politics and security. In this climate, Russia must be prepared to let go of certain trade benefits and financial conveniences that the West is willing to provide to its more pliant partners. If security is, once again, on the top of the agenda, military preparations must go hand in hand with information warfare, defensive diplomacy and alliance building. The use of the country's strategic resources cannot but be strategic. This centrally applies to the choice of trade partners, export routes and long-term deals. Exploration and development of Russia's hydrocarbons, just like Russia's participation in the production of petroleum abroad, Russia's access to the export markets West and East, and Russia's ability to package its energy politics with international concessions on other issues of vital importance will remain central to the country's security strategy for years to come.

Note

1 Both the Russian and the Ukrainian sides were aware of the so-called unsanctioned taking of gas on both sides of the border and accepted it as routine practice. Assigning accountability and calculating the exact amount of theft of the Russian gas in transit has been grossly complicated by the fact that the Russian exporters, as well as the Ukrainian middlemen, availed themselves of this opportunity freely and with little or no consequences.

References

Alekperov, V. (2011). *Oil of Russia: Past, present & future.* Minneapolis, MN: Eastview.

Bilgin, M. (2011). 'Energy security and Russia's gas strategy: The symbiotic relationship between the state and firms'. *Communist and Post-Communist Studies, 44*(2), 119–127.

Bonin, H. (2007). 'Business interests versus geopolitics: The case of the Siberian pipeline in the 1980s'. *Business History, 49*(2), 235–254.

Bushuyev, V., and Mastepanov, A. (2015). 'Geopolitika v razreze globalnoi energetiki'. *Nezavisimaya gazeta*, 13 October, www.ng.ru/energy/2015-10-13/9_geopolitik.html

Casier, T. (2016). 'Great game or great confusion: The geopolitical understanding of EU-Russia energy relations'. *Geopolitics, 21*(4), 763–778.

Closson, S. (2011). 'A comparative analysis on energy subsidies in Soviet and Russian policy'. *Communist and Post-Communist Studies, 44*(4), 343–356.

Committee on Foreign Relations. U.S. Senate (2012). *Energy and security from the Caspian to Europe: A minority staff report.* Washington, DC: U.S. Government Printing Office.

Crane, K. (1988). *Soviet economic policy towards Eastern Europe.* A Rand Note N-2861-RC. Santa Monica, CA: Rand, www.rand.org/pubs/notes/2007/N2861.pdf

Dike, J. C. (2013). 'Measuring the security of energy exports demand in OPEC economies'. *Energy Policy, 60*, 594–600.

Dugin, A. (2012). 'Energeticheskaia geopolitika'. *Geopolitika.ru*, 3 July, www.geopolitika.ru/article/energeticheskaya-geopolitika

Elek, P. S. (1982). 'Europe's new road to serfdom'. *Eastern Economic Journal, 8*(3), 163–176.

Evans, R., and Hencke, D. (2003). 'US and UK in joint effort to secure African oil'. *The Guardian*, 14 November, www.guardian.co.uk/politics/2003/nov/14/uk.freedomofinformation

Fairgrieve, J. (1915). *Geography and world power.* London: University of London Press.

Goldthau, A., and Boersma, T. (2014). The 2014 'Ukraine-Russia crisis: Implications for energy markets and scholarship'. *Energy Research & Social Science, 3*, 13–15.

Grigas, A. (2012). *The gas relationship between the Baltic states and Russia: Politics and commercial realities.* University of Oxford: The Oxford Institute for Energy Studies.

Heinrich, A., and Pleines, H. (Eds.). (2014). *Export pipelines from the CIS region: Geopolitics, securitization, and political decision-making.* Stuttgart: ibidem-Verlag.

Högselius, P. (2013). *Red gas: Russia and the origins of European energy dependence.* New York: Palgrave Macmillan.

Jackson, M. (1986). 'When is a price a price? The level and patterns of prices in the CMEA'. *Soviet and Eastern European Foreign Trade, 22*(1), 100–112.

Jirušek, M., and Vlček, T. (2015). *Energy security in Central and Eastern Europe and the operations of Russian state-owned energy enterprises.* Brno: Masaryk University.

Johnson, C. A. (2004). *The sorrows of empire: Militarism, secrecy and the end of the Republic.* London: Verso.

Jonsson, D. K., Johansson, B., Månsson, A., Nilsson, L. J., Nilsson, M., and Sonnsjö, H. (2015). 'Energy security matters in the EU energy roadmap'. *Energy Strategy Reviews, 6*, 48–56.

Judge, A., Maltby, T., and Sharples, J. D. (2016). 'Challenging reductionism in analyses of EU-Russia energy relations'. *Geopolitics, 21*(4), 751–762.

Lenin, V. I. (1920). 'Report on the work of the Council of People's Commissars. Eighth All-Russia Congress of Soviets'. *Collected Works*, 31, http://marxists.org/archive/lenin/works/1920/8thcong/ch02.htm

Lippert, W. D. (2011). *The economic diplomacy of Ostpolitik: Origins of NATO's energy dilemma.* New York: Berghahn Books.

Mackinder, H. (1919). *Democratic ideals and reality.* New York: H. Holt.

Mankoff, J. (2009). *Eurasian energy security.* Council Special Report No. 43. February 2009. New York: Council on Foreign Relations.

Marrese, M., and Vanous, J. (1983). *Soviet subsidization of trade with Eastern Europe.* Berkeley: University of California Press.

Marrese, M., and Vanous, J. (1988). 'The content and controversy of Soviet trade relations with Eastern Europe, 1970–1984.' In J. C. Brada, E. A. Hewett and T. A. Wolf (Eds.), *Economic adjustment and reform in Eastern Europe and the Soviet Union: Essays in honor of Franklyn D. Holzman* (pp. 185–217). Durham, NC.: Duke University Press.

McDonald, D. (2007). 'Domestic conjunctures, the Russian state and the world outside, 1700–2006'. In R. Legvold (Ed.), *Russian foreign policy in the twenty-first century and the shadow of the past* (pp. 145–203). New York: Columbia University Press.

Meyer, H., Arkhipov, I., Kravchenko, S., and Reznik, I. (2018). 'Putin claims mandate in record win amid conflict with West.' *Bloomberg*, 18 March, www.bloomberg.com/news/articles/2018-03-18/putin-sweeps-to-new-term-in-russia-as-tensions-spiral-with-west

Molchanov, M. A. (2002). *Political culture and national identity in Russian-Ukrainian relations.* College Station: Texas A&M University Press.

Molchanov, M. A. (2015). *Eurasian regionalisms and Russian foreign policy.* New York: Routledge.

Molchanov, M. A. (2016). 'Energy security and the revival of geopolitics'. In S. F. Krishna-Hensel (Ed.), *New security frontiers: Critical energy and the resource challenge* (pp. 9–30). New York: Routledge.

Newnham, R. (2011). 'Oil, carrots, and sticks: Russia's energy resources as a foreign policy tool'. *Journal of Eurasian Studies, 2*, 134–143.

Nygren, B. (2008). *The rebuilding of greater Russia: Putin's foreign policy towards the CIS countries.* London and New York: Routledge.

Orttung, R., and Overland, I. (2011). 'A limited toolbox: Explaining the constraints on Russia's foreign energy policy'. *Journal of Eurasian Studies, 2*, 74–85.

Ray, J., and Esipova, N. (2017). 'Russians happier with Putin than with country's direction'. *Gallup*, 8 December, http://news.gallup.com/poll/223382/russians-happier-putin-country-direction.aspx

Reuters (2018). 'EU even more dependent on Russian gas'. *The National*, 14 January, www.thenational.ae/business/energy/eu-even-more-dependent-on-russian-gas-1.695131

RIA Novosti (2008). 'Gazovye konflikty Rossii za poslednie 15 let'. Spravka [Russia's gas conflicts over the last 15 years. A reference]. 12 February, http://ria.ru/spravka/20080212/99021453.html

Shafranik, Y. K. (Ed.). (2015). *Globalnaya energetika i geopolitika (Rossiia i mir).* Moscow: Energiia.

Smith Stegen, K. 2011. 'Deconstructing the "energy weapon": Russia's threat to Europe as case study'. *Energy Policy, 39*(10), 6505–6513.

Sotiriou, S. (2014). *Russian energy strategy in the European Union, the former Soviet Union region, and China.* Lanham: Lexington.

Stern, J. P. (2006). 'Natural gas security problems in Europe: The Russian-Ukrainian crisis of 2006'. *Asia-Pacific Review, 13*(1), 32–58.

The National Security Strategy of the Russian Federation (2015). Approved by the President of the Russian Federation Decree No. 683 on 31 December, http://kremlin.ru/acts/bank/40391

Tkachev, I., and Feinberg, A. (2017). 'Skrytyi schet na $100 mlrd: kak Rossiia soderzhit belorusskuyu ekonomiku'. *RBK*, 2 April, www.rbc.ru/economics/02/04/2017/58e026879a79471d6c8aef30

Wigell, M., and Vihma, A. (2016). 'Geopolitics versus geoeconomics: The case of Russia's geostrategy and its effects on the EU'. *International Affairs, 92*(3), 605–627.

World Bank. (2017). *Russia's recovery: How strong are its shoots?* Russia Economic Report 38, November 2017. Moscow: The World Bank in Russia.

Xinhua (2017). 'Oil imports through Sino-Kazakh pipeline hit 100 mln tonnes', 29 March, www.xinhuanet.com/english/2017-03/29/c_136168316.htm

Xinhua (2018). '38.7 bln cubic meters of gas piped to China from Central Asia', 5 January, www.xinhuanet.com/english/2018-01/05/c_136874692.htm

Yergin, D. (2006). 'Ensuring energy security'. *Foreign Affairs, 85*(2), 69–82.

Yergin, D. (2012). *The quest: Energy, security, and the remaking of the modern world.* Rev. and updated. New York: Penguin Books.

16

THE INTELLIGENCE AGENCIES AND PUTIN

Undermining Russia's security?

Kimberly Marten

In the popular imagination, the Russian intelligence services are a frightening and seamless tool used by former KGB officer President Vladimir Putin to consolidate his power at home and wreak havoc on his opponents abroad. Whether collecting compromising material on political opponents, murdering those who dig too deeply or reveal too much, or using cyber technology to interfere in elections in the U.S. and Europe, these agencies are often seen as all-powerful and invincible.

As in Soviet times, Putin is once again using Russia's intelligence agencies domestically to undermine political opposition and support his authoritarian rule. The Russian state's working definition of 'security' confuses the security of the Putin regime's hold on state power with the protection of the Russian people from harm. Any analysis of the effect of Russian intelligence agencies on security must start by recognising that they often violate human rights, and hence human security. The effort to quash domestic Russian dissent may also end up weakening the Russian state, if as a result there is no meaningful pushback against the inevitable errors and idiosyncratic policy choices of authoritarian leaders.

Moreover, a close reading of the literature on both Soviet and Russian intelligence agencies reveals that they were never quite as effective historically as they wished to portray themselves as being and that at least some of these problems probably continue to undermine real state security today. Russian intelligence agencies have always suffered from infighting and factionalism, made worse in the 1990s by the forays of intelligence officers into the commercial and criminal worlds. The Kremlin, therefore, finds itself with a classic principal-agent problem, where individual officers and even whole units have both the motive and the economic means to act beyond centralised monitoring and control, failing to align with state interests (Jensen and Meckling, 1976). Furthermore, in Soviet times, the intelligence collected on foreign opponents was always heavily politicised, bent to the wishes of what Communist Party leaders wanted to hear. This trend is likely continuing under Putin, providing him with inadequate information for making significant foreign policy decisions, and perhaps skewing Russian actions in ways that align with Putin's overly risk-acceptant personality. For all of these reasons, the Russian intelligence agencies and their current and former officers today may be undermining long-term Russian security.

Information about Russian intelligence agencies

The attempt to understand any secretive actor anywhere in the world is fraught with difficulties. All intelligence agencies wish to keep their activities (and especially their weaknesses) hidden from opponents and can use the excuse of classification to evade scrutiny from even loyal domestic audiences. In an authoritarian state like Russia, the task is made much harder because state agencies are not held accountable to oversight by independent legislative or judicial processes.

Historical knowledge about the roots of today's Russian intelligence agencies is also constrained. Unlike many former Soviet allies in East-Central Europe and the Baltics, Russia never underwent lustration: the archives of the Communist-era Committee for State Security (KGB) in Moscow were never fully opened after the USSR collapsed, and no attempt was made to name and shame collaborators with the Soviet system's brutality. A law passed in 1991 (and amended several times thereafter) has allowed family members to obtain some documents about Soviet repression of their relatives, but its attachment to a victim compensation programme has leant it the air of a contested social welfare programme (Frierson, 2014). There was one official effort in the early 1990s to give a Russian journalist, Alexander Vassiliev, partial access to files concerning Soviet intelligence operations in the U.S. during the Stalin era. Vassiliev's notebooks summarising thousands of those documents (but not copies of the documents themselves) are housed at the U.S. Library of Congress and have offered a fertile (if controversial) trove for historians (Haynes, Klehr, and Vassiliev, 2009). More recently, the KGB archives located in the former Soviet republics of Estonia, Latvia, Lithuania, and Ukraine have been opened, and many documents from them (mostly covering domestic and regionally specific operations) are available on the Internet. The Ukrainian documents will likely prove the most fruitful, given the special role of the region in much Soviet intelligence work, but they have only been available since 2015 and are just beginning to be plumbed. Some Soviet intelligence documents were also unsealed in the West. In 1995, Washington declassified a trove of intercepted and decoded messages from Soviet intelligence operatives working in the U.S. during World War II (Haynes and Klehr, 1999). In addition, a junior KGB officer, Vasili Mitrokhin, who was banished to do archival work by Stalin as punishment for his heterodox views, was later given responsibility for sorting and boxing up the KGB archives in 1972, when they were moved to a new location outside Moscow. Mitrokhin used that opportunity, and the fact that he controlled access to those files for the next 12 years until his retirement, to copy a huge number of the documents by hand, squirrel them away at home, and later smuggle them to London (Andrew and Mitrokhin, 1999, 2005). Over time, a number of former Soviet intelligence officers have also published memoirs.

These rich, if limited, historical sources matter for understanding the Russian intelligence services today because the KGB and its military intelligence counterpart, the Main Intelligence Directorate (GRU) of the Soviet Armed Forces General Staff, were never reformed. Following the failed coup attempt against him in August 1991, the last Soviet leader, Mikhail Gorbachev, split the KGB into separate functional organisations, but nothing else was really changed about them, including their personnel, training or sense of mission (Bakatin, 1992). The first post-Soviet Russian president, Boris Yeltsin, continued this reorganisation effort, but the new pieces of the old organisation were never purged of old thinkers or forced to change their organisational mindsets. As a result, the cultures and behaviour patterns of those Soviet agencies may be influencing Russian choices today (Marten, 2017).

While information about today's Russian intelligence operations is even thinner, there are some intrepid Russian journalists, such as Andrei Soldatov and Irina Borogan, who have dedicated their careers to unearthing whatever information is available. In 2005, they founded a non-governmental centre for journalists on this subject, with findings published on their website (agentura.ru) and commentary disseminated in other media. Somehow they have managed to continue their work despite the Putin regime's crackdown against independent media. There are also some Western analysts who have what appears to be remarkable inside access, including Mark Galeotti, now based at the Institute of International Relations in Prague. Although Galeotti's high-quality analysis does not always reveal his source material, he has published an explanation of how he has managed to interview many high-ranking Russian organised crime figures—if not Russian intelligence officers (Galeotti, 2018b). Then, too, cases where members of Russian intelligence organisation are investigated for crimes or corruption by another, a rather regular occurrence in the Putin era, have been covered in great detail in the Russian media. Finally, Western investigations (including the British inquiry into the murder by polonium-210 poisoning of former KGB agent Alexander Litvinenko, and the ongoing Robert Mueller investigation into Russian interference in the 2016 U.S. presidential campaign) have brought much to light about Putin-era intelligence activities.

The limits inherent in these published sources mean that specific 'facts' about any Russian intelligence agency or operation may be selectively planted, creatively invented or just plain wrong. Yet, the consistency in overall patterns of behaviour reported by all of these sources provides a degree of confidence about our ability to understand the basic relationship between Russian intelligence agencies and security under Putin, even if the details remain murky.

Putin, the KGB, and the FSB

Putin began his career in the KGB in 1975. While his various roles over time have not all been confirmed, he is believed to have served briefly in counter-intelligence and, possibly, in the branch responsible for rooting out Soviet dissidents, before relocating to Dresden, East Germany. In Dresden, he may have been responsible for recruiting agents among those wishing to travel to see relatives in West Germany (Hill and Gaddy, 2013; Myers, 2015). When the Warsaw Pact collapsed, and Germany reunified in 1990, Putin returned to Russia to work in the KGB active reserves, where his task may have been to recruit foreign scholars working at Leningrad State University. Putin officially resigned from the KGB during the attempted coup against Gorbachev in 1991, but may have continued working in the post-KGB reserves even after accepting a position on the staff of St. Petersburg Mayor Anatoli Sobchak (Treisman, 2011; Hill and Gaddy, 2013; Dawisha, 2015; Myers, 2015). Putin once famously said, 'There is no such thing as a former KGB man' (Nemtsova, 2006).

Putin held a variety of responsibilities within Sobchak's office, including brokering and approving licenses for all foreign trade and investment contracts. That would have given him a treasure trove of information about key businesses, a financial investigative skill set, and perhaps an early set of kickbacks useful both for his future political career and on behalf of his intelligence service colleagues. Within months of Sobchak's failed re-election campaign in 1996, Putin was offered work in the Kremlin. Later that year, he brought in two old friends to work with him on the presidential staff who were also believed to be from the intelligence services: Sergey Chemezov, now chief executive officer (CEO) of the giant state-owned Rostec defence industrial conglomerate, who was Putin's neighbour in his building in Dresden; and Igor Sechin, now CEO of Rosneft, the huge state-controlled oil and energy conglomerate, who was thought by many actually to be working for the KGB when he served as a Soviet military translator in Mozambique and Angola (Myers, 2015). By 1998, Putin had risen to lead the Federal Security Service (FSB), the Russian successor to the domestic intelligence directorate of the KGB. In 1999, President Boris Yeltsin appointed Putin Prime Minister, and when Yeltsin resigned on 31 December, Putin became acting president. In 2000 he was elected to his first presidential term. He has been in charge ever since, despite switching his presidential title for the prime ministership once again when Dmitry Medvedev (his colleague from the St. Petersburg Mayor's office) was elected president from 2008 to 2012. While it is clear that Putin used connections, worked hard, and demonstrated loyalty to get ahead (Myers, 2015), his meteoric rise from being a rather ordinary KGB officer to the modern equivalent of a tsar has never been fully explained.

As Putin rose to power, he brought additional members of his old KGB and FSB network into positions of power and wealth both in the Russian government itself and in the state enterprises that he renationalised and recentralised. A key figure in the consolidation of this 'siloviki' (power ministry) control has been Nikolai Patrushev, connected by family, financial or historical career ties to a huge swathe of the Kremlin elite (Taylor, 2007). Patrushev, who worked in the local security services when Putin started in Mayor Sobchak's office, helped defend Putin from an investigative report launched by the St. Petersburg city council that accused him of misappropriating commodities meant to be exchanged for food aid (Hill and Gaddy, 2013). After Patrushev followed Putin to Moscow, he was named in 1999 to succeed Putin as FSB director. In 2008, Patrushev left that post to become the ultrapowerful secretary of Russia's Security Council.

Along the way the FSB—originally the inheritor only of the domestic functions of the old KGB—has expanded its mandate to include a significant part of foreign intelligence, especially (but not only) in the post-Soviet space. It also oversees a significant component of signals intelligence work, including cyber hacking and influence operations, under the oversight of Putin's circle from St. Petersburg (Tsypkin, 2007; Soldatov and Borogan, 2010; Haslam, 2015). The FSB currently also commands three of the Russian state's many organised armed groups: the Alpha elite counterterrorism special forces, used most infamously under Putin in response to the Dubrovka Moscow theater (2002) and Beslan school (2004) hostage crises, when their choices led to the death of many innocent hostages; the Vympel special counterterrorism and nuclear facilities forces; and the Russian border guards (Galeotti, 2013).

The intelligence agencies and domestic security

Russian domestic intelligence agencies perform the same functions as criminal investigation agencies do in other countries around the world: reacting against such things as violent riots, treason by those with security clearances, organised crime, terrorism, cyberattacks, smuggling, and drug trafficking. Some of these agencies, like the FSB, are former directorates of the KGB, including the Federal Protection Service (the FSO). The FSO, beyond its role of guarding political leaders and buildings, controls the Special Communications and Information Service, responsible for both foreign signals intelligence and domestic cyber defence. It is also reportedly used to monitor and prevent potential coup attempts arising inside other Russian armed organisations, and as an alternative source of intelligence analysis (Galeotti, 2013). Other key domestic intelligence agencies include the Interior Ministry (the MVD), and the Investigations Committee, established by Putin in 2011 as an anti-corruption agency reporting directly to the president and charged with investigating the police and other agencies and forces (it was formerly under the Federal Prosecutor's Office).

Yet some of their current roles have come to resemble those of their Soviet counterparts, as state intelligence has been used against peaceful protestors, human rights advocates, opposition political candidates, and even prominent businesspeople who have fallen out with Putin. An example is the use of the System for Operative Investigative Activities (SORM) programme, under FSB authority but accessible to other agencies as well, which allows the collection, storage, and analysis of all electronic data transiting Russian networks (Soldatov and Borogan, 2015). SORM was used for mass surveillance during the 2014 Sochi Olympics and has been officially and legally used to collect *kompromat* (compromising information) against various of Putin's opponents (Lewis, 2014). State investigations related to tax evasion, fraud, and other financial crimes have also been used with devastating effects against oligarchs who have offended Putin, including Boris Berezovsky, Vladimir Gusinsky, and Mikhail Khodorkovsky (Taylor, 2007). A 2016 investigation felled Putin's own Minister of Economic Development, Aleksei Ulyukaev, who was sentenced at age 62 to eight years' hard labour for supposedly extorting a bribe from Rosneft's Sechin. Recently, groups of Cossacks (who are recognised by the state, but may have little actual connection to their historical counterparts) have begun whipping protestors and other opposition figures on the street. At least one of their leaders is a retired FSB general, Ivan Mironov, who has strong personal and financial links to Rostec's Chemezov (Vavina and Coalson, 2018).

The re-emergence of what observers in Soviet times called the 'intelligence state' is a response to Putin's perception that he is vulnerable to domestic 'regime change' efforts by external opponents in the West. In the view of Putin and his supporters, the security of Putin's autocratic rule, including the need to protect it from mass protests and potential democratic challengers, is equivalent to the security of the Russian state. This likely has its roots in the KGB mindset. The KGB's work was premised on the notion that external enemies were constantly trying to undermine the USSR from within (Primakov, 2006). This mindset became especially ingrained under KGB director (and later Soviet leader) Yuri Andropov, who as Soviet ambassador to Hungary in 1956 had witnessed the attempted anti-Soviet revolution there. Andropov established a new KGB directorate focused on rooting out internal dissidents (Andrew and Mitrokhin, 1999; Khlobustov, 2006). The hard-line KGB director who led the 1991 coup attempt against Gorbachev was Vladimir Kruchkov, an Andropov protégé who believed that reformers of the Soviet perestroika ('restructuring') era were Western agents (Remnick, 1993; Andrew and Mitrokhin, 1999; Garthoff, 2015).

One major difference between the KGB in Soviet times and the FSB under Putin is that in the past, the Communist Party bureaucracy and the Politburo at the top played a countervailing role to check the power of the KGB as an institution (Petrov, 2011). The Soviet Union was also a patron-client political system, where power was exercised through informal personal networks, but at least in the post-Stalin era formal bureaucratic institutions provided a brake on the decision making of individual Soviet leaders. The KGB and the Communist Party reached a modus vivendi where they were able to balance each other for the sake of stability. In contrast, Russia's post-Soviet patronal presidency has allowed a singular pyramid of personal networks, all focused on Putin's leadership, to dominate the levers of power (Hale, 2014).

The North Caucasus

Russia has a unique domestic threat setting it apart from most other states: insurgency and terrorism emanating from its own restive North Caucasus region. Russian police and intelligence agencies in the region have been quick to use excessive violence and abusive practices in response (for one set of recent detailed examples, see Human Rights Watch, 2015). Actions taken following terrorist attacks have also fuelled concerns that innocent Muslims from the North Caucasus and Central Asia who are living elsewhere in Russia face repression by the state, undercutting the security of one group of Russian residents in the name of protecting the population as a whole (Filipov, 2017). Meanwhile, radicalised Russian citizens have provided an outsized number of foreign fighters in both Al-Qaeda and the Islamic State, amidst evidence that the FSB and its border guards service encouraged them to leave for Turkey (Sanderson, Oliker, Markusen, and Galperin, 2017). While only a fraction of these hardened militants is believed to have returned home to Russia thus far, the FSB has expressed worry about their eventual impact (Reuters, 2017).

Putin consolidated power in 1999 in large part by launching Russian forces into a second round of devastating Civil War in Chechnya, which had originally begun shortly after the Soviet collapse. One extreme consequence has been Putin's decision effectively to outsource security in Chechnya to its strongman local ruler, Ramzan Kadyrov. In reward for Kadyrov's loyalty, and in recognition of his success in pacifying the republic through a combination of bribery, torture, and brutal collective punishment, Putin allowed Kadyrov's forces gradually to take control over the intelligence agencies on Chechen territory, including the FSB (Marten, 2012; Yaffa, 2016a). Putin may have given up the ability to monitor what is happening inside Chechnya as a result, potentially undermining long-term Russian security. This was brought to the surface most vividly with the murder of opposition politician Boris Nemtsov outside the Kremlin in 2015. Putin assigned the FSB to investigate the killing, and while many such investigations drag on without result, this led within days to the arrest and indictment of several of Kadyrov's men (Yaffa, 2016b). Some observers, including Nemtsov's family, doubt that the real killers and the motive for the assassination have been identified, but at a minimum this example illustrates the lack of cohesion among Russian security forces.

Infighting

Below the surface the Russian intelligence state is not what it seems. Various agencies have been given overlapping mandates and regularly engage in bitter infighting (Taylor, 2007, 2011; Galeotti, 2013; Galeotti, 2016). In addition to those responsible for domestic security, the rivals include the Foreign Intelligence Service (the SVR), the former KGB international directorate whose mandate to carry out foreign espionage and operations has been encroached by an expanding FSB under Putin's watch. The military intelligence agency of the Armed Forces General Staff (the GRU) has a long history of mutual antagonism towards the KGB and its predecessors. This is at least in part because their foreign espionage and operational duties have always significantly overlapped (Penkovsky, 1965; Suvorov, 1984, 1986; Richelson, 1986; Andrew and Mitrokhin, 1999).

Indeed, in Soviet times, especially under Stalin, the infighting between and even within various intelligence services was often deadly. When Stalin's blood purges turned against the security forces, whole clans of personal patronage networks were murdered together when their leaders were accused of crimes by other such clans (Getty, 2013). Competing blood purges between the predecessor of the GRU and the Chekists (the various predecessor organisations to the KGB) reportedly began in Lenin's time and intensified under Stalin (Suvorov, 1984). During the Soviet Great Fatherland War against Nazi Germany in Fall 1941, rival Moscow and Odessa groups within the Chekists (then known as the NKVD), who were vying over command in Odessa, began killing each other when they were supposed to be cooperating to win the war (Andrew and Mitrokhin, 1999).

A new element in the rivalry was added in the early 1990s when KGB officers entered private commerce. In the face of budget and personnel cuts, as well as the desire to get some benefit for themselves from Russia's new and wild capitalism, many officers retired from the KGB to provide security, muscle, and investigation of potential partners for Russia's new private businesses. Others kept their state intelligence jobs while moonlighting in the private sector (Volkov, 2002). Provision of such services was necessary even for legitimate businesses in the absence of strong state legal institutions, but they cemented a long-standing link between Soviet intelligence agencies and organised crime (Handelman, 1997). Galeotti calls this relationship today the 'spook-gangster nexus', where intelligence agencies and criminals cooperate when it is in their interests to do so, including in the 2014 Russian takeover of Crimea and continuing military action in eastern Ukraine (Galeotti, 2018a). Not surprisingly, continuing opportunities for ill-gotten gains have further stoked the rivalries between Russian intelligence forces, who have continued to provide protection and information for favoured clients, and sometimes fall afoul of each other (Taylor, 2007, 2011). Known cases of sometimes deadly commercial rivalry have affected FSB relations with the Investigations Committee, the MVD, and the FSO (Taylor, 2011; Galeotti, 2014; Aslund, 2016).

On the one hand, this infighting benefits Putin. By keeping each other in check, these various agencies ensure that none of them will become powerful enough to challenge Putin's rule. And keeping his advisors off balance, including through the selective use of *kompromat* he has gathered against them, may help ensure their personal loyalty. But once more we are confronted with the fact that what provides for the security of Putin's regime may be undermining the security of Russia more broadly: corruption and infighting detract from the ability of Russian intelligence agencies to use their resources to protect the Russian state.

Skewed analysis, risky operations

As a result of Putin's unchallenged control of the so-called power vertical in Russia, even his close advisers may be reluctant to disagree with him (Zygar, 2016). Meanwhile, the current and former intelligence officers who surround Putin and feed him analysis may be telling him what he wants to hear. In particular, they may be encouraging his tendency toward short-term thinking and recklessness in foreign affairs (Galeotti, 2017; Marten, 2018a).

One possible example of this is suggested in the controversial Steele Dossier, the opposition research report compiled by a former British intelligence officer on behalf of Donald Trump's opponents in the 2016 U.S. presidential campaign. Although some of the report's claims have been contested and are accused of having been politicised, some former U.S. intelligence officers believe that at least parts of the document may prove accurate and useful (Sipher, 2017). One claim made by the Dossier has nothing whatsoever to do with Trump, so is unlikely to have been politicised. It is that Putin approved Russian intelligence agencies' interference in the campaign against the advice of his foreign ministry and two former Russian ambassadors to the U.S. (who thought it would likely be discovered and have negative consequences for Russian interests), but on the urging of the SVR and one of Putin's closest advisors, Sergei B. Ivanov (Steele Dossier, 2016). Ivanov is a retired KGB general who befriended Putin during KGB training school in Leningrad.

If the intelligence agencies are skewing analysis to fit what Putin wants to hear, they would be following yet another pattern set by the KGB in Soviet times. The KGB international directorate, especially its offices in Western countries, had a difficult time obtaining real intelligence about politics and policy decisions. It, therefore, tended to repackage local media reports as 'intelligence' and to twist its analysis to conform to Soviet ideology and confirm what Soviet Communist Party leaders wanted to hear (Bakatin, 1992; Garthoff, 2015). Today, what the Kremlin wants to hear is unlikely to be tied to any particular ideology, but may confirm Putin's tendencies towards highly risk-acceptant aggression carried out by Russian intelligence agencies.

The GRU in particular appears to be following very risky practices abroad. For example, it has employed technically illegal private military forces like the Wagner Group in Ukraine and Syria, as well as in Sudan and the Central African Republic (Gostev and Coalson, 2016; Brown, 2018; Marten, 2018b; Marten, 2018c). The Wagner Group is led by retired GRU officers and trains next to GRU facilities, even though its existence is not recognized under Russian law. So-called "volunteer" forces, including self-described Cossacks, were active under the Yeltsin regime too, including in Chechnya, in Georgia and Moldova, and in the former Yugoslavia. But under Putin their use has skyrocketed. The use of these forces provides a number of benefits to the Putin regime. They can be sent into dangerous situations in place of regular Russian armed forces, preventing the kind of political backlash that might ensue if Russian soldiers were being killed in large numbers abroad. They can also contribute to plausible deniability, if Russia is engaged in foreign actions that it wishes to disavow. But the use of such forces magnifies the principal-agent problem (Avant, 2005). In Russia's case, their commercial interests may sometimes interfere with broader state security goals. This appears to have happened in eastern Syria in February 2018, when Wagner crossed the agreed U.S.-Russia deconfliction zone and became embroiled in a firefight with U.S.-backed Kurdish forces guarding a Conoco gas plant. The Russian military denied that the Wagner Group forces were under Russian command, and there is good evidence that they were acting under a commercial contract for the benefit of Putin's close colleague, Yevgenii Prigozhin, to seize oil and gas fields back for the Syrian regime (Malkova, Stogney, and Yakoreva, 2018). The U.S. called in airstrikes against them, killing dozens. It is fortunate that the use of the deconfliction hotline prevented this from becoming a militarized crises between Moscow and Washington.

Now there is overwhelming evidence from multiple sources that GRU officers carried out the attempted assassination of former GRU double agent Sergei Skripal in Salisbury, England in March 2018, using a perfume bottle filled with the Russian nerve agent Novichok (RFE/RL, 2018). The question of who ordered the attack and why remains subject to speculation. The fact that it killed one innocent British civilian and injured another (in addition to injuring Skripal and his daughter), nonetheless, demonstrates that the GRU has become extraordinarily risk-acceptant in carrying out attacks in the West in peacetime. The event led to a massive uptick in Western sanctions against Russia, once again also demonstrating a disconnect in Putin's Russia between the risks intelligence agencies take, and the results they obtain for Russian interests.

Conclusion

Putin has created a Russian intelligence state not only by replicating and updating but also by corrupting the model he experienced in his career as a KGB officer and FSB leader. The Soviet model itself had many flaws in its ability to provide for the real security of Russian citizens—and those flaws, too, have been replicated and even deepened under Putin's reign.

Despite their apparent successes in dampening dissent inside Russia, putting down terrorism in Chechnya, and attempting to interfere in foreign elections, it is questionable whether Putin's intelligence services are truly serving a coherent Russian security strategy, much less one that benefits and protects the Russian citizenry. Instead, they are securing Putin's personalistic and autocratic regime, while enriching themselves in the process. Their factional infighting and commercial interests are already undermining Russian security. It may be only a matter of time before a truly major crisis results from their actions.

References

Andrew, C., & Mitrokhin, V. M. (1999) *The Sword and the Shield: The Mitrokhin Archive and the Secret History of the KGB.* New York: Basic.

Andrew, C., & Mitrokhin, V. (2005) *The World Was Going Our Way: The KGB and the Battle for the Third World.* New York: Basic.

Aslund, A. (2016) Dismissal of Putin's Top Aide Reveals Rifts in Kremlin Security Services. *Atlantic Council blog*, August 12. www.atlanticcouncil.org/blogs/new-atlanticist/dismissal-of-putin-s-top-aide-reveals-rifts-in-kremlin-security-services

Avant, D. (2005) *The Market for Force: The Consequences of Privatizing Security.* New York: Cambridge University Press.

Bakatin, V. (1992) *Izbavlenie ot KGB.* Moscow: Novosti.

Brown, D. (2018) 3 Countries Where Russia's Shadowy Wagner Group Mercenaries Are Known to Operate. Business Insider, April 27. www.businessinsider.com/russia-wagner-group-mercenaries-where-operate-2018-4

Dawisha, K. (2015) *Putin's Kleptocracy: Who Owns Russia?* New York: Simon and Schuster.

Filipov, D. (2017) Russia's Aggressive Response to the St. Petersburg Subway Bombing Is Raising Questions. *Washington Post*, May 7.

Frierson, C. (2014) *Russia's Law "On Rehabilitation of Victims of Political Repression," 1991–2011.* Washington, DC: National Council for Eurasian and East European Research Working Paper.

Galeotti, M. (2013) *Russian Security and Paramilitary Forces since 1991.* New York: Osprey.

Galeotti, M. (2014) A 'Spook War' May Be Brewing Moscow Times. *Moscow Times*, June 17.

Galeotti, M. (2016) Putin's Hydra: Inside Russia's Intelligence Services. European Council on Foreign Affairs Policy Brief. www.ecfr.eu/publications/summary/putins_hydra_inside_russias_intelligence_services

Galeotti, M. (2017) The Spies Who Love Putin. TheAtlantic.com. www.theatlantic.com/international/archive/2017/01/fsb-kgb-putin/513272/

Galeotti, M. (2018a) *The Vory: Russia's Super Mafia.* New Haven, CT: Yale University Press.

Galeotti, M. (2018b) How Do You Talk to a Russian Gangster? *Yale Books Blog*, April 10. https://yalebooksblog.co.uk/2018/04/10/how-do-you-talk-to-a-russian-gangster/

Garthoff, R. (2015) *Soviet Leaders and Intelligence: Assessing the American Adversary during the Cold War.* Washington, DC: Georgetown University Press.

Getty, J. A. (2013) *Practicing Stalinism: Bolsheviks, Boyars, and the Persistence of Tradition.* New Haven, CT: Yale University Press.

Gostev, A., & Coalson, R. (2016) Russia's Paramilitary Mercenaries Emerge from the Shadows. *RFE/RL*, December 16. www.rferl.org/a/russia-paramilitary-mercenaries-emerge-from-the-shadows-syria-ukraine/28180321.html

Hale, H. E. (2014) *Patronal Politics: Eurasian Regime Dynamics in Comparative Perspective.* New York: Cambridge University Press.

Handelman, S. (1997) *Comrade Criminal: Russia's New Mafiya.* New Haven, CT: Yale University Press.

Haslam, J. (2015) *Near and Distant Neighbors: A New History of Soviet Intelligence.* New York: Farrar, Straus and Giroux.

Haynes, J. E., & Klehr, H. (1999) *Venona: Decoding Soviet Espionage in America.* New Haven, CT: Yale University Press.

Haynes, J. E., Klehr, H., & Vassiliev, A. (2009) *Spies: The Rise and Fall of the KGB in America.* New Haven, CT: Yale University Press.

Hill, F., & Gaddy, C. G. (2013) *Mr. Putin: Operative in the Kremlin.* Washington, DC: Brookings Institution Press.

Human Rights Watch. (2015) Invisible War: Russia's Abusive Response to the Dagestan Insurgency. www.hrw.org/report/2015/06/18/invisible-war/russias-abusive-response-dagestan-insurgency

Jensen, M. C., & Meckling, W. H. (1976) Theory of the Firm: Managerial Behavior, Agency Costs and Ownership Structure. *Journal of Financial Economics, 3*(4), 305–360.

Khlobustov, O. M. (2006) Fenomen Andropova. In *Trudy Obshchestva Isucheniia Istorii Otechestvennykh Spetssluzhb* (Vol. 1, pp. 192–202). Moscow: Kuchkovo Pole.

Lewis, J. A. (2014) Reference Note on Russian Communications Surveillance. Center for Strategic and International Studies, April 18. www.csis.org/analysis/reference-note-russian-communications-surveillance

Malkova, I., Stogney, A., & Yakoreva, A. (2018) Russian Mercenary Army Financier Made an Oil Deal with Syria Just Before Clash with U.S. Troops. *The Bell*, February 27. https://thebell.io/en/russian-mercenary-army-financier-made-oil-deal-syria-just-clash-u-s-troops/

Marten, K. (2012) *Warlords: Strong-Arm Brokers in Weak States*. Ithaca, NY: Cornell University Press.

Marten, K. (2017) The 'KGB State' and Russian Political and Foreign Policy Culture. *Journal of Slavic Military Studies, 30*(2), pp. 131–151.

Marten, K. (2018a) Reckless Ambition: Moscow's Policy toward the United States, 2016/17. *International Politics*. doi: 10.1057/s41311-018-0163-z

Marten, K. (2018b) The Puzzle of Russian Behavior in Deir al-Zour. *War on the Rocks*, July 5. https://warontherocks.com/2018/07/the-puzzle-of-russian-behavior-in-deir-al-zour/

Marten, K. (2018c) Semi-state Security Actors and Russian Aggression. Lawfare, July 8. www.lawfareblog.com/semi-state-security-actors-and-russian-aggression

Myers, S. L. (2015) *The New Tsar: The Rise and Reign of Vladimir Putin*. New York: Alfred A. Knopf.

Nemtsova, A. (2006) A Chill in the Moscow Air. *Newsweek*, February 5. www.newsweek.com/chill-moscow-air-113415

Penkovskiy, O. (1965) *The Penkovsky Papers*. New York: Avon.

Petrov, N. (2011) The Excessive Role of a Weak Russian State. In M. Lipman, & N. E. Petrov, *Russia in 2020: Scenarios for the Future* (pp. 303–328). Washington, DC: Carnegie Endowment for International Affairs.

Primakov, E. M., ed. (2006) *Ocherki Istorii Rossiiskoi Vneshnei Razvedki* (Vol. 6). Moscow: Mezhdunarodnyi Otnosheniia.

Remnick, D. (1993) *Lenin's Tomb: The Last Days of the Soviet Empire*. New York: Random House.

Reuters. (2017) Return of Defeated IS Fighters 'Real Threat' to Russia: RIA Cites FSB Chief, December 12. www.reuters.com/article/us-mideast-crisis-syria-russia-militants/return-of-defeated-is-fighters-real-threat-to-russia-ria-cites-fsb-chief-idUSKBN1E60PA

RFE/RL (2018). Bellingcat Names Second Skripal Poisoning Suspect As Russian GRU Agent, October 8. www.rferl.org/a/bellingcat-names-second-novichok-suspect/29532554.html

Richelson, J. T. (1986) *Sword and Shield: Soviet Intelligence and Security Apparatus*. Cambridge, MA: Ballinger.

Sanderson, T., Oliker, O., Markusen, M., & Galperin, M. (2017) *Russian-Speaking Foreign Fighters in Iraq and Syria*. Center for Strategic and International Studies. www.csis.org/analysis/russian-speaking-foreign-fighters-iraq-and-syria

Sipher, J. (2017) The Steele Report, Revisited. *Slate*, September 11. www.slate.com/articles/news_and_politics/jurisprudence/2017/09/a_lot_of_the_steele_dossier_has_since_been_corroborated.html

Soldatov, A., & Borogan, I. (2010) *The New Nobility: The Restoration of Russia's Security State and the Enduring Legacy of the KGB*. New York: Public Affairs.

Soldatov, A., & Borogan, I. (2015) *Red Web: The Struggle between Russia's Digital Dictators and the New Online Revolutionaries*. New York: Public Affairs.

Steele Dossier. (2016) *Company Intelligence Report 2016/80*. https://assets.documentcloud.org/documents/3259984/Trump-Intelligence-Allegations.pdf

Suvorov, V. (1984) *Inside Soviet Military Intelligence*. New York: Macmillan.

Suvorov, V. (1986) *Inside the Aquarium: The Making of a Top Soviet Spy*. New York: Macmillan.

Taylor, B. (2007) *Russia's Power Ministries: Coercion and Commerce*. Syracuse, NY: Syracuse University Institute for National Security and Counterterrorism.

Taylor, B. D. (2011) *State Building in Putin's Russia: Policing and Coercion After Communism*. New York: Cambridge University Press.

Treisman, D. (2011) *The Return: Russia's Journey from Gorbachev to Medvedev*. New York: Free Press.

Tsypkin, M. (2007) Terrorism's Threat to New Democracies: The Case of Russia. In T. C. Bruneau & S. C. Boraz (Eds.), *Reforming Intelligence: Obstacles to Democratic Control and Effectiveness* (pp. 269–300). Austin: University of Texas Press.

Vavina, Y., & Coalson, R. (2018) KGB General In Cossack's Clothing: Meet The Man Behind The Whips. *Radio Free Europe/Radio Liberty*, May 21. www.rferl.org/a/kgb-general-in-cossack-s-clothing-meet-the-man-behind-the-whips/29240578.html

Volkov, V. (2002) *Violent Entrepreneurs: The Use of Force in the Making of Russian Capitalism*. Ithaca, NY: Cornell University Press.

Yaffa, J. (2016a) Putin's Dragon: Is the Ruler of Chechnya out of Control? *The New Yorker*, February 8 and 15.

Yaffa, J. (2016b) The Unaccountable Death of Boris Nemtsov. *The New Yorker*, February 26.

Zygar, M. (2016) *All the Kremlin's Men: Inside the Court of Vladimir Putin*. New York: Public Affairs.

17
RUSSIAN INFORMATION SECURITY AND WARFARE

Carolina Vendil Pallin

Introduction: information warfare and security in Russia

Anyone hoping to find a description of Russian offensive strategy in the cyber or information sphere in official documents or statements will be duly disappointed. The Russian position is that it does not interfere in the internal affairs of other countries and this includes information operations. Russia does, however, see itself as a victim of undue meddling in its own internal affairs. Everything from hacker attacks to unfavourable news coverage is considered part of this unwanted activity. From the above, it is obvious that the Russian definition of what constitutes information warfare is broad – and so is the realm of national security in the information sphere. The definition available on the website of the Russian Ministry of Defence states that information warfare takes place between states, which use

> measures of dangerous influence on its information sphere, the destruction or disruption of information and communications systems from functioning normally, of security of information resources, getting unsanctioned access to these, and also mass-informational-psychological influence on the personnel of the Armed Forces and the population of the adversary in order to destabilize society and the state.
>
> *(http://encyclopedia.mil.ru)*

The very wide definition of information warfare makes it difficult to grasp analytically. This chapter focuses on information warfare in the information technology (IT) sphere. Electronic warfare, which is included in the definition, will not be treated here, nor will psychological operations and public diplomacy except indirectly.

A natural point of departure for an analysis of Russia's strategy in the information sphere is to describe the main tenets available in the country's official security documents. This is done in the first section, which also outlines the main decision-making bodies concerned with information security and warfare in the Russian policy system. One of the most important documents is Russia's Doctrine on Information Security (2016). Its content, as well as the implementation of its goals, is analysed in more detail in the second section. Russia's offensive measures in the information sphere are not described in official documents, but there are nevertheless good grounds for assuming that such measures are not only undertaken but also coordinated and developed by Russia. This is the topic of the final analytical section.

The bureaucratic framework for information security and warfare

Russia regularly publishes security strategies, doctrines and concept. The most important of these are documents have been coordinated between relevant ministries and government agencies, as well as signed into force by the president. There is a hierarchy among these documents, while the National Security Strategy (2015) bridges all security spheres. Other key documents, such as the Military Doctrine (2014), the Foreign Policy Concept (2016) and the Doctrine on Information Security (2016), are thus in line with the National Security Strategy.[1]

The Doctrine from 2016 follows the format by now established for Russian strategic documents and is part of Russia's strategic planning system. It is divided into five sections. The first section provides definitions and positions the document within the legislation and the system of strategic planning (§§1–6). The second section provides a list of Russian national interests in the information sphere (§§7–9), whereas the third describes the main information threats and the information security situation (*sostoianie*) in Russia (§§10–19). This then feeds into the fourth section, where the strategic goals for information security are identified (§§20–29). The last section details the organizational base for ensuring information security (§§30–38).

In addition to the doctrine, there is a number of policy documents that outline Russia's overall goals and concerns in the information sphere. For example, there is the government programme 'Digital Economy' (2017), a Strategy for the Development of the Information Society (2017), as well as a specific Concept for Children's Information Security (2015). Such documents are usually operationalized through roadmaps.

When it comes to formulating and implementing information and communication technology (ICT) policy, there is an intricate web of responsible authorities and decision-making bodies. Both the government and parliament initiate and adopt legislation, but semi-official as well as business organizations put forward initiatives and even perform a role in carrying out policy. At the apex of the decision-making system is the President and the Security Council, which the president chairs. The Presidential Administration is instrumental in coordinating policy together with the Security Council apparatus. The 2016 Information Security Doctrine was hammered out between representatives of the Security Council apparatus, state authorities as well as members of the scientific, expert and business communities in its Commission on Information Security. As the previous one in 2000, work on the new doctrine on information security was most likely coordinated by a deputy secretary of the Security Council.

Inside the Ministry for Foreign Affairs, Andrei Krutskikh is 'Special Presidential Representative for Questions of International Cooperation in the Sphere of Information Security', with ambassador's rank since 2014. He is responsible not least for promoting Russia's views on global Internet governance in international organizations. In addition, there is the Institute for Information Security Issues (IISI) at Moscow State University, strongly linked to the Security Council (Soldatov and Borogan, 2015, 226) and the Federal Security Service (FSB). The IISI also conveys the Russian view on information security to an international audience (Nocetti, 2015, 119). The Ministry of Defence is active foremost in formulating information security policy in its own realm when developing information, digital and communication technologies. Within the Ministry for Internal Affairs, Directorate K is responsible for combatting crime on the Internet.

The Ministry for Digital Development (until 2018 the Ministry for Telecom and Mass Communications) is the policymaking and implementing organ within the sphere of IT, electronic communication, mass communication, mass media and processing of personal data. The government service *Roskomnadzor* (The Federal Service for Supervision of Communications, Information Technology and Mass Media) is under the ministry's purview. Since it is not a ministry, *Roskomnadzor* cannot initiate legislation, but it has a key role in supervising the Internet and blocking websites, accounts and individual posts with unwanted content.

Until 2003, most aspects of information warfare and security were handled inside the Federal Agency of Government Communications and Information (FAPSI). This agency was responsible for signal intelligence and secure communications inside Russia. The notion that the Internet was a threat appeared to have been firmly entrenched inside FAPSI (Giles, 2012a, 73). When FAPSI was disbanded, most of it was absorbed into the FSB as was the view that the Internet needed to be controlled and managed by the state. The FSB is also responsible for the ICT surveillance system SORM (System for Operative Investigative Activities), which all operators are required to install. In practice, this gives the FSB 'direct remote access to all data' that passes through the internet service providers' (ISPs) networks SORM (Soldatov and Borogan, 2016, 398). In 2013, the FSB's powers to detect and counteract attacks on Russian information security were extended when it was given responsibility for a nationwide system for ensuring security in state information infrastructure. In addition, the FSB has been influential in pushing for and drafting legislation, even though formally the profile ministry for these questions is the Ministry of Digital Development. Finally, the FSB has been implicated as one of the organizations probably running IT attack groups and has actively recruited young people, for example, by visiting competitions for young programmers and hackers (Turovskii, 2017).

The Federal Protection Service (FSO) took from FAPSI in 2003 the Service for Special Communication and Information, which today is one of its largest departments. It is mainly responsible for secure government communications and the FSO has two higher education centres, which train specialists in IT. In addition, the FSO has centres for monitoring the media and public opinion (Nikolsky, 2013, 35–38) as well as activity on the Internet.

Within Russia's Parliament, both the Duma and the Federation Council play a role. The role of parliament is mainly to initiate and adopt legislation, including the federal budget. The Duma Committee on Information Policy is one of the most important vehicles for introducing new or amending existing legislation. Among the initiatives are the *Yarovaia Package* (see below), a draft bill on creating a filter or a 'white list', a National System for Filtrating Internet Traffic (NaSFIT) and legislation to increase control over social media in 2018. In reality, much legislation such as the *Yarovaia Package* was probably initiated by the FSB. Within the Federation Council, a Temporary Commission on the Development of Information Society developed a draft Concept for a Cyber Security Strategy in 2014. This document was shelved, however, perhaps because it advised against isolating a Russian segment of the Internet. Since 2016, there is also a Temporary Commission on Information Politics, and since 2017 a Temporary Commission for Protection of State Sovereignty and Prevention of Interference in Russia's Internal Affairs. Both latter commissions are active in promoting Russia's view of information security as well as pointing to the numerous national security threats in this sphere.

A number of semi-official societal organizations, such as the League for a Safe Internet, at times create the impression that initiatives to increase control over ICT come about as a result of pressure from below. However, there are also organizations such as RosKomSvoboda and the human rights organization AGORA that work actively to promote freedom of expression on the Internet. In addition, there are Internet business organizations that have tried to influence policy. The tendency since 2014 is that few major ICT companies challenge the increasing control from above. There are even differences in nuances between and even within the agencies and organizations described above (Nocetti, 2015, 118) as well as regular turf wars that go on between different agencies for influence (Giles, 2011, 51ff). However, there are few markedly dissenting voices in the web of policy-makers, legislators, government agencies, semi-official organizations and ICT companies.

Information security in practice

The information security of the Russian Federation is defined in the 2016 Doctrine as

> a situation where the individual, society and state is protected against domestic and external information threats, [a situation] in which the constitutional rights and freedoms of the person and citizen, a dignified quality and level of life of citizens, sovereignty, territorial integrity and robust social-economic development of the Russian Federation, defence and security of the state are provided for.
>
> (§2)

An information threat, meanwhile, refers to 'the aggregate of measures and factors that create a danger of damaging national interests in the information sphere' (§2). As is evident from the definitions above, the terms are broad, catch-all ones and, in fact, the word 'cyber' (*kiber*) does not appear at all in the doctrine. The word 'Internet' does, however, which it did not in the 2000 Doctrine. The 2016 definition of the information sphere thus includes objects of computerization; information systems; websites; communication networks; IT; entities that create and process information, that are involved in the development and use of ICTs, that provide information security; as well as the entire setup of mechanisms that regulate these societal relations (§1). It is difficult to think of a wider definition of the information sphere (Pynnöniemi and Kari, 2016), but ICT is certainly more in focus.

One of the main concerns is to protect the 'critical information infrastructure ... and the unified electric system of the Russian Federation in peacetime, in a period of direct threat of aggression and during war' (§8). The key threats are identified as emanating from foreign countries that use IT means for 'military goals' (§11), but the Doctrine also notes that terrorist and extremist organizations are developing means to attack critical information infrastructure (§13). The need to protect critical infrastructure was an important theme in the 2000 Doctrine on Information Security as well, but this concern appears to have intensified. At a Security Council meeting in October 2014, which seems to have been important in establishing the main directions for Russia's information security strategy, Putin pointed first to the need to protect Russian communication networks and information resources. He noted that the number of computer attacks had increased sharply ('Zasedanie Soveta Bezopasnosti', 2014). Indeed, in common with other countries, Russia was registering an increased incidence of IT attacks. It needed to develop mechanisms to detect and warn against information threats as well as mitigate the consequences. In addition, the 2016 Doctrine singled out 'foreign control' of the management of critical information infrastructure objects as something to avoid (§23).

In 2013, the FSB was tasked with ensuring the security of state information system. This became the unified State System for Detecting, Preventing and Eliminating Consequences of Computer Attacks (GosSOPKA, 2014). The system will consist of a network of centres at the regional, territorial level, as well as centres within government agencies and at state companies. GosSOPKA was primarily aimed at government structures and state-owned companies. When the doctrine was published in 2016, there was still not a system of demands on operators within the private sector and other constituent parts of the critical information infrastructure. However, in July 2017, the federal law 'On Security of Critical Information Infrastructure of the Russian Federation' was adopted – an important step towards fulfilling the goals in the doctrine.

One of Russia's main concerns, however, was that it was vulnerable to outside pressure and influence. This was why Russia conducted an exercise in July 2014, in which it explored how RuNet – primarily domains ending with.ru or.рф – would manage if detached from the global Internet (Golitsyna, 2014). At the very heart of Russia's concern – heightened by the Western sanctions introduced after Russia's annexation of Crimea – was the fact that critical infrastructure of the global Internet was located in the West. This meant that, at least in theory, Russia could be pressured by the West through threats of disconnecting it from the Internet. The three critical components of the global Internet infrastructure that Russia singled out were:

- the 13 root servers which handle the top domains – including the domain .ru;
- the Internet Routing Registry, which is a database of the hierarchy between objects that route traffic on the Internet (for Russia's ISPs, this is done through the Dutch regional registry RIPE NCC, a non-profit organization);
- the Domain Name System (DNS) list, in other words, the list of which domain name corresponds to which individual IP address.

The basic idea was to create copies of these three critical components of the global Internet. In addition to this, physical control over what international Internet traffic entered into Russia through increased control over ownership of cables was introduced, together with an overall goal of decreasing the share of 'foreign traffic' from 10 per cent to 1 per cent by 2020 (Sukharevskaia and Yuzbekova, 2016). Furthermore, in the autumn of 2017, Roskomnadzor and the MFA was tasked with initiating a discussion within the BRICS framework (Brazil, Russia, India, China and South Africa) to create a system of DNS root servers independent of ICANN. If realized, this would in practice create a parallel Internet (Kolomychenko, 2017).

Developing the Russian ICT industry is another national interest identified in the 2016 Doctrine on Information Security. The national industry remains dependent on foreign technology, especially when it comes to electronic components, programmes, digital technology and communications. To Russia, this signifies being dependent 'on geopolitical interests' of countries with a superior technological level in the field (§17–18). Similar concerns were present in the 2000 Doctrine on Information Security, but relatively little progress has been made (Pynnöniemi and Martti, 2016). At the Security Council meeting in October 2014, Putin pointed to the need to develop Russian IT as one of four prioritized directions of policy in the information security field. In particular, state agencies were to be encouraged to use Russian companies ('Zasedanie Soveta Bezopasnosti', 2014). This is a goal in the 2016 Doctrine on Information Security that will be difficult to implement. Research and innovation is not best achieved 'from above' and through legislation. In fact, some of the most talented people in the software industry, like Pavel Durov who developed the social network

VKontakte and the messaging service Telegram, left Russia as pressure and ownership control from authorities increased (Vendil Pallin, 2017). It will be difficult for Russia to realize this goal in isolation from other leading nations in the industry. Subsidizing innovation from above while imposing heavy regulation risks only fuelling corruption.

At the heart of Russian security thinking, however, is establishing control over information that is circulated on RuNet. Concerns about cyberthreats are interwoven with a general one that certain information can undermine Russia's stability and political system. The 2016 Doctrine states that 'special services of certain states increasingly use means of information-psychological influence in order to destabilize the domestic and social situation in different regions of the world', something that undermines the sovereignty and even the territorial integrity of the countries targeted (§12). The younger section of the population is considered especially susceptible to harmful influence (§12). This concern with the young Russian mind is not only present in a number of key security documents but also the main target for the programme 'Patriotic Education of the Citizens of the Russian Federation 2016–2020' (2015, see also the National Security Strategy, 2015, §76, 82; the Military Doctrine, 2014, §13; and the Concept for Children's Information Security, 2015).

This leads Russia to emphasize the need to control what information is available through ICT – the actual content on RuNet. The stated aim to secure the constitutional rights and freedoms of Russian citizens is qualified by an identified national interest to use 'information technology to preserve the cultural, historic and spiritual-moral values of the multinational people of the Russian Federation' and to bring 'reliable information about the policy of the Russian Federation and its official position to the Russian and international community' (§8). Western dominance on the Internet is thus framed as a geopolitical threat against Russia's sovereignty and even its national identity (Giles, 2012a, 72).

The concern about the information to which the Russian public is exposed was present in the 2000 Doctrine on Information Security (Skillen, 2017, 48–49, 287ff) and events such as the Arab Spring and the demonstrations in 2011–2012 only served to intensify the concern of the Russian political leadership that the Internet could be used to distribute information that could undermine Russia's political system (Soldatov and Borogan, 2015, 163ff; Giles, 2016, 36ff). A number of measures were introduced to increase control over the Internet in Russia, something that has raised more debate and concern internationally than inside Russia. In 2016, Freedom House's ranking of Internet freedom in Russia deteriorated from 'partly free' to 'not free' and the Russian branch of the non-governmental organization AGORA (2018) has monitored how rights and freedoms on the Internet have deteriorated over a ten-year period (see Table 17.1). The sections of the 2016 Doctrine on Information Security that deal with the rights and freedoms of citizens to receive and distribute information have thus become moderated by perceived threats to Russian sovereignty.

The so-called Yarovaia Package, a set of legislative amendments, was passed in July 2016, named after the Duma deputy, Irina Yarovaia, who initiated the process. This package, among other things, tasked the ISPs with storing personal data, as well as traffic content. The costs for Internet industry would be substantial, but the changes to legislation would also impinge on human rights and freedoms as data about users would be automatically available to the FSB through SORM (Rozhkov and Tishina, 2017). Moreover, Russian authorities appear to have encountered difficulties in overcoming encryption networks. This task has in effect been passed on to ISPs, who are expected to block virtual private networks and mastermind the engineers of anonymizing tools. From 2018, the law 'On Information' stipulates that users must identify themselves on messenger services, such as Telegram, Snap and Yandex. The amendments also meant that *Roskomnadzor* could block messenger services – something

Table 17.1 AGORA Internet freedom in Russia, 2011–2017

Type of Infringement	2011	2012	2013	2014	2015	2016	2017
Murder	1	–	1	1	–	–	1
Violence (threats)	10	3	23	26	28	50	66
Proposals for regulation	5	49	75	87	48	97	114
Criminal prosecution/ actual imprisonment	38	103	226	132	202/18	298/32	411/48
Administrative pressure	173	208	514	1,448	5,073	53,004	22,523
Access restrictions[a]	231	609	236	947	1,721	35,019	88,832
Court injunction on information	–	124	624	72	7,300	24,000	2,196
Cyberattacks	31	47	63	10	30	122	15
Civil legal actions	11	26	37	60	49	170	39
Other	–	28	34	168	570	3,343	1,509
Total	**500**	**1,197**	**1,832**	**2,951**	**15,021**	**116,103**	**115,706**

a AGORA notes that its data on access restrictions are based on official statistics. According to RosKomSvoboda (2018), the actual number of blocked resources was over ten million.

that happened when Russia tried to block Telegram in April 2018, leading to considerable collateral damage as sections of RuNet became unavailable to regular users. The result is that the right to privacy – articles 23 and 24 in the Russian Constitution – only applies to foreign states' accessing these data, while Russian authorities have increased their access to personal data and content with little or no possibility for individuals to control this.

Russia has also pursued its own vision on how to establish international information security especially within the United Nations (Franke, 2015, 17ff). US pre-eminence in the ICT field has led to a situation where, according to Russia's 2016 Doctrine, 'the distribution of resources necessary for a safe and stable functioning of the network "Internet" does not allow a joint, fair governance based on principles of trust' (§19). This goal is, furthermore, expressed in the Foreign Policy Concept (2016), which states that Russia takes all necessary measures to ensure international information security, to withstand the meddling in internal affairs of states and to 'develop universal rules of responsibility under the auspices of the UN', including the internationalization of the governance of the Internet (§28).

A Russian suggestion for a Convention on International Information Security was published in September 2011. Two major differences stand out between the approach of the West and that of Russia when it comes to the question of global Internet governance and security. First, Russia proposes an information security regime that would include how content – the information transmitted – influences society, whereas the West insists that what should be at the centre are questions of security and robustness of the ICT infrastructure. Second, Russia is pursuing a future international agreement that will be government-centred rather than the multi-stakeholder approach that the West wants to retain. The different approaches are mirrored in the different terminology that the West and Russia uses. Whereas the West uses the term cyber security, Russia uses the wider term of information security (Demidov, 2016, 37–39; Giles, 2012b).

Russia has been waging an uphill battle when it comes to persuading the Euro-Atlantic community, but has been more successful on the regional level, for example, inside the

Shanghai Cooperation Organization and the Collective Security Treaty Organisation (Franke and Vendil Pallin, 2012, 62–64; Giles, 2011, 50; Giles, 2012a, 77). Russia has found sympathetic voices among a group of countries that to varying degrees share its concern that the global nature of the Internet undermines the ability of governments to control information flows within their own territory or national 'information space'. The delicate problem of defining what constitutes a national information space is usually not discussed in detail, nor is the difficulties that government regulators tend to encounter with keeping up with technological development (Brown and Marsden, 2013, ix).

Russia and information warfare

Russian official documents and statements are rich on details on the need to defend itself against information warfare. Almost as prevalent are statements to the effect that Russia does not interfere in the internal affairs of other countries. In common with other countries, Russia thus does not admit to IT attacks. Moreover, it generally tends to rebut accusations by claiming that there is a tendency to implicate Russia, in order to weaken the country, that it is all part of a Western policy to contain Russia. In other words, incriminating circumstances – such as the fact that IT attack codes were written in a Russian-language environment, that attacked entities could be logically assumed to be preferred Russian targets and that the compiling of code and attacks take place during Moscow office hours – are all explained by this being part of a larger plan to blame Russia. While this cannot be excluded, it is not the most likely one. Moreover, some of what falls under Russia's wide definition of information warfare are measures that Russia openly engages in and even encourages as part of official policy.

Russia's Foreign Policy Concept (2016, §9) explicitly mentions 'soft power' as one of the methods of achieving foreign policy objectives. Since Russia considers much information biased in favour of the West, it emphasizes the need to deliver objective information as an important element of Russian foreign policy and actively involves non-governmental organisations, think tanks, cultural exchanges and academics in its public diplomacy efforts (§§46–48; see also Vendil Pallin and Oxenstierna, 2017, 11–12). Russia is thus active in promoting its view within the sphere of public diplomacy and propaganda (see the following chapter). In addition to this, Russia has created media outlets, most notably the television channel RT and the Internet-based news agency *Sputnik*, to compete with the leading Western television networks with a global reach. The editorial policy is to promote a Russian view of events. Another aspect of Russian efforts to influence the information sphere that has been widely debated is that of using bots and trolls to influence the discussion on social media networks. Not least the so-called 'troll factory', the Internet Research Agency, in St. Petersburg, has been implicated in attempts to influence the US presidential election. Certainly, data collected through unauthorized access to IT facilities appear to have been transferred to groups such as the Internet Research Agency, in order to construct effective messages in social media. In 2018, the Internet Research Agency and people working there were included in the US sanctions list as a result of this (US Department of the Treasury, 2018).

While Russia has never acknowledged that it has offensive IT operations capabilities, IT forensics have often pointed in Russia's direction and there is evidence of the government's recruiting skilled personnel in IT security and hacking. At least the FSB probably also uses affiliated resources in the form of criminal hackers and trolls on more or less ad hoc basis, but these are not part of Russia's military organization. Russia has been identified as one of the top five countries when it comes to IT warfare resources (Zecurion, 2017). There is a close link between building IT defensive and offensive capabilities, and Russian officials have explained the need to buy malware by pointing to the need to examine these to build defence mechanisms. Most likely, Russia engages in offensive IT measures as do other countries, such as the US, China, the UK and Germany.

The problem of attributing an IT attack is well researched and plagues the field as well as international relations (Demidov, 2016, 99). Nevertheless, some of the most successful cyberattack groups have been connected with Russia with a high degree of probability. Two IT operations groups that have most frequently been pointed to are closely affiliated to or run by Russia are APT28 (also often referred to as Fancy Bear) and APT29 (also referred to as Cozy Bear). These groups use a technique where emails and websites are carefully tailored to elicit interest of a targeted user. The malware they use tend to contain advanced counter-analysis techniques to hinder detection. The acronym APT stands for 'advanced persistent threat', and these groups consist of a highly skilled team that collect intelligence that is useful to a government (FireEye, 2014, 3; see also Muller, Gjesvik and Friis, 2018).

Russia sees information warfare as an integrated entity, where propaganda, electronic warfare and IT operations are all used simultaneously. There is probably a degree of coordination when it comes to developing IT capabilities and strategic targets. However, there is also evidence of a certain degree of cooperation between the constituent parts of Russia's information warfare organization. It seems likely that Russia does indeed have considerable capabilities to execute advanced IT operations against selected targets consistent with Russian security policy interests. One attractive feature of IT attacks is the difficulty to attribute an attack with 100 per cent reliability. There is, so far, no international court where such allegations can be tried and it will be a challenge to establish a powerful international institution for such investigations (Davis, 2017).

Conclusion

Russia's broad definition of information warfare and security provides it with a holistic view of what it considers not only threats to the country's national security but also an extensive toolbox for enhancing its security. While it does not single out cyberthreats specifically, it is evident not least from the 2016 Information Security Doctrine that threats especially in the ICT sphere are considered a challenge. Russia has committed considerable resources to realizing its goals when it comes to protecting critical information infrastructure and controlling content on RuNet. It also has ambitious goals for building a national ICT industry so as to get away from its import dependence, goals that probably will prove difficult to fulfil. On the international arena, Russia is painstakingly building alliances with countries like China in order to challenge the current dominance of the West, most notably the US, and to promote a Russian agenda for governance of the global Internet.

While promoting a wide definition of information security, Russia rarely discusses the conflicts of interests that arise and how to strike a balance between them. For example, Russia's efforts to control the Internet could make RuNet's infrastructure more vulnerable when it comes to bottlenecks as traffic is channelled through a limited number of exchange points. The balance between state interests of control, on the one hand, and protecting Internet users' freedom and privacy, on the other, has become decidedly skewed towards the former. A more nuanced debate on the role of global Internet companies in Internet governance and the negative effects of restricting the flow of information within and between countries is also almost absent. Finally, it is worth noting that Russia probably is developing capabilities for conducting IT attacks and that attributing such attacks will continue to be a moot point.

Note

1 These documents are regularly overhauled. For an overview and analysis of earlier versions of these documents, see Franke (2015, 11–17) and also Thomas (2014).

References

AGORA (2018) *Svoboda interneta 2017: polzuchaia kriminilizatsiia*, Annual Report, February 2018. Accessed on (1 May 2018) at http://meduza.io/static/0001/Agora_Internet_Freedom_2017_RU.pdf.

Brown, Ian and Marsden, Christopher T. (2013) *Regulating Code: Good Governance and Better Regulation in the Information Age*. Cambridge; MA: MIT Press.

'Concept for Children's Information Security' [in Russian], Government Resolution no. 2472, 2 December 2015. Accessed on (25 September 2017) at http://static.government.ru/media/files/mPbAMyJ29uSPhL3p20168GA6hv3CtBxD.pdf.

'Concept for a Cyber Security Strategy for the Russian Federation', Federation Council, February 2014. Accessed on (31 January 2018) at http://council.gov.ru/media/files/41d4b3dfbdb25cea8a73.pdf.

'Convention on International Information Security', Ministry of Foreign Affairs of the Russian Federation, 22 September 2011. Accessed on (10 March 2017) at www.mid.ru/en/foreign_policy/official_documents/-/asset_publisher/CptICkB6BZ29/content/id/191666.

Davis, John S. II et al. (2017) *Stateless Attribution: Toward International Accountability in Cyberspace*. Santa Monica, CA: RAND Corporation. Accessed on (28 May 2018) at www.rand.org/pubs/research_reports/RR2081.html.

Demidov, Oleg (2016) *Global'noe upravlenie Internetom i bezopasnost' v sfere ispol'zovaniia IKT*. Moscow: PIR-PRESS.

'Digital Economy of the Russian Federation – Programme' [in Russian], Government Regulation no. 1632, 28 June 2017. Accessed on (14 September 2017) at http://static.government.ru/media/files/9gFM4FHj4PsB79I5v7yLVuPgu4bvR7M0.pdf.

'Doctrine on Information Security of the Russian Federation' [in Russian], Presidential Instruction no. 1895, 9 September 2000. Accessed on (15 September 2000) at www.scrf.gov.ru/Documents/Decree/2000/09-09.html.

'Doctrine on Information Security of the Russian Federation' [in Russian], Confirmed through Presidential Decree no. 646, 5 December 2016. Accessed on (11 August 2017) at http://static.kremlin.ru/media/acts/files/0001201612060002.pdf.

Federal Law no. 187, 'On Security of Critical Information Infrastructure of the Russian Federation', 26 July 2017.

FireEye (2014) 'APT28: A Window into Russia's Cyber Espionage Operations?' *FireEye Special Report*. Accessed on (21 February 2018) at www.fireeye.com/content/dam/fireeye-www/global/en/current-threats/pdfs/rpt-apt28.pdf.

'Foreign Policy Concept of the Russian Federation' [in Russian], Presidential Decree no. 640, 30 November 2016. Accessed on (26 September 2017) at http://static.kremlin.ru/media/events/files/ru/ZIR5c3NHwMKfbxUqKvNdqKhkA4vf3aTb.pdf.

Franke, Ulrik (2015) *War by Non-Military Means: Understanding Russian Information Warfare*, FOI Report, FOI-R--4065--SE, March, Stockholm.

Franke, Ulrik and Vendil Pallin, Carolina (2012) *Russian Politics and the Internet in 2012*, FOI Report, FOI-R--3590--SE, December, Stockholm.

Giles, Keir (2011) '"Information Troops" – A Russian Cyber Command', in Czosseck, C., Tyugu, E. and Wingfield, T. (eds.), *3rd International Conference on Cyber Conflict*, NATO CCD COE Publications, Tallinn, pp. 45–60.

Giles, Keir (2012a) 'Russia and Cyber Security', *Nação e Defesa*, no. 133–5, pp. 69–88.

Giles, Keir (2012b) 'Russia's Public Stance on Cyberspace Issues', in Czosseck, C., Ottis, R. and Ziolkowski, K. (eds.), *4th International Conference on Cyber Conflict*, NATO CCD COE Publications, Tallinn, pp. 63–75.

Giles, Keir (2016) 'Handbook of Russian Information Warfare', *Fellowship Monograph, Research Division – NATO Defense College*, no. 9 (November).

Golitsyna, Anastasiia (2014) 'Sovet bezopasnosti obsudit otkliuchenie Rossii ot global'nogo interneta', *Vedomosti*, 19 September. Accessed on (28 May 2018) at www.vedomosti.ru/politics/articles/2014/09/19/suverennyj-internet.

GosSOPKA (2014) 'Concept for State System for Detecting, Preventing and Eliminating Consequences of Computer Attacks on Information Resources of the Russian Federation (excerpt)' [in Russian], Confirmed by the President, no. K 1274, 12 December 2014. Accessed on (15 September 2017) at www.fsb.ru/files/PDF/Vipiska_iz_koncepcii.pdf.

Kolomychenko, Mariia (2017) 'Sovbez Rossii poruchil sozdat' "nezavisimyi internet" dlia stran BRIKS', *RBK*, 28 November. Accessed on (30 April 2018) at www.rbc.ru/technology_and_media/28/11/2017/5a1c1db99a794783ba546aca.

'Military Doctrine of the Russian Federation' [in Russian], Presidential Instruction no. 2976, 25 December 2014. Accessed on (26 September 2017) at www.scrf.gov.ru/security/military/document129/.

Ministry of Defence of the Russian Federation (2011) 'Kontseptual'nye vzgliady na deiatel'nost' vooruzhennykh sil Rossiiskoi Federatsii v informatsionnom postranstve'. Accessed on (19 January 2018) at http://ens.mil.ru/science/publications/more.htm?id=10845074@cmsArticle.

Muller, Lilly Pijnenburg, Gjesvik, Lars and Friis, Karsten (2018) *Cyber-weapons in International Politics: Possible Sabotage against the Norwegian Petroleum Sector*. NUPI Report, no. 3, Oslo. Accessed on (10 April 2018) at http://hdl.handle.net/11250/2486814.

'National Security Strategy of the Russian Federation' [in Russian], Presidential Decree no. 683, 31 December 2015. Accessed on (26 September 2017) at www.scrf.gov.ru/security/docs/document133/.

Nikolsky, Aleksey (2013) 'Federal Protection Service – FSO', *Moscow Defense Brief*, no. 4, pp. 35–39.

Nocetti, Julien (2015) 'Contest and Conquest: Russia and Global Internet Governance', *International Affairs*, Vol. 91, no. 1, pp. 111–130.

'Patriotic Education of the Citizens of the Russian Federation 2016–2020' [in Russian], Adopted through Government Resolution, no. 1493, 30 December 2015.

Pynnöniemi, Katri and Kari, Martti (2016) *Russia's New Information Security Doctrine: Guarding a Besieged Cyber Fortress*, FIIA Comment, no. 26 (December), Helsinki. Accessed on (11 August 2017) at www.fiia.fi/en/publication/646/russia_s_new_information_security_doctrine/.

RosKomSvoboda (2018) 'Infografika'. Accessed on (18 May 2018) at https://reestr.roskomsvoboda.org/.

Rozhkov, Roman and Tishina, Yuliia (2017) '"Paket Yarovoi" napolniat psevdonimami', *Kommersant*, 12 August. Accessed on (2 October 2017) at www.kommersant.ru/doc/3383396.

Skillen, Daphne (2017) *Freedom of Speech in Russia: Politics and Media from Gorbachev to Putin*. New York: Routledge.

Soldatov, Andrei and Borogan, Irina (2015) *The Red Web: The Struggle between Russia's Digital Dictators and the New Online Revolutionaries*. New York: Public Affairs.

'Strategy for Development of the Information Society in the Russian Federation 2017–2030' [in Russian], Adopted by Presidential Decree, no. 203, 9 May 2017.

Sukharevskaia, Alena and Yuzbekova, Irina (2016) 'Lishnego ne utechet: kak immeno chinovniki namereny obesopasit' Runet', *RBK*, 17 June. Accessed on (17 June 2016) at www.rbc.ru/technology_and_media/17/06/2016/57613a4b9a794724f3e07644.

Thomas, Timothy (2014) 'Russia's Information Warfare Strategy: Can the Nation Cope in Future Conflicts', *The Journal of Slavic Military Studies*, Vol. 27, no. 1, pp. 101–130.

Turovskii, Daniil (2017) 'V Moskve sushchestvuet kruzhok shkolnikov-programmistov pod FSB, gde uchenikam raskazyvaiut pro evreiskii zagovor', *Meduza*, 25 May. Accessed on (29 May 2017) at https://meduza.io/feature/2017/05/25/v-moskve-suschestvuet-kruzhok-shkolnikov-programmistov.

US Department of the Treasury (2018) 'Changes to the Specially Designated Nationals and Blocked Persons List since January 1, 2018', *Office of Foreign Assets Control*. Accessed on (16 March 2018) at www.treasury.gov/ofac/downloads/sdnnew18.pdf.

Vendil Pallin, Carolina (2017) 'Internet Control through Ownership: The Case of Russia', *Post-Soviet Affairs*, Vol. 33, no. 1, pp. 16–33.

Vendil Pallin, Carolina and Oxenstierna, Susanne (2017) *Russian Think Tanks and Soft Power*, FOI Report, FOI-R-4451-SE, August, Stockholm.

'Zasedanie Soveta Bezopasnosti', *Prezident Rossii*, 1 October 2014. Accessed on (18 September 2017) at http://kremlin.ru/events/president/news/46709.

Zecurion (2017) 'Kibervoiny 2017: balans sil v mire', *Zecurion Analytics*, January. Accessed on (22 March 2018) at www.zecurion.ru/upload/iblock/cb8/cyberarmy_research_2017_fin.pdf.

18
INFORMATION-PSYCHOLOGICAL WARFARE IN RUSSIAN SECURITY STRATEGY

Katri Pynnöniemi

Introduction

The research on information-psychological warfare has been one of the major themes of Russian military science since at least the 1960s and the development of the reflexive control theory (Thomas, 2004). One can go even further in the history, to Chinese strategist Sun-Tzu, or to the publication of Lenin's essay *On Guerrilla Warfare* in 1906, where he anticipated practices and strategies to be used in the political struggle for power. The set of measures ranged from assassination of political enemies to the stimulation of mass consciousness for active, but controlled, actions supporting the Bolshevik Revolution in Russia (Pynnöniemi, 2016, 31–32). Much later, these tactics became known as 'organisational weapon'. This term refers to organisations or organisational practices that are torn from their 'normal' context and used in the ways that are 'unacceptable to the community as legitimate mode of action' (Selznick, 1960, 2). These practices include, but are not limited to, the creation of unconventional tools of intervention, the direct weakening of the propaganda targets and the neutralisation of the opposition. As concluded in a study first published in 1950s, these tools were used 'to control directly the *arena* of conflict' (Selznick, 1960, 7).

Western research in the 1980s renamed the concept 'organisational weapon' as 'active measures' that refer to 'certain overt and covert techniques for influencing events and behaviour in, and the actions of, foreign countries'. One of the pioneering works emphasised information and the psychological nature of these actions, such as attempts to deceive the target and distort the target's perceptions of reality (Shultz and Godson, 1984, 198; see also Clews, 1964, 23). With the collapse of the Soviet Union, the research on propaganda and disinformation was rebranded anew and partly, forgotten. However, in the context of military studies, comparative research on Russian and US views on information operations and other forms of information warfare continued (Thomas, 1998).

The use of 'political technologies' was an important part of the struggle for political and economic power in the 1990s, although research on these phenomena was not articulated in the framework of information warfare. The adoption of a law on information security in 1995 and the subsequent information security doctrine in 2000 signalled the importance given to this sphere in Russia. From the Russian perspective, a series of 'colour revolutions' in the former Soviet countries starting with the 2003 Rose Revolution in Georgia and the 2004 Orange Revolution in Ukraine, became a game-changer. These events demonstrated the possibilities vested in the information-psychological techniques and other non-conventional measures. Since then, the term 'colour revolution' has stuck in the Russian foreign policy parlance and research literature. After 2014, it is used in describing the events in Ukraine and is often used interchangeably with the term 'hybrid war'.

Information-psychological warfare comes in many disguises. Each of the terms briefly discussed above is a product of its time. Some of these terms have been forgotten, whereas others seem to travel through time and become revitalised in a new era. This chapter analyses assumptions underlying the contemporary Russian debate on information warfare. The focus is on research literature and other writings that contribute to the formation of the Russian conceptualization of information security policy, and especially on information-psychological warfare as the information-technological (cyber) sphere was already examined in the previous chapter. The purpose is to illuminate assumptions guiding the official policy that in turn help us to understand differences and similarities between Russian and the Western thinking on this topic. The downside of this choice is that critical voices that challenge the official policy line or conspiratorial interpretations of information warfare that dominate the public debate are not discussed in full (see Berzina, 2018). However, some works from this latter genre are included in the analysis (Panarin, 2010, 2017; Brychkov and Nikonorov, 2017). The argument put forward in this article is that attention to nuances, even in translation, can create new knowledge about the roots of Russian thinking on threats to information security and assumptions guiding Russia's security strategy in this sphere.

Conceptualisation of information-psychological warfare in Russia

A study[1] published by the Primakov Institute of World Economy and International Relations of the Russian Academy of Sciences (IMEMO) notes that

> the ambiguity of the term "information warfare" defined and developed in the doctrines of the USA, gave rise to a *discrepancy in its translation*, resulting in the emergence of a large number of other definitions existing nowadays in the Russian journalistic and scientific sources.
>
> *(Romashkina, 2016, 19, emphasis added)*

Instead of addressing these problems in translation, the authors review the US terminology on information warfare, as well as numerous definitions provided by different Russian authorities.

The definition of 'information war' used in the study is taken from *the Intergovernmental Agreement of the SCO Member States on Cooperation in the Information Space* (Agreement, 2009). Actually, this same definition[2] appears later in the Russian Defence Ministry document known as the *Conceptual Views on the Activities of the Armed Forces of the Russian Federation in Information Space* (Conceptual Views, 2011). Accordingly, information war is

> *Confrontation between two or more states* in the information space for damaging the information systems, processes and resources, which are of critical importance, and other structures, to undermining the political, economic and social system, and massive brainwashing of the population for *destabilizing the society and the state*, and also *forcing the state to make decisions in the interests of the confronting party*.
>
> *(Conceptual views, 2011, emphasis added)*

This definition of information warfare addresses key assumptions in the Russian debate. First, information war is a strategic-level confrontation between two or more states. With this, it is understood as a geopolitical struggle for power (Derbin, 2017). Second, information war provides the means to destabilise society and state, and finally, is a coercive tool with which the target (country) can be forced to make decisions that favour the attacking party. Each of these assumptions will be addressed in more detail in the following three chapters.

Information warfare as a form of counter-struggle

The dictionary (encyclopedia) of information-psychological operations published in 2011 provides a good starting point for the analysis of concepts guiding Russian thinking on information warfare. It contains, as the title suggests, terminological explanations for the phenomenon and technologies relevant for waging information warfare. Thus, 'information warfare' is translated as *armed informational confrontation*, aka *information war (voina)*, whereby two (or more) antagonistic systems make use of 'open or hidden targeted informational influences with the purpose of gaining an advantage in material sphere' (Venprintsev et al., 2011, 68). This definition originates from the theory developed by Professor Sergey Rastorguyev who is considered one of the most prominent Russian theorists of information warfare (Berzina, 2018, 164). Later, the entry on 'information confrontation' (*informatsionnoe protivoborstvo*) defines it as rivalry (*sopernichestvo*) between social systems in the information sphere, aimed at gaining control of the strategic resources, as a result of which one participant in the competition acquires advantage required for further development, whereas others will lose that chance (Venprintsev et al., 2011, 318–319).

The two above-mentioned definitions do not distinguish between peace and war, but indicate that information confrontation is a continuous and comprehensive process affecting the whole of society. One of the authors of the dictionary, Andrei Manoilo,[3] later specified that 'information-psychological confrontation' may take any form of social and political competition (*konkurentsii*) and comprises a wide spectrum of conflict situations, from individual-level conflicts to open confrontation of social systems (Manoilo, 2015, 184). The underlying idea, put forward in the dictionary, is that information confrontation is about competition for (strategic) resources and ultimately for (state) power.

The literary translation of the term 'information confrontation' (*informatsionnoe protivoborstvo*) is 'counter-struggle', 'counteraction', or 'countermeasure'. As noted earlier by Ristolainen, 'the verb *protivoborstvovat* can be found in common dictionaries and is translated as "to oppose", or "to fight against"'. Thus, the correct translation would be 'information counter-struggle'. The translation of Russian term as 'information warfare' misses the underlying rhetorical game, aimed at portraying Russia as the one 'under attack' (Ristolainen, 2017, 10–11). The original Russian concept underlines the active role of other countries in the information sphere and, at the same time, masking the ways in which Russia wages information war. Accordingly, Russian academic and popular literature discuss extensively the Western experiences of conducting information warfare and only rarely refer to Russia's own operations (Gapich and Lushnikov, 2014; Gryzlov and Pertsev, 2015; Manoilo, 2015; Brychkov and Nikonorov 2017; Kokoshin, 2017).

Although the general context is different, the argumentation is familiar from the Soviet era when the textbook on psychological war declared that only imperialist countries were conducting psychological warfare, whereas 'the Soviet Union did not need the help of defamation, disinformation and lies', for it had historical truth on its side (Volkogonov, 1983, 8). This did not, however, prevent the Soviet Union from systematically manipulating and mobilising mass movements and other political forces for the sake of the creation and facilitation of tensions internationally and within the capitalist countries (Morozov et al., 1978; Aspaturian, 1980; see also Pynnöniemi and Rácz, 2016). The underlying logic of these 'active measures' (Shultz and Godson, 1984) derived from the relative weakness of the Soviet Union in face of the US military and industrial potential. Consequently, the use of 'non-military factors' was expected to play in favour of the Soviet Union in the overall equation of the 'correlation of forces' (Aspaturian, 1980, 10).

The above-mentioned study published by the Russian research institute IMEMO exemplifies how this logic applies in the current context. The authors of the study argue that *confrontation* in the information space takes place between two groups of states: the Shanghai Cooperation Organisation (SCO) member-states (Russia, Kazakhstan, China, Kyrgyz Republic, Tajikistan and Uzbekistan) and the 'the developed countries'. The latter states 'have established authorities and special committees that are responsible for providing information technology and information-psychological security, as well as for conducting information operations'. Having characterised what is required for a level playing field, authors conclude that 'information security is an integral and increasingly important part of the process of ensuring *strategic stability*' (Romashkina 2016, 21, emphasis added).

The rhetoric used in the above characterisation is typical for the Russian debate. The developed countries are deemed active both in defence of information space and in conducting offensive information operations. Russia, in turn, is represented as passive (especially with regard to the conflicts in Georgia and Ukraine). What is emphasised instead is Russia's role in building a legal basis for the protection of international information security. The study argues that Russia does this because it

> supports demilitarisation of the international information space, the necessity of completion and adaptation of the mechanism of international law in relation to IT, and also creation of new norms, emphasizing that the arms race in information space is capable of destabilising the developed agreements on disarmament and international security in other spheres.
>
> *(Romashkina 2016, 104)*

A more mundane explanation for this interest in rewriting international agreements and policies in the information sphere is that, in this way Russia seeks to 'alleviate dangers posed by its own underdevelopment and to increase the monitoring of information sphere inside Russia' (Pynnöniemi and Kari, 2016; see also Thomas, 2014, 128). Although these concerns are real, and Russia is keen on advancing its interests in the international legal sphere, much of the current debate focuses on the dangers the information warfare poses for the societal and state security.

The colour revolution as information warfare technology

On the eve of the Russian presidential elections in 2018, the Russian Federation Council established a special commission tasked to study 'foreign interference into Russia's internal affairs'. The committee was tasked to offer recommendations how to mitigate this threat. The annual report of the commission identified several types of interference including the foreign financing of Russian non-governmental organisations, the spread of foreign ideas through educational programs, the creation of a negative image of Russia in the foreign media, politisation of the sport events (read World Cup) and stimulation of ethnic and social antagonism within Russia (Doklad, 2018). The report merely registered the mainstream interpretation according to which threat towards Russian information security were increasing. As stated in the Russian military doctrine,

> It is noteworthy that military dangers and threats are also moving into the information space and within the Russian Federation. Against this background, although the likelihood of a major war on the Russian Federation has declined, the military threats to Russia are on the rise.
>
> *(Military Doctrine, 2014, Article 11)*

The underlying assumption is that information technologies are used for the purpose of destabilising society and the state. This basic starting point is expressed with the concept of 'colour revolution' that refers to the set of information-psychological technologies manipulated outside the target country and used for the purpose of initiating a state coup. The typical argument states that the Western countries use colour revolutions as instruments to create a (neo)liberal order at the global scale (Novikov et al., 2017). The most evident use of this rhetorical strategy is among the popular literature intended for wider audiences. In recent publications, the colour revolution concept is replaced with the reference to 'hybrid war' (Panarin, 2016, 2017). Both in the academic literature and in official documents, Western governments, in particular the US, are accused of 'weaponisation of information' and, consequently, for the creation of conditions that have led to the emergence of local armed conflicts and uprisings in different parts of the world (Gryzlov and Pertsev, 2015; National Security Strategy, 2015; see also Thomas, 2014).

Some researchers compare the 'colour revolution technologies' to 'irregular warfare' (Gapich and Lushnikov, 2014, 7), whereas others, such as Andrei Manoilo, suggest that local wars and armed conflicts manifest the objectives and logic rooted in the information-psychological war that ultimately is about 'political struggle for power and authority […] conducted with the means of information weapons' (Manoilo, 2015, 185). In this context, Russia's own experiences in using information and other non-military measures are rarely mentioned. The war in Georgia in 2008 stands out as an exception to this general rule, for it has been identified both as a success story (Novikov, 2017, 30) and a failure (Gareev, 2008; Evseev and Idayatov, 2016). Little is also said about the use of these methods in the conflicts in Ukraine or Syria, apart from 'showing' their Western origin (National Security Strategy, 2015).

Russian activities in the information sphere are often framed with the concept of 'soft power'. As the original concept suggests (Nye, 2004), soft power (*myahkaya sila, vlast'*) is not coercive but designed to influence the target through attraction. The Russian government agency established for promoting the interests of Russian speakers abroad is used as an example of Russia's attempts in this sphere. Sometimes his concept is used interchangeably with the term colour revolution to underline that the phenomenon in question has negative repercussions for Russia. What is more common, however, is that debate on colour revolution does not address issue of 'soft power' and vice versa (Borisova, 2016, 7).

Reflexive control at the time of war and peace

The third aspect of information warfare, identified in the above definition, refers to a situation where the target is forced to make decisions in the interests of the confronting party (Conceptual Views, 2011). In accordance with this new form of warfare, an attack is successful when it leads to the 'self-disorganisation' and 'self-disorientation' of the adversary, and the subsequent capture of the enemy's resource base and its usage to the benefit of the attacker (Ovtchinskii and Sundiev, 2013, 1). The theory of reflexive control, intensively developed by Soviet military and civilian theorists since the early 1960s, explains and provides practical means for achieving the 'self-disorganisation' of the enemy. According to V. A. Lefebvre, one of the thinkers behind the theory, reflexive control is 'a process by which one enemy transmits the reasons or bases for making decisions to another' (cited in Thomas, 2004, 2). As explained by Tim Thomas, an expert on Russian information war:

> Reflexive control occurs when the controlling organ conveys (to the objective system) motives and reasons that cause it to reach the desired decision, the nature of which is maintained in strict secrecy. A "reflex" itself involves the specific process of imitating the enemy's reasoning or imitating the enemy's possible behavior and causes him to make a decision unfavorable to himself.
>
> *(Thomas, 2004, 5)*

The task, so to speak, is to find a weak link in the enemy's 'filter' and exploit it. The filter is 'made up of concepts, knowledge, ideas and experience', and it can be targeted by an information weapon defined as a 'specially selected piece of information capable of causing changes in the information processes of information systems in accordance with the intent of the entity using the weapon' (Thomas, 2004, 11; see also Pynnöniemi and Rácz, 2016).

This is what in Soviet terminology was meant by *disinformation*. As described by Ladislav Bittman in an essay published in 1985, disinformation is 'a carefully constructed, false message that is secretly introduced into the opponent's communication system to deceive either his decision-making elite or public opinion' (Bittman, 1987, 113). For this purpose, various channels were used, including rumours, forgeries, manipulative political actions, agents of influence, front organisations and other means (Shultz and Godson, 1984, 195). As explained by Bittman, Soviet disinformation operations were,

> Acts of opportunity reflecting the long-term interests of the Soviet Union. Their primary objective is to add another drop of venom to the opponents' internal system which the expectation that eventually, after a certain period of time, quantity will become quality and the patient will die.
>
> *(1987, 119)*

Given this theoretical background, it is perhaps not surprising that many Russian works interpret the demise of the Soviet Union and the subsequent end of the Cold War as a Western victory in the information struggle. According to the popular conspiratorial argumentation, the Soviet Union lost the 'first information war' because the country's leadership acted upon false premises, in other words, was under foreign influence (Panarin, 2010).

In the context of more theoretical debate, a distinction is drawn between 'standard information war' that takes place as a part of a military operation (e.g. use of camouflage) and 'strategic information war' that refers to information-psychological operations aimed to change the perception of the target in a way that is favourable to the attacker (Venprintsev et al., 2011, 72). Researchers identify three general features of what they call 'strategic information war'. First, it is asymmetrical, making it difficult to predict the direction and means of possible attack. Second, different layers of society are attacked separately, while the appearance of peace is maintained (Venprintsevm et al., 2011, 73). With the use of non-military methods, the appearance of peace can be maintained without jeopardising the main objectives (Derbin, 2017, 15–16). Third, the same person can be attacked by multiple attackers simultaneously with each targeting a different sphere of cognition. Consequently, the clear distinction between 'friend' and 'enemy' (e.g. marked by the use of military uniform) is lost, making it more difficult to recognise the direction and the form of attack. This leads to the loss of the sense of danger, which is, in turn, the most dangerous aspect of the information war (Venprintsev et al., 2011, 74).

The definition of the term 'information weapon' offers additional insight on Russian thinking on information war. The dictionary defines information weapon as 'special means, technologies and information that are used in influencing the information space of the target society and in achieving significant damage to political, military, economic and other strategically significant state interests' (Venprintsev et al., 2011, 234). The dictionary, like other Russian studies on the subject, distinguishes between information-psychological weapons and information-technical (cyber) weapons. These two general categories are further specified by distinguishing between programming weapons (computer, or cyber sphere); psychological weapons; chemical, biological and biochemical weapons; electromagnetic weapons; infrasound weapons; and psychophysiological weapons (Venprintsev et al., 2011, 236).

Vladimir Novikov, a professor at the Russian military academy, provides one of the most extensive descriptions of information-psychological weapons (Novikov, 2017). Professor Novikov specifies different categories of information-psychological weapons, including 'mass-media weapons', 'virtual information-psychological weapons' (e.g. mobile games like Tamagotchi), 'energy-informational psychological weapons' (ultrasound technologies harming physical systems and human organisms), 'psychotropic information weapons', 'bioenergy information weapons' (control of another person through hypnosis), 'information-genetic weapons' and 'somatotropic-psychoinformation weapons' (use of chemical and biological entities to affect human body). Furthermore, he identifies in this category also translation as form of struggle for linguistic meaning, as well as neurolinguistics influence, virtual money, flashmob and finally, geolocation technology (Novikov, 2017, 150; see also Thomas, 2014, 123–124, on other Russian authors discussing nonlethal and cognitive attacks).

What makes information weapons different from other types of weapons is explained with reference to three functions: asymmetry, mimicry and adaptation. *Asymmetry* refers in this context to idea that one element of the system can out-manoeuvre the whole system, thus leading to unpredictability. *Mimicry* is a root concept of deception. It refers to situation where appearance (or form) is maintained, but the content has changed. Thus, recognition of the form and direction of attack, as noted in above, becomes a challenge. And finally, *adaptation*, that refers to the transformation of context to fit the objectives of attacker (Venprintsev et al., 2011, 236). Taken together, these weapons can be used in a controlled manner, provide means to achieve quick results relatively cheaply, and due to their universal character, can be applied in different political and situational contexts (Manoilo, 2015, 197–198).

The main goal of the information struggle is to ensure the protection of the national interests in the information-psychological sphere. This refers, in particular, to the protection of the information-psychological security of the state (Venprintsev et al., 2011, 318). The Russian national security documents define what this means concretely.

The strategic context of information-psychological confrontation

Already in 1996, the Federal Agency of Governmental Liaison and Information (FAPSI), announced that 'the effect produced by information weapons can be compared only with weapons of annihilation', and therefore, in 1997, 'the Duma and the CIS Inter-Parliamentary Assembly had appealed to the UN, OSCE, and Council of Europe with a proposal to pass international ban on information wars and demanded that the turnover of information weapons be limited'. According to Andrei Soldatov, an expert on Russian information security, the security authorities in Russia had succeeded to lobby the government for allocating funding to develop such weapons, that were, subsequently, identified among the 'three priority factors deterring possible aggressions together with the Strategic Nuclear Force and the systems of high-precision weapons' (Soldatov, 2000, 1). Today, Russia considered among the most advanced countries when it comes to the development of state-of-the-art cyber capabilities (see previous article by Carolina Vendill Pallin).

More recently, the Russian National Security Strategy (2015) identifies information warfare among the risks (and dangers) to Russian national security. It states that the 'polycentric world' is shaped by the open-ended struggle for 'resources, access to markets, and control over transportation arteries'. Furthermore, 'competition between states is increasingly encompassing social development values and models and human, scientific, and technological potentials'. The Strategy reflects an idea that traditional military power, although important in intimidating Russia's weaker neighbours, is not sufficient for protecting Russia's strategic interests amid changing security landscape. The new situation requires 'asymmetric approach', where Russia's strengths (weaponisation of information, technology and organisations) are coupled with relative weakness in military-technological (force) development. The main objective of this approach is expressed in Article 36, where it is stated that

> Interrelated political, military, military-technical, diplomatic, economic, informational, and other measures are being developed and implemented in order to ensure strategic deterrence and the prevention of armed conflicts. These measures are intended to prevent the use of armed force against Russia, and to protect its sovereignty and territorial integrity.

This paragraph summarises Russia's strategy of active defence, where a set of non-military measures (informational, political, economic, organisational and cyber resources) are activated in order to neutralise a potential threat to Russia's national interests.

The information security doctrine identifies risks, dangers and threats to Russian national security in four distinct spheres: state defence; state and public security; economy, science, technology and education; and in the sphere of strategic stability and equal strategic partnership (Information Security Doctrine, 2016). The main forms of action in the protection of the information-psychological security of the state and society include:

- neutralisation of information and psychological impact, including aimed at undermining the historical foundations and patriotic traditions associated with the protection of the Motherland;
- the countering (*protivodeistvie*) of the use of information technologies for the propaganda of extremist ideology, the spread of xenophobia, the ideas of national exclusiveness, in order to undermine sovereignty, political and social stability, violent change of the constitutional order, violation of the territorial integrity of the Russian Federation;
- neutralisation of information impact aimed at eroding traditional Russian spiritual and moral values (Information Security Doctrine, 2016, Articles 21d, 23a, k).

Here again a similar rhetoric strategy is adopted, as was discussed in the first section. Russian actions are framed as counteraction against the (aggressive) foreign information-psychological influence. Since this obviously is not the whole picture, the last section of this article will briefly discuss how Russia's opportunities and challenges in this sphere are defined in the context of Russian research literature.

Towards a Russian model of information-psychological warfare

The concept of 'geoinformational threat', developed by Russian researchers, refers to global geopolitical antagonism (*protivostoyaniya*), in the conditions of which 'financial-economic, political groups, and elites of different countries' aim to 'change the balance of political space within particular societies or in the world society at large'. The 'network technologies', first and foremost the Internet, are identified as 'the most important manipulative-propagandistic channel that has both disinformation and destructive potential' (Kochekova and Opaleva, 2018, 104–105, 122–23). Given the high level of development in the Western countries, they are in a better position to 'control and influence information space' and, therefore, form a major threat to Russian information security. Accordingly, the Internet is viewed as a resource that is controlled by the Western states and used 'for the resolution of political missions' against the interests of the Russian state (Kochekova and Opaleva, 2018, 106).

Another strand of argumentation interprets the geopolitical meaning of information space with reference to Russian exceptionalism and its civilisational mission. In their work on state information policy in the framework of information-psychological war, Andrei V. Manoilo, Anatolii I. Petrenko and Dmitri B. Frolov argue that

> real threats to Russia's national interests are not linked to the use of exotic information weapons against Russia, but stem from the danger of Russia losing her current status in the world politics. Authors call for mitigation of information-cultural expansion and consolidation of Russian national-intellectual potential in the global information space and alternative to the Western paradigm of globalisation.
>
> *(Manoilo et al., 2013, 85, 106)*

This Russian alternative is distinguished from four other models of information-psychological warfare, namely the Anglo-Saxon, Middle Eastern, East-Asian and Romano-German models (Manoilo, 2015, 218–270). Manoilo explicitly warns against imitation of the Anglo-Saxon model (a complete control of the information sphere supported by the military dominance) because this would lead to the instrumentalisation of the UN norms and thus would go against the Russian foreign policy principles. Furthermore, the use of 'colour revolution' technology (considered as the core of the Anglo-Saxon model) would make Russia an aggressor in the eyes of international society (Manoilo, 2015,[4] 301–304).

The specific Russian model should be based on Russian mentality and national traditions, as well as on the Russian schools of thought in political, psychological and sociological research spheres. Although Russia has not yet chosen a specific model, its basic features are already emerging. These include the following:

- formation of positive image of Russia as a country that is effectively solving international conflicts;
- conduct of psychological operations at the individual and mass consciousness level both in the conflict zone and beyond;
- the role of Russian special services in conducting psychological operations;

- protection of the domestic audience and state decision-making bodies from the foreign information-psychological influence (Manoilo, 2015, 307–310).

Taking into account later developments, most importantly Russia's actions during the war in Ukraine and Syria, this list provides quite comprehensive view on Russia's 'model' of information-psychological warfare. During the critical periods of conflict, especially in Ukraine, Russia has been able to systematically craft an image of itself as the one 'outside' the conflict, rather than the principal aggressor (Pynnöniemi, 2016). At the same time, the state-owned media companies have 'protected' the Russian domestic audience by creating and maintaining enemy images from Ukrainian 'fascists' to all-encompassing portrayal of the West as a threat to Russia (see, e.g., Giles, 2016; Pynnöniemi and Rácz, 2016). The active participation of Russian special services in specific psychological operations is more difficult to confirm. However, in the course of recent years, there is more and more public evidence about this. From the individual research reports (Aaltola, 2016; Conley, 2016; Kivimäki, 2017), systematic reporting (EUvsDisinfo, 2018) to official acknowledgement by the US authorities about the Russian meddling during the presidential elections in 2016 (ICA, 2017).

Conclusion

In the Western context, the term 'information warfare' usually describes 'limited, tactical information operations carried out during hostilities'. The Russian approach takes a holistic view of information warfare, seeing it as 'an ongoing activity regardless of the state of relations with the opponent' (Heickerö cited in Giles, 2016, 4). In the Russian context, information 'is both the subject and the medium of the conflict' (Giles, 2016, 4).

The deep-rooted image of Russia as a 'besieged fortress' is an important part of the argumentation on information security. The conceptualisation of information warfare as a counter-struggle implies that Russia is in a defensive posture. The comparative disadvantage that Russia has in specific high-technology sectors is sometimes highlighted to further support this claim. The underlying assumption is that information warfare is a struggle for geopolitical power between state actors. This idea is highlighted, especially in those works that see the information warfare in long-term perspective as a form of competition between different cultural-civilisational entities. Thus, the argumentation about information-psychological counter-struggle is construed as a discourse on the Otherness and incompatibility of Russian and Western social-political models. This is particularly the case with present-day academic and, most importantly, policy-oriented research that seeks to contribute to the formation of Russian information security policy. However, this conclusion remains incomplete since the studies that challenge the current policy line are not included in this analysis.

Notes

1 One of the reviewers of this work is Colonel Anatolii Streltsov, who is an author of several authoritative books on information security strategy and has been attached to the Russian National Security Council since 1995 (Franke, 2015, 28).
2 The Ministry of Defence documents provide more accurate translation of original Russian definition and are, therefore, used here.
3 Andrei Manoilo is a professor of Moscow State University and defended his doctoral dissertation in 2008 on the role of information-psychological technologies in the conflict resolution and is a member of the Russian Security Counsel scientific board (Auvinen et al., 2018, 14).
4 The first edition of the textbook was published in 2008.

References

Aaltola, Mika (2016) 'Cyber Attacks Go Beyond Espionage. Strategic Logic of State-Sponsored Operations in the Nordic-Baltic Region, *FIIA Briefing Paper* 200. Accessed on (May 28, 2018) at www.fiia.fi/en/publication/cyber-attacks-go-beyond-espionage.

Aspaturian, Vernon V. (1980) 'Soviet Global Power and the Correlation of Forces', *Problems of Communism*, Issue 9, May–June, pp. 1–18.

Auvinen, Toni, Martti J. Kari, Toni Puranen, and Anu Shibutani ja Juho Salminen (2018), *Venäjä informaatiovaikuttamisen kohteena*, Jyväskylän yliopisto, informaatioteknologian tiedekunta, KYBS7022, Informaatiovaikuttamisen erityiskysymyksiä, 7 May 2018.

Berzina, Ieva (2018) 'The Narrative of 'Information Warfare against Russia' in Russian Academic Discourse', *Journal of Political Marketing*, Vol. 17. No. 2, pp. 161–175.

Bittman, Ladislav (1987) 'The Language of Soviet Disinformation', in *Contemporary Soviet Propaganda and Disinformation: A Conference Report*, United States Department of State.

Borisova, E.G. ed. (2016) *Soft Power. Mezhdistsiplinnarnyi Analiz*. Moskva: Izdatelstvo Nauka.

Brychkov, A.S. and G.A. Nikonorov (2017) 'Colored Revolutions in Russia: Possibility and Reality', *Vestnik Akademii Voennyh Nauk*, No. 3 (60), pp. 4–9.

Clews, J. C. (1964) *Communist Propaganda Techniques*. London: Methuen.

Conceptual Views Regarding the Activities of the Armed Forces of the Russian Federation in the Information Space (2011). Accessed on (May 5, 2018), Originally Published in Russian Language at: http://ens.mil.ru/science/publications/more.htm?id=10845074%40cmsArticle#1.

Conley Heather et al. (2016) *The Kremlin Playbook. Understanding Russian Influence in Central and Eastern Europe*. A Report of the CSIS Europe Program and the CSD Economics Program. Accessed on (May 28, 2018) at https://csis-prod.s3.amazonaws.com/s3fs-public/publication/1601017_Conley_KremlinPlaybook_Web.pdf.

Derbin, E.A. (2017) 'Methodological Aspects of Analyzing Modern Warfare', *Vestnik Akademii Voennyh Nauk*, Vol. 1, No.58, pp. 11–18.

Doctrine on Information Security of the Russian Federation (2016) Confirmed through Presidential Decree No. 646, 5 December 2016. Accessed on (August 11, 2017) at http://static.kremlin.ru/media/acts/files/0001201612060002.pdf.

Doklad (2018) 'Ezhegodnyi doklad vremennoi komissii Soveta Federatsii po zashcite gosudarstvennoi suvereniteta i predotvrashcheniyu vmeshatel'stva vo vnutrennie dela Rossiiskoi Federatsii', 5 March, 2018, Accessed on (April 2, 2018) at http://council.gov.ru/media/files/G6hNGZ3VbQNiMdZki1BKbrsrvuRxPwim.pdf.

EUvsDisinfo (2018) 'Everyone against Russia: Conspiracy Theories on the Rise in Russian Media', 22 May 2018, News and Analysis. Accessed on (May 28, 2018) at https://euvsdisinfo.eu/everyone-against-russia-conspiracy-theories-on-the-rise-in-russian-media/.

Evseev, V.V. and A.K. Idayatov (2016), 'Georgian – South-Ossetic Conflict in 2008: Lessons from the Information Warfare', in Romashkina, N.P. and A.V. Zagorskii, eds. *Information Security Threats During Crises and Conflicts of the XXI Century*, Moscow: IMEMO, Accessed on (January 15, 2018) at www.imemo.ru/files/File/en/publ/2016/2016_001.pdf.

Franke, Ulrik (2015) *War by Non-military Means, Understanding Russian Information Warfare*, The Swedish Defence Research Agency, March.

Gapich, A.E. and D.A. Lushnikov (2014) *Technology of Color Revolutions*. Moskva: RIOR, INFRA-M.

Gareev, Makhmut (2008) 'Strategicheskoe Sderzhivanie: problemy i resheniya', *Krasnaya Zvezda*, 8 October.

Giles, Keir (2016) 'The Next Phase of Russian Information Warfare', NATO Strategic Communications Center of Excellence, Accessed on (May 6, 2018) at www.stratcomcoe.org/next-phase-russian-information-warfare-keir-giles.

Gryzlov, B.M and A. B. Pertsev (2015) 'Information Confrontation. History and Modernity', *Vestnik Akademii Voennyh Nauk*, No. 2 (51), pp. 124–128.

ICA (2017), 'Assessing Russian Activities and Intentions in Recent US Elections', *Intelligence Community Assessment*, 7 January. Accessed on (May 28, 2018) at www.dni.gov/files/documents/ICA_2017_01.pdf.

The Intergovernmental Agreement of the SCO Member States on Cooperation in Providing International Information Security (2009). Accessed on (April 23, 2018) at http://docs.pravo.ru/document/view/20364925/19329178.

Kivimäki, Veli-Pekka (2017), 'The Cyber-Enabled Information Struggle. Russia's Approach and Western Vulnerabilities', *The FIIA Briefing Paper* 220. Accessed on (May 28, 2018) at www.fiia.fi/julkaisu/the-cyber-enabled-information-struggle.

Kochetkova, Aleksandra and Opaleva, Alekandra, eds. (2018) *Natshionalnaya bezopasnost' Rossii v usloviyah globalizattsii*. Geopoliticheskii podhod, Moskva: Unity.

Kokoshin, A.A. (2017) *Politologiya i Sotsiologiya Voennoi Strategii*. Moskva: URSS. Third edition. First published in 2005.

Manoilo, A.V. (2015) *Tekhnologii Nesilovogo Razresheniya Sovremennyh Konfliktov*. Moskva: Goryachaya liniya – Telekom, Second edition. First published in 2008.

Manoilo, A.V., A. I. Petrenko, and D. B. Frolov, eds. (2013) *Gosudarstvennaya Informatsionnaya Politika v Usloviyah Informationno-psihologicheskoi Voiny*. Moskva: Goryachaya liniya – Telekom, Second edition. First published in 2003.

Morozov, G.I., ed. (1978) *Obshchestvennost' i Problemy Voiny i Mira*. Moskva: Mezhdunarodnye Otnoshenie.

Novikov, V. K. (2017) *Informatsionnoe Oruzhie – oruzhie sovremennyh i budushchii voin*. Moskva: Goryachaya liniya – Telekom. Third edition. First published in 2011.

Novikov, V. K., S.V. Golubhinov, and V.V. Zakharov (2017) 'The Main Reasons and Conditions for Initiation and Waging of an Information War', *Vestnik Akademii Voenniyh Nauk*, Vol. 4. No. 61, pp. 28–32.

Nye, Joseph S. (2004), *Soft Power. The Means to Success in World Politics*. NY: Public Affairs.

Ovtchinskii, V.S. and I.Yu. Sundiev (2013), 'Organizatsionnoe Oruzhie: funktsionalnyi genesis i Sistema tehnologii XXI veka', *Izborskii klub*. Accessed on (October 23, 2013) at http://www.dynacon.ru/content/articles/1466/.

Panarin, Igor (2010) *Pervaya Mirovaya Informatsionnaya Voina*. Razval SSSR. Moskva: Piter.

Panarin, Igor (2016) *Informatsionnaya Voina i Kommunikatsii*. Moskva: Goryachaya liniya – Telekom. Second edition. First published in 2014.

Panarin, Igor (2017) *Gibridnaya Voina Protiv Rossii 1816–2016*. Moskva: Goryachaya liniya – Telekom. Second edition. First published in 2016.

Pynnöniemi, Katri (2016) 'The Metanarratives of Russian Strategic Deception', in Pynnöniemi, Katri and András Rácz, eds., *Fog of Falsehood. Russian Strategy of Deception and the Conflict in Ukraine*, The Finnish Institute of International Affairs, Report No. 45, Accessed on (May 6, 2018) at www.fiia.fi/fi/publication/588/fog_of_falsehood/.

Pynnöniemi, Katri and András Rácz, eds. (2016) *Fog of Falsehood. Russian Strategy of Deception and the Conflict in Ukraine*, The Finnish Institute of International Affairs, Report No. 45, Accessed on (May 6, 2018) at www.fiia.fi/fi/publication/588/fog_of_falsehood/.

Pynnöniemi, Katri and Martti J. Kari (2016) 'Russia's New Information Doctrine: Guarding the Besieged Fortress', *The FIIA Comment* No. 26, The Finnish Institute of International Affairs, Accessed on (April 12, 2018) at: www.fiia.fi/en/publication/russias-new-information-security-doctrine.

Ristolainen, Mari (2017) 'Should 'RuNet 2020' Be Taken Seriously? Contradictory Views about Cybersecurity between Russia and the West', in Kukkola, Juha, Mari Ristolainen and Juha-Pekka Nikkarila, eds., *Game Changer: Structural Transformation of Cyberspace*, Puolustusvoimien tutkimuslaitos, Julkaisuja 10, Tampere: Juvenes Print.

Romashkina, N. P. (2016) 'Modern Information Security Threats: from Practice to Theory', in Romashkina, N.P. and A.V. Zagorskii, eds. *Information Security Threats During Crises and Conflicts of the XXI Century*, Moscow: IMEMO, Accessed on (January 15, 2018) at www.imemo.ru/files/File/en/publ/2016/2016_001.pdf.

Russian Military Doctrine (2014) Presidential Edict N2976N, Approved 25 December 2014, Accessed on (May 5, 2018) at www.scrf.gov.ru/security/military/document129/.

Russian National Security Strategy (2015) Approved by Decree of the President of the Russian Federation, 31 December, 2015, No. 683, Accessed on (May 5, 2018) at www.scrf.gov.ru/security/docs/document133/.

Selznick, Philip (1960) *The Organisational Weapon. A Study of Bolshevik Strategy and Tactics*. Chiago, IL: The Free Press of Glencoe. First Published 1952 by the RAND Corporation.

Shultz, R. and R. Godson (1984) *Dezinformatsia. Active Measures in Soviet Strategy*. New York: Bergamon Brassey's.

Soldatov, Andrei (2000) 'The Riders of the 'Psychotropic' Apocalypse', *Segodnya*, 11 February.

Thomas, Timothy L. (1998) 'Dialectical versus Empirical Thinking. Key Elements of the Russian Understanding of Information Operations', *The Journal of Slavic Military Studies*, Vol. 11, No. 1, pp. 40–62.

Thomas, Timothy L. (2004) 'Russia's Reflexive Control Theory and the Military', *Journal of Slavic Military Studies*, Vol. 17, pp. 237–256.

Thomas, Timothy L. (2014) 'Russia's Information Warfare Strategy: Can the Nation Cope in Future Conflicts?', *The Journal of Slavic Military Studies*, Vol. 27, No. 1, pp. 101–130.

Venprintsev V.B. et al. (2011) *Operatsii informatsionno-psihologicheskoi voiny. Kratkii entsiklopedicheskii slovar-spravochnik*. Moskva: Goryachnaya Linya - Telekom.

Volkogonov, D. A. (1983) *Psikhologicheskaya Voina. Podryvniye deistviya imperializma v oblasti obshchestvennogo soznaniya*. Moskva: Voennoe Izdatelstvo.

19
OUTER SPACE IN RUSSIA'S SECURITY STRATEGY

Nicole J. Jackson

Today, the Russian Federation is a major actor in space and outer space governance. Its presence in space is second only to that of the US. Meanwhile, the challenges of keeping outer space 'secure' is growing in importance and complexity in the current context of globalisation, rapid technological change, and the increasing access to space for state and non-state actors. Russia considers outer space as a strategic region to enhance its military capabilities on earth, provide intelligence and communication functions, and achieve international status and prestige as a space power. It is sensitive to US strategy and actions and has developed counter-space technologies (e.g. electronic weapons that can jam satellites) to provide Russia with an asymmetrical edge to offset US military advantages. However, Russia's outer space rhetoric and policy are also driven by domestic and identity issues. Outer space strategy is an instrument through which Russia pursues its goal to be a 'great power' and to shape the international system more closely to the new multipolar world as it sees it. It may also bring Russia economic benefits and mask internal challenges.

President Vladimir Putin has taken both symmetric and asymmetric actions in outer space and increased Russia's investment in new technologies (satellites, electronic warfare,[1] strategic offensive weapons, etc.) and simultaneously pursued diplomatic initiatives to control weapons in space. During the Cold War, despite military tensions and serious concern about a possible arms race in outer space, Russia and the US negotiated internationally binding agreements related to the governance of space activities. Today, both powers are again warning of a new arms race in outer space while continuing to strengthen the roles of their militaries in the field.

Since 2000, Russia has actively pursued both binding laws and non-binding norms to ban and control weapons in outer space and has advocated for non-binding, voluntary transparency and confidence-building measures (TCBMs). Sometimes it has done this in cooperation with other states, sometimes in opposition to them. This diplomatic endeavour may seem somewhat at odds with Russia's growing militarisation; however, the dual role on outer space fits well within Russia's overall foreign and security strategy which is both reactive to US policy and simultaneously pro the United Nations (UN) and consensus-based multilateral negotiations. Russia is strengthening its comprehensive power, including military, diplomatic and normative global influence, in order to make its voice heard on the international stage. Russia's diplomatic activism is that of an aspirational great power, but it also reflects the limits of its current economic and military weaknesses. International negotiations enable Russia to be recognised as a key player in global affairs, while also benefiting from an opportunity to highlight the US/West's declining influence and the rise of a multipolar world.

This chapter examines why outer space is so important for Russia. Then, it shows how and why the Russian government's outer space strategy and capabilities have evolved since the 1990s. The paper concludes with an appraisal of Russia's recent diplomatic initiatives on outer space governance.[2] No longer economically competitive in the race for control of outer space, Russia has attempted several strategies to enable it at least to keep in the running. It has placed its space strategy in the context of defence requirements and state military control. It is using diplomacy – working with international organisations affiliated with the UN – to discuss, cooperate on and influence the race for the militarisation of space. It works with disarmament organisations to influence and promote a collective approach to the problem, rather than one dominated by the richer and more powerful states.

Russia's securitisation of outer space: threats and opportunities

The Russian state defines threats largely in traditional terms of territorial protection from military challenges and views space assets as vital for military communication and defence. Russia's geography highlights the need to protect its extensive borders and military and economic assets and infrastructure scattered over its vast territory (Barvinenko, 2007). The state has traditionally assessed that it is surrounded by hostile powers and thus needs 'buffers' or a 'sphere of influence' to protect itself. Today, Russia has expanded this rhetoric of vulnerability to include attacks from outer space. Russians use the term 'aerospace' rather than outer space because of the interrelatedness of airspace and outer space in the context of contemporary threats and conflicts, and because there is no distinct boundary between the two concepts (Kupriyanov, 2005). Russia's rhetoric on outer space broadly mirrors that of the US, stressing urgency to prepare for a possible future war there. In 2017, US Navy Vice Admiral Charles Richards, deputy commander of US Strategic Command, argued that 'With rapidly growing threat of a degraded space environment, we must prepare for a conflict that extends into space' (quoted in Daniels, 2017).

Rapid technological advancements in the space industry have influenced perceptions that there are economic benefits from being a space power. At the same time, they have given rise to concerns about threats stemming from the militarisation of space. For example, the development of cheap miniature satellites promises speedy replacement of disabled satellites in the event of attack. Theoretically, this could allow the US military (or other actors) to use such space constellations to support operations during a conflict.[3] Through technology outer space has become integrated with other domains – land, sea, air and cyber. Most recently, the first generation of hypersonic weapons has 'set the conditions for the merger of air and missiles defence and the air and outer space domains' (Charron and Fergusson, 2018). Of course, a healthy space industry also provides strategic resources for a state's military and economy. In Russia's case, the announcement of new technological developments also masks unaddressed structural and systemic weaknesses, and confers domestic and international legitimacy on Russia's aspiration to be a 'great power'.

Russia's official perceptions today are not very different from those of the Soviet period. Outer space has long been significant to Russia, and now it again has the resources to be a major contender. Under Putin, as in Soviet times, Russia seeks global strategic parity with the US and securitises the US threat to its nuclear deterrence. Russia perceives a US first strike against its nuclear forces from space-based weapons as the key security threat from space. Its 2010 and 2014 Military Doctrines classify both the deployment of strategic missile defences (the intention to place weapons in space) and the deployment of strategic conventional precision weapons as key military dangers to Russia. Other threats listed include impeding state command and control and disruption of strategic nuclear forces, missile early warning systems, and systems for monitoring outer space. Both these doctrines and the 2016 Foreign Policy Concept highlight the US and North Atlantic Treaty Organisation (NATO) as potential enemies at a time of 'increased global competition' and conclude that Russia needs to focus not only on the credibility of its nuclear deterrent but also on conventional and non-conventional elements in a complex toolkit of responses (The Military Doctrines of the Russian Federation, 2010, 2014; Russia's Foreign Policy Concept, 2016).

Russia has also adamantly opposed US plans for ballistic missile defence (BMD), which it perceives as opening a door towards space-based weapons integrated into BMD architecture and in turn could threaten Russia's strategic missiles forces. The 2002 US withdrawal from the 1972 ABM Treaty paved the way for deployment of intercept missiles, and Russians interpreted this move as undermining the consensus on the strictly peaceful use of space. In this context, in 2015 Russia threatened that 'Any action undermining strategic stability will inevitably result in counter measures' (Russian Government, 2015). Russia's key security preoccupation has been the prospect of space-based interceptors and the US refusal to accept constraints on BMD. It continues to denounce the US withdrawal from the ABM Treaty and argues that the development of US ground- and sea-based missile defence have increased tensions and led to increased missile proliferation which Russia directly links to space-based threats.

The Russian (and Chinese) governments also believe that their missiles and satellites are targeted by US anti-missiles.[4] Russia perceives anti-satellite weapons tests (ASATs) by China (2007) and the US (2008) to be precursors to the weaponisation of space. ASAT capabilities are those that target an adversary's satellites with the intention of disabling their function – communications; intelligence, surveillance and reconnaissance (ISR); navigation; positioning – through interference or damaging/destroying the satellite entirely. The latter creates a second-order effect of creating space debris that threatens other space assets and activities in that spatial region.

The Russian government argues that these multiple developments are leading to a new arms race that disrupts broader arms control and disarmament processes and requires Russia's huge expenses for its space program (Luzin, 2015). In March 2018, Putin announced the development of some 300 new 'strategic weapons' which he said was a response to US missile defence capabilities and then unveiled several at the annual Victory Day military parade (RFE/RL, 2018).[5] Such showmanship was not new, but Putin's hyperbole and critique of the West has intensified, and Western concern about Russia's intentions and growing, if overblown, capabilities are likely to continue.

The evolution of Russia's outer space strategy 2000–2008: Russia's securitisation and militarisation of outer space

The Soviet Union had been a pioneer and military superpower in outer space. The 1990s in Russia were characterised overall by economic stagnation, military disintegration and dependency on the West. This was reflected in a dramatic decrease in Russia's space budgets and space assets (Arbatov, 2011). The Russian economic recovery in the 2000s coincided with a political emphasis on space as a strategic sector and subsequent increases in its state budget. Space became a symbol of Russia's revived international standing, and attempts were made to restore its former space glory and prestige (Facon and Sourbes-Verger, 2007). For Putin, space policies became a central tool in Russia's rebirth as a great power and its drive for independence from the West, and he prioritised rebuilding and modernising Russia's military space capabilities. Clearly, he aimed to reduce Russia's dependencies on West (especially on technology and military data) and ensure strategic autonomy and independent access to space.

Russia began restructuring its space industry in the early 2000s, increasing the role of the state (as it did in other strategic sectors). Space and defence industries reoriented production away from export markets towards national armed forces. Both sectors were place under the new Military-Industrial Commission (*Voenno-promychlennaia komissiia*, VPK). Venet writes that this led to mixed results, including some 'spectacular failures', e.g. the loss of military and dual-use satellites, foreshadowing President Medvedev's call for more extensive military reforms (Venet, 2015, 360). Russia's policies on space militarisation (use of space assets to support military actions on Earth) continued to focus on the territory of Russia and the former Soviet Union. According to Venet, Russia could not return to the Soviet global approach (i.e. maintain the 'high number of military launches and… extensive constellations of military spacecraft needed for all for military communications, navigation, surveillance, early warning, signals intelligence etc') (Venet, 2015, p. 363).

During Putin's first two terms, many state programmes[6] and presidential decrees brought Russia into a leading position in the space industry, developed new public-private partnerships and expanded international cooperation (Edelkina, Kraasev and Velikanova, 2015). However, even with steady economic growth during these years, space spending remained precarious, prompting Roskosmos (The Federal Space Agency) to petition President Putin for more funding. In the early 2000s, GLOSNASS was revived and new satellites were launched (Honkova, 2013). This provided a source of prestige and a symbol of independence from the US in positioning, timing, information and navigation.

Concurrently, Russia began to modernise its ground infrastructure (important for satellite control, space surveillance networks and cosmodromes). It brought ground-based assets back to Russian territory, and militarised space assets already there. For example, Roskosmos took over the Baikonur Cosmodrome in Kazakhstan, and the Plesetsk Cosmodrome in Northern Russia was set to become Russia's major military spaceport. Russia also revived its ASAT system program (not co-orbital ASAT system) and made substantial advances in ballistic missiles, radars and missile defence interceptors (details below).

2008–2013: Halting modernisation and growing ambitions following the Russia-Georgia conflict

After Russia's war in Georgia in 2008, and with President Medvedev in power, the push for space modernisation resumed; however, uncertainty over funding and overambitious plans continued. Russia's space industry did survive the 2008 world economic crisis, declining oil revenues, and foreign capital flight thanks to government subsidies. However, the war in Georgia highlighted the limits of Russia's military capabilities and the failure of its command and control system. Space-based intelligence was deficient and satellite communications facilities were not useable. There was no situational awareness and satellite targeting was not operational (for artillery or precision-guided munitions).

Russia's early warning system (crucial for nuclear deterrence) improved in subsequent years, but still lacked global detection. Then, it then lost its last major satellites in 2014. GLONASS regained full operational capacity only in December 2011 when the second-generation

GLONASS-MA entered service, but difficulties with the technology, and political disputes over its deployment lingered. However, there is evidence that the Russian government during these years increasingly perceived space-based systems as highly important and essential for integration of command, control, communications, information, surveillance and reconnaissance (C31SR), and also for what Russians call the 'information-strike operations' – which consist of 'information-strike battles, information-weapons engagements and strikes with the goal of disrupting enemy troop command and control of weapons systems and the destruction of its information resource' (Johnson-Freese, 2017, 44).

The 2011 Presidential decree on science and technology, which provides the current legal basis for technological development of the Russian economy, included plans for space, information and communications systems (President of the Russian Federation, 2011). However, many of the projected missions and launches were postponed, and a gap between stated goals (e.g. creation of a unified, information, command and control system) and realities remains (Samoylova, 2013). Many experts question the quality of Russia's space-based communication system as well as the required infrastructure on the ground. As a result, it has often been suggested that the Russian armed forces did not evolve relative to new combat realties and that Russia should focus more on reconnaissance, electronic warfare capabilities, command and control, data processing and information distribution systems (Gareyev, 2009; McDermott, 2012; Roffey, 2013).

2014 and beyond: moving to the offensive?

Since Russia's annexation of Crimea in 2014 and its military involvement in Syria, tensions between Russia and the West have dramatically increased. Russia's 2014 military doctrine included in its list of key external threats: 'global strike',[7] the intention to station weapons in space and strategic non-nuclear precision weapons (Russia's Security Council, 2014). Russia continues to argue that to preserve the strategic balance of power, it must respond to US actions. It, therefore, seeks to limit the technical superiority of the US by focusing on counter-space activities such as cyber and electronic warfare while fostering uncertainty about its own intentions. The potential threat to Russia's strategic nuclear deterrent and the US pursuit of 'global strike' conventional precision missile systems are frequently cited as the main reasons that Russia can't consider further reductions of offensive forces at this time Overall, while Russian rhetoric has become increasingly bellicose, Russia continues to militarise and centralise its policies on outer space with an emphasis on the importance of information. The stated strategic priorities of its current Security Strategy include 'Strengthening the country's defence, ensuring the inviolability of the Russian Federation's constitutional order, sovereignty, independence and national and territory integrity' and 'consolidating the Russian Federation's status as a leading world power, whose actions are aimed at maintaining strategic stability and mutually beneficial partnerships in a polycentric world' (The National Security Strategy of the Russian Federation, 2015).

Some argue that a close reading of Russia's current space documents reveals confusion about different goals and budgets (Zak, 2018). However, the documents also reveal Russia's key principles on space policy, including the protection of state interests such as the right to self-defence; the promotion of economic development, including the development of space assets, launch vehicles, ground infrastructure; the development and use of space technology and goods and services in the interests of Russia's socio-economic sphere and the space and rocket industry; and maintenance of Russia's primary position in piloted flights. Public documents include plans to create a new generation of space complexes and systems to be competitive in the world market and, once again, the completion of the GLONASS system Russian Federal Government, 2014.

The Federal Space Program, a long-term planning document (Space Activity of Russia in 2013–2020, 2014), listed three goals: contributing to the development of the economy, enhancing national security and strengthening Russia's position in the world, and increasing the welfare of Russia citizens The subsequent Federal Space Program 2016–2025 continues to prioritise the competitiveness and large-scale use of the GLONASS system as well as ground infrastructure for space activities (Interfax, 2015).

Since 2014, the centralisation of Russia's space industry has advanced. It reverted to state ownership in the 2000s, but the heads of companies retained their autonomy and were involved in bureaucratic fights with Roscosmos. Then, Roscosmos merged with state-owned United Rocket and Space Corporation to create the Roscosmos state corporation. This new state corporation has been criticised as being similar to the old Soviet model with no incentive other than to follow instructions from political leaders (Luzin, 2015). Other recent developments include Russian plans for a new space system including systems for intelligence and warning of air and space attacks, and destruction and suppression of forces and means of air and space attack. In 2015, the Russian Space Forces (established in 1992) was merged as a new branch of Russia's Aerospace Defence Forces responsible for monitoring space objects, identifying potential threats to the nation from space and preventing 'attacks as needed' (Jotham, 2018). This branch combines elements of space forces, air forces, as well as air and missile command. (Meanwhile, US President Trump is moving to separate space activities from the Air Force with his executive order in June 2018 to create a new Space Force.)

Russia has continued to work on ground facilities to control orbit and wage electronic warfare by targeting space communication and navigation systems. It allegedly jammed global positioning system (GPS) signals during the Crimean conflict in 2014 (Harrison, Johnson and Roberts, 2018). Luzin wrote in 2016 that outer space communications and reconnaissance remain the Achilles' heel of the Russian Army (Luzin, 2016). However, during the Syrian conflict, Russia used reconnaissance aircraft in addition to Soviet-era Vishnya-class intelligence gathering vessels (AGIs) and ground-based SIGINT facilities on Syrian territory (Hendrickx, 2017). Nevertheless, for now Russia remains dependent on airborne, sea-based and ground-based reconnaissance assets to compliment satellite data. Future plans include investment in counter-drone and electromagnetic warfare capabilities, as part of an 'automated reconnaissance and strike system' towards advanced communications, reconnaissance and targeting capabilities (Tucker, 2018). US Director of National Intelligence, Daniel Coats, concluded in 2018 that 'Russia aims to improve intelligence collection, missile warning, and military communications systems to better support situational awareness and tactical weapons targeting… Russia plans to expand its imagery constellation and double or possibly triple the number of satellites by 2025' (Coats, 2018).

Russia also allegedly has, or is developing, new ASAT capabilities, including direct energy lasers,[8] interceptor missiles, manoeuvrable satellites, robotics and electronic warfare (Weeden, 2015; Mizokami, 2018). Although many of these remain unverified or denied by the Russian government, US experts believe that the biggest threats from outer space are 'non-kinetic threats such as jamming satellite-based capabilities such as GPS and communications' and that Russia has sent micro-satellites into space which could be used to ram another satellite or snoop on it to collect data or interfere with its capabilities (Daniels, 2017). Russia is also developing BMD capabilities, which are now centred around Moscow with plans for a national missile defence dome (Bodner, 2018; Luzin, 2018). Missile defence capabilities may have dual function as ASATs, particularly systems deployed around the

Kremlin. Russia has reportedly carried out the world's longest test of a surface-to-air missile system (The Moscow Times, 25 May 2018). Its efforts to develop hypersonic glide vehicles are argued to be explicitly aimed at evading US missile defence systems (Podvig quoted in Live Science, 2018).

Addressing the Russian Military Academy of the General Staff in March 2018, Army General Valery Gerasimov announced that the next phase of Russia's new high-tech approach will focus on robotics, artificial intelligence, the information and space spheres as well as on economic and non-military targets (quoted in Tucker, 2018). This approach is likely to continue. It is reactive to increases in the US' military budget, as well as to rapid technological developments, and is part of a larger effort to move possible conflicts into areas of 'non-traditional warfare'. However, despite all of its modernisation programs, upgrades and plans, Russia continues to be weak in many space systems and many argue that long-term structural weaknesses affecting the broader economy, such as an ageing workforce, inefficiency and brain drain, have still not been solved.[9]

Russia's strategy on outer space security issues since 2000 has also included diplomacy, just as it did in the Soviet period. Previously, the Soviet Union co-sponsored the Partial Test Ban of 1963 and the landmark Outer Space Treaty (OST) of 1967. Soviet delegates were active at the Conference on Disarmament (CoD) to promote discussion on the 'Prevention of an Arms Race in Outer Space' (PAROS).[10] Under Putin, Russia has used the UN and its affiliated bodies to attempt to develop binding laws, non-binding norms and TCBMs to prevent and control the use of weapons in space. Russia's official rhetoric is that it cooperates with states that share its goals and preference for multilateral and inclusive negotiations at the UN. Certainly, Russia's diplomatic activism reflects a desire to participate in international organisations and fora to shape international rules, but it may also be a strategy to hedge its comparative economic and military weaknesses. Russia participates in the UN as part of a broader attempt to develop relations with other states of the emerging 'multipolar international system' and as a platform to denounce what Russia perceives as the US' role in undermining the international rules of the game (e.g. The US 'unilateral pulling out of the ABM treaty but also Western military operations that lack the UN Security Council's mandate, Iraq and Kosovo).

Russia introduced a working paper in 2002 and then two more in 2004 at the CoD. These became the basis for the 2008 Russia-Chinese Draft Treaty on 'Prevention of the Placement of Weapons in Outer Space and the Threat or Use of Force Against Outer Space Objects' (PPWT). This draft treaty extended the OST prohibitions on placement of weapons of mass destruction (WMD) to all forms of weapons. It sought to ban 'any device placed in Outer Space, based on any physical principle, specially produced or converted to eliminate, damage or disrupt normal function of objects' (Conference on Disarmament, 2008). As Paul Meyer explains, 'the termination of the ABM treaty meant the elimination of the only prohibition on space-based weapons agreed upon beyond the ban on WMD in the 1967 Outer Space Treaty' (Meyer, 2016). As mentioned above, Russia equates space weapons with WMD and has consistently argued that their deployment would have a destabilising effect on the global strategic balance. The US and other critics of the PPWT argued that the Russia-China Treaty did not include a verification mechanism, it only limited deployment not building of weapons; did not include terrestrial-based ASAT weapons[11] and did not resolve the problem of how to define a 'weapon'. In response, in June 2014, Russia and China presented a revised version of the PPWT, which included a new article acknowledging the need for verification measures and suggested that these could be elaborated in a subsequent protocol to the treaty.

However, further consideration of the PPWT has been prevented by the general blockage of the CoD, and Russia and China have not taken the draft to another forum. They prefer the CoD which protects their interests and gives them a voice and legitimacy (Lavrov, 2017). Unsurprisingly, Russia also opposed the 2008 European Union (EU) Draft Code of Conduct for Outer Space (and its latest draft of March 2014) arguing that the EU code is undermining the work of the UN on space security. Russia and the BRICS argue that the proper format for such deliberations must be 'inclusive and consensus-based multilateral negotiations within the framework of the UN,' and to 'take into account the interests of all States' (BRICS, 2015).

Since 2005, Russia has also solicited and proposed ideas for non-legally binding and voluntary TCBMs at the UN General Assembly. A UN Group of Governmental Experts (GGE), chaired by Victor Vasiliev, head of the Russian delegations to the UN GGE, produced a report in 2013 that enumerates several potential TCBMs, including information exchange, risk reduction measures, visits to space-related facilities and consultative mechanisms (UN General Assembly, 2013). This report led to subsequent UN General Assembly resolutions encouraging states to review it. To quote Vasiliev (2015), '...we tried to put forward proposals that were practical, implementable, did not undermine sovereign rights or security of States'. In 2018–2019, a new GGE will make recommendations on creating international legally binding instruments to prevent an arms race in outer space, including the prevention of the placement of weapons in outer space. Since the Conference on Disarmament remains in a state of paralysis, this means that Russia and China have finally shown some creativity and found another platform for official work on their PPWT and other possible legal instruments. As a final example of Russia's active diplomacy, Russia has also been pushing a 'no first placement of weapons in outer space' resolution which was adopted by the UN General Assembly in 2015. This resolution, critiqued by the US for not being truly transparent, encourages states to adopt a political commitment not to be the first to place weapons in outer space. In 2016, Russia and Venezuela (after years of Russian loans and weapon deals to Venezuela) released a joint statement to the CoD, declaring that they will not be the first to deploy any type of weapon in outer space (CoD, 4 April 2016).

Conclusion

For Russia, outer space has become an important area through which to respond to or negate Western strategy and capabilities and influence global norms. Its economic, military and technological weaknesses compared to the US and NATO have led it to pursue asymmetrical tactics including working through bodies affiliated through the UN which give it publicity and some legitimacy but little ability to make real progress. Asymmetrical tactics adopted to advance their goals include traditional and new military capabilities, use of denial and uncertainty about Russian intentions, psychological aspects, diplomatic negotiation and cooperation and legal means (including attempting to develop or reinforce norms). The separation between global security and governance is not distinct. Russia's outer space strategy fits within its security and foreign policy efforts which focus on asserting Russia's authority and prestige. Military efforts are but one part of a complex set of tools, which include not only outer space and new technology such as electronic warfare but also non-military means (negotiation, finance, propaganda, etc.) employed to navigate what Russia perceives as an increasingly hostile world.

This situation is likely to become even more complicated. Outer space is increasingly interrelated with land, sea and air and cyber domains. It is also increasingly congested with other state and non-state actors, including private companies. This proliferation of actors is taking place just as military strategies are increasingly forced to consider the 'battlefield' as a seamless whole.

Today, tensions between Russia and the US are high, and each recognises what is sometimes called 'an integrated multi-domain threat' coming from the other. This is reinforced by recent technological advances and significant distrust about each other's intentions. The result is the growing militarisation of space. A pressing challenge for the future will be how to reconcile different security perceptions of states as well as non-state actors and their understandings about how the laws of armed conflict apply to military (and even civilian) space activities. For example, how does one define proportionality of response to an attack on a satellite? Is radio jamming a use of force or an armed attack? Which activities are legitimate, and which are not? There is a plethora of ambiguity. The goal of creating the sustainable use of space for peaceful purposes and for the benefit of all humankind seems ever elusive.

Notes

1. Electronic warfare plays a role in counter-space in terms of interfering with the functioning of satellites used for ISR and other communications activities and thus overlaps with ASATs.
2. Word constraints mean that this paper does not examine Russia-US international space cooperation which focuses on the International Space Station, nor on scientific cooperation in the exploration of space, in which Russia professes keen interest.
3. Space X Falcon 9 is another breakthrough technology that would allow precision rocket landings after orbital flight. The concern is that such technical breakthroughs could facilitate the militarisation of space by greatly decreasing the cost for landing and providing maintenance to space-based weapons and manned bases (Stratfor, 2015).
4. There is a similar assessment from the US about Russia. See Director of National Intelligence's (DNI) assertion that that 'Russia and China continue to pursue weapons systems capable of destroying satellites in orbit, placing US satellites at greater risk in the next few years' (Coats, 2018).
5. The West is particularly concerned about new anti-access/area-denial (A2/AD) capabilities (air and missile defences; surface-to-surface ballistic missiles; land-, air- and sea-launched cruise missiles batteries-layered anti-submarine capabilities).
6. These included four major space policy documents: Federal Space Program (FSP) (2005–2015), Federal Program on Global Navigation Systems (GLONASS) (2002–2011), Federal Special Program for the Development of Russia's Cosmodromes (DRC) (2006–2015) and Federal Target Program for GLOSNASS development (2013–2020).
7. Prompt Global Strike is the Pentagon's strategy of being able to strike anywhere in world with a conventional warhead in less than an hour.
8. These are designed to blind US intelligence and BMD satellites.
9. Details about Russia's development of a long-term strategy since 2012 can be found on Anatoly Zak's website RussianSpaceWeb.com.
10. The CoD, a 65-member body in Geneva, is supposed to serve as a UN's forum for discussing multilateral agreements on arms control and disarmament. Since 1994, the CoD has been deadlocked due to competing priorities. CoD needs unanimous agreement to move forward on issues and set agenda. PAROS gained near-universal support in annual UN General Assembly resolutions, but the US has consistently objected arguing that space weapon cannot be defined or effectively verified.
11. Although given the inherent ASAT capability of ballistic missile interceptors, any effort to include ground-based systems runs up against US commitment to deploy BMD.

References

Arbatov, Alexei (2011) 'Russian Perspective on Spacepower', in C. Lutes and P.L. Hayes (eds.), *Towards a Theory of Spacepower*. Washington, DC: National Defence University Press, pp. 441–449.

Barvinenko, V.V. (2007) 'Aerospace Defense: Modern Aspects', *Military Thought*, Vol. 16, No. 1.

Bodner, Matthew (2018) 'Russia Releases Video of its Modernised Ballistic Missile Defense System', *Defense News*, 20 February. Accessed on 4 April 2018 at www.defensenews.com/land/2018/02/20/russia-releases-video-of-its-modernised-ballistic-missile-defense-system/

Charron, Andrea and James Fergusson (2018) 'From NORAD to NOR [A] D: The Future Evolution of North American Defence Cooperation', *Policy Paper*, May, Toronto, ON: Canadian Global Affairs Institute.

Coats, Daniel (2018) *Worldwide Threat Assessment of the US Intelligence Community*, Congressional Testimonies, 13 February. Accessed on 02 April 2018 at www.dni.gov/index.php/newsroom/congressional-testimonies/item/1845-statement-for-the-record-worldwide-threat-assessment-of-the-us-intelligence-community

Conference on Disarmament (2008) 'Draft 'Treaty on the Prevention of the Placement of Weapons in Outer Space, the Threat or Use of Force Against Outer Space Objects', February 29, 2008, CoD/1839.

Conference on Disarmament (2016) 4 April 2016, CoD/12060.

Daniels, Jeff (2017) 'Space Arms Race as Russia, China Emerge as 'rapidly growing threats' to US', *CNBC*, 29 March. Accessed on 2 April 2018 at www.cnbc.com/2017/03/29/space-arms-race-as-russia-china-emerge-as-rapidly-growing-threats-to-us.html

Edelkina, Anastasia, Oleg Kraasev, and Natalia Velikanova (2015) 'Space Policy Strategies and Priorities in Russia', *Basic Research Program Working Paper*, Moscow: National Research University Higher School of Economics.

Facon, Isabelle and Sourbes-Verger (autumne 2007) 'La Cooperation Spatiale Russie-Europe – Une Entreprise Inarchevee', *Géoéconomie*, Vol. 43, pp. 75–89.

Gareyev, M.A. (April 2009) 'Issues of Strategic Deterrence in Current Conditions', *Military Thought*, Vol. 18, No. 2.

Gent, Ed (2018) 'Here's What We Know About Russia's Hypersonic Waverider Weapon', *Live Science*, 20 May. Accessed on 21 May 2018 at www.livescience.com/62653-russia-hypersonic-weapon.html

Harrison, Todd, Kaitlyn Johnson, and Thomas G. Roberts (2018) *Space Threat Assessment*, Washington, CSIS, April.

Hendrickx, Bart (2017) 'Update: Apparent Identification of Classified Russian Military Satellite', *Jane's Intelligence Review*, 12 July. Accessed on 19 May at www.janes.com/images/assets/764/71764/Russia_encounters_hurdles_in_satellite_development_and_expansion.pdf

Honkova, Jana (2013) 'The Russian Federation's Approach to Military Space and Its Military Space Capabilities', *Policy Outlook*, November.

Interfax (2014) Russia's Space Program to Cut Back by Another 500 Billion Rubles, *Interfax*, 9 October. Accessed on 2 May at www.interfax.ru/business/472276

Jackson, Nicole (2017) 'NATO's and Canada's Responses to Russia since the Crimea Annexation of 2014: A Critical Literature Review', *Simons Papers in Security and Development*, no. 6. Online at http://summit.sfu.ca/item/17651

Johnson-Freese, Joan (2017) *Space Warfare in the 21st Century: Arming the Heavens*. Abingdon: Routledge.

Jotham, Immanuel (2018) 'Russia's 'Space Forces' Just Completed the Construction of Two New Radar Facilities', *International Business Times*, 1 February. Accessed on 2 March 2018 at www.ibtimes.co.uk/russias-space-forces-just-completed-construction-two-new-radar-facilities-1657957

Kupriyanov, G.P. (2005) 'Principal Trends in the Evolution of Space Warfare', *Military Thought*, 14 January. Accessed on 2 May 2018 at www.highbeam.com/doc/1G1-136342873.html

Lavrov, Sergey (2017) Speech to CoD Informal Session Dedicated to the 110th Anniversary of the Second Hague Peace Conference, 1 March, 2017.

Luzin, Pavel (2015) 'Russia's Space Program-2025: Will Russia Be Capable of Cosmic Exploits given the Crisis and Its Political Isolation?' *Intersection*, 2 November. Accessed on 4 May 2018 at http://intersectionproject.eu//article/economy/space-program-2025

Luzin, Pavel (2016) 'Russia's Position in Space', *Foreign Affairs*, September. Accessed on 2 March 2018 at www.foreignaffairs.com/articles/2016-09-21/russias-position-space

Luzin, Pavel (2018) 'Russia's Tactical Nuclear Weapons: A Reality Check', *Riddle*, 1 May. Accessed on 5 May 2018 at www.ridl.io/en/russias-tactical-nuclear-weapons-a-reality-check/

McDermott, Roger (2012) 'Russia's 'New Look' Military Reaches Out to Space', *Eurasia Daily Monitor*, Vol. 9, No. 140. Acced on 7 May 2018 at https://jamestown.org/program/russias-new-look-military-reaches-out-to-space/

Meyer, Paul (2016) 'Dark Forces Awaken: The Prospects for Cooperative Space Security', *The Nonproliferation Review*, Vol. 23, No. 2–3, pp. 495–503.

Mizokami, Kyle (2018) 'Russia, China Will Have Anti-Satellite Weapons 'Within a Few Years'', *Popular Mechanics*, 15 February. Accessed on 2 May 2018 at www.popularmechanics.com/military/weapons/a18197465/russia-china-anti-satellite-weapons/

President of the Russian Federation (2010) 'The Military Doctrine of the Russian Federation' Approved by Russian Federation Presidential Edict on 5 February 2010.

President of the Russian Federation (2011) The Presidential Decree 'On the Approval of the Priority Directions of Science and Technologies of the Russian Federation' Approved by the President of the Russian Federation on July 7, 2011, no. 899.

President of the Russian Federation (2015) 'The Russian Federation's National Security Strategy', 31 December 2015.

RFE/RL (March 1, 2018) 'I'm Not Bluffing': Putin Touts New Advanced Russian Arsenal',. Available at www.rferl.org/a/putin-new-advanced-russian-arsenal-nuclear-capable-weapons/29071274.html; 'Russia Conducts World's Longest Surface-to-Air Missile Test with New S-500', *Moscow Times*, 28 May. Available at https://themoscowtimes.com/news/russia-conducts-worlds-longest-surface-to-air-missile-test-with-new-s-500-media-reports-61577

Roffey, Roger (2013) 'Russian Science and Technology is Still Having Problems – Implications for Defence Research', *The Journal of Slavic Military Studies*, Vol. 26, No. 2, pp. 162–188.

Russia Federal Government (2014) 'Space Activity of Russia in 2013–2020' Approved by the Federal Government on April 15, 2014 (no. 306).

Russia's Ministry of Foreign Affairs (2016) 'Russian Foreign Policy Concept', 30th November 2016.

Russian Government (2015) 'Russian Assessment of the US Global ABM Defence Programme – International Security and Disarmament', 5 March 2015.

Russian Security Council (2010) 'The Military Doctrine of the Russian Federation', 5 February 2010.

Russian Security Council (2014) 'The Military Doctrine of the Russian Federation', 25 December, 2014.

Samoylova, Svetlana (2013) 'Space 'Scare Tactic' for Medvedev', *Politkom.ru*, 15 April.

Stratfor (2015) 'The Battle to Militarise Space has Begun', 11 November. Accessed on 1 May at www.stratfor.com/analysis/battle-militarise-space-has-begun

Tucker, Patrick (2018) 'Russian Military Chief Lays Out the Kremlin's High Tech War Plans', *Defense One*, 28 March. Accessed on 2 April 2018 at www.defenseone.com/technology/2018/03/russian-military-chief-lays-out-kremlins-high-tech-war-plans/147051/

UN General Assembly (2013) 'Group of Governmental Experts on Transparency and Confidence building Measures in Outer Space Activities', A/68/189, Sixty-Eighth Session, July 29, 2013.

Vasiliev, Victor (2015) *Statement at the Joint Ad hoc Meeting of the First and Fourth Committees of the 70th Session of the UN General Assembly*, 22 October 2015, Accessed on 2 May 2018 at www.reachingcriticalwill.org/images/documents/Disarmament-fora/1com/1com15/statements/22October_SpaceGGE.pdf

Venet, Christoph (2015) 'Space Security in Russia' in K.U. Shrogl et al. (eds.), *Handbook of Space Security*, New York: Springer, pp. 355–370.

Weeden, Brian (2015) 'Dancing in the Dark Redux: Recent Russian Rendezvous and Proximity Operations in Space', *The Space Review*, 5 October.

Zak, Anatoly (2018) *Russian Space Program in the 2010s: Decadal Review*, 6 April. Accessed 8 April at www.russianspaceweb.com/russia_2010s.html

PART IV

Global and regional aspects of Russian security strategy

Introduction

Roger E. Kanet

The chapters that comprise the fourth section of the *Handbook* focus on Russian security policy as it relates to specific regions or countries of the world, from the US and the European Union (EU) to Eurasia and the Arctic. In the first of these, Chapter 20, Kathryn E. Stoner and Michael A. McFaul, both of Stanford University, focus on 'Russian Security Policy toward the United States'. They argue that the deterioration of Russian relations with the US is primarily the result of decisions made by and policies pursued by Vladimir Putin after the demonstrations against him in 2011 and 2012 – in other words, as a means to generate a form of Russian nationalism targeted on the outside world that would contribute to support for the authoritarian system that he had been constructing and for his continuing dominance of that system. As they argue, 'Putin's pivot toward anti-Americanism, anti-liberalism, nationalism, and an ever more aggressive foreign policy toward his neighbours is a consequence of Russian domestic developments, and first and foremost the preservation of Putin's hold on power'.

Chapter 21, by Alberto Priego of Universidad Pontificia, treats 'NATO Enlargement: A Security Dilemma for Russia'. Framing his argument within the concept of 'the security dilemma', he maintains that Russian relations with North Atlantic Treaty Organisation (NATO) have gone through three periods of increasing hostility and that today they have reached the level of 'offensive spiral', which implies reciprocal and expanding forms of conflict. Priego concludes that

> [t]he approval of a series of aggressive military doctrines, the construction of an A2/AD strategy or the implementation of military exercises (ZAPAD) that violate OSCE codes are clear evidence that Russia has entered an offensive spiral that could be very dangerous, not only for the Alliance, but also for Russia itself.

'Russia's Regional and Global Counterterrorism Strategies: How Moscow's Vision of the New Global Order Affects Its Approach to Terrorism', by Mariya Omelicheva of National Defense University, is examined in Chapter 22. She begins by discussing the increasing paranoid versions of Russia's national security strategy and their impact on policy both in Russia and in Russia's relations with the outside world. In the remainder of the chapter, she 'provide[s] an overview of Russia's regional and global security and counterterrorism strategies and account for Moscow's tactical choices prioritising the use of force as well as inconsistencies in counterterrorism measures used by Moscow'.

Chapter 23, by Licínia Simão and Maria Raquel Freire, both of the University of Coimbra, concerns 'Security Challenges in Russia-European Union Relations'. It begins by identifying the many issues involved in the security relations between the EU and Russia, as well as the factors that have resulted in a deterioration of those relations over recent years. They conclude that the prospects for a substantial improvement are 'not bright', in part because of domestic political dynamics in both the Russian Federation and the countries of the EU.

In Chapter 24, John Berryman, a member of the faculty of Birkbeck College of the University of London, examines 'Russian Security Strategy and the Geopolitics of Eurasia'. Unlike most of the other chapters, it provides a more extensive historical examination of the topic, which provides an historical overview of Tsarist Russian, Soviet and more recent Russian security relations.

> [W]ithin the increasingly competitive and transactional environment of the new Greater Eurasia, Russia has re-established its position as a normal Great Power and is once more exercising its influence in not only Europe but parts of the Middle East, Eastern Mediterranean, and the Arctic.

'The Impacts of Climate Change on Russian Arctic Security', by Stacy Closson, a Global Fellow at the Kennan Institute, is the topic of Chapter 25. She points out that 'Russia's security objectives in the High North are socio-economic development and maintaining sovereignty over its territory', and discusses both of these issues throughout the chapter. She notes that

> the Arctic serves as a flagship for nationhood as Russian authorities perceive the nation to be under siege from the West and South. The answer, according to Russian strategic doctrine, is to fortify and then exploit Russia's vast natural resources in its High North.

She also emphasises the fact that in many ways competing interests are at play in Russia's attempts to securitise its Far North.

In Chapter 26, entitled 'Caucasian Chess or The Greatest Geopolitical Tragedy of the Twentieth Century', Lilia Arakelyan of Florida International University argues that for Russia the Caucasus – both that portion which is part of the Russian Federation and the South Caucasus, are of strategic importance to Moscow and that an important element of Russian policy is playing off regional rivals against one another as a means of maintaining Russian dominance. This policy has its roots in the policies of both Tsarist and Soviet Russia.

In Chapter 27, Graeme Gill and Yelena Zabortseva, both of the University of Sydney, examine 'Russian Security Strategy in Central Asia'. Moscow has been especially concerned about Western, including US, involvement in the post-Soviet states of the region, especially in the burgeoning energy field. The Russians have also been opposed to US and EU involvement in the region in the area of civil society development. Russia has not voiced opposition to China's 'belt and road' project which aims at strengthening China's role in Central Asia and in building the overall infrastructure to facilitate China's access to both resources and markets in the Middle East, South Asia and Europe. The authors conclude that 'unless Russia

Aspects of Russian security strategy

is able to develop a coherent and focused security policy for the region, its ability to shape events will be limited'.

Chapter 28, entitled 'Russian-Chinese Security cooperation: the Bear and the Dragon', by Marcel de Haas of Leiden University, traces the evolution over the past quarter century of the basically cooperative security relationship between Russia and China. It then points to the areas in which the objectives of the two countries diverge and the fact that China is able to devote a far greater amount of resources to its relevant military and economic development. De Haas concludes that, because of differing objectives and a growing difference in economic base, 'more and more signals have appeared, which demonstrate that the Sino–Russian strategic partnership is crumbling'.

In the final chapter in this section of the *Handbook*, Chapter 29, entitled 'The BRICs and Russian Foreign and Security Policy: Changing the Narrative', Rachel Salzman of Johns Hopkins University is interested in the ways in which Moscow has tried to use its relations with other emerging states, the BRICS, to enhance its ability to challenge the dominant West. She notes that 'Russia played a critical role in effecting BRICS's transformation from economic concept to a political group'. Since the group's basic support for Russia in its dispute with the West over Russia's absorption of Crime, the BRICS have begun discussing future cooperation that would challenge Western domination over the international system.

20
RUSSIAN SECURITY POLICY TOWARDS THE UNITED STATES[1]

Kathryn E. Stoner and Michael A. McFaul

The debate about the United States' flawed approach to Russia, first heard in the 1990s, is replaying today. Many, not only in Moscow but in Washington, New York, Berlin, Tallinn, and Beijing—are blaming the West, and the United States in particular, for a return to Cold War confrontation between the United States and Russia following the Maidan Revolution in Ukraine in 2014, Russia's subsequent annexation of Crimea, ongoing intervention in Eastern Ukraine, and alleged interference in the American presidential elections of 2016.

The contemporary 'too much' camp resuscitates many of the old arguments from the 1990s, insisting that the United States pressed Russia too hard, both on its domestic and foreign policy, forcing President Putin to finally strike back (Mearsheimer, 2014). The updated 'too little' camp blames President Obama and his administration for acting too softly on Moscow and also President Trump for similarly doing too little to counter Russian re-insertion into international politics. According to this line of analysis, the 'reset' in United States-Russia relations that Obama initiated in 2009 was a mistake, signalled U.S. weakness, and therefore invited Russian aggression. Putin knew he could annex Crimea in 2014, intervene in Syria in 2015, and meddle in the U.S. presidential election in 2016, so this argument goes because Obama would not stop him.

In the 1990s, U.S. policies of both varieties—doing too much and doing too little—may have influenced Russian domestic reforms and foreign policy responses. But these experiences from the past cannot be invoked as analogies to explain the ongoing United States-Russia conflict. Russia today is not the same country as it was in the 1990s. Nor do U.S. policies since 2012 towards Russia or the rest of the world have much in common with this earlier era. Specifically, President Putin's annexation of Crimea and proxy war in Eastern Ukraine are *not* a natural or inevitable reaction to either a 'too hard' or 'too soft' approach from Washington. Nor are recent Russian foreign policy decisions a natural result of Russia doing what it has always historically done (Graham, 2015). Russia has not always annexed territory, propped up dictators, or intervened in the domestic politics of other countries. Russian culture, history, and power did not always compel clashes with the West.

Instead, Putin's pivot towards anti-Americanism, anti-liberalism, nationalism, and an ever more aggressive foreign policy towards his neighbours is a consequence of Russian domestic developments, and first and foremost the preservation of Putin's hold on power. The change in leadership in the Kremlin from President Yeltsin to President Putin initiated this shift in direction in Russian foreign policy. After a period of cooperation between the Russia and the United States during the Obama-Medvedev era, Russia's turn against the West accelerated once again in 2012 when Putin returned to the Kremlin during a period of popular mobilisation against his regime. By 2012, a different U.S. policy towards Russia—a more confrontational stance or a more pliant approach—would have had only marginal effects on the current condition of U.S.-Russia relations.

To develop this argument, we begin this chapter by refuting the claim that U.S. aggression provoked the Russian intervention in Ukraine in 2014, and election interference in 2016. The following section interrogates the converse claim—that the United States was too soft on Russia during the 'reset', which in turn invited Russian aggression. The final section develops our explanation for the negative turn in United States-Russia relations: Russian domestic politics.

The 'too much' school

The 1990s was a tough decade for Russians. The economy contracted by nearly 50 per cent, and then collapsed in August 1998 (World Bank, 1998). Regional and national elections took place on a regular basis (with elections in 1991 and 1999 being the most competitive), and society certainly liberalised, but democracy did not consolidate. The standoff between President Yeltsin and the parliament in September–October 1993 ended tragically in military conflict, inspiring few about the virtues of democracy. Gradually, a narrative inside Russia took hold which blamed the West for intentionally imposing bad economic policies on Russia that caused this hardship, all in an attempt to keep Russia down. According to the purveyors of this argument, U.S. and European leadership also looked the other way on unfair privatisation schemes, exploding corruption, and Yeltsin's bombing of the parliament in October 1993, which reinforced the idea of Western hypocrisy and indifference (Cohen, 2000). Some argued that what the United States really wanted was not a vibrant Russian economy or functioning democracy, but a weak Russia. With Russia out of the great power loop, the United States and its allies could expand NATO, attack Serbia, ignore Russian interests in the Middle East, and foment revolution against regimes considered close to Moscow.

U.S. foreign policy most certainly influenced the course of Russian internal reforms in the 1990s, but did not determine it. Decades ago, in fact, some analysts worried that the United States was not doing enough to help Russia's transition to democracy and markets succeed. One of us (McFaul), for instance, wrote this dire prediction on August 19, 1990, one year to the date before the August 1991 coup that triggered the collapse of the Soviet Union six months later,

> Failure [by the West] to embrace and defend the upstart [Russian] leadership [after the fall of Gorbachev] would provide the real opportunity for a counterrevolutionary backlash. If economic decline and civil strife were to continue under a new regime, calls for order and tradition flavored with nationalist slogans will resonate with a suffering people. At this future but avoidable stage in the drama of the Soviet revolution, the specter of dictatorship will be real.
>
> *(McFaul, 1990)*

More aid—meaning more focus on strengthening democratic and market institutions—might have made a difference. In turn, a democratic Russia, more fully integrated into the West, would have been less likely to turn so dramatically away from the United States by 2012 (Doyle, 1996; Owen, 1996; Russett, 1996). Other post-communist countries, like Poland, Latvia, Lithuania, Estonia and the Czech Republic, for example, which *did* make the transition to democracy and capitalism more quickly and more successfully, are now American allies in Europe.

Undeniably, some U.S. foreign policy decisions in the 1990s and 2000s also triggered tensions in United States-Russia relations. Neither 'democrat' Boris Yeltsin in 1999 nor 'autocrat' Vladimir Putin in 2004 reacted indifferently to NATO expansion. Likewise, NATO's aerial assault on Serbia in 1999, as well as the U.S.-led invasion of Iraq in 2003, sparked further strains. In addition, President Bush's unilateral decision to withdraw from the ABM Treaty threatened Russian security interests, or so many Russian officials and analysts have claimed. Putin would add to this list the colour revolutions in Georgia (2003) and Ukraine (2004), which he blamed Washington for orchestrating.

Nonetheless, U.S. actions or inactions in these earlier two decades cannot explain later tensions with Russia for one simple reason: the reset. For the first several years of his presidency, President Barack Obama's reset with Russia yielded genuine cooperation between Russia and the United States. During the reset, President Obama and Russian President Dmitri Medvedev worked together on several projects, which improved the security and prosperity of both countries. In 2010, they signed and then ratified the New Start Treaty, which reduced by 30 per cent the number of nuclear weapons allowed to be deployed in the United States and Russia (Bernstein, 2010), while also keeping in place a comprehensive inspections regime to verify compliance. In that same year, the White House and the Kremlin worked together to pass UN Security Council Resolution 1929, the most comprehensive set of sanctions against Iran ever. Together, the United States and Russia greatly expanded the Northern Distribution Network (NDN)—a mix of air, rail, and truck routes through Russia and other countries in Central Asia and the Caucasus to supply U.S. soldiers in Afghanistan and reduce U.S. military dependency on the southern route through Pakistan. NDN grew from just a trickle of supplies to U.S. forces fighting in Afghanistan to over 50 per cent by 2011 (Katzman, 2013). This dramatic shift was essential in allowing the United States to risk disruptions to the southern supply route, most importantly after the operation to kill Osama bin Laden in May 2011.

The United States and Russia also collaborated in avoiding conflict during the reset era. There was no second Russian-Georgian war after 2008. When another popular uprising toppled President Bakiev in Kyrgyzstan in 2010, the United States and Russia could have squared off again. After all, dozens of people died in the initial fighting (almost as many as were shot in Maidan Square in Kyiv in 2014), and tens of thousands of ethnic Uzbeks fled southern Kyrgyz cities when it looked like this regime change might unleash an ethnic civil war (*New York Times*, June 14, 2010). In response to this crisis, though, Obama and Medvedev worked together to help diffuse a very dangerous situation.

Perhaps most remarkably, President Medvedev agreed to abstain on UN Security Council Resolutions 1970 and 1973, thereby authorizing the use of force against the Libyan regime of Muammar Gaddafi in the spring of 2011. No Russian leader had ever acquiesced to an external military intervention into a sovereign country.[2]

In addition to security issues, the Obama and Medvedev governments collaborated on several projects to increase trade and investment between the United States and Russia during the reset years. The United States helped Russia obtain membership in the World Trade Organisation (WTO). Trade between the United States and Russia also increased dramatically between 2009 and 2012, as did foreign direct investment (U.S. Census Bureau, n.d.). A new visa regime expanded the number of Russians traveling to the United States, and vice versa. And even bigger plans were afoot, including the massive joint venture between Exxon-Mobil and Rosneft, Russia's largest oil company, owned by the government.

And the dreaded issue of NATO expansion that somehow provoked Russia into grabbing Crimea and intervening in Eastern Ukraine? It was not an issue of contention during the reset. Aside from the addition of Croatia and Albania in 2009, two countries far away from Russia, NATO did not expand in the Obama-Medvedev era. Despite pressure from George W. Bush at the 2008 NATO Bucharest Summit, other NATO allies refused to allow Georgian membership. After Russia's invasion of Georgia in August 2008, the issue within the alliance died. Even under President Yushchenko, the leader of the Orange Revolution in 2004, Ukraine never pushed for NATO membership. There was simply no support within Ukrainian society at that time. After President Yanukovych was elected Ukraine's new president in 2010, the idea faded completely. Consequently, during the reset years, neither President Medvedev nor Prime Minister Putin ever objected to NATO expansion because there was nothing to which to object.

Indeed, when President Medvedev attended the NATO Summit in Lisbon in November 2010, he echoed other Western leaders in waxing effusively about NATO-Russia relations. 'Incidentally', he said,

> even the declaration approved at the end of our talks states that we seek to develop a strategic partnership. This is not a chance choice of words, but signals that we have succeeded in putting the difficult period in our relations behind us now.
>
> *(Medvedev, 2010)*

In his last meeting with Obama in his capacity as President in March 2012 in Seoul, Medvedev also praised the reset, saying, '[W]e probably enjoyed the best level of relations between the United States and Russia during those three years than ever during the previous decades' (2012). This new level of cooperation between the Russian and U.S. governments even impacted public opinion in both countries. In 2010, nearly 60 per cent of Russians had a positive view of the United States, and roughly the same number of Americans had a positive view of Russia (Pew Global, 2010).

Again, all of these successful initiatives during the reset occurred *after* the bombing of Serbia, *after* the Orange Revolution in Ukraine in 2004, *after* the U.S.-led intervention in Iraq beginning in 2003, and *after* NATO expansion. Previous rounds of NATO expansion or U.S. military intervention cannot explain the era of cooperation that followed. Nor, therefore, can they be cited to explain the current era of confrontation. Other factors—more proximate variables—must be added to the analysis.

The 'too weak' school

A second critique of U.S. foreign policy blames the current U.S.-Russian confrontation on U.S. weakness. One variant of this argument posits that Russia is belligerent today because the regime in Moscow is autocratic and U.S. presidents allowed Russian dictatorship to develop (McFaul, 1997/98). Clinton was too soft on Yeltsin, calling him a democrat when he bombed the parliament in 1993, and comparing him to Lincoln when he invaded Chechnya. Bush also went soft on Putin at their very first meeting when he infamously proclaimed, 'I looked the man in the eye. I found him to be very straightforward and trustworthy. We had a very good dialogue. I was able to get a sense of his soul' (Bush, 2001). During Putin's first eight years in the Kremlin, many U.S. analysts, including one of us, criticised both the Clinton and Bush administrations for their indifference to growing Russian autocracy (Goldgeier and McFaul, 2005). For some, U.S. inattention to democracy and human rights continued during the Obama administration. He did not push hard enough to democratise Russia, critics say, and therefore an autocratic Russia became more bellicose and anti-Western in the conduct of its foreign policy (Kramer, 2010). More than any other president, President Trump seems completely indifferent to Russian autocracy. Although it is too early to judge, this acceptance of Russian autocracy may well permit even more belligerent Putin foreign policies.

The more damning claim, however, was that Obama's 'reset' invited bad Kremlin behaviour abroad, including most dramatically, Putin's invasion of Ukraine. Obama showed weakness, so this line of analysis contends, and therefore Putin took advantage, in Ukraine, Syria, and then even the American presidential elections of 2016. Other commentators have even suggested a direct connection between Obama's backing down on his threat to use force against Syrian leader Bashar al-Assad after he used chemical weapons and Putin's decision to annex Crimea. Obama undermined U.S. credibility by backing away from his own red line. Therefore, Putin thought he could do what he wanted, where he wanted, and when he wanted.

This claim about Obama's 'reset' mixes causation and correlation. The reset came before Putin's invasion of Ukraine, but did not cause it. This argument also conveniently forgets a lot of history. The reset ended in 2012—two years before Putin intervened in Ukraine. In December 2011, immediately after the Russian parliamentary election, Secretary of State Hillary Clinton expressed 'serious concerns about the conduct of the election' and called for a 'full investigation' of irregularities (Clinton, quoted by Labott, 2011). Putin and other Russian leaders strongly reacted, blaming Clinton for fomenting the massive public demonstrations that followed the parliamentary vote. As discussed in detail in the next section, Putin's need for a new enemy to help him address his domestic challenges compelled him to reject the reset.

After a few failed attempts to engage the new Russian president on a substantive agenda, the Obama administration eventually responded and changed policy towards Russia. The U.S. administration cut off talks with the Russians on missile defence, did not invite Putin to the 2012 NATO Summit, eventually stopped pursuing arms control, signed into law the Magnitsky Act (even though the Obama administration had initially objected to this law, it was designed to punish Russian officials for the death in prison of Russian lawyer Sergei Magnitsky), cancelled a two-day summit planned in Moscow in September 2013, met with human rights activists on the sidelines of Putin's G20 Summit in St. Petersburg in 2013 (the only head of state to do so), and then sent a White House delegation to the Sochi Olympics in February 2014 with a strong message of support for LGBT rights in response to Russia's 'anti-gay propaganda' law.[3] These were not policies of weakness, but strong responses to Putin's increasingly aggressive foreign policy stances and growing autocratic tendencies at home. After Putin intervened in Ukraine in 2014, the United States, together with European allies, did respond aggressively: first, by sanctioning Russian individuals and companies deemed to be involved in the invasion; second, by strengthening NATO; and third, by providing military and economic aid to Ukraine.

The end of the reset and the more confrontational approach towards Russia by the U.S. government after 2012 failed to deter Putin's invasion of Ukraine. But has *any* U.S. policy over the last 70 years deterred Russian aggression—direct or through proxies—against its neighbours in Eastern Europe and or the former republics of the Soviet Union? In February 2014, Putin could have reviewed the 70-year history of Russian military interventions in neighbouring countries and correctly concluded that the United States and NATO were not willing to stop his invasion plans into Ukraine. For instance, when Russia invaded Georgia in 2008, George W. Bush did little. He did send the USS *McFaul* (a naval destroyer ship named after Chief Petty Officer Donald L. McFaul, a Navy SEAL killed in action in 1989, and no relation to either author) to troll the waters off the coast of Georgia, as well as provide humanitarian assistance to Georgia, but there were no sanctions of Russian government officials or Russian companies, no NATO troop movements, and no lethal assistance besides transporting Georgian troops back to Georgia from Afghanistan. In Afghanistan and Iraq, Bush had bolstered his credentials for using force, but that reputation did not deter Russia's invasion of Georgia in 2008.

President Ronald Reagan could not be accused of being weak on the Soviet communist regime. Yet, when Soviet leader Leonid Brezhnev colluded with Polish General Jaruzelski to crush Solidarity (the Polish labour movement led by Lech Walesa) and implement martial law in December 1981, Reagan could not deter this brutal crackdown. President Carter, of course, did not stop the Soviet invasion of Afghanistan, just as President Johnson did not prevent Brezhnev from intervening Czechoslovakia in 1968, and President Eisenhower, even armed with his rhetorically muscular 'rollback' of communism policy, failed to stop Soviet tanks from rolling into Hungary in 1956. And obviously, President Roosevelt had no ability to push the Red Army back to Soviet borders at the end of World War II. The pattern of Russian aggression and U.S. response is clear. Whether Democrat or Republican, no U.S. president has ever succeeded in deterring Soviet/Russian military intervention in Eastern Europe and Afghanistan.

Wag the bear: domestic determinants of Russian foreign policy

Russia's foreign policy towards the West, including specifically the annexation of Crimea and military intervention in Eastern Ukraine, did not change in response to U.S. foreign policy, strong or weak. Rather, Russian foreign policy changed in large measure as a result of Putin's response to new domestic political and economic challenges inside Russia.

For his first eight years as president, from 2000 to 2008, President Putin enjoyed solid public support because of economic performance. After a ten-year depression, Putin moved into the Kremlin in 2000, just as the Russian economy started to grow for this first time since the collapse of the Soviet Union (see Figure 20.1). Between 2000 and 2008, Russia's gross domestic

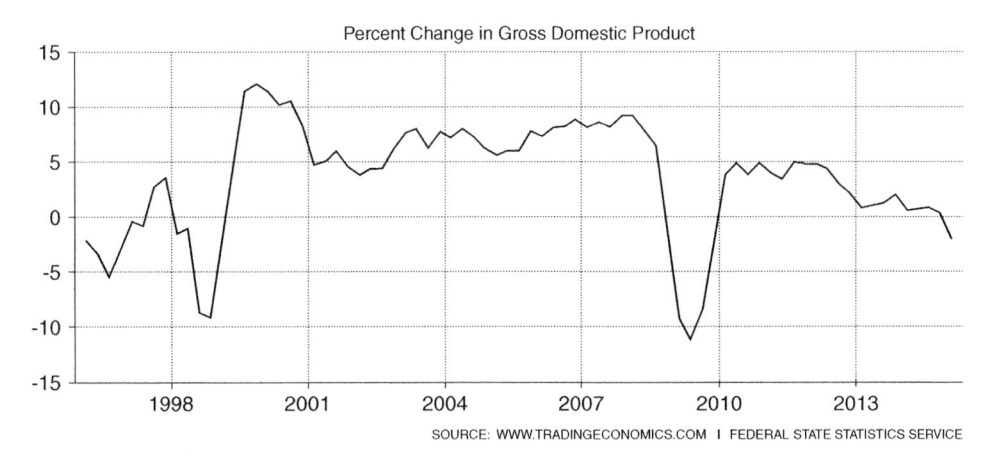

Figure 20.1 Russian GDP annual growth rate, 1996–2014

Source: Annual GDP growth rates are available at 'Russia GDP' (n.d.), accessed June 10, 2015. Data come from the Russian Federal Statistical Service and the World Bank (1998).

product (GDP) per capita grew 7 per cent per year on average. In contrast to the 1990s, when the economy declined steadily, such that public sector wages and pensions went unpaid for months, this growth produced huge positive changes in the lives of average Russian citizens. Wages increased 400 per cent between 2004 and 2008 ('Russia Average', n.d.).

Some of Putin's first-term reforms (e.g. introduction of a flat income tax, lower corporate taxes, and creation of sovereign wealth funds) contributed to this economic turnaround. But rising energy prices were the real driver (McFaul and Stoner, 2007). In the 1990s, as Yeltsin's government was undertaking dramatic structural reform, Russia's main export, oil, cost about $17 per barrel on average, bottoming out at $12.76 in 1998. But by 2002, oil prices had doubled in the ensuing four years and then shot up further to $132, an all-time high in June 2008, just as the global financial crisis hit (US Energy Information Administration, n.d.).[4] Whatever the true reasons were for Russian economic growth, they didn't really matter to the Russian people. Putin got the credit. He was in the right place at the right time.

At the same time that Russia's economy began to boom, Putin contracted political rights. Almost as soon as he assumed office, he cracked down on the Russian media, taking back broadcasting licenses to make the media 'more responsible', that is more responsive to the state, and specifically to perpetuating his regime. Independent media were virtually eliminated, except for a handful of radio, print, and television stations. Civil society also became a target, as did oppositional political activity. Putin's preferred political party, United Russia, dominated parliament after the 2003 elections. He began to appoint regional governors. Russia was becoming increasingly autocratic, but Putin remained popular, his approval rating hovering around 70 per cent during his first two terms as president (see Figure 20.2).

As Figure 20.2 indicates, during his years as prime minister (2008–2012), Putin's popular support fell slightly. His numbers dipped to their lowest point since the summer of 2000 in the fall of 2011, when they hit 63 per cent after Putin announced unexpectedly at the United Russia Congress that he planned to return to the presidency. Putin clearly expected most Russian citizens to welcome news of his return to the Kremlin. In fact, the reaction was less than enthusiastic. In November 2011, he was publicly booed at a martial arts match as he jumped into the ring in front of 20,000 people to congratulate the winner. In the

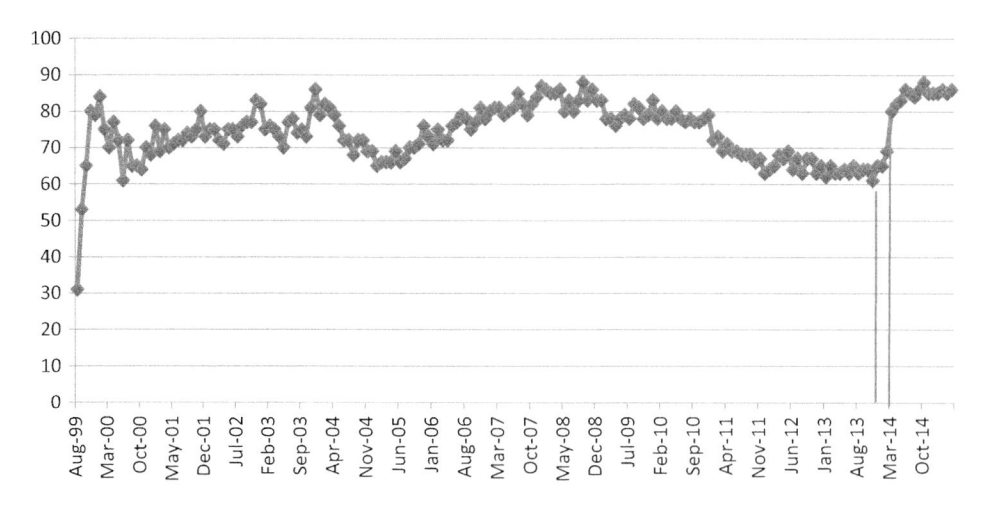

Figure 20.2 Responses to monthly question: do you approve of the Job President (Prime Minister) Putin is doing?[25] (Levada Center Data, August 1999 to April 2015, percentage approval rating)

parliamentary elections a few weeks later, Putin's party, United Russia, performed well below expectations, even with the help of complete control of national television stations, unlimited financial resources, the backing of regional governments, and a bump up from falsification in United Russia's favour.

The extent of falsification was probably no more than in previous Russian elections. But in 2011 the proliferation of smartphones, better organised election monitoring organisations, Twitter, Facebook, and VKontakte (the largest Russian social network in Europe) combined to expose it (Schwirtz and Herszenhorn, 2011). Compelling evidence that this election had been stolen in favour of Putin's party in turn triggered popular demonstrations, numbering at first in the thousands and then tens of thousands, and occasionally hundreds of thousands. The last time so many Russians had taken to the streets for a political act was in 1991, the year the Soviet Union collapsed. Moreover, these demonstrations in Russia in 2011 were occurring in the same year that massive demonstrations were toppling regimes in the Arab world.

At the same time, the Russian economy was not growing at the same clip as during Putin's first eight years in office. As Figure 20.1 indicates, the global economic meltdown in 2008 hit Russia particularly hard as demand for oil fell. In 2009, the Russian economy contracted by 8 per cent, and only grew at around 4 per cent in the three years before Putin's 2012 presidential campaign.

The social contract that Putin had struck implicitly with the Russian people—high growth in return for political passivity—appeared to be unravelling. The Kremlin was not delivering on its part of the deal. Moreover, the newly emerging Russian middle classes, which took to the streets in Moscow and St. Petersburg, wanted more from their government than just economic growth. These protestors first demanded cleaner elections and lamented Putin's decision to run for a third term, but eventually increased their demands by calling for a change in government and the removal of Putin himself (CNN, 2012; Parfitt, 2012).

The growing popular unrest meant that Putin needed a new argument, in order to achieve re-election as President of Russia for a third time, in 2012 (and eventually a fourth, in 2018). To counter this new wave of social mobilisation, Putin revived an old Soviet-era argument as his new source of legitimacy—defence of the motherland against the evil West, and especially the imperial, conniving, threatening United States. In particular, Putin argued that the United States was seeking to topple his regime. As in the old days, the United States was interfering in Russia's internal affairs,

> We know, regrettably, that ... some representatives of some foreign states are gathering those to whom they are paying money, so-called grant recipients, carrying out instruction sessions with them and preparing them to do the relevant "work", in order to influence, ultimately, the election campaign process in our country.
> *(Putin, as quoted in Elder, 2011)*

Putin, his aides, and his media outlets accused the leaders of Russian demonstrations of being U.S. agents, traitors from the so-called 'fifth column' (internal enemies whose goal is to bring the regime down).

Putin's campaign against protestors, opposition parties, and civil society did not end after his re-election. Opposition leaders were arrested or placed under detention for extended periods. For example, Putin's most feared opponent, anti-corruption blogger Alexei Navalny has been in and out of jail any time there is a large public protest against the regime. Laws introduced since 2012 restricted the activity of non-governmental organisations (NGOs) and independent media outlets, and the introduction of significant fines for participation in protests have dissuaded many (although not all) Russians from taking to the streets in opposition to the regime. (Notable exceptions were protests organised by Navalny and others that were largely led by Russians in their teens an early twenties in 2017 and 2018.)

Putin's particular response to his domestic challenges was not inevitable. Other Russian leaders before him chose a different course. In fact, following the mass demonstrations held in Bolotnaya Square in Moscow to protest the results of the December 2011 parliamentary elections, and other popular protests in the winter of 2012, President Medvedev initially tried to negotiate with the opposition and introduce some limited political reforms. He met with protest leaders and appeared on the independent television station *Dozhd*. He reinstated direct elections for regional governors, introduced a new electoral law, made it easier for opposition parties to register, and even proposed a public television station that would have considerable independence from the state, like the BBC in the United Kingdom or the Canadian Broadcasting Corporation (CBC) in Canada (Stanovaya, 2012). Putin, however, in 2012, reversed this engagement and squelched these incremental reforms. Instead of working with opposition leaders, he crushed them.

In parallel to this crackdown on domestic dissent, Putin and his government expanded media attention to the supposed U.S. threat. Echoing the Cold War era, the Kremlin propaganda machine portrayed the United States as an imperial, predatory state, which constantly undermined international stability and violated the sovereignty of other states. Different from the Cold War, however, Putin's regime added a new dimension to the ideological struggle—conservative Russia versus the liberal West. Russian state-controlled media asserted that Putin had nurtured the rebirth of a conservative, Orthodox Christian society. By contrast, these same media outlets presented the West as decadent, hedonistic, godless, and homosexual. Russians needed protection from these dangerous Western ideas. This is why the Kremlin passed a law against homosexual 'propaganda'—while decadent Western countries like the United States and Ireland legalised gay marriage. His growing embrace of the Russian Orthodox Church has been another part of his campaign to champion Russia as a culturally conservative alternative to a hedonistic Western culture. The Russian government also shut down the United States Agency for International Development (USAID) in the country, chased several American NGOs out of Russia, and banned adoptions of Russian orphans by U.S. citizens. Increasingly, Russian television, where most of the population receives their news, painted the United States as an enemy, out to weaken and ultimately to destroy the resurrected Russia.

Putin's domestic turn against the United States made cooperation more difficult. After all, he could not be seen as resetting relations with the enemy. Moreover, his distrust of the United States was not just on display for domestic consumption. Putin seemed to genuinely believe that the United States represented a threat to Russian stability. In his view, the United States sparked the Arab Spring, and so he firmly resisted U.S. proposals to negotiate a political transition in Syria. When Edward Snowden appeared unexpectedly in Moscow, Putin deliberately sought to embarrass the United States by giving him asylum in 2013. His new domestic agenda and new foreign policy priorities supported each other.

In response, the Obama administration found it increasingly difficult to work with Putin, although there were compartments of cooperation with Russia. Between 2012 and 2014, the Rosneft-Exxon-Mobil deal kept on course. The various working groups within the Bilateral Presidential Commission between the U.S. and Russian governments continued to meet. The FSB (the Russian Internal Security Service) assisted the FBI's investigation of the Tsarnaev brothers, Chechen immigrants who killed two innocent Americans and wounded hundreds of others at the Boston Marathon on April 15, 2013. The P5+1 negotiations with Iran continued uninterrupted until the successful conclusion of a deal. Most dramatically, Presidents Obama and Putin agreed in September 2013 to work together to remove and eliminate Syria's chemical weapons stockpiles. In addition, Putin seemed to still care somewhat about Western perceptions during the first two years of his third presidential term. In December 2013, he released Russian billionaire Mikhail Khodorkovsky (jailed on trumped up charges of money laundering and corruption) after ten years in prison, and freed the Pussy Riot singers (a group of three women arrested for singing a few lines of an anti-Putin punk rock song in Christ the Saviour Cathedral in Moscow). These actions were designed to display to the world the new, modern Russia just prior to the 2014 Sochi Olympics.

But most of the pockets of cooperation ended or were significantly disrupted after the fall of the Yanukovych government in Ukraine in February 2014 and the subsequent Russian invasion of Eastern Ukraine and the seizure of Crimea. (Amazingly, Russian cooperation in the P5+1 negotiations with Iran endured during this period.) In November 2013, Ukrainian President Yanukovych refused to sign the Ukraine-EU Association Agreement. The Agreement had been drafted in March 2012 and committed both the EU and Ukraine to closer political and economic ties, but contained no promise of future Ukrainian membership in the EU. Since the agreement had been so long in the making, Yanukovych's sudden decision not to sign it triggered massive demonstrations on the streets of Kyiv. The United States supported European efforts to negotiate a deal between Yanukovych and the opposition. In the early morning of February 21, 2014, the two sides signed an agreement to cease hostilities and hold new elections later that year ('Agreement on the Settlement of Crisis in Ukraine', 2014).

For a while it appeared that a major confrontation between the government and the protestors had been avoided. Several hours after signing the agreement, however, Yanukovych fled the country, eventually showing up in the southern Russian city of Rostov. The Ukrainian Rada (parliament) filled the political vacuum by impeaching Yanukovych and electing Oleksandr Turchynov as interim president and Arseniy Yatsenyuk as prime minister. In May 2014, Ukrainian voters elected a new president, Petro Poroshenko.

The Obama administration, along with other European governments, had pushed hard to get both Yanukovych and opposition leaders to sign an agreement. When it fell apart, Western governments recognised the decisions of the Rada and supported the new transition plan. Putin did not. What happened in Ukraine was exactly what Putin feared for Russia—hundreds of thousands of demonstrators flooding the streets and demanding that their corrupt, autocratic president step down. And he did! Putin described the events in Kyiv as a U.S.-backed coup, while his media outlets described the transition in government as Nazi-led regime change (Dimitri Kiselev, as quoted by the BBC, 2014). In Putin's view, the same foreign forces, which had attempted to overthrow his government in December 2011 and the spring of 2012 were now at work in Ukraine. Allowing them to succeed would encourage them to mobilise again against his regime. So, he struck back, first using special operations forces to seize and then annex Crimea, and then supporting separatist forces in Eastern Ukraine in a proxy war against the new government in Kyiv.

In parallel to Russian military actions in Ukraine, anti-American propaganda on Russian state-controlled media outlets reached a fevered pitch. For instance, on his evening programme broadcast to tens of millions on Channel One, Dmitri Kiselev, a prominent pro-Putin TV journalist and head of the *Russia Today* news agency, compared Obama's ideology to that championed by Islamic State of Iraq and Levant (ISIS) leader Abu-Bakr al-Baghdadi. Kiselev also noted, in what seemed like a thinly veiled threat, that Russia is the only country that can turn the United States into radioactive dust (Kiselev, as reported by the BBC, 2014). Putin suppressed independent sources of information even further. The Kremlin effectively kicked *Dozhd* off the air, increased penalties for 'unauthorised' protests, and signed a law which allows the state to label as 'undesirable' (a purposely flexible term) foreign organisations, including even businesses, 'posing a threat to Russia's defense capabilities, security, public order, [or] public health' (Radio Free Europe, 2015).

As Figure 20.2 indicates, during the first two years of his third term, before his annexation of Crimea, Putin's popular approval rating was stuck. For most of this period, fewer than half of Russian voters reported that they wanted to re-elect him to a fourth term (*The Moscow Time*, 2013). Moreover, while most Russians maintained a positive perspective on Putin personally, they also expressed real dismay with the general trajectory of their country. Half of those polled thought the country was on the wrong path. In the wake of annexation, Putin's popularity soared. As Figure 20.2 shows, his popular approval rating rose from an almost all-time low of 61 per cent in November 2013 to 80 per cent in March 2014 as Russian forces took control of Crimea. By June 2014, following the referendum in Crimea, his approval rating reached an all-time high of 86 per cent, where it remained until the time of writing in 2018 (Levada Center, n.d.).

Putin's perceived success among Russians in battling neo-Nazis in Ukraine, the evil Americans, and the decadent West more generally will make it hard for him to change course. To maintain his argument for legitimacy at home, Putin needs perpetual conflict with external enemies—not full-scale war, not a direct clash with the United States or NATO, but a low-level, yet constant confrontation that supports the narrative that Russia is under siege from the West, that Russia is at war with the United States.

Staying the course of neo-containment, selective engagement

To Putin's annexation of Crimea and military intervention in Eastern Ukraine, the Obama administration, together with NATO allies and EU friends, responded forcefully. In his speech in Tallinn on September 2, 2014, Obama explained that Russian intervention in Ukraine

> is a brazen assault on the territorial integrity of Ukraine—a sovereign and independent European nation. It challenges that most basic of principles of our international system—that borders cannot be redrawn at the barrel of a gun; that nations have the right to determine their own future. It undermines an international order where the rights of peoples and nations are upheld and can't simply be taken away by brute force. This is what's at stake in Ukraine. This is why we stand with the people of Ukraine today.
>
> *(Office of the Press Secretary, 2014)*

Obama's response to Russia's latest military intervention in Europe compared in scale and scope to Reagan's vigorous reaction to the Soviet-ordered crackdown on Solidarity in Poland in 1981, and was considerably more robust than Bush's response to the Russian invasion of Georgia in 2008, or President Lyndon B. Johnson's reaction to Soviet intervention in Czechoslovakia in 1968, or President Eisenhower's reaction to the Soviet invasion of Hungary in 1956.

First, the Obama administration (in concert with the EU) sanctioned dozens of Russian individuals and companies. Not even Ronald Reagan slapped sanctions on the Kremlin chief of staff, as Obama did. The G7 also agreed to kick Russia out of their club, a decision not made after the Russian invasion of Georgia in August 2008. Western leaders have promised additional sanctions in response to future Russian military aggression in Ukraine.

Second, the Obama administration (again in close coordination with the EU and the International Monetary Fund [IMF]) pledged billions of dollars to help reform and rebuild the Ukrainian economy. The IMF pledged $17.5 billion, and roughly $40 billion over four years (Francis and Trindle, 2015). The EU has provided three macro-financial assistance (MFA) packages to Ukraine for a total of €3.41 billion, while the United States has added $1 billion in loan guarantees as well as tens of millions in humanitarian assistance (European Commission, 2015). The Obama administration also provided non-lethal military assistance, including training and equipment to Ukraine's military. The Trump administration has gone even further and provided lethal military assistance, including most importantly, anti-tank Javelin missiles (Baker, June 8, 2018).

Third, NATO moved rapidly to make credible the Article 5 commitment that an attack on one of the 28 members is an attack on all. In direct response to Russia's annexation and continuing support of unrest in Eastern Ukraine, the alliance also doubled the size of its NATO Response Force, which is 'NATO's high-readiness force comprising land, air, sea and Special Forces units capable of rapid deployment wherever needed.' At its core is a new brigade known as Very High Readiness Joint Task Force (VJTF), which is the 'spearhead' that can rapidly deploy within 48 hours and is comprised of 5,000 troops. For the first time, NATO has a rotating force in the seven alliance members that border Russia. NATO Secretary General Jens Stoltenberg called the Readiness Action Plan 'the biggest reinforcement of our collective defense since the end of the Cold War' when the programme was introduced after the NATO Summit in Wales in September 2014 (Bendavid, 2014; NATO, 2014; Stoltenberg, 2015). NATO also created six new command centres in Eastern Europe, to better connect local military forces to NATO (Schmitt and Meyers, 2015).

This three-pronged strategy is smart and comprehensive, but more could be done to counter current and future behaviour. The West, for instance, is not adequately explaining its policies to people in Eastern Ukraine, let alone to Russians in Russia. Even in some allied countries, the U.S. perspective is losing out to the Russian propaganda machine (Baker, 2015). In particular, the White House needs to explain why some Russian business people are being sanctioned, and others are not. Ukrainian leaders also need more help from Western leaders to restructure the country's debt, deepen economic reforms, fight corruption, and attract new investment. If the Ukrainian economy implodes, Putin wins. Providing the Ukrainian military more sophisticated radar and drones, as well as sharing intelligence, could help reduce civilian casualties should fighting flare substantially again. And over time, the Ukrainian military must receive the weapons, training, and equipment they need to deter future Russian military threats. The West also could be doing more to reach out, nurture, and support directly the people in the Donbass, including the 1.2 million of them currently displaced in other parts of Ukraine. They need immediate humanitarian assistance, as well as long-term support—education, housing, and retraining—to rebuild their futures. Similarly, independent and objective reporting in the Russian language needs support and resources.

Beyond Ukraine, if the United States and its allies are to maintain a balance with Russia, they must seek to contain belligerent Russian foreign policy actions more generally. Cybersecurity for the computers and networks which count votes in the United States and Europe must be enhanced. More sophisticated regulation of Russian disinformation must be adopted globally. At a minimum, consumers of Russian propaganda on television and social media platforms must know that the Russian state is producing this content. The United States—together with democratic allies—must develop better ways to disseminate the truth. More generally, leaders of the democratic West must reinvigorate their commitment to mutual defence of members of NATO and to liberal, democratic values. Today, Putin is winning supporters throughout Europe and even inside the United States for his brand of conservatism. This influence is eroding the liberal international order and must be contained.

While deterring Putin's anti-Western foreign policies, American and European leaders also can cooperate with the Kremlin on a limited agenda of mutual interests. First and foremost, American and Russian diplomats must re-engage on arms control, since the New Start Treaty expires in 2021. Further, threats by the Trump administration in the autumn of 2018 to withdraw from the 1987 Intermediate Nuclear Forces (INF) Treaty signed in 1987 between the United States and the Sovie Union, rather than renegotiating the deal with Russia forfeit an opportunity for positive engagement. If constructive, Russian cooperation on North Korean denuclearisation should be welcomed. Intelligence sharing on counterterrorism is another area of possible cooperation worth exploring. In parallel to limited engagement with the Russian government, the United States and its European allies also should increase efforts to engage directly with the Russian people, including students through exchanges and scholarships, peer-to-peer dialogue with NGOs, and allowing Russian companies not tied to the state to continue to work with Western partners (although we recognize disentangling some Russian businesses from the state is difficult to do).

The greatest worry for the future is that U.S. and European leaders will not fully implement their own declared policies. So far, sanctions have not only remained, but expanded since 2016. U.S. attention, always hard to maintain for complex foreign policy issues, could wane in light of our deepening domestic divisions. In Europe, several governments already have begun to call for lifting sanctions and normalising relations with Russia, even though Putin has not changed his behaviour. Dangerously, even President Trump has called to reinstate Russia's membership in the G8, evidently without demanding anything in return from Putin regarding Ukraine (Baker, June 8, 2018). Others assert that the policy is not working: sanctions on Russia are not biting; Ukrainian reforms are failing; and only some NATO members are willing to spend additional resources on defence, while Putin is supported and beloved by his people as witnessed by is stunning 77 per cent of the vote in his re-election to the presidency on March 14, 2018. The impulse to just move on—forget about Putin's past egregious behaviour and re-engage—is growing. Mystifyingly, one of the most vocal proponents of this approach is President Donald Trump.

Such a pivot towards rapprochement with Moscow, without any change in Russian behaviour, would be a mistake. Instead, the West needs to remain committed to selective containment of the Russian government under Putin, while continuing to selectively engage Russian society. After all, in the Cold War, containment alone—a policy now celebrated as strategic wisdom—did not produce results a mere three to four years after its adoption, or even a decade later, or even several decades later. The current U.S. and European policy of selective containment and selective engagement also will take time to yield intended outcomes. Putin has locked Russia in to his current confrontational course, especially given the domestic political and economic environment that he has created. Tragically, but necessarily, we too must lock in and patiently stay the course, as well.

Notes

1 This chapter is a revised and updated version of an article by the authors entitled 'Who Lost Russia (This Time)? Vladimir Putin,' *The Washington Quarterly* (2015), 38, no. 2, pp. 167–187; copyright © The Elliott School of International Affairs and reprinted by permission of Taylor & Francis Ltd, www.tandfonline.com, on behalf of The Elliott School of International Affairs.

2 Gorbachev did not try to stop the first Gulf War, but the U.S. response there, in cooperation with many other countries, was in response to Iraqi intervention in Kuwait.
3 Known as the anti-gay propaganda law, the official name of the law is 'The defense of children from information and propaganda promoting non-traditional family relationships' and is available in Russian at http://pravo.gov.ru:8080/page.aspx?50556.
4 Historical oil price data are also available at 'Crude Oil Prices' (n.d.).
5 Every month, the Levada Center carries out omnibus surveys in order to make current and accurate data available on a constant basis. The results of the nationwide polls are based on a representative sample of 1,600 over-18s from 130 sampling points across 45 regions of the Russian Federation. Data available at Levada-Center, 'Indexes,' www.levada.ru/eng/indexes-0.

References

'Agreement on the Settlement of Crisis in Ukraine – full text' (2014) *The Guardian*, February 21, www.theguardian.com/world/2014/feb/21/agreement-on-the-settlement-of-crisis-in-ukraine-full-text

Baker, Peter, June 8, 2015 in *New York Times*.

Baker, Peter (2018) 'Trump Shakes Up World Stage in Break with U.S. Allies,' June 8, 2018, *The New York Times*, https://www.nytimes.com/2018/06/08/us/politics/trump-russia-g7-readmitted-tariffs.html, accessed December 10, 2018.

BBC (2014) 'Dmitri Kiselev: Russia's Spin Doctor', April 2. BBC.com

Bendavid, Naftali (2014) 'NATO Completes Plans for Spearhead Force,' *The Wall Street Journal*, 15 June, www.wsj.com/articles/nato-pledges-support-for-ukraine-no-word-on-weapon-1423139719

Bernstein, Aron (2010) 'Is President Obama Reducing the Probability of Nuclear War?' *MIT Faculty Newsletter*, 22, no. 4 (March/April/May), http://web.mit.edu/fnl/volume/224/bernstein.html

Bush, George W. (2001) 'Bush and Putin: Best of friends,' BBC, 16 June, http://news.bbc.co.uk/2/hi/europe/1392791.stm

CNN (2012) 'Russians Call for Putin's Resignation,' CNN International, June 12, www.cnn.com/2012/06/12/world/europe/russia-protest/index.html

Cohen, Stephen F. (2000) *Failed Crusade: America and the Tragedy of Post-Communist Russia* (New York: W.W. Norton).

'Crude Oil Prices' (n.d.) www.topoilnews.com, accessed June 10, 2015.

Doyle, Michael (1996) 'Liberal Legacies, and Foreign Policy,' in Michael Brown, Sean Lynn-Jones, and Steven, eds. *Debating the Democratic Peace* (Cambridge: MIT Press).

Elder, Miriam (2011) 'Vladimir Putin Rallies Obedient Crowd at Party Congress,' *The Guardian*, November 27, www.theguardian.com/world/2011/nov/27/vladimir-putin-party-congress

European Commission (2015) 'Antitrust: Commission sends Statement of Objections to Google on Comparison Shopping Service; Opens Separate Formal Investigation on Android,' April 15, 2015, http://europa.eu/rapid/press-release_MEX-15-4784_en.htm

Francis, David and Jamila Trindle (2015) 'Will New U.S. Aid and an IMF Bailout Be Enough to Save Ukraine?' *Foreign Policy*, March 11, http://foreignpolicy.com/2015/03/11/will-new-u-s-aid-and-an-imf-bailout-be-enough-to-save-ukraine/

Goldgeier, James and Michael McFaul (2005) 'Putin's Authoritarian Soul: The First Test of Bush's Liberty Doctrine,' *The Weekly Standard*, 10, no. 22 (February 28), pp. 14–16

Graham, Thomas (2015) 'Europe's problem is with Russia, not Putin Moscow is not a rising revolutionary force but one seeking to restore power,' *The Financial Times*, May 31, 2015, http://www.ft.com/cms/s/0/f0ff7324-03b5-11e5-a70f-00144feabdc0.html - axzz3cb6030PB, accessed June 9, 2015.

Katzman, Kenneth (2013) 'Afghanistan: Post-Taliban Governance, Security, and U.S. Policy,' (Washington, DC: Congressional Research Service, April), p. 31.

Kramer, David (2010) 'America's Silence Makes Us Complicit in Russia's Crimes,' *The Washington Post*, September 20, www.washingtonpost.com/wp-dyn/content/article/2010/09/19/AR2010091902893.html

Labott, Elise (2011) 'Clinton Cites 'serious concerns' about Russian Election,' CNN, www.cnn.com/2011/12/06/world/europe/russia-elections-clinton/

Levada Center (n.d.) 'Indexes,' www.levada.ru/eng/indexes-0, accessed June 12, 2018.

McFaul, Michael (1990) '1789, 1917 Can Guide '90s Soviets,' *San Jose Mercury News*, August 19.

McFaul, Michael (1997/98) 'The Precarious Peace: Domestic Politics in the Making of Russian Foreign Policy,' *International Security*, 22, no. 3 (Winter), pp. 5–35.

McFaul, Michael and Kathryn Stoner (2007) 'The Myth of the Authoritarian Model: How Putin's Crackdown Hurt Russia,' *Foreign Affairs*, 87, no. 1 (Winter), pp. 68–84.

Mearsheimer, John (2014) 'Why the Ukraine Crisis is the West's Fault: The Liberal Delusions that Provoked Putin,' *Foreign Affairs*, 93, no. 5 (September/October), www.foreignaffairs.com/articles/russia-fsu/2014-08-18/why-ukraine-crisis-west-s-fault

Medvedev, Dimitri (2010) 'Medvedev is "more optimistic" about Russia-NATO Relations after Summit', www.rt.com/politics/russia-nato-summit-medvedev/

Medvedev, Dimitri (2012) 'Medvedev Press Conference Seoul, South Korea,' March 27 2012, transcript available in English at: http://en.kremlin.ru/events/president/news/14859

Moscow Times (2013) 'Who Will Replace Vladimir Putin in 2018?' November 18, www.themoscowtimes.com/who will replace news/article/who-will-replace-vladimir-putin-in-2018/489793.html

NATO (2014) 'NATO's Readiness Action Plan,' factsheet, December 2014, www.nato.int/nato_static_fl2014/assets/pdf/pdf_2014_12/20141202_141202facstsheet-rap-en.pdf

New York Times (2010) 'Ethnic Uzbeks Flee Violence in Kyrgyzstan,' slideshow, June 14, 2010, www.nytimes.com/slideshow/2010/06/14/world/0614-Kyrgyzstan.html?_r=0

Office of the Press Secretary (2014) 'Remarks by President Obama to the People of Estonia,' Nordea Concert Hall, Tallinn, Estonia, The White House, September 3, www.whitehouse.gov/the-press-office/2014/09/03/remarks-president-obama-people-estonia

Owen, John, IV (1996) 'Why Democratic Peace', in Michael Brown, Sean Lynn-Jones, and Steven Miller, eds. *Debating the Democratic Peace* (Cambridge: MIT Press).

Parfitt, Tom (2012) 'Anti-Putin Protesters March Through Moscow,' *The Guardian*, February 4, www.theguardian.com/world/2012/feb/04/anti-putin-protests-moscow-russia

Pew Global (2010) 'Opinion of the United States,' www.pewglobal.org/database/indicator/1/country/181/Bussh

Radio Free Europe (2015) 'Russia's Putin Signs 'Undesirable' NGOs Bill,' May 23, www.rferl.org/content/russia-law-undesirable-organizations/27032975.html

Russett, Bruce (1996) 'The Fact of Democratic Peace,' in Michael Brown, Sean Lynn-Jones, and Steven Miller, eds. *Debating the Democratic Peace* (Cambridge: MIT Press).

'Russia Average Monthly Wages' (n.d.) www.tradingeconomics.com/russia/wages accessed June 4, 2018.

'Russia GDP Annual Growth Rate' (n.d.) www.tradingeconomics.com/russia/gdp-growth-annual and, http://www.tradingeconomics.com/russia/wages

Schmitt, Eric and Steven Lee Meyers (2015) 'U.S. Poised to Put Heavy Weaponry in East Europe,' *New York Times*, June 14, p. A1.

Schwirtz, Michael and David Herszenhorn (2011) 'Russians Look at Election Results and Corruption is What they See,' *New York Times*, December 5, www.nytimes.com/2011/12/06/world/europe/russian-parliamentary-elections-criticized-by-west.html?_r=0, accessed June 10, 2015.

Stanovaya, Tatiana (2012) 'Why Russia Can't Have a Public Television Network,' Institute of Modern Russia,' July 25, http://imrussia.org/en/analysis/politics/270-russias-newest-state-controlled-television-network

Stoltenberg, Jens (2015) 'Adapting to a Changed Security Environment,' Speech by NATO Secretary General Jens Stoltenberg at the Center for Strategic and International Studies (CSIS) in Washington D.C., May 27, www.nato.int/cps/en/natohq/opinions_120166.htm

U.S. Census Bureau (n.d.) 'Trade in Goods with Russia,' www.census.gov/foreign-trade/balance/c4621.html

US Energy Information Administration (n.d.) 'Historical Oil Data 1989–2013,' www.eia.gov/dnav/pet/hist/LeafHandler.ashx?n=PET&s=RBRTE&f=D. Historical oil price data is also available at: www.topoilnews.com hit (US Energy Information Administration (n.d.), accessed June 10, 2015.

World Bank (1998) 'Data: Russian Federation,' http://data.worldbank.org/country/russian-federation

21
NATO ENLARGEMENT
A security dilemma for Russia?

Alberto Priego

Introduction

Relations between Russian and North Atlantic Treaty Organisation (NATO) have never been easy, although it is true that shortly after the dissolution of the USSR, there were some years in which cooperation was the standard. Nevertheless, after the publication of the 1995 Study on NATO enlargement, relations worsened significantly until reaching their current state. The key in the relationship has always been the enlargements by the Atlantic Alliance to the East, an aspect that Russian views as a threat against its national security. In this sense, relations between Russian and NATO can be divided into three periods that coincide with two security dilemmas and one offensive spiral.

The first period (1991–2004), which we have considered as a dormant *security dilemma*, came into full effect in 1995 when the aforementioned enlargement study led to progressively deteriorating relations between both parties. This situation, which was not exempt of measures to improve confidence, was the spark for tense moments like the incorporation of Hungary, Czech Republic and Poland and of crises like the one provoked after the NATO's intervention in Kosovo. The point of maximum tension that provoked the transformation from a dormant security dilemma to an imperialist one came in 2004 with the NATO enlargement to the East.

The *second security dilemma* (2004–2007), the *imperialist security dilemma* (Snyder, 1985), began in 2004 with the previously mentioned enlargement and concluded in 2007 at the Munich Security Conference when Putin announced the move from defensive security to a more offensive and hostile form. This marked the beginning of the end of the second dilemma and its evolution towards the offensive spiral that opened the third and last stage.

The third stage (2007–present) – the *offensive spiral* – is marked by Russian interference in the internal affairs of NATO members and of the Alliance itself. In regard to NATO enlargements, Moscow went from passive rejection to a more active role, to the point of even invading the territory in Georgia and Ukraine as a way of deterring the Alliance from integrating these members.

This chapter is developed as follows: first, we discuss the current state of research that has analysed the main developments between NATO and Russia. In the second section, we focus on the security dilemma regarding NATO-Russia relations by considering the main conditioning factor as Atlantic Alliance enlargements (Lukin, 2016, 98). In this sense, in order to verify how the enlargements have affected Russia's national security, we analyse aspects such as defence budgets, acquired capacities, military exercises or approved security doctrines.

NATO-Russia relations: the current state of research

If there is one subject that has monopolized research about NATO after the fall of the USSR it is, without a doubt, relations between the Alliance and Russia. This research, to a great extent, has been inspired by the complicated issue of enlargement. It would be impossible to discuss the current state of research that covers all contributions regarding NATO-Russia relations or even the repercussion of enlargements between Moscow and Brussels. The first research papers dealing with this issue were written by Blank (1998), Yost (1999), Hunter, Rogov, and Oliker (2001), Szayna (2001) and Asmus (2002), while recently we have witnessed the appearance of new authors such as Williams and Neumann (2000), Ringsmose and Rynning (2017), Pothier (2017) and Zapfe (2017).

While it is true that some authors, such as Deni (2016), Yilmaz (2016) and Duke and Gebhard (2017), have used the security dilemma to explain relations between Russia and NATO, none of their results have indicated the offensive spiral as the evolution of the security dilemma. In fact, most papers have focused on the security dilemma theoretical approach, insisting on the issue of missile defence systems as the central point, thus paying less attention to other aspects such as military manoeuvres, military doctrines or hybrid warfare.

From the dormant security dilemma to the offensive spiral in NATO-Russia relations

The security dilemma has been used to explain a diversity of issues, such as ethnic conflicts (Posen, 1993), arms races (Glaser, 2004) or even the emergence or the decline of powers (Collins, 1998). The most classic definitions can be attributed to Butterfield (1951, 1960), Herz (1950, 1951, 1966) and Jervis (1976, 1978, 1982, 1999, 2001) and the most recent authors such as Tang (2009), Glaser (1997) and Booth and Wheeler (2008). The latter researchers, while not having abandoned the claims of their predecessors, have updated the concept by adjusting it to the current reality.

These and other authors have pointed out a multitude of elements as vital to a security dilemma, that, according to Tang (2009, 595), can be summed up in the following points Tang calls essential and that will be used to develop the theoretical approach to this paper.

a   The anarchic nature of international relations
b   The absence –at least in the origin – of malice of those involved
c   The accumulation of power as a way to guarantee security.

In other words, due to the lack of a global and common authority, survival becomes the only motivation of states in a continuous and untiring search for security. In this endless dynamic, states became distrustful of other states, bringing about a new and more dangerous situation: the security dilemma.

The dormant security dilemma (1991-2004)

We understand that the situation in 1991 was a dormant security dilemma because both parties had adopted positions of defensive realism like those developed at the end of the 1980s by Presidents Bush and Gorbachev.

Therefore, in 1991, the relations between Russian and NATO, although they cannot be defined as cooperative, were at least not conflictual, as was the case of the Russian military doctrine of 1993, whose main objective was preventing war (Palacios and Arana, 2002, 84). Some of the Alliance's cooperation initiatives like the Partnership for Peace (PfP), although they tried to increase the security of former members of the Warsaw Pact, they generated a progressive deterioration in relations between Brussels and Moscow. This deterioration provoked an increase in tension, and finally did not only activate the security dilemma, but also transformed it into with one with imperialistic characteristics, which will be explained later. We can highlight two important disagreements with Russia that caused the aforementioned deterioration in relations between NATO and the Kremlin: the first one was related to potential Alliance expansion and the second to changes of regime supported by the West.

The first disagreement, related to expansion, occurred in 1995 with the publication of the Alliance's Study of NATO Enlargement, which opened the door to the Czech Republic, Hungary and Poland (Goldgeier, 1999). This event made Russia reconsider not only its security policy but also its relations with the Alliance. The first decision after the publication of the report was to suspend its participation in the PfP cooperation programme. Despite Russian apprehension, the Alliance was able to generate confidence through different means such as the signing of the *NATO-Russia Founding Act*, the *Permanent Joint Council* (PJC) or the participation of Russian troops in the Stabilisation Force in Bosnia and Herzegovina (SFOR). All these initiatives sought to improve cooperation with Russia and, overall, overcome misperceptions built upon both sides.

The second disagreement, the one related to the change of regime, took place in 1999 when NATO, after approving a new strategic concept, led an airstrike against Yugoslavia. Although the objective was to defend the Kosovar population from Serbian forces, the Russian perception was that NATO initiated the first of a series of political changes whose first step was always an airstrike. This perception will be very much present in subsequent actions taken by Russia, such as improving its air defence systems or even its commitment to an A2/AD (anti-access and area denial) strategy in order to deter the effect of NATO expansion to the East. Russia even shared these arms improvements with allies like Iran, whom they consider to be susceptible to suffering a military aggression and subsequent political change (Charap and Shapiro, 2015, 39).

Despite the fact that 9/11, the attack on the US in New York and Washington, meant a decrease in tension between both parties, which to some extent favoured the expansion to the East, the American invasion of Iraq and subsequent change of regime, reactivated Russian fears. Therefore, the fall of Saddam Hussein prompted the start of the second phase, the imperialist security dilemma. In any event, and in response to the enlargements, Russia adopted a policy with the objective, on one hand, to limit the damage of the expansions, and on the other hand, to obtain maximum guarantees from the Alliance (Palacios and Arana, 2002, 86) in regard to its own security.

The imperialist security dilemma (2004-2007)

The imperialist security dilemma is a concept coined by Snyder (1985, 155–156) to describe a reality during the end of the Cold War. Nevertheless, in my opinion, this situation was repeated in the framework of relations between NATO and Russia between 2004 and 2007 (Priego, 2010). Snyder pointed out three characteristics as elements making up the imperialist's security dilemma that do not appear in other security dilemma approaches:

a   First, it occurs when at least one of the parties wants to expand, even if that expansion puts its security at risk.
b   Second, in this particular security dilemma, the final objective is not exclusively military, but rather the competition between powers extends to other areas such as economic, political or even ideological. Therefore, military development is provoked by the need of the parties to show their capacities in other areas.
c   Third and lastly, it is necessary to mention that both parties prefer a compromise before a war (Snyder, 1985, 165–166).

The change from a classic (dormant) security dilemma to an imperialist one is conditioned by the two facts present in Russia's new foreign policy direction.

1   *The activation of the security dilemma*. First, one should point out that the activation of the security dilemma was provoked by NATO's integrating seven former Warsaw Pact states and three that were part of the USSR (the Baltics); this expansion of NATO was interpreted by Moscow as an attempt by NATO to accumulate offensive power.
2   *The imperialist dimension of the security dilemma*. The difference between the classic security dilemma and the imperialist one is the existence of three aspects mentioned earlier and which are present in the analysed case:

   a   *One of the parties wants to expand*, even when expanding could jeopardize its security. In the current matter, the two parties had the desire to expand. On the one hand, during the period of 2004–2007, NATO finalized the large expansion and prepared the integration of Albania and Croatia (Priego, 2007). It was also during this period when Georgia, Ukraine and FYROM (Macedonia) prepared their applications to became Alliance members. Thus, it is confirmed that the West in general and NATO in particular tried to broaden their influence in the space that Russia used to dominate.
   On the other hand, leaving aside the cases of South Ossetia, Abkhazia and Crimea, we must point out the Russian efforts to revitalize the Tashkent Pact, which in 2002 was the foundation for the creation of the *Collective Security Treaty Organization* (CSTO). Since CSTO, Russia prepared to bring states like Uzbekistan (which joined in 2006) closer or Serbia and Afghanistan that were incorporated as observers in 2013.
   b   *The competition between the parties is not reduced to the area of security*, but extends, as well, to economics, politics and, especially, ideology. With respect to the economy, projects like the Eurasian Economic Community (EurAsEC) directly competed and compete with Western economic approaches like the *European Neighbourhood Policy* (ENP) and *The Eastern Partnership* (EAP) which, although they are not developed by NATO, in the eyes of Russia are initiated by the same actor performing, namely, the West. Perhaps the place where that competition is seen most clearly is in Ukraine, as can be observed in the Maidan Revolution that ended Victor Yanukovych's government. In the political ring, some of the states that aspired to be NATO members, like Georgia or even Ukraine, created a political organization – the GUAM (Georgia, Ukraine, Azerbaijan and Moldova) – which, with the support of the US, looked to bring its

members into the Western circle. We can thereby conclude that the competition with Russia extended to sectors other than only that of security (Shapovalova, 2010).

c *The parties prefer compromise before war*, as recognized in the agreements made in the NATO-Russia Council framework established in Rome in 2002. Some examples of these compromises were the logistic agreements for supplying International Security Assistance Force (ISAF), the cooperation against narcotics in Central Asia and the joint support of the Afghan army. Although it is true that Russia changed its attitude in 2007 and the Atlantic Alliance continued moving within this logic until the crisis in Ukraine, as demonstrated in the continuous invitations to cooperation launched by NATO to Russia in the Lisbon Summit in 2010.

Moreover, from a pure assessment point of view, authors like Trenin (2007, 36) and Cross (2015) have pointed out that since the arrival on the scene of Vladimir Putin in the Kremlin, Russia has adopted a foreign policy with imperialist shades more characteristic of the Tsarist era than of Soviet Russia. This conception, which takes us back to the nineteenth century and distances us from the twenty-first century (Carter, 2017, 53), has been embodied in the concept *Novorossiya*, a term that was publicly invoked by Putin in 2014 (Taylor, 2014) to justify Russia's annexation of Crimea.

Although it is true that one of the commonly accepted elements of the security dilemma is the lack of malice in the behaviour, some authors such as Collins (2000), Wheeler (2009) and Booth (2008) convey, at least, the difficulty of assessing their real intentions. The inclusion of a supposed malicious intention in the behaviour of those involved is not distant from the classic authors' vision of the dilemma because Christian realism authors like Niebuhr (2002, 2010) already established human nature as malicious, which logically conditioned the intentions among those involved. While it is true that this difficulty is widely accepted, in the case of the imperialist dilemma, it is even more so.

This adjustment of intentions from benign to malign is what marks the transition of the security dilemma to the offensive spiral and, although demonstrating it is not easy, in the case of the Russian Federation, it was clearly proven in Putin's speeches in the Munich Security Conference (2007), in the Valdai International Discussion Club in Sochi (2014) and in the United Nations in New York (2015).

The offensive spiral (2007–today)

Although many authors have signalled the invasion of Ukraine as the moment of change in Russia's foreign policy, in my opinion this happened implicitly in 2007 with President Putin's speech at the Munich Security Conference and explicitly in 2008 with the invasion of Georgia. One of the clearest points in which to appreciate the offensive spiral is the radicalization of the Russian Federation's security and military doctrines. The fundamental change took place with the approval of the 2010 Military Doctrine (Russian Presidency, 2010) which identified NATO as an 'external danger' (Cross, 2015, 159), especially in regard to future enlargements, improvement of capacities and ballistic missile defence (BMD) systems. The 2014 doctrine (Russian Presidency, 2014) follows the path of the previous one, although it elevates the tone (Trenin, 2015), as this document was approved right after the Crimea invasion and the measures approved by the Alliance in the Wales Summit. The main difference from the previous document is NATO's qualification as a 'main external military danger'. In any case, since 2010, a change in Russia's attitude can be recognized, a change which is included in the military doctrines approved by the Kremlin in this period.

Another aspect of Russian behaviour that has been affected by the radicalization of the Russian position is the use of military exercises carried out by the federal army, especially the so-called ZAPAD, a word used by the Kremlin when referring to the West. The first of these exercises was held in 1999, but the hostility and symbolism has increased over the years. In 2009, ZAPAD simulated the reaction by Russia and Belarus faced with an insurrection by the Polish minority in Belarus and four years later in 2013 the invasion of Poland and the Baltic states (Zdanavičius and Cezkaj, 2015, 5). In 2017, a new edition of the ZAPAD exercises was held; on this occasion, the simulation was an occupation operation of a territory (Veshnoriya) very similar to the Baltic states (Boulègue, 2017). In this case, the Russian forces fought against an enemy made up of interoperable forces, very similar to those of NATO.

It must be mentioned here that since 2007, Russian naval and airspace violations have greatly increased in a number in NATO member-countries. The period with the greatest number of incidents was from March 2014 to November 2015 (Frear, 2015). During those 20 months, which coincide with the period of maximum tension due to the Ukrainian crisis, 66 incidents took place, of which 11 were described as 'Serious Incidents with Escalation Risk'. Because of their exceptional seriousness, these events should also be pointed out: a Russian nuclear submarine was sighted on the coast of Stockholm (18 October 2014), the kidnapping of an Estonian intelligence officer (26 September 2015) and especially a Russian combat jet without a transponder that flew over the Malmö airport, which almost crashed into a Swedish commercial airplane (12 December 2014).

However, if there is something that can confirm that Russia has decided to leave the security dilemma to enter an offensive spiral, it is its A2/AD strategy, which began in 2008 with the invasion of Georgia and concluded in 2014 with the annexation of Crimea. In fact, the creation of an A2/AD strategy is aimed at stopping the Alliance forces in a potential theatre of war. In the case of Russia, the Kremlin would have created an A2/AD that would go from St. Petersburg to Crimea, passing through Kaliningrad, Abkhazia, South Ossetia and even Tartus (Syria). In this manner, by means of long-range anti-aircraft, anti-shipping and surface-to-surface missiles (Frühling and Lasconjarias, 2016, 96) in the mentioned enclaves, action and access by NATO troops, even mobilization in their own territory, would be restricted. Therefore, the effect of the latest NATO enlargements would be reduced, and thus, the potential threat of a change of regime in Russia would be diminished.

The creation of an A2/AD strategy would give Russia – in a supposed confrontation with NATO – a significant advantage in the first days of the crisis (Pothier, 2017, 74). This situation would lower the Alliance's credibility, because it would not be able to respond decisively to the supposed Russian aggression. In this manner, it would reduce the effect of some of the leading measures approved in Wales like the 'Very High Readiness Joint Task Force' (VHRJTF).

Faced with this aggressive policy, the Atlantic Alliance has adopted an original measure called 'Enhanced Forward Presence' (EFP). It consists of four-battalion–sized battle groups deployed in the Baltic states and Poland, each one commanded by one nation that leads the mission. Germany is responsible for the mission in Lithuania, the US in Poland, Canada in Latvia and the UK in Estonia. The deterring effect of the EFP is being contested by Russia through the use of hybrid warfare actions (Radin, 2017) trying to provoke the people of these states to rebel against the presence of 'occupation' troops. In February 2017, information was spread about the rape of a teenage girl in Lithuania at the hands of a German soldier (Zapfe, 2017, 151). These actions are in line with the well-known Gerasimov Doctrine, whose main objective is to provoke instability in the NATO member-societies.

Conclusions

We can establish that relations between NATO and Russia have been marked by Alliance expansions to the East. Since 1995, when the Study of NATO Enlargement was published, four rounds of enlargements have taken place (1999, 2004, 2008, and 2017), incorporating 13 new members. This has caused relations between NATO and Russia to go from a dormant security dilemma to the current offensive spiral in which we are immersed. The turning point was President Putin's speech in Munich in 2007 and, especially, the invasion of Georgia in 2008 that gave rise to the creation of an aggressive policy that has continued in Ukraine and Syria.

The approval of a series of aggressive military doctrines, the construction of an A2/AD strategy or the implementation of military exercises (ZAPAD) that violate Organization for Security and Cooperation in Europe (OSCE) codes are clear evidence that Russia has entered an offensive spiral that could be very dangerous, not only for the Alliance but also for Russia itself.

References

Asmus, Ronald (2002) *Opening NATO's Door. How the Alliance Remade Itself for a New Era*. New York: Columbia University Press.
Blank, Stephen (1998) 'Russia, NATO Enlargement and Baltic States', *World Affairs*, Vol. 160, no. 3, pp. 115–125.
Booth, Kenneth and Wheeler, Nicholas (2008) *The Security Dilemma. Fear, Cooperation and Trust in World Politics*. Basignstoke: Palgrave.
Bosworth, Kara (2002) 'The Effect of 11 September on Russia-NATO Relations', *Perspectives on European Politics & Society*, Vol. 3, no. 3, pp. 361–387.
Boulègue, Mathieu (2017) 'Five Things to Know About the Zapad-2017 Military Exercise', *Chatham House*, www.chathamhouse.org/expert/comment/five-things-know-about-zapad-2017-military-exercise
Butterfield, Herbert (1951) *History and Human Relations*. London: Collins.
Butterfield, Herbert (1960) *Christianity and History*. London: Bell.
Carter, Ash (2017) 'A Strong and Balanced Approach to Russia', *Survival*, Vol. 58, no. 6, pp. 51–62.
Charap, Samuel and Shapiro, Jeremy (2015) 'Consequences of a New World War', *Survival*, Vol. 57, no. 2, pp. 37–45.
Collins, Alan R. (1998) 'GRIT, Gorbachev and the End of the Cold War', *Review of International Studies*, Vol. 24, no. 2, pp. 201–219.
Collins, Alan R. (2000) *Security Dilemma in Southeast Asia*. London: Palgrave Macmillan.
Cross, Sharyl (2015) 'NATO-Russia Security Challenges in the Aftermath of Ukraine Conflict: Managing Black Sea Security and Beyond', *Southeast European and Black Sea Studies*, Vol. 15, no. 2, pp. 151–177.
Deni, John (2016) 'A Security Dilemma in Northeastern Europe? *Atlantic Council*, July, available at http://www.atlanticcouncil.org/blogs/new-atlanticist/a-security-dilemma-in-northeastern-europe
Duke, Simon and Gebhard, Carmen (2017) 'The EU and NATO's Dilemmas with Russia and the Prospects for Deconfliction', *European Security*, Vol. 26, no. 3, pp. 1–35.
Frear, Thomas (2015) 'List of Close Military Encounters Between Russia and the West, March 2014–March 2015', European Leadership Network, www.europeanleadershipnetwork.org/wp-content/uploads/2017/10/ELN-Russia-West-Full-List-of-Incidents.pdf
Frühling, Stephan and Lasconjarias, Guillaume (2016) 'NATO A2/AD and the Kaliningrad Challenge', Vol. 58, no. 2, pp. 95–116.
Glaser, Charles L. (1997) 'The Security Dilemma Revisited', *World Politics*, Vol. 50, no. 1, pp. 171–201.
Glaser, Charles L. (2004) 'When Are Arms Races Dangerous? Rational versus Suboptimal Arming', *International Security*, Vol. 28, no.4, pp. 44–84.
Goldgeier, James (1999) *Not Whether but When: The U.S. Decision to Enlarge NATO*. Washington, DC: Brookings Institution Press.
Herz, John H. (1950) 'Idealist Internationalism and the Security Dilemma', *World Politics*, Vol. 2, no. 2, pp. 157–180.

Herz, John H. (1951) *Political Realism and Political Idealism*. Chicago: Chicago University Press.
Herz, John H. (1966) *International Politics in the Atomic Age*. New York: Columbia University Press.
Hunter, Robert, Rogov, Sergey, and Oliker, Olga (2001) *NATO and Russia. Bridge-Building for the 21st Century Report of the Working Group on NATO-Russia Relations*. Santa Monica: RAND.
Jervis, Robert (1976). *Perception and Misperception in International Politics*. Princeton; Princeton University Press.
Jervis, Robert (1978) 'Cooperation under security dilemma' *World Politics*, Vol. 40, no. 1, pp. 167–214.
Jervis, Robert (1982) 'Security Regimes' International Organization, 1982, Vol. 36, no. 2, pp. 357–378.
Jervis, Robert (1999) 'Realism, Neorrealism and Cooperation' *International Security*, Vol. 21, no 1, pp. 42–63.
Jervis, Robert (2001) 'Was the Cold War a Security Dilemma?' *Journal of Cold War Studies*, Vol. 3, no. 1, pp. 36–60.
Lukin, Alexander (2016) 'Russia in the Post-Bipolar World', *Survival*, Vol. 58, no. 1, pp. 91–112.
Niebuhr, Reinhold (2002). *Moral Man and Immoral Society: A Study of Ethics and Politics*. Louisville: Westminster John Knox Press.
Niebuhr, Reinhold (2010). *Moral Man and Immoral Society: A Study in Ethics and Politics*. Whitefish: Kessinger Publishing.
Palacios, José Miguel and Arana, Paloma (2002) 'Doctrina militar rusa: herencia soviética, realidades postsoviéticas, perspectiva europea', *Revista CIDOB d'Afers Internationals*, Vol. 11, no. 59, pp. 81–103.
Posen, Barry, R. (1993) 'The Security Dilemma and Ethnic Conflicts', *Survival*, Vol. 35, no. 1, pp. 27–47.
Pothier, Fabrice (2017) 'An Area-Access Strategy for NATO', *Survival*, Vol. 59, no. 3, pp. 73–80.
Priego, Alberto (2004) 'NATO Cooperation Towards South Caucasus', *Caucasian Review of International Affairs*, Vol. 2, no. 1, pp. 1–8.
Priego, Alberto (2007) 'La OTAN tras la Cumbre de Riga: la puerta sigue abierta', *UNISCI Discussion Papers*, Vol. 5, no. 13, pp. 71–89.
Priego, Alberto (2010) 'The Atlantic Alliance in Eurasia: A Different Player?' in Freire, Raquel and Kanet, Roger, eds. *Key Players and Regional Dynamics in Eurasia*. Basingstoke: MacMillan, pp. 215–237.
Radin, Andrew (2017) *Hybrid Warfare in the Baltics: Threats and Potential Responses*. Santa Monica: RAND Corporation.
Ringsmose, Jens and Ryning, Sten (2017) 'Now for the Hard Part: NATO's Strategic Adaptation to Russia', *Survival*, Vol. 59, no. 3, pp. 129–146.
Russian Presidency (2010) 'The Military Doctrine of the Russian Federation', approved by Russian Federation presidential edict on 5 February 2010. Available at https://carnegieendowment.org/files/2010russia_military_doctrine.pdf
Russian Presidency (2014) 'The Military Doctrine of the Russian Federation', approved by Russian Federation. Available at www.offiziere.ch/wp-content/uploads-001/2015/08/Russia-s-2014-Military-Doctrine.pdf
Shapovalova, Alexandra (2010) 'Political Implications of the Eastern Partnership for Ukraine: A Basis for Rapprochement or Deepening the Rift in Europe', *Romanian Journal of European Affairs*, Vol. 10, no. 3, pp. 70–80.
Snyder, Jack, L. (1985) 'Perceptions of the Security Dilemma 1914', in Jervis, Robert, Lebow, Richard N., and Stein, Janice G., eds. *Psychology and Deterrence*. London: The John Hopkins University Press.
Szayna, Thomas (2001) *NATO Enlargement, 2000–2015. Determinants and Implications for Defense Planning*. Santa Monica: RAND.
Taylor, Adam (2014) 'Novorossiya: The Latest Historical Concept to Worry About in Ukraine', *Washington Post*, April 18.
Tang, Shiping (2009) 'The Security Dilemma: A Conceptual Analysis', *Security Studies*, Vol. 18, pp. 587–623.
Trenin, Dimitri (2007) 'Russia's Threat Perception and Strategic Posture', *Strategic Studies Institute*, November, pp. 35–49. Accessed on (2 March 2018) at www.StrategicStudiesInstitute.army.mil/
Trenin, Dimitri (2015) '2014: Russia's New Military Doctrine Tells It All', http://carnegie.ru/commentary/57607

Williams, Michael C. and Neumann, Iber B. (2000) 'From Alliance to Security Community: NATO, Russia, and the Power of Identity', *Millennium: Journal of International Studies*, Vol. 29, no. 2, pp. 357–387.

Yilmaz, Serdar (2016) 'NATO and Russia's Security Dilemma Within the European Union's Far Neighbors', *International Relations and Diplomacy*, Vol. 4, no. 10, pp. 650–665.

Yost, David (1999) *NATO Transformed: The Alliance's New Roles in International Security*. Washington, DC: United States Institute of Peace.

Zapfe, Martin (2017) 'Deterrence from the Ground-up: Understanding NATO's Enhanced Forward Presence', *Survival*, Vol. 59, no. 3, pp. 147–160.

Zdanavičius, Liudas and Czekaj, Matthew (2015) *Russia's Zapad 2013. Military Exercise Lessons for Baltic Regional Security*. Washington, DC: Jamestown Foundation, National Defence Academy of Latvia.

22
RUSSIA'S REGIONAL AND GLOBAL COUNTERTERRORISM STRATEGIES

How Moscow's vision of the new global order affects its approach to terrorism

Mariya Y. Omelicheva

The struggle against international terrorism has been declared among Russia's chief foreign policy and national security goals. The 2000 National Security Concept of the Russian Federation signed by then Acting President Vladimir Putin asserted that international terrorism was waging an open campaign to destabilise Russia (The Ministry of Foreign Affairs of the Russian Federation, 2000). Traditionally, the threat of international terrorism has been identified with insurgent and militant activities on the southern border of the former Soviet Union. Russia has viewed Afghanistan as a source of destabilisation in Central Asia and warned about Islamist groups exploiting these countries' ethnic, sectarian and other fault lines to spread insurgency to this volatile region. Georgia's tumultuous territories of Abkhazia and South Ossetia were named as the breeding grounds of extremism, and safe havens for the training camps of terrorist organisations.

The 9/11 attacks on the U.S. provided Moscow with an opportunity to reframe the Chechen conflict as part of the global jihadist crusade and renew its call for a broad-based global coalition against international terrorism. Russia offered the U.S. cooperation in the area of intelligence sharing and opened its airspace for the anti-Taliban coalition aircraft. These efforts at forging cooperative counterterrorism connections with the West were, however, short-lived. Two years later, Moscow turned into a staunch opponent of Washington's intervention in Iraq. In the following decade, considerable differences in the Russian and American counterterrorism practices, disagreements over the issues of governance, and mutual mistrust stood in the way of Moscow-Washington practical counterterrorism cooperation.

Although the 2009 version of Russia's National Security Concept downgraded the threat of international terrorism to national security, possibly reflecting the declared end of the 'counterterrorism operation in Chechnya', the Russian leadership expressed concerns with the deteriorating security situation in Central Asia because of the growing threat of terrorism from Afghanistan. To deal with this problem, Moscow strengthened its military presence in Kyrgyzstan and Tajikistan by reinforcing the military bases of the Collective Security Treaty Organisation (CSTO) located in these countries. It also argued for strengthening the military component of the Shanghai Cooperation Organisation (SCO) whose members include Russia, China, and several Central Asian states.[1]

A new National Security Concept of Russia adopted in 2015 names the threat of international terrorism among the top threats to state and public safety, second only to the threat of subversive activities by foreign states and their agents (Russian National Security Strategy, 2015). This clearly reflects the elevated fears of the jihadist destabilisation at home engendered by the sprawling Islamist networks connected to the Islamic State of Iraq and Levant (ISIS) established in 2014. The election of Donald Trump as the 45th President of the U.S. in November 2016 opened a window of opportunity for Moscow's joining its forces with those of Washington in fighting for a common cause of transnational terrorism in the Middle East. However, the use of chemical weapons by the regime of Syrian President Bashar al-Assad and the U.S. missile strikes against the Ba'athist Syrian government that ensued pushed Washington-Moscow counterterrorism cooperation into limbo.

The goal of this chapter is to provide an overview of Russia's regional and global security and counterterrorism strategies and account for Moscow's tactical choices prioritising the use of force as well as inconsistencies in counterterrorism measures used by Moscow. Among these inconsistencies are Russia's rhetorical exaggeration of the threat of terrorism, the backing of insurgent groups involved in terrorist operations, and support for institutions and practices that themselves give rise to terrorism. The chapter argues that Russia's regional and global counterterrorism strategy must be understood in the context of broader foreign policy and security goals assessed through the critical geopolitics lens. The critical geopolitics perspective views foreign policy as a discursive and political practice of constructing, defending and living the alternative claims about the 'truths' of global politics. How these geopolitical visions of international life and Russia's place in it are defined and redefied by the Kremlin matters crucially in explaining its counterterrorism measures in the neighbourhood and beyond (Omelicheva, 2016).

The chapter begins with an overview of Moscow's regional and global counterterrorism activities followed by the discussion of alternative explanations of Russia's counterterrorism policies. Next, the chapter offers an analysis of Russia's counterterrorism responses followed by the discussion of the findings.

Russia's counterterrorism responses (2000–2017)

The threat of terrorism in Russia has evolved from a tactic used by the Chechen rebels fighting for national independence into the sprawling Islamist insurgency under the umbrella of the Caucasus Emirate seeking to establish a sharia-based Islamic state in Russia's North Caucasus (Dannreuther, 2010; Kim and Blank, 2013; Pokalova, 2015). The evolution of Russia's counterterrorism policy has trailed the Kremlin's experiences with fighting the Chechen resistance and outbreaks of insurgency in the broader North Caucasus region. The Russian authorities have adopted extensive counterterrorism legislation, established and modified institutions responsible for combating terrorism, and streamlined the leadership and conduct of counterterrorist operations (Baev, 2018; Omelicheva, 2017).

The global and regional dimensions of Russia's counterterrorism policy developed concurrently with the Kremlin's domestic counterterrorism efforts and were part of President Putin's broader security and military policy. From the beginning of his first presidency in January 2000, Putin insisted on the operational ties of the Chechen fighters with Al-Qaeda and ventured to portray the second military campaign in Chechnya launched in 1999 as a part of the international war against terrorism. He raised alarm over the linkages between the militant and criminal groups in Europe, Eurasia, and Afghanistan and advocated for a joint Euro-Atlantic counterterrorism effort (Hill, 2002).

Following the 9/11 terrorist attacks, the Kremlin actively supported the U.S. and the Northern Alliance in their struggle with the Taliban and continued drawing world attention to the threat of transnational terrorism through various international and regional forums. President Putin seized on Russia's rapprochement with the West, which softened its position on Russia's warfare in Chechnya, to accuse Azerbaijan and Georgia of supporting global terrorism and the Chechen rebels (Cornell, 2017). Russia laid demands on the Georgian government to allow Russian troops into Georgian territory to stage attacks on the Chechen rebels in 1999. That year, several thousand Chechens, including some fighters, crossed into Georgia's Pankisi Gorge area near Chechnya's border. In 2002, President Putin sent notes to the members of the United Nations Security Council (UNSC) and Organisation for Security and Cooperation in Europe (OSCE) condemning Tbilisi for harbouring terrorists and threatened the use of military force against Georgia in Russia's 'self-defence' (Nichol, 2003). Russia's intervention was averted by a U.S.-sponsored $64-million Train and Equip Program (GTEP) for the Georgian armed forces, which enabled the Georgian military to reassert control over its territory.

Central Asia became another theatre of Russia's regional counterterrorism efforts. Political and economic circumstances of the transitional period – civil war in Tajikistan (1992–1997), pervasive poverty and inequality defining everyday experiences of many Central Asians, and the heavy-handed tactics of authoritarian regimes – have encouraged the emergence of a number of violent non-state actors. Criminal infiltration of these states aggravated by porous borders and weaknesses of law enforcement institutions turned Central Asia into an important site for drug trafficking and organised crime (Burnashev, 2007; UNODC, 2012). Since the late 1990s, the Russian government and security services have been pouring out warnings about the imminent threat of Islamist insurgency powered by the Afghan opioids in Central Asia. The Russian leadership spearheaded the adoption of a series of documents related to the implementation of joint measured for combating international terrorism in the region. The signed agreements laid platform for the creation of several regional counter-terrorism structures, including the Anti-Terrorist Centre (ATC) of the Commonwealth of Independent States established in 2000 with a structural subdivision in Bishkek, Kyrgyzstan, and the Regional Anti-Terrorism Structure (RATS) of the SCO established in 2004 in Tashkent, Uzbekistan. In 2001, Russia launched the Central Asian Regional Collective Rapid Deployment Force staged at the Kant military based in Kyrgyzstan and the 201st Military Base in Tajikistan. In 2009, Moscow spearheaded a more powerful and mobile Collective Rapid Reaction Force, a joint combined arms task force consisting of independent military units from the CSTO member-states, with the main purpose of fighting terrorism, drug trafficking, and countering a limited military aggression against the CSTO members (Omelicheva, 2011).

The establishment of ISIS elevated the threat of transnational terrorism for the Russian government. By different accounts, between 900 and 2400 Russian foreign fighters had left for Iraq and Syria by 2015 (The Soufan Group, 2015). In 2014, several high-ranking field commanders of the Caucasus Emirate pledged the oath of allegiance to ISIS (Youngman, 2016). The prospects of the battle-hardened and competent militants returning to Russia and staging jihadist violence at home became a major source of concern for the Russian regime. Concurrently, multiple jihadist cells radicalised by the ISIS online propaganda and autonomous from the Caucasus Emirate popped up in different parts of Russia. Using the pretext of combating the terrorist threat in Syria, the Kremlin launched a military intervention in the Syrian Civil War in September 2015, the first military operation in Russia's post-Soviet history carried out outside Eurasia. President Putin delivered a high-profile speech at the United Nations emphasising the counterterrorism purpose of Russia's air strike in Syria and seeking to build a broad international coalition to defeat the terrorist threat in the Middle East (Baev, 2018).

Similarly to domestic counterterrorism policy, Russia's regional and global counterterrorism efforts have predominantly relied on the military modus operandi. Whether in Georgia in 2002, where Russia threatened a military intervention in pursuit of the Chechen rebels, or more recently in Ukraine, where Moscow deployed its special operations forces in Crimea allegedly to prevent the recruitment of Crimeans for terrorist networks and possible attacks on the Russian population, Russia's actions have been limited to military force and threats of force (Baev, 2018). Joint counterterrorism operations and security drills held under the auspices of the CSTO and SCO have become a regular feature of Russia-Central Asia counterterrorism cooperation (Omelicheva, 2011). In Syria, the singular focus of the military campaign has been the physical liquidation of the insurgents and purported terrorists. Not only have these measures lacked a strategic dimension, they have also been inconsistent with the stated goal of fighting international terrorism.

First, both the Taliban and Al-Qaeda have few tactical, strategic, or ideological reasons in crossing over into the post-Soviet region (Stepanova, 2000). The threat of the spillover of Islamist violence from Afghanistan to Central Asia is, therefore, vastly exaggerated. And, while the transborder movement of criminals, fighters, and illicit goods in Central Asia poses a challenge to regional security, the upsurge of Islamist activity, including some acts of terrorist violence, has been largely a product of internal factors, rather than external Islamic influences (Omelicheva, 2015). The Kremlin's rhetoric and counterterrorism initiatives designed to halt the spread of Islamist violence from Afghanistan to Central Asia have diverted attention from the chief causes of public discontent in the region. Those include growing economic disparity and impoverishment in many parts of Central Asia, demographic pressures, and criminal and kleptocratic nature of the ruling authoritarian regimes.

Second, not only have the Russian counterterrorism projects failed to address the domestic root causes of terrorism, by emboldening and strengthening the governing regimes, they have furthered the very political and security malformations responsible for engendering them. Moscow's backing of institutions and practices responsible for socio-political instability is clearly evidenced in Syria, where Moscow has openly backed the repressive regime of Bashar al-Assad. Russia's own air strikes and, more importantly, the attacks by the Syrian military have shown blatant disregard for civilian casualties, thus contributing to radicalisation of the Syrian population (Carpenter, 2017).

Last, but not least, in both Syria and Afghanistan, the Kremlin has worked with the forces of international terrorism which it avows to defeat. Bashar al-Assad's allies in Syria include Hezbollah and the Iranian Revolutionary Guards. By enabling sectarian tensions between the Assad regime, Hezbollah, and other Iran-sponsored Shia militias, on the one side, and Sunni Arab groups, on the other, Moscow has been contributing to the conflict in Syrian and beyond (Baev, 2018; Carpenter, 2017). In Afghanistan, Russia has forged ties with the Taliban that continues threatening the security of the Afghan government as well as the U.S. and North Atlantic Treaty Organisation (NATO) forces. While the extent of Russian support for the Taliban is debated, including whether the Kremlin has been arming the group, its relationship with the group has both empowered and legitimised it (Gurganus, 2018).

Mariya Y. Omelicheva

Explaining Russia's regional and global counterterrorism strategies

What explains the glaring inconsistences in Russia's global and regional counterterrorism efforts? While Russia's foreign policy has been scrutinised for determinants of its foreign policy behaviour, Moscow's global and regional counterterrorism policy has received less systematic evaluation. It is possible, however, to discern the sources of Russia's counterterrorism actions abroad from the general accounts of Russia's foreign and security policy. For an analytical purpose, these explanations can be divided into two large groups emphasising either pragmatic (rational) or ideology-driven logic of Moscow's foreign policy and security actions. Furthermore, the idea of Putin's foreign policy as pragmatic has been linked to the international relations tradition of political realism (Casier, 2006; Isakova, 2005; Lynch, 2001).

Proceeding from a set of shared core assumptions, realist thinking produced several explanations of Russian foreign policy conduct. From the standpoint of defensive realism, Russia has been viewed as a status quo power balancing the U.S. in order to preserve its regional and global status. Throughout the 1990s, Russia saw a decline of its influence in the post-Soviet space. From the early days of Putin's presidency, the Kremlin has sought a revival of Russia as an economic and military heavyweight in the post-Soviet region and looked for a rationale in support of a more assertive posture there. In Central Asia and, to a lesser extent, the South Caucasus, Russia exploited the threat of terrorism to reinvigorate its military-security influence under the counterterrorism banner. The deployment of the U.S. and NATO forces in the region following the 9/11 attacks amplified its concerns with the threat to Russia's interest posed by the U.S. and Moscow intensified its security, military, and counterterrorism initiatives to contain and balance Washington (Allison, 2004).

From the perspective of offensive realism, Russia has been portrayed as a revisionist power with aggressive intentions. Moscow's invasion and the subsequent annexation of Crimea enabled the transfer of control over a vital military and security asset to Moscow (Omelicheva, 2016). Russia's continued backing of the anti-regime separatist militias implicated in violence against civilians, including terrorism, has sought to impair the prospect of Kiev joining the Western security and economic institutions. In both Syria and Afghanistan, Russia has ramped up its support for anti-American insurgents under the guise of counterterrorism in pursuit of its goal of power aggrandisement when the opportunity presented itself.

The literature on counterterrorism has also illuminated the role of historical and cultural-institutional context in counterterrorism policymaking, and the constructed identity of states as determinants of national security and foreign policies (Miyaoka, 1998; Pedahzur and Ranstorp, 2001). Russia's foreign policy and counterterrorism efforts have been traced to its imperialist ideology and authoritarian political culture, which have shaped its policies towards the neighbours (Tsygankov, 2012; Van Herpen, 2014). Enduring beliefs rooted in the Russian imperial tradition have reinforced its practice of imperial preservation and expansion and strengthened Moscow's resolve in the effectiveness of the use of force as the primary means of combatting the perceived threat of transnational and domestic terrorism (Omelicheva, 2017).

Although increasingly popular, both pragmatic and ideological explanations of Russia's foreign and counterterrorism policy have limitations. The imperialist accounts are typically deployed to critique Russia's aggressive policies, rather than explain the diversity of ideas and images that make up Moscow's ideology and how the Putin regime manipulated the nationalist and imperialist sentiments to garner public support for its foreign policy agendas (Lankina and Watanabe, 2017; Laruelle, 2012). The pragmatist/realist presentations, on the other hand, confer legitimacy to Russia's foreign and counterterrorism policy in the neighbouring nations and are insufficient for explaining inconsistencies between the Russian foreign and security policy objectives and actions.

This chapter concurs with the dominant perspectives on Russia's foreign policy conduct in that Moscow's regional and global counterterrorism policy has to be understood in the context of its foreign policy and security aims. It departs from these perspectives postulating power competition or imperial ideology as a priori sources of Russia's foreign policy by shifting focus on Russia's own beliefs about the nature of international politics, power, ideas, and threats. A critical geopolitics perspective[2] used in the analysis of Russia's counterterrorism policy emphasises the role of 'geopolitical imaginations', the co-called 'truths' of global politics, in states' foreign policy actions. How these geopolitical visions of international life and Russia's place in global affairs are defined, redefined, and deployed by the Russian leadership helps in understanding Moscow's counterterrorism measured in its neighbourhood and beyond.

For the Russian leadership, the main 'truth' of global politics is that Russia is (and has always been) a great power by virtue of its size, geostrategic position, immense natural wealth, historical legacy, and cultural superiority. Russia finds itself in the world plagued by a systemic crisis triggered by the U.S. While Russia has always favoured a Westphalian model of global order emphasising the principles of sovereignty and territorial integrity, it has viewed the U.S.-led international liberal order as inimical to its national interests (Omelicheva, 2016). Subsequently, one of the visions of Russia's role in global affairs is that of a rebuilder of the global order on terms that are compatible with Russia's interests and status-related aspirations. To restructure the global order means weakening the existing one, including its main champion, the U.S. Because the current competition between the U.S. (and the West, in general) is not only the contest of crude power but also the struggle of ideas and ideologies, the threats to Russia's sovereignty and integrity are not limited to traditional concerns with the military attack. Any attempt at imposing Western values on Russia has been viewed as imminently dangerous.

Critical geopolitics on Russia's counterterrorism policies

How can a critical geopolitics perspective emphasising countries' own geopolitical imaginations inform our understanding of Russia's global and regional counterterrorism policies? Looked at through the lens of the Russian leadership, global politics are undergoing a transition to a new 'polycentric' model of world order.[3] Russia's increasingly important role in shaping the new world order has been met with opposition by the U.S. and its allies. According to Russian National Security Strategy (2015), the West has applied economic, political, military, and informational pressure to contain Russia's resurgence in international politics. Russia's conventional capabilities are insufficient for balancing against the U.S. Subsequently, the Russian leadership has endeavoured to undermine the U.S. through the triage of information- and cyber warfare, support for the extremist forces in Europe, and subversive activities in the Middle East, Southeast Asia, and Ukraine carried out under the counterterrorism banner. Concurrently, Russia has sought to position itself as a key global and regional player on a par with other heavyweights like the U.S.

Russia's collaboration with Hezbollah, designated as a terrorist group by the U.S. Department of State, and other Iran-sponsored Shia militias backing the Syrian government should be examined on the backdrop of Moscow's views of global affairs and the chief threats to its national security. From the operational standpoint, Russia's military actions in Syria, framed as a counterterrorism campaign, did more to constraint the U.S. forces and destroy the country's opposition to President Assad rather than to fight the terrorist threat posed by ISIS. The Kremlin chose to deploy a Russian-made air defence system in Syria to deter and intercept possible U.S. air strikes against the Assad forces. Washington has been fighting ISIS in Syria but shown willingness to deploy its military assets against the Syrian regime (Baev, 2018).[4] The purported goal of helping Damascus in fighting terrorists has been secondary to presenting Russia as an active geopolitical player capable of projecting its military force outside its traditional operational theatre and frustrating the plans of the U.S. (Trenin, 2018).

Russia's counterterrorism interventions in both Syria and Afghanistan have also sought to promote an image of a weakened and faltering U.S. Similarly to its strategy in Syria, where the Russian government has been shaping the situation on the ground, in Afghanistan it chose to build relations with the key political players, including the Taliban, to make sure it can impact any future settlement. These actions carry the promise of Russia's long-term influence in the Middle East and Southeast Asia and force Washington to recognise Moscow's role in these regions (Korostikov, 2017).

The second reason for Russia's patronage of authoritarian regimes and support for violent non-state actors has to do with the Kremlin's trepidation over 'colour revolutions' orchestrated by the U.S. The Russian National Security Strategy (2015) places the threat of 'intelligence and other activity by special services and organisations of foreign states' before the threat associated with activities of terrorist and extremist groups. Notably, the document links the emergence of ISIS and spread of its influence in the Middle East to intrastate instability and conflict provoked by 'the practice of overthrowing legitimate political regimes' (Russian National Security Strategy, 2015). Russia's president has repeatedly denounced Washington's meddling in the sovereign affairs of other states and avowed to counter those interventions.

Moscow's support for the anti-government rebels fighting in eastern Ukraine and its military actions Syria, both framed as an effort to root out terrorism, have been part of Russia's counter-revolution strategy. In the Kremlin's initial interpretation, the Arab Spring's events were a malicious plan orchestrated by the West with the goal of decreasing Russia's influence in the region. Although Putin has had little personal affinity towards the Syrian president, the survival of his regime has been deemed necessary for turning the tide of colour revolutions (Miller, 2016). The Syrian and Russian governments have dubbed Assad's opponents as 'terrorists' and 'extremists' and justified their deadly air campaigns that resulted in high civilian casualties by the exigencies of counterterrorism operation (RFE/RL, 2018). Although, the Kremlin's narrative concerning the sources of revolts in the Arab world has changed over time,[5] Moscow's government has been vexed by the diminished standing of Russia in the Middle East in the aftermath of the Arab revolutions. Syria presented the Kremlin with an opportunity for strengthening Russia's position in the region (Malashenko, 2013).

Status-linked concerns and fears of regime overthrow have guided Russia's counterterrorism policy in Central Asia. Having witnessed the Taliban's success in challenging the authoritarian regime in Afghanistan, the Kremlin has expressed concerns over the mobilisation of religious identity against the ruling administrations in Central Asia (Stepanova, 2000). And, while Russia's counterterrorism policy in Central Asia has been influenced by the state of United States-Russia relations, as argued by political realism, the details of Russia's counterterrorism and security assistance to the region can only be discerned through the analysis its own geopolitical imagery of Central Asia. The lasting historical legacy of invasions from the Central Asian steppes continues shaping Russian views on Central Asia. Improving the defence of Russia's eastern borders has become a strategic imperative for the Kremlin. When the Central Asian territories were absorbed in the Soviet Union, Russia enjoyed a strong defensive position shored up in the favourable topography of the region. The only exception was a stretch of the Tajik-Afghan border, where the difficult terrain made it virtually impossible to stage a large military force. This enkindled a long-lasting unease with the Afghan threat still playing out in the modern Russia. Its 201st Military Base, previously known as the 201st Motor Rifle Division in Tajikistan, is its largest military contingent abroad. The division constitutes the core of the CSTO's rapid deployment force and has been continually reinforced by the Kremlin (Omelicheva, 2018). The largest to date military reconnaissance exercise under the auspices of the CSTO took place in Tajikistan in 2016, where about 1,500 servicemen from the CSTO member-states practiced a scenario of an army of insurgents crossing into Tajikistan from Afghanistan (McDermott, 2016).[6]

Discussion and conclusions

On 3 April 2017, a bomb detonated in St. Petersburg's subway killing 15 people and injuring dozens of others. It was the first attack on the public transport system in Russia since the 2010 Moscow Metro bombing and the first of its kind in the St. Petersburg metro. In advance of the attack, ISIS circulated heavy propaganda encouraging supporters to launch strikes on Moscow and St. Petersburg. The suicide bomber was identified as Akbarzhon Jalilov, a naturalised Russian citizen born in Kyrgyzstan (BBC News, 2017). Less than five months later, the Secretary of Russia's Security Council, Nikolai Patrushev, announced that the threat of international terrorism inside Russia was 'practically resolved', although the problem had increased around the world (Sputnik, 2017).

Despite the politicisation of the transnational terrorist threat and heavy propaganda on its tireless efforts to root out terrorist networks, the Russian leadership takes the risks associated with transnational terrorist activity seriously. It has channelled considerable resources to build up its domestic security and law enforcement structures and invested lavishly in sustaining security and counterterrorism cooperation in its immediate neighbourhood and beyond. These efforts, however, have not abated the terrorist danger. In fact, the threat of homegrown and international terrorism in Russia has become more challenging and complex. Social discontent triggered by disastrous economic conditions, rampant corruption, and lack of opportunity in the authoritarian states of Central Asia and Russia's own republics of the North Caucasus have been exported outside their borders. The routine counterterrorism exercises with the Central Asian partners and Moscow-led counterterrorism operations with the local security forces in Russia's restive regions only aggravated the public discontent. The Russian leadership and law enforcement and security structures have been less prepared to avert the spread of ISIS influence through the networks of migrants and other sympathisers and remiss of their own role in furthering international terrorism (Baev, 2018).

The geopolitical loyalty of the Central Asian republics to Moscow has come at the expense of practical outcomes of Russia's counterterrorism efforts in the region. While there have been tenuous economic and ideological ties between the Central Asian Islamists and radical Islamic elements from Afghanistan and the Middle East, religious violence has remained a local project fuelled by rampant corruption, pervasive poverty, lack of effective governance, and repression by security forces. Russia has ignored the Central Asian states' internal dynamics that are conducive to political instability, terrorism, and organised crime. The Kremlin-led regional security projects have had a negligible impact on the root causes of security problems that continue plaguing these states. While Russia can stage a show of force by practicing large military reconnaissance exercise of the CSTO's rapid deployment force, it cannot address the weaknesses and instability of the Central Asian governments.

Whether in Central Asia or Syria and Afghanistan, Russia's counterterrorism policy has fostered security challenges by empowering repressive regimes responsible for social frictions. Its preferred strategy of repression and force has also contributed to long-term radicalisation of local communities.

Moscow's regional and global counterterrorism policy has jeopardised one of the remaining avenues for meaningful cooperation between Russia and the West. Russia has long been regarded as a significant part of the problem of domestic insurgency in eastern Ukraine. Terrorism has been a by-product of this war, and the Kremlin's denial of its involvement in the conflict has severely aggravated prospects for counterterrorism cooperation between Russia and the West. From Washington's perspective, Russia's actions in Syria have stoked tensions between the Sunni extremist groups and Iran-sponsored Shia militias and fuelled the Syrian conflict, rather than contributed in meaningful way to the defeat of ISIS (Carpenter, 2017). From the Brussels' standpoint, Russia's support for the regime of Bashar al-Assad has been inimical to the European policies. Despite the official rhetoric of the Russian leadership calling on the Western partners to engage in counterterrorism cooperation, Russia has been less than cooperative in allowing for full transparency of money flows in and out of Russia that is necessary for interdiction of financial assistance to terrorism. And, its long-standing tradition of the heavy-handed responses to the threat of terrorism and homegrown radicalisation by instituting a wide range of criminal offenses and launching prosecutions on the flimsiest of evidence of individuals' involvement in terrorism hinders Russia-European Union cooperation in the suppression of jihadist propaganda (Baev, 2018; Vaino 2013).

Disclaimer: The views expressed in this paper are those of the author and are not an official policy or position of the National Defense University, the Department of Defense or the U.S. Government.

Notes

1. India and Pakistan joined the SCO as new members in summer 2017.
2. Critical geopolitics combines a range of diverse perspectives united by their rejection of classical geopolitical reasoning. They emphasise the construction of the 'world' by the ideas, beliefs, and assumptions about global politics held by the intellectuals of statecraft and ordinary people, and how these 'imaginations' influence and reinforce political behaviour and policy choices (for further information, see Dodds, Kuus, and Sharp, 2016; O'Tuathail, 1996).
3. A 'polycentric' world order, according to the Russian leadership, denotes the emergence of new economic and financial centres of power playing a growing role in managing the world economy and political processes (Lavrov, 2014).
4. Neither ISIS nor other Sunni militias in Syria have access to airpower.
5. The Foreign Policy Concept of the Russian Federation approved in 2013 describes the 'Arab Spring' as evidence of the Arab people's desire 'to return to their civilisational roots' and states that 'political and socioeconomic renewal of [their] society has been frequently carried out under the banner of asserting Islamic values' (The Ministry of the Foreign Affairs of the Russian Federation, 2013).
6. This trend continued in 2017, when Russia carried out large-scale operational-strategic exercises across Central Asia and the South Caucasus (McDermott, 2017).

References

Allison, Roy (2004) 'Strategic Reassertion in Russia's Central Asia Policy', *International Affairs*, 80(2), pp. 277–293.
Baev, Pavel (2018) 'From Chechnya to Syria: The Evolution of Russia's Counter-Terrorist Policy', *Notes de L'Ifri: Russie.Nei.Visions*, 107, pp. 1–32.
BBC News (2017) 'St Petersburg Attack: What We Know,' *BBC News*, 19 April 2017. Accessed on 28 May 2018 at www.bbc.com/news/world-europe-39481067.

Burnashev, Rustam (2007) 'Terrorist Routes in Central Asia: Trafficking Drugs, Humans, and Weapons', *Connections*, 6(1), pp. 65–70.
Carpenter, Michael (2017) 'Russia: Counterterrorism Partner or Fanning the Flames', Congressional Testimony for the Committee on Foreign Affairs, United States House of Representatives, Subcommittee on Terrorism, Nonproliferation, and Trade, and Subcommittee on Europe, Eurasia, and Emerging Threats, 7 November 2017. Accessed on 24 May 2018 at https://foreignaffairs.house.gov/hearing/joint-subcommittee-hearing-russia-counterterrorism-partner-fanning-flames/.
Casier, Tom (2006) 'Putin's Policy Towards the West: Reflections on Russian Foreign Policy', *International Politics*, 43, pp. 384–401.
Cornell, Svante (2017) 'Russia's Relationship to Insurgent and Terrorist Groups', Congressional Testimony for the Committee on Foreign Affairs, United States House of Representatives, Subcommittee on Terrorism, Nonproliferation, and Trade, and Subcommittee on Europe, Eurasia, and Emerging Threats, 7 November 2017. Accessed on 24 May 2018 at https://docs.house.gov/meetings/FA/FA18/20171107/106596/HHRG-115-FA18-Wstate-CornellS-20171107.pdf.
Dannreuther, Roland (2010) 'Islamic Radicalization in Russia: An Assessment', *International Affairs*, 86(1), pp. 109–126.
Dodds, Klaus, Kuus, Merje, & Sharp, Joanne, eds., (2013) *The Routledge Research Companion to Critical Geopolitics*. New York: Routledge.
Gurganus, Julia (2018) 'Russia's Afghanistan Strategy', *Carnegie Moscow Center*. Accessed on 24 May 2018 at http://carnegie.ru/2018/01/02/russia-s-afghanistan-strategy-pub-75160.
Hill, Fiona (2002) 'Putin and Bush in Common Cause? Russia's View of the Terrorist Threat After September 11', Accessed on 24 May 2018 at www.brookings.edu/articles/putin-and-bush-in-common-cause-russias-view-of-the-terrorist-threat-after-september-11/.
Isakova, Irina (2005) *Russian Governance in the Twenty-First Century: Geo-strategy, Geopolitics, & Governance*. New York: Frank Cass.
Kim, Younkyoo, & Blank, Stephen (2013) 'Insurgency and Counterinsurgency in Russia: Contending Paradigms and Current Perspectives', *Studies in Conflict & Terrorism*, 36(11), pp. 917–932.
Korostikov, Mikhail (2017) 'Russia Is the Honey Badger of International Relations', *Carnegie Moscow Center*. Accessed on 24 May 2018 at https://carnegie.ru/commentary/75051.
Lankina, Tomila, & Watanabe, Kohei (2017) '"Russian Spring" or "Spring Betrayal"? The Media as a Mirror of Putin's Evolving Strategy in Ukraine', *Europe-Asia Studies*, 69(10), pp. 1526–1556.
Laruelle, Marlene (2012) *Russian Eurasianism: An Ideology of Empire*. Baltimore, MD: John Hopkins University Press.
Lavrov, Sergey (2014) 'Remarks by Foreign Minister Sergey Lavrov during an Open Lecture on Russia's Current Foreign Policy', *The Ministry of Foreign Affairs of the Russian Federation*. Accessed on 24 May 2018 at www.mid.ru/en/web/guest/foreign_policy/news/-/asset_publisher/cKNonkJE02Bw/content/id/716270.
Lynch, Allen C. (2001) 'The Realism of Russia's Foreign Policy', *Europe-Asia Studies*, 53 (1), pp. 7–31.
Malashenko, Andre (2013) *Russia and the Arab Spring*. Moscow: Carnegie Center. Accessed on 28 May 2018 at https://carnegieendowment.org/files/russia_arab_spring2013.pdf.
McDermott, Roger N. (2016) 'Poisk-2016: CSTO Stages Intelligence and Reconnaissance Exercise', *The Central Asia-Caucasus Analyst*, 31 May. Accessed on 28 May 2016 at www.cacianalyst.org/publications/analytical-articles/item/13366-poisk-2016-csto-stages-intelligence-and-reconnaissance-exercise.html.
McDermott, Roger N. (2017) 'Russia Rehearses Military Intervention in Central Asia and the Caucasus', *The Central Asia-Caucasus Analyst*, 31 May. Accessed on 28 May 2016 at www.cacianalyst.org/publications/analytical-articles/item/13484-russia-rehearses-military-intervention-in-central-asia-and-the-caucasus.html
Miller, James (2016) 'What Vladimir Putin Learned from the Arab Spring', *The Interpreter*, 14 March. Accessed on 28 May 2018 at www.interpretermag.com/what-vladimir-putin-learned-from-the-arab-spring/.
The Ministry of Foreign Affairs of the Russian Federation (2000) 'National Security Concept of the Russian Federation', *The Ministry of Foreign Affairs of the Russian Federation*. Accessed on 24 May 2018 at www.mid.ru/en/foreign_policy/official_documents/-/asset_publisher/CptICkB6BZ29/content/id/589768.
The Ministry of the Foreign Affairs of the Russian Federation (2013) 'The Concept of the Foreign Policy of the Russian Federation', approved by the President of the Russian Federation,

V. Putin, on 12 February 2014. Accessed on 28 May 2018 at www.mid.ru/en/foreign_policy/official_documents/-/asset_publisher/CptICkB6BZ29/content/id/122186

Miyaoka, Taiji (1998) 'Terrorist Crisis Management in Japan: Historical Development and Changing Response (1970–1997)', *Terrorism and Political Violence*, 10(2), pp. 23–52.

Nichol, Jim (2003) 'Georgia's Pankisi Gorge: Russian Concerns and U.S. Interests', *CRS Report for Congress*. Accessed on 24 May 2018 at http://congressionalresearch.com/RS21319/document.php?study=Georgias+Pankisi+Gorge+Russian+Concerns+and+U.S.+Interests.

Omelicheva, Mariya (2011) *Counterterrorism Policies in Central Asia*. New York: Routledge.

Omelicheva, Mariya (2015) 'The Multiple Faces of Islamic Rebirth in Central Asia', in Clowes, Edith, & Bromberg, Shelly, eds., *Area Studies in the Global Age: Community, Place, Identity*. Dekalb, IL: Northern Illinois University Press, pp. 143–158.

Omelicheva, Mariya (2016) 'Critical Geopolitics on Russian Foreign Policy: Uncovering the Imagery of Moscow's International Relations', *International Politics*, 53(6), pp. 708–726.

Omelicheva, Mariya (2017) 'Russia's Counterterrorism Policy: Variations on an Imperial Theme', in Romaniuk, Scott, et al., eds., *The Palgrave Handbook of Global Terrorism Policy*. London: Palgrave MacMillan, pp. 515–534.

Omelicheva, Mariya (2018) 'Central Asia', in Tsygankov, Andrei, ed., *Routledge Handbook of Russian Foreign Policy*. New York: Routledge, pp. 325–337.

O'Tuathail, Gearóid (1996) *Critical Geopolitics: The Politics of Writing Global Space*. London: Routledge.

Pedahzur, Ami, & Ranstorp, Magnus (2001) 'A Tertiary Model for Countering Terrorism in Liberal Democracies: The Case of Israel', *Terrorism and Political Violence*, 13(2), pp. 1–26.

Pokalova, Elena (2015) *Chechnya's Terrorist Network: The Evolution of Terrorism in Russia's North Caucasus*. Santa Barbara, CA: ABC-CLIO.

RFE/RL (2018) 'Amid Outcry over Ghouta, Russia Vows to Back Assad against "Terror Threat"', Radio Free Europe Radio Liberty, 28 February. Accessed on 28 May 2018 at www.rferl.org/a/syria-russia-vows-back-assad-vs-terror-threat-ghouta-bloodshed/29067479.html.

Russian National Security Strategy (2015) Approved by the President of the Russian Federation on 31 December 2018. Accessed on 28 May 2018 at www.ieee.es/Galerias/fichero/OtrasPublicaciones/Internacional/2016/Russian-National-Security-Strategy-31Dec2015.pdf.

The Soufan Group (2015) 'Foreign Fighters: An Updated Assessment of the Flow of Foreign Fighters into Syria and Iraq', *The Soufan Group*. Accessed on 24 May 2018 at http://soufangroup.com/wp-content/uploads/2015/12/TSG_ForeignFightersUpdate3.pdf.

Sputnik (2017) 'Terrorism in Russia Nearly Defeated – Security Council Head', *Sputnik*, 12 September. Accessed on 28 May 2018 at https://sputniknews.com/russia/201709121057319071-terrorism-russia-defeated/.

Stepanova, Ekaterina (2000) 'International Terrorism in the Southern Tier: Perceived or Real Threat to Russian Security?', *PONARS Eurasia*. Accessed on 24 May 2018 at www.ponarseurasia.org/memo/international-terrorism-southern-tier-perceived-or-real-threat-russias-security.

Trenin, Dmitri (2018) 'Avoiding U.S.-Russia Military Escalation during the Hybrid War', *Carnegie Moscow Center*. Accessed on 24 May 2018 at http://carnegie.ru/2018/01/25/avoiding-u.s.-russia-military-escalation-during-hybrid-war-pub-75277.

Tsygankov, Andrei (2012) 'Assessing Cultural and Regime-Based Explanations of Russia's Foreign Policy. "Authoritarian at Heart and Expansionist by Habit"?' *Europe-Asia Studies*, 64(4), pp. 695–713.

UNODC (2012) 'Opiate Flows through Northern Afghanistan and Central Asia: A Threat Assessment', *Brookings*. Accessed on 24 May 2018 at www.unodc.org/documents/data-and-analysis/Studies/Afghanistan_northern_route_2012_web.pdf.

Vaino, Davis (2013) 'Can Russia and the West Cooperate More Closely on Counterterrorism?', *Carnegie Moscow Center*. Accessed on 26 May 2017 at https://carnegieendowment.org/files/Article_Vaino_Eng.pdf.

Van Herpen, Marcel (2014) *Putin's Wars: The Rise of Russia's New Imperialism*. Lanham, MD: Rowman & Littlefield.

Youngman, Mark (2016) 'Between Caucasus and Caliphate: The Splintering of the North Caucasus Insurgency', *Caucasus Survey*, 4(3), pp. 194–217.

23
SECURITY CHALLENGES IN RUSSIA-EUROPEAN UNION RELATIONS

Maria Raquel Freire and Licínia Simão

Introduction

Russia-European Union (EU) relations encompass a broad spectrum of issues across multiple levels of interaction, evidencing a mature and dense relationship between the two neighbours. Security issues remain one area where relations have encountered greater challenges, reflecting an evolving understanding of security matters, as well as the distinct nature of both actors. In this chapter, we advance a broad understanding of security as necessary to address the many aspects that the EU and Russia have defined as relevant in their perceptions of and interactions with each other. Although many of these security dimensions are not new, as they were already developed in the context of the Helsinki Process in the 1970s, they acquire new relevance depending on the interactions between both actors and the broader regional and international context. We argue therefore that there is no linearity in the assessment of Russia-EU security relations. On the one hand, we can see both cooperative and uncooperative behaviours coexisting in the same period of time across different issues. On the other hand, within one same issue we can also see evolving patterns of relations across time. This suggests that Russia-EU security relations, particularly in the wider European context, remain largely dependent on domestic factors, including the specificities of decision-making of each actor, as well as on external factors, particularly regional dynamics in the post-Soviet space and great Middle East, and relations with the US. This chapter addresses EU member-states' policies only when relevant to understand EU policymaking.

The chapter starts with a mapping exercise, identifying the many issues covered by the spectrum of security relations between the EU and Russia. It addresses the main academic views on the topic, including those from different theoretical traditions, as well as the priorities established by the two actors. This literature varies considerably in its assessment of the elements structuring these relations, as well as of the achievements reached. Authors addressing energy security, for instance, might underline how both actors have managed to develop a system where mutually beneficial relations were established, despite the difficulties being experienced since the gas crisis of 2006 in Ukraine. However, authors dealing with security in the shared neighbourhood have put forward a dismay picture of uncooperative behaviour and competition, which has resulted in an unprecedented level of insecurity since the Cold War. Nuclear issues have also been an area where both the EU and Russia have cooperated, in order to bring about denuclearisation both regionally in Europe and globally, as the joint efforts in the Iranian nuclear deal illustrate. They have, nevertheless, sponsored opposing views of the elements needed to assure societal security in their respective societies. This complex picture seems to suggest that different understandings have been favoured at different points in time, depending on a series of factors.

The chapter then engages more directly with the ways in which issues have been placed on the bilateral EU-Russia security agenda, and how the different policy documents and options have addressed these varying priorities. We identify major tensions in the bilateral security agenda, including divisions over the US global interventionist policies following 9/11, suspicion over the colour revolutions in the post-Soviet space, the North Atlantic Treaty Organisation (NATO) enlargement policy, Kosovo, and Russia's military intervention in Georgia and in Ukraine, among others. Many of these issues evidence the strong impact that the regional and global context bears on these relations. Finally, the chapter discusses future challenges regarding cooperative and uncooperative trends in Russia-EU security relations, including issues on cybersecurity, hybrid warfare, and popular mobilisation, in a context of tensions over Ukraine and uncertainty at home.

Mapping the field: security issues in EU-Russia relations

Security remains one of the most complex and contested concepts in International Relations, especially due to the continuous enlarging of its scope and meaning. Security no longer relates exclusively to national (state) security and has come to include other referent objects (individuals, communities, multinational corporations, the environment). It is no longer assured mainly by military means, since the threats to security have grown more complex, as have the number of issues considered relevant for security (Buzan, Wæver, and de Wilde, 1998). EU-Russia security relations are not an exception to this evolving field of study. An analysis of the historical development of Russia's and EU's security policies evidences not only largely distinct starting points and frameworks of reference but also a trend towards approximation and complexification of each actor's security policies.

For the EU, developing a common security policy has been a complex process, due to the unique features of its supranational integration. Peace and security through functional cooperation and dialogue have resulted in important security gains for EU member-states and for countries in the EU's neighbouring regions, namely those dealing with conflicts and which have been granted membership perspectives (Diez, Stetter, and Albert, 2006; Bremberg, 2015). The EU has thus advanced a normative conception of regional security based on the principles enshrined in EU founding treaties, including liberal democracy, human rights, the rule of law, and market economies. The EU's late development of integrated mechanisms to manage military capabilities and increased spending in defence cooperation through Permanent Structured Cooperation (PESCO), followed this historically placed emphasis of its security policies on normative and economic means. The promotion of a norms-based international order constitutes the EU's main contribution to European security (Manners, 2002; Telò, 2011).

Russia's security approach in the 1990s was very much focused on internal threats arising from 'economic decline, instability and societal problems' (Lomagin, 2016, 127; see also Military Doctrine, 1993; National Security Concept, 1997), and external challenges to Russian security were to be addressed in '"partnership" with the West', allowing a focus on non-military security (ibid.). The Russian Federation's territorial integrity as well as the ability of the state structures to safeguard national institutions, including economic and financial ones, were major concerns (Clark and Graham, 1995; Stepanov, 2000). A further issue that was rather prominent during the 1990s was management (or rather the mismanagement) of the military arsenal of the former Soviet Union, including its nuclear facilities (Booth, 1992; Coté et al, 1996). Nuclear security was also on the agenda well into the early 2000s regarding non-proliferation issues and Russia's important role in this regard, as well as the potential links between nuclear weapons and terrorism (Bunn, 2005). For most of this period, the EU was not a privileged interlocutor with Moscow for military issues, but rather the US and leading European powers, like France and the UK. The EU became increasingly relevant in financial and economic issues, especially as the 1990s advanced and a new Partnership and Cooperation Agreement between the two partners came into force in 1997.

The 2000s brought a change in Russia's political leadership with Vladimir Putin coming to power and developments in Russia's relations with the West that prompted a revision of Moscow's security policy. The wars in Yugoslavia and NATO's intervention in 1999, the ongoing Chechen Wars, lack of agreement with the West on offensive and defensive weapons, the Iraq war, and later projects such as the US defence missile shield and the antagonising issue of NATO enlargement, all set the stage for the development of a more independent and self-assuring security policy that would reflect Russia's status as a great power, accompanied by the means to face domestic and external threats. The focus on the internal-external security nexus has remained central in Russian security policy, and nontraditional security issues have featured on the agenda despite Moscow's traditional national security concerns very much focused on preserving its sovereignty, and its focus on military means as a source of power projection, as seen in Georgia (2008) and, more recently, Ukraine (2014) and Syria (2015) (Mearsheimer, 2014; Freire and Heller, 2018). In this context, discussions on the level of Russia and the EU partnership became prominent (Timmins, 2002), namely due to their divergent identities and self/mutual perceptions (Ispa-Landa, 2003; Diez, 2004). The inability to renegotiate a new framework agreement with the EU since 2007 and the consequences of the war in Ukraine (2014 to present), including the imposition of sanctions, have rendered discussion on security matters between these two parties even more complex, particularly regarding the so-called third common space, of external security.[1]

In this setting, a major issue in the literature dealing with EU-Russia security relations has been the impact of the EU's enlargement and neighbourhood policies on Russia's regional strategic interests and its self-perception as a regional and global power (Light, White, and Löwenhardt, 2000; Averre, 2005; O'Brennan, 2006; Freire, 2018a). The overlapping neighbourhood has grown into an area of high-intensity confrontation between the two actors, as evidenced in Georgia (2003, 2008) and Ukraine (2004, 2014). The critical geopolitical readings of the shared space between Russia and the EU, and the distinctive narratives constructed demonstrate how relevant the overlapping neighbourhood is in EU-Russia security relations. The heterogeneity and agency that is recognised to the states in the common neighbourhood of the EU and Russia, along with the interplay of perceptions (including ontological security approaches), have been identified as most relevant to understand and interpret EU-Russia security relations in their neighbourhood (Simão, 2011; Dias, 2013; Pop, 2016; Rieker and Gjerde, 2016; Smith, 2016; Svarin, 2016; Browning, 2018).

Energy security also gradually made its way onto the common EU-Russia agenda, especially as a reflection of the important political role ascribed to energy development in Vladimir Putin's foreign policy. However, the different contexts in the EU and Russia where energy policies have been developing paved the way for difficulties in finding agreement over a common energy policy (Locatelli, 2013; Talseth, 2017). Some authors even argue that in the process the EU revealed incapable of defining a unified policy and speaking at one voice in energy-related matters (Kuzemko, 2014). This meant that only with a regulatory framework reflecting all stakeholders' interests and a fair distribution of risks it would be possible to assure predictability in energy relations between these actors (Van Der Meulen, 2009; Kaveshnikov, 2010). The energy crises involving Ukraine in 2006 and 2009 disrupted gas supplies from Russia to the EU transiting through Ukraine due to lack of agreement on the new prices for gas supplies from Russia to Ukraine. Authors addressing these issues underlined the risks associated to Moscow's political use of energy, as a tool for leverage over the post-Soviet countries (Helén, 2010), with Nygren (2008) defining the policy's two main strategies as the 'tap weapon' and the 'transit weapon'. The negative impacts on Russia's credibility as an energy supplier to the EU were immediately visible, leading the Union to look for diversification strategies. These same dynamics became present in Russia's policy of diversification. Moreover, asymmetrical interdependence would highlight the fragility of one of the parties whereas conferring added leverage to the other (Krickovic, 2015), leading to the need to redefine policy goals. Nevertheless, Milatschew (2012) makes the case that in its relations with the EU, Russia's power only affects cooperation between these two actors in a marginal way, contrary to what is often argued. In this same critical line, Lukáš Tichý and Petr Kratochvíl (2014) add that the narratives implied in energy security integration, liberalisation, and diversification show a more complex picture than the usual cooperation/ confrontation binary analysis (see also Casier, 2016).

The normative dimensions of security have also remained an important element in analyses of EU-Russia relations (Haukkala, 2010; Sakwa, 2017). The contestation to the liberal regimes in Western Europe, which is increasingly visible in Russia (Jankovski, 2017; Freire, 2018b; Romanova, 2018), but also inside the European countries with the rise of radical political parties, has been addressed as a potential security issue on the common agenda. If democracy and free market economies are a central part of the Union's self-perceived role in stabilising Europe, the undermining of these principles, namely since the financial crisis of 2008, pose significant challenges to the EU's central role in providing for European security. Derek Averre (2016) claims that a security governance framework helps in explaining how EU-Russia relations have developed, particularly considering Russia's revisionism of the Western order and criticism of its institutional arrangements, which has had a clear impact on readings about security in the wider Europe, with the case of Ukraine illustrating this dynamic process.

Russia has also increasingly perceived the importance of addressing the normative and soft dimensions of power, articulating an alternative vision to Western leadership, based on multipolarity and conservative values. Although initially multipolarity included the EU as an alternative pole of power to the US, several authors have highlighted the disappointment in Moscow regarding the inability of the EU to balance US global interventionist policies and to defend principles of international law (Makarychev and Morozov, 2011; Tsygankov, 2011). Despite a similar normative rhetoric, the meanings attributed by the two actors to norms and their role in providing for security vary considerably. According to some authors, this has prevented the development of a multilateral setting for security issues (Fernandes, 2011). The definition of Russia in the European security architecture as 'an object of security', as argued by Diesen (2017a), contributes to exacerbate a collision trajectory based on a zero-sum game. According to the author, this is linked to the development of the EU and NATO as 'inter-democratic security institutions', which Russia has been reading as following an antagonistic path. The issue of NATO enlargement has been in the agenda for a long time, with Russia understanding the further extension of the Atlantic Alliance as a major external threat to its security. In this context, Russia has been pursuing a selective approach in its relations with the EU that became both cooperative and competitive in its nature (Kropatcheva, 2012). The images of national identity, honour, international power, and global role, although shared by both authors as important elements, articulate largely different images of international politics and its development (Tsygankov, 2014; Diesen, 2017b; Nitoiu, 2017).

Security challenges to EU-Russia relations in a regional and global setting

The European 'security architecture' has evolved around the central role of NATO, the marginal role of the Organisation for Security and Cooperation in Europe (OSCE) and a limited contribution from the EU. In the process, the NATO-Russia Council was established in 2002 (replacing the 1997 Permanent Joint Council), but Russia never considered itself fully integrated in the European security system (de Haas, 2010; Kortunov, 2016; Lavrov, 2018). Moreover, the structural policies of regional integration, namely NATO and EU enlargements and the development of the EU Neighbourhood Policy, have, nevertheless, remained largely disarticulated from EU discourse on security. 'Civilian power Europe' (Bull, 1982; Stavridis, 2001; Telò, 2006) only recently engaged with the challenges of thinking and developing its security policies, namely with the establishment of a Common Foreign and Security Policy (CFSP) and a European Security and Defence Policy (ESDP). Also, the adoption of the European Security Strategy (ESS) of 2003 (Council of the European Union, 2003) contributed to clarifying the perceived threats and priority fields, but did not articulate a clear definition of what EU security is or should be. In the absence of a consensus in this regard, different conceptions of security emerged both from the various institutional actors and among EU member-states, combining structural approaches and crisis and conflict management tools (Freire and Simão, 2018).

The role of Russia in these emerging EU security policies was surprisingly marginal, at least until 2008. The ESS refers to Russia's role in four areas, including energy security, managing the stabilisation of the Western Balkans, of the Israeli-Arab conflict, as well as the importance of developing a strategic partnership with Moscow that 'Respect[s] […] common values' (Council of the European Union, 2003, 14). The conflicts in the shared neighbourhood with Russia are marginally referred in the 2003 document, but emerge as a central concern in the 2008 Report on the Implementation of the European Security Strategy (Council of the European Union, 2008), in view of the deterioration of relations with Russia following the 2008 Russian-Georgian War. Similarly, the 2016 Global Strategy of the EU raises the concerns of the Union vis-à-vis Russia, explicitly identifying Moscow as one of the biggest security concerns for the EU and its member-states and stating that 'Russia's violation of international law and the destabilisation of Ukraine, on top of protracted conflicts in the wider Black Sea region, have challenged the European security order at its core' (European Commission and High Representative of the EU for Foreign Affairs and Security Policy, 2016, 33). Relations with Russia have remained largely strained since the annexation of Crimea, in 2014, both at high political level and intermediate ones. Tatiana Romanova (2016) addresses the negative impacts of the imposition of Crimea-related sanctions by the EU, underlining how relations have been negatively affected, even at the more horizontal technical level. In the aftermath of difficult relations with Russia, in March 2016, the EU put forward the five principles for guiding relations with Russia, which reflect this difficult security atmosphere. These principles include full implementation of the Minsk agreements, closer ties with Russia's former Soviet neighbours, strengthening EU resilience to Russian threats, selective engagement with Russia on certain issues such as counterterrorism, and support for people-to-people contacts (Russell, 2016). The principles sum up what are different security understandings in the EU and Russia, with Moscow voicing criticism of EU conditions.

This analysis evidences how Russia is simultaneously a security concern for the EU and other European actors and is a security actor in its own terms. Moscow's policies have reflected this dual status and have incorporated the effects of these external perceptions. Russia's conceptualisation of security has maintained a strong focus on military issues and national security, gradually incorporating other strategic dimensions, including energy, food, and environmental security, among others. The linkages between the rights of citizens, sustainable economic development, and the traditional values of 'sovereignty, independence, state and territorial integrity' have been recurrent in official Russian security documents (see RNSS, 2015, §6). The identification of diversified threats to Russia's security leads to a listing of military and non-military measures to respond to current challenges, while also clearly linking internal development in different spheres (economic, cultural, social) to external security, by addressing issues such as corruption or ideological use of systems of communication and information, among others (RNSS 2015, §43; Freire and Simão, 2018).

Russia's own views regarding the ordering of European security and its place in it have thus been a central element in its security policies, as mentioned. The feeling of encirclement, mainly driven by NATO enlargement and reinforced by the EU's Neighbourhood Policy, has been a central element sustaining the drive towards a new military build-up and an arms race, both by EU-NATO countries and Russia. In fact, Russia has advanced alternative visions for the reordering of European security. Both in its 1999 Medium Term Strategy for Development of Relations with the EU, and later with the European Security Treaty Proposal advanced by then President Dmitry Medvedev in 2008 (RFE/RL, 2009; The Kremlin, 2009), Russia underlined the importance of keeping the principles of cooperative security as drafted back in 1975, while recognising the limits of the OSCE and of the need to bring forward something new. 'Overall, the proposal meant to refurbish old principles and bring Russia back into the European security discussion and decision-making' (Freire and Simão, 2018).

There are valid reasons for Russia to be invested in the materialisation of a new more inclusive European security regime, where Russia would have voice, vote, and veto, and which would be based on shared principles of sovereignty and respect for the territorial integrity of states, as core norms binding the parties into the common framework proposed. However, difficulties remain in finding a balance between the current contested order and new proposals to reshape it. The Ukraine conflict and the annexation of Crimea questioned the very foundations of the security regime Russia has been promoting, given the violation of the very basic principles that were at the core of this security order. The end result has been not only the imposition of sanctions but also contradictory dynamics regarding Russia's inclusion in the European security system. It is a formal part of this architecture, but it is not a member of the institutions that have come to dominate the management of European security, namely NATO and the EU. The annexation of Crimea and the crisis in Ukraine represent a definitive shift with regard to Russia's position in the European security order, distancing Moscow from agreed norms and shared principles, including on border regimes. Regionalism, in the shape of traditional spheres of influence, seems to be back and it is informing the erosion of the European security regime.

Since the Ukrainian crisis began in 2013, the management of security relations between the EU, including its member-states, and Russia has sharply deteriorated. This crisis also illustrates rather well how EU-Russia security relations are exposed to regional and global dynamics. US policies towards Russia and European security more broadly have been major factors, shaping the approximation of both actors (as was partly the case with the US decision to invade Iraq in 2003) (Gordon and Shapiro, 2004), or further setting them apart, as was the case with Kosovo's unilateral declaration of independence, in 2008 (Antonenko, 2017). US policies of global intervention, which became particularly active after 9/11, have been at the heart of Russian criticisms, as famously voiced by President Putin in Munich in 2007 (Putin, 2007). Calls for the EU to distance itself from these policies have only marginally led to a more fruitful dialogue between Moscow and Brussels. Regional dynamics further impact on this relation, as illustrated by the management of the Iranian nuclear programme. Russia has remained a crucial element on this issue, both as a supplier of nuclear technology to Iran and as a critical element in the negotiations (Omelicheva, 2012). In fact, as the Trump administration decided to withdraw from the Nuclear deal with Iran and restate the sanctions regime, Russia-EU relations have found new ground on which to improve (Thomson and Kulesa, 2017; Viscusi and Meyer, 2018). Despite the positive alignment of interests on Iran, EU-Russia relations remain divergent regarding the Astana process over Syria, which is managed by Russia, Turkey, and Iran, without EU or US participation, and remain divergent regarding the implementation of the Minsk Agreements over Ukraine.

Looking ahead: EU-Russia security challenges

Delinking the regional dimension of security in EU-Russia relations from the more global context where relations take place is difficult. In fact, the regional challenges relate to the narratives associated with the 'shared' neighbourhood, which have become increasingly antagonistic, or to counterterrorism activities, which have provided ground for closer collaboration, mingle with the role of other players and spaces such as the US, Turkey, or even China. This means that the internal-external nexus applies both to security readings within the EU and Russia and to those regarding their relationship. Challenges at the structural level will remain with the redefinition of the European security order providing ground for competitive and cooperative relations. Transnational threats to security coming from criminal organisations, cybersecurity threats, or terrorist groups, with a transnational dimension, will keep adding to the security challenges these players face. At the actor's level, overcoming the mistrust, even in face of a military build-up scenario and hostile discourse, and reaching the political conditions for the normalisation of relations will remain on the agenda. These points to the fact that the security challenges ahead might bring in new dimensions, but in essence they are not new. The way cybersecurity, propaganda and fake news, and new-armaments' development have made it to EU-Russia relations poses new challenges not so much in their novelty, but more regarding the need for sophisticated answers that these technological changes require, as visible, for example, in the creation by Russia and the EU of active responsive bodies to propaganda.

The ways forward are, however, not bright. An attempt to reinstate the old status quo through a 'reset-type' exercise would be insufficient in face of the inadequacy of this very old order that revealed to be limited. 'Moscow's answer to the EU's mantra, [that] "there is no return to the business as usual for Russia" is: we do not want business as usual' (Romanova, 2016). A deeper reassessment needs, therefore, to be made. Starting anew might mean the need for the joint definition of policies and actions, and joint monitoring of results – i.e. co-ownership of decisions (Casier et al., 2016) and processes. The recognition that security and integration mean different things to Russia and the West must be at the basis of the identification of the structural causes that need to be tackled. Ad hoc and small-scale initiatives might ease tensions, but they will not solve crystalised differentials. For these, confidence-building measures and constructive dialogue need to be built from scratch. Moreover, engaging 'constructively with geopolitics through gradual and selective economic cooperation with the Eurasian Economic Union and by preparing the way for a robust diplomatic process on European security with Russia' (Koenig, 2016, 1) might prove useful in overcoming opposing narratives, policies, and actions whereas providing ground for the sharing of security approaches in EU-Russia relations.

A major challenge to these potentially positive steps remains the domestic dynamics both within the EU and its member-states and in Russia. The incorporation of domestic dynamics into the analysis is fundamental, in order to account for intra-EU pressures for greater military investment, which have been largely legitimised as a response to a perceived revisionist-Russian stance (Nielsen, 2017). Moreover, pressures on the EU's democratic institutions and the election of extremist parties have been interlinked with accusations of Russian interference in domestic political processes, raising tension over a new field of perceived insecurity in EU-Russia relations (Dobrokhotov, 2017). The ways in which the Russian regime will manage the pressures associated with the economic and political impact of the existing sanctions regime and the future of Russia after Putin remain important challenges to EU-Russia security relations. Overcoming mistrust and addressing the important issues on the common security agenda will require a reassessment of Russia's current role as a major threat to EU member-states, as well as a new assessment in Moscow of the role of the former Soviet space in its regional and global affirmation strategies.

Note

1 EU-Russia relations have been structured on the existing Partnership and Cooperation Agreement (PCA) as well as on the 2003 agenda on the development of four common spaces: a common economic space; a common space of freedom, security, and justice; a common space of cooperation in the field of external security; and a common space of research, education, and culture.

References

Antonenko, Oksana (2007) 'Russia and the Deadlock over Kosovo', *Survival*, Vol. 49, no. 3, pp. 91–106.

Averre, Derek (2005) 'Russia and the European Union: Convergence or Divergence?', *European Security*, Vol. 14, no. 2, pp. 175–202.

Averre, Derek (2016) 'The Ukraine Conflict: Russia's Challenge to European Security Governance', *Europe-Asia Studies*, Vol. 68, no. 4, pp. 699–725.

Booth, Ken (1992) 'Loose Nukes and the Nuclear Mirror: The Dangers and Opportunities Resulting from the Breakup of the Soviet Union', *Arms Control*, Vol. 13, no. 1, pp. 140–150.

Bremberg, Niklas (2015) 'The European Union as Security Community-Building Institution: Venues, Networks and Co-operative Security Practices', *Journal of Common Market Studies*, Vol. 53, no. 3, pp. 674–692.

Browning, Christopher S. (2018) 'Geostrategies, Geopolitics and Ontological Security in the Eastern Neighbourhood: The European Union and the "New Cold War"', *Political Geography*, Vol. 62, no. 1, pp. 106–115.

Bull, Hedley (1982) 'Civilian Power Europe: A Contradiction in Terms?', *Journal of Common Market Studies*, Vol. 21, no. 2, pp. 149–170.

Bunn, Matthew (2005) 'Preventing a Nuclear 9/11', *Issues in Science & Technology*, Vol. 21, no. 2, pp. 55–62.

Buzan, Barry; Wæver, Ole; de Wilde, Jaap (1998) *Security: A New Framework for Analysis*. Boulder, CO: Lynne Rienner Publishers.

Casier, Tom (2016) 'Great Game or Great Confusion: The Geopolitical Understanding of EU-Russia Energy Relations', *Geopolitics*, Vol. 21, no. 4, pp. 763–778.

Casier, Tom et al. (2016) 'Policy Report. EU-Russia Relations: Which Way Forward?', Jean Monnet Multilateral Research Group, EU-Russia Relations: Developing a Transnational Perspective. Available at www.kent.ac.uk/brussels/studying/research/projects/jeanmonnet.html (accessed 20 May 2018).

Clark, Susan L. and Graham, David R. (1995) 'The Russian Federation's Fight for Survival', *Orbis*, Vol. 39, no. 3, pp. 329–352.

Coté, Owen R.; Allison, Graham; Miller, Steven E.; Falkenrath, Richard A. (1996) *Avoiding Nuclear Anarchy. Containing the Threat of Loose Russian Nuclear Weapons and Fissile Material*. Cambridge, MA: The MIT Press.

Council of the European Union (2003) *European Security Strategy - A Secure Europe in a Better World*. Brussels, 12 December.

Council of the European Union (2008) *Report on the Implementation of the European Security Strategy - Providing Security in a Changing World*. S407/08, Brussels, 11 December.

De Haas, Marcel (2010) 'Medvedev's Alternative European Security Architecture', *Security and Human Rights*, Vol. 21, no. 1, pp. 45–48.

Dias, Vanda Amaro (2013) 'The EU and Russia: Competing Discourses, Practices and Interests in the Shared Neighbourhood', *Perspectives on European Politics and Society*, Vol. 14, no. 2, pp. 256–271.

Diesen, Glenn (2017a) *EU and NATO Relations with Russia: After the Collapse of the Soviet Union*. London: Routledge.

Diesen, Glenn (2017b) 'The EU, Russia and the Manichean Trap', *Cambridge Review of International Affairs*, Vol. 30, no. 2–3, pp. 177–194.

Diez, Thomas; Stetter, Stephan, Albert, Mathias (2006) 'The European Union and Border Conflicts: The Transformative Power of Integration', *International Organization*, Vol. 60, no. 3, pp. 563–593.

Diez, Thomas (2004) 'Europe's Others and the Return of Geopolitics', *Cambridge Review of International Affairs*, Vol. 17, no. 2, pp. 319–335.

Dobrokhotov, Roman (2017) 'Is Russia a Real Threat to the West?', *Aljazeera*, 31 July. Available at www.aljazeera.com/indepth/opinion/2017/07/russia-sanctions-united-states-170729121726556.html (accessed 20 May 2018).

European Commission and High Representative of the EU for Foreign Affairs and Security Policy (2016) *Shared Vision, Common Action: A Stronger Europe - A Global Strategy for the European Union's Foreign and Security Policy*. Brussels, June.

Fernandes, Sandra (2011) 'European Security through EU-Russian Relations: Towards a New Multilateral Order'? *Journal of Contemporary European Research*, Vol. 7, no. 2, pp. 195–215.

Freire, Maria Raquel (2018a) 'The Quest for Status: How the Interplay of Power, Ideas, and Regime Security Shapes Russia's Policy in the Post-Soviet Space', *International Politics*, doi: 10.1057/s41311-018-0164-y.

Freire, Maria Raquel (2018b) 'Political Dynamics within the BRICS in the Context of Multilayered Global Governance'. In John Kirton and Marina Larionova (eds.), *BRICS and Global Governance*. London: Routledge, pp. 70–88.

Freire, Maria Raquel and Heller, Regina (2018) 'Russian Power Politics in Ukraine and Syria: Status-Seeking between Identity, Opportunity and Costs', *Europe-Asia Studies*, Vol. 70, no. 8, pp. 1185–1212.

Freire, Maria Raquel and Simão, Licínia (2018) 'EU-Russia Relations and the Unravelling of the European Security Regime in the Context of the Ukraine Crisis'. In Tom Casier and Joan DeBardeleben (eds.), *EU-Russia Relations in Crisis. Understanding Divergent Perspectives*. London: Routledge, pp. 159–177.

Gordon, Philip H. and Shapiro, Jeremy (2004) *Allies at War: America, Europe, and the Crisis over Iraq*. New York: McGraw-Hill.

Haukkala, Hiski (2016) *The EU-Russia Strategic Partnership. The Limits of Post-Sovereignty in International Relations*. London: Routledge.

Helén, Henry (2010) 'The EU's Energy Security Dilemma with Russia', *POLIS Journal*, Vol. 4. Available at www.polis.leeds.ac.uk/assets/files/students/student-journal/ma-winter-10/helen-e.pdf (accessed 20 May 2018).

Ispa-Landa, Simone (2003) 'Russian Preferred Self-Image and the Two Chechen Wars', *Demokratizatsiya*, Vol. 11, no. 2, pp. 305–319.

Jankovski, Aleksandar (2017) 'The Russian Federation and the West: The Problem of International Order'. In Roger E. Kanet (ed.), *The Russian Challenge to the European Security Environment*. Cham, Switzerland: Palgrave Macmillan.

Kaveshnikov, Nikolay (2010) 'The Issue of Energy Security in Relations between Russia and the European Union', *European Security*, Vol. 19, no. 4, pp. 585–605.

Koenig, Nicole (2016) 'Taking the ENP beyond the Conception-Performance Gap', *Jacques Delors Institut Policy Paper* no. 160, 22 March.

Kortunov, Andrey (2016) 'How Not to Talk with Russia', 1 April. Available at www.ecfr.eu/article/commentary_how_not_to_talk_with_russia_6053 (accessed 20 May 2018).

Krickovic, Andrej (2015) 'When Interdependence Produces Conflict: EU-Russia Energy Relations as a Security Dilemma', *Contemporary Security Policy*, Vol. 36, no. 1, pp. 3–26.

Kropatcheva, Elena (2012) 'Russian Foreign Policy in the Realm of European Security through the Lens of Neoclassical Realism', *Journal of Eurasian Studies*, Vol. 3, no. 1, pp. 30–40.

Kuzemko, Caroline (2014) 'Ideas, Power and Change: Explaining EU-Russia Energy Relations', *Journal of European Public Policy*, Vol. 21, no. 1, pp. 58–75.

Lavrov, Sergei (2018) 'Russia's Foreign Policy in a Historical Perspective', *Russia in Global Affairs*, 20 March. Available at http://eng.globalaffairs.ru/number/Russias-Foreign-Policy-in-a-Historical-Perspective-19445 (accessed 20 May 2018).

Light, Margot, White, Stephen and Löwenhardt, John (2000) 'A Wider Europe: The View from Moscow and Kyiv', *International Affairs*, Vol. 76, no. 1, pp. 77–88.

Locatelli, Catherine (2013) 'Les enjeux de sécurité dans la relation gazière UE-Russie', *Revue d'économie industrielle*, Vol. 3, no. 143, pp. 35–69.

Lomagin, Nikita A. (2016) 'Russia's CIS Policy and Economic and Political Transformations in Eurasia'. In Roger E. Kanet and Rémi Piet (eds.), *Shifting Priorities in Russia's Foreign and Security Policy*. Oxon: Routledge, pp. 115–140.

Makarychev, Andrey and Morozov, Viatcheslav (2011) 'Multilateralism, Multipolarity, and beyond: A Menu of Russia's Policy Strategies', *Global Governance*, Vol. 17, no. 3, pp. 353–373.

Manners, Ian (2002) 'Normative Power Europe: A Contradiction in Terms?', *Journal of Common Market Studies*, Vol. 40, no. 2, pp. 235–258.

Mearsheimer, John J. (2014) 'Why the Ukraine Crisis Is the West's Fault. The Liberal Delusions That Provoked Putin', *Foreign Affairs*, September/October. Available at www.foreignaffairs.com/articles/russia-fsu/2014-08-18/why-ukraine-crisis-west-s-fault (accessed 20 May 2018).

Milatschew, Valentina (2012) *EU-Russian Energy Relations: How Russia's Power Affects Its Willingness to Co-operate with the European Union in Gas-Related Matters*. Saarbrücken: Lambert Academic Publishing.

Military Doctrine (1993) 'The Basic Provisions of the Military Doctrine of the Russian Federation'. Available at https://fas.org/nuke/guide/russia/doctrine/russia-mil-doc.html (accessed 20 May 2018).

National Security Concept (1997) 'Concept of National Security of the Russian Federation'. Approved by Presidential Decree of 17 December 1997, no. 1300. Available at www.prlib.ru/en/node/354146 (accessed 20 May 2018).

Nielsen, Nikolaj (2017) 'Russia Threat Triggers European Military Spending Hike', *EUObserver*, Brussels, 24 April. Available at https://euobserver.com/foreign/137645 (accessed 20 May 2018).

Nitoiu, Cristian (2017) 'Aspirations to Great Power Status: Russia's Path to Assertiveness in the International Arena under Putin', *Political Studies Review*, Vol. 15, no. 1, pp. 39–48.

Nygren, Bertil (2008) *The Rebuilding of Greater Russia: Putin's Foreign Policy towards the CIS Countries*. London: Routledge.

O'Brennan, John (2006) '"Bringing Geopolitics Back In": Exploring the Security Dimension of the 2004 Eastern Enlargement of the European Union', *Cambridge Review of International Affairs*, Vol. 19, no. 1, pp. 155–169.

Omelicheva, Mariya Y. (2012) 'Russia's Foreign Policy toward Iran: A Critical Geopolitics Perspective', *Journal of Balkan & Near Eastern Studies*, Vol. 14, no. 3, pp. 331–344.

Pop, Adrian (2016) 'From Cooperation to Confrontation: The Impact of Bilateral Perceptions and Interactions on the EU-Russia Relations in the Context of Shared Neighbourhood', *Eastern Journal of European Studies*, Vol. 7, no. 2, pp. 47–70.

Putin, Vladimir (2007) 'Speech and the Following Discussion at the Munich Conference on Security Policy', February 10, Munich. Available at http://archive.kremlin.ru/eng/speeches/2007/02/10/0138_type82912type82914type82917type84779_118123.shtml (accessed 20 May 2018).

RFE/RL (2009) 'Russia Unveils Proposal for European Security Treaty', 30 November. Available at https://www.rferl.org/a/Russia_Unveils_Proposal_For_European_Security_Treaty/1891161.html (accessed 20 May 2018).

Rieker, Pernille and Gjerde, Kristian Lundby (2016) 'The EU, Russia and the Potential for Dialogue – Different Readings of the Crisis in Ukraine', *European Security*, Vol. 25, no. 3, pp. 304–325.

RNSS (2015) 'Russian National Security Strategy, December 2015 [Text of 31 December Russian Federation Presidential Edict 683 approving appended text of 'The Russian Federation's

National Security Strategy']'. Available at www.ieee.es/Galerias/fichero/OtrasPublicaciones/Internacional/2016/Russian-National-Security-Strategy-31Dec2015.pdf (accessed 20 May 2018).

Romanova, Tatiana (2016) 'Russia and Europe: Somewhat Different, Somewhat the Same?', *Russian International Affairs Council* Policy Brief no. 5. Available at http://russiancouncil.ru/common/upload/Russia-Europe-Policybrief5-en.pdf (accessed 20 May 2018).

Romanova, Tatiana (2018) 'Russia's Neorevisionist Challenge to the Liberal International Order', *International Spectator*, Vol. 53, no. 1, pp. 76–91.

Russell, Martin (2016) 'The EU's Russia Policy. Five Guiding Principles', *European Parliament Research Service (EORS)* Briefing, PE 589.857, October.

Sakwa, Richard (2017) *Russia against the Rest: The Post-Cold War Crisis of World Order*. Cambridge: Cambridge University Press.

Simão, Licínia (2011) 'Discursive Differences and Policy Outcomes: EU-Russia Relations and Security in Europe', *Eastern Journal of European Studies*, Vol. 2, no. 1, pp. 81–95.

Smith, Nicholas Ross (2016) *EU-Russian Relations and the Ukraine Crisis*. Cheltenham: Edward Elgar Publishing.

Stavridis, Stelios (2001) '"Militarising" the EU: The Concept of Civilian Power Europe Revisited', *The International Spectator*, Vol. 36, no. 4, pp. 43–50.

Stepanov, Valery (2000) 'Ethnic Tensions and Separatism in Russia', *Journal of Ethnic & Migration Studies*, Vol. 26, no. 2, pp. 305–332.

Svarin, David (2016) 'The Construction of "Geopolitical Spaces" in Russian Foreign Policy Discourse before and after the Ukraine Crisis', *Journal of Eurasian Studies*, Vol. 7, pp. 129–140.

Talseth, Lars-Christian U. (2017) *The Politics of Power: EU-Russia Energy Relations in the 21st Century*. Cham, Switzerland: Palgrave Macmillan.

Telò, Mario (2006) *Europe: A Civilian Power? European Union, Global Governance, World Order*. Basingstoke: Palgrave Macmillan.

Telò, Mario (2011) 'The European Union, Regionalism, and World Order: Five Scenarios', *Fédéralisme Régionalisme*, Vol. 11, no. 2. Available at https://popups.uliege.be/1374-3864/index.php?id=1090&format=print (accessed 20 May 2018).

The Kremlin (2009) 'The draft of the European Security Treaty', 29 November. Available at http://en.kremlin.ru/events/president/news/6152 (accessed 20 May 2018).

Thomson, Adam and Kulesa, Lukasz (2017) 'Support for the Iran Nuclear Deal Brings the EU and Russia Closer Together', *European Leadership Network Commentary*, 14 November. Available at www.europeanleadershipnetwork.org/commentary/support-for-the-iran-nuclear-deal-brings-the-eu-and-russia-closer-together/ (accessed 20 May 2018).

Tichý, Lukáš and Kratochvíl, Petr (2014) 'The EU-Russia Energy Relations under the Prism of the Political Discourse', *Perspectives*, Vol. 22, no. 1, pp. 5–32.

Timmins, Graham (2002) 'Strategic or Pragmatic Partnership? The European Union's Policy towards Russia since the End of the Cold War', *European Security*, Vol. 11, no. 4, pp. 78–95.

Tsygankov, Andrei P. (2011) 'The Russia-NATO Mistrust: Ethnophobia and the Double Expansion to Contain "the Russian Bear"', *Communist and Post-Communist Studies*, Vol. 46, no. 1, pp. 179–188.

Tsygankov, Andrei P. (2014) 'The Frustrating Partnership: Honor, Status, and Emotions in Russia's Discourses of the West', *Communist and Post-Communist Studies*, Vol. 47, no. 3–4 pp. 345–354.

Van Der Meulen, Evert Faber (2009) 'Gas Supply and EU-Russia Relations', *Europe-Asia Studies*, Vol. 61, no. 5, pp. 833–856.

Viscusi, Gregory and Meyer, Henry (2018) 'Macron Heads to Russia in European Effort to Salvage Iran Deal', *Bloomberg*, 22 May. Available at www.bloomberg.com/news/articles/2018-05-22/macron-heads-to-russia-in-european-effort-to-salvage-iran-deal (accessed 22 May 2018).

24
RUSSIAN SECURITY STRATEGY AND THE GEOPOLITICS OF EURASIA

John Berryman

Introduction

Of the world's land masses, the supercontinent of Eurasia remains the largest and most dynamic, containing around 75 per cent of the world's peoples, 60 per cent of the world's gross national product (GNP), about three-fourths of the world's known energy resources, and after the United States the next six largest and biggest spenders on military equipment (Brzezinski, 1997: 31; Macaes, 2018). This chapter explores the ways in which the geopolitics of Eurasia – the influence of the geographical location and features of states on the politics of the region – has helped shape, but not determine, Russia's security strategy. (Implications of the grand theories of classical geopolitics for Russian foreign policy are explored in Berryman, 2012, 2018.)

The security strategy of Muscovy 1480–1682: the geopolitics of the periphery

After enduring more than two centuries of the 'Tatar Yoke' (*Tataro-Mongolskoye Igo*) of the Mongol Empire, from 1480 the lands of the Grand Duchy of Muscovy began to re-secure their independence. Located within what Halford Mackinder would later term the 'Eurasian Heartland', a vast plain lacking natural geographical barriers or easy access to the world's oceans, Muscovy looked to compensate for its geostrategic shortcomings by means of territorial expansion, moving outward to pre-empt external attack. Tsar Ivan IV initially moved East to annex the Volga Tatar Khanates of Kazan in 1552 and Astrakhan in 1556. However, Muscovy's southern and western borderlands remained vulnerable, and in 1571 Crimean Tatars besieged and partly burned Moscow, while during the Time of Troubles Polish forces briefly occupied Moscow (1610–1612). Undeterred by these incursions, meeting negligible resistance from nomadic tribes and a Chinese Empire recovering from the collapse of the Ming Dynasty, Muscovite Rus extended its rule thousands of miles east across 11 time zones to Siberia, establishing a settlement on the coast of the Pacific Ocean at the Bay of Okhotsk in 1648. By virtue of its geopolitical location on the eastern periphery of Europe, Muscovy was, therefore, able to expand easily and rapidly eastward across Eurasia without posing a challenge to any significant neighbour (Samokhvalov, 2017: 15). Russia's vast space (*prostranstvo*) would henceforth underpin its 'strategic solitude' on the eastern flank of the European states system. As an emerging continental state with severely restricted outlets to the wider oceans, in a far from benign security environment Russia could not but be ever-conscious of the constraints of geography (Haslam, 2002: 166).

The security strategy of Imperial Russia 1682–1825

Peter I and after (1682–1762)

Unhappy with Russia's limited access to the wider oceans through the port of Arkhangelsk, which was frozen for much of the year, Peter the Great looked for outlets through the Baltic Sea and Black Sea. Following the failure of Turkish forces to take Vienna in 1683, Peter chose initially to move south. In 1696, the Turkish fortress of Azov at the mouth of the Don River was seized and Taganrog established as a naval base for a southern fleet on the Sea of Azov. However, at the conclusion of another Russo-Turkish War in 1711, with Turkish forces at Kerch and Enikale barring entrance to the Black Sea, Peter abandoned his southern project, dismantling the fortress at Taganrog and destroying the Azov fleet. His focus of interest now shifted northwest to the Baltic (LeDonne, 1997: 23–24, 89–90; Hosking, 2012: 192–195; Berryman, 2017a: 57).

With the onset in 1700 of the Great Northern War between the Swedish Empire and the Russian Empire, the great victory of Russian forces at the Battle of Poltava 1709 signalled the termination of Sweden's hegemonic position in Northern Europe. Peter had already founded St. Petersburg in 1703 on the shores of the Baltic Sea as Russia's new capital and 'window to Europe', and with the signing of the Peace of Nystad in 1721, Sweden recognised the loss of most of its Baltic provinces. Alongside a powerful new Russian Baltic Fleet based at Kronstadt on Kotlin Island protecting St. Petersburg, a heavy defensive military presence was now deployed in the Baltic borderlands of Estland, Livonia and Ingria. Russia was now the dominant power within the Baltic Sea – albeit a seaway to the wider oceans still controlled by the Danish Straits. And over subsequent decades, Russia would become a member of the European diplomatic scene, albeit perceived as a somewhat feared semi-Asian 'Other' on the periphery of Europe (Kennedy, 1988: 122–123, 139; LeDonne, 1997: 25–27, 99–100; Coones, 2005: 72; Neumann, 2008: 24–27).

Catherine II (1762–1796)

Switching Russia's focus of attention to the southwest, from 1762 Catherine II acquired the steppe grasslands of 'New Russia' (*Novorossiya*), and following a six-year Russo-Turkish War (1768–1774) in 1782, a Russian Black Sea Fleet was established. With Russia's annexation of the Crimea in the following year, the main base of the fleet was established at Sevastopol. And at the conclusion of another Russo-Turkish War (1787–1792), by the Treaty of Jassy, Russia's control of much of the northern Black Sea littoral was recognised. As well as the Baltic Sea Russia had now secured an even more valuable ice-free outlet through the Black Sea, albeit one dependent on the movement of Russia's ships through the Turkish Straits and the Mediterranean Sea (Schroeder, 1994: 22–23; Ruhl, 1997: 35; Coones, 2005: 72, 218; Berryman, 2017a: 57–58; Samokhvalov, 2017: 85).

Paul I (1796–1801) and Alexander I (1801–1825)

In response to the ideological and power political challenge of the 1789 French Revolution, the Great Powers pursued a strategy of containment. Occupying a peripheral geopolitical position, Russia was initially able to pursue a 'buck-passing' security strategy, committing Russian military forces for only one year in the War of the Second Coalition (1798–1802). Although Russia rejoined the struggle to contain Napoleon, following Russian military reverses a short-lived modus vivendi was reached by Napoleon and Tsar Alexander I at Tilsit in1807 (Schroeder, 1994: 200–202, 217–223; Lieven, 2003: 214–215; Haas, 2005: 40–68; Mearsheimer, 2014: 274–281). Thanks to the strategic depth provided by the 'cushion' of its vast territories, Imperial Russia found that it was able to ride out Napoleon's invasion of 1812, and the remnants of his retreating *Grande Armee* were pursued across Europe by Russian and Prussian forces. In recognition of Russia's contribution to the collective defeat of Napoleon, Russia was now formally recognised as a Great Power at the 1815 Congress of Vienna (Ruhl, 1997: 28; Neumann, 2008: 30).

Maintaining armed forces of around 800,000 men, nearly triple the size of any other Great Power, after 1815 there were fears that Russia might displace France as the European hegemon (Kennedy, 1988: 197). Such fears were exaggerated. With the absorption of most of the former Polish provinces of Prussia into a new Kingdom of Poland within the Russian Empire, Alexander I was satisfied with the territorial settlement reached in Vienna. But continued Russian expansion into the Transcaucasus aroused British and French fears that their routes through the Mediterranean to the Near East and India would be threatened (Schroeder, 1994: 558–559, 590–591; Haas, 2005: 75–90; Tsygankov, 2012: 71–74).

The security strategy of Imperial Russia 1825–1917

Nicholas I (1825–1855)

In what was in effect the first 'Cold War' between Russia and the West, the harsh internal suppression of the Polish revolt of 1830–1831 by Nicholas I and his assistance to Austria in its suppression of the 1848 Hungarian revolt, sharpened Western liberal perceptions of Russia as the despotic 'gendarme of Europe'. Paradoxically, it was only when its relative Great Power position in Europe was in fact declining that Russia's invasion of the Danubian principalities in the initial stage of another Russo-Turkish War in 1853 triggered the intervention of the United Kingdom and France (Malia, 2000: 7–8, 91–103, 146–159; Haas, 2005: 90–104; Otte, 2013: 20–23; Samokhvalov, 2017: 15).

The Anglo-French expeditionary force was despatched through the Bosphorus to destroy the Russian Black Sea base at Sevastopol and deny Russia the naval dominance of the Black Sea and the Turkish Straits. However, the hopes of Palmerston and other liberals and Russophobes that an international coalition could drive Russia's western borders back to those it had occupied before the reign of Catherine the Great were not realised. Once Sevastopol was taken by British, French and Turkish forces in September 1855, Austria threatened to intervene in support of Russia's enemies, an announcement which 'astonished the world with its ingratitude', while preparations were made by the Royal Navy to despatch a coastal assault fleet of more than 300 vessels to bombard and burn Kronstadt, the world's largest naval fortress complex, followed by St. Petersburg. In these circumstances the Tsar concluded that Russia should seek peace. By the 1856 Treaty of Paris the demilitarisation of the Black Sea and the Aaland Islands in the Baltic Sea diminished Russia's sea power in both theatres (Lambert, 2011: chapters 22 and 23; Tsygankov, 2012: 145–146, 200–215; Berryman, 2017a: 59–60).

Alexander II (1855–1881), Alexander III (1881–1894) and Nicholas II (1894–1917)

After more than 150 years of military success as a rising power, defeat in the Crimean War represented a shocking reversal for St. Petersburg, highlighting the geostrategic dilemma of how Russia could protect both its land borders with Austria and Prussia and its Baltic and Black Sea coastlines. While all of these theatres posed defensive demands, none of them were mutually supporting. Hence, of the 1.2 million men mobilised by Russia for the Crimean War, just 320,000 were deployed in the Crimean theatre. An additional 260,000 guarded the Baltic Coast and St. Petersburg, 293,000 held Poland and West Ukraine, 121,000 were stationed in Bessarabia and the northern Black Sea coast, and 183,000 fought the Turks and the Caucasian mountaineers in the Caucasus (Fuller, 1992: 94–105; Kokoshin, 1998: 111; Kagan, 1999: 243–244).

In the post–Crimean War decades, a grand strategy of 'concentration' (*recueillement*) was pursued by Tsar Alexander II's foreign minister, Count Aleksandr Gorchakov, in order that 'Great Reforms' could be driven through to accelerate Russia's modernisation and restore Russia as a Great Power. By 1870, Russia was in a position unilaterally to renounce the Black Sea clauses of the Treaty of Paris, re-establish a Russian Black Sea Fleet and in another war with Turkey (1877–1878) secure the establishment of an enlarged Bulgarian dependency with an Aegean Sea coastline. However, in an exercise of coercive diplomacy, the 1878 Congress of Berlin stripped Bulgaria of its Aegean Sea coastline, blocking Russia's hopes of an advanced base for its naval forces in the Eastern Mediterranean (Fuller, 1992: 265–327; Coones, 2005: 73; Hosking, 2012: 315–316; Otte, 2013: 28–30).

Meanwhile, taking advantage of the Second Anglo-Chinese War (1858–1860), Russia acquired from China the half million square miles of the Amur and Maritime Districts, and at the extreme end of these territories established Vladivostok on the Pacific coast as a naval base for Russia's Pacific Fleet. Russia's imperial overstretch into these additional territories in the Far East resulted in a disastrous 1904–1905 war with Japan, by which time Russia had pushed south to carve out an equally vast geopolitical salient in Central Asia (Gillard, 1977; Fuller, 1992: 289–292, 452; LeDonne, 1997: 130–136; Lieven, 2003: 210–211, 286).

With the signing of the Austro-German Dual Alliance in 1879, ending generations of Austro-Prussian rivalry which had enhanced Russia's power and security, St. Petersburg now recognised the geopolitical logic of securing arrangements with republican France to contain the powerful military challenge posed by the two Central Powers. Between 1892 and 1894, the fateful Franco-Russian Alliance was forged to address the primacy of this security challenge to Russia's western borders (Fuller, 1992: 350–360; Lieven, 2003: 286; Mearsheimer, 2014: 213–215).

The outbreak of war in 1914 saw the advance of German troops into Russia, albeit an incursion limited by Germany's simultaneous invasion of France. When the Ottoman Empire and Bulgaria subsequently entered the war alongside Germany from 1915 an uninterrupted front was established on Russia's western flank from Riga to Baghdad. Anxious to maintain Russia's commitment to the war, the April 1915 Treaty of London indicated that the United Kingdom and France would now raise no objection to the Russian annexation of the Turkish Straits, while an ill-fated Anglo-French Dardanelles expedition was mounted to turn Germany's flank and open a southern route to Russia. Russia's military performance on the Eastern Front exceeded many expectations, but thanks to the botched 1917 revolution and the collapse of Russia's war effort, her Western allies were able to escape any obligations to honour their promises. Having made a significant contribution to the collective containment of Imperial Germany's bid for Eurasian hegemony, Russia received no reward for its sacrifice of 1.7 million dead and almost 5 million casualties (Ruhl, 1997: 37–38; Lieven, 2003: 286–287; Samokhvalov, 2017: 87–88, 109). Reflecting on Russia's history at the end of World War II, Stalin complained to Molotov that the West was accustomed to use Russia as cannon fodder, lure them to fight with promises of major strategic gains, and leave them empty-handed in the end. As he put it, 'Russians are remarkable warriors but they do not know how to make peace. They are deceived and underpaid' (Pechatnov, 2013: 21).

The security strategy of the Soviet Union 1917–1991

The Soviet Union and World War II (1917–1945)

With the advance of German forces on Petrograd following the seizure of power by the Bolsheviks in October 1917, to buy time for possible military or revolutionary developments, Lenin insisted upon the signing of the draconian March 1918 Treaty of Brest-Litovsk. Soviet Russia now relinquished all the western borderlands it had acquired since Peter the Great, and one million German and Austrian troops occupied the former Russian territories of Finland, Poland, the Baltic, Ukrainian and Belorussian provinces, plus Crimea and Georgia. Following the Allied victory in November 1918, with the assistance of remaining German military units in the Baltic, Finland and the Baltic states established their independence and formed an anti-Soviet cordon sanitaire. Western intervention prolonged and exacerbated the Russian Civil War, but, half-hearted and chaotic, it failed to dislodge the Bolsheviks (Mawdsley, 2008).

Fearful of 'capitalist encirclement' and renewed Western intervention, through the 1920s, a weakened Soviet Union pursued a security strategy of 'peaceful coexistence', negotiating non-aggression and friendship treaties with its Western neighbours. However, with the Japanese occupation of Manchuria in the East and the rise of Nazi Germany in the West, by the 1930s Moscow confronted for the first time the possibility of a major war on two fronts. Having accelerated military production, much of it located beyond the Urals, and established massive strategic reserves (a policy which Putin has followed), Stalin pursued a balance of power strategy which would enable the Soviet Union to stand on the periphery and stay out of any forthcoming war (Sonnenfeldt and Hyland, 1979: 5–7; Hill and Gaddy, 2013: 81–93).

August 1939 saw the signing of the Nazi-Soviet Non-Aggression Pact, clearing the way for the German-Soviet invasion and fourth partition of Poland, followed by a brief Soviet-Finnish War to secure the approaches to Leningrad and the re-absorption of the Baltic states and Bessarabia into the Soviet Union. These rushed measures, in many cases accompanied by harsh policies of deportation, purges and collectivisation, only marginally improved the Soviet security presence in the Baltic and Black Seas and at the mouth of the Danube, and Germany's swift conquest of most of Western Europe cleared the way for Hitler's 'war of annihilation' (*Vernichtungskrieg*) of the Soviet Union (Gorodetsky, 1999; Hosking, 2012: 417, 420, 486–491).

In a sensational change of policy, having signed a Neutrality Pact with the Soviet Union in April 1941, in December 1941 Tokyo initiated a strike south to establish a Greater East Asia Co-Prosperity Sphere – a course of action which would lead Japan to war with the United States (Calvocoressi et al., 1972: 915–926). Freed from the prospect of a coordinated two-front pincer attack on the Soviet Union by Nazi Germany and the Japanese Empire, Soviet forces were able to push back the *Wehrmacht* and drive across Eastern Europe into the heart of Germany, establishing an extended Soviet sphere of influence containing 95 million people, more than half the population of the Soviet Union itself (Kramer, 1996; Berryman, 2018: 64–65). Unlike the positive recognition in 1815 of the value of the cooperation between Russia and the West in the joint defeat of Napoleon, the onset of fierce rivalry between the Soviet Union and its former allies after 1945 was similar to that which had followed Russia's withdrawal from the war in 1917.

The Soviet Union and the Cold War 1947–1989

With the British withdrawal from India in 1947, the Soviet Union emerged as 'unquestionably the greatest single power in Eurasia with far more capacity to influence events throughout the continent than either the British or Russian governments had possessed in the nineteenth century' (Gillard, 1977: 180). Having deployed enormous resources in a two hemisphere war to deny German hegemony in western Eurasia and Japanese hegemony in eastern Eurasia, the Cold War strategy of the United States was based on a 'containment consensus'. The view from Washington was that in relation to Eurasia as a whole, the United States was an island power with inferior resources and that its position would not be secure if the markets and raw materials of Eurasia fell under the domination of a hostile hegemonic power or group of powers. Washington accordingly mobilised a global chain of U.S. air and naval bases around the perimeter of the potential Soviet 'heartland' and forward deployed U.S. forces in Europe and East Asia, offering bilateral security guarantees to East Asian states and multilateral security guarantees to member-states of the North Atlantic Treaty Organisation (NATO) (Berryman, 2018: 66).

Aware of the global threat posed by the United States, the greatest military and economic power in the history of the world, Stalin prudently adopted an asymmetric, continental, 'Hostage Europe' survival strategy. Thirty Soviet divisions were forward deployed in East Germany and Eastern Europe as compared to the ten or so divisions deployed in Western Europe, and to protect the Soviet heartland from U.S. strategic air power dense Soviet air defence systems were deployed in both Eastern Europe and along the borders of the Soviet Union (Wolf, 1970: Part One; Sonnenfeldt and Hyland, 1979: 7–10; Barrass, 2009: 34, 62).

With the subsequent development of its nuclear forces, plus naval and air power, the Soviet Union moved from a position of a regional Eurasian Great Power into the position of a global superpower (Sonnenfeldt and Hyland, 1979: 10–15). However, from the 1960s the Sino-Soviet conflict opened the door to several decades of a 'parallel Cold War' between Moscow and Beijing in which 52 Soviet divisions (25 per cent of Soviet ground forces), plus tactical and strategic nuclear forces, confronted 70 Chinese divisions across the Sino-Soviet border. And given the still strained character of post-war Soviet-Japanese relations over the Kurile Islands and the development of a Sino-American detente, by the 1980s the Soviet Union once more faced the prospect of potential encirclement on the Eurasian continent, this time by NATO on its western flank and a Sino-American-Japanese Anti-Soviet Triple Alignment on its eastern flank. The signal success of Gorbachev in securing the normalisation of Sino-Soviet relations, the withdrawal of Soviet forces from Afghanistan, and the termination of the Cold War division of Europe in 1989–1990 was unfortunately overshadowed by his less well-judged role in the subsequent self-liquidation of the Soviet Union (Zagoria, 1982; Barrass, 2009; 174–175; Berryman, 2010: 126–127).

The security strategy of the Russian Federation 1992–2018

As a consequence of this second implosion of the Russia state in the twentieth century, although its borders now approximated those of Muscovy before the conquests of Peter the Great and his successors, the Russian Federation still remained the world's largest country. Lacking the former buffer zones provided by the borderlands of the Baltic states, Ukraine, and Moldova, as well as the dominant position formerly occupied by the Soviet Union in the Caucasus and Central Asia, the Russian Federation nonetheless remained far stronger militarily and economically than any of the other 14 newly independent states (Suny, 2007: 66; Trenin, 2011: 20; Friedman, 2012).

In 1990 President Yeltsin pledged that Russia would not seek to re-create any sort of new empire or seek any advantages over any of its former republics. However, with armed conflicts emerging in some former republics, in February 1993 Russia's new Minister of Foreign Affairs, Andrei Kozyrev, called for all international organisations, including the United Nations, to recognise Russia's special responsibilities for the despatch of peacekeeping missions to guarantee peace and stability within all of the other 14 states of the former Soviet Union – the 'near abroad' (McNabb, 2016: 43, 60, 174–175). Moscow's response was seen by some as that of an imperial expansionist power, reverting to its historical preference to secure its geopolitical objectives in the borderlands by annexation of territory or the creation of satellite states (Hill and Jewett, 1994). However, the replacement of Kozyrev as Foreign Minister by Evgenii Primakov in January 1996 signified the victory of statist forces committed to the re-establishment of Russia as a Great Power rather than a revived Imperial Russia (Trenin, 2011: 11–17; Toal, 2017: 71–87).

Russia's initial expectations of cooperation and even integration with the West were to be disappointed. At the point when the last remaining Soviet garrisons had just left Germany, Eastern Europe, and the Baltic states, and Russia's military presence in Europe was at its lowest point in three centuries, in 1994 a triumphalist Washington took the decision to initiate the post–Cold War eastward enlargement of NATO (Trenin, 2016: 25). Driven by a hedging strategy of 'soft containment' of a potentially resurgent re-imperialising Russia, over the next two decades the eastward enlargement of NATO, a Cold War alliance, has helped perpetuate Cold War mentalities. And coupled with Washington's support for colour revolutions, Moscow has concluded that the United States is ultimately seeking to dismantle Russia's political system and its territorial integrity (Berryman, 2014, 2017b: 168–172; Tsygankov, 2018). Moreover, following Washington's unilateral abrogation of the ABM Treaty in 2002, NATO's eastward expansion was accompanied by the progressive deployment in Europe of NATO's missile defence system with an offensive potential to jeopardise the viability of Russia's key land-based strategic nuclear forces – posing a more significant security challenge than NATO's largely symbolic military deployments (Sakwa, 2017: 90–93, 210–215; Diesen and Keane, 2018).

Following the 1992 transformation of the European Community into the European Union (EU), NATO's eastward enlargement would also be accompanied by the eastward enlargement of the EU. Apart from its adoption of an increasingly tutelary approach to Russian officials, imbued with a self-congratulatory conviction of the superiority of its post-modern identity and procedures, in response to the belated efforts of Putin to construct a Eurasian Economic Union to reinforce Russia's regional position in the new Greater Eurasia vis-à-vis the EU, Turkey, China, and the United States, the securitised EU quickly developed a 'forward' European Neighbourhood Policy and an Eastern Partnership Initiative (Sakwa, 2017: 137–152, 249–276; Macaes, 2018: 187–191). Still located as a 'Lonely Power' or 'Other' civilisation on the periphery of Europe, a position it has occupied for several centuries, Russia has seen all independent states in the 'grey zone' close to its borders to be potential weapons in the hands of the Western powers (Shevtsova, 2010; Kotkin, 2016: 4). Although their accession to NATO was blocked at the critical 2008 Bucharest NATO Summit, in the view of much of the security community in Washington, Georgia and Ukraine remain key target states for eventual NATO membership (Toal, 2017: 291–297). By contrast, with the exposure of the limitations of the EU as a foreign policy actor in the Ukraine crisis, the President of the European Commission, Jean-Claude Juncker, has indicated that Brussels anticipates that Ukraine will not join the EU (or NATO) for 25 years (Sakwa, 2017: 263–265).

Against the background of this dual eastward advance of NATO and the EU over the past two decades, with the exception of the defensive annexation of Crimea, Moscow has displayed no imperial appetite to absorb fresh territories into the Russian Federation. As a modernising multinational state engaged in the process of post-imperial transition, Russia has looked instead to become a regional Great Power, not an imperial overlord (Suny, 2007: 68). But like all Great Powers, Russia has displayed a sensitivity to security challenges that are geographically proximate to its borders. The priority concern for Moscow's security strategy in post–Cold War Eurasia, spelled out in the December 2014 Military Doctrine of the Russian Federation, has therefore been to deny potentially hostile forces the availability of strategically sensitive territories for the discretionary deployment of military infrastructures. Russia's pre-emptive annexation of the vital strategic complex of Crimea in 2014 reflected such strategic, rather than imperial, concerns (Berryman, 2015; Triesman, 2016; Toal, 2017: 214–236). Moreover, like other Great Powers, including the United States, China, and France, Russia has also sought to maintain 'regions of privileged interests' or security zones to provide strategic depth without the requirement to meet the economic or ideological overhead costs of empire – as was required by the maintenance of the 'tight' Cold War Soviet bloc in Eastern Europe. Within such zones, the expectation is that, while states may retain their own domestic priorities, they should pursue neutral foreign and security policies (Berryman, 2011; Friedman, 2012; see also Haslam, 2002: 175–176; Hast, 2014). Shortcomings in Moscow's treatment of its close neighbours within its spheres of interests have certainly not escaped notice by Western commentators (Sherr, 2013). Leaving aside the question of how the modalities of Moscow's exercise of influence within its spheres may compare to those exercised by Washington or Beijing within their respective spheres, what can be noted are the limits of Moscow's efforts. Since there is no evidence of plans to destabilise and annex former Soviet territories, Dmitri Trenin concludes, 'The Russian Empire is definitely not making a comeback' (2016: 43–45).

Following Russia's 2014 annexation of Crimea and support for rebel forces in eastern Ukraine, concerned to bolster the security of its Baltic member-states, in 2016 NATO announced that a rapid-reaction force of four multinational battalions (4,000 troops) would be forward deployed to the western borders of Russia, just 100 miles from St. Petersburg. In response, apart from a concentration of Russian military forces on its western borders with the Baltic states and Ukraine, Russia's ongoing modernisation of its nuclear and conventional military forces has focused on the development and deployment of defensive anti-access/area denial and hybrid warfare systems (Gorenberg, 2017; Berryman, 2017b; Sakwa, 2017: 192–207). But with the prospect of more Western economic sanctions and a further build-up of Western military forces in the Baltic Sea and Black Sea, an additional option open to Moscow is the strengthening of Russian-Chinese cooperation.

Despite talk of a 'strategic partnership' between Russia and China, Chinese finance and investment has done little to compensate for Western sanctions, while China has been vigorously developing its own Greater Eurasia project – the Belt and Road Initiative – at Russia's expense and with its cooperation. The challenge of China to the triangular balance of Russia, the EU, and the United Sates in Eurasia is, therefore, not so much its fast developing military power as the gravitational pull of its economic strength, as compared to the continued economic weakness of the Russian economy and the retrenchment of the United States in Eurasia (Kotkin, 2016: 7; Macaes 2018: 57–58). In the longer term, as one Russian commentator has warned, a consolidation of the Russia-China alliance would lead to precisely the geopolitical configuration that the United States has been trying to prevent at all costs since at least the beginning of the 20th century, namely, the emergence of a unified centre of power in Eurasia that is opposed to the United States and which has a superior resource, demographic and (eventually) economic base. The fact that Moscow would likely be the junior partner in such a configuration is little consolation for the strategists in Washington.

(Kortunov, 2018)

In sum, within the increasingly competitive and transactional environment of the new Greater Eurasia, Russia has re-established its position as a normal Great Power and is once more exercising its influence in not only Europe but parts of the Middle East, Eastern Mediterranean, and the Arctic. However, rather than pursuing a place within a Greater Europe, the goal initially identified by Gorbachev at the end of the Cold War, Moscow is now pursuing a geo-economic strategy within a Greater Eurasia (Diesen, 2017). With the continued rise of China and the possible disaggregation of NATO and the EU, Russia may become the 'West of the East' (Trenin, 2016: xi–xii, chapter 2).

References

Barrass, G. S. (2009) *The Great Cold War: A Journey Through the Hall of Mirrors*. Stanford, CA: Stanford University Press.

Berryman, J. (2010) 'Russia and China in Eurasia: The Wary Partnership', in M. R. Freire and R. E. Kanet, eds., *The Return of the 'Great Game'*. Basingstoke: Palgrave Macmillan, pp. 126–145.

Berryman, J. (2011) 'Russia, NATO Enlargement, and 'Regions of Privileged Interests', in R. E. Kanet, ed., *Russian Foreign Policy in the 21st Century*. Basingstoke: Palgrave Macmillan, pp. 228–246.

Berryman, J. (2012) 'Geopolitics and Russian Foreign Policy', *International Politics*, 49(4): 530–544.

Berryman, J. (2014) '"Fear and Loathing" in the Kremlin: Russia and the Challenge of Intervention', in R. E. Kanet and R. Piet, eds., *Shifting Priorities in Russia's Foreign and Security Policy*. Farnham: Ashgate, pp. 51–72.

Berryman, J. (2015) 'Russian Grand Strategy and the Ukraine Crisis: An Historical Cut', in M. Sussex and R. E. Kanet, eds., *Power, Politics and Confrontation in Eurasia: Foreign Policy in a Contested Area*. Basingstoke: Palgrave Macmillan, pp. 186–209.

Berryman, J. (2017a) 'Crimea: Geopolitics and Tourism', in D. Hall, ed., *Tourism and Geopolitics: Issues and Concepts from Central and Eastern Europe*. Wallingford, Oxfordshire: CABI, pp. 57–70.

Berryman, J. (2017b) 'Russia and the European Security Order: Impact and Implications of the Ukraine Crisis', in R. E. Kanet, ed., *The Russian Challenge to the European Security Environment*. Basingstoke: Palgrave Macmillan, pp. 167–188.

Berryman, J. (2018) 'Geopolitics and Russian Foreign Policy', in A. P. Tsygankov, ed., *Routledge Handbook of Russian Foreign Policy*. London and New York: Routledge, pp. 60–78.

Brzezinski, Z. (1997) *The Grand Chessboard: American Primacy and Its Geostrategic Imperative*. New York: Basic Books.

Calvocoressi, P., G. Wint and J. Pritchard (1972) *The Penguin History of the Second World War*. London: Penguin.

Coones, P. (2005) 'The Heartland in Russian History', in B. W. Blouet, ed., *Global Geostrategy: Mackinder and the Defence of the West*. London and New York: Frank Cass, pp. 64–89.

Diesen, G. (2017) *Russia's Geoeconomic Strategy for a greater Eurasia*. London: Routledge.

Diesen, G. and C. Keane (2018) 'The Offensive Posture of NATO's Missile Defence System', *Communist and Post-Communist Studies*, 51: 91–100.

Fuller, W. C. (1992) *Strategy and Power in Russia 1600–1914*. New York: The Free Press, Macmillan.

Friedman, G. (2012) 'Russia's Strategy', *Geopolitical Weekly*. April. www.stratfor.com/weekly/russias-strategy?utm-source=freelist-f&utm_medium..... Accessed 3 June 2018.

Gillard, D. (1977) *The Struggle for Asia 1828–1914: A Study in British and Russian Imperialism*. London: Methuen.

Gorenberg, D. (2017) 'Russia's Military Modernisation Plans: 2018–2027', *Ponars Eurasian Policy Memo No. 495.*

Gorodetsky, G. (1999) *Grand Delusion: Stalin and the German Invasion of Russia.* New Haven and London: Yale University Press.

Haas, M. L. (2005) *The Ideological Origins of Great Power Politics, 1789–1989.* Ithaca and London: Cornell University Press.

Haslam, J. (2002) *No Virtue Like Necessity: Realist Thought in International Relations since Machiavelli.* New Haven and London: Yale University Press.

Hast, S. (2014) *Spheres of Influence in International Relations: History, Theory, and Politics.* Farnham: Ashgate.

Hill, F. and P. Jewett (1994) *Back in the USSR: Russia's Intervention in the Internal Affairs of the Former Soviet Republics and the Implications for United States Policy towards Russia.* Strengthening Democratic Institutions Project, John F. Kennedy School of Government, Harvard University, January.

Hill, F. and C. G. Gaddy (2013) *Mr. Putin: Operative in the Kremlin.* Washington, DC: Brookings Institution Press.

Hosking, G. (2012) *Russia and the Russians: From the Earliest Times to the Present.* Second Edition. London: Penguin Books.

Kagan, F. W. (1999) *The Military Reforms of Nicholas I: The Origins of the Modern Russian Army.* New York: St Martin's Press.

Kennedy, P. (1988) *The Rise and Fall of the Great Powers: Economic Change and Military Conflict from 1500 to 2000.* London: Fontana.

Kokoshin, A. A. (1998) *Soviet Strategic Thought, 1917–1991.* Cambridge, MA: The MIT Press.

Kortunov, A. (2018) 'How Do We Get Out of the Chelyabinsk Disco?' *Russian International Affairs Council,* 1 March. http://russiancouncil.ru. Accessed 23 June 2018.

Kotkin, S. (2016) 'Russia's perpetual geopolitics: Putin returns to the historical pattern', *Foreign Affairs,* 95(3): 2–9.

Kramer, M. (1996) 'The Soviet Union and Eastern Europe: Spheres of Influence', in N. Woods, ed., *Explaining International Relations since 1945.* Oxford: Oxford University Press, pp. 98–125.

Lambert, A. D. (2011) *The Crimean War: Britain's Grand Strategy against Russia, 1853–1856.* Second Edition. Farnham: Ashgate.

LeDonne, J. P. (1997) *The Russian Empire and the World, 1700–1917: The Geopolitics of Expansionism and Containment.* New York: Oxford University Press.

Lieven, D. (2003) *Empire: The Russian Empire and Its Rivals.* London: Pimlico.

Macaes, B. (2018) *The Dawn of Eurasia: On the Trail of the New World Order.* London: Penguin.

Malia, M. (2000) *Russia Under Western Eyes: From the Bronze Horsemen to the Lenin Mausoleum.* Cambridge, MA: The Belknap Press of Harvard University Press.

Mawdsley, E. (2008) *The Russian Civil War.* Edinburgh: Birlinn Ltd.

McNabb, D. E. (2016) *Vladimir Putin and Russia's Imperial Revival.* Baton Rouge, FL: CRC Press, Taylor & Francis Group.

Mearsheimer, J. J. (2014) *The Tragedy of Great Power Politics.* Updated Edition. New York and London: W. W. Norton.

Neumann, I. V. (2008) 'Russia's Standing as a Great Power, 1494–1815', in T. J. Hopf, ed., *Russia's European Choice.* Basingstoke: Palgrave Macmillan, pp. 13–34.

Otte, T. (2013) "A Very Internecine Policy': Anglo-Russian Cold Wars before the Cold War', in C. Baxter and M.L. Dockrill and K. Hamilton, eds., *Britain in Global Politics. Volume 1. From Gladstone to Churchill.* Basingstoke: Palgrave Macmillan, pp. 17–49.

Pechatnov, V. (2013) 'A Soviet perspective on Cold War Origins', in M. R. Fitzgerald and A. Packwood, eds., *Out of the Cold: The Cold War and Its Legacy.* New York and London: Bloomsbury Academic, pp. 19–23.

Ruhl, L. (1997) 'The Historical Background of Russian Security Concepts and Requirements', in V. Baranovsky, ed., *Russia and Europe: The Emerging Security Agenda.* Oxford: Oxford University Press for the Stockholm International Peace Research Institute, pp. 21–41.

Sakwa, R. (2017) *Russia Against the Rest: The Post-Cold War Crisis of World Order.* Cambridge: Cambridge University Press.

Samokhvalov, V. (2017) *Russian-European Relations in the Balkans and Black Sea Region: Great Power Identity and the Idea of Europe.* Cham: Palgrave Macmillan.

Schroeder, P. (1994) *The Transformation of European Politics, 1763–1848.* Oxford: Clarendon Press.

Sherr, J. (2013) *Hard Diplomacy and Soft Coercion: Russia's Influence Abroad*. London: The Royal Institute of International Affairs.

Shevtsova, L. (2010) *Lonely Power: Why Russia Has Failed to Become the West and the West is Weary of Russia*. Washington, DC: Carnegie Endowment for International Peace.

Sonnenfeldt, H. and W. G. Hyland (1979) *Soviet Perspectives on Security*. Adelphi Paper 150. London: International Institute for Strategic Studies.

Suny, R. (2007) 'Living in the Hood: Russia, Empire, and Old and New Neighbours', in R. Legvold, ed., *Russian Foreign Policy in the Twenty First Century and the Shadow of the Past*. New York: Columbia University Press, pp. 35–70.

Toal, G. (2017) *Near Abroad: Putin, The West and The Contest Over Ukraine And the Caucasus*. Oxford: Oxford University Press.

Trenin, D. (2011) *Post-imperium: A Eurasian Story*. Washington, DC: Carnegie Endowment for International Peace.

Trenin, D. (2016) *Should We Fear Russia?* Cambridge: Polity Press.

Triesman, D. (2016) 'Why Putin Took Crimea', *Foreign Affairs*, 96(3): 46–54.

Tsygankov, A. P. (2012) *Russia and the West from Alexander to Putin: Honour in International Relations*. Cambridge: Cambridge University Press.

Tsygankov, A. P. (2018) 'The Sources of Russia's Fear of NATO', *Communist and Post-Communist Studies*, 51: 101–111.

Wolf, T. W. (1970) *Soviet Power in Europe 1945–1970*. Baltimore and London: The John Hopkins Press.

Zagoria, D. S. (1982) *Soviet Policy in East Asia*. Baltimore and London: The John Hopkins Press.

25
THE IMPACTS OF CLIMATE CHANGE ON RUSSIAN ARCTIC SECURITY

Stacy Closson

Climate scientists suggest that changes are occurring faster in the polar regions of the planet than elsewhere. Russia's Arctic region – the territory above the Arctic Circle – is one-fifth of Russia's landmass. This heightens the challenge of climate change to Russia. In Russia, an official summary of peer-review research has concluded that temperatures are warming more in Russia than elsewhere (Roshydromet, 2014). Moreover, Russian scientists have projected a further warming into the future and warn that urban sustainability will be hampered by more precipitation and more flooding. As the majority of Russia's High North are coastal cities located on the sea or rivers, the population is directly impacted by climate change (Anisimov and Kokorev, 2017, 142–143).

Russia's security objectives in the High North are socio-economic development and maintaining sovereignty over its territory. The security architecture is bolstered by maritime transportation, energy production and export, and development of the High North for industry and the military. Transportation is critical to economic development of the High North as Russia has to get its natural resources to the market, and this requires road, rail, air, and sea. Russian authorities anticipate a huge growth in the use of its maritime Northern Sea Route, connecting European and Asian markets and providing expanded opportunity to the approximately two million Russians residing near the Arctic coast.

However, climate change will continue to have profound impacts on Russian Artic security. Climate change is affecting the reliability of these transportation routes and, in the longer term, sustained development of the High North. The changing physical environment and infrastructure sensitive to the environment require a sustained and well-funded plan to adapt and mitigate to consequences (Stephenson, 2017).

This long-term vision for the Arctic, however, is impeded by several challenges. These include, first, a political climate in Russia that more often denies the impact of climate change and therefore delays adaption and mitigation measures. Second, competing Russian stakeholders with different priorities locked in a competition for limited resources.

This chapter first theorises security of Russia's Arctic. While realism captures Russia's policy and actions, the securitisation of climate is a competing important approach. The chapter then addresses how climate change is expected to have a profound impact on Russian Arctic security, including in the areas of transportation and energy production. The chapter next reviews Russia's position in international climate negotiations on climate change. The fourth section addresses two challenges to addressing climate security in an effective way in Russia, from climate denial to competing interests. The final section discusses whether outside actors, from the United Nations, to the Arctic Council, to Nordic and Asian countries may assist or desist in Russia's Arctic climate security challenges.

Securitisation of the Arctic

Russia must contend with several geographical groupings of Arctic states. There is the North American contingent of the United States and Canada, both with sparsely populated Arctic territory, credible claims to energy deposits, and capable of deploying strategic forces. There is the Arctic Ocean 5 (the United States, Canada, Denmark/Greenland, Norway, and Russia). There is the Western 7 (North Atlantic Treaty Organisation's [NATO] United States, Canada, Denmark, Iceland, and Norway; plus Finland and Sweden), who are harmonious in strengthening a security community in response to Russia. There are the four Nordic countries bordering Russia, whose northern regions are the most densely populated and developed part of the Arctic. There is Russia's vast Arctic zone, covering one-fifth of the Arctic Circle, and home to two-thirds of the world's Arctic population, among them 27 indigenous groups. Finally, the Arctic as a "global commons" draws in non-Arctic states wanting a greater role in determining its development, among them China.

These geographical groupings have resulted in the creation, since the 1990s, of several multilateral organisations focused on the Arctic. In practice, the organisations do not address hard security issues, and instead foster through consensus cooperative efforts on softer security issues. The Arctic Council is the pan-Arctic organisation that includes all 8 states (Western 7 and Russia), plus 6 indigenous organisations and over 30 non-Arctic observers. The Arctic Council meets at the national, parliamentary (including the European Union [EU] parliament), and regional governmental levels. The Barents Euro-Arctic Council (BEAC) includes the four Nordic countries, the EU, Iceland, and Russia. Related is the Barents Regional Council (BRC) that links up 13 local administrative and territorial entities in Russia, Norway, Finland, and Sweden, including Russia's Karelia, Komi, Arkhangelsk, Murmansk, and Nenets. Other northern non-governmental regional organisations such as the Nordic Council of Ministers and the Northern Dimension Environmental Partnership (NDEP) also promote regional cooperation.

Arctism, hailing Russia's return to the Northern Motherland, is a glorification of the Arctic as the last territory on earth to be conquered. The exploration of the Soviets in the High North, a period known as the Red Arctic of 1932–1964, saw the rapid and impressive social, economic, and military development of Russia's High North (Laruelle, 2013). Russia's return to the Arctic in the past decade is meant to overcome the trauma of the end of the Soviet Union and to reclaim Russia as a Great Power.

According to official Russian doctrine, the realist school of theory dominates relations in the Arctic; conflict among nations in the pursuit of power. Today, the Arctic serves as a flagship for nationhood as Russian authorities perceive the nation to be under siege from the West and South. The answer, according to Russian strategic doctrine, is to fortify and then exploit Russia's vast natural resources in its High North. In the Russia Arctic Strategy, the Government of Russia (2013) named NATO as the primary national security threat in the Arctic and declared countering NATO as a top priority. In Russia's Military Doctrine, the Government of Russia (2014) named the Arctic a strategic priority and the military as the protector of natural resources. In Russia's latest National Security Strategy, the Government of Russia (2015) envisions a global competition to secure and develop Arctic resources.

Russia has bolstered its military forces and permanent bases in the High North, including the nuclear triad of submarines, bombers, and missiles as part of a broader military modernisation programme (Klimenko, 2016).

However, while the Arctic serves to bolster Russia's greatness, Russia is not the dominant regional power, and it is not clear from Russian doctrine or discourse that it desires this role. In both the pan-Arctic and the Barents Sea region, all of the states are wealthy, highly developed, and not dependent on Russia for trade or security. There are EU members (Denmark, Finland Iceland, and Sweden) and NATO members (U.S. Canada, Denmark, Iceland, and Norway). Hence, Russia's position is rather one of several regional powers engaged with different economic and security communities (Closson, 2017).

Most relevant to this study is the securitisation of the Arctic as constructed around new norms of climate change. The Copenhagen School (Buzan et al., 1998) of security studies discusses how an issue becomes labelled an existential threat and securitised. Over decades of international negotiations to reduce greenhouse gas emissions, increasingly alarming findings from climate science on global warming, and a growing pattern of severe weather events, experts have securitised the climate as a direct threat, as opposed to treating it only as an environmental or political challenge (Scott, 2012). As the climate threat has become more urgent, it has gained the attention of appropriate audiences to address the issue.

Climate change impacts on Russia's Arctic

Russia's High North areas constitute over half of its landmass stretching across 11 time zones from Europe to Asia. During the Soviet period, new technologies and ideologies brought new waves of people and new cities to Russia's Arctic, despite the remoteness and harsh climate. Today, Russia's High North is highly urbanised and contains almost two-thirds of the Arctic population. The North is a large source of economic development, from the transportation hub of Murmansk, to the energy cities of Novy Urengoy, Rugut, and Nadym, to industrial cities such as Norilsk for the mining of nickel and platinum (Reisser, 2017).

These frontline cities are experiencing both challenges and benefits of climate change and melting Arctic ice. The instability of the permafrost is already testing the structural integrity of buildings and infrastructure in the region. While warmer temperatures require less heat for buildings, it also means less accessible roads as surfaces. For Russia, anticipation of melting ice leading to more profitable seaports and easier oil and gas exploration can also mean the flooding of cities, creating economic loss and human suffering.

One potentially positive result for Russia is the accessibility of the Northern Sea Route (NSR) and the major rivers leading to it, such as the Ob, Yenisei, and Lena. Recent research suggests that the route across the polar north from Asia to Europe may be available on a more regular basis by mid-century (Smith and Stephenson, 2013). But the commercial viability of the NSR is questionable due to variability of ice melt, future trade patterns, and unknown costs (Humpert, 2011). There is a need for greater technology and partnerships, but economic development is further complicated by sanctions against Western companies operating with Russian firms in relation to Russia's invasion of Ukraine in 2014.

Reliable transportation within the Arctic is crucial for Russia's future energy growth. The energy industry has been the prime economic enterprise over the past several decades, but needs enhanced infrastructure to reach markets. State-owned energy firms, such as Gazprom and Rosneft, have a dominant presence in Yamal Nenets, which provides more than 80 per cent of Gazprom's total extractive wealth, while tax revenue from energy companies makes up the majority of the region's budget. Russia is still very dependent on oil and gas for two-thirds of its exports, 20 per cent of its gross domestic product (GDP), and 6 per cent of its state budget. New Arctic fields will keep output up given a decline in other inland Soviet-era fields. The majority of the 61 large oil and gas fields discovered in territory north of the Arctic Circle in Canada, Norway, Russia, and the United States are in Russia (Budzik, 2009).

Russia and climate change negotiations

In Russia, the securitisation of climate change, in relation to the Arctic, has been slow, marked by periods of greater and lesser urgency. This has been due, in part, to Russia's overall oscillating position on climate change. In 1992, Russia was one of the first countries to sign the UN Framework Convention on Climate Change and ratified it in 1994. However, Russian government officials soon expressed concern as to how climate mitigation efforts would harm the energy sector. During negotiations on the Kyoto Protocol, at first Russia expressed support for lower emission restrictions for industrialised countries. However, once again, by the time Russia signed the Kyoto protocol, Russian industrial leaders were openly expressing opposition to it. The government signed the agreement only after concessions were made and support for Russia's accession to the World Trade Organisation was promised (Poberezhskaya, 2016, chapter 3). However, ultimately Russia did not ratify the agreement and withdrew in 2013, citing the unfair advantage other major producers such as the United States and China had in not committing to pollution reductions.

At the same time, target reductions for climate emissions in Russia benefitted for a long time from the collapse of the Soviet Union. A combination of losing 14 Soviet Socialist Republics and a collapse in the economy, most especially the industrial complex, meant that Russia did not emit nearly as much as its Soviet predecessor. This left Russia in between the two established categories of emitters – developed and developing. Russian media portrayed Russia in the lead up to Kyoto as a 'Great Environmental Power' providing environmental solutions rather than contributing to them. Tynkkunen (2010) suggests that this diverted attention from Kyoto and its lack of meaningful contributions in emissions reductions. When targets were set for Kyoto, Russia set its baseline for reduction at 1991 and not earlier when the Soviet Union was arguably one of the most polluting nations in the world. As a result, reductions in greenhouse gas emissions in the 1990s declined significantly (Poberezhskaya, 2016, chapter 3).

Going into the United Nation Framework Convention on Climate Change [UNFCCC] talks on a successor agreement to Kyoto, President Medvedev released the Russian Climate Doctrine (Government of Russia, 2009). It was a declaratory and definitive statement of Russia's belief in anthropogenic influence and the risks posed to Russia, as well as the actions it must take. However, at the 2015 UN Conference in Paris dedicated to stopping average global temperatures from increasing by more than 2 degrees Celsius by the year 2050, Russia's proposed commitment to greenhouse gas emissions reductions allowed for growth from current levels (Climate Analytics, 2017). Russian leaders realise the benefit and burden they have in this case; while the exploitation of vast natural resources degrades the environment, it also gives Russia power in international discussions of climate change regulation (Poberezhskaya, 2016, 73–77).

Russia's Intended Nationally Determined Contribution (INDC) for the Paris Agreement was once again not set from post-Soviet levels. Russia would not need to implement any new policy to achieve its INDC target of 25–30 per cent below 1990 levels by 2030. Not only were the targets significantly above current policy projections, but the government also made it clear that their achievement was conditional on the accounting rules advantageous to Russia, such as "the maximum possible account of the absorbing capacity of forests" (UNFCCC, 2015). As of 2018, Russia had not yet ratified the agreement, remained one of the top five emitters of carbon dioxide in the world, and Russian industry was projected to be the world's most energy intensive until at least 2030 (Deutsche Welle, 2017).

Russia also changed its bureaucratic structures to weaken oversight of environmental protection by eliminating the State Committee on Environmental Protection and placing responsibilities under the Ministry of Natural Resources. This was indicative of President Putin's design to centralise the energy sector by strengthening ties to the elite and gaining ownership over assets. In turn, business leaders in Russia were not forced to curb emissions by policy or public pressure, despite understanding the implications of non-action.

Challenges to Russia addressing climate security

There are two challenges to addressing climate security in an effective way in Russia from politicising climate science to competing interests among stakeholders.

The first challenge is a growing discourse denying climate change from leading Russian politicians. Russia's engagement in climate science began during the Soviet period in 1969 when Russian Professor Mikhail Budyko developed a climate model and linked anthropogenic combustion of fossil fuels with the growing atmospheric concentration of carbon dioxide and global air temperatures. Forty years later, during international talks to update the Kyoto Protocol, Andrei Illarionov, economic advisor to President Putin, rebuffed scientific consensus and questioned the data taken from Russia's weather stations for the United Nation's intergovernmental Panel on Climate Change report. At that time, Russia was allied with China against the efforts by the Western developed countries to set new targets for greenhouse gas emissions at the Copenhagen Summit (Anisimov and Kokorev, 2017, 142–143).

Three Russian documents set out Arctic policy, which reflect Russia's weaker relationship to international climate science and international climate change politics (Wilson Rowe, 2013). They are the 2008 Fundamental Policy of State Policy of the Russia Federal in the Arctic in the Period up to 2020 and Beyond (Government of Russia, 2008), the Strategy for Socio-economic Development of Siberia towards 2020 (Government of Russia, 2010), and the Strategy for the Development of the Arctic Zone of the Russian Federation (Government of Russia, 2013). The 2008 document emphasised the Arctic as a source of natural resources, and only secondly mentioned protecting the environment, as well as peace, militarisation, and transportation. The 2010 document is more focused on domestic development. As in the first document, the environment is listed among numerous developmental priorities. The 2013 document lists challenges to sustainable development, including the change in climatic conditions. The "minimalisation of environmental damage" is addressed as primarily an issue of monitoring. Adaptation to the ongoing climate change effects is scarcely mentioned.

There is also a broad scepticism of Western climate science in general, and as applied to Russia's High North, in particular. This region is a highly securitised area, including sensitive nuclear and other military assets, as well as oil and gas development. Only after a severe winter in Siberia in 2007 and fires in southwestern Russia in 2010 did Russian leaders begin to consider anthropogenic climate change as an explanation (Tynkkunen, 2010). More recently, a spate of extreme weather events has propelled society to ask the government to protect them from future incidences and propelled politicians to start planning for adaptation, but has not led to an admission of the need to mitigate against climate change (Davydova, 2017). Instead, President Putin has actually argued that climate change is likely a global phenomenon that cannot be countered and that it will help Russian economic development in the long run (Jurčová, 2017).

That said, Russian authorities have begun work on a national climate change adaptation strategy. Ministries and regional officials were tasked to assess the risks of adverse impacts and possible adaptation measures. Due in part to an escalation in severe weather events, melting ice could swallow parts of islands that Russia uses for military purposes, including bases, but also radar stations and rocket sites. It could also necessitate the relocation of communities, which could contribute to domestic instability. Deforestation in parts of Russia's High North have already hampered Russia's ability to lower carbon emissions and could have further harmful effects on the environment. And, changing migratory patterns of fisheries will impact jobs in the Arctic.

Second, Russia's role in the Arctic is affected by differing priorities among governmental agencies; between the centre and peripheral governmental institutions in Russia; and between civil society and the regional governments. Debates can get heated between different Russian stakeholders and result in policy shifts.

Russia's domestic climate policy has remained ill-defined, despite international diplomacy to forward cooperation in reducing greenhouse gases. At the federal level, the reorganisation of agencies and weak enforcement powers hinder the effort at creating a coherent domestic policy. The regions are beholden to federal budgets, and progress in addressing environmental issues in general, and climate change, specifically has stagnated (Graybill, 2017, 226–227).

There is a push and pull between federal agencies in Moscow which stress the importance of security – the FSB, MOD, and other elements of the military industrial complex – versus the ministries focused on regional development, natural resources, transportation, fishing, industry, and social welfare (Laurelle, 2013). In a display of the seriousness, the federal government in Moscow puts on the Arctic that it established an Arctic Commission in 2015 and named Deputy Prime Minister Dmitry Rogozin to be in charge of it, in addition to his duties as head of defence and space issues. The 'losers' in this struggle have arguably been the environmentalists, who have remained weak political actors throughout much of the post-Soviet period (Yablokov, 2010). The term 'sustainable development' is featured throughout the government's Arctic development strategies, but the actual practice is inconsistent and remains contested among the parties mentioned above (Wilson Rowe, 2017).

Citizen groups critical of the energy and industrial sectors advocating for more regulations and safeguards have been particularly burdened. Non-governmental organisations (NGOs) have faced increasing pressure from the Russian government to limit their activities. Since 2012, NGOs in Russia have faced a new law that lists them 'foreign agents' for receiving external funding and individuals and they can be prosecuted. Russian authorities sometimes engage in a conflict with environmental activists in their High North, including indigenous groups. Indigenous groups continue to struggle to have their voices heard on issues of sustainable development where minerals and hydrocarbon production are prioritised. This fight is tied into the government's concerns over separatism from minority groups who have long felt left behind from development projects in their regions.

Role of outside actors

The Barents Sea region above the Arctic Circle demonstrates the trade-offs in Russia's efforts to securitize its High North. On the one hand, Russia demonstrates its military prowess by violating air and sea space, staging large-scale exercises, reopening Soviet bases, and prepositioning forces. Russia also tests boundaries around Norway's Svalbard archipelago and protests NATO activity that it perceives as a threat. On the other hand, Russian officials consistently underscore the need to depoliticise cooperation in the region and keep channels of high-level communication open. Russia requires the support of Nordic countries for investment, finance, and technology to enhance its own energy production and regional development (Closson, 2017).

Representatives of the Barents region meet at every level, from civil society to subregional, regional, and state levels. They meet in governmental and non-governmental capacities. As the main regional organisation, BEAC's goals are to create a favourable environment for trade and investment, develop stable integration links, upgrade border and customs infrastructure, and create new transport routes. Russia has chaired the BEAC twice, most recently in 2015–2017, and prioritises environmental issues and socio-economic development. Russia also chairs the Barents Regional Council. Typically, this province-level group is most concerned with people-to-people ties, promoting culture and tourism.

These myriad and overlapping regional organisations have been generous in funding projects in Russia's northwest Arctic region. Individual Nordic country financing (led by Norway), co-Russian financing with the EU and participating countries, and leveraging monies from international financial institutions have enhanced the environment and economic development in Russia's Arctic.

However, the imposition of international sanctions against Russia over the Ukraine crisis has slowed down Barents regional cooperation. Prior to the sanctions, Russia received funding for a variety of Barents projects from several European development and investment banks. However, after 2014, the bigger infrastructure projects have stopped or been postponed, and some smaller projects have failed to receive matching funds from the Russian government. Cooperation is further harmed by Russia's labelling of various groups as foreign agents, including the Nordic Council of Ministers in St. Petersburg and several indigenous and environmental groups in Russia's Barents region.

Nevertheless, Russia continues to demonstrate readiness to act in collaboration with other states. In the Arctic Council, Russia has recently led or co-led three task forces at the Arctic Council: one on marine oil pollution and prevention that led to a binding agreement, another on business that led to the establishment of the Arctic Economic Council, and a third on scientific cooperation with the United States that also led to a binding agreement. Importantly, all of these agreements will enhance Russia's national interests by establishing Russia as an even more important regional player in the Arctic.

In the end, Russia must strike a balance in developing its High North. On the one hand, it is increasingly securitising the region, building euphemistic walls around growing military facilities, and working less collaboratively with its Nordic neighbours in cleaning up and developing the region. This lack of cooperation is further hampered by Western sanctions against working with Russian companies to finance and develop new projects in Russia. In the Barents region, a decreased Russian budget for cooperation and the aforementioned designation of certain cooperative groups as "foreign agents" have limited both the level and types of international contact.

The crackdown on climate activists has also pitted Russian authorities against the Russian Association of Indigenous Peoples of the North (RAIPON) and, by extension, the United Nations. Founded 1990 at the First Congress of Indigenous Peoples, RAIPON has had the largest representation of Arctic indigenous population at the Arctic Council. Russia's 2008 Arctic Strategy addressing sustainable development challenges provided a domestic platform for their efforts to contest oil and gas development on or near sacred lands. In 2012, indigenous groups from across the Arctic took up this cause and RAIPON presented their case to the United Nations and the Arctic Council on violations of their basic rights. The Russian Ministry of Justice subsequently suspended RAIPON and changed the leadership.

The pan-Arctic region is also being reshaped by the slow, but gradual, inclusion of extra-regional states with interests in developing natural resources in the Arctic. It is unclear how increased activity from non-Arctic states in the region may affect overall cooperation. Already Chinese state-owned companies have financed the Yamal Nenets LNG terminal with Russia's Novatek, made use of the Northern Sea Route, invested in mining in Greenland, and conducted oil and gas exploration offshore of Iceland. Increasing interest from other Asian states in Russia's Arctic zone will affect both the pan-Arctic and Barents cooperation.

China, an observer of the Arctic Council since 2013, has named its Dalian port in its northeastern region as part of its broader efforts to develop infrastructure from the east to west on land and sea known as the Belt and Road Initiative. In 2017, the research vessel Xue Long became the first Chinese ship to navigate the three major Arctic shipping routes: The Northwest Passage, Northeast Passage, and Transpolar Sea Route. China self-identifies as a 'Near-Arctic State' and released an Arctic Strategy in 2018, which discussed a Polar Silk Road. The focus of China's efforts remains on research, but stress a role for encouraging commercialisation of the sea passage by building ships, ports, and navigational aids along the Northern Sea Route.

Conclusion

In the end, the future of Russia's High North is a caught between several paradoxes. First, there is a need to develop on a sustainable basis while relying on oil and gas to fund it. Russia has the largest Arctic population and some of the poorest urban areas, whose inhabitants increasingly demand better socio-economic conditions. Russia also has the largest amount of proven oil and gas of any of the Arctic states. Estimates vary, but Russia's Arctic is predicted to generate about 20 per cent of its GDP and 22 per cent of its exports in the future. As western Siberian hydrocarbons wane, Russia hopes to tap into the estimated 13 per cent of the world's oil, 30 per cent of the world's natural gas, and rare earth minerals located within in its Arctic zone (U.S. Geological Survey, 2008). However, decades of Soviet-era industrial growth have marred the landscape and polluted the environment, and Russians do not wish to repeat this.

Second, Russia signed the UNFCCC Agreement and has agreed to reduce its greenhouse gas emissions; however, the domestic discourse questions anthropomorphic impacts of climate change and the urgency to curb emissions. Russia has been engaged for decades in global negotiations within a UN framework to address climate change. But, Russia's emissions targets still fall short and the global climate agreement remains unratified by the Duma. Instead, Russian officials discuss the 'benefits' of climate change, particularly the melting of ice in the High North and a hoped-for gain in maritime transport.

Third, outside actors could assist Russia in developing and securitising its Arctic region, but long-running suspicions of outsiders, compounded by sanctions against Russia, hamper this effort. Countries in the Barents Sea region could continue to assist Russia in addressing environmental issues and providing the finance, technology, and infrastructure for the growth of Russia's High North. However, these countries, NATO and/or EU members, pose a perceived threat to Russia, and its military posturing in the Arctic is a direct response. Moreover, EU sanctions on Russia after the invasion of Ukraine in 2014 have halted many Arctic projects. China has invested in enhancing Russia's northern maritime route and energy projects on the Yamal Peninsula. But, some Russian officials remain concerned about indebtedness to China in the future.

Ultimately, Russia's securitisation of the climate in its High North may be overtaken by a few factors. Policy aside on climate emissions, continued economic stagnation in Russia, combined with an uptick in renewable energy generation means that Russia could very likely slow emissions growth (Climate Analytics, 2017). Paralleling a general global trend, Russia has realised the contribution renewable energy brings to economic growth, diversity of supply, and a cheaper alternative in remote areas (IRENA, 2017). Finally, increasing extreme weather events could harm economic development and plans for infrastructure in the Arctic, as well as human health and services. Retaining population and enhancing the economy will depend on predictability, which, in turn, depends on the climate.

References

Anisimov, Oleg and Vasily Kokorev (2017) 'Cities of the Russian North in the Context of Climate Change,' in Orttung, Robert, ed., *Sustaining Russia's Arctic Cities: Resource Politics, Migration, and Climate Change*. New York: Berghahn, chapter 7.

Budzik, Phillip (2009) *Arctic Oil and Gas Potential*. Washington, DC: US Energy Information Administration, Office of Integrated Analysis and Forecasting (Accessed on 3 May 2018) at www.akleg.gov/basis/get_documents.asp?session=28&docid=741

Buzan, Barry, Ole Wæver, and Jaap de Wilde (1998) *Security: A New Framework for Analysis*. London: Lynne Rienner.

Climate Analytics (2017) 'Russian Federation,' Climate Action Tracker (Accessed on 7 May 2018) at https://climateactiontracker.org/media/documents/2018/4/CAT_2017-11-06_CountryAssessment_RussianFederation.pdf

Closson, Stacy (2017) 'Russian Foreign Policy in the Arctic: Balancing Cooperation and Competition,' Kennan Cable 24, Woodrow Wilson Center, Washington, DC, 26 June (Accessed on 22 June 2018) at www.wilsoncenter.org/publication/kennan-cable-no24-russian-foreign-policy-the-arctic-balancing-cooperation-and

Davydova, Angelina (2017) 'Russia Wants to Protect itself from Climate Change without Reducing Carbon,' Science Magazine, 21 September (Accessed on 3 May 2018) at www.sciencemag.org/news/2017/09/russia-wants-protect-itself-climate-change-without-reducing-carbon-emissions

Deutsche Welle (2017) 'Where Russia Falls Short in Fight against Climate Change,' 11 April (Accessed on 5 May 2018) at www.dw.com/en/where-russia-falls-short-in-fight-against-climate-change/a-41240610

Government of Russia (2008) 'The Fundamentals of State Policy of the Russian Federation in the Arctic in the Period up to 2020 and Beyond.' Retrieved from www.scrf.gov.ru'documents/98.html

Government of Russia (2009) 'Climate Doctrine of the Russian Federation' (Accessed on 16 May 2018) at http://archive.kremlin.ru/eng/text/docs/2009/12/223509.shtml

Government of Russia (2010) 'Strategy for Socio-Economic Development of Siberia towards 2020' (Accessed 5 May 2018) at www.rg.ru

Government of Russia (2013) 'Strategy for the Development of the Arctic Zone of the Russian Federation to 2020' (Accessed on 11 April 2017) at https://minec.gov-murman.ru/activities/strat_plan/arkticzone/

Government of Russia (2014) 'Military Doctrine of the Russia Federation' (Accessed on 11 April 2017) www.offisiere.ch/wp-content/uploads-001/2015/08/Russia-s-2014-Military-Doctrine.pdf

Government of Russia (2015) 'Russia National Security Strategy' (Accessed on 11 April 2017).

Graybill, Jessica K. (2017) 'Urban Vulnerability to Climate Change in the Russian Arctic,' in Orttung, Robert, ed., *Sustaining Russia's Arctic Cities: Resource Politics, Migration, and Climate Change*. New York: Berghahn, chapter 10.

Humpert, Malte (2011) 'The Future of the Northern Sea Route: A 'Golden Waterway' or Niche Trade Route?' The Arctic Institute, Center for Circumpolar Studies (Accessed on 4 April 2015) at https://issuu.com/thearcticinstitute/docs/future_northern_sea_route

IRENA (2017) 'Renewable Energy Prospects for the Russian Federation,' April (Accessed on 6 June 2018) at www.irena.org/publications/2017/Apr/Renewable-Energy-Prospects-for-the-Russian-Federation-REmap-working-paper

Jurčová, Alžběta (2017) 'The Consequences of Climate Change: Will Russia Emerge as an Unlikely Winner from Lack of Action?' BlogActive EU, 10 July (Accessed 5 May 2018) at http://europeum.blogactiv.eu/2017/07/10/the-consequences-of-climate-change-will-russia-emerge-as-an-unlikely-winner-from-lack-of-action/

Klimenko, Ekaterina (2016) 'Russia's Arctic Security Strategy: Still Quiet in the High North,' SIPRI, 48, February (Accessed 5 May 2018) at https://www.sipri.org/publications/2016/sipri-policy-papers/russias-arctic-security-policy-still-quiet-high-north.

Laruelle, Marlene (2013) *Russia's Arctic Strategies and the Future of the Far North*. New York: Routledge.

Poberezhskaya, Marianna (2016) *Communication Climate Change in Russia: State and Propaganda*. London: Routledge.

Reisser, Coline (2017) 'Russia's Arctic Cities: Recent Evolution and Drivers of Change,' in Orttung, Robert, ed., *Sustaining Russia's Arctic Cities: Resource Politics, Migration, and Climate Change*. New York: Berghahn, chapter 1.

Roshydromet (2014) 'Second Report of Roshydromet on Climate Changes and Consequences for the Territory of the Russian Federation' (Accessed on 5 May 2018) at https://public.wmo.int/en/media/news-from-members/second-roshydromet-assessment-report-climate-change-and-its-consequences

Scott, Shirley (2012) 'The Securitisation of Climate Change in World Politics: How Close have We Come and would Full Securitisation Enhance the Efficacy of Global Climate Change Policy?' *Review of European Community and International Environmental Law*, Vol. 21, No. 3, pp. 220–230.

Smith, Laurence and Scott Stephenson (2013) 'New Trans-Arctic Shipping Routes Navigable by Midcentury,' *Proceedings of the National Academy of Sciences*, Vol. 110, pp. 4871–4872.

Stephenson, Scott (2017) 'Access to Arctic Urban Areas in Flux: Opportunities and Uncertainties in Transport and Development,' in Orttung, Robert, ed., *Sustaining Russia's Arctic Cities: Resource Politics, Migration, and Climate Change*. New York: Berghahn, chapter 8.

Tynkkunen, Nina (2010) 'A Great Ecological Power in Global Climate Policy? Framing Climate Change as a Policy Problem in Russian Public Discussion,' *Environmental Politics*, Vol. 10, No. 2, pp. 179–195.

U.S. Geological Survey (2008) 'Circum-Arctic Resource Appraisal: Estimates of Undiscovered Oil and Gas North of the Arctic Circle' USGS Fact Sheet 2008–2049 (Accessed 5 May 2018) at https://pubs.usgs.gov/fs/2008/3049/fs2008-3049.pdf.

UNFCCC (2015) 'Russian Federation Submission of Intended Nationally Determined Contributions' (Accessed 5 May 2018) at https://www4.unfccc.int/sites/submissions/indc/Submission%20Pages/submissions.aspx.

Wilson Rowe, Elana (2013) 'Climate Science, Russian Politics and the Framing of Climate Change,' *WIREs Climate Change*, Vol. 4, No. 5, pp. 457–465.

Wilson Rowe, Elena (2017) 'The Arctic in Moscow,' in Orttung, Robert, ed., *Sustaining Russia's Arctic Cities: Resource Politics, Migration, and Climate Change*. New York: Berghahn, chapter 2.

Yablokov, Alexey (2010) 'The Environment and Politics in Russia,' *Russian Analytical Digest*, Vol. 79, pp. 2–4.

26
CAUCASIAN CHESS OR THE GREATEST GEOPOLITICAL TRAGEDY OF THE TWENTIETH CENTURY

Lilia A. Arakelyan

The meaning of the concept of security is constantly changing due to technological progress and globalisation. There is no single definition of the term security; however, the traditional approach to security in International Relations during the Cold War era has focused on military aspects of national security, mainly associated with the state's sovereignty and independence, in regard to sustaining the conventional balance of power in world politics. While for realists of all strands, world politics is a constant struggle among nations over power and security in the absence of an international authority, liberals argue that cooperation is a key to maintain peace among the states in an anarchic world. Meanwhile, a broader understanding of security that goes beyond the military-political element of the subject includes economic, environmental, cultural, human, ideological, societal and other aspects. For instance, the state's security concerns can reflect the nation's economic power, if the poor countries' security needs would be the provision of food and clean water, the developing countries may deal with ethnic conflicts and military interventions, and the developed countries may face industrial espionage, cyberwar or pollution. Moreover, states' perception of security concerns may vary depending on regime types, whereas current threat of terrorism can be regarded as either a threat to the very existence of the nation or a legitimate tool of one's foreign policy (Spiegel, Matthews, Taw, and Williams, 2009, 239). With the changing nature of threats, the concept of security in International Relations can no longer be associated solely with the military aspect of the subject and must include new elements that will reflect current issues and challenges in world politics.

Prior to discussing Moscow's security policy in the Caucasus, it is useful to examine Russia's security challenges from a historical perspective. The geographic placement of Russia and its desire to expand to the south towards the open sea (Black Sea) can be considered as one of the most decisive factors in Russian foreign and security policy in the Caucasus starting with the Tsarist conquest of the region in the seventeenth century (see Figure 26.1). Hence, regional location plays a vital role in whether neighbours will be strong or weak, many or few, whereas the topography of the area determines the nature of those relations with neighbouring states (Spykman, 1938, 213). Hegemony over the Black Sea steppe was crucial for Tsarist Russia in determining the political fate of Moldavia and Walachia in the West and the Caucasus in the East. However, steppe colonisation carried heavy protection costs since it was an apple of discord among the Crimean Khanate, the Ottoman Empire,

Figure 26.1 Caucasus Mountains Map
Source: FreeWorldMaps.net

Poland-Lithuania, and Russia. Consequently, the main feature of Russian state policy from the reign of Ivan the Terrible (1533–1584) to Peter the Great (1689–1725) was an attempt to control the steppe despite the challenge by the Tatar Khans and the Ottomans (Arakelyan, 2017, 83). Nevertheless, what began as a defensive policy of Russia's security changed over the course of the eighteenth century into an expansionist approach that has dominated the state's foreign policy in the region over the last four centuries.

The Caucasus has always occupied a special place not only in Russian politics but also in its literature. Gavrila Derzhavin, Aleksandr Griboedov, Aleksandr Pushkin, Mikhail Lermontov, and Leo Tolstoy just to name a few prominent Russian writers and thinkers inspired by the rough natural beauty of the region, which they depicted in their work. However, for some of those writers, the Caucasus represented also a violent land in need of a taming hand. After all, Russians believed that the locals epitomised a warrior culture, no wonder that the conquest of the Caucasus became the longest-running military conflict in its history. Charles King writes that more than two generations of generals and soldiers were consumed with the battle that affected Russian culture and Moscow's geopolitics (King, 2013). Yet, the North Caucasian territory (the part of Russia that considered to bridge Europe with Asia) never produced a modern nation-state, unlike the South Caucasus where three nation-states were formed as Armenia, Azerbaijan, and Georgia.

Moreover, the North Caucasian Federal District, one of the most ethnically and geographically diverse regions of the Russian Federation, was colonised by Tsarist Russia in the nineteenth century and has been a subject of imperial conquest and local resistance for centuries – before, during, and after the annexation by the Empire. The region still presents governance and counterterrorism challenges to the Putin administration, since the resistance movement was superseded by Islamic extremism[1] that allows Russia security forces to undertake counterterrorist operations often marked by human rights violation. According to the Human Right Watch report, Russian law enforcement and security forces, involved in counter-insurgency, often treating all adherents of Salafism, an Islamic religious denomination in Dagestan, as criminals, and, in general, pursue ruthless counter-insurgency methods (Lokshina, 2016).

With this in mind, Russian security policy in the Caucasus[2] can be analysed through the analytical lenses of what Barry Buzan calls regional security complex, which holds that, in order to study the national security of a given state, we should look at the international pattern of security interdependence in which it is meshed (Buzan, 1991, 187). Moscow's security approach in the North and South Caucasus should be viewed as an issue of regional security, since the primary interests of Russia, Turkey, Iran, and the European Union (EU) are situated in the region in the spheres of military and economic security. Moreover, given the rise of Islamic extremism in the North Caucasus, the latter has been a source of instability for Russia since the Tsarist conquest of the region during the period of 1600–1850s, Moscow will be viewed not only as an actor but also as a target in terms of security and its counter-insurgency efforts in the region.

Russian traditional foreign policy in the Caucasus

After the end of the Cold War, the concepts of security and security threats underwent significant transformations due to the change from bipolarity to unipolarity, and more recently to multipolarity within the international system. The collapse of the bipolar security order initiated a balance between the economic, political, and military requirements of security, as well as brought attention of International Relations scholars and policymakers upon the institutions and international regimes. In addition, the emergence in the international system of newly independent states, which had little experience in enforcing national security on their own, presented a challenge for Russia and the West to maintain a partnership after the disintegration of the Soviet Union. According to regional complex theory, there is a difference 'between the system level interplay of the global powers, whose capabilities enable them to transcend distance, and the subsystem level interplay of lesser powers whose main security environment is their local region' (Buzan and Wæver, 2003, 9). As the following analysis suggests, Russia's security policy in the Caucasus presents a clear example of Moscow's ability to create security interdependence within the region, since local players' securitisation and/or desecuritarisation are so interlinked that their security issues cannot be examined apart from one another. In addition, this chapter uses four levels of analysis: domestic level, state-to-state relations, region's interaction with neighbouring regions, and the role of global powers in the regions to examine Russia's security policy in the Caucasus.

The Russian expansion into the Caucasus that was concluded in the nineteenth century was meant to strengthen the Empire's presence on the Black Sea coast, in order to have a gateway to the Mediterranean. It coincided with the decline of the Ottoman Empire and the fading power of Persia. The Greater Caucasus, from a geopolitical perspective, was an insecure frontier that had been considered dangerous to Russians, as well as providing opportunities to weaken Iran and Turkey. The region served as a buffer zone among the three major powers bordering it: Russia, Turkey, and Iran, which had competed to establish its influence in the Caucasus over the prior three centuries.

It is no surprise that the Caucasus has long been a region of geopolitical struggle between the East and the West, since it is situated between two economically and strategically important regions, the Caspian Basin and the Black Sea. The outside actors, Turkey, Iran, Russia, Britain, and Germany, tried to invade the land, assimilate the local people, and exploit the natural resources of the area. Throughout the nineteenth century, Russia was seen by Western states as an equal partner; however, with the creation of the Soviet Union in 1917, when a revolutionary regime was established on the European landmass with the intention to change the state system and to erase the class barriers, the perception of Russia by the outside world changed. As previously discussed, the original military aspects of security were changed to include political, economic, social, and environmental threats (Buzan, Wæver, and de Wilde, 1998). Considering that the theory of regional security complexes focuses on the four levels of relations in the region: the vulnerability of the individual states in the region, the relations between the states in the region, the interaction of the region with the neighbouring regions, and the role of global superpowers in the region, it becomes clear that Bolsheviks desperately needed to be recognised not only by the outside world but also by the nations within the Russian Empire.

Thus, one of the hallmarks of Soviet foreign policy became a principle of self-determination of nations within the Russian Empire, although Vladimir Lenin used this concept selectively, mainly to destroy the Tsarist regime. After the Bolsheviks' victory, when the new Soviet government was able to bring back into the Union the former imperial territories, including the Caucasian states, Lenin found the idea of establishment of ethno-territorial federalism attractive, since it enabled his government to rebuild damaged Russia's authority and to win political loyalty in the ethnic Russian regions. Bolsheviks used the Tsarist 'divide-and-rule' strategy in order to undercut organised and effective opposition to the Soviet regime, by tailoring the boundaries among the Soviet states according to their loyalty to communist principles and their government rather than by reflecting their ethno-national make-up. Thus, administrative territorial divisions formed in 1917–1918 represented one of the most powerful tools of Soviet foreign and security policy, which overlapped traditional territories and administrative boundaries to create 'fifth columns' within the Union to foment ethnic conflicts and divisions in the Caucasus, as well as in other parts of the USSR (Arakelyan, 2017, 100). In regard to the Caucasus, in order to tighten its grip on the region, over the centuries Tsarist Russia, the Soviet government, and lately Putin's administration have all instigated hostility among the local actors, while St. Petersburg and then Moscow served as a saviour of last resort to 'solve' all the disputes among the regional rivals. For instance, in the Caucasus, there were quite a few issues to unravel thanks to the Stalin legacy, such as the Nagorno-Karabakh conflict, the disputes over South Ossetia and Abkhazia, as well as the Soviet crimes perpetrated against the Chechen people followed by the two Chechen Wars in 1994–2004. On February 23, 1944, Joseph Stalin deported one million Chechens to Siberia and Central Asia, under the charge that they were Nazi sympathisers. One-third of the population died on the journey, others did not survive the exile.

The peculiarity of the Russian security approach in the Caucasus has rested on the concept of great pragmatism borrowed by the Soviet government from Tsarist authorities. An example of this pragmatism can be seen in the formation of the Nagorno-Karabakh Autonomous Oblast in July 1923 that was followed by more than two years of intense argument among Nariman Narinamov and Alexander Miasnikian (representing, respectively, the newly formed governments of Soviet Azerbaijan and Soviet Armenia) and Sergo Ordzhonikidze and Sergei Kirov (the emissaries of Central Soviet power in the Caucasus), Georgi Chiherin (the Soviet People's Commissar for Foreign Affairs), and Joseph Stalin (People's Commissar for the Affairs of Nationalities at the time). The first settlement was to recognise the disputed territories of Zangezur and Nakhichevan as integral parts of Soviet Armenia and grant Nagorno-Karabakh, with a predominantly Armenian population, the right to self-determination,[3] the latter was further confirmed by a decision of the plenary session of the Caucasian Bureau of the Russian Communist Party Central Committee

(Kavbiuro) on June 3, 1921. However, under pressure from Stalin, whose main concerns were to appease Kemal Ataturk and Azerbaijan with its oil-rich resources and the truculent Muslim population, which was being subdued by the Bolsheviks, the final decision to attach Karabakh and Nakhichevan (the latter located on Armenia's southwestern side) to Azerbaijan was made at another plenary session of Kavbiuro on July 5, 1921 (Zverev, 1996, 18–19). Thus, the ethnic Armenian region situated in the heart of Azerbaijan was given to Baku as a way of cementing the Kremlin's role as arbiter between the two nations.

To analyse the dispute over Abkhazia, one should consider the ethnic affiliations of the peoples concerned. Thus, the Abkhazians are closely related to the Abazinians, who live in the foothills of the northwest Caucasus, and distantly to both the Circassians and the Ubykhs. The latter along with many Circassians, Abkhazians, and other North Caucasian people migrated (by some accounts they were forcefully removed) to the Ottoman Empire following Russia's annexation of the North Caucasus in 1864 (Hewitt, 1996, 190–194). It is important to add that Abkhazian rulers were in nominal vassalage to various Georgian kingdoms and princedoms until Abkhazia came under the control of Tsarist Russia's in 1810, when administrative regions were formed and altered in various ways thereafter. Despite the fact that an independent Soviet Socialist Republic of Abkhazia was proclaimed on March 31, 1921, this status lasted until 1931, when the republic was incorporated into the Georgian state as an autonomy and the Abkhaz alphabet was changed to a Georgian base by 1944–1945. Furthermore, all Abkhazian schools were closed and replaced by Georgian ones, and the Abkhaz language was banned from administration and publication. Abkhazians also made a few attempts to secede from Georgia and join Russia during the period of the Soviet rule (Potier, 2001, 10).

Ossetians were Christianised in the nineteenth century as a result of ongoing political and cultural alliances with Russia and migrated from the North Caucasus to the neighbouring region, which is now South Ossetia. Ossetians were always a majority within their own territory and fought against Georgians in support of Bolsheviks. In 1922, the Bolsheviks divided Ossetia between the South Ossetian autonomous region in Georgia and North Ossetian autonomous region in Russia. On the one hand, South Ossetians always considered Russians as their allies against Georgians, on the other, the latter conceived of Ossetians as late-coming colonists lacking the Abkhaz's historical roots (Horowitz, 2005, 92). After Georgia accepted new laws aimed to restore a national identity in 1989, the Ossetians, who did not speak Georgian, reacted in a series of protests and violent clashes as well as voted to upgrade South Ossetia's autonomous status within Georgia. In order to oppress the Ossetian opposition, Gamsarkhudia organised a march of Georgian citizens on the South Ossetian capital, Tskhinvali. However, Soviet troops prevented large-scale clashes, although there were numerous small-scale clashes between two ethnic groups (Horowitz, 2005, 96). Ossetians continued to demand for more autonomous and, on September 20, 1990, declared South Ossetia a democratic republic within the USSR (Potier, 2001, 14).

Post-Soviet regional security in the Caucasus

The demise of the Soviet Union left institutional, political, and power vacuums in post-Soviet space. In the case of the South Caucasus, weakened state structures along with political and economic crises, as well as centuries-old animosities between local ethnic groups, have created permissive conditions for the outbreak of ethnic conflict in the region. As a result, despite the fact that Russia, along with the key external actors in the region – Turkey Iran, the EU, and the United States – has tried to establish new approaches to conflict management in the region, a nationalist genie came out of the bottle and there was no way to put it back.

Current Russian security policy in the Caucasus features the similar trends that were used before: the policy of *prestige, leadership,* and *provocation*. Mr. Putin approved a new national security strategy for the Russian Federation on December 31, 2015. According to the prestige and leadership strategies, the Russian government is not only solving all the important international problems with which the United States and the EU are not able to deal but also taking care of maintaining 'peace' in the former Soviet space. While we will analyse the policy of provocation below, it is worth mentioning that Vladimir Putin follows in the footsteps of its spiritual masters, such as Empress Catherine, in seeking to re-establish Russia as a great nation in the world and the leader in the former USSR territory, including the Caucasus, to show the state's prestige and leadership in the international system. Thus, the current Russian government also turned its gaze inwards rather than westwards when it came to deal with civil or military disobedience in its former empire.

Meanwhile, the Soviet government's behaviour in the dispute over the Nagorno-Karabakh region during Gorbachev's rule was very suspicious, to say the least. Existing literature on ethnic conflicts in the former USSR focuses on the role of the KGB, stating that the conflict had occurred under mysterious circumstances not without the participation of the KGB's Fifth Chief Directorate that was responsible for the infiltration of minority groups within the Soviet Union (see Hill and Jewett, 1994; Leitzinger, 1997; Shafir, 1995).

This chapter adds to the existing literature by proposing that the Russian government is successfully continuing the policy of *provocation* of its predecessor and has been intervening in the conflict over the Nagorno-Karabakh territory in such a way to promote its escalation and continuation instead of cessation. Russia provides weapons to Armenia at a discount as its Collective Security Treaty Organisation (CSTO) partner and maintains its military base in Gyumri. Simultaneously, Moscow supplied over 80 per cent of the armaments recently purchased by Azerbaijan, citing 'a strategic partnership' with the two Transcaucasian countries, and, arguably, using arms trade to maintain parity while assuming the role of a peacekeeper in the region. It is safe to suggest that the Kremlin uses its strategy of *provocation* to maintain *leadership* and *prestige* not only in world politics but also in the Near Abroad with the intention to decline the outside actors' aspirations through pressures.

The North Caucasus

With the fall of the Iron Curtain, Russia lost more than 20 per cent of the Soviet territory, almost half of the population of the USSR, and quite a few strategic regions, including resource-rich Caucasus and South Asia (Arakelyan, 2017). Although, Boris Yeltsin, then the head of the Russian Soviet Socialist Federative Republic, gave regional leaders a green light to acquire as much sovereignty as they could 'swallow' in 1990, Moscow could not afford losing a tiny, oil-rich province in the North Caucasus, Chechnya, whose new leader, Dzhokhar Dudaev, proclaimed independence from Russia as soon as he came to power in 1991. In the beginning, the Soviet Russian government, just fresh from surviving an attempted coup d'état, did not pay much attention to Dudayev's proclamations. However, after the dissolution of the Soviet Union in 1991, the Provisional Council of the Chechen Republic, led by Umar Avturkhanov, the pro-Russian head of the Upper Terek region, was appointed to act as a counterweight to Dzhokhar Dudaev. Avturkhanov appealed to the Russian government for support when on August 2, 1994, fighting broke out between supporters and opponents of Dudaev. As a result, Boris Yeltsin, then the president of the Russian Federation, signed a decree to restore constitutional law and order across Chechnya. On December 11, 1994, Russian troops crossed the border into the region, war had been declared that lasted a decade, and considered to be one of the most brutal in contemporary history that created severe instability in the Caucasus (Muratov, Shchekhochikhin, and Sokolov, 2014).

Meanwhile, since the mid-1990s, radical Islamists from the North Caucasus, spurred by historical grievances, have been behind the majority of terrorist attacks that hit Russia's main cities. Chechnya, Ingushetia, Kabardino-Balkaria, and Dagestan republics have been an Al-Qaida's hotbed in the region with transnational ties between Islamist militants across the North Caucasus and their Arab and Central Asian counterparts (Dugulin, 2016). The decline of the Caucasus Emirate, and the formation of a new Islamic State's governorate, Vilayat Kavkaz (the Caucasus Province), in June 2015, created a new power shift in the North Caucasus. While most insurgent groups in the region had sworn their allegiance to the Islamic State, there are still small groups in Kabardino-Balkaria and Dagestan that remained loyal to the Caucasus Emirate. The strict security measures undertaken by the pro-Russian President of Chechnya Ramzan Kadyrov shifted the Islamist insurgency's operational centre to Dagestan, and with Russia's involvement in the Syrian conflict, both the Islamic State and Al-Qaida have called for continued attacks against Russia. Yet, there is also a threat of the potential return of violent extremists who had been radicalised by the Islamic State of Iraq and Syria (ISIS) in Syria and Iraq. According to the Soufan Group, there is a significant rise of foreign fighters from the former Soviet states traveling to Syria and Iraq to join the Islamic State and other violent groups in the region. Some estimates suggest a near 300 per cent increase in known fighters since 2014 ('Foreign Fighters', 2015).

We shall note that Soviet policies of the twentieth century contributed to the present instability in the North Caucasus. The Soviet government formed the autonomous republics for ethnic groups, codifying ethnic divisions in the region, and thus ultimately planted the seeds for interethnic animosity. For instance, many Chechens found their land distributed upon their return from the exile, which, in return, inflamed many interethnic tensions (Laub, 2005).

The South Caucasus

As mentioned above, another tool of Russia's security policy in the Caucasus is *provocation*, when the Kremlin instigates one or more independent actors, in this case, Armenia, Azerbaijan, and Georgia, to commit acts that are then will be condemned, and followed by the desired counter-reaction. As a matter of fact, *provocation* is followed by *cover-ups*, when Moscow seems to be neutral, but will employ 'peacekeepers' to keep the rival countries under its radar. Thus, Russian troops appear at the scene as 'mediators' to pacify the conflict they caused.

The South Caucasus during the last 30 years has mainly been associated with frozen conflicts. The region remains war-torn in Nagorno-Karabakh, Ossetia, and Abkhazia. Moreover, a sharp escalation in fighting between Armenia and Azerbaijan over the disputed territory of Nagorno-Karabakh in 2014–2016 is considered to be the deadliest since the two states signed a ceasefire in 1994. Despite the strategic alliance between Moscow and Yerevan, Russia pursues political-military cooperation with Azerbaijan, which means that the Kremlin will be hesitant to defend Armenia in case of war with its neighbour. There is speculation that Putin offered to return some part of Artsakh to Azerbaijan if the country joins the Eurasian Union. For instance, during the four-day war in April 2016, which considered to be an unprecedented escalation of the Nagorno-Karabakh conflict, both sides accused each other in launching the military action. Given that Armenia defeated Azerbaijan in 1994 and since then controls not only Nagorno-Karabakh but also the surrounding territories, it seems clear that Baku took the initiative and managed to shift the front line in its favour. The recent escalation of the conflict between Yerevan and Baku is beneficial for Moscow, since it will definitely impede the current cooperation between the West and Azerbaijan in the energy sector and will highlight Russia's role as a peacemaker and a guarantor of the stability in the South Caucasus. After all, the fighting ended as suddenly as it began, and President Vladimir Putin held telephone conversations with then President of Armenia, Serzh Sargsyan, and President of Azerbaijan, Ilham Aliyev. The latter used the symbolic victory to boost his declining popularity in the country and to divert attention from the difficult socio-economic situation in Azerbaijan.

There is a possibility that Azerbaijan did not act alone, since the Kremlin has been trying to enhance its influence over the region for quite a while to no avail with the exception of Armenia, which, besides being a member of the Moscow-led Eurasian Economic Union, is a traditional Russia's ally and heavily depends on Moscow in the military, economic, and political spheres. Thus, to strengthen its grip on power in the South Caucasus, Russia needed to change the status quo and the format of the ceasefire in Nagorno-Karabakh to impose a resolution on the warring sides, including the introduction of Russian peacekeeping forces in the conflict zone, which only Moscow could guarantee. Recently, Azerbaijan became the 17th largest importer of conventional weapons and bought more than 80 per cent of its weapons from Russia, the main strategic ally of Armenia. Moreover, Moscow sold the Smerch and Solnsepek fire systems that Azerbaijan used against Armenian side in the four-day war, as well as T90S tanks, Mi-35M helicopters, BMP-3 armoured vehicles, and other military equipment to Baku (Galstyan, 2018). It is important to note that the four-day war occurred while the Presidents of Armenia and Azerbaijan were in Washington D.C. at the nuclear summit, and despite the fact that Putin immediately called for the armed clashes to cease, Moscow let the fighting to run its course. Yerevan, one of the members of the military-political bloc, did not receive any support from its allies in the Collective Security Treaty Organisation, despite the continued escalation of the fighting. Suddenly, the Russian media (not Armenian or Azerbaijani) announced the ceasefire, which was reached between the chiefs of staff of Armenia and Azerbaijan during their meeting in the Russian capital (Jarosiewicz and Falkowski, 2016). Moscow not only managed to pose itself as a conciliator, and to prove the powerlessness of the Organization for Security and Co-operation (OSCE) Minsk group, but also gained the popularity among the citizens of the de facto state Nagorno-Karabakh, who over the span of 30 years see Russia as their protector and might follow the fate of Abkhazians and South Ossetians in the near future.

The regional security complex includes the principles of power, rivalry, and alliances among the key actors in the region. The cooperation or hostility at the regional level is impacted by historical and political factors, and material conditions. Georgia, for instance, remains the country where Russia exercises its so-called hybrid tactics, including the use of military force, diplomatic pressure using Moscow's control over the two breakaway regions Abkhazia and South Ossetia, and economic dependencies as the means to punish or reward Tbilisi. Despite the fact that Georgia signed the Association Agreement with the EU in 2013, and established a visa-free regime in 2016, Tbilisi is doing its best not to aggravate Moscow, in order to avoid the fate similar to that of Ukraine. The 2008 Russian-Georgian War left a sense of distrust between Tbilisi and Moscow and the two breakaway states, Abkhazia and South Ossetia that are under Kremlin's control. In fact, the Georgian government treats these conflicts as Moscow's attempts to continue its assertive foreign and security policy in the South Caucasus rather than the struggle for independence by Abkhazians and Ossetians.

Abkhazia won a secessionist war with Georgia in 1992–1993, and formally declared independence in 1999. After the Russia-Georgia War of 2008, Russia became one of the few states which formally recognised Abkhazian independence. Moreover, in 2014, Moscow and Sukhumi signed a 'strategic partnership' agreement, thus establishing official ties between Russia and Abkhazia in the social, economic, and humanitarian spheres. In addition, the agreement also foresaw a joint 'defence and security' space with a unified group of Russian-Abkhazian forces. As a result, the Russian influence on the region's economic, political, and social developments cannot be underestimated.

South Ossetia proclaimed its independence from Georgia in 1991 and is recognised by five states, including Russia, Venezuela, Nicaragua, Nauru, and Tuvalu. In 2011, Moscow and Tskhinvali signed a 49-year agreement allowing Russia to build a new military base (with about 4,000 Russian troops) on its territory, while the Kremlin continues to exercise total control over the de facto state.

Analysing the regional security complex in the Caucasus

Arguably, the ex-Soviet bloc states of Central and Eastern Europe considered Soviet Russia as the main guarantor of stability and peace in the region over the seven decades of its existence. With the fall of the Iron Curtain in 1991, the international choices and political behaviour of the former Soviet states (the FSU states) have changed. Whereas some of the states became members of the EU or maintain close relations with the West (the Baltic states, Georgia, Ukraine), others joined the Moscow-led Eurasian Union (Armenia, Belarus, Kazakhstan, Kyrgyzstan), and finally, the rest of the former Soviet republics are either playing off both sides against each other to maintain a favourable foreign policy (Azerbaijan), or are governed by friendly authoritarian regimes and present no threat to the Kremlin's security policies in the region (the Central Asian states). The changing nature of the international system, which shifted from bipolarity to unipolarity after the end of the Cold War, and then headed towards a multipolar world order after Putin's Russia gained economic and political power in the beginning of the 2000s, in addition to the rise of the BRICS countries, contributed to the continuation of the Kremlin's foreign and security approach in the Caucasus, that featured a 'divide-and-rule policy', adopted by the Tsarist Russia in the nineteenth century. This well-calculated strategy ensured imperial peace and cemented hostility among the regional actors, who, instead of rebelling against the Russians, fought with each other.

Consequently, the regional security complex in the Caucasus is built, in part at least, on enmity between Armenia and Azerbaijan due to the Nagorno-Karabakh conflict, between Georgia and Russia (which controls Abkhazia and South Ossetia) over the two de facto states, and among the North Caucasian nations, such as the Chechens, Dagestani, and Ingushetians, and Russians over the discriminatory policies of the Kremlin, as well as the terrorist threat. The Caucasus represents a classic example of the interrelatedness of security concerns, which defines the security of a given state as directly related to that of other states situated in the same region.

Russia as the top target of Jihadists

The security environment in the South Caucasus is also affected by Islamic radicalisation in the Middle East and the North Caucasus. For instance, the Islamic influences from Iran (Shia) and Turkey (Sunni) create new dividing lines between Azerbaijani Shia and Sunni Muslims. Thus, Azerbaijan, one of the three states of the South Caucasus, found itself on the edge of religiously inspired civil protest. In November 2015, Azerbaijani law enforcement carried out a special operation in Nardaran, a township located 25 kilometres (15 miles) northeast of the capital's centre, to break the backbone of the Muslim Unity Group, a military Shiite organisation. The authorities seized from the group's members four sub-machine guns, 12 grenades, 3 explosive devices, and 10 Molotov cocktails. Two police officers and four extremists were killed during the operation, the group's Shiite cleric and leader, Taleh Bagirov, was arrested along with 14 accomplices, which led to mass protests in Nardaran (Suleimanov, 2015).

The Caucasus region has become an important recruiting ground for the Islamic State. As mentioned previously, the number of foreign fighters from the former Soviet Union has increased since June 2014: from the Russian Federation alone, 2,400 Russians had joined the Islamic State by September 2015. The Soufan Group calculates that there are at least 4,700 fighters from the post-Soviet space. The majority of fighters come from Chechnya and Dagestan (the North Caucasus). However, some estimates have put the combined total from Azerbaijan and Georgia at around 500 (Paul, 2015). There is a general pattern within Azerbaijan by which Islamic State recruits come from several towns such as Sumgait, Shabran, and Quasar. According to other sources, an estimated 1,500 people from Azerbaijan joined the Islamic State in Syria, and many of them are returning home where they pose a serious threat not only to their nations but also to other neighbouring states. Anton Bredikhin claims that many young Azerbaijanis have been encouraged by ISIS to believe that if they serve its ranks, they will liberate the Nagorno-Karabakh region, which is controlled by Armenians since the end of the war in 1994 (Bredikhin, 2015). It is important to note that many of the fighters from Azerbaijan came from predominantly Sunni districts in the northern part of the country (Azerbaijan is traditionally two-thirds Shiia), and they claim that the Azerbaijani government itself, with it harsh policy against the Salafis, is driving them into the hands of ISIS (Goble, 2015).

Pankisi, situated in northeastern Georgia, is home to 8,000 ethnic Kists, a Muslim minority group related to Chechens in the North Caucasus which had already gained a reputation as a refuge for militants during the Chechen Wars in the 1990s–2000s. Currently, Pankisi has once again become a jihadist hotbed. Sergey Lavrov, the Russian Foreign Minister, claims that the Islamic State of Levant and Syria fighters are using the town as its training base 'to train, rest and restock their supplies' (Lavrov, 2016). While Zurab Abashidze, the Georgian Prime Minister's Special Envoy for relations with Russia, rejected these claims, stating that the Georgian government is in control of the region, he also admitted that up to 30 locals from the area travelled to Syria to join the Islamic State ('ISIS Fighters', 2016). Moreover, one of the most famous commanders of the Islamic State, Abu Omar al-Shishani, came from a small village in Georgia's Pankisi.

The Islamic State has created a powerful recruitment machine that attracts a global following and encourages Muslims around the world to join them in their battle against Christian and Jewish 'unbelievers' and Western 'crusaders'. While Georgian Muslims (just 10 per cent of the total population) are not traditionally devout, they became an easy target for ISIS because of the Georgian government's failure to develop an appropriate policy on religion that could avert the alienation of Georgian Muslims from the rest of the predominantly Christian country, which, in turn, could prevent their radicalisation. The foreign fighters from Azerbaijan and Georgia are joining ISIS, in order to find the solution to the religious, social, and economic grievances that they face in their home countries.

Conclusion

The Caucasus is still the most turbulent region for Russia. The security concerns of the three Transcaucasian states are linked to the neighbouring countries, while for Moscow, Tehran, and Ankara, the Greater Caucasus remains an important part of their foreign and security policies. In this chapter, we have analysed Russian security policy in the Caucasus through the analytical lens of Buzan's regional security complex. In order to study the national security of the Kremlin, we examined the international pattern of security interdependence in which it is meshed – the primary military, economic and security interests of Russia, Turkey, Iran, and the EU overlap in the region. In addition, given the rise of Islamic extremism in the North Caucasus, Russia was analysed not only as an actor but also as a target in terms of security-wise and its counter-insurgency efforts in the area. Russia's security policy in the Caucasus presented a clear example of regional security complex theory, since there was a difference between the system-level interplay of Moscow, Tehran, Ankara, and Brussels, whose capabilities enabled them to transcend distance, and the subsystem-level interplay of the South Caucasian and North Caucasian states whose main security environment is their local region. As the following chapter suggested, Russia's security policy in the Caucasus presented an empirical evidence of Moscow's ability to create the security interdependence within the region, since local players' securitarisation and/or desecuritarisation are so interlinked that their security issues cannot be examined apart from one another. We showed that Russia's security policy in the Caucasus is better studied through a four-level analytical framework: domestic level, state-to-state relations, region's interaction with neighbouring regions, and the role of global powers.

Notes

1 The Caucasus Emirate (the local branch of Al-Qaeda) was an Islamist military organisation in the North Caucasus founded by a Chechen separatist warlord, Doku Umarov, in 2007. The group aimed to establish an independent Islamic State in the North Caucasus ruled via sharia law. The Caucasus Emirate declared allegiance to the global jihadi movement in April 2009, but Russia remained the main enemy. By 2015, Russian security forces eliminated the key leaders of the group, including Doku Umarov, virtually destroying the Caucasus Emirate. However, after several North Caucasus commanders transferred their allegiance to Islamic State, Abu Muhammad al-Adnani, an ISIS spokesman, announced the creation of the 'Vilayat Kavkaz', or Caucasus Province, on June 23, 2015.
2 The South and North Caucasus, or the 'Big Caucasus', include Armenia, Azerbaijan, Georgia, the disputed regions of South Ossetia, Abkhazia and Nagorno-Karabakh, and Russia's seven North Caucasus republics: Dagestan, Chechnya, Ingushetia, North Ossetia-Alania, Adygea, Kabardino-Balkaria, and Karachaevo-Cherkessia.
3 At the same meeting, Ordzhonikidze spoke about ceding Nagorno-Karabakh to Armenia; later Stalin did the same in the issue of Pravda of December 4, 1920 (Zverev, 1996, 19).

Bibliography

Arakelyan, Lilia A. (2017) *Russian Foreign Policy in Eurasia: National Interests and Regional Integration*. London, UK: Routledge.
Bredikhin, Anton (2015) 'Ne Otstupaet Azerbaijan', *Nauchnoe Obschestvo Kavkazovedov*, 6 November 2015. Accessed on 15 March 2016. www.kavkazoved.info/news/2015/11/06/ig-otstupaet-v-azerbajdzhan.html
Buzan, Barry (1991) *People, States, and Fear: An Agenda for International Security Studies in the Post-Cold War Era*. Hertfordshire, UK: Harvester Wheatsheaf
Buzan, Barry, Ole Waever, and Jaap de Wilde (1998) *Security: A New Framework for Analysis*. Boulder, Colorado: Lynne Rienner Publishers.
Buzan, Barry and Ole Wæver (2003) *Regions and Power: The Structure of International Security*. Cambridge, UK: Cambridge University Press.
Dugulin, Riccardo (2016) 'The Emerging Islamic State Threat in the North Caucasus', *Global Risk Insights*. 3 April. Accessed on 3 July 2018. https://globalriskinsights.com/2016/04/the-emerging-islamic-state-threat-in-the-north-caucasus/

FreeWorldMaps.net (2018) 'Caucasus Mountains Map', Accessed on 12 September 2018. www.freeworldmaps.net/asia/caucasus/map.html
'Foreign Fighters' (2015) 'Foreign Fighters: An Updated Assessment of the Flow of Foreign Fighters into Syria and Iraq', The Soufan Group report, December.
Galstyan, Areg (2018) 'Armenia is Rethinking Relations with Russia', *Intersection*, 30 January. Accessed on 10 July 2018. http://intersectionproject.eu/article/russia-europe/armenia-rethinking-relations-russia
Goble, Pavel (2015) 'ISIS Fighters Returning to Azerbaijan Seen Creating Serious Problems for Baku', *Window on Eurasia-New Series*, 7 November 2015.
Hewitt, B.G. (1996) Abkhazia: A Problem of Identity and Ownership', in John F.R. Wright, Suzanne Goldenberg, and Richard Schofield (eds.), *Transcaucasian Boundaries*. New York, NY: St. Martin's Press.
Hill, Fiona and Pamela Jewett (1994) *Back in the USSR': Russia's Intervention in the Internal Affairs of the Former Soviet Republics and the Implications for United States Policy Toward Russia*. Washington, DC: The Brookings Institution.
Horowitz, Shale (2005) *From Ethnic Conflict to Stillborn Reform: The Former Soviet Union and Yugoslavia*. College Station: Texas A&M University Press.
International Crisis Group (2016) 'The North Caucasus Insurgency and Syria: An Exported Jihad?' *Report no. 238 Europe and Central Asia*, 16 March.
'ISIS Fighters' (2016) 'ISIS Fighters Use Georgia's Pankisi Gorge to Train & Rest – Lavrov', *RT*, 26 January 2016. Accessed on 31 March 2017. www.rt.com/news/330234-georgia-pankisi-isis-lavrov/
Jarosiewicz, Aleksandra and Maciej Falkowski (2016) 'The Four-Day War in Nagorno-Karabakh', *Osrodek Studiow Wschodnich im. Marka Karpia*, 6 April. Accessed on 8 June 2016. www.osw.waw.pl/en/publikacje/analyses/2016-04-06/four-day-war-nagorno-karabakh
King, Charles (2013) 'What to Read on the Caucasus', Foreign Affairs, 25 April. Accessed on August 20, 2018
https://www.foreignaffairs.com/articles/eastern-europe-caucasus/2013-04-25/what-read-caucasus
Lavrov, Sergey (2016) 'Lavrov rasskazal ob otdykhe i trenirovkakh boevikov IG v Pankisskom uschel'e', *RosBusinessConsulting (RBK)*, 26 January 2016. Accessed on 31 March 2016 www.rbc.ru/rbcfreenews/56a763599a79475100a12282
Laub, Zachary (2005) 'Instability in Russia's North Caucasus Region', *Council on Foreign Relations*, 13 October. Accessed on 16 September 2017. www.cfr.org/backgrounder/instability-russias-north-caucasus-region
Leitzinger, Antero (1997) 'Kristallnacht' – Russian-Style', in Antero Leitzinger (ed.), *Caucasus and an Unholy Alliance*. Vantaa, Finland: Kirja-Lietzinger.
Lokshina, Tatyana (2016) 'Human Rights Violations in Russia's North Caucasus', *Human Rights Watch* report, 28 January 2016. www.hrw.org/news/2016/01/28/human-rights-violations-russias-north-caucasus
Muratov, Dmitrii, Iurii Shchekochikhin, and Sergei Sokolov (2014) 'Chislo Pogibshikh Neizvestno', *Novaya Gazeta*, N. 139, 10 December 2014. httpspyks://www.novayagazeta.ru/articles/2014/12/10/62288-chislo-pogibshih-neizvestno
Paul, Amanda (2015) 'Foreign Fighters from the Caucasus', *NRT News*, 21 July. http://nrttv.com/EN/birura-details.aspx?Jimare=1358
Potier, Tim (2001) *Conflict in Nagorno-Karabakh, Abkhazia and South Ossetia: A Legal Appraisal*. The Hague, The Netherlands; Boston, MA: Kluwer Law International.
Shafir, Gershon (1995) *Immigrants and Nationalists: Ethnic Conflict and Accommodation in Catalonia, the Basque Country, Latvia and Estonia*. Albany, NY: State of New York.
Spiegel Steven L., E.G. Matthews, J.M. Taw, and K.P. Williams (2009) *World Politics in a New Era*. Oxford, UK: Oxford University Press.
Spykman, Nicolas J. (1938) 'Geography and Foreign Policy, II', *The American Political Science Review*, vol. XXXII, N. 2, April, pp. 213–236.
Suleimanov, Emil A. (2015) 'Azerbaijan, Islamism and Unrest in Nardaran', *The Central Asia-Caucasus Analyst*, 27 December.
https://www.cacianalyst.org/publications/analytical-articles/item/13316-azerbaijan-islamism-and-unrest-in-nardaran.html
Zverev, Alexei (1996) 'Ethnic Conflicts in the Caucasus 1988–1994', in Bruno Coppieters (ed.), Contested Borders in the Caucasus. Brussels, Belgium: VUB University Press.

27
RUSSIAN SECURITY STRATEGY IN CENTRAL ASIA

Graeme Gill and Yelena Nikolayevna Zabortseva

The collapse of the USSR in 1991 transformed Central Asia (CA) into a zone of increased uncertainty in the eyes of Russian policymakers. Historically, this region had been economically and politically tied to Russia, with foreign powers largely excluded. With the Soviet collapse and the independence of the five constituent states – Kazakhstan, Kyrgyzstan, Tajikistan, Turkmenistan and Uzbekistan – and with the large energy resources in the region, it became a zone of geopolitical and geoeconomic competition in a way it had not been before (e.g. Rumer et al., 2017). Domestic regional problems also became more salient. Despite the 'relative peace' that the region had been said to experience since 1991 (Robinson, 2012), it has seen Civil War in Tajikistan, a colour revolution in Kyrgyzstan, civil violence in Uzbekistan, and military conflict or unrest on its borders in Afghanistan and Sinjiang. It is a region of highly authoritarian states with significant levels of corruption, generally weak domestic governance and poor human rights records (Hallgren & Ghiasy, 2017, 8). It is a principal component of the land-based corridors between China, Europe and the Middle East, and is a region of vast differences, underdeveloped infrastructure and significant security issues (Hauff, 2015). It is an area of significant challenge to Russia (e.g. SIPRI, 2015) and one with which it has had strong historic ties. Thus, while Russia's interest in the region has been described as nationalist and chauvinist (MacHaffie, 2010, 374), Russia was bound to seek to protect its interests in the region in the face of these new challenges.

Challenges and interconnections

CA is not specifically identified as a particular focus of foreign policy concern[1] in the most recent Foreign Policy Concept of the Russian Federation (Kontseptsiya, 2016), but it is subsumed within the discussion of the Commonwealth of Independent States (CIS), which is listed first among regional foreign policy priorities, the Shanghai Cooperation Organisation and the Eurasian Economic Union. All of the foreign policy problems identified in the Foreign Policy Conception document are to be found in CA. But what is probably the most important Russian concern, external involvement in CA, is addressed only indirectly, in terms of regional stability.

Significant foreign involvement in CA began in the last years of the Soviet period. This concerned commercial interest in the energy market and revived memories of the 'great game' of the nineteenth century (Fatima & Zafar, 2014; Freire & Kanet, 2010). With independence, this interest became both more active and broader. At the time of the Soviet collapse, the Yeltsin government tried to claim the right to act as general peacekeeper in the CIS. This perception of the countries of the former USSR as being in its sphere of influence was immediately challenged, not only rhetorically by the West but also by the entry of the former Baltic republics into the European Union and North Atlantic Treaty Organisation (NATO) and by the growth of external interest in other states, including those of CA. Most concerning here was the growth of the American presence. One form this took was attempts to support the development of civil society in the countries of the region, action which was not welcomed by the regimes and which Russia blamed for the colour revolution in Kyrgyzstan and elsewhere in the CIS (Bunce & Wolchik, 2011). The American presence gained a military dimension in the lead-up to the 2001 invasion of Afghanistan when the US leased air bases in Uzbekistan and Kyrgyzstan, which lasted until June 2014. More significant has been economic involvement and the associated growth of corruption. Most foreign interest has been in the energy sphere. The large reserves of energy possessed by some of the states of CA – in terms of proven reserves, Kazakhstan is said to rank 12th internationally on oil and 15th on gas, Turkmenistan 45th and 6th, and Uzbekistan 47th and 20th (CIA, n.d.) – have made this region attractive to foreign energy companies seeking to expand their sources of supply (for energy security and the region, see Chapter 15). Foreign involvement has been central to the construction of pipelines to carry both oil and gas from the region to Europe, China and the Indian Ocean bypassing Russia (for the breaking of Russia's monopoly, see Coburn, 2010).

The effect of American involvement is exacerbated by the interest shown in the region by other external powers. Although India has some undeveloped interests in CA (Lee & Gill, 2015), the main potential challenge comes from China. As outlined in Chapter 28, China has major interests in the region. Not only is this seen as a central component of President Xi Jinping's 'belt and road' project, but ever since the collapse of the USSR, China has sought to expand its presence in the region, principally through the projection of Chinese soft power. China's membership of the Shanghai Cooperation Organisation, a body officially meant to enhance cooperation in security, economy and culture (Trofimov, cited in Zabortseva, 2016, 140) rather than to bring about closer integration, reflects this intent to remain involved in the region. While China generally has not sought directly to challenge Russia's influence in the region, Moscow remains wary of Chinese intentions. Most of the countries of the region share Russia's concern about increased Chinese involvement and see Russia as a potential guarantor of stability and protector against this. However, the squeezing of the Russian position with regard to controlling the transit of oil and gas through CA, allied to the imposition of Western sanctions on Russia in 2014, has led Russia to establish closer relations with China (Chenoy & Kumar, 2017, 247), including proposals for a common gas market by 2025 and intensified trade ties. Nevertheless, Moscow remains cautious about Chinese intentions in CA.

Russian concern about external involvement thus has had both economic and geopolitical dimensions. Economically, non-Russian producers compete against Russian producers, and the stronger they are, the more difficult Russia finds it to play a dominating role in the energy market. Foreign involvement in the construction of pipelines is seen as a strategic challenge for Russia, not only because they insert those powers into the region but because they threaten to weaken the existing European dependence upon Russia for their energy supplies, thereby eroding Russia's strategic position. But there is also concern about the political and potential military presence. As well as the fear that external powers may displace Russia from what it sees as its natural role as regional hegemon, and thereby create a shift in the overall geostrategic balance, there is also the fear that external involvement could exacerbate existing problems in the region which the regional states may not be able to control.

One area of concern is that the Western, especially the US, support for grassroots civil society organisations (e.g. Henderson, 2003; Bunce & Wolchik, 2011) will contribute to destabilisation and potentially regime change, both of which are seen as antithetical to Russia's interests. Such instability could both decrease central state controls in the region and increase feelings of popular insecurity, which would strengthen other challenges. One such challenge is terrorism, which Russia acknowledges as a significant issue (Kontseptsiya, 2016, #14; Baev, 2006). CA has been described as a 'sitting duck' for Islamic State (IS), which is claimed to have allocated US$70 million for the organisation of terrorist acts in the Fergana Valley, an area divided both linguistically and politically between Uzbekistan and Tajikistan (Haas, 2016, 214; Akhtar, 2010). These are the two states where Islam has historically had most influence. Several Afghanistan- and Pakistan-based terrorist groups are active in CA, while the growth of IS and other extremist groups in the Middle East and North Africa has had reverberations in CA (UNRCCA, 2015): the Party of Islamic Liberation, the Islamic Movement of Uzbekistan and its splinter group the Islamic Jihad Union, the Islamic Movement of Eastern Turkestan and some other smaller groups have all been present in the region (Akhtar, 2010, 43). In 2015, the UN Security Council's Counter-Terrorism Committee stated that the senior commanders of IS in Syria and Iraq included militants from several of the CA extremist groups (Haas, 2016, 214), while some 4,000 fighters from the Islamic Movement of Uzbekistan are estimated to have been in Afghanistan. The conflict in Afghanistan, where more than 10 million Tajiks, three million Uzbeks and one million Turkmen live (MGIMO, 2017, 232), shows no sign of a negotiated settlement, and the spillover impacts of the conflict continue to be felt across the porous CA borders.

The drug trade has been a major source of funding for terrorist activity in CA. Afghanistan cultivates enough opium to produce approximately 75 per cent of the world's supply, with CA being a transit route for criminal groups smuggling narcotics to markets in Russia and Europe; some 20 per cent of opiates leaving Afghanistan are reported to pass through CA, mainly Tajikistan (UNODC, 2007, 22), while the Fergana Valley is seen as a focus of such international drug trafficking. In recent decades, the number of drug users in CA has skyrocketed with heroin addiction levels rising significantly (Akhtar, 2010, 44; Hamidreza, 2018). This is linked to organised crime, another acknowledged challenge (Kontseptsiya, 2016, #16), and corruption.

Border problems have been significant (ICG, 2011, 10; Kontseptsiya, 2016, #17). Turkmenistan and Azerbaijan have an outstanding dispute over oil and gas resources in the Caspian Sea, about 40 per cent of Kyrgyzstan's border with Uzbekistan remains to be demarcated and is subject to dispute (Nichol, 2010), while the Fergana Valley remains a source of tension. There have been significant disputes between Uzbekistan and Tajikistan, particularly as the latter seeks to free itself from energy dependency on its neighbour (Musiol, 2015, 65). The Tajik-Afghan border area is a constant source of concern, characterised by ethnic communities straddling that border and the fear that this is an avenue for infiltration by jihadi fighters. Access to water supplies remains contentious, particularly in terms of the implications this has for food supply and human welfare (Martin & Angel, 2017). The Tajik Civil War and civil violence in Uzbekistan resulted in large numbers of refugees and displaced persons whose quest for safety overwhelmed formal international borders, generating further worries about the possible infiltration of terrorist elements.

The movement of populations in this way reflects the underlying serious situation with regard to human security concerns. CA's basic human and physical infrastructure has been eroding. All countries are to some degree affected, with the two poorest – Kyrgyzstan and

Table 27.1 Immigration to Russia

	2000	2010	2016
Kazakhstan	124,903	27,862	69,356
Rest of Central Asia	74,127	65,472	149,097
Ukraine	74,748	27,508	178,274
Total	359,330	191,656	575,158

Source: Goskomstat (2018).

Tajikistan –most severely so. Seventy per cent of AIDS cases across CA are linked to intravenous drug use (Hamidreza, 2018, 44–45). International crime groups collude with local ones to transport people to the Middle East or Europe where they enter forced labour or prostitution rings. There have been reports of cases in Tajikistan where children have been trafficked out of the country and subsequently killed for their organs (UNODC, 2007, 40). A wide range of environmental threats to the human right to water and sanitation (HRWS) have also been identified, including desertification, use of harmful insecticides and risks of nuclear pollution (Martin & Angel, 2017, 39). Poor social conditions and associated health issues, especially in rural areas, have been a potent cause of migration, with the region acting as both a transit and source area of such action; according to the Russian Federal Migration Service, in December 2014, over 4.5 million citizens from CA lived in Russia (Cooley, 2017, 7–8). In 2013, Russia was the second largest migrant-receiving state internationally (UN, n.d.). Levels of immigration from the region into Russia have been high throughout the post-Soviet period.

These figures show that the CA region constitutes the largest, if declining, source of legal migration into Russia, providing 55.4 per cent of all immigrants in 2000, 48.7 per cent in 2010 and 38 per cent in 2016. While a proportion of these will be ethnic Russians, many will be of CA nationality, and this feeds into the fears about terrorist infiltration held especially (but not exclusively) by rightist political forces in Russia. The use of illegal workers in Russia has been used to fuel such concerns (for migration, see Bartolomeo et al., 2014).

The Russian diaspora in the countries of CA has been a potentially challenging issue. Repeatedly throughout the post-Soviet period, human rights non-governmental organisations (NGOs) have expressed concern about the violation of the rights of the Russian-speaking populations in the region. The fate of these people has also been a matter of concern to the Russian government, at least rhetorically; the official Russian position is 'to protect the rights and legitimate interests of compatriots living abroad ... so as to enable them to better realise their rights in the countries of residence...' (Kontseptsiya, 2016, #45e & f). On occasions, they have used this to utter veiled threats to neighbouring states about their perceived responsibility to act in defence of such people. The CA states have also at times sought to play the 'diaspora card' in relations with Russia. When political tensions are high, immigration levels to Russia tend to increase, raising associated security concerns.

The continuing degradation of the human environment, especially in terms of environmental problems including guaranteed access to food and water, was seen as threatening not only in terms of people movement, but potentially popular unrest. This was a particular concern given the history of such conflict in the post-Soviet period, including the overthrow of leaders through non-constitutional means in the Tajik Civil War, the Kyrgyz colour revolution of 2005 and the uprising of 2010, and the outbreak of ethnic conflict including in Uzbekistan in 2005 and more generally in the Fergana Valley where Kyrgyzstan, Tajikistan and Uzbekistan intersect. The danger as seen from Moscow was not only that popular mobilisation like that in the 'colour revolutions' could result in regional political instability, but that it could provide a stimulus for oppositional forces within Russia itself.

As well as these potential geopolitical threats, Russia also has an economic interest to protect in the region. Trade with CA amounts to around 4 per cent of Russia's total foreign trade (Sinitsina, 2012, 10) and has been growing in volume; between 2000 and 2016, exports grew from a value of US$7,974 million to US$26,544 million (Rossiya v tsifrakh, 2017, 470). If China is included, this constitutes about 18 per cent of Russian trade; between 2003 and 2014, trade with China increased around five-fold (Chenoy et al., 2017, 247) and has continued to grow. This is also a region of Russian foreign direct investment (FDI). While it is difficult to get exact figures on the scale of FDI because of the extensive use of offshore jurisdictions, official Russian FDI in CA exceeds US$15 billion (MGIMO, 2017, 12) but may in practice be significantly higher (Zabortseva, 2016, 147–152). The Russian desire to maintain its global position as an energy superpower also has implications for CA as Russia has sought to exert control over both the exploitation and shipment of the immense energy reserves in the region; for example, a 2003 agreement saw Russian companies gain rights to all gas produced in Turkmenistan for 25 years (Sussex, 2012, 52). Russia also has a continuing interest in the Baikonur cosmodrome in Kazakhstan for the maintenance of its space program, an issue of considerable strategic importance. This importance for Russia is reflected in the fact that it was not until an agreement was signed to extend the Russian lease until 2050 that agreement could be reached on the Russian-Kazakh border.

CA remains an area of strategic concern for Russia. This is a region with weak states and significant problems, a proliferation of non-state (principally terrorist) actors, and potential external actors that could challenge the dominant position Russia has generally had. It is also a region where the constituent states have been unable to construct lasting international organisations to address common issues. How has Russia reacted to the manifold security challenges in this region?

Strategies for dealing with the region and its challenges

The Russian approach to protecting its security interests in the region is linked to its perception of its place in the world and its broader foreign policy outlook. In the initial post-Soviet period, the Yeltsin administration's focus lay primarily on relations with the West, with the result that CA did not appear as a major area of concern, despite the instability suggested by the outbreak of the Tajik Civil War in 1992. Yeltsin did seek to claim Russia's right to exercise a broadly hegemonic role over the territory of the former Soviet Union, a claim that was rebuffed, and from time to time concern was expressed about the fate of ethnic Russians living outside Russia (Heleniak, 2004, 111–112), but these did not translate into a sustained interest in the region (Allison, 2008). There was more interest when Primakov became Russian foreign minister in 1996, but it was not until the election of Vladimir Putin as president in 2000 and the straining of relations with the West over Ukraine in 2014 that this region gained a higher profile. This was part of Putin's attempt to reorient Russian foreign policy to make the CIS a major priority, a change which promoted CA as an area of foreign policy concern. This does not mean that it displaced the West as the principal focus of Russian interest, but that it was recognised as more important than it had been in the 1990s.

This was accompanied by an ideological shift. Described as a transfer from pro-Western to post-Western (Owen et al., 2018, 289), this is more accurately seen in terms of a rejection of the view that Russia is just like the major states of the West but has a unique history, culture and trajectory that clearly sets it apart from the West. This has been described principally in terms of the concept of 'Eurasianism', which in the view of one observer was a contemporary version of the 'Monroe Doctrine' (Kubicek, 2004, 208), and seemed to gain official status when the Foreign Policy Concept adopted in July 2008 described Russia as a Eurasian rather than a European country (Foreign Policy Concept, 2008), although this did not appear in the 2016 version. Eurasianism sees Russia as being a unique historical and cultural amalgam of Slav, Turkic and Muslim components (Laruelle, 2004, 115) and as having a historically unique role in acting as a bridge between Europe and Asia, with a foot in both camps. The adoption of this view naturally cast Russia as having much in common with CA and, at least in the view of those who accepted Eurasianism (and the extent to which Putin believes in this as opposed to viewing it instrumentally is not clear), elevated this region in importance.

Another ideological aspect of the approach to CA is also rooted in the view that Russia is following a unique path, and this involves the rejection of Western forms of liberal democracy in favour of a claimed political system consistent with Russia's traditions. Sometimes called 'sovereign democracy' (e.g. Suverennaya demokratiya, 2006), although Putin has rarely used this term, this is something that has been common in regimes claiming a special quality for their political systems that accorded with national traditions and differed from the principles of Western democracy. In counterposing its own system to that of the West, Russia gained a rationale not only for not introducing changes that might weaken the authoritarian elements of its own system but also for supporting other regimes that claimed a similar nativist heritage. This has translated into an active policy of supporting such regimes, including in CA, a policy which is paradoxically consistent with Western support for these regimes. In Russia, there has been little official criticism of these regimes for things like human rights abuses or anti-democratic behaviour. The Russian authorities, especially in the wake of the colour revolutions in Georgia, Ukraine and Kyrgyzstan in 2003–2005, have been anxious to do what they could to sustain the existing regimes in power, principally because they have been worried about potential spillover effects in Russia itself. They have also sought to support these regimes through a combination of economic, political, diplomatic and military aid (Ambrosio, 2009).

As well as providing regime support, aid has been significant in addressing some of the region's pressing social problems. According to Russian Foreign Minister Sergei Lavrov, in October 2017, over the preceding decade, Russia had given six billion dollars in aid to the countries of the region (Lavrov, 2017). Russia has financed projects to reduce poverty, improve health outcomes, promote education and ecology (Zolotova, 2018) and upgrade law enforcement agencies. Military assistance has also been extensive, including the provision of military equipment; the training of military officers; joint military exercises; cooperation in the production of military wherewithal such as air defence systems, torpedoes and anti-ship mines (Kumar, 2017); and the deployment of Russian troops in the border area of Tajikistan/Afghanistan in 1993; Russian troops also helped end the Tajik Civil War in 1997. There are also Russian bases in Kazakhstan, Kyrgyzstan and Tajikistan, and Russian troops are stationed in Tajikistan under a 25-year basing agreement (MGIMO, 2017, 225).

An important part of the strategy to maintain stability is collective organisation, and Russia has been active in fostering this in the region. The initial such organisation was the CIS, which was formed at a meeting in Kazakhstan at the time of the end of the Soviet Union. Of the CA states, only Turkmenistan was not a full member, and it was an associate, reflecting its stated desire to be a neutral country. While some may have had aspirations for this to provide the framework for the reconsolidation of a substantial part of the USSR, such hopes were always ill-founded. None of the new states' leaders, including the Russian, was willing to forego their newly found sovereignty in favour of such a transnational organisation, and accordingly the CIS has been little more than a talking shop and has not been an effective vehicle for the pursuit of Russian security concerns in the region.

The most prominent organisation has been the Shanghai Cooperation Organisation established in 2001 and uniting Russia, China, Kazakhstan, Kyrgyzstan, Tajikistan, Uzbekistan, India and Pakistan, with Mongolia, Iran, Belarus and Afghanistan as observer members (there are also six 'dialogue partners': Armenia, Azerbaijan, Cambodia, Nepal, Sri Lanka and Turkey). Most members are, therefore, not from CA, but this is an important collective organisation for the region and one which brings together Russia and China in an organisation that by some is seen as being a challenger to the West (Scholl & Westphal, 2017, 7). It is discussed in Chapter 28.

In 2002, the Collective Security Treaty Organisation (CSTO) was formed, building on a collective security treaty initially signed in 1992 (and which underpinned the role of Russian troops in helping end the Tajik Civil War). In 2018, the CSTO comprised Russia, Armenia, Belarus, Kazakhstan, Kyrgyzstan and Tajikistan, with Afghanistan and Serbia as observer states. In 2006, Uzbekistan joined the CSTO but following a dispute with Tajikistan in which Russia was perceived to support the latter, withdrew in 2012. This organisation, which has been dominated by Russia, which had the largest military and whose military spending far exceeded that of the other members, has been Russia's preferred instrument for regional security cooperation; it is officially described as 'one of the key elements of the current security framework in the post-Soviet space' (Kontseptsiya, 2016, #52). In October 2016, it adopted a 'Collective Security Strategy 2025' which identified anti-terrorism and peacekeeping activities as its major tasks. The formal aim of the organisation was development of the aggregate military capacity of the member-states in order to protect those states from external danger, including from terrorist organisations. To this end, special forces were established, including a collective rapid reaction force in 2009 and a peacekeeping force in 2010. It was also decided that member-states' militaries could purchase Russian weapons at the same price as Russia, a decision designed both to enhance the sale of Russian weaponry and to increase the capacity for military integration. Regular military exercises are conducted, with the aim of improving coordination between the different forces. As a bulwark against external involvement in the region, the CSTO agreed that the official consent of all member-states was required before a military base of a third country could be established on the territory of a member-state. This decision effectively gave Russia (and the other states) a veto power over the establishment of new foreign military bases.

The CSTO has sought the coordination of military activity rather than the integration of national military forces into a single supranational force. It has been reluctant to deploy forces in response to domestic crises in the member-states. For example, when in April 2010 riots broke out in Kyrgyzstan in connection with the ousting of the president from office and two months later ethnic conflict erupted in the south of the country, calls by Kyrgyz leaders for CSTO troops to put down the disturbances were rejected. Some action has been taken with regard to the drug trade (Molchanov, 2015, 143), illegal migration and human trafficking (Nikitina, 2009, 6), the identification of extremist organisations (MGIMO, 2017, 229) and cyber security, but this has not been a particularly active body. In part this has been because of the continued difficulty in getting common agreement in the leading circles of the alliance. Nor has it been called upon to respond to external attack of any sort. So, while on paper it may appear to be an effective military organisation and a counterbalance to NATO or a replacement for the Warsaw Pact (Stratfor, 2009), in practice it has had limited effect or utility in the CA region; one author has described it as 'a weak form of local coordination rather than a robust institution' (Sussex, 2012, 47).

The most comprehensive attempt at collective organisation has culminated in the Eurasian Economic Union (EEU). The idea of a Eurasian Union had been first mooted by Kazakh President Nursultan Nazarbayev in 1994, but it did not gain any momentum until taken up by Vladimir Putin in 2011 (Putin, 2011). Following preparatory work, an EEU Treaty was signed in May 2014 and came into effect on 1 January 2015. The treaty effectively codified the principles that had underpinned the earlier established Customs Union and Single Economic Space, creating free movement of goods, capital and labour and bringing about regulatory harmonisation in some 19 areas of economic activity. There is also a programme stretching into the future to bring other sectors of the economy into such a harmonised structure, culminating in the transformation of the EEU into a more rounded Eurasian Union. This remains a central plank of Russia's approach to the region; according to the 2016 Foreign Policy Conception document, 'Russia considers a key task to be the deepening and widening of integration in the Eurasian Economic Union' (Kontseptsiya, 2016, #51; Putin, 2018).

The EEU comprises Russia, Armenia, Belarus, Kazakhstan and Kyrgyzstan. It covers 75 per cent of the post-Soviet space, has a population of 183 million, a total gross domestic product (GDP) of some US$2.7 trillion (cf. the EU US$16.6 trillion), and has 20 per cent of global reserves of gas and 15 per cent of oil (Sakwa, 2017, 148). This is a solid, although in comparative terms not large, economic basis for future regional consolidation, but it is not clear how extensive this might become. The absence of Ukraine, the second state of the former Soviet Union and currently estranged from any perceived Russian efforts at achieving greater integration, is a major barrier, while the absence of China too creates some uncertainty. Furthermore, there is resistance within the EEU to tighter integration. In the view of the earliest proponent of such a Union (Nazarbayev, 2011), membership and integration within the Union should be voluntary and member-states should retain responsibility for their own internal development with the Union's supranational organs operating on the basis of consensus and clearly defined (and therefore limited) authority. This view seems to have gained general assent among the member-states judging by the differences that have been aired in the supranational organs over various policy proposals, including water access, the transit of oil resources and energy policy.

The limitations of integration thus far achieved reflect the fact that the member-states, including Russia, remain protective of their national sovereignty. They do not favour the surrender of that sovereignty in the interests of greater economic coordination or harmonisation, and their stubbornness on this issue also represents a real barrier to any Russian aspirations to use the EEU to draw the other members more closely into its orbit. The reaction to Russian action in Ukraine in 2014 seems to have hardened this position.

Conclusion

Russia faces significant security challenges in the CA region. These arise both from within that region itself – including terrorist threat, humanitarian insecurity, the position of the diaspora, weak states, and disputes over water access, food supply and borders – and also from the incursion into the region of external powers, including the continuing instability in Afghanistan, US and Western attempts to displace Russian influence, and the uncertainties surrounding China's future role. Russia's response has been multifaceted, including providing support for the local regimes against both internal and external challenge, trade and aid, the deployment of military force and the construction of supranational organisations. But this has not been a coherent programme. Nor is it able, alone, to combat fully the challenges arising from the region. Given the deterioration in relations with the West, the potential threats that could emanate from this region, and the economic potential that is in some of the CA countries, it is likely that we will see greater Russian attention being devoted to this region in the future. But unless Russia is able to develop a coherent and focused security policy for the region, its ability to shape events will be limited.

Note

1 In contrast to Belarus, Ukraine, Abkhazia, South Ossetia, Transdnistr, Nagorno-Karabakh, Georgia and the Black Sea-Caspian Sea region.

References

Akhtar, Uzma (2010) 'Central Asia Security: Issues and Implications for US Interests', *ISSRA Papers*, Vol. 2, no. 11, pp. 37–63, www.ndu.edu.pk/issra/issra_pub/articles/issra-paper/ISSRA_Papers_Vol2Issue11_2010/04-Central-Aisa-Security-UZMA-Akhtar.pdf [sic] (accessed 28 May 2018).

Allison, R. (2008) 'Virtual Regionalism, Regional Structures and Regime Security in Central Asia', *Central Asian Survey*, Vol. 27, no. 2, pp. 185–202.

Ambrosio, Thomas (2009) *Authoritarian Backlash. Russian Resistance to Democratization in the Former Soviet Union*, Farnham: Ashgate.

Baev, Pavel (2006) 'Turning Counter-Terrorism into Counter-Revolution: Russia Focuses on Kazakhstan and Engages Turkmenistan', *European Security*, Vol. 15, no. 1, pp. 3–22.

Bartolomeo, Anna Di, Shushanik Makaryan, & Agnieszka Weimar (eds.) (2014) *Regional Migration Report: Russia and Central Asia*, Florence: European University Institute.

Bunce, Valerie J. & Sharon L. Wolchik (2011) *Defeating Authoritarian Leaders in Postcommunist Countries*, Cambridge: Cambridge University Press.

Chenoy, Anuradha M. & Rajan Kumar (2017) *Re-emerging Russia: Structures, Institutions and Processes*, Singapore: Springer Singapore.

CIA (n.d.) *The World Fact Book*, www.cia.gov/library/publications/the-world-factbook/ (accessed 25 May 2018).

Coburn, Leonard L. (2010) 'Central Asia: Pipelines Are the New Silk Road', *International Association for Energy Economics Newsletter*, 4th Quarter 2010, pp. 19–21, www.iaee.org/en/publications/newsletterdl/aspx?id=113 (accessed 28 May 2018).

Cooley, Alexander (2017) 'Whose Rules, Whose Sphere? Russian Governance and Influence in Post-Soviet States', Carnegie Endowment for International Peace, Task Force White Paper 30 June 2017.

Fatima, Qamar & Sumera Zafar (2014) 'New Great Game: Players, Interests, Strategies and Central Asia', *South Asian Studies*, Vol. 29, no. 2, pp. 627–655.

Foreign Policy Concept (July 2008) www.kremlin.ru/eng/text/docs/2008/07/204750.shtml (accessed 20 May 2018).

Freire, Maria & Roger Kanet (eds.) (2010) *Key Players and Regional Dynamics in Eurasia: The Return to the 'Great Game'*, Basingstoke: Palgrave Macmillan.

Goskomstat (2018) www.gks.ru/wps/wcm/connect/rosstat_main/rosstat/ru/statistics/population/demography/# (accessed 27 May 2018).

Haas, Marcel de (2016) 'Security Policy and Developments in Central Asia: Security Documents Compared with Security Challenges', *The Journal of Slavic Military Studies*, Vol. 29, no. 2, pp. 203–226.

Hallgren, H. & R. Ghiasy (2017) *Security and Economy on the Belt and Road: Three Country Case Studies*, Stockholm: Stockholm International Peace Research Institute.

Hamidreza, Azizi (2018) 'Analysing the Impacts of Drug Trafficking on Human Security in Central Asia', *Strategic Analysis*, Vol. 42, no. 1, pp. 42–47.

Hauff, Luba (2015) 'The Value of Alternatives: Why the EU is Indispensable to Central Asian Security', *DGAP Working Paper*, www.ssoar.info/ssoar/bitstream/handle/document/55733-7 (accessed 3 March 2018).

Heleniak, Timothy (2004) 'Migration of the Russian Diaspora after the Breakup of the Soviet Union', *Journal of International Affairs*, Vol. 57, no. 2, pp. 99–117.

Henderson, Sarah L. (2003) *Building Democracy in Contemporary Russia. Western Support for Grassroots Organizations*, Ithaca, NY: Cornell University Press.
ICG (2011) 'Crisis Group Asia Central Asia: Decay and Decline', *Asia Report* No. 201, 3 February.
'Kontseptsiya vneshnei politiki Rossiiskoi Federatsii' (30 November 2016) www.mid.ru/en/foreign_policy/official_documents/_/asset_publisher/CptlCkB6BZ29 (accessed 27 May 2018).
Kubicek, Paul (2004) 'Russian Energy Policy in the Caspian Basin', *World Affairs*, Vol. 166, no. 4, pp. 207–217.
Kumar, Yogendra (2017) 'Afghanistan-Central Asia Relations', *Himalayan and Central Asian Studies*, Vol. 21, no. 2/3, pp. 38–49.
Laruelle, Marlene (2004) 'The Two Faces of Contemporary Eurasianism: An Imperial Version of Russian Nationalism', *Nationalities Papers*, Vol. 32, no. 1, pp. 115–136.
Lavrov, Sergei (2017) 'Rossiya-Tsentral'naya Aziya: partnerstvo, ispytannoe vremenem', *Rossiiskaya gazeta*, 4 October.
Lee, Lavina & Graeme Gill (2015) 'India, Central Asia and the Eurasian Union. A New Ballgame?', *India Quarterly*, Vol. 7, no. 2, pp. 110–125.
MacHaffie, J. (2010) 'China's Role in Central Asia: Security Implications for Russia and the United States', *Comparative Strategy*, Vol. 29, no. 4, pp. 368–380.
Martin, Peres & Miquel Angel (2017) *Security and Human Right to Water in Central Asia*, New York: Palgrave Macmillan.
MGIMO (2017) *Rossiya i TsA: novye perspektivy: mezhdunarodnaya nauchnaya konferentsiya 25-letiyu ustanovleniya diplomaticheskii otnoshenii mezhdu RF i TsA*, 14 June, Moscow: Ministry of Foreign Affairs.
Molchanov, Mikhail A. (2015) 'Eurasian Regionalism: Ideas and Practices', in Roger E. Kanet & Matthew Sussex (eds.), *Power, Politics and Confrontation in* Eurasia. Foreign Policy in a Contested Region, New York: Palgrave Macmillan, 135–157.
Musiol, M. (2015) 'Post-Soviet Central Asia as a Unique Regional Security Complex', *The Polish Quarterly of International Affairs*, Vol. 24, no. 5, pp. 59–78.
Nazarbayev, Nursultan (2011) 'Evraziiskii soyuz: ot idei k istorii budushchego', *Izvestiya*, 25 October.
Nichol, J. (2010) 'Central Asia's Security: Issues and Implications for U.S. Interests', CRS Report for Congress, https://fas.org/sgp/crs/row/RL30294.pdf (accessed 7 January 2018).
Nikitina, Yu. A. (2009) *ODKB i SHOS: Modeli regionalisma v sfere bezopasnost*, Moscow: Navona.
Owen, C., J. Heathershaw, & I. Savin (2018) 'How Postcolonial Is Post-Western IR? Mimicry and Metis in the International Politics of Russia and Central Asia', *Review of International Studies*, Vol. 44, no. 2, pp. 279–300.
Putin, Vladimir (2011) 'Novyi integratsionnyi proekt dlya Evrazii – budushchee, kotoroe rozhdaetsya segodnya', *Izvestiya*, 4 October.
Putin, Vladimir (2018) 'Poslaniye Prezidenta Federal'nomu Sobraniyu', 1 March, http://kremlin.ru/events/president/news/56957 (accessed 7 May 2018).
Robinson, Neil (2012) 'Why Not More Conflict in the Former USSR? Russia and Central Asia as a Zone of Relative Peace', in Sussex (ed.), *Rossiya v tsifrakh*, 2017, Moscow: Federal State Statistical Service, 118–145.
Rumer, Eugene, Richard Sokolsky, Paul Stronski, & Andrew S. Weiss (2017) *Illusions vs Reality: Twenty-Five Years of U.S. Policy toward Russia, Ukraine, and Eurasia*, February, Washington DC: Carnegie Endowment for International Peace.
Sakwa, Richard (2017) *Russia against the Rest. The Post-Cold War Crisis of World Order*, Cambridge: Cambridge University Press.
Scholl, Ellen & Kirsten Westphal (2017) *European Energy Security Reimagined. Mapping the Risks, Challenges and Opportunities of Changing Energy Geographies*, Berlin: German Institute for International and Security Affairs.
Sinitsina, Irina (2012) *Economic Cooperation between Russia and Central Asian Countries: Trends and Outlook*, Bishkek: University of Central Asia, Institute of Public Policy and Administration, Working Paper No. 5.
SIPRI (2015) 'Central Asian Security'. Roundtable. www.sipri.org/research/conflict-and-peace/asia/central-asian-security
Stratfor (2009) *Russia: Using CSTO to Claim Influence in the FSU*, 23 February, https://worldview.stratfor.com/article/russia-using-csto-claim-influence-fsu
Sussex, Matthew (ed.) (2012) 'The Shape of the Security Order in the Former USSR', *Conflict in the Former USSR*, Cambridge: Cambridge University Press, pp. 35–63.

Suverennaya demokratiya: ot idei – k doctrine (2006) Moscow: Evropa.

UN Department of Economic and Social Affairs, Population Division, www://un.org/en/development/desa/population/migration/data/index.shtml (accessed 29 May 2018).

UNODC (2007) *On Drugs and Crime an Assessment of Transnational Organized Crime in Central Asia*, New York: UNODC.

UNRCCA (2015) *UN Regional Centre for Preventive Diplomacy for CA the Impact of External Factors on Security and Development in Central Asia*, Ashgabat: UNRCCA.

Zabortseva, Yelena Nikolayevna (2016) *Russia's relations with Kazakhstan: rethinking ex-Soviet transitions in the emerging world system*, London: Routledge.

Zolotova, Ekaterina (2018) 'Central Asia Steps Out of Russia's Shadow', GPF/Geopolitical Futures, 8 February 2018, https://geopoliticalfutures.com/central-asia-steps-russias-shadow/ (accessed 23 May 2018).

28
RUSSIAN-CHINESE SECURITY COOPERATION

The Bear and the Dragon

Marcel de Haas

Introduction

This chapter elaborates on the development, current status and likely future of Sino-Russian cooperation in the field of security, as it has advanced since the start of Putin's presidency in 2000. Security is understood in a broad context – that is, in addition to the military-political domain, energy security will also be discussed, since energy is a strategic asset (for the survival) of a state. First, the military, demographic, social and economic cooperation and challenges of the strategic security partnership between Moscow and Beijing are analysed. The next section describes how Russia and China operate in Central Asia, a strategic region for both of them. Subsequently, the Shanghai Cooperation Organisation (SCO), a political, economic and security entity, is on the agenda, with China and Russia as the leading actors. Finally, evaluating the aforementioned areas of cooperation, the question arises whether Russia's security could become under threat from China.

Moscow and Beijing: cooperation and challenges

After the downfall of the Soviet Union, a comprehensive improvement of bilateral relations developed between China and Russia in the 1990s. For instance, the long-standing border disputes between both states were settled in agreements. Moreover, Russia agreed to provide China with oil and gas. China also became one of the best customers of Russian arms and equipment, and Moscow and Beijing issued joint statements on rejecting (US) dominance in the international arena. Furthermore, both powers conducted joint war games (Blua, 2005; 'Putin Stresses', 2005; 'Russian, Chinese President', 2005). Today, Russia and China maintain a strategic partnership consisting of comprehensive cooperation in the areas of bilateral and international politics, defence and security, as well as energy.

Initially, Russia took the lead in the relationship between Beijing and Moscow – in political, economic and military might – but this has gradually turned around: China has become more powerful, especially in the areas of economic growth and military power. Pertaining to population size, with some 140 million Russians but 1.4 billion Chinese, China outstrips Russia nearly ten times ('Total Population', 2017). In 2012, China's economy was already four times the size of Russia's and was the second largest economy in the world after the

USA ('Economy-GDP: Countries Compared', 2017). Moreover, Beijing's defence budget is the second biggest in the world (the USA is number one), while Moscow's accounts for the third largest. China's defence budget is three times as much as that of Russia ('Military Balance', 2017). Russia outnumbers China in nuclear weapons; however, its conventional armed forces, less than 800,000, are only a third of China's more than 2.2 million soldiers ('Active Military Manpower', 2017). The development of the relationship between Moscow and Beijing, in which China has come to overrule Russia in many areas, undoubtedly has affected the cooperation between both actors: cracks have become visible in the mirror of their strategic partnership.

During the past decade, more and more signals have appeared, demonstrating that the Sino-Russian teamwork is crumbling. Political disputes have occurred in recent years. Furthermore, the importance of energy and arms deals – the core of their cooperation – is steadily decreasing because China has found alternative energy suppliers – to avoid dependency on Russia – and because Beijing nowadays is manufacturing weapon systems itself. When China has reached enough independence from Russia in military technology and has created sufficient alternative ways of gaining energy, Beijing might well put aside Russia as a 'strategic' partner, although a united front against the USA will be maintained for mutual benefit (Baev, 2017).

As to *bilateral cooperation*, an important aspect of the partnership has been the settlement of the border regions. However, the bilateral covenant in this field already revealed differences, with China considering the handing over of territory by Russia as a sign that Moscow is the weaker party in the partnership (Blagov, 2008). Furthermore, in recent years, Beijing's increasing intrusion into Russia's Far East province has alerted the Kremlin. Russia considers protection of its Far East region as a main concern ('LDPR', 2016). By deploying reinforcements of defence forces and other (power ministries') troops in the Far East, and by implementing measures to enhance the socio-economic development of this region, Moscow has provided evidence that it takes a possible Chinese threat seriously (McDermott, 2010). However, at the same time, Russia's Far East economy is depending on Chinese investments (Blank, 2013; Shtepa, 2016). Moscow has been investing heavily in its Far East region in order to counterbalance the population decline, as well as China's economic and demographic 'takeover' of this region. Russia's shift in policy emphasis from Europe to the Asia-Pacific region was therefore not only because of economic profits in the area. This geopolitical change of course was also taken to guard itself against growing Chinese influence in the South-East Asian region, and in the Russian Far East province in particular. The bilateral cooperation mainly consisted of mutual foreign policy statements and actions, not on intensive (socio-) economic cross-border ties. Moreover, China's rapid military build-up has raised awareness in Moscow of a threat from China.

Sino-Russian *foreign political cooperation* has primarily focused on an anti-Western (US) stance when needed. Examples of their geostrategic mutual-beneficial approaches are China's support for Russia's intervention in Syria, as well as the common refrain that both powers are strongly opposed to U.S. deployment of an anti-missile system in South Korea. Russia's immense natural resource base is also quite relevant to Beijing's foreign policy stance. But nevertheless, to keep its policy options open, China chooses ad hoc cooperation with Russia, instead of an alliance (Goldstein, 2017). The foreign policy cooperation has also demonstrated bias, such as, on the one hand, joint declarations in crises such as Syria, as part of their mutual interest in sovereignty and non-intervention in domestic issues, but, on the other hand, disputes, such as on Russia's support of separatism (as in Georgia) and China's increasingly dominating role in 'Moscow's Central Asia'. The good relationship between Moscow and Beijing deteriorated between 2005 and 2010, probably in particular as a consequence of China's rejection of Russia's war against Georgia and Moscow's subsequent recognition of the Georgian separatist regions in 2008 (Wagstyl, 2008). Moscow's support for the separatist regions in East Ukraine since 2014 forms another obstacle, since China considers (support to) 'separatism' as a direct threat to its national security, given its problems with Tibet and Taiwan.

Russo-Chinese economic cooperation has only been substantial in the areas of energy and arms, with Russia as supplier and China as recipient. Economic (trade) ties in other areas have not been significant. Moreover, the importance of energy and arms sales is steadily decreasing because China has sought and found other energy suppliers – to avoid dependency on Russia – and because China is itself more and more manufacturing weapon systems (Dobbs, 2014). Sino-Russian cooperation in the field of energy was a combination of teamwork, as well as of competition. A number of ambitious joint efforts were launched, but disputes between both parties arose in due course, especially over energy prices. However, after 10 years of talking, in May 2014, Russia finally agreed with China to deliver gas for a period of 30 years. With its disputes with the West on Ukraine, it was likely that Moscow had given in to China's demand for a lower price, to foster ties with Beijing in reply to its clash with the West (Johnson, 2014). Furthermore, to avoid dependency on Russia, China also focused on Central Asia for its energy needs. China no longer needs Russia as much for energy and arms. Moreover, by supplying China with military technology, Russia has created a strong competitor to its own military industry on the world market.

Additionally, Moscow and Beijing are rivals in trade routes. An example of this can be seen in the railway networks from China via Central Asia to Europa. In November 2017, the Baku-Tbilisi-Kars (BTK)[1] railway was opened, the shortest route providing China direct access to Europe. Moscow is suspicious of this rail route, which bypasses Russia and is a competitor to its Trans-Siberian railway (Sharip, 2017). Another example of trade route competition between Moscow and Beijing is that China is working to bypass Russia's Northern Sea Route in the Arctic, to establish a cheaper sea route from Asia to Europe (Goble, 2017). Nevertheless, Russia has to follow a cautious course towards China, since it has become highly dependent on Beijing, with China's financial role in Russian firms and towards Russian economy in particular. Moreover, billions in Sino-Russian financing deals are covering budget holes in Moscow. Clearly, Chinese money forms a lifeline for Moscow's economy (Trickett, 2017). Therefore, China is appeased by Russia in its South-East Asian naval expansion and in its endeavours in Central Asia: Moscow is forced to keep silent.

In addition to arms sales, the other part of Sino-Russian *military cooperation* consists of joint military exercises. On first sight – and in public statements – this area displays unity, a combined effort of military power to show the USA and others that China and Russia follow a united security course. It is exactly this that led Moscow to invite the Chinese Navy to participate in joint drills in the Baltic Sea in July 2017 ('Na Baltike', 2017). Hence, China and Russia demonstrate their willingness to help each other in case of military conflict. Likewise, it was not surprising that their joint manoeuvres in 2016 were held in the South China Sea, considering Beijing's naval power projection in this region (Golts, 2017). However, the joint exercises also serve to gain more insight into the military capabilities of the other 'partner'. Moreover, a closer look reveals disputes on the content of the bilateral war games. Both sides also conduct unilateral exercises, with scenarios in which the other party is considered the potential adversary. Interestingly, whereas Russia's 'Vostok-2005' exercise included military cooperation with China, at 'Vostok-2010' the relationship with Beijing had already cooled. 'Vostok-2010' and 'Vostok-2014' were meant as a warning from Russia to China, with the latter portrayed as potential adversary (Dobbs, 2014). Clearly, war games, also disclose feelings of fear and threat, especially from the Russian side since Moscow has become the inferior military party.

Russia and China in Central Asia

Beijing is acquiring more and more economic and, consequently, also political influence in the former Soviet Central Asian states. China is replacing Russia as the 'imperial' power in Central Asia, economically but also politically, pushing Moscow out of the Central Asian Commonwealth of Independent States (CIS) republics, its traditional realm. In the past, Russia was afraid of meddling by the West, especially in Central Asia, after the deployment of Western troops to Afghanistan as a result of the terrorist attacks of 9/11. At Russia's instigation, the SCO Summit in 2005, therefore, encouraged the West to withdraw its forces from the Central Asian region (Katz, 2008). However, it is China, and not the West, that is taking over Central Asia from Russia. In addition to – and connected with – energy deals, China brought its own population: more than 300,000 Chinese are living in Kazakhstan, some 200,000 are housed in Kyrgyzstan and approximately 150,000 are found in Uzbekistan, Turkmenistan and Tajikistan together (Orozobekova, 2011).

A major security concern in its relations with China concerns whether and how Russia can maintain its *sphere of influence* in the former Soviet Union's area. China has increased its economic clout in the former Soviet Central Asian states, especially in the energy domain. Moscow, for its part, initially disapproved of Beijing's emergent energy ties with Central Asian states, and by way of its Gazprom firm tried to convince these states to engage in closer energy cooperation with Russia (Blagov, 2012). However, this policy seemed to be less and less successful, whereas China has continued its march into Central Asia. With its booming economy, growing population and increasing demand for energy, China needs Central Asia for reasons of energy security as well as for expanded trade. The nucleus of China's operations from Asia to Europe is the Belt and Road Initiative (BRI), first proposed by Chinese President Xi Jinping in 2013. It has since then grown into an ambitious transcontinental project aimed at asserting China's new formative role in Eurasian affairs. Unlike the West, China makes neither political demands nor complaints about human rights. In the Central Asian states, China mostly focuses on infrastructure building and natural resource extraction. Although these Chinese investments are more than welcome and beneficial to the economies of the Central Asian countries, Central Asia actually has no alternatives besides accepting the Chinese offers. All five Central Asian states need significant investments to modernise their economies after years of neglect (Voloshin, 2017). Hence, it also makes them increasingly dependent on Beijing, possibly also politically. Moscow's concerns about China's operations in Central Asia are likely to go beyond economic aspects. The BRI already demonstrates expanding Chinese soft power, whereas Russia's intervention in Ukraine and disputes with the West over Syria and other issues have alienated many former allies in Central Asia. Consequently, Moscow's dominance over Central Asia is probably already a matter of the past.

Russia maintains *military bases* in Kyrgyzstan and Tajikistan. In September 2011, Russia and Tajikistan agreed to extend the Russian military base, founded in 2005, with some 6,000 troops, for another 49 years. The Kremlin had the same extension in mind for its airbase Kant in Kyrgyzstan, which was opened in 2003 for a period of 15 years (Marat, 2011). In December 2012, Bishkek ratified an agreement with Moscow for a period of 15 years, as of 2017, with which the four separate Russian military facilities in Kyrgyzstan (a weapons test range, a signals centre, a radio-seismic laboratory and an airbase at Kant) were united into an integrated Russian military base ('Kyrgyzstan okays', 2012). These bases are necessary for the security survival of these weak states, but also provide Moscow with military power projection options in that region, as well as with political clout on these governments. Whereas military and political influence are Russia's traditional objective, China seeks markets, trade and energy resources in Central Asia. Although it does not have any military bases in that region, China does maintain military cooperation with Central Asian countries. With Kazakhstan, Kazakh military received education and training at Chinese military academic institutions. Furthermore, since 2002, Kazakh and Chinese defence and other security forces have been engaged in joint and multilateral exercises. Nevertheless, Russia remained Kazakhstan's main supplier of arms. Moreover, military cooperation overall with Russia was much more intensive than with China (Weitz, 2012). China is developing military cooperation not only with Kazakhstan but also with Uzbekistan. Cooperation was established on high-level visits, technical exchanges and training programmes. Both countries share visions of non-interference and rejection of foreign military bases in the region (Saipov, 2012a).

The Chinese shift from Russian towards *Central Asian gas* undermines Russia's regional and economic influence. China has been constructing and expanding pipelines through all five Central Asian states, which had historically been dominated by the Russians. China has also become Central Asia's largest trade partner, as Central Asia is the only friendly front to China's expansionist policies. Replacing Russia, China has picked Central Asia to provide the lion's share of its natural gas demands. Allegedly, already in 2014 China received nearly half of its natural gas supply from Central Asia (Michel, 2014). China concentrates its efforts in Central Asia on Kazakhstan, Uzbekistan and Turkmenistan, all of which possess energy resources, with Tajikistan and Kyrgyzstan on the sidelines. In December 2005, the Atasu-Alashankou oil pipeline between Kazakhstan and China was opened, and in May 2006 oil pumped from Kazakhstan reached China, thus marking the first direct pipeline import of oil to China. In 2011 China already had a bigger stake in the Kazakh energy sector than did Russia (Orozobekova, 2011). China's objective is to avoid energy dependency on Russia. Another argument is that by redirecting Kazakh oil pipelines through China instead of through Russia, China's influence over Kazakhstan and Central Asia will increase at the expense of Russia's position. Since August 2012, Uzbekistan has been supplying China with gas on a regular basis (Saipov, 2012b). Furthermore, China seeks to monopolise Turkmen natural gas exports. In 2006, China and Turkmenistan signed a 30-year contract of Turkmen gas deliveries, starting in 2010, and in December 2009 the first branch of the Turkmenistan-Uzbekistan-Kazakhstan gas pipeline became operational (Orozobekova, 2011). Turkmenistan is the biggest supplier of piped natural gas to China and heavily relies on Chinese loans for large-scale infrastructure projects (Voloshin, 2017). During the June 2012 SCO Summit, China also discussed with Tajikistan, Kyrgyzstan and Afghanistan the possibility of branch-offs from the existing gas transit pipeline through these countries, to end in China (Socor, 2012). Other than Uzbekistan, Turkmenistan and Kazakhstan, these three transit countries lack natural gas resources and infrastructure, but nevertheless are included in China's energy and political plans for Central Asia.

China and Russia are also both involved in developing *railway networks* in Central Asia. Beijing already longer aimed at the construction of a railroad to connect China, Kyrgyzstan and Uzbekistan (Saipov, 2012b). At the 2017 SCO Summit, the new Uzbek President Mirziyaev and his counterpart from Kyrgyzstan resurrected the idea of constructing a China-Kyrgyzstan-Uzbekistan railway. The project was first conceived in the late 1990s (Sharip, 2017). Furthermore, China urged Kyrgyzstan and Uzbekistan to readjust their

Russian/Soviet broad-gauge rail networks to the narrow-gauge standard used by China (and most of Europe). Russian experts recognise a military-strategic objective in this, Chinese-fit rail lines extended from China into Central Asia would allow Beijing to quickly dispatch its troops to the region in a potential future conflict with Moscow (Shustov, 2017). In November 2017, plans were announced for a new railway route from China to Europe via the territories of Russia and Kazakhstan. The announcement was made ten days after the official launch of the earlier mentioned BTK railroad, which bypasses Russia (Aliyev, 2017; Sharip, 2017). Hence, this might have well been Russia's reply to China's BTK plans. Kazakhstan and Uzbekistan are eager to seek alternative trade routes free of Russian control. However, the two countries are being actively 'encouraged' by Moscow to join transit corridors through Russia. As with energy resources, obviously, transport networks also constitute an area of competition between Beijing and Moscow.

The SCO: China takes over the lead from Russia

In the SCO, China and Russia have different sometimes opposing interests. China is seeking Central Asian markets for the products of its expanding economy and energy sources to keep its economy going. Russia is eager to solidify its leadership status within the former Soviet area, hence also in Central Asia, as well as to promote itself as a superpower in the international arena. Since the SCO partners in general regard the economy as their first priority, China is more attractive than Russia, and thus China is gradually becoming the sole leader of the SCO. This is yet another policy discrepancy between Beijing and Moscow. The SCO is a *regional international organisation* comprising states in Europe, the Near East, Central Asia and South-East Asia (De Haas and Van der Putten, 2007).[2] The SCO consists of three types of participants. First, eight member-states: China (1996),[3] Russia (1996), Kazakhstan (1996), Kyrgyzstan (1996), Tajikistan (1996), Uzbekistan (2001), India (2017) and Pakistan (2017) ('About SCO', 2017). Second, four observer states: Mongolia (2004), Iran (2005), Belarus (2010) and Afghanistan (2012). And third, six dialogue partners: Sri Lanka (2009), Turkey (2012), Nepal (2015), Cambodia (2015), Azerbaijan (2015) and Armenia (2015). Traditionally, Russia and China have been the leading actors of the SCO. In the SCO, Russia, China, India and Pakistan bring together four nuclear powers. The size of the armed forces of China and Russia belongs to the top three lists of the world.[4] Comprising the larger part of the territory of Eurasia, half of the world population, energy sources, nuclear arms and significant armed forces, the SCO in theory has a formidable economic, political and military potential. However, in addition to a growing number of controversies between Moscow and Beijing, SCO member-states hold divergent interests, which prevent this organisation from becoming a dominating economic and/or military alliance.

Regarding *objectives*, according to its website, the SCO promotes cooperation in ensuring peace, security and stability in the region, politics, trade and economy, science and technology, culture as well as education, energy, transportation, tourism, environmental protection and other fields ('About SCO', 2017). Important ingredients of economic cooperation are (conventional) arms trade – with Russia as supplier – and energy, in which Russia, Kazakhstan, Uzbekistan and Iran are big exporters – and China and India are significant importers. Cooperation in the domain of defence and security comprises aspects such as security policy concepts and agreements, counterterrorism activities, armament deals, as well as military exercises ('SHOS vpervyye', 2015). Although the SCO started as a security organisation – extending from confidence-building measures at the borders to antiterrorist activities – the SCO members frequently state that this organisation nowadays primarily is meant for political and economic cooperation and that military coordination – focussing on domestic security – plays only a minor role.

The cooperation between Russia and China is also waning in the SCO. A first example of disagreement between these two actors is SCO membership. China always wanted Pakistan in as full member of the SCO, but Russia preferred India. Thus, it took some 15 years before these two countries could join as member-states, in 2017. The full membership of Iran is a similar issue of disagreement, with Russia as solid proponent and China reluctant to say the least ('SCO to Study', 2016). Iran's aggressive reputation towards the West might be detrimental for the SCO and hence also for China's economic interests. Furthermore, since Putin's second term as President (2004–2008), Moscow has been a more powerful player in the international arena and demanded not only to be part of discussions on international security but also to influence the global agenda in this field. The Kremlin could best achieve this endeavour by starting from its 'own backyard', the former Soviet area, especially in Central Asia, as manifested in the SCO. However, in addition to China's growing leverage over this region, these Russian ambitions were counteracted because the SCO's member-states and observers were often short of constructive, common objectives but full of disputes. More importantly, Moscow and Beijing sometimes took contrasting viewpoints in the SCO forum, for instance, on the military feature of this organisation – enhanced by Russia but opposed by China – and on Russia's support for the separatist regions in Georgia, but not endorsed by the SCO forum, and certainly not by China (Larsen, 2017). Regarding separatism, China condemned Russia for recognising the Georgian separatist regions of Abkhazia and South Ossetia, as contradicting the SCO's principle of considering separatism as one of its main threats.

In the SCO, China's star has been rising above that of Russia. Supported by its economic (investment) input into the Central Asian states of the SCO, China has been able to strengthen its influence in this organisation, at the expense of Russia, thus becoming the more dominating actor in this organisation. The dominating role of both Russia and China in the SCO is also reflected in the military exercises of this organisation. As long as the new 'Cold War' between Russia and the West – as a result of the former's interventions in Ukraine – goes on, so will Russia's deepened interest of conducting war games with China, to show the world that it has a powerful military partner. However, Beijing keeps all options opened (Goldstein, 2017). With its growing economic cooperation in Central Asia, in due course, as a result of its emergent military power, China might also expand its military cooperation in this region, thus further ousting Moscow from its traditional (Soviet/Russian) sphere of influence in Central Asia and hence also from the SCO.

Russia's security threatened by China?

As to threat perception, the joint Russo-Chinese military exercises are not only a show-of-force towards the USA but also serve to gain more insight into the military capabilities of the other 'partner'. Both sides also conducted unilateral exercises, including scenarios in which the other was considered the potential adversary ('V Rossii …', 2010; Rousseau, 2012). Clearly, war games also disclose feelings of fear and threat, especially from the Russian side, since Moscow had become the inferior military party, i.e. in conventional arms and troop strength, for which a Russian surplus in nuclear capabilities cannot compensate.

The Kremlin is keeping up the appearance that Chinese rising military might does not pose any threat towards Russia. The deployment by China of intercontinental ballistic missiles near Russia's border, in 2016–2017, was formally seen as no threat to Russian national security interests ('Kreml' otreagiroval', 2017). Nevertheless, at least a part of the Russian security elite, also in Parliament, is evidently upset by China's military build-up. As mentioned, Russia conducts military exercises, in which it clearly uses a scenario with China as adversary. Instead of formal political statements against Chinese military build-up, such war games are an indirect way of providing a message of discontent. For instance, on February 13, 2017, on the border with China, Russia's Armed Forces launched military exercises employing Iskander-M tactical (short-range) ballistic missile complexes (Sukhankin, 2017).

By deploying additional military forces in the Far East, and by implementing measures to enhance the socio-economic development of this region, President Putin has given evidence that it takes a possible Chinese threat of a takeover of its Far East seriously (Goble, 2018). However, it is doubtful whether these measures can stop Chinese increasing clout on this region.

Another major security concern of Moscow in its relations with China was how Russia could maintain its sphere of influence in the former Soviet Union's area, and in Central Asia in particular. China's economic strength and beneficial economic offers are pushing Russia out of Central Asia (Kassenova, 2017). Fed by the threat of an overwhelmingly powerful China in the region, Russia's fear of China could eventually cause the Kremlin to draw back from closely cooperating with China and to seek an intensification of political, economic and security ties with the West.

Conclusions

During the past decade, more and more signals have appeared, which demonstrate that the Sino-Russian strategic partnership is crumbling. Political disputes have occurred in recent years, for instance, on energy (prices), separatism (Georgia), military exercises (scenarios of mutual opposing forces), SCO membership (Iran) and territory (Russia's Far East). With China as the regional power-to-be and Russia as the regional power-of-the-past, it is likely that their cooperation will dwindle further and possibly turns into a hostile relationship.

In Central Asia, China is replacing Russia as the 'imperial' power, economically but also politically. As a more attractive partner, Beijing is pushing Moscow out of the Central Asian former Soviet republics, Russia's traditional realm. Currently, China and Russia are in particular competing in Central Asian gas and in the development of railway networks in that region. Only with the deployment of military forces in Central Asia is Moscow in the lead, simply because China does not (yet) have such an intention.

In the SCO since its foundation, China and Russia, the two leading actors of this body, regularly have opposing views and objectives. China is seeking markets for its products and energy sources for its economy. Russia, however, is eager to enhance its status of Great Power in the international arena, first through the organisations which it leads. Since the SCO partners in general regard the economy as their first priority, China is more interesting for them than Russia, and thus China is gradually becoming the sole leader of the SCO.

Could China become a threat for Russia? Yes indeed. Perhaps not military, but certainly in terms of regional political and economic influence. It is questionable if Moscow can stop China's rising demographic and socio-economic clout of Russia's Far East. It is not inconceivable that in a couple of decades Beijing de facto will reign over this Russian region, because of the large number of Chinese citizens and Chinese enterprises located there. And if continuing its grip on the former Soviet republics in Central Asia is considered by Moscow as a national security issue, then Chinese dominating economic role in this region is felt by Russia as another threat by Beijing. If China's leverage over Russia's Far East and over Central Asia by the Kremlin is felt as a threat to its national security, Moscow might consider aligning itself with the West – hence against China – in the field of security cooperation, in order to keep its territorial integrity intact and to keep some influence in Central Asia. Although currently such a policy watershed from Moscow seems highly unlikely, it should be taken into account for the coming decades. What will the West then do, receive Russia with open arms or consider beneficial economic ties with China as more important?

Notes

1 A regional rail link project to directly connect Azerbaijan, Georgia and Turkey.
2 For a more detailed description of the SCO, see this source.
3 Year of access.
4 With the USA as number two in size.

References

EDM   Eurasia Daily Monitor
RFE/RL   Radio Free Europe/Radio Liberty

'About SCO'. 2017. *sectsco.org*. Accessed on 24 December 2017 at http://eng.sectsco.org/about_sco/.
'Active Military Manpower'. 2017. Total Available Active Military Manpower by Country. *globalfirepower.com*. Accessed on 12 December 2017 at www.globalfirepower.com/active-military-manpower.asp.
Aliyev, Nurlan. 2017. 'New Railway Route from China to Europe Through Russia: Bluff or Tactical Ploy?', *EDM*, 27 November, Volume: 14, Issue: 152.
Baev, Pavel. 2017. 'Russia and China Part Company in Davos', *EDM*, 23 January, Volume: 14, Issue: 5.
Blagov, Sergei. 2008. 'Russia, China Establish Stronger Economic Ties', *EDM*, 30 October, Volume: 5, Issue: 208.
Blagov, Sergei. 2012. 'Russia Eyes New Far Eastern Gas Export Hub, Reassesses Central Asia', *EDM*, 21 November, Volume: 9, Issue: 214.
Blank, Stephen. 2013. 'Moscow Talks Business, Beijing Answers with Geo-strategy', *China Brief*, 7 November, Volume: 13, Issue: 22.
Blua, Antoine. 2005. 'Joint Exercises Underscore Growing Ties between Moscow and Beijing', *RFE/RL Russian Political Weekly*, 9 August, Volume: 5, Issue: 28.
De Haas, Marcel & Van der Putten, Frans-Paul. 2007. *The Shanghai Cooperation Organisation: Towards a Full-Grown Security Alliance?* Clingendael Security Paper 3, The Hague: Clingendael Institute, November 2007.
Dobbs, Joseph. 2017. 'Guest Post: Russia and China – Friends or 'Frenemies'?', *Financial Times*, 11 December 2014.
'Economy-GDP: Countries Compared'. 2017. *NationMaster*. Accessed on 12 December 2017 at www.nationmaster.com/country-info/stats/Economy/GDP#-date.
Goble, Paul. 2017. 'China Preparing to Bypass Russia's Northern Sea Route in Arctic', *EDM*, 3 October, Volume: 14, Issue: 122.
Goble, Paul. 2018. 'Russians Are Not Fools'—Moscow Failing to Encourage Significant Migration to Far East', *EDM*, 25 January, Volume: 15, Issue: 12.
Goldstein, Lyle. 2017. 'A China-Russia Alliance?', *The National Interest*, 25 April.
Golts, Aleksandr. 2017. 'The Russian Navy: To Deter the US and to Compete with China', *EDM*, 1 August, Volume: 14, Issue: 102.
Johnson, Luke. 2014. 'What You Need to Know about Russia and China's Gas Deal', *RFE/RL*, 22 May.
Kassenova, Nargis. 2017. 'Central Asia as Russia's "Near Abroad": Growing Ambiguities', *Bishkek Project*, 22 March. Accessed on 28 January 2018 at https://bishkekproject.com/memos/15.
Katz, Mark. 2008. 'Russia and the Shanghai Cooperation Organization: Moscow's Lonely Road from Bishkek to Dushanbe', *eurasianet.org*, 2 September. Accessed on 20 December 2017 at www.eurasianet.org/departments/insight/articles/pp090308f.shtml.
'Kreml' otreagiroval na kitayskiy rakety u rossiyskoy granitsy'. 2017. *vlasti.net*, 24 January. Accessed on 31 January 2018 at http://vlasti.net/news/254685?mc_cid=419008cda7&mc_eid=7d6771189c.

'Kyrgyzstan okays "integrated" Russian military base'. 2012. *RIA Novosti*, 18 December.
Larsen, Joseph. 2017. 'Georgia-China Relations Are about More Than Economics', *Civil Georgia*, 12 October. Accessed on 24 December 2017 at www.civil.ge/eng/article.php?id=30514.
'LDPR: resheniye o razmeshchenii kitayskikh zavodov na Dal'nem Vostoke – oshibka'. 2016. *Amurpress.ru*, 12 April. Accessed on 19 December 2017 at http://amurpress.ru/politics/629/.
Marat, Erica. 2011. 'Russia Seeks Long-Term Military Presence in Tajikistan and Kyrgyzstan', *EDM*, 22 September, Volume: 8, Issue: 174.
McDermott, Roger. 2010. 'Reflections on Vostok 2010: Selling an Image', *EDM*, 13 July, Volume: 7, Issue: 134.
Michel, Casey. 2014. 'Russia Has Lost Control of Central Asian Gas', *The Moscow Times*, 14 July.
'Military Balance'. 2017. *International Institute for Strategic Studies* (IISS). Accessed on 12 December 2017 at www.iiss.org/-/media//images/publications/the%20military%20balance/milbal%202017/final%20free%20graphics/mb2017-top-15-defence-budgets.jpg?la=en.
'Na Baltike nachinayetsya aktivnaya faza rossiysko-kitayskikh voyenno-morskikh ucheniy'. 2017. *TASS*, 25 July. Accessed on 12 December 2017 at http://tass.ru/armiya-i-opk/4437085?mc_cid=8dbd8574d4&mc_eid=7d6771189c.
Orozobekova, Cholpon. 2011. 'Beijing's Stealthy Expansion in Central Asia', *RFE/RL*, 12 January.
'Putin Stresses Importance of Sino–Russian Economic, Military Cooperation'. 2005. *RFE/RL Newsline*, 10 August, Volume: 9, Issue: 150, Part: I.
Rousseau, Richard. 2012. 'Will China Colonize and Incorporate Siberia?', *Harvard International Review*, 27 June. Accessed on 28 January 2018 at http://hir.harvard.edu/article/?a=2949.
'Russian, Chinese President Discuss Expanding Political, Economic, Military Cooperation'. 2005. *RFE/RL Newsline*, 1 July, Volume: 9, Issue: 125.
Saipov, Zabikhulla. 2012a. 'Common Concerns and Threat Perceptions Force China and Uzbekistan to Closely Coordinate their Positions', *EDM*, 5 October, Volume: 9, Issue: 182.
Saipov, Zabikhulla. 2012b. 'China's Economic Strategies for Uzbekistan and Central Asia', *EDM*, 21 September, Volume: 9, Issue: 172.
'SCO to Study Iran's Full Membership after India, Pakistan: Chinese FM'. 2016. *tasnimnews.com*, 25 May. Accessed on 24 December 2017 at www.tasnimnews.com/en/news/2016/05/25/1083914/sco-to-study-iran-s-full-membership-after-india-pakistan-chinese-fm.
Sharip, Farkhad. 2017. 'Controversial Railway Project Consolidates China's Foothold in Central Asia', *EDM*, 17 November, 2017, Volume: 14, Issue: 149.
'SHOS vpervyye provodit ucheniya po bor'be s terrorizmom v Internete'. 2015. *sputnik.ru*, 14 October. Accessed on 24 December 2017 at https://ru.sputnik.kg/world/20151014/1019275281.html.
Shtepa, Vadim. 2016. 'Moscow Invites Chinese Factories to Move to the Russian Far East', *EDM*, 28 April, Volume: 13, Issue: 83.
Shustov, Aleksandr. 2017. 'Iran i Kitay khotyat perekroit' geopoliticheskuyu kartu Tsentral'noy Azii', *eurasia.expert*, 23 January. Accessed on 20 December 2017 at http://eurasia.expert/iran-i-kitay-khotyat-perekroit-geopoliticheskuyu-kartu-tsentralnoy-azii/?mc_cid=df7edbcfa3&mc_eid=7d6771189c.
Socor, Vladimir. 2012. 'China to Increase Central Asian Gas Imports', *EDM*, 9 August.
Sukhankin, Sergey. 2017. 'Russia Sells S-400 Complexes to China: Smart Move or a Mixed Blessing?', *EDM*, 24 February, Volume: 14, Issue: 24.
'Total Population – Both Sexes. World Population Prospects, the 2017 Revision'. 2017. *United Nations Department of Economic and Social Affairs, Population Division, Population Estimates and Projections Section*. June. Accessed on 12 December 2017 at https://esa.un.org/unpd/wpp/Download/Standard/Population/.
Trickett, Nicholas. 2017. 'China Quietly Looms over Zapad 2017 Exercises; Any Russian Aggression out of the Exercises Could Hurt Sino-Russian Relations.' *thediplomat.com*, 28 August. Accessed on 12 December 2017 at http://thediplomat.com/2017/08/china-quietly-looms-over-zapad-2017-exercises/.
'V Rossii nachinayetsya masshtabnyye voyennyye ucheniya "Vostok-2010"'. 2010. *Vesti/ RBK*, 29 June.
Voloshin, George. 2017. 'Central Asia Ready to Follow China's Lead Despite Russian Ties', *EDM*, 24 May, Volume: 14, Issue: 71.
Wagstyl, Stephan. 2008. 'Russia Fails to Secure Regional Backing', *Financial Times*, 28 August.
Weitz, Richard. 2012. 'Kazakhstan–China Military Exchanges Continue', *EDM*, 9 November, Volume: 9, Issue: 206.

29

THE BRICS AND RUSSIAN FOREIGN AND SECURITY POLICY

Changing the narrative[1]

Rachel S. Salzman

The BRICS group (Brazil, Russia, India, China, South Africa) is a core symbol of Russian discontent with the international system. It has not, however, always served a critical purpose or filled a security need. Russia initially brought the group together as a rhetorical feint against Western dominance of institutions of global governance. In the decade of BRICS' institutional existence before the onset of the crisis in Ukraine in 2014, Russian political leadership spoke about the role of BRICS as a keystone of a new, democratic world order, but they invested little in the substance of the group itself. In the immediate aftermath of the onset of the Ukraine crisis, that changed. From 2014 to 2015, BRICS served as a key organ of security. Since 2015, with the lessening of international focus on the Ukraine crisis and the diversion of interest in BRICS from China and India, BRICS is once again a rhetorical device for Russia, but one that has proved its worth in times of need.

It is worth taking a moment to define 'security' in this context. When looking at BRICS as part of Russian security policy, the question is one first and foremost of what might be called 'status security.' The primary objective of Russian foreign policy since the late 1990s has been the recognition and acceptance of Russia as a great power by other great powers, especially the United States. Concomitant with that goal has been the aim of creating a multipolar (now polycentric) world, or a world where no single great power can dictate the actions of another great power. What underlies both of those goals is a sense of alienation from the Western-led international system since the end of the Cold War and accompanying status insecurity about Russia's role in the world. BRICS, with its cachet of 'rising powers' and its singular focus (initially) on moving global economic governance away from U.S. dominance, gave Russia a path for achieving great power influence that was less dependent on acceptance by Western countries.

Both political and economic security are part of the story as well, particularly in the period immediately following the onset of the Ukraine crisis in 2014. Political security in this context means protection from political isolation, including protection of Russia's seat at the table in international institutions. Economic security means the willingness of BRICS countries to do business with Russia and the diversification of trading partners more broadly. Political and economic security, however, have never displaced status security as the Russia's most important takeaway from the BRICS group.

This chapter tells the story of the rise and fall of BRICS in Russian foreign policy from the advent of the group in 2005 through 2017. It begins with a brief institutional history of the BRICS group to give the reader context for the foregoing discussion. It then looks at BRICS in Russian policy first before Ukraine, from 2008 to 2014, and then after Ukraine, from 2014 to 2015. The chapter concludes with a discussion of BRICS and its role in Russian policy since 2015.

BRICS: a brief history

The term 'BRIC' originated in a 2001 analysis by Goldman Sachs economist Jim O'Neill entitled 'Building Better Global Economic BRICS' (O'Neill, 2001). Looking at gross domestic product (GDP) growth, population, and GDP per capita, the goal of the paper was to identify the likely future leaders of the global economy and was targeted primarily at investors. While O'Neill's analysis suggested that global growth patterns might eventually necessitate a reshuffling of the G7, he did not intend his paper to have geopolitical consequences.

However, the idea took hold beyond the private sector in ways O'Neill never envisioned. Although he was not the first to notice the economic performance of the world's largest states, his acronym became the shorthand for both shifts in the global economic landscape and the presumed geopolitical rebalancing that would follow (Stuenkel, 2014; Tett, 2010). It then became a banner under which those states began to coordinate. The first meeting of BRIC representatives was a meeting of deputy foreign ministers in 2005 (Andreev, 2013, p. 127). The following year, in what is normally hailed as the first official BRIC meeting, the foreign ministers of the BRIC countries met at the sidelines of the 2006 United Nations General Assembly (UNGA). Since 2009, the group has held regular independent summits at the heads of state level. In 2011, after sustained lobbying by President Jacob Zuma, South Africa formally became a member and BRIC became BRICS (Shubin, 2012, p. 198). This accession is notable not only for the change in acronym, but because the inclusion of South Africa, a state that would not qualify for membership on O'Neill's original criteria, marks the completed transformation from O'Neil's 'global economic BRICs' to a geopolitical BRICS group.

Russia played a critical role in effecting BRICS's transformation from economic concept to political group. Russian intellectuals were thinking about BRICS more as a political than an economic question from very early in the 2000s. In 2004, the Institute of Latin America of the Russian Academy of Sciences sponsored a conference about how the rise of the Giant Emerging Countries, and first and foremost the BRICs, could impact the creation of a new world order (Bobrovnikov and Davydov, 2005, p. 4; Davydov, 2014). While Brazilian research centres were also beginning to engage with similar questions at around the same time, it was Russia that really pushed the initiative forward. This is most evident in then President Vladimir Putin's initiative to bring the foreign ministers together at the 2006 UNGA. The proposal for a stand-alone BRIC Summit also came from Russia, and the first summit was held in Ekaterinburg in 2009.

Russian academics also engaged early with how best to develop BRIC. In advance of the Ekaterinburg Summit, Russian political scientist and Duma member Vyacheslav Nikonov organised a meeting of scholars from BRIC countries to think about the future of the group (Toloraya, 2014). Russia wanted to institutionalise the group from the beginning, and Russian Foreign Minister Sergei Lavrov is often credited as 'the intellectual architect of the politicisation of the BRICs platform' (Stuenkel, 2014, p. 103). Further, while the other partners joined the grouping for economic reasons, Russia's motivations in pushing for meetings were primarily related to politics and security (Unnikrishnan, 2014). The combination of the early push for institutionalisation and the alternative motivations for cooperation suggest both that Russia had a distinct narrative it wished the BRIC group to represent and that it sought to control and shape that narrative in a way that served Russia's own international priorities.

While Russia was a key force in bringing BRICS together, it was helped along considerably by global events, particularly the onset in 2008 of the global financial crisis. Indeed, although the BRIC countries began meeting in 2005, they forged as a group only in the crucible of the 2008 crisis. They quickly became an important subgroup in the newly prominent G20 (Stuenkel, 2013, p. 612). At Brazil's initiative, the finance ministers began meeting as a group following the 2008 G20 in São Paolo. In 2009, the finance ministers met twice to coordinate their positions for upcoming G20 meetings (Larionova, 2012, p. 2). That coordination paid dividends. The high-water mark of BRIC visibility and success within the G20 came at the 2009 Pittsburgh Summit, when the group was able to push through significant reforms on weights and quotas within the International Monetary Fund (IMF). As a mark of their influence at the time, the then U.S. Treasury Secretary Timothy Geithner met with the countries as a group, the only time a U.S. official has met with BRIC(S) (Panova, 2013, p. 51).

2009 was the apogee of BRIC's influence on the global stage, but 2014 marked the apex of BRICS's internal cohesion as a political group. The group began to discuss forming its own institutions, in particular a BRICS development bank, at the Delhi Summit in 2012. The idea came to fruition in 2014 with the creation of both the New Development Bank (NDB) and the Contingency Reserve Arrangement (CRA), a currency pool for BRICS members. Both institutions are small by international standards, but each is now open and operational. In conjunction with the new institutions China has opened independently, most importantly the Asian International Infrastructure Bank (AIIB), they represent a constellation of international financial institutions that operate independently from the umbrella of the Western-dominated international development system

In addition to the foundation of its own institutions, BRICS has seen its number of working groups and meetings multiply since the first summit in 2009. In 2008, the year of the first leaders' sideline meeting, the group held five meetings, all at the ministerial level or above. In 2017, China oversaw 98 BRICS-related events, of which 31 were at the ministerial level ('BRICS 2017 Calendar,' 2017). While some of the BRICS working groups seem more interested in photo ops than substantive cooperation, others are active and productive. The result of the combination of the founding of its own institutions, its proliferating working groups and its resilience in the face of leadership transitions, economic downturns and political crises is that BRICS is now a group that is both more and less than the sum of its parts. It has not accomplished nearly what it set out to do, whether in terms of boosting intra-BRICS economic ties or turning global governance on its head. It has, however, proven itself to be an established and at times influential coalition in both formal and informal global economic governance.

BRICS in Russian foreign policy, 2008–2013

The years 2003–2008 saw a sustained decline in U.S.-Russian relations. What began as cordial and even warm relations between U.S. President George W. Bush and Russian President Vladimir Putin, with a summit in 2001 and close cooperation following the terrorist attacks of September 11, 2001, soured following the U.S. invasion of Iraq in 2003 and a simultaneous turn in Russian politics away from democracy and economic reform.

Part and parcel of these shifts was a gradual redefinition of Russian national identity away from Russia as part of European civilisation to the idea of Russia as a distinct Eurasian civilisation. Russia has long held a divided national identity, torn between Westernisers (or Atlanticists) who saw Russia's future with Europe and Slavophiles (or Eurasianists) who argued that Russia's distinct Eurasian identity mandated an independent and non-Western path to development (Stent, 2007, pp. 397, 419). While the Atlanticists dominated in the early post-Soviet era, by the late 1990s foreign policy consensus had settled around the idea of Russia as a great power that would work with the West, but would not be of the West. This consensus solidified and moved further away from Atlanticism over the course of Vladimir Putin's first two terms in office.

The most famous public announcement of this shift, and the first public statement by a Russian leader on the BRICS group, came in Putin's 2007 address at the Munich Security Conference. The Munich speech in some ways simply laid bare at a global-level rhetoric that Putin had been using for some time domestically (Salzman, 2019, chap. 3). It also, however, was a clear renunciation of the Western order in favour of one where the BRIC countries would be ascendant. Putin proclaimed,

> The combined GDP measured in purchasing power parity of countries such as India and China is already greater than that of the United States. And a similar calculation with the GDP of the BRIC countries – Brazil, Russia, India and China – surpasses the cumulative GDP of the EU…. There is no reason to doubt that the economic potential of the new centres of global economic growth will inevitably be converted into political influence and will strengthen multipolarity.
>
> (2007)

The year 2008 brought with it more tension, both in the bilateral U.S.-Russian relationship and at the broader level of Russian discontent with the international system. First, the five-day war between Russia and Georgia in August 2008 vividly demonstrated Russian concerns over Western interference in its neighbourhood and the extent to which the possibility of Georgian membership in North Atlantic Treaty Organisation (NATO) had increased Russia's threat perception. Second, the onset of the acute phase of the financial crisis with the collapse of Lehman Brothers on September 15, 2008, seemed to underscore that Russia was correct in its long-standing lamentations that Western countries were irresponsible stewards of the global system.

By the time these events occurred, Dmitri Medvedev had taken over the presidency from Vladimir Putin. At least initially, Medvedev followed his predecessor's lead. During his 2008 Address to the Federal Assembly, Medvedev spoke of BRIC as an equal in Russian foreign policy to the G8 (Medvedev, 2008). This was the highpoint of Russian reference to BRIC as an alternative to the Western system before the onset of the crisis in Ukraine. After that mention, BRIC receded from Russian political rhetoric and strategic planning for most of Medvedev's time in office. Part of this had to do with the Obama administration's Reset policy. The Reset depended on a pragmatic approach to Russia, with an emphasis on cooperation on issues of mutual concern (Salzman, 2010, p. 10). The Reset initially succeeded in calming tensions inflamed by the Bush 'Freedom Agenda' and Russian provocations in its neighbourhood. Russian rhetoric on BRICS tends to spike in inverse correlation to the state of relations with West. The steadying of U.S.-Russian relations decreased Russia's sense of isolation from the current order and minimised dependence on the construction of BRICS as an alternative.

The other reason rhetoric about BRICS decreased under Medvedev's tenure was his focus on economic development. This focus stemmed in part from the damage the global financial crisis wrought on the Russian economy. After first appearing to be an 'island of stability,' the Moscow Stock Exchange lost 80 per cent of its value between May and November 2008 (Åslund et al., 2010, p. 1). Russia was the hardest hit among Group of 20 (G20) economies, with GDP dropping 7.9 per cent between 2008 and 2009. To recover and grow, Russia needed foreign investment, of which the West was the best source (Stott, 2010).

The shift away from BRICS was not only born of economic necessity; Medvedev's preferences tended to run towards economic security through economic development. This is visible most clearly in three documents produced during his first two years in office. The first was a new Foreign Policy Concept, the first since 2000, that emphasised economic stability and integration into the global economy to a far greater extent than its predecessor (Ministry of Foreign Affairs, 2000, 2008). The second was *Rossiia vpered!* (Forward Russia!), an article that appeared under Medvedev's byline in September 2009 (Medvedev, 2009). The article focused on domestic economic development, especially turning Russia into a modern knowledge economy. Finally, the leaked 2010 survey of Russian foreign policy, 'Program for the Effective Exploitation on A Systemic Basis of Foreign Policy Factors for the Purposes of the Long-Term Development of the Russian Federation' (Ministry of Foreign Affairs, 2010). The Program details the need for strong economic relations with Western countries to give Russia a technological boost and then carefully goes through the ideal economic relationship with core countries in every region of the world. Despite the fact that the BRICS had already held two leaders' summits, the sections on economic cooperation with all three other BRIC countries are remarkably short (Salzman, 2019, chap. 4). The picture from these three documents, both individually and as a set, is that of a Russia, while still bent on strategic independence and increasing its voice in global governance, was less set on doing so at the expense of the current order.

The positive trend in U.S.-Russian relations slowed and then ceased in 2011, with the breakdown in cooperation on ballistic missile defence and the announcement that Vladimir Putin would return to the presidency in 2012. Putin, however, did not pick up where he had left off with BRICS in 2008. Instead, his focus shifted to the Eurasian Economic Union (EEU). The idea of a customs union in Eurasia dates back to the 1990s, but Putin revived it in 2009 during the St. Petersburg International Economic Forum and then expanded upon it in one of a series of articles he wrote in the run up to the 2012 elections (Putin, 2011).

BRICS remained primarily in the realm of rhetoric. The discussion of BRICS and its role in global affairs in Putin's 2012 and 2013 addresses to the Federal Assembly recalled the rhetoric of his 2007 speech in its emphasis on BRICS over Western organisations. However, his statements reflected neither advancement in the approach towards the group nor the strides the group had made towards institutionalisation over the preceding years (Putin, 2012, 2013). Similarly, although the foreign policy concept Putin approved in 2013 highlighted BRICS over the G8 in the discussion of how Russia would use its international connections to build a new world order, the Concept ignored BRICS in the details of Russian foreign policy plans and priorities (Ministry of Foreign Affairs, 2013a).

The result is that the 2013 'Concept of participation of the Russian Federation in BRICS' reads as vague and almost pro-forma (Ministry of Foreign Affairs, 2013b). While the BRICS Concept elaborates a long-term vision for BRICS and its role in Russian foreign policy, it is neither specific nor ambitious. The text foresees some level of institutionalisation, but it emphasises keeping the group informal and ensuring that group dynamics never override bilateral relations.

This lack of conceptual innovation, especially from the country that sees itself as the intellectual architect of BRICS, is revealing. It underscores that through the end of 2013, Russian policies and intentions towards BRICS remained both narrow and shallow. BRICS was another table to sit at and a useful theoretical alternative to Western clubs. It was also a convenient rhetorical weapon to show both domestic and international audiences that Russia had other friends besides Europe and the United States. It was not taken seriously, however, as a real alternative option for Russia. Indeed, the 2013 Concept in some ways confirmed the inverse: that the real value of BRICS to Russia before 2014 was in the ability to speak about and tout its existence and maturation as an international group as a way of pushing back against global norms with which it disagreed. The substance of cooperation was less important.

BRICS in Russian foreign policy after Ukraine, 2014–2015

BRICS might have stayed permanently in the realm of rhetoric in Russian foreign policy were it not for the onset of the crisis in Ukraine in November 2013 and its escalation in February 2014. The revolution in Ukraine began when President Viktor Yanukovych refused to sign a Deep and Comprehensive Free Trade Area agreement with the European Union (EU). It spiralled as a result of violence against the protesters in Kyiv and the revelation of astonishing levels of corruption in the Yanukovych government. The conflict over Ukraine's future alignment quickly became as much a proxy fight between Russia and the West as it was over domestic politics in Ukraine. The revolution culminated in the ouster of Yanukovych on February 21, 2014, immediately after signing a peace agreement with the leaders of the protest movement. Yanukovych fled to Russia, gave one final statement and faded from the scene (Marson et al., 2014).

Yanukovych's ouster terrified the Kremlin. Russian leadership has long accused the West of meddling in elections in its borderlands. Putin became especially sensitive to the issue following the colour revolutions in Georgia and Ukraine in 2003 and 2004, respectively. The revival of this perceived threat, its recurrence in a country Russia sees as critical to its security, integral to its national identity, and core to the success of the Eurasian Union, activated a deep paranoia in the leadership and spurred it to unexpected action.

On February 27, 2014, unmarked military personnel began seizing Ukrainian military bases in Crimea and took control of the Crimean Parliament building. Within two weeks, the Russians had named a new leader of the Crimean Parliament and orchestrated a referendum on Crimean independence from Ukraine and incorporation into Russia. Vladimir Putin formally announced the Russian annexation of Crimea in a landmark speech on March 18, 2014 (Putin, 2014a).

It is unclear what precipitated Russia's annexation of Crimea. The Russian leadership contends that it was a direct and spontaneous reaction to instability in Kyiv. Documents revealed in February 2015, however, suggest that Russia had been planning for a post-Yanukovych scenario for several weeks before his ouster and that part of that planning included a blueprint for the seizure of Crimea (Novaia gazeta, 2015). Given Russian security concerns in Crimea – among other things, Sevastopol has been the home of Russia's Black Sea Fleet for centuries – it is not altogether surprising that the leadership had contingency plans for if and when things deteriorated. What is surprising, however, is the implementation of those contingency plans; even if the Russian threat perception is believed, the annexation of Crimea was an overreaction to the dangers the situation presented. The subsequent invasion of the Donbas and ongoing support to those fighting Ukrainian sovereignty further belies the claim of self-defence.

Russia's annexation of Crimea took the West by surprise, but the response was swift. Between Russia's initial invasion of Crimea and the annexation three weeks later, the United States and Europe imposed successive rounds of coordinated sanctions on people within Putin's inner circle and Bank Rossiia, the bank favoured by the Russian political elite. Western leaders declared that Russian actions were condemned by the international community and were in direct contravention of international law (European Parliament, 2014; Obama, 2014). On March 24, 2014, the G7 announced the suspension of Russia from the G8, despite its being the planned summit host in 2014 (Borger and Watt, 2014). On March 27, 2014, the United States, the EU and other countries passed resolution 68/242 in the UNGA, which declared the annexation of Crimea invalid (United Nations General Assembly, 2014).

What the reaction to the Western response made clear, however, is that the West no longer controlled the narrative of rule makers and rule breakers in the international system. Of the 193 members of the UNGA, only 100 voted in favour of the resolution on the territorial integrity of Ukraine. Eleven countries, including Russia, voted against it, and 58 members, including all of the other BRICS countries, abstained (24 countries were absent). President Obama may have declared that the international community rejected Russian actions in Ukraine, but only half of that community stood up and agreed with that assessment.

The UN vote was not Russia's only victory. Three days before the UN vote, at the Nuclear Security Summit in the Hague, BRICS offered a quiet rebuke to those countries trying to isolate Russia. In response to rumoured efforts to ban President Putin from the November 2014 G20 Summit in Brisbane, Australia, the BRICS foreign ministers issued a statement reminding observers that no G20 member has the authority to exclude another unilaterally (BRICS Foreign Ministers, 2014; Cox, 2014). This was the first statement the BRICS made on Russian actions in Ukraine, and it placed them firmly against efforts to make Russia an international pariah.

The combination of isolation from the West and a willingness to look the other way by the BRICS countries brought BRICS to the fore of Russian foreign policy in a way it had not been before the onset of the crisis in Ukraine. This manifested itself in two primary ways. First, the period of 2014–2015 witnessed a strengthened focus on ways the BRICS group could support Russian efforts in its broader efforts to build an alternate world order not dominated by Western countries and institutions. Second, there was a renewed emphasis on maintaining economic security through increasing trade with BRICS.

The most visible example of Russia's sharpened focus on concrete benefits BRICS could bring is the 2015 'Concept of the Russian Federation's Presidency in BRICS in 2015–2016' (Ministry of Foreign Affairs, 2013b, 2015). As discussed above, the 2013 BRICS Concept outlines a long list of areas where Russia would like to see BRICS cooperation but displays little interest in either firm institutionalisation or pushing the boundaries of how BRICS could evolve. The 2015 Concept, by contrast, focused on building BRICS into a full-fledged player in global governance. It linked BRICS initiatives to specific Russian policy goals, including cooperation in the UN Security Council and assisting Russia in circumventing Western sanctions (Ministry of Foreign Affairs, 2015). Where the 2013 Concept is long in length and short on details, the 2015 Concept proposes fewer projects, but each one is sharper and more implementable than any presented in the predecessor document.

In part, this difference is due to the different goals of each Concept: the 2013 Concept was a vision for the group, whereas the 2015 Concept was a one-year plan for action while Russia held the chair. Indeed, holding the chair is itself an intervening variable in comparing the two documents. Russia tends to be event-oriented, putting focus on its next major diplomatic event (such as hosting APEC in 2012 and the Olympics in 2014) and then moving on once the event has passed (Gabuev, 2014). Even with those caveats, however, the 2015 Concept is evidence of clearer thinking in the Russian bureaucratic apparatus about the particularities of the BRICS platform and how it could best be leveraged towards broader Russian foreign policy aims. The 2015 Concept is considered in its aims given its audience, balancing long-term ambition with short-term objectives.

As a case in point, the 2015 Concept specifically references Western sanctions on Russia as an impetus for strengthening intra-BRICS economic cooperation (Ministry of Foreign Affairs, 2015). Indeed, many of Russia's suggestions for the BRICS are aimed at creating a parallel system to that controlled by Western states, perhaps as a way of circumnavigating the West's attempted isolation of Russia. During his statement at the Fortaleza Summit, Putin suggested that BRICS use Russia's GLONASS navigation system, which is an alternative to the U.S. Global positioning system (GPS) (Putin, 2014b). In May 2015, the Central Bank of Russia suggested that the BRICS discussed creating their own version of the SWIFT system (TASS, 2015).

Whether or not any of these proposals ultimately come to fruition (BRICS has a long incubation period), they are indicative of two important developments. First, they show that the combination of the Ukraine crisis and the chairmanship forced those involved in making Russia's BRICS policy to think seriously about how the forum could help Russia navigate its new global context. Second, the efforts to create a parallel system indicate that the rhetoric of building a new world order translated into Russia's operational approach to BRICS, at least during its tenure at the helm of the organisation.

One other note is important. To Western ears, these proposals seem outlandish, particularly the proposal that BRICS created their own SWIFT system, which is the backbone of international financial transactions. For the other BRICS, though, these proposals are not outlandish, they are ambitious. China began exploring its own international payment system, Cross-Border Inter-Bank Payment System (CIPS), long before Russia proposed BRICS do the same. CIPS opened on a small scale in 2015 and rolled out a second phase in 2017 (Xinhua, 2017). Russia also launched its own modified version and has proposed that it be available for both BRICS and members of the EEU (Alekseevskikh, 2018). The point here is not that either of these systems is a credible alternative to SWIFT on a large scale. Instead, it is that the proposals Russia put forward in 2015 both showed a concretisation of its ambitions for BRICS and also jived with plans that other BRICS were already undertaking for their own reasons.

The concretisation of goals leads to a discussion of Russian efforts to boost trade and economic relations with other BRICS nations. The high point of that effort was the May 2014 $400 billion gas deal between Russia and China, as well as the inauguration in September 2014 of the construction of the Power of Siberia pipeline (Hornby, 2015). The 2015 agreement between Russia and China to coordinate China's Belt and Road Initiative (BRI) with Russia's EEU is another example and puts Russia at the centre of the largest infrastructure investment scheme in the region (Charap *et al.*, 2017) There have also been efforts to increase trade with India, long a prime export market for Russian arms and import market for Indian pharmaceuticals (Confederation of Indian Industry, 2017). In addition, in 2014, a group of Indian businessmen met with the Russian-nominated leader of Crimea to discuss investment during Putin's visit to Delhi (Barry, 2014).

These economic deals have more import than the rubles they bring in, and this is where the concretisation of goals and the efforts to increase economic ties come together. More important than the dollar amount of deals, which ultimately cannot make up for the loss of revenue from trade with Europe, is the optics. The willingness of China, India and the other

BRICS to engage in business and summitry with Russia during the height of the Ukraine crisis was ample evidence that the West had not succeeding in isolating Russia either on the world stage or in global markets. BRICS bolstered that story, not only through the willingness of its members to trade with Russia, but through the fortunate timing of being ready to debut independent institutions right when Russia most needed an alternative narrative. As noted in the first section, the creation of both the NDB and the CRA was announced during the 2014 Summit in Fortaleza. That timing was not intentional; the group had been working towards that aim for two years. Nevertheless, the announcement of the agreement in Fortaleza to create the first BRICS institutions underscored that Russia was not without international partners. Russia's chairmanship of BRICS the following year, and the succession of BRICS-related events throughout Russia over the course of 2015 reinforced that message, giving Russia an alternative narrative to Western isolation just when it needed it most.

Conclusions: Russia and BRICS since 2015

The apex of BRICS cooperation in creating new institutions and presenting itself as a credible alternative to the Western-led international system occurred in 2014. This resulted from a number of factors, including economic slowdown across the BRICS beginning in 2014 and political and economic crises in Brazil and South Africa. Most important has been the loss of interest in BRICS in China and India. China has turned its attention to the BRI and the AIIB, both of which are iterative of BRICS projects. India, since the 2014 election of Narendra Modi, has focused instead on building relations with the United States. This is due primarily to an increased threat perception from China and a conviction that India can only achieve its economic development goals through strong relations with advanced economies (Pant and Joshi, 2017, p. 134). Russia too has begun to focus elsewhere. The EEU is the preferred institution through which to exercise Russian foreign policy goals. BRICS is still a part of the story, but it has been de-emphasised in recent years. The BRICS countries still meet regularly and hold both leaders' summits and numerous ministerial and sub-ministerial-level meetings per year, but the momentum that seemed evident in 2014 is gone.

BRICS may yet make a comeback, if its members decide that it is in their individual national interests. Even if it never regains its narrative or institutional impact, however, it has served its purpose for Russia. BRICS as a political concept began as something for Russian leaders to talk about as a way of showing that its lack of power in Western-led organs of global governance in no way diminished its status as a great power. BRICS became instead a group that changed how Russia experienced Western backlash after the onset of the crisis in Ukraine by blunting both the effect of economic sanctions and the attempt by Western powers to isolate Russia on the world stage. BRICS has allowed Russia to change the dominant narrative about its place in global order and thereby protect and preserve its status as a great power.

Note

1 This chapter draws heavily on three previous works: Salzman, Rachel S. 'From Bridge to Bulwark: The Evolution of BRICS in Russian Grand Strategy,' *Comillas Journal of International Relations*, 2015, 0(3):1–13. doi:10.14422/cir.i03.y2015.001; Salzman, Rachel S. 'BRICS in Russian Foreign Policy before and after the Onset of the Crisis in Ukraine,' PhD Thesis, Johns Hopkins University, 2016; and Salzman, Rachel S. *Russia, BRICS, and the Disruption of Global Order*, Washington, DC: Georgetown University Press, 2019.

References

Alekseevskikh, A. (2018) BRIKS bez SWIFT [WWW Document]. *Izvestiia*. https://iz.ru/743886/anastasiia-alekseevskikh/briks-bez-swift (accessed 5.18.18).

Andreev, Y.V. (2013) 'BRIKS: Cherez sotrudnichestvo – k bezopasnosti?', *Puti k miru i bezopasnosti* 45, 127–128. http://new.imemo.ru/files/File/magazines/puty_miru/2013/13026_andreev.pdf

Åslund, A., Guriev, S., and Kuchins, A.C., eds. (2010) *Russia after the Global Economic Crisis*. Peterson Institute for International Economics Center for Strategic and International Studies New Economic School, Washington, DC; Moscow.

Barry, E. (2014) 'Putin and Modi Reaffirm Bond between Russia and India', *The New York Times*, 11 December. www.nytimes.com/2014/12/12/world/asia/putin-and-modi-reaffirm-bond-between-russia-and-india.html

Bobrovnikov, A. and Davydov, V. (2005) Voskhodiashchie strany-giganty na mirovoi stsene XXI veka', *Latinskaia Amerika* 4–20. No. 5. There is no volume number.

Borger, J. and Watt, N. (2014) 'G7 Countries Snub Putin and Refuse to Attend Planned G8 Summit in Russia', *The Guardian*, 24 March. www.theguardian.com/world/2014/mar/24/g7-countries-snub-putin-refuse-attend-g8-summit-russia

BRICS 2017 Calendar [WWW Document] (2017) BRICS 2017 China. www.brics2017.org/English/China2017/BRICSCalendar/ (accessed 2.22.18).

BRICS Foreign Ministers (2014) 'BRICS Ministers Meet on the Sidelines of the Nuclear Security Summit in the Hague', *BRICS*, 24 March. http://brics.itamaraty.gov.br/press-releases/21-documents/190-brics-ministers-meet-on-the-sidelines-of-the-nuclear-security-summit-in-the-hague

Charap, S., Drennan, J., and Noël, P. (2017) 'Russia and China: A New Model of Great-Power Relations', *Survival* 59, 25–42. doi: 10.1080/00396338.2017.1282670.

Confederation of Indian Industry (2017) 'India-Russia Trade and Investment Relations', *CII Blog*. https://ciiblog.in/india-russia-trade-and-investment-relations/

Cox, L. (2014) 'Russian President Vladimir Putin May Be Banned from G20 Summit in Brisbane', *The Sydney Morning Herald*, 20 March www.smh.com.au/politics/federal/russian-president-vladimir-putin-may-be-banned-from-g20-summit-in-brisbane-20140320-353t9.html

Davydov, Vladimir Mikhailovich. 2014 Interview by Rachel S. Salzman. Personal Interview. Moscow, Russia.

European Parliament (2014) 'European Parliament Calls on Russia to Withdraw Military Forces from Ukraine' [WWW Document]. European Parliament. www.europarl.europa.eu/news/en/newsroom/content/20140312IPR38707 (accessed 6.1.15).

Gabuev, A. (2014) Personal Interview, Moscow, Russia.

Hornby, L. (2015) 'China and Russia Set to Finalise Gas Deal', *Financial Times*. www.ft.com/intl/cms/s/0/c0c385ea-c55f-11e4-bd6b-00144feab7de.html#axzz3cavrbqxI

Larionova, M. (2012) 'BRIKS v sisteme globalnogo upravleniia', *Mezhdunarodnaia zhizn* 2–14. http://dlib.eastview.com/browse/doc/27160066

Marson, J., Cullison, A., and Kolyandr, A. (2014) 'Ukraine President Viktor Yanukovych Driven from Power', *Wall Street Journal*. www.wsj.com/articles/SB10001424052702304914204579398561953855036

Medvedev, D. (2009) 'Rossiia, vpered!', *Gazeta.ru*. http://kremlin.ru/events/president/news/5413

Medvedev, D. (2008) 'Address to the Federal Assembly of the Russian Federation'. http://en.kremlin.ru/events/president/transcripts/1968

Ministry of Foreign Affairs (2015) 'Concept of the Russian Federation's Presidency in BRICS in 2015–2016 [WWW Document]', *Official Website of Russia's Presidency in BRICS*. http://en.brics2015.ru/russia_and_brics/20150301/19483.html (accessed 6.17.15).

Ministry of Foreign Affairs (2013a) 'Concept of the Foreign Policy of the Russian Federation'. http://www.mid.ru/brp_4.nsf/0/76389FEC168189ED44257B2E0039B16D

Ministry of Foreign Affairs (2013b) 'Concept of participation of the Russian Federation in BRICS'. http://eng.news.kremlin.ru/media/events/eng/files/41d452b13d9c2624d228.pdf

Ministry of Foreign Affairs (2010) 'O programme effektivnogo ispolzovaniia na sistemnoi osnove vneshnepoliticheskikh faktorov v tseliakh dolgosrochnogo razvitiia Rossiiskoi Federatsii', *Russkii Newsweek*. http://perevodika.ru/articles/13590.html

Ministry of Foreign Affairs (2008) 'The Foreign Policy Concept of the Russian Federation'. http://kremlin.ru/acts/news/785

Ministry of Foreign Affairs (2000) 'Foreign Policy Concept of the Russian Federation', Russian. http://kremlin.ru/acts/news/785

Novaia gazeta (2015) 'Predstavliaetsia pravilnym initsiirovat prisoedinenie vostochnykh oblastei Ukrainy k Rossii', *Novaia gazeta*. www.novayagazeta.ru/politics/67389.html

Obama, B. (2014) 'Statement by the President on Ukraine'. https://obamawhitehouse.archives.gov/the-press-office/2014/03/20/statement-president-ukraine

O'Neill, J. (2001) 'Building Better Global Economic BRICs', *Goldman Sachs*. www.goldmansachs.com/our-thinking/archive/archive-pdfs/build-better-brics.pdf

Panova, V. (2013) 'BRIKS: Mesto Rossii v Gruppe, videnie i prakticheskie rezultaty, sovmestnaia deiatelnost "piaterki" v ramkakh mnogostoronnikh institutov', in: Nikonov, V.A., Toloraya, G.D. (Eds.), *Strategiia Rossii v BRIKS: tseli i instrumenty*, Rossiiskii Universitet Druzhby Narodov, Moscow, 19–55.

Pant, H.V. and Joshi, Y. (2017) 'Indo-US Relations under Modi: The Strategic Logic Underlying the Embrace', *International Affairs* 93, 133–146. www.chathamhouse.org//node/27169

Putin, V. (2014a) 'Address by President of the Russian Federation'. http://en.kremlin.ru/events/president/news/20603

Putin, V. (2014b) 'Speech at BRICS Summit Plenary Session'. http://eng.kremlin.ru/transcripts/22677

Putin, V. (2013) 'Address to the Federal Assembly of the Russian Federation'. http://en.kremlin.ru/events/president/news/19825

Putin, V. (2012) 'Address to the Federal Assembly of the Russian Federation'. http://en.kremlin.ru/events/president/news/17118

Putin, V. (2011) 'Novyi integratsionnyi proekt dlia Evrazii – budushchee, kotoroe rozhdaetsia sigodnia', *Izvestiia*. http://izvestia.ru/news/502761

Putin, V. (2007) 'Putin's Prepared Remarks at 43rd Munich Conference on Security Policy', *The Washington Post*. www.washingtonpost.com/wp-dyn/content/article/2007/02/12/AR2007021200555.html

Salzman, R.S. (2019) *Russia, BRICS, and the Disruption of Global Order*, Georgetown University Press, Washington, DC.

Salzman, R.S. (2010) 'U.S. Policy toward Russia: A Review of Policy Recommendations', for the project 'Designing U.S. Policy towards Russia', American Academy of Arts & Sciences, Cambridge, MA. www.amacad.org/russia/recommendations.pdf

Shubin, V.G. (2012) 'Ot BRIK k BRIKS: rol IuAR v sostave gruppy i v kontinentalnom kontekste', in: Okuneva, L.S., Orlov, A.A. (Eds.), *Voskhodiashchie gosudarstva-giganty BRIKS: rol v mirovoi politike, strategii modernizatsii – sbornik nauchnykh trudov*, MGIMO – Universitet, Moscow, Russia, 198–206.

Stent, A. (2007) 'Reluctant Europeans', in: Legvold, R. (Ed.), *Russian Foreign Policy in the Twenty-First Century and the Shadow of the Past*, Columbia University Press, New York, 393–441.

Stott, M. (2010) 'Russia's New Foreign Policy Puts Business First', *Reuters*. www.reuters.com/article/2010/05/25/us-russia-policy-idUSTRE64O28020100525

Stuenkel, O. (2014) 'Emerging Powers and Status: The Case of the First BRICs Summit', *Asian Perspective* 38, 89–109. http://search.proquest.com/docview/1501333974/abstract?accountid=11752

Stuenkel, O. (2013) 'The Financial Crisis, Contested Legitimacy, and the Genesis of Intra-BRICS Cooperation', *Global Governance* 19, 611–630. http://search.ebscohost.com/login.aspx?direct=true&db=mth&AN=92015918&site=ehost-live&scope=site

TASS (2015) 'Tsentrobank Rossii predlagaet obsudit ideiu sozdaniia analoga SWIFT v ramkakh BRIKS', *Vedomosti*. www.vedomosti.ru/finance/news/2015/05/29/594387-tsentrobnak-rossii-predlagaet-obsudit-ideyu-sozdaniya-analoga-swift-v-ramkah-briks

Tett, G. (2010) 'The Story of the Brics', *Financial Times*. www.ft.com/intl/cms/s/0/112ca932-00ab-11df-ae8d-00144feabdc0.html#axzz2hRROifdt

Toloraya, G. (2014) Personal Interview, Moscow, Russia.

United Nations General Assembly (2014) '68/262: Territorial Integrity of Ukraine'. www.un.org/en/ga/search/view_doc.asp?symbol=A/RES/68/262

Unnikrishnan, N. (2014) Personal Interview, Moscow, Russia.

Xinhua (2017) 'China to Launch 2nd Phase of Cross-Border Interbank Payment System [WWW Document]', *China Daily*. www.chinadaily.com.cn/business/2017-06/22/content_29842105.htm (accessed 5.18.18).

PART V

Case studies of Russian security strategy

Introduction

Roger E. Kanet

In this fifth and final section of *The Handbook*, the authors examine cases of direct Russian involvement in security conflict situations. In all the cases discussed the conflicts involve other peoples and/or states. Russia has gotten directly involved because of its support for one side or the other or its interest in challenging external actors involved in the region.

In Chapter 30, 'Instrumentalising the Frozen Conflicts of the Greater Black Sea Region', Thomas Ambrosio of North Dakota State University examines the ways in which the Russian leadership has used the ongoing conflicts in the Caucasus to further its own foreign policy and security objectives. The primary objective is to counter the influence of external states and to facilitate continued Russian dominance over former Soviet space, especially in this region so central to Russian concerns and interests. Ambrosio then outlines Russia policy in each of the frozen conflicts – Transdnistria, Abkhazia, South Ossetia and Nagorno-Karabakh – to demonstrate the ways in which Russian policy has been implemented.

Chapter 31, entitled 'Russian Security Strategy in the Balkans', by Nadia Boyadjieva of the Institute for Balkan Studies of the Bulgarian Academy of Sciences, traces Russia's efforts since the demise of the former Soviet Union to maintain its influence in that part of Europe once dominated by the Ottoman Empire. This includes the challenge to the West at the time of the crisis over Kosovo, as well as the Russian opposition to more recent entry of several Balkan states into North Atlantic Treaty Organisation (NATO).

In Chapter 32, Bertil Nygren, retired from the Swedish National Defence College and the University of Stockholm, examines the place of 'The 2008 Russia-Georgia War' in overall Russian security strategy. He agrees that Russia's primary goal was to thwart Western advances into the region, more specifically to send both Georgian and NATO leaders the message that Georgia would not become a NATO member. He provides a brief, but detailed description of the factors that led to fighting and a discussion of the various arguments about whose forces moved first to initiate hostilities.

Chapter 33, by Yury Fedorov, formerly of the Moscow State Institute of International Relations (MGIMO), concerns 'Russia's "Hybrid" Aggression against Ukraine'. He begins by noting that 'Russia's annexation of Crimea and proxy war in Donbas are often seen as the classic or at least the first case of "hybrid" warfare..., a mix of conventional military operations with non-military methods of corrosion of an opponent such as economic pressure, fomenting political and social conflicts, subversive activities and massive propaganda campaigns'. He then discusses the factors that led Russia to attack Ukraine, including its place in overall Russian strategy, and the development and implementation of the concept of 'hybrid warfare'.

In the final chapter in this volume, Chapter 34, entitled 'Russia, the Middle East and the conflict in Syria', Derek Averre of the University of Birmingham analyses the most recent and ongoing example of Russian military intervention, in the civil war that has raged in Syria since 2011. Western support for the 'colour revolutions', followed by the 'Arab spring' were important factors in the development of Russia's increasingly hostile approach to relations with the West. Thus, when the civil war in Syria expanded and the United States and other Western states intervened, Russia took a strongly opposed position, one that evolved into full and direct support of the Assad regime. This is part of a broader commitment to challenge Western efforts to export liberal political institutions, to rebuild Russia's place in the international political system, especially in a region of strategic importance for Russia.

30
INSTRUMENTALISING THE FROZEN CONFLICTS OF THE GREATER BLACK SEA REGION

Thomas Ambrosio

The greater Black Sea region contains several unresolved secessionist conflicts which developed as a consequence of the disintegration of the Soviet Union. Conditions in Abkhazia, South Ossetia, Transnistria, and Nagorno-Karabakh are often called *frozen conflicts* because progress on resolving these disputes has stagnated for decades and a militarised status quo has been established, with these areas possessing de facto independence from their respective parent states. While each has different dynamics, a common thread is Russia's strategy of instrumentalising these conflicts in order to advance its own security interests in its self-declared region of 'privileged interests' (Reynolds, 2008). This extends Moscow's influence within the former Soviet space and counters the external influence of the US and the European Union (EU). It is perhaps no surprise that these frozen conflicts are located in the same area: where Russia perceives itself to be under the greatest threat from the Western powers.

This chapter provides an overview of this strategy before turning to the case studies. Because there is so much ground to cover, each treatment will necessarily be brief, with an emphasis on identifying Moscow's role in the frozen conflict and how its actions correspond to this larger strategy. Additional detail on each of these conflicts can be found in other contributions in this volume. The conclusion discusses how Russia appears to be utilising a similar strategy in eastern Ukraine.

Before beginning, three quick points need to be made. First, the reason for the non-settlement of these conflicts is overdetermined and includes historical, ethnic, and political factors – all in addition to Russia's involvement. However, Russia certainly plays a crucial role in perpetuating these situations through its support for these secessionist regions, as well as demonstrating little interest in moving toward a resolution. Second, one cannot always assume that the Kremlin has a master plan. Its specific policies are often reactive, ad hoc, and opportunistic. Nonetheless, Russia's strategy of instrumentalising each of these conflicts for its own ends ties to Russian security interests in common ways. Lastly, Russian involvement in each frozen conflict is unique. Therefore, not every aspect of Russian policy will be found in each case.

Enhancing and countering influence

Since the Russian Federation emerged as an independent country, it has sought to create a near-exclusive sphere of influence within the former Soviet space, excluding the Baltics. This is at the very heart of Russian security strategy: shaping conditions under which Russia can establish strategic depth against military, geopolitical, and ideological threats. To this end, it has promoted a series of Russian-dominated institutions to bind these countries to Moscow – most recently through the Eurasian Economic Union (EEU) and the Collective Security Treaty Organisation (CSTO) – rather than allow them to orient themselves elsewhere. In those countries less amenable to Russia's advances, it has used economic and diplomatic tools to both pressure and punish them. Most relevant for this chapter, it has sought to enhance its influence in the former Soviet Union and counter external powers from spreading their influence into this region by prolonging the frozen conflicts of the greater Black Sea area.

The parent states within which these frozen conflicts are contained – Georgia, Moldova, Azerbaijan, and, now, Ukraine – are unable to assert their rule over the whole of their territory because of the ever-present threat that Russia could act militarily to counter any forcible reunification of their country, as it did against Georgia in 2008. Not only does this undermine these states' sovereignty, but it can also have economic, geographical, and political effects. For example, the geographic concentration of certain industries enacted under Soviet central planning means that, in some cases, the separation of territories has effectively removed these industries from the parent states' economy, given that there is little trade across the demilitarised zone.[1] This separation may also mean that transit lines, access to the sea, or other strategic locations are cut off without any chance of being restored. These frozen conflicts have also stunted the political development of these parent states by derailing their state-building and governmental reform processes. These unsettled situations act to 'drain economic resources and political energies from these weak countries', which could be better used elsewhere (Socor, 2004, 127). Moreover, the desire for reunification creates incentives for nationalist outbidding by political elites in the parent states, which constantly distracts them 'from successfully pursuing reforms to reduce corruption and build representative institutions' (Orttung and Walker, 2015). All of this keeps the parent states weak and more open to Russian pressures.

These frozen conflicts also provide additional opportunities for Russia to extend its influence more directly along its southwestern periphery. In some cases, Russian soldiers were introduced into these secessionist regions as peacekeepers, ostensibly as part of multilateral forces. However, these operations very quickly became Russian-exclusive affairs, serving Russian interests without working to resolve these conflicts. This has legitimised Russia's military presence in these territories and permitted their consolidation into de facto statehood – which, in turn, means that they are highly dependent upon Moscow for their survival. This military presence has also led to permanent military bases outside Russia, extending its force projection capabilities within the region. In some instances, Moscow has also broadened its political reach into the secessionist regions by providing residents with Russian passports and citizenship over the objections of the parent states. This provides Russia with legal cover for actions which it can claim are intended to protect its citizens. More generally, Russia's deep involvement in these conflicts ensures that they remain 'three-sided and not bilateral conflicts', guaranteeing that Moscow has a seat at the table in any possible settlement and that all parties to the conflict must take Russian interests into account (Tudoroiu, 2012, 137). This latter point applies to issue areas not directly related to these conflicts.

Russian authorities believe that a central security interest of their state is to obstruct outside powers from encroaching on its sphere of influence without its consent. In Central Asia, Russia has acquiesced to China having economic and political influence, but only under the umbrella of the Shanghai Cooperation Organisation, which it co-founded in 2001.

Russia has been less willing to tolerate the intrusion of external powers in the greater Black Sea area, where it feels particularly vulnerable, given that the states of this region could potentially join Western military, economic, and political institutions. This would not only extend the West's reach further along Russia's borders, but would pull these states out of Moscow's orbit permanently, as had happened with the Baltic states. Perpetuating the frozen conflicts fulfils this goal of countering the West in three ways. First, Russia's deep involvement in these countries sends a clear message to the US and EU that it considers these states within its sphere of influence and as a red line that, if crossed, will precipitate a Russian response, including the use of force. Russia has also made it understood that any resolution of these conflicts must occur in accordance with Moscow's security needs – meaning that Russia would wield an effective veto over any Western shift by these states. Second, the continuation of these conflicts also effectively blocks these states from joining Western institutions. Neither the North Atlantic Treaty Organisation (NATO) nor the EU wish to bring these problems into their respective organisations. In fact, NATO released guidelines on enlargement in 1995, which explicitly cited the peaceful resolution of all ethnic disputes as a requirement for membership. The EU was willing to make an exception for the frozen Cyprus-North Cyprus dispute, but that was only because Greece threatened to block any expansion unless Cyprus was admitted. Such conditions do not apply to the present frozen conflicts and it is difficult to imagine Brussels being willing to confront Moscow over them. Furthermore, the lack of progress on democratisation and solidifying the rule of law in these states, caused in part by the political effects of the frozen conflicts, means that they will have difficulty meeting the political criteria for NATO or EU membership anyway. Lastly, Western encroachment along Russia's borders is not just military and economic, it is also ideological. Since moving toward authoritarianism under President Vladimir Putin, the Russian government has sought to insulate itself from democratic pressures at home and in the 'near abroad' (Ambrosio, 2009). Some scholars have pointed to the frozen conflicts as advancing this agenda: not only is the democratic development of the parent states hampered, and therefore undermining the possibility that democratic contagion could affect Russia itself (Bunce and Hozić, 2016), but Russian support for the authoritarian tendencies of the secessionist regions also allows 'pockets of autocracy' to persist within the region (Tolstrup, 2015a, 109).

In short, the frozen conflicts have been instrumentalised by Russia to further its goals of dominating the former Soviet space and creating an additional bulwark against the West. The subsequent sections of this chapter provide an overview of how this has occurred.

Abkhazia and South Ossetia

Although their levels of independent agency and dependency on Russia differ (Ambrosio and Lange, 2016), it is appropriate to cover Abkhazia and South Ossetia together, given the similarities in their relationship with their parent state and Russia's involvement there. The introduction of Russian peacekeepers into these regions followed ethnic violence in the early 1990s and these territories have been outside Georgian control ever since. Georgia was seen as 'the most staunchly anti-Russian republic in the former Soviet Union' and, therefore, Moscow needed to ensure both Tbilisi's compliance over Georgia's membership in the Commonwealth of Independent States and a continuance of Russian basing rights in the country (Lukic and Lynch, 1996, 362). Despite acceding to both demands, relations between Russia and Georgia remained troubled throughout the 1990s and early 2000s, with the flashpoints of Abkhazia and South Ossetia occasionally at its core. During this time, Russia aided in the construction of independent government institutions in these territories, while, at the same time, entrenching its own influence there. Russian involvement rose to new levels after the 2003 Rose Revolution, in part because Georgia's new government was seen as an ideological threat to Russia's emerging authoritarianism (Ambrosio, 2009, 136–145). Russia also began strengthening its position in Abkhazia and South Ossetia after the removal of Russian bases from Georgia-proper in 2005. Georgian demands that Russia withdraw from these territories as well were rejected. After Georgia re-established control over the Adjara region[2] in 2004, Russia began issuing passports to Abkhazian and South Ossetian residents. By the time of the 2008 August War between Russia and Georgia, nearly all had become Russian Federation citizens (Artman, 2013). Moscow then used the argument that it was protecting its citizens as justification for acting so forcefully against Tbilisi.

The origins of the August War are still a matter of dispute, but what is certain is that Russia increasingly saw its security interests as being threatened by the possibility that Western influence would spread into the South Caucasus. The Rose Revolution opened the door for a closer relationship between Georgia and the EU, which intensified after the signing of an "action plan" between Tbilisi and Brussels in 2006. Furthermore, Georgia's geopolitical value to the West improved significantly following completion of the Baku-Tbilisi-Ceyhan pipeline in 2005, which now allowed oil to bypass Russia en route to European markets. This likely meant that Western powers would be more inclined to protect their foothold in the Caucasus region at Russia's expense. However, the most immediate threat to Russian interests came just four months before the war began when NATO members issued a communiqué which stated that Georgia could become a member of the alliance once it had met all the necessary requirements. Although this did not formally invite Georgia to join at that time, a path to NATO expansion along Russia's southern border appeared open. For Russia, this was simply intolerable and a clear message had to be set to the West. According to Allison (2008, 1165), Russia's military action against Georgia was just such a message: 'In this way Russia is also trying to make the case of Georgia appear to European NATO states as a touchstone for assessing the sobriety of US policy in broader plans for NATO enlargement'.

In the wake of the August War, Russia's involvement in Abkhazia and South Ossetia increased considerably. The terms of the ceasefire effectively legitimised the Russian troop presence there, since its peacekeeping force was permitted to remain and even take additional measures to maintain the peace. Moreover, Russia's recognition of their independence, an act which was overwhelmingly rejected by the international community (and even by Russia's closest allies), afforded Moscow with the legal veneer to enter into scores of agreements with these governments on border security, economic relations, social issues, and military cooperation (Ambrosio and Lange, 2016). These agreements codified Russian influence in these territories and, especially in the case of South Ossetia, their growing integration with the Russian Federation itself. The agreements which attracted the most attention were those involving Russia's basing rights, which allow for the long-term hosting of thousands of Russian troops in these territories, the construction and expansion of Russian military installations, and the establishment of joint groupings of forces under Russian command (German, 2012). Russia also expended significant resources in these territories for welfare, economic development, and reconstruction, as well as to heavily subsidise their government budgets, with hundreds of millions of US dollars spent there in the years after the war. This amounted to a substantial investment by the Russian Federation and should also be seen as sending a powerful signal to both Georgia and the West that Moscow considers these territories firmly part of its sphere of influence and that its security interests there should not be challenged.

For Georgia, the effects of this frozen conflict have been substantial. First, Georgia remains disadvantaged geographically. Georgia lost nearly two-thirds of its coastline along the Black Sea, which makes it vulnerable to a Russian naval blockade, and Russia's continued troop presence in these regions deprives Georgia of any strategic depth. Moscow took advantage of both of these in August 2008 and could easily do so again. In addition, Russia engaged in a process of creeping territorial claims around South Ossetia after 2008, calling into question the security of the Baku-Tbilisi-Ceyhan pipeline (German, 2016, 162–163). This, in turn, has suppressed interest in expanding energy transit lines across Georgia.

Second, the hardening of borders between these territories and Georgia has exacerbated the problems associated with Georgia's post-Soviet economic transition. Tax revenues from South Ossetia's mineral resources and Abkhazia's agricultural and tourism industries have been lost to Tbilisi for decades, and nearly all trade to and from these regions goes through Russia, depriving Georgia of cross-border economic benefits and customs revenue. Furthermore, Georgia has had to bear the cost of supporting hundreds of thousands of internally displaced persons who fled their homes in the 1990s and will likely not return.

Third, the effects on Georgia's nation- and state-building have also been significant. In terms of identity, Kabachnik (2012) noted how the impact of losing these territories on Georgian national consciousness has enflamed nationalist sentiments, kept alive by political elites who have utilised it to counter alternative viewpoints on this and other issues. For example, opposition leaders relentlessly attack the government whenever proposals are made to normalise relations with Russia or whenever Moscow takes some action to help reinforce the separation of these territories. This helps to polarise the Georgian political system (Delcour and Wolczuk, 2015, 472). Moreover, despite the surge of liberalism associated with the Rose Revolution, the process of Georgian democratisation has long been distracted by the fact that territory, rather than reform, is often at the centre of Georgia's political debates (Wertsch, 2005, 523–524). This, in turn, undermines Georgia's political development.

Lastly, Georgia's westward shift has been stymied. Russia's greatest strategic success in the August War was not on the battlefield, but rather in preventing Georgia's ascension to NATO. Unless Georgia was to relinquish its claims to South Ossetia and Abkhazia – which, in Georgia's current political climate, is impossible – then this territorial dispute will effectively block Georgian membership. In fact, Medvedev cited this as one of the most significant outcomes of Russia's military action (Dyomkin, 2011). Georgia's prospects in regard to the EU are much better, with Tbilisi and Brussels signing an Association Agreement (EUAA) over Russia's strong objections (Antidze and Tanas, 2014). Nevertheless, ascension to the EU is highly unlikely in the short-to-medium term as the EU, which is already showing signs of strain, does not appear to be interested in making this frozen conflict their own.

Transnistria

Transnistria separated from Moldova after clashes between Moldovan and local forces in 1992 prompted the intervention by the Russian 14th Army, which had been stationed in the region since the collapse of the USSR. Afterwards, Russia supported the consolidation of Transnistrian governmental institutions as a means to pressure Moldova and undermine its westward alignment. Nonetheless, this is often seen as the most solvable of the frozen conflicts of the former Soviet Union for three reasons (Secrieru, 2011, 241–242; Istomin and Bolgova, 2016, 172). First, Moldova appears genuinely interested in reintegrating the region on the basis of a multi-ethnic national identity. Second, Transnistria is physically isolated and geographically vulnerable – a thin strip of land located between Moldova and

Ukraine without access to the sea. Lastly and most importantly, Russia has gone the furthest in voicing its support for a resolution, pledging to withdraw Russian forces from Transnistria at the 1999 Istanbul Summit of the Organization for Security and Co-operation in Europe.[3] However, Russia's incentives for maintaining the status quo remain and it has been willing to pay a reputational price for violating its 1999 pledge (Devyatkov, 2012, 555). Consequently, little progress has been made on reintegrating the region.

Russia has two key security interests in Moldova/Transnistria: strategic and geopolitical. Although Russia does not have many troops in Transnistria (approximately 1,500), it has reportedly located significant store of munitions in the region (Secrieru, 2011, 243). It, therefore, serves as a potential 'forward operations base' which Russia could utilise to project its military reach into southeast Europe (Sanchez, 2009, 175). It could also be used to pressure Ukraine from its western flank if Russia so choose (Istomin and Bolgova, 2016, 185). However, Transnistria's primary value to Moscow is how it is used to hamper Moldova's Western geopolitical orientation. Since most Moldovans wish to see Transnistria reintegrated, in part because it would reaffirm the country's multi-ethnic identity and distinctiveness from Romania, Moldova's room to manoeuvre between Russia and the West is limited by the fact that Moscow has explicitly linked a resolution with Moldova's continued neutrality between the East and the West (Devyatkov, 2012, 55; Tudoroiu, 2012, 149). This is a central reason why Moldova, unlike Georgia, has not sought to join NATO – in fact, Moldova's constitution includes an explicit requirement that the country remain neutral. By contrast, there is far more support in Moldova for having a close relationship with the EU, including possible future membership. It is in regard to this issue that Russia sees the most significant security threat to its influence in the country. The EU is more deeply involved in Moldova than in Georgia because it directly abuts EU territory, possesses cultural connections with EU member country Romania, and elected a pro-Western government in 2009 (Tudoroiu, 2012, 136). In an effort to counter further EU-Moldova progress, Moscow has supported pro-Russian candidates in parliamentary and presidential elections, in part by implying that these individuals would be better positioned to help resolve the Transnistria situation (Tolstrup, 2015b, 685–687). After its setback in the 2009 election, Russia imposed a series of escalating sanctions upon Moldova in order to dissuade the country from entering into its own EUAA, and, later, to punish the country for doing so in 2014 (Secrieru, 2011, 255; Cenusa, et al., 2014, 5–6). The election of a pro-Russian president in October 2016 – an election in which Transnistria citizens were allowed to vote – led to a somewhat softening of Russia's position. However, in a press conference with Moldova's new president, Putin was explicit in discussing the inverse relationship between improvements in EU-Moldovan relations, on the one hand, and Russian-Moldovan relations, on the other, and connecting the latter with the potential for progress on Transnistria (President of Russia, 2017). The implication was clear: if Moldova wanted to ever reintegrate Transnistria, it had to orient itself away from the West.

Russian support for Transnistria has been extensive, though not as great as that in South Ossetia and Abkhazia. The Transnistria government would not have been able to survive without Moscow's direct financial aid, its backing of Transnistria's currency, extensive building projects, and Gazprom subsidies. Much of this has been through loans which Transnistria simply will never pay back. Devyatkov (2012, 58) referred to the region as a financial 'black hole' for Russia. Nevertheless, Moscow's support continues. Furthermore, Russia has provided Transnistrian citizens with Russian passports, allowing them to work in Russia and send remittances back to the region, which amounts to approximately 17.3 per cent of its gross domestic product (GDP) (Istomin and Bolgova, 2016, 179–180). Russia has also encouraged private investment in Transnistria – a source of much-needed capital which further deepens Russian influence there (Secrieru, 2011, 244). It is notable, however, that Russia's relationship with Transnistria has been more troubled than that with the secessionist regions of Georgia. Moscow has recognised neither the overwhelming results of Transnistria's 2006 independence referendum nor the 2016 decree by the regional president endorsing unification with Russia. This is likely for three reasons. First, it would guarantee Moldova's geopolitical orientation westward by making its balancing act moot, as had happened to Georgia and, most likely, current-day Ukraine. Second, Transnistria's geographic isolation would make Russian annexation physically difficult to protect. Third, the EU's interest in Moldova means that the international consequences for Russia would likely be greater there than in Georgia (or even Ukraine) if Russia were to annex this region.

The effects on Moldova of Transnistria's de facto independence have been considerable. Moldova's economic development has been undermined by the fact that the region was the location of much of Moldova's heavy industry, relegating the country to a more agricultural economic base and without the tax and export revenues from these industries (Tudoroiu, 2012, 139). Moldova's transportation and communications lines with Ukraine run through Transnistria and it receives most of its electricity from the region, making it vulnerable to pressure from Transnistrian authorities (Eurasianet.org, 2016). Moreover, exports that travel through Transnistria are often subject to extra-legal fees and delays.

According to Tudoroiu (2012, 139) restoring Moldova's territorial integrity has become 'the main political preoccupation of the Moldovans', not 'democratization, EU accession, or relations with Romania'. In this way, the situation is similar to that in Georgia in that liberal reforms and anti-corruption policies have become secondary to resolving this frozen conflict. However, the desperate need to reunify the country has often led to the opposite of the situation in Georgia: rather than nationalist outbidding, the Transnistria issue has often necessitated pro-Russian attitudes amongst some elites. This has been in conflict with those who think that Moldova's future lies with the West, creating tensions amongst a population that appears evenly split between the two orientations (International Republican Institute, 2017, 54). As noted above, this is reflected in Moldova's inability to shift decisively toward the West – an outcome which well suits Russia's strategic needs.

Nagorno-Karabakh

The dispute over Nagorno-Karabakh has some similarities to the other cases examined in this chapter: it was a consequence of the collapse of the USSR, its frozen status was ensured through Russian intervention,[4] and it has negatively affected the participants. However, there are crucial differences which make this case quite dissimilar and impact how Russian security interests intersect with this situation. First, this is an interstate conflict between Armenia and Azerbaijan, rather than one between a parent state and a secessionist region. Armenia and Azerbaijan are locked in a zero-sum game with mutually incompatible goals and while their bilateral dynamic is influenced by their respective relationship with Russia, it is largely independent of it (Özkan, 2008). Second, Russia's involvement there is qualitatively different. Russia neither directly funds the region, nor do its troops shield it from attack. While Russia provides extensive support to Armenia, Nagorno-Karabakh's survival is not based on direct Russian patronage or protection. Moreover, Moscow has sought to have good relations with both sides and has been able to 'keep both countries, to varying degrees, in its orbit of influence' (Valiyev, 2012, 199). In fact, Russia is involved in peace talks along with the US and France,[5] as well as conducting its own independent mediation between Armenia and Azerbaijan. While these talks have gone on for decades without bearing fruit, it means that Russia is not in a position of openly undermining Azerbaijan's by directly supporting the secessionist region, as we have seen in the other frozen conflicts. Third, the potential threat to Russia's security interests from the West is less serious here. Armenia has a positive relationship with the US and the EU, but is very close to Russia. It has, therefore, eschewed a westward alignment and instead joined the Russian-dominated EEU and CSTO, placing itself firmly within Moscow's sphere of influence. While Azerbaijan had aligned itself more closely with the US and NATO, the West's weak reaction to the 2008 August War make it appear to be 'a fair weather friend', which could not be relied upon in the face of Russian military activities (Sherr, 2017, 59). Baku then understood that it needed a better relationship with Russia and subsequently pursued a multi-vector foreign policy between Russia and the West. Regardless, Azerbaijan's firmly authoritarian political system precludes its membership in the EU and NATO, which inadvertently advances Russian interests. Consequently, Russia has little to fear from Western encroachment into these countries.

Because of these differences, Russia has instrumentalised the Nagorno-Karabakh conflict in a different manner than in the other cases. For example, Russia has used this conflict to consolidate its already strong influence over Armenia. Although joining the EEU made better economic sense than signing an EUAA, Yerevan had actually considered the latter (Rinna, 2014). In response, Moscow reportedly made a not-so-veiled threat to shift its support toward Baku if this were to occur. Immediately thereafter, Armenian officials declared that they would join the EEU, reinforcing the leverage that Moscow has over Yerevan (Sherr, 2017, 61). In addition, Armenia's incentive to join the CSTO was predicated upon that organisation's mutual defence obligations – meaning that Russia would come to Armenia's aid if it were attacked by Azerbaijan. While it is unclear whether this would apply to an Azeri campaign in Nagorno-Karabakh exclusively, Moscow utilises this ambiguity to ensure that Armenia feels itself reliant upon Russia for its security (German, 2012). Russia has leveraged this to acquire long-term basing rights in Armenia for 3,000–5,000 troops and two air force squadrons until at least 2044, providing Moscow with crucial power projection capabilities in the southern Caucasus (Baev, 2017, 79). This relationship is not completely one-sided, however. Russia has delivered much-needed financial assistance, energy supplies, and transportation infrastructure to Armenia. More importantly, Russia has supplied Armenia with significant amounts of high-tech military equipment, which allows Armenia to maintain 'parity' with Azerbaijan (Sherr, 2017, 59). This means that the Armenia/Nagorno-Karabakh military, in conjunction with the possibility of Russia coming to Armenia's defence, has effectively cancelled out Azerbaijan's oil-fuelled defence spending, which amounts to Armenia's entire governmental budget (German, 2012, 218). Thus, while Armenia certainly benefits from this relationship, the country's dependency on Russia has deepened over time.

Russia has had a more difficult relationship with Azerbaijan, as Baku remains wary of Russian domination and has long sought to assert its independence from Moscow. Therefore, rather than attempt to secure a pro-Russian alignment, Russia has instead utilised the conflict to reinforce Azerbaijan's multi-vector foreign policy. Russia knows that Azerbaijan needs to remain friendly toward it to prevent Moscow from fully backing Armenia and completely foreclosing the possibility that Azerbaijan could resolve the Nagorno-Karabakh conflict on its terms. Given its role as an official mediator in the conflict, Russia has come to expect certain concessions from Azerbaijan – referred to by Valiyev (2012, 199) as 'gifts' provided in an attempt 'to win the Kremlin's favour'. However, Russia has also made clear that it is willing to reciprocate Baku's attempts to improve relations with Moscow. For example, because of Baku's more balanced foreign policy following the 2008 August War, Russia reiterated its support for Azerbaijan's territorial integrity and has even discussed the possibility of forming a strategic partnership, expanding trade, and strengthening military cooperation on the Caspian (Ramani, 2016; Baev, 2017, 77). Moreover, Russia has opened up arms sales to Azerbaijan. Although this makes neither party to the conflict happy, in that Moscow is arming both sides, it emphasises the fact that Russia could tilt the military balance toward one party should it so choose. The implication of all this is that Russia could impose real costs on Azerbaijan should Baku deviate too far from Russian desires, not only in regard to Nagorno-Karabakh, but more broadly. This ensures that Azerbaijan takes Russian security interests into account and pursues a more balanced foreign policy.

Conclusion

Russia has instrumentalised the frozen conflicts of the greater Black Sea to extend its geopolitical influence and military reach along its southwestern periphery, as well as to counter Western influence there. While Russia's specific policies and roles in each case, and the effects on the involved parties, remain unique, there is a common thread which links this strategy to its security goals. This is the key to understanding why Russia has an interest, not in resolving these conflicts, but rather in perpetuating them.

It remains to be seen if this pattern will be replicated in Ukraine, where Russia has annexed Crimea and supported the secessionist regions of Donetsk and Luhansk. Though, this is likely to be the case, given the country's geographic location and the danger seen by the Kremlin from its geopolitical orientation westward. Although Russia's Ukraine policy could ultimately be considered a failure – given that its intervention has inflamed Ukrainian nationalism and effectively removed Ukraine from Russia's orbit for the foreseeable future – it has had its successes. Russia loss of influence in Kiev already occurred with the fall of President Viktor Yanukovych, so it had to be satisfied with severely damaging Ukraine and creating whatever bulwark it could against further Western expansion. For example, Russia secured its military reach into the Black Sea by placing that the naval base in Sevastopol permanently under its control. Ukraine's economy has suffered through the detachment of the heavy industries of eastern Ukraine, the costs of fighting against Donetsk/Luhansk, and the scaring off foreign investors. It has also undermined Ukraine's post-Maidan political development and scuttled any real chance of fighting corruption as the war has distracted elites from the necessary business of reform. This, in turn, compounds the endemic problem of Ukraine's entrenched oligarchy. Although Ukrainian support for joining NATO is at an all-time high and a Ukrainian EUAA was approved by EU members in July 2017, neither organisation appears willing to confront Russia directly by extending membership to Ukraine while matters remain unsettled in the east. The prospect of truly neutral peacekeepers being introduced into eastern Ukraine, raised by Putin himself in September 2017, is almost certainly a ruse intended to divide Western opinion and relieve international pressure against Russia. Nothing will probably come of this plan, as the logic for Russia of maintaining its current policy in Ukraine is similar to that in the other cases reviewed in this chapter. Thus, Russia's strategy of instrumentalising frozen conflicts to enhance its security interests will undoubtedly continue and will likely be extended.

Notes

1 Other than black marketeering.
2 This region had also broken away from Tbilisi's control in the early 1990s.
3 One possibility floated by the Kremlin was to replace Russian forces with Russian police. Russia has not fulfilled this pledge.
4 In this case, diplomatic, rather than military.
5 France is effectively representing the EU.

References

Allison, Roy (2008) 'Russia Resurgent? Moscow's Campaign to 'Coerce Georgia to Peace', *International Affairs*, vol. 84, no. 6: 1145–1171.

Ambrosio, Thomas (2009) *Authoritarian Backlash: Russian Resistance to Democratization in the Former Soviet Union*. Farnham: Ashgate.

Ambrosio, Thomas and Lange, William (2016) 'The Architecture of Annexation? Russia's Bilateral Agreements with South Ossetia and Abkhazia', *Nationalities Papers*, vol. 44, no. 5:673–693.

Antidze, Margarita and Alexander Tanas (2014) 'Defying Russian Warnings, Moldova and Georgia Head for EU Pact', *Reuters*, 10 June. Accessed on 17 October 2017 at www.reuters.com/article/us-moldova-georgia/defying-russian-warnings-moldova-and-georgia-head-for-eu-pact-idUSKBN0EL1BP20140610.

Artman, Vincent (2013) 'Documenting Territory: Passportisation, Territory, and Exception in Abkhazia and South Ossetia', *Geopolitics*, vol. 18, no. 3: 682–704.

Baev, Pavel (2017) 'Russia: A Declining Counter-Change Force', in Cornell, Savante, ed., *The International Politics of the Armenia-Azerbaijani Conflict*. New York: Palgrave-Macmillan, pp. 71–87.

Bunce, Valerie and Aida Hozić (2016) 'Diffusion-Proofing and the Russian Invasion of Ukraine', *Demokratizatsiya*, vol. 24, no. 4: 435–446.

Cenusa, Denis, et al. (2014) 'Russia's Punitive Trade Policy Measures towards Ukraine, Moldova, and Georgia', CEPS Working Document, no. 400. Accessed on 20 October 2017 at www.ceps.eu/system/files/WD%20300%20Punitive%20Trade%20Measures%20by%20Russia_0.pdf.

Delcour, Laure and Wolczuk, Kataryna (2015) 'Spoiler or Facilitator of Democratization? Russia's Role in Georgia and Ukraine', *Democratization*, vol. 22, no. 3: 459–478.

Devyatkov, Andrey (2012) 'Russian Policy Toward Transnistria: Between Multilateralism and Marginalization', *Problems of Post-Communism*, vol. 59, no. 3: 53–62.

Dyomkin, Denis (2011) 'Russia Says Georgia War Stopped NATO Expansion', *Reuters*, 21 November. Accessed on 9 October 2017 at http://in.reuters.com/article/idINIndia-60645720111121.

Eurasianet.org (2016) 'Moldova: No Support for NATO Involvement in Transnistria Dispute', 28 July. Accessed on 23 October 2017 at www.eurasianet.org/node/79901.

German, Tracey (2012) 'Securing the South Caucasus: Military Aspects of Russian Policy towards the Region since 2008', *Europe-Asia Studies*, vol. 64, no. 9: 1650–1666.

German, Tracey (2016) 'Russia and South Ossetia: Conferring Statehood or Creeping Annexation?' *Southeast European and Black Sea Studies*, vol. 16, no. 1: 155–167.

International Republican Institute (2017) 'Public Opinion Survey: Residents of Moldova', February-March. Accessed on 23 October 2017 at www.iri.org/sites/default/files/iri_moldova_poll_march_2017.pdf.

Istomin, Igor and Bolgova, Irina (2016) 'Transnistrian Strategy in the Context of Russian-Ukrainian Relations: The Rise and Failure of 'Dual Alignment', vol. 16, no. 1: 169–194.

Kabachnik, Peter (2012) 'Wounds that Won't Heal: Cartographic Anxieties and the Quest for Territorial Integrity in Georgia', *Central Asian Survey*, vol. 31, no. 1: 45–60.

Lukic, Reneo and Lynch, Allen (1996) *Europe from the Balkans to the Urals*. Oxford: Oxford University Press.

Orttung, Robert and Walker, Christopher (2015) 'Putin's Frozen Conflicts', *Foreign Policy*, 13 February. Accessed on 9 October 2017 at http://foreignpolicy.com/2015/02/13/putins-frozen-conflicts/.

Özkan, Behlül (2008) 'Who Gains from the "No War No Peace" Situation? A Critical Analysis of the Nagorno-Karabakh Conflict', *Geopolitics*, vol. 13, no. 3: 572–599.

President of Russia (2017) 'Joint News Conference with President of Moldova Igor Dodon', 17 January. Accessed on 20 October at http://en.kremlin.ru/events/president/news/53744.

Ramani, Samuel (2016) 'Why the Russia-Azerbaijan Alliance Is Weaker Than It Looks', *Huffington Post*. Accessed on 7 November 2017 at www.huffingtonpost.com/samuel-ramani/why-the-russiaazerbaijan-_b_11608854.html.

Reynolds, Paul (2008) 'New Russian World Order: The Five Principles', *BBC*, 1 September. Accessed on 9 October 2017 at http://news.bbc.co.uk/2/hi/europe/7591610.stm.

Rinna, Anthony (2014) 'Yerevan's Choice: Armenia and Its Integration into the Eurasian Customs Union', *Iran and the Caucasus*, vol. 18, no. 4: 395–404.

Sanchez, W. Alejandro (2009) 'The "Frozen" Southeast: How the Moldova-Transnistria Question has Become a European Geo-Security Issue', *The Journal of Slavic Military Studies*, vol. 22, no. 2: 153–176.

Secrieru, Stanislav (2011) 'The Transnistrian Conflict: New Opportunities and Old Obstacles for Trust Building', *Southeast European and Black Sea Studies*, vol. 11, no. 3: 241–263.

Sherr, James (2017) 'Nagorno-Karabakh between Old and New Geopolitics', in Cornell, Savante, ed., *The International Politics of the Armenia-Azerbaijani Conflict*. New York: Palgrave-Macmillan, pp. 49–69.

Socor, Vladimir (2004) 'Frozen Conflicts: A Challenge to Euro-Atlantic Interests', in Asmus, Ronald, et al., eds., *A New Euro-Atlantic Strategy for the Black Sea Region*. Washington, DC: German Marshall Fund of the United States, pp. 127–137.

Tolstrup, Jakob (2015a) 'Subnational Level: Russian Support for Secessionism and Pockets of Autocracy', in Obydenkova, Anastassia and Libman, Alexander, eds., *Autocratic and Democratic External Influences in Post-Soviet Eurasia*. Farnham: Ashgate.

Tolstrup, Jakob (2015b) 'Black Knights and Elections in Authoritarian Regimes: Why and How Russia Supports Authoritarian Incumbents in Post-Soviet States', *European Journal of Political Research*, vol. 54, no. 4: 673–690.

Tudoroiu, Theodor (2012) 'The European Union, Russia, and the Future of the Transnistrian Frozen Conflict', *East European Politics and Societies*, vol. 26, no. 1, pp. 135–161.

Valiyev, Anar (2012) 'Nagorno-Karabakh: Twenty Years Under Damocles' Sword', *Demokratizatsiya*, vol. 20, no. 2: 197–202.

Wertsch, James (2005) 'Georgia as a Laboratory for Democracy', *Demokratizatsiya*, vol. 13, no. 4: 519–535.

31
RUSSIAN SECURITY STRATEGY IN THE BALKANS

Nadia Boyadjieva

Over the past two centuries the Balkans — the region also known as 'southeastern Europe' consisting of countries on the Balkan Peninsula — have often loomed large in Russian foreign policy. This was the case in the 1870s when Russia defeated Turkey in a war that helped Bulgaria, Montenegro, Romania, and Serbia break away from Ottoman rule. In 1914, the Balkans again had a profound impact on Russian foreign policy, triggering a chain of events that led to Russia's military mobilization, the mobilization of other European powers, and the start of the First World War (McMeekin, 2011). For some 20 years after the First World War, the new Soviet Communist regime in Russia devoted little attention to the Balkans, working mostly through the Communist International (Comintern) to support underground Communists in the region. But that changed with the outbreak of the Second World War. As the war was ending, Soviet forces occupied Bulgaria and Romania and swiftly installed Communist regimes in those countries (Kramer, 2013). Communist leaders also came to power in Yugoslavia and Albania in 1945 after the Red Army drove back Nazi Germany's forces.

Elsewhere in the Balkans, however, the Soviet Union faced major challenges. Two important Balkan countries — Greece and Turkey — soon became allies of the United States against the USSR. In the latter half of the 1940s, the Soviet leader Joseph Stalin had backed Communist guerrillas in Greece's Civil War, but he ultimately refrained from using military force to bring the Greek Communists to power (Iatrides, 2005; Marantzidis, 2014). Turkey, for its part, was never in danger of falling under Communist rule. Successive Turkish governments, including several military regimes, maintained a close alliance with the United States throughout the Cold War. Both Greece and Turkey were admitted to the North Atlantic Treaty Organisation (NATO) in 1952.

Even in the Balkan countries in which Communists gained power at the end of Second World War, Soviet influence came under challenge both during and after Stalin's lifetime. Two of the countries — first Yugoslavia and then Albania — ended up leaving the Soviet bloc. Stalin provoked a rift with Yugoslavia in 1948 in the expectation that he would be able to remove the Yugoslav leader Josip Broz Tito and subjugate Yugoslavia fully to Soviet will (Kramer, 2017). But, as it turned out, Tito was able to withstand Soviet pressure and keep Yugoslavia outside the Soviet Union's sphere of influence in subsequent decades. Albania split with the Soviet Union in the early 1960s, siding with the People's Republic of China (PRC) in the Sino-Soviet conflict and formally renouncing its membership in the Warsaw

Pact in 1968. In the 1970s, Albania also broke ties with the PRC and staked out a position independent of all external powers (Mëhilli, 2017).

The two other Balkan countries that were under Communist rule — Bulgaria and Romania — remained members of the Warsaw Pact until 1991, but Romania from the mid-1960s on loosened its ties with the Soviet Union and pursued a maverick position. Although Romania continued to side with the USSR on most matters, Romanian leaders defied Soviet preferences on some important issues (Braun, 1978). Only Bulgaria remained a fully reliable Balkan ally of the USSR through 1989.

The end of the Cold War in 1989–1990, the disintegration of the Soviet Union in late 1991 and the violent dissolution of Yugoslavia in the 1990s drastically changed the relationship between Russia and the Balkans. This essay discusses how the Russian government under President Boris Yeltsin (1991–1999) and his successor, Vladimir Putin, has dealt with individual Balkan countries and with the region as a whole.[1] Under Yeltsin, the wars of Yugoslav separation preoccupied Russian officials. Under Putin, Russia has continued to pay close attention to the former Yugoslavia, but has also forged relationships with far-left and far-right elements in Greece and with the Islamist government in Turkey, in order to counter U.S. and NATO influence. The Russian government has also striven to maintain Russia's role as the dominant energy supplier in the region.

National security documents under Yeltsin

When Yeltsin was elected president of Russia in June 1991 — six months before the Soviet Union broke apart — he had little experience in foreign affairs (Colton, 2008). His two initial prime ministers in post-Soviet Russia, Egor Gaidar (1992) and Viktor Chernomyrdin (1992–1998), also had little background in foreign policy. However, the momentous changes in international politics that led to the end of the Cold War in 1989–1991 helped to shape the new Russian government's foreign policy agenda, including initial cooperation with Western countries on most matters (Boyadjieva, 2013).

In April 1993, the Russian authorities officially enacted the Foreign Policy Concept of the Russian Federation, which laid out Russia's foreign policy priorities in the post–Cold War international environment ('Kontseptsiya vneshnei politiki RF', 1993). The document mentioned most of the individual Balkan countries, calling for 'the reestablishment of bi-lateral relations with Albania' and the strengthening of ties with Bulgaria and Romania. With regard to the disintegration of Yugoslavia, the Concept pledged 'cooperation with the United Nations [UN], the Organization for Security and Cooperation in Europe [OSCE], the European Union [EU], and other interested sides to continue active participation in peacekeeping efforts'. The document indicated that Russia would not only establish bilateral relations with all of the individual Yugoslav republics but would also 'maintain a permanent channel of contact with the leadership of the Federal Republic of Yugoslavia [i.e., Slobodan Milošević] to devise ways of ending the Yugoslav crisis'.

Seven months later, the Russian authorities published the Basic Propositions of the Military Doctrine of the Russian Federation, which dealt with numerous military issues that could affect the Balkans, such as Russia's approach to military conflicts and the types of forces that should be deployed to this end ('Osnovnye polozheniya voennoi doktriny', 1993). The document did not link any of the principles specifically to the Balkans, but references to the resolution of conflicts and peacekeeping had obvious relevance to Yugoslavia, which was being torn apart at the time by wars between Serbia and Croatia and increasingly between Serbia and Bosnia and Hercegovina (BiH).

The Balkans, especially the former Yugoslav republics, also figured in other basic national security documents of the Yeltsin period. In December 1997, Yeltsin approved a draft National Security Concept affirming that Russia's interests in the international sphere 'require the implementation of an active foreign policy course aimed at consolidating Russia's positions as a great power and as one of the influential centers of the developing multipolar world'. The document pledged that Russia would foster 'dialogue and all-around cooperation with the countries of Central and Eastern Europe', including the Balkan states ('Kontseptsiya natsional'noi bezopasnosti RF', 1997).

Russia and the Yugoslav wars

During the initial limited violence in Yugoslavia between Serbia and Slovenia in mid-1991 (the so-called Ten-Day War), Russia was still part of the USSR. Neither the Soviet nor the Russian government was in a position to play any role in Yugoslavia. At that same time, a separate war began between Serbia and Croatia, which, like Slovenia, was seeking to break away and establish independence. Serbia's war with Croatia was far more violent than the brief conflict with Slovenia, and fighting between Serbs and Croats was still escalating by the time the Soviet Union broke apart.

In January 1992, at Germany's urging, all member-states of the European Communities recognized Slovenia and Croatia, and a month later Russia followed suit. Contrary to Germany's hopes, however, recognition of the independence of the former Yugoslav republics did not stem the violence. The war between Serbia and Croatia intensified further, and then a much more destructive war in BiH erupted in June 1992, with the external involvement of both Serbia and Croatia.

Relations with Western countries, especially the United States and Germany, influenced Russia's decisions about the Yugoslav wars and international intervention in the region. The Russian government sought to establish a larger role in the Balkans and to take part in diplomatic efforts to resolve the conflicts there. Because neither the OSCE nor the EU proved capable of mitigating the warfare, the two bodies increasingly looked to the United States and NATO. Both George H. W. Bush and Bill Clinton were very hesitant about getting deeply involved, but the Clinton administration in 1993 and 1994 did begin regularly discussing the issue with Russian officials, hoping to find common ground.

Russia, as the 'legal successor state' to the Soviet Union and thus a permanent member of the UN Security Council, wanted the United Nations (and later the so-called Contact Group) to be the main forum for dealing with the former Yugoslavia, including with peacekeeping. As enunciated in the 1993 Foreign Policy Concept, the Russian government was willing to work with other countries on peacekeeping in the Balkans, contributing some 1,400 troops to Sector East of the UN Protection Force (UNPROFOR) in Yugoslavia during its mandate from 1992 to 1995. However, the Russian contingent, despite its political significance, was a net burden. In April 1995, the commander of Russian forces in UNPROFOR, General Aleksandr Perelyakin, was ousted from his post by the UN after overwhelming evidence of corruption, smuggling, and other egregious abuses came to light (Cohen, 1995, p. A16). Many other Russian officers serving under Perelyakin on UNPROFOR also engaged in arms trafficking, human smuggling, and illegal narcotics dealing. UNPROFOR had many problems during its three-year existence and proved wholly ineffective in keeping the peace in either Croatia or BiH. Even though the deleterious impact of the Russian contingent was only one of many reasons for UNPROFOR's woeful record, the Russian forces' performance in Sector East did not get Russia's role in peacekeeping off to a good start.

The peacekeeping scandals with Russian forces in Croatia and BiH were symptomatic of a larger trend — the extent to which the positions of Russia and NATO countries increasingly diverged. Russia, for example, opposed NATO's ultimatum to the Bosnian Serbs in 1994 and also opposed the follow-up ultimatum in 1995. However, the common strategic goal of ending the fighting in BiH and containing the conflict ultimately spurred all major parties to unite their diplomatic efforts (Boyadjieva, 2003). Within the UN Security Council, Russia endorsed the U.S.-mediated Dayton accords that put an end to the warfare in BiH, and the Russian government contributed a brigade to the NATO-led peacekeeping Implementation Force in 1995–1996 and Stabilisation Force (SFOR) from 1997 on that operated on behalf of the UN (Lambert, 2002).

In line with NATO and EU countries, Russia adhered to the policy of maintaining the sovereignty and integrity of BiH and rejecting 'any model based on the principle of creation of three separate states'. Russian diplomats worked to try to keep the Bosnian Serbs in the peace process, adding to the NATO and UN efforts. Cooperation on the matter frayed, however, as a result of the bitter disagreements that emerged between NATO and Russia over Serbia's province of Kosovo.

Russia, the Kosovo War, and its aftermath

The conflict in Kosovo and its culminating phase in 1999 engendered severe tension between Russia and NATO. After the Serb leader Slobodan Milošević revoked the autonomous status of Kosovo in 1990, unrest rapidly built up there among ethnic Albanians, who accounted for roughly 90 per cent of the population. A peaceful movement led by Ibrahim Rugova pushed for Kosovo's independence, but neither the Russian authorities nor the NATO governments paid any heed, choosing instead to deal directly with Milošević at Dayton (Glaurdić, 2011). In 1997, as discontent in the province mounted, the Kosovo Liberation Army resorted to a campaign of guerrilla warfare and terrorist violence against Serb forces and paramilitaries, hoping to provoke grisly reprisals that would prompt external powers, especially NATO, to intervene (Kuperman, 2008).

The resulting civil war escalated over the next year, leading to a NATO ultimatum to Milošević at Rambouillet in early 1999, a step that Russian leaders strongly opposed. When, as NATO governments expected, Milošević was unable to comply with the ultimatum, the United States and other NATO countries geared up for military action to compel Serbia to fulfil their demands. Russian officials did whatever they could to prevent military action, but, unlike in the case of Bosnia in 1995 when NATO acted in accordance with UN Security Council resolutions (and therefore with Russia's consent), U.S. and NATO military action in 1999 against Serbia was undertaken entirely outside the UN Security Council's auspices over the vehement opposition of Russia.

NATO's two-and-a-half-month war against Serbia, from 24 March to 9 June 1999, killed large numbers of civilians in Serbia and sparked intense anti-Western sentiment in Russia, both among elites and in the wider public. Russian leaders argued that NATO's military operations were hasty, unnecessary, and illegal, but those objections ultimately proved futile. Seeking to prevent a complete breakdown of relations, U.S. officials made overtures to their Russian counterparts, hoping to work with them in bringing an end to the conflict. In response, Yeltsin's personal envoy, Viktor Chernomyrdin, agreed to push Milošević to consent to a ceasefire that would entail the withdrawal of all Serb military and security forces from Kosovo. Although the Serb leader was extremely reluctant to accept this demand, Chernomyrdin managed to bring him around, leading to the Kumanovo military-technical accord on 9 June 1999 that put an end to NATO's bombardment.

Russia joined with other UN Security Council members the next day in adopting Resolution 1244, which established Kosovo as an independent administrative, political, and defence structure. For a brief while, however, the Kumanovo accord and UN Security Council Resolution 1244 seemed on the verge of coming undone as a result of an incident at Pristina airport — an incident provoked by the Russian government partly out of frustration with NATO's heavy-handed approach vis-à-vis Serbia and partly because of disagreements within the UN Security Council over the arrangements for external peacekeeping forces in Kosovo (KFOR). Yeltsin and his aides had expected that Russian peacekeeping forces would be deployed in their own sector of Kosovo outside NATO's command. But NATO governments refused to establish a separate zone for Russia, fearing that if they did so it might lead over time to a formal partition between northern areas controlled by ethnic Serbs and the rest of Kosovo controlled by ethnic Albanians.

Disagreements over the matter prompted the Russian government to dispatch an armoured column of 250 Russian peacekeeping forces from Bosnia (part of SFOR) into Kosovo on 11 June 1999, just hours after UN Security Council Resolution 1244 had been adopted. Moscow's aim was to gain control of the airport before NATO forces could be brought in. Once NATO troops did arrive on 12 June, an armed confrontation briefly appeared imminent, especially after NATO's top brass learned that the Russians were preparing to fly in reinforcements (Jackson, 2007). However, urgent diplomacy, combined with the decision by Bulgaria, Romania, and Hungary to deny overflight rights for the Russian reinforcements, permitted a makeshift compromise to be worked out (Bitkova, 2016). Under this arrangement, the Russian peacekeeping forces did not receive their own zone but did not have to report directly to NATO commanders. With the confrontation peacefully defused, the Russian KFOR contingent worked with NATO forces to secure Pristina airport and reopen it to civilian air traffic.

UN Security Council Resolution 1244 had envisaged that negotiations would later be held to determine the final status of Kosovo, but in the meantime the region was turned into a de facto independent entity under NATO (and later EU) supervision. Even when Kosovar Albanians carried out atrocities and ethnic cleansing against ethnic Serbs in Kosovo, NATO failed to step in. The Russian government condemned the abuses, but Kosovo increasingly moved toward formal independence.

When UN Special Envoy Martti Ahtisaari launched final status talks for Kosovo in February 2006, Putin and his advisers reacted warily, suspecting that the talks were little more than a subterfuge to establish and consolidate Kosovo's independence. The Russian government made clear it would not accept any outcome that did not uphold the principle of state sovereignty and did not meet with the approval of Serbia as well as the Kosovar Albanians. Several times, U.S., British, and French diplomats at the UN rewrote a draft UN Security Council Resolution to try to overcome Russia's objections, but none of the drafts gained Moscow's consent. In the summer of 2007, U.S. and EU representatives launched a separate negotiation with Russian diplomats on the disposition of Kosovo, but this effort, too, proved of no avail and collapsed altogether once it became clear that the Kosovar government was preparing to issue a unilateral declaration of independence — a declaration that came on 17 February 2008, just after Serbia's presidential election.

A few days before the Kosovar government issued its proclamation, Putin denounced the imminent move as 'illegal, ill-conceived, and immoral' and accused Western countries of 'double standards'. But he stopped short of saying what Russia would do in response, and he emphasized that Russia did not intend to 'act like fools. If someone makes an illegal and ill-conceived decision [about Kosovo], it does not mean we should act the same way' about Abkhazia and South Ossetia, two regions of Georgia that had long exercised de facto independence despite remaining nominally a part of Georgia. Putin added that Russia would simply 'react to preserve our interests' ('Transcript of Annual', 2008).

Just six months later, however, the Russian army responded to provocations against its forces in South Ossetia by moving en masse into Georgia and formally detaching South Ossetia and Abkhazia from Georgia's main territory. Shortly thereafter, Putin and Russian President Dmitry Medvedev announced they would be recognizing the two regions as independent countries. Putin brushed aside Western criticism by explicitly referring to the precedent NATO had set vis-à-vis Serbia, and he scolded Western leaders for condemning 'the sort of international behaviour you yourselves were eager to engage in. Two can play at this game' (Questions and Answers, 2008).

Thus, even though the new National Security Concept adopted by Putin in 2000 made only passing mention of the Balkans, the text with its anti-Western orientation was profoundly shaped by NATO's war against Serbia (Fawn, 2008). The war and its repercussions also had long-term consequences for Russia's foreign policy that induced Russia leaders to invoke Balkan analogies far outside the region ('Kontseptsiya natsional'noi bezopasnosti RF', 2000).

The Balkans, NATO enlargement, and Russia

Although the Soviet-dominated Warsaw Pact was dismantled in mid-1991, the alliance that had long confronted it — NATO — not only survived the end of the Cold War but began to bring in new members. The process, especially early on, was driven not by NATO itself but by the former Communist states in Central and Eastern Europe, which did not want to be left without a solid guarantee of their security in the post–Cold War world. In the early 1990s, they repeatedly urged the leading NATO powers to expand the alliance. After initially being reluctant, the United States and other major NATO countries moved ahead with enlargement, specifying numerous criteria for new members.

In two stages — in 1999 and 2004 — all of the USSR's former Warsaw Pact allies were granted NATO membership. The admission of new members in 2004 included Bulgaria and Romania, the first Balkan countries that had been brought into the alliance since Greece and Turkey were admitted 52 years earlier.[2] Subsequently, in 2009 and 2017, Croatia, Albania, and Montenegro also gained NATO membership. The Republic of Macedonia was invited to join in 2009 under its provisional name 'Former Yugoslav Republic of Macedonia', but its formal entry into the alliance was held up when Greece refused to drop its decades-old objection to the country's name, insisting that the use of 'Macedonia' implied a claim on Greece's region of that name. The dispute was not resolved until June 2018 when the two countries tentatively agreed that Macedonia would be renamed the Republic of Northern Macedonia (*Republika Severna Makedonja*), subject to approval in popular referendums in both countries. The compromise did not please either side and provoked angry nationalist complaints in both, but it seemed the only plausible way of enabling Macedonia to join NATO and the EU.

The Russian government's response to the extension of NATO into Central and Eastern Europe, including the Balkans, was extremely negative. Russian leaders repeatedly tried to discourage NATO from enlarging. Their objections slowed the process but did not derail it, much to Moscow's consternation (Fraser, 2003). Although Russian officials did not seek to punish former Warsaw Pact countries that had joined NATO, politicians and journalists in both Bulgaria and Romania reported that Russian diplomats had informed them that their countries were no longer regarded as 'friendly' (see also Fenenko, 2001, p. 61). Similar warnings were conveyed after they joined the EU in 2007.

Curiously, some observers in the United States, Great Britain, and other long-time NATO countries had the opposite concern about enlargement into the Balkans, especially Bulgaria. They worried that Bulgaria, with its deep historical ties to Russia, cultural affinities, orthographic similarities, and heavy dependence on Russian energy supplies, would become a kind of 'Trojan horse' for Putin (Stanishev, 2009). Bulgarian leaders did their best to counter this perception by tangibly demonstrating their contributions to NATO, including its warfighting in Afghanistan, and by emphasizing Bulgaria's quest for alternative energy supplies. Even as they did this, however, they had to strike a fine line between reassuring their NATO allies and avoiding comments and actions that would further inflame relations with Russia and potentially result in manipulation of gas shipments.

Romania was also cited in the Western press as a potential security risk within NATO that might benefit Russia. In May 2002, *The Wall Street Journal* published a lengthy article claiming that many NATO governments were wary of sharing highly sensitive information with Romanian intelligence services, for fear that Communist-era holdovers in those services would divulge the information to hostile powers, notably Russia (Shishkin, 2002, p. A9). The article generated a furor in Romania, where it was widely republished in translation (Matei, 2008, p. 15). Ultimately, though, these sorts of concerns did not prevent Romania from being invited in November 2002 to join the alliance and then formally admitted along with Bulgaria in 2004.

The continued extension of NATO into the Balkans in 2009, 2017, and 2018 came as a new irritant in relations with Russia, where Putin and other policymakers worried that Kosovo and BiH might also eventually be brought in, thereby 'surrounding' Serbia. Some in Russia also worried that over time even Serbian officials might think about joining NATO despite the bad feelings left by NATO's aerial bombardment in 1999 and by the alliance's crucial role in forcibly separating Kosovo and establishing it as an independent country. To be sure, a far-reaching reorientation of Serbia could not happen easily or quickly (Dronina, 2018). The political barriers to such a move in Serbia are still formidable, and Serbia is still heavily dependent on Russia for weapons supplies and military training.

Nonetheless, Serb experts have occasionally floated the idea of a rapprochement with NATO that could pave the way for an eventual effort by Serbia to apply for membership. No matter how ethereal these proposals may be, they have drawn notice in Russia. From Moscow's perspective, any significant indication that Serb leaders were contemplating the pursuit of NATO membership would be cause for alarm, signalling a potentially fatal threat to Russia's most durable foothold in the Balkans.

Russia's scramble for influence

Until recently, Russia's role as the dominant natural gas supplier to Balkan countries gave Moscow potential leverage it could exert there. However, that prospect has become more complicated for Russia since 2014. After Russia's annexation of Crimea in early 2014 and instigation of a destructive conflict in eastern Ukraine from 2014 on, the transit of Russian natural gas across southern Ukraine — the traditional route for shipments to Balkan countries — plummeted (Pirani, 2018). Bulgaria's decision to stay out of the planned underwater South Stream route, a decision that marked the death knell of the project, further reduced options for Russian energy shipments to the Balkans. Moreover, the advent of U.S. liquefied natural gas exports as a result of the shale revolution offers an alternative that could eventually cut significantly into Russia's market share.

Even if the two projected Turkish Stream pipelines come on line in 2019–2021 (which is by no means certain), the maximum expected capacity of the two routes combined will not be enough to make up for more than a relatively small fraction of the decline in Russian natural gas transiting Ukraine's southern corridor. For some time to come, Bulgaria, Serbia, and most other Balkan countries will remain heavily dependent on Russian natural gas, but Russian experts who want to maintain Russia's dominant supply presence in the region have begun to speculate that in coming years Gazprom might find itself increasingly under challenge in the region (Ponomareva, 2018).

As Russia strives to maintain influence in the Balkans, the role of Turkey will be especially important. Because Recep Tayyip Erdoğan's Islamist rule in Turkey and mercurial defiance of the United States have left Turkey relatively isolated within NATO, Putin has sought to enlist Erdoğan in a wider anti-American coalition (Trenin, 2013). The repressive crackdown Erdoğan implemented in the wake of the Turkish military's attempted coup d'état in July 2016 alienated most EU countries, providing further inroads for Putin. Erdoğan's own sense that the EU will never seriously consider Turkey's membership has given him ample incentive of his own to lean toward Russia.

Nevertheless, over the longer historical perspective, Turkey has been mostly a rival of Russia in the Balkans, not an ally. If Erdoğan someday is forced out of power, Turkey's policy could shift back to the closer alignments with NATO it embraced before Erdoğan altered the country's posture. Even with Erdoğan still in power, Russia and Turkey have often been sharply at odds over the civil war in Syria. Putin has been intent on preserving Bashar al-Assad's regime through unbridled violence, whereas the Turkish government has consistently demanded Assad's removal. The potential for trouble was illustrated in November 2015 when a Turkish fighter pilot near the Syrian-Turkish border shot down a Russian aircraft, sparking a prolonged, severe downturn in Russian-Turkish relations. Although Erdoğan ultimately gave in on the matter and offered an abject apology to Putin that allowed bilateral relations to be mended, the crisis underscored the ease with which Russian-Turkish ties could be disrupted by major events in the region.

Some other Balkan countries also offer tempting opportunities for Russia. In September 2014, Russian officials warned that any prospect of Montenegro's entry into NATO would be a 'major provocation' (Bieri, 2015). Yet, despite Russian browbeating, the Montenegrin government persisted with its bid for NATO membership, gaining admission into the alliance in June 2017 (Morrison, 2018). However, Montenegro's accession to NATO came only eight months after Russian intelligence operatives had plotted for months to thwart Montenegro's overtures to NATO by overthrowing the Montenegrin government and assassinating the country's then Prime Minister Milo Djukanović (Farmer, 2017). The plot was only narrowly averted after British and U.S. intelligence officials tipped off the Montenegrin security services hours before the plot was to be implemented. Even so, the very fact that the conspiracy proceeded as far as it did was a sobering reminder of Russia's capacity to wreak havoc in the Balkan countries that are members of NATO or the EU or both.

Greece is another country that has attracted Russian interest, though the record has been mixed. Even though Greece has been a member of NATO since 1952, its relationship with the alliance has often been problematic, in part because of Greece's long-standing hostility toward fellow NATO member Turkey and in part because populist leaders in Greece have seen benefit in defying the alliance. Much the same applies to Greece's membership in the EU, which drastically worsened after the financial crisis beginning in 2011 plunged Greece into a debilitating recession. Rightly or wrongly, many Greeks suspected that Germany and the European Central Bank were content to leave Greece mired in an endless recession. As a result of these tensions, Russian Foreign Minister Sergei Lavrov in 2015 sensed an opportune moment to cultivate close ties with Greece, a country in which sentiment toward Russia with its Orthodox tradition has long been favourable.

On numerous occasions, Lavrov praised the Greek government headed by the far-left Syriza party for its opposition to the EU sanctions that had been imposed against Russia in 2014 after it seized Ukrainian territory and instigated deadly warfare in eastern Ukraine. Greek Prime Minister Alexis Tsipras and other radical leftists in Syriza had repeatedly denounced the EU and NATO and seemed ready to forge much closer relations with Russia. Putin likewise went out of his way to praise Syriza.

The marked warming of ties between Russia and Greece proceeded smoothly for a few years but suddenly came to a halt in July 2018, when Greece expelled two Russian diplomats and denied entry to others (Konstandaras, 2018). Ironically, the breakdown was connected to the long-standing dispute between the Greek and Macedonian governments over Macedonia's name. The accord signed by Greece and Macedonia in mid-2018 proposing Republic of Northern Macedonia as the new name would allow the renamed country to enter NATO, an outcome Putin was hoping to block. With official Russian encouragement, pro-Kremlin elements in both Greece and Macedonia were trying to fuel enough public opposition to defeat the proposal, putting an end for the time being to the prospect that a renamed Macedonia would join NATO (Konstandaras, 2018). In June 2018, U.S. officials provided highly classified intercepted communications to the Greek government revealing the Russian authorities' efforts to thwart the Greek-Macedonian agreement (Cooper and Schmitt, 2018). The Kremlin's heavy-handed interference in Greece's internal politics on such a sensitive issue prompted the Greek government's retaliation against Russia, a stunning setback for Moscow after years of notable progress.

The record of Russia's security strategy in the Balkans more generally reflected mixed outcomes. Russia maintained its one close relationship, with Serbia, but its attempts to strengthen ties with other countries too often proved fleeting. The spread of NATO and the EU into the Balkans was incomplete and was not always effective, but it did put a crimp on Russia's more grandiose aspirations.

To the extent that Russia and NATO have often been on opposite sides in the Balkans, the responsibility can be attributed to both parties. Neither of them could fully abandon its Cold War-era images of the other. Zero-sum conceptions proved resilient. NATO's decision in 1999 to wage war against Serbia outside UN Security Council auspices poisoned the alliance's relationship with Russia almost beyond repair, and many of Russia's actions from 2008 on have inflicted further damage. Even if greater cooperation proves feasible in the future, Russia and NATO will likely maintain a broadly competitive relationship in the Balkans for many years to come.

Notes

1 Vladimir Putin has been the highest leader in Russia from the end of 1999 to the present. He first served two terms as president (2000–2008) and then, for constitutional reasons, served four years as prime minister while Dmitry Medvedev served as president (2008–2012). Putin then returned to the presidency in 2012 and is currently in his fourth term, extending to 2024. Even when Putin was 'only' prime minister, he remained the dominant leader in the country. Medvedev nominally outranked Putin during those years, but no one either inside or outside Russia doubted that Putin had the final say.
2 Slovenia, which was also admitted into NATO in 2004, can be deemed a Balkan country as a former Yugoslav republic, but, unlike almost all the rest of the Balkan countries, Slovenia was

never under Ottoman rule. Hence, some scholars do not regard it as a true Balkan country. There is no universally accepted definition of 'Balkans', and therefore the question of whether to include Slovenia is up to the individual.

References

Bieri, Matthias (2015) 'The Western Balkans between Europe and Russia,' *CSS Analyses in Security Policy*, No. 170, March, pp. 1–4.
Bitkova, Tatyana (2016) *Vneshnepoliticheskie orientiri Ruminii: Analiticheskii obzor*. Moscow: Institut nauchnoi informatsii po obshhestvennym naukam RAN.
Boyadjieva, Nadia (2003) *NATO on the Balkans: Patterns of Peace-keeping in the Post-Cold War Era (The Cases of Bosnia-Herzegovina and Kosovo)*, NATO Research Fellowships Programme, Sofia, available at: www.nato.int/acad/fellow/01-03/boyadjieva.pdf
Boyadjieva, Nadia (2013) *Rusya, NATO i sredata na sigurnost sled Studenata voina 1989–1999* [Russia, NATO and the Security Environment after the Cold War], 1989–1999. Sofia: D. Ubenova Publishers.
Braun, Aurel (1978) *Romanian Foreign Policy since 1965*. Westport, CT: Praeger Publishers.
Cohen, Roger (1995) 'U.N. Dismisses Russian from Croatia Peacekeeping Post,' *The New York Times*, 12 April, p. A16.
Cooper, Helene and Eric Schmitt (2018), 'Work of U.S. Spies Uncovers Russian Link in Key Balkans Vote,' *The New York Times*, 10 October, pp. A1, A8.
Colton, Timothy J. (2008) *Yeltsin: A Life*. New York: Basic Books.
Dronina, Irina (2018) 'Strategicheskie plani Serbii i Rossii,' *Nezavisimaya Gazeta*, 2 January, p. 3.
Farmer, Ben (2017) 'Russia Plotted to Overthrow Montenegro's Government by Assassinating Prime Minister Milo Djukanovic Last Year,' *The Sunday Telegraph* (London), 19 February, p. 8.
Fawn, Rick (2008) 'The Kosovo and Montenegro: Effect,' *International Affairs* (London), Vol. 84, No. 2, pp. 269–294.
Fenenko, Aleksei (2001) 'Balkanskii krizis i rossiiskie vneshepoliticheskie prioriteti,' *Pro et Contra*, Vol. 6, No. 4, Fall, pp. 59–73.
Fraser, John M. (2003) 'Serbia and Montenegro: How Much Sovereignty? What Kind of Association?' *International Journal*, Vol. 58, No. 2, pp. 373–388.
Glaurdić, Josip (2011) *The Hour of Europe: Western Powers and the Breakup of Yugoslavia*. New Haven, CT: Yale University Press.
Iatrides, John O. (2005) 'Revolution or Self-Defense? Communist Goals, Strategy, and Tactics in the Greek Civil War,' *Journal of Cold War Studies*, Vol. 7, No. 3, pp. 3–33.
Jackson, General Sir Mike (2007) *Soldier: The Autobiography*. New York: Random House.
'Kontseptsiya natsional'noi bezopasnosti Rossiiskoi Federatsii' (1997) *Rossiiskaya Gazeta*, 19 December, pp. 1–3.
'Kontseptsiya natsional'noi bezopasnosti Rossiiskoi Federatsii' (2000) *Nezavisimoe voennoe obozrenie*, No. 2, 14 January, pp. 1–2.
'Kontseptsiya vneshnei politiki Rossiikoi Federatsii' (1993) *Diplomaticheskii vestnik*, No. 1–2, Spetsvypusk, pp. 3–23.
Kramer, Mark (2013) 'Stalin, Soviet Policy, and the Establishment of a Communist Bloc in Eastern Europe, 1941–1949,' in Mark Kramer and Vít Smetana, eds., *Imposing, Maintaining, and Tearing Open the Iron Curtain: East-Central Europe and the Cold War, 1945–1990*. Lanham, MD: Rowman & Littlefield, pp. 3–37.
Kramer, Mark (2017). 'Stalin, the Split with Yugoslavia, and Soviet-East European Efforts to Reassert Control, 1948–53,' in Svetozar Rajak et al., eds., *The Balkans in the Cold War*. London: Palgrave Macmillan, pp. 29–63.
Konstandaras, Nikos (2018) 'Athens and Moscow's Stunning Falling-Out,' *The New York Times*, 23 July, p. A17.
Kuperman, Alan J. (2008) 'The Moral Hazard of Humanitarian Intervention: Lessons from the Balkans,' *International Studies Quarterly*, Vol. 52, No. 1, March, pp. 49–80.
Lambert, Nicholas J. (2002). 'Measuring the Success of the NATO Operation in Bosnia and Herzegovina, 1995–2000,' *European Journal of Operational Research*, Vol. 140, No. 2, pp. 459–481.
Marantzidis, Nikos (2014) 'The Greek Civil War (1944–1949) and the International Communist System,' *Journal of Cold War Studies*, Vol. 15, No. 4, pp. 25–54.

Matei, Florina Cristiana (2008) *Romania's Transition to Democracy: Press's Role in Intelligence Reform*, Working Paper, Research Institute for European and American Studies, Athens, Greece, February.

McMeekin, Sean (2011) *The Russian Origins of the First World War*. Cambridge, MA: The Belknap Press of Harvard University Press.

Mëhilli, Elidor (2017) *From Stalin to Mao: Albania and the Socialist World*. Ithaca, NY: Cornell University Press.

Morrison, Kenneth (2018) 'Change, Continuity and Crisis. Montenegro's Political Trajectory (1988–2016),' *Sudosteuropa*, No. 2, pp. 153–181.

'Osnovnye polozheniya voennoi doktriny Rossiiskoi Federatsii' (1993) *Roiisskaya Gazeta*, 4 November, pp. 2–3.

Pirani, Simon (2018) 'The Decline and Fall of the Russia-Ukraine Gas Trade' *Russian Analytical Digest*, No. 221, 11 June, pp. 1–6.

Ponomareva, Elena (2018) *Balkanskii rubezh Rossii: Vremya sobirat' kamni*. Moscow: Knizhnyi mir.

Questions and Answers (2008) Putin meeting with Valdai Club, in Rostov-on-Don, September.

Shishkin, Philip (2002) 'Among NATO Applicants, Romania Draws Particular Scrutiny – Its Communist Police State Was Especially Ruthless, Can It be Trusted?' *The Wall Street Journal*, 3 May, p. A9.

Stanishev, Sergei (2009) 'Building Cooperation: Bulgaria's Essential Role in Regional Integration,' *Harvard International Review*, Vol. 30, No. 4, Winter, p. 84.

'Transcript of Annual Big Press Conference,' 14 February 2008, The Kremlin, available online at http://en.kremlin.ru/events/president/transcripts/24835.

Trenin, Dmitry (2013) 'From Damascus to Kabul: Any Common Ground between Turkey and Russia?' *Insight Turkey*, Vol. 15, pp. 37–49.

32
THE 2008 RUSSIA-GEORGIA WAR

Bertil Nygren

Introduction: the Georgian conflict with its two breakaway republics and Russia – the longer-term political history of the conflict

This chapter tells the briefest possible story of the short Russia-Georgia War of August 2008, from an initial intrastate war between Georgian and South Ossetian armed forces and militias over the jurisdiction of South Ossetia (judicially within the state of Georgia) to a full-blown international war between Russian and Georgian regular armed forces. Historically, the Caucasus region with its complex mix of languages, ethnicities and religions has in recent centuries been a security problem to neighbouring regional powers, Russia, Persia/Iran and Turkey. Russia has been both a security provider and a conqueror, and Russia gradually annexed the Georgian territory in the nineteenth century. After a short period of independence in 1918, Georgia was invaded by the Red Army in 1921, and in 1922, Georgia joined Armenia and Azerbaijan in the Transcaucasian Republic of the USSR, and again, in 1936, Georgia was transformed into one of the Soviet Republics with its present legally recognised borders.

The break-up of the USSR in December 1991 (the Belavezh Accords) made very clear that the 12 republics should remain territorially intact, and Georgia emerged with two separatist regions, South Ossetia and Abkhazia. In the much weaker South Ossetia, with a population of approximately 25,000 Ossetians and 20,000 Georgians, the civil war that followed between 1990 and 1992 resulted in some 1,500 casualties and ended with a *de facto* secession after an independence vote in 1992. The much stronger Abkhazia also broke free after a more severe civil war in which Georgia was defeated in 1993 with some 10,000 casualties, and with several hundred thousand ethnic Georgians exiting, leaving the population at approximately 250,000 (mostly Abkhazians) (Tagliavini, 2009, P2, 79). In both separatist regions, Commonwealth of Independent States (CIS) (or in effect, Russian) peacekeepers with a UN mandate kept peace, not always impartially, and tensions remained.

The run-up to the war

A brief chronology of the rising tension between Russia and Georgia from the 'Rose Revolution' in December 2003 and up to the war is appropriate and necessary to understand the context of the 2008 war. In early 2004, Saakashvili swore to establish Georgia's 'territorial integrity', i.e. to take control of Abkhazia and South Ossetia. After a short period of thaw, relations with Russia deteriorated again, though, and hit a low in summer 2006 when Russia even warned Georgia of attacking South Ossetia (Nygren, 2008, 149). In both Abkhazia and South Ossetia, Russia intensified its policy (since 2002) to grant Russian passports to the citizens of the two breakaway republics (by 2008, most residents in South Ossetia had Russian passports), and Russia continued to act in its own interests, despite its formal peacekeeping role. From 2006, Georgia also set up alternative administrations in the two breakaway republics in addition to the long-established Abkhazian and South Ossetian ones (Tagliavini, P1, 2009, 29–30). Differences between the two breakaway republics existed: while Abkhazia was fairly well divided up territorially, South Ossetia was a patchwork of control with many villages under *de facto* Georgian state control. Peace plans were presented by Georgia both in summer 2005 and in spring 2007, but were rejected by South Ossetia. In November 2006, two referendums took place on South Ossetian independence (Nichol, 2009, 3–4).

Several incidents severed the relationship. For example, in September 2006, after Georgia detained four Russian spies, Russia introduced an air, land and sea transport and mail blockade of Georgia, expelling more than 2,000 Georgians living in Russia. In March 2007, Russian helicopters attacked Georgian administration buildings in Kodori Valley. In summer 2007, the South Ossetian administration initiated a blockade of Georgian villages, and in August, a Russian aircraft bombed a Georgian radar station (Illarionov, 2009, 65–66; Cohen and Hamilton, 2011, 20).

In the spring of 2008, the situation deteriorated further. In March, a former Russian general was appointed Minister of Defence of South Ossetia, and the South Ossetian and Abkhazian Parliaments called on the UN to recognise their independence. In April, Russia withdrew from the sanctions imposed by the CIS in 1996 and opened formal direct relations between Russian and corresponding ministries in the two *de jure* Georgian, but *de facto*, independent republics (Chivers, 2008b; Tagliavini, P1, 2009, 1). Georgia, in turn, continued to block Russian World Trade Organization (WTO) membership.

In the summer months that followed, both Georgian and South Ossetian forces engaged in violent attacks, including artillery shelling of civilian homes. In July, Russia acknowledged four overflights of Georgian territory, in response to which Georgia recalled its ambassador from Moscow. Several bomb explosions and mortar shelling around Tskhinvali then resulted in a total mobilisation in South Ossetia. Furthermore (on 6 July), the Russian 'Caucasus Border' 2008 military exercises began, involving some 8,000 troops, paralleled with Georgian military exercises ('Immediate Response 2008') near Tbilisi. Further exchanges of fire and artillery shelling took place in late July, accompanied by a bomb explosion in Tskhinvali (Illarionov, 2009, 70–72; Nichol, 2009, 4; Tagliavini, P2, 2009, 205–206).

Since April 2008, the situation in Abkhazia had also deteriorated. In May, Russia added about a thousand peacekeeping forces to Abkhazia, with tanks, artillery and air defence weapons, and the Russian Black Sea Fleet held several exercises (Illarionov, 2009, 68–69). Furthermore, some 400 Russian Railroad Troops began to repair a disused railroad line connecting Sukhumi with Ochamchire on the border of Georgia proper, without the Georgian government permission, finalising it by late July.

The days immediately preceding the large-scale Russian military invasion is still a matter of some controversy, but some facts are irrefutable. On 1 August, an Ossetian bomb attack on Georgian policemen was followed by Georgian snipers killing six South Ossetian police officers. Ossetian shelling of Georgian villages in South Ossetia followed, and Georgian forces amassed along the *de facto* administrative border to South Ossetia with mortar exchanges, in turn resulting in several casualties. On 2 August, Russia's 'Caucasus 2008' exercises formally ended, although troops did not withdraw (Illarionov, 2009, 73). Intensified firing and mortar shelling in South Ossetia also followed, and on 4 August, volunteers were mobilised and some 300 irregulars passed into South Ossetia from Russia. By 6 August, the entire informal front line between Georgia proper and South Ossetia experienced intense firing, resulting in more than two dozen killed and wounded, and there were significant Georgian troop movements close to South Ossetia (Nichol, 2009, 5; Tagliavini, P2, 2009, 208). Direct preparations for war were obvious.

The Russia-Georgia War of August 2008

By 7 August, 12,000 Georgian troops gathered close to the South Ossetian border, supported by some 75 tanks and armed vehicles. In the early night of 7–8 August, South Ossetian artillery shelling of Georgian villages took place, and resumed again at approximately 2:00 PM, to which Georgian peacekeepers responded. The UN Security Council (UNSC) called a nightly emergency session requested by Russia. Later in the afternoon, at approximately 6:00 PM, Georgian air fighters attacked South Ossetian forces and Georgian forces entered South Ossetia from the Gori direction with tanks and heavy artillery and pounded Tskhinvali. According to Georgian sources, mercenaries from Russia that were trying to reach Tskhinvali were battled (Antidze, 2008). At about 7:00 PM, Saakashvili called for a unilateral ceasefire which lasted for about three hours (Finn, 2008c; Tagliavini, P2, 2009, 209; Up in flames, 2009, 22). At approximately 11:00 PM, South Ossetian artillery fire purportedly resumed (according to the Georgian side but denied by the Russian side and by present OSCE observers). Russia claimed not to have any forces in South Ossetia at this time (Finn, 2008c). At 11:50 PM, Saakashvili then unquestionably ordered resumed fire and Georgian military forces initiated massive artillery shelling. According to Georgian official sources, invading Russian forces through the Roki tunnel at about 00:45 AM was shelled (Felgenhauer, 2009, 169).

By 2:00 AM on 8 August, Georgian forces began shelling the city itself with the highly inaccurate BM-21 multiple rocket system. The firing and shelling from both sides continued all through the night and early morning of 8 August, when Georgian regular forces entered Tskhinvali and street fighting with South Ossetian forces and militias erupted. Russian peacekeepers also responded, purportedly to defend Russian citizens (Finn, 2008a). At this time, there were about 9,000 Georgian troops in the war theatre around Tskhinvali. At some time during the night or very early morning of 8 August, Russian regular forces must have entered South Ossetia through the Roki tunnel and moved southward towards Tskhinvali some 30 kilometres to the south, under artillery fire from Georgian forces (ICG, 2008). The run-up to the war was now over and the international war was to begin. Russian artillery and air strikes now pushed Georgian troops back from Tskhinvali within two more hours. In the morning, Russian aircraft bombed villages in Georgia proper and destroyed several airfields, including two close to Tbilisi (Nichol, 2009, 5). A renewed Georgian attack on Tskhinvali a couple of hours later resulted in yet another Russian counter-attack with air strikes and artillery fire, and by 11:00 PM on that Friday 8 August, the Georgian troops retreated for the second time from Tskhinvali (Finn, 2008c; Felgenhauer, 2009, 170). Russia's Ministry of Defence stated that Russian troops had been sent to South Ossetia to assist the peacekeepers and Russian state television showed pictures of troops and tanks already in South Ossetia (Finn, 2008a). Saakashvili ordered a full military mobilisation (including reservists) and asked for an emergency meeting of the UNSC and also called home its 2,000 soldiers from Iraq. Putin stated that 'war has started' and Saakashvili accused Russia of a 'well planned invasion' (Schwirtz, 2008). Medvedev summoned the Russian Security Council. This is probably the closest we get to a true history of the first full day of regular warfighting in South Ossetia. The alternatives will be dealt with later. The first interstate war in the former Soviet territory had begun and the security order established in Europe after the disastrous Balkan wars in the 1990s was seriously threatened.

Generally, official Georgian sources (and some unofficial Russian sources) afterwards claim that several thousand Russian troops from the Caucasus 2008 exercises entered the Roki tunnel already in the morning of 7 August, i.e. 24 hours earlier (Felgenhauer, 2009, 163), while the Russian side claimed that this early advancement did not occur, although it admitted that a normal rotational unit of Russian peacekeepers in South Ossetia had crossed the tunnel that day (Felghenhauer, 2009, 169). More importantly, the Georgian side afterwards claimed that they attacked South Ossetia only after Russian forces had already invaded South Ossetia, while the Russian side claimed that they entered only after the Georgian forces had attacked Tskhinvali (Finn, 2008c). During the next couple of days, Russian troops advanced into South Ossetia with the help of South Ossetian forces and militias. On 9 August, Russian aircrafts bombed also Upper Kodori Valley, which was part of Georgia proper (Nichol, 2009, 6). By the end of 9 August, the situation for the Georgian forces had become increasingly hopeless. A military force was being assembled in Abkhazia and the Russian Black Sea Fleet began patrolling the Abkhazian coastline. Russian infantry and armour was being moved into Abkhazia through the newly repaired railway line and Abkhazian forces entered Kodori Valley in the evening. The UNSC failed for the second time to respond.

In the morning of 10 August, most Georgian troops retreated from South Ossetia to Gori in Georgia proper. Russia also bombed the Gori military garrison and airfields in the Tbilisi area (including the civilian airport of Tbilisi) and the military base at Vaziani. Later the same day, Georgia declared a unilateral ceasefire and called on Lavrov for a mutual ceasefire (Nichol, 2009, 6). Russia landed 4,000 paratroopers at Ochimchire in south Abkhazia and linked up with the heavy equipment coming by rail on the recently restored railroad (Donovan, 2009, 15). Abkhazian forces were mobilised. The war stage had expanded.

On 11 August, Georgian forces retreated on all fronts, including from Gori, to defend Tbilisi some 40 miles away. The war had now clearly entered Georgia proper (Felgenhauer, 2009, 174), and Saakashvili claimed that Russia was occupying Georgia and asked for assistance from abroad, while Putin complained that Cold War thinking dominated in the West and claimed its operations to be nothing but peace-enforcing (Schwirtz et al., 2008). This day Russia attacked along two axes into Georgia proper, towards Gori from South Ossetia and threatened Tbilisi, to gain operational depth south of Tskhinvali ('Russian Imperialist ...', 2008; Donovan, 2009, 16–17).

On 12 August, Russian forces entered deep into Georgia proper, both from South Ossetia and from Abkhazia, and Gori itself was surrounded (but never actually occupied) and other Russian forces moved through Abkhazia and continued during the next few days to take other military bases and small cities (Poti, Zugdidi, Senaki) closer to Tbilisi. The Georgian Senaki base was taken by Russian forces on a 'preventative mission'. Russian operations along the Abkhazian coast and further south into Georgia proper continued, with the likely goal to cut the east-west transport and railroad corridor, and to take the ports of Poti (Georgia's largest port) and the oil and gas export ports of Supsa and Batumi (Donovan, 2009, 17). Abkhazian forces entered Upper Kodori Valley after Georgian troops had retreated (Tagliavini, P1, 2009, 21–22). Georgian forces had now been assembled outside Tbilisi for a last stand, but the Russian troops stopped some 30 kilometres outside the capital (Felgenhauer, 2009, 175). Russian troops generally seemed to have exercised some restraints in avoiding civilian targets.

On the same day, the French President (and at the time Chairman of the European Council) Nicolas Sarkozy visited Moscow and Tbilisi and managed to draw a six-point cease fire or stablilisation plan aiming at the withdrawal of troops to positions prior to the war (Owen and Lomsadze, 2008b; Tagliavini, P1, 2009, 22). Medvedev explained that 'mopping up operations' would continue (which, as it later turned out, also included aerial bombing and occupation of villages and destruction of military facilities) (Nichol, 2009, 7).

On 13 August, the EU foreign ministers endorsed the peace plan, and on 14 August, Medvedev met with the Abkhazian and South Ossetian *de facto* presidents in Moscow to sign the agreement (Nichol, 2009, 8). Accusations of later breaches of the ceasefire were many, and Russia obviously continued to destroy Georgian military facilities. By 16 August, Saakashvili and Medvedev signed a second ceasefire agreement also brokered by Sarkozy, according to which all forces should withdraw to the positions held before 6 August. Only on 22 August did all Russian troops retreat and an implementation agreement was signed on 8 September (Nichol 2009, 7; Tagliavini, P1, 2009, 22). The 'five-day war' was now finally and formally over.

At the end of the war, Russian forces had destroyed Georgian military equipment at three military bases and established 'buffer security zones' in and around Abkhazia and South Ossetia (Felgenhauer, 2009, 176). The estimated Russian costs for the war was about half a billion dollars (Larsson, 2008, 40). One immediate consequence of the war was Georgia's withdrawal from the CIS (first *de facto* and a year later *de jure*). Another was the Russian formal recognition of the independence of the two breakaway republics on 25 August (two weeks later Nicaragua did the same). The Shanghai Cooperation Organisation (SCO) met in late August without an approval of the Russian stand, and a meeting with the Collective Security Treaty Organisation (CSTO) in September yielded the same result. Thus, no close Russian ally recognised the two breakaway republics (Nichol, 2009, 9). A third effect, positive in the eyes of Russia, was the increased resistance in Europe for a speedy NATO accession process for Georgia (and Ukraine).

Combat performance

In the end, the Russian army had overwhelmed a third-rate military power by using four times as many soldiers in the combat zone. Generally speaking, at the strategic level, Russia used a combined politico-military strategy that isolated Georgia from its Western partners. At the operational level, the early commitment to a decisive amount of forces yielded results, and at the tactical level, offensive mindedness, superior numbers and speed of Russian forces resulted in battlefield victory and finally in military victory. In other words, Russia had superior strategic and operational planning, while Georgian forces had greater tactical advantages (Cohen and Hamilton, 2011, 9).

The Russian army troops performed well, despite the fact that some conscripts were added to the contract soldiers (Larsson, 2008, 30–31; Vendil and Westerlund, 2009, 407). Some weaknesses of the Russian military operations were obvious, however. First, the use of motorised infantry units to secure terrain for the advancing infantry was missing and, instead, airborne and Spetsnaz units were used. Second, the limited options for the terrain advance forced the Russian units to operate in smaller units, which, in turn, resulted in unnecessary losses. Third, protection of tanks and armed vehicles was inadequate and, as a result, Russian soldiers preferred to ride on top of the vehicles rather than inside them. Fourth, artillery units lacked precision ammunition, which resulted in the use of larger amounts of ammunition than otherwise would have been needed. Fifth, inefficient communications could be noted (at times, even mobile phones were used by military staff to connect units). Sixth, Russian intelligence also seemed to have been somewhat inadequate in the early phases of the conflict (Larsson, 2008, 32–33, 36; Vendil and Westerlund, 2009, 407ff). The Russian air force enjoyed great superiority with its combat aircraft (including Su-24, Su-25, Su-27, and Tu-22) and between 200 and 400 sorties (with some 36 targets) were made (Vendil and Westerlund, 2009, 408; Cohen and Hamilton, 2011, 10–11). The results were mixed, however, and, despite Georgia's lack of air defence, at least four Russian aircrafts were shot down, or at least ten damaged (Larsson, 2008, 33; Vendil and Westerlund, 2009, 408). The Russian air support of its land forces was also weak, and even the inadequate Georgian air force managed to inflict damage to Russian land troops all through the war.

The complexity of the war is partly explained by the fact that the war was a combination of an interstate conflict between Georgia and Russia as well as an intrastate conflict within Georgia with a mix of regular armed forces and less controllable militia forces, as well as irregular armed groups – the war thus involved many types of actors (Tagliavini, P1, 2009, 36). Russia used airborne troops, motorised infantry units, artillery units, attack aircrafts and medium bombers, attack helicopter units, surface naval forces, marine infantry and special units from the Armed Forces and the Ministry of Internal Affairs (Larsson, 2008, 30). Another complexity had to do with the media reporting and the war of information – many Western journalists in Georgia and none in Russia followed the war on the ground (they were not allowed on the scene). Attempts at cyberattacks were also made by Russia on the Georgian state administration home pages, without any significant effects.

Although figures are notoriously imprecise, some suggest that approximately 10,000 Russian troops were used in South Ossetia and another 9,000 in Abkhazia (Felgenhauer, 2009, 170; Vendil and Westerlund, 2009, 406; Cohen and Hamilton, 2011, 12). Others suggest much higher numbers, claiming that the overall number of Russian troops that moved into Georgia was probably 25,000 (supported by some 1,200 pieces of armour and artillery, up to 200 aircraft and 40 helicopters), in addition to which some 10,000–15,000 separatist militia fighters may have been involved. The total figure of all Russian and assisting forces thus amounts to 35,000–40,000 (Felgenhauer, 2009, 141–143, 173; Asmus, 2010, 165). In comparison, the 17,000-member Georgian army, together with approximately 5,000 Georgian police officers, took part in the war (Felgenhauer, 2009, 170).

The military losses were not as severe as could have been expected, however. Georgia claimed losses of 170 servicemen, 14 policemen, 228 civilians and 1,747 wounded, while Russia claimed losses of 67 servicemen killed and 283 wounded. South Ossetia claimed 365 persons killed, both civilians and servicemen. Thus, a total of 850 were killed in the war. In addition, more than 110,000 fled their homes (Tagliavini, P1, 2009, 5).

Russia's strategic war objectives

The most important Russian strategic goal was probably to show the West and NATO that 'Russia was back' and ready to defend its backyard, and to force Georgia to give up its NATO aspirations (Donovan, 2009, 6–7; Felgenhauer, 2009, 177; Nichol, 2009, 12; Cohen and Hamilton, 2011, 13–14). A most important backdrop to the war was quite evidently the possibility of Georgian membership in NATO, which Russia regarded as totally unacceptable

(Tagliavini, P1, 2009, 31). Since the late 1990s, Russia had felt marginalised in the face of NATO's eastern enlargement and NATO's cooperation with some CIS states. Georgia was a prime actor in this, and in November 2002 Georgia applied for NATO membership. A bilateral security pact was also signed between Georgia and the United States in April 2003. In late 2004, Georgia concluded the IPAP with NATO and in September 2006, an 'Intensified dialogue' was decided upon. In January 2008, Russia officially warned that an invitation to a Membership Action Plan (MAP) might result in Russian recognition of the two breakaway republics in Georgia and military basing of Russian troops there. In February the same year, Georgia officially requested participation in a MAP at the upcoming summit in April 2008, and only because several European NATO members opted for a postponement (largely based on the assumed negative response from Russia), no MAP was offered to Georgia at the summit. A review of the membership plans of Georgia and Ukraine was then to be made before the next NATO summit in November 2008. The invasion thus simply showed the dangers of a Georgian NATO membership (Socor, 2008b).

Another important goal was to force Georgia to give up Abkhazia and South Ossetia, and a third to cripple Georgia's armed forces. Other possible goals include unseating Saakashvili (Krauthammer, 2008; Felgenhauer, 2009, 179; Nichol, 2009, 12; Vendil and Westerlund, 2009, 403). The Kosovo connection was important, too, best seen in how arguments on Georgia were moulded in Russia – if Kosovo could break free of Serbia, so could the two Georgian breakaway republics break free of Georgia (Tagliavini, P1, 2009, 1). Saakashvili had supported NATO's military intervention in Kosovo, and Russia warned that its support for the two breakaway republics would increase if Kosovo was offered independence (Chivers, 2008a). Talbot notes that Russia generally claimed that its peacekeeping operations aimed to end Georgian 'genocide' and 'ethnic cleansing of South Ossetia' which, although falsely, echoed US and NATO language claims in justifying bombing Serbia over Kosovo (Talbott, 2008).

International law and the war – and who started the war

International law is fairly clear on the right to go to war and the reasons why – defensive war is accepted, but aggression against another state is not. It is not very specific about the right to use violence in domestic conflicts, however, and the UN R2P (Responsibility to Protect) has confused the issue further. In short, the shelling and firing on Tskhinvali and its surroundings, including Russian peacekeepers, by Georgian regular forces was clearly neither proportionate nor necessary. Georgian troops thus used indiscriminate and disproportionate force. The South Ossetian forces initial response was legal as self-defence, but the violence later used as well as the looting and ethnic cleansing violated international law and often also human rights (Up in flames, 2009, 3–4). The immediate Russian reaction to defend its peacekeeping forces in South Ossetia was legal, as self-defence, while the Russian military invasion of Georgia proper was unjustifiable on all accounts of self-defence and proportionality. In conclusion, as far as international law is concerned, both the Georgian and Russian regular forces, as well as the South Ossetian and Abkhazian and other irregular forces did not act according to international law (Tagliavini, P1, 2009, 19–31).

One of the most common questions with respect to any international war is 'who started the war?' (see, for example, Finn, 2008c; Illarionov, 2009, 77ff). The EU FFM report from 2009 states that there is 'no conclusive evidence' for any simple explanation and basically blames Georgia for the initiation of the intrastate war in South Ossetia and Russia for the interstate war on Georgia (Tagliavini, P1, 2009, 21). The fact that many actors were involved in the war makes it difficult to answer the question in any simple or dichotomous way. Apart from the regular armed forces of Russia and Georgia, there were also the 'regular' South Ossetian and Abkhazian military forces, in addition to which a variety of irregular militias and armed gangs should be added as well as irregular forces from outside (two regular Chechen battalions) and voluntary irregular warriors – some of whom were fighting under the colours of Islam against orthodox Georgians. Proxy forces might thus very well have been in operation (Felgenhauer, 2008). Certainly, events and activities in this case escalated, seemingly without centralised control, both in Georgia and Russia (Larsson, 2008, 29).

In terms of individual decision makers, the 'blame game' was quite clear though – the Georgian or Russian Presidents were the major culprits, respectively. Bowker (2011) gives a fair description of the arguments used by the two sides. Criticism of the somewhat hesitant EU conclusion on 'the guilt issue' has been common with the claim that Russia was behind the entire chain of events and activities (Cohen and Hamilton, 2011, 37). One of the basic arguments is simply based on the fact that the planning for such a massive military invasion must have been done well ahead of the invasion (Felgenhauer, 2009, 165–166). Timing is thus a key issue: although Russian regular troops must have entered South Ossetia no later than early morning of 8 August, some claim that Russian troops entered the Roki tunnel already on the evening of 7 August (Nichol, 2009, 14), while others suggest that advance elements of some regiments entered South Ossetia even before 7 August (in addition to the two Chechen battalions) (Cohen and Hamilton, 2011, 20–21).

This argument of an earlier Russian attack is sometimes followed by the claim of a Russian general plan already from 1999 or at least from the inauguration of the colour revolutions in 2003–2005, or in any event from 2006 (Kagan, 2008; Illarionov, 2009, 50–51; Cohen and Hamilton, 2011, 3). In any event, a general plan for war does not necessarily suggest a plan for its actual fulfilment or initiation – military war plans in conflict zones are part of military routines and obligations to its governments (Larsson, 2008, 27; Vendil and Westerlund, 2009, 405–406). There is a difference between military and political planning for a war. In this interstate war, the Russian military planning for how (and possibly also why) there would be a future war must have taken place at least from spring 2008. The political planning for a war, especially the when and why, is another matter, although it seems likely that some political planning for a war with Georgia had come quite far by early summer 2008. The question of when the actual political decision to go to war was taken is more complicated, since it was affected by the situation on the ground and also on activities of other actors. August is a fair guess for an invasion, however, the decision probably taken in April 2008, just after the NATO summit (Felgenhauer, 2008). Putin's arrival in Vladikavkaz on the evening of 9 August most likely resulted in the final decision to invade Georgia proper the next day (Felgenhauer, 2009, 163, 171). Medvedev later claimed that preparations for war had indeed been made, although the very decision to go to war was made quite quickly (Civil Georgia, 2008).

One of the major arguments for an actual military plan is the conduct of the Caucasus-2008 exercises and the lingering of troops in the region and the fact that the exercises seemed much more similar to war preparations on foreign soil than to the purported goal of chasing terrorists. These troops were in the right place at the right time, and they had been training for much of the war situations later to become real. The fairly rapid involvement of large numbers of Russian forces on the ground at the time of the invasion, as well as the type of military activities engaged in simply had to be pre-planned. Another strong argument for a military plan is the entirely illegal repair of railroads in Abkhazia (*de jure* in Georgia) for heavy transports by Russian military railway troops (Vendil and Westerlund, 2009, 405).

Arguments against a Russian political or military plan for the actual invasion around 7–8 August focus on the seeming unpreparedness of the Russian political leadership: Medvedev cancelled his holiday cruising on the Volga river on 8 August and Putin flew from Beijing to Vladikavkaz on late 9 August. Another argument is that the Russian Federation Council did not get involved in the decision (despite requirements by the Russian constitution) and that the Russian Security Council was convened only after Russian troops had already entered South Ossetia (Larsson, 2008, 27; Vendil and Westerlund, 2009, 406). These circumstances might suggest that Russia (at least) had not planned to attack at this particular time. As for Georgia, Saakashvili obviously made a great mistake in attacking South Ossetia. He obviously never believed that the Russian response would be a full invasion. The greatest Georgian tactical mistake was not to block the Roki tunnel in the beginning of the war (Donovan, 2009, 30).

In conclusion, although not decisively, Georgia indeed played a crucial role in the actual initiation of the international war at this very time (as the Tagliavini report suggests), although it was not at all prepared for the violent Russian response (Larsson, 2008, 28). Georgia offered the opportunity for a war maybe already pre-planned and therefore actually invited Russia, which could not resist the temptation to hit back, in the typical Great Power manner. To be a small power bordering on a revanchist great power is always dangerous. To challenge it is to ask for disaster, however legally or formally correct. A lesson well-worth remembering.

Russia also learned some military lessons from the war, seen in the military reforms taking place in the following years. Maybe the most useful lesson for Russia should be sought, not in the conduct of military operations as such, but rather in the preparations for quasi-military operations: what followed in early 2014 in Crimea and in eastern Ukraine is a showcase of military-political operations where the strategic goals were achieved with a minimum of military losses. Simply to border on Russia may not in itself be as dangerous as to have Russian citizens living on your territory, and organised, as militias found in Abkhazia and South Ossetia.

The West, finally, also should draw some lessons from the war. Most important, Putin's so-called Munich speech of early 2007 revealed not only the challenges ahead but also that Russia was back on the old imperial track of subjugating neighbours, regardless of Western moral reactions. The West has once again become the major enemy in the contest for Russian security space, and no soft power response by the West will change that. Russia's renewed imperial design creates obvious military and political threats to Russia's small power neighbours. The question is how far Russia will go in its attempt to rectify the 'geopolitical disaster' of 1989, and what the West can do about it, given the present cracks in the idea of a united Europe.

References

Antidze, Margarita (2008) 'Georgian Troops, Warplanes, Pound Separatists', *Washington Post* 8 August. Accessed on 7 December 2017 at www.washingtonpost.com/wp-dyn/content/article/2008/08/07/AR2008080700402_2.html

Asmus, Ronald (2010) *A Little War that Shook the World. Georgia, Russia and the Future of the West*. New York: Palgrave.

Bowker, Mike (2011) 'The War in Georgia and the Western Response', *Central Asian Survey*, 30:2, 197–211. Accessed on 7 December 2017 at doi: 10.1080/02634937.2011.570121

Chivers, C.J. (2008a) 'Russia Warns It May Back Breakaway Republics in Georgia', *New York Times* 16 February. Accessed on 12 November 2017 at www.nytimes.com/2008/02/16/world/europe/16breakaway.html

Chivers, C.J. (2008b), 'Russia Expands Support for Breakaway Regions in Georgia', *New York Times* 17 April. Accessed on 3 October 2017 at www.nytimes.com/2008/02/16/world/europe/17georgia.html

Civil Georgia (25 December 2008) (Medvedev on war with Georgia). Accessed on 4 January 018 at http://civil.ge/eng/artice.php?id=20192

Cohen, Ariel, and Hamilton, Robert E. (2011) *The Russian Military and the Georgian War: Lessons and Implications*. Strategic Studies Institute, Carlile, PA: The US Army War College.

Donovan Jr., Georgie T. (2009) 'Russian Operational Art in the Russo-Georgian War of 2008', UAAWC, Carlisle Barracks, PA 17013-5050, USAWC Class of 2009.

Felgenhauer, Pavel (2008) 'The Russian-Georgian War Was Preplanned in Moscow', *Eurasia Daily Monitor* 14 August (Volume 5, Issue 156). Accessed on 11 December 2017 at https://jamestown.org/program/the-russian-georgian-war-was-preplanned-in-moscow/

Felgenhauer, Pavel (2009) 'After August 7: The Escalation of the Russia-Georgia War', in Cornell, Svante E. and Starr, Frederick (Eds.), *The Guns of August 2008. Russia's War in Georgia*. New York, London: M.E. Sharpe, pp. 162–180.

Finn, Peter (2008a) 'Russian-Georgian Troops Clash in South Ossetia', *Washington Post* 8 August. Accessed on 13 October 2017 at www.washingtonpost.com/wpdyn/content/article/2008/08/08/AR2008080800285_4.html?hpid=topnews&sid=ST2008080802320&pos

Finn, Peter (2008b) 'Russia-Georgia War Intensifies. Civilian Deaths on Increase in Conflict over South Ossetia', *Washington Post* 10 August. Accessed on 15 October 2017 at www.washingtonpost.com/wpdyn/content/article/2008/08/09/AR2008080900238_3.html

Finn, Peter (2008c) 'A Two-Sided Descent into Full-Scale War', *Washington Post* 17 August. Accessed on 3 September 2017 at www.washingtonpost.com/wpdyn/content/article/2008/08/16/AR2008 1081600502_4.html

Human Rights Watch (2009) *'Up in Flames – Humanitarian Law Violations and Civilian Victims in the Conflict over South Ossetia'*, New York: Human Rights Watch. Accessed on 12 August 2017 at www.hrw.org/report/2009/01/23/flames/humanitarian-law-violations-and-civilian-victims-conflict-over-south

Illarionov, Andrei (2009) 'The Russian Leadership's Preparation for War, 1999–2008', in Cornell, Svante E. and Starr, Frederick (Eds.), *The Guns of August 2008. Russia's War in Georgia*. New York, London: M.E. Sharpe, pp. 49–84.

International Crisis Group (2008) *Russia & Georgia: The Fallout* 22 August. Accessed on 8 January 2018 at www.crisisgroup.org/europe-central-asia/caucasus/georgia/russia-vs-georgia-fallout

Kagan, Robert (2008) 'Putin Makes His Move', *Washington Post* 11 August. Accessed on 15 August 2017 at www.washingtonpost.com/wp-dyn/content/article/2008/08/10/AR2008081001871.html

Krauthammer, Charles (2008) 'How to Stop Putin', *Washington Post* 14 August. Accessed on 12 November 2017 at www.washingtonpost.com/wp-dyn/content/article/2008/08/13/AR2008081303365_2.html?sid=ST2008081401253&s_pos=

Larsson, Robert L. (ed.) (2008) 'Det kaukasiska lackmustestet: konsekvenser och lärdomar av det rysk-georgiska kriget i augusti 2008', Stockholm, *Research Report* FOI-R--2563--SE, September. (The Caucasian Test Case: Consequences and Lessons Learned of the Russian-Georgian War in August 2008). Accessed on 13 August 2017 at http://webbrapp.ptn.foi.se_pdf_0128cf7c-fbdb-4ffc-bb59-68d837b1cac7.pdf

Nichol, Jim (2009) 'Russia-Georgia Conflict in August 2008: Context and Implications for U.S. Interests', 3 March. CRS *Report for Congress*, CRS 7–5700. Accessed on 11 August 2017 at http://edition.cnn.com/2014/03/13/world/europe/2008-georgia-russia-conflict/index.html

Nygren, Bertil (2008) *The Re-building of Greater Russia*. London: Routledge.

Owen, Elisabeth and Lomsadze, Giorgi (2008a) 'Georgian Troops Withdraw from South Ossetia, Russia Bombs Tbilisi Airport', *Eurasia Insight* 10 August. Accessed on 10 August 2017 at www.eurasianet.org/departments/insight/articles/eav081008.shtml

Owen, Elisabeth and Lomsadze, Giorgi (2008b) 'Georgia: Scene of the Outbreak of Cold War II?', *Eurasia Insight* 12 August. Accessed on 2 September 2017 at www.eurasianet.org/departments/insight/articles/eav081208.shtml

'Russian "Imperialist Boots" stomping on Georgia – President' (2008) *Eurasia Insight* 11 August. Accessed on 8 January 2018 at www.eurasianet.org/departments/insight/articles/eav081108.shtml

Schwirtz, Michael (2008) 'Russia Sends Troops into Rebel Enclave in Georgia', *New York Times* 8 August. Accessed on 15 August 2017 at www.nytimes.com/2008/08/09/world/europe/09georgia.html

Schwirtz, Michael, Barnard, Anne and Kramer, Andrew E. (2008) 'Russian Forces Capture Military Base in Georgia', *New York Times* 11 August. Accessed on 14 December 2017 at www.nytimes.com/2008/08/12/world/europe/12georgia.html?pagewanted=2

Socor, Vladimir (2008a) 'Russia Deploys Railway Troops to Abkhazia', *Eurasia Daily Monitor* 3 June (Volume 5, Issue 105). Accessed on 13 December 2017 at https://jamestown.org/program/russia-deploys-railway-troops-to-abkhazia/

Socor, Vladimir (2008b), 'Moscow Orchestrates War Scare in South Ossetia', *Eurasia Daily Monitor* 4 August (Volume 5, Issue 148). Accessed on 8 January 2018 at https://jamestown.org/program/moscow-orchestrates-war-scare-in-south-ossetia/

Tagliavini Commission (2009) 'IIFFMCG – Independent International Fact-Finding Mission on the Conflict in Georgia', Part1, Part 2. September. Accessed on 19 August 2017 at www.ceiigf.ch/

Talbot, Strobe (2008) 'Russia's Ominous New Doctrine?', *Washington Post* 15 August. Accessed on 12 December 2017 at www.washingtonpost.com/wp-dyn/content/article/2008/08/14/AR2008081403124.html

Vendil Pallin, Carolina and Westerlund, Fredrik (2009) 'Russia's War in Georgia: Lessons and Consequences', *Small Wars & Insurgencies*, 20:2, 400–424, doi:10.1080/09592310902975539. Accessed on 12 December 2017 at doi:10.1080/09592310902975539

33
RUSSIA'S 'HYBRID' AGGRESSION AGAINST UKRAINE

Yury E. Fedorov

Russia's annexation of Crimea and proxy war in Donbas are often seen as the classic or at least the first case of 'hybrid' warfare, the trendy term today to denote what is a mix of conventional military operations with non-military methods of corrosion of an opponent, such as economic pressure, fomenting political and social conflicts, subversive activities and massive propaganda campaigns. Since many believe that 'hybridity' will be a predominant trait of armed conflicts in the twenty-first century, analysing Moscow's invasion of Ukraine could be helpful for comprehension of the future security environment as well as for assessing strategy and methods of Russia's power projection in nearby regions. With this in view, the chapter exposes the Russian concept of a hybrid warfare, describes Moscow's strategic goals towards Ukraine, outlines evolution of its war plans from 'traditional' to hybrid operations and analyses tactics and efficiency of Russian interventionism in that country.

Ukraine in Russia's 'grand strategy'

Conventional wisdom often deems that Russia's aggression against Ukraine was caused by a mix of transient factors, such as the views of a few people at the very top, President Vladimir Putin above all, suffering from a wounded *amour-proper*, post-Imperial syndrome and a parochial mentality. These drivers of Russia's international behaviour are valid, indeed. However, Moscow's hybrid war on Ukraine results also from some fundamentals of Russian political thinking typical both of the elites and the majority of society. It combines historical myths with a few elements of the Kremlin's 'grand strategy'.

Russians often, yet falsely, perceive Ukraine not as a separate country, but as a part of a single Russian political and cultural entity united by common values based on Orthodoxy and by common descent from Kievan Rus. Albeit this concept contradicts historical facts since late eighteenth century, it became one of the cornerstones of Russia's imperial policy and philosophy. Within this intellectual and psychological framework, Ukrainian national self-identification and desire for national independence was – as it is now – seen as a nonsense, something unnatural and perverted, which has no right to exist. In addition, by the annexation of Crimea and fuelling the separatist mutiny in Donbas, Moscow wanted to meet a number of geopolitical ends, above all, to stop Ukraine's drive to Europe and to turn it, or at least a part of it, into a de facto Russian protectorate. This is seen as the first step in implementation of the Russian 'grand strategy' aimed at building a new international architecture comprising Moscow's spheres of influence in the vast area between Russia and so-called 'old Europe' and to redraw 'the lines of power running through Eastern and Southern Europe, which would secure new borders and frontiers for the coming decades and protect them from challenges arising from either side' (Inozemtzev, 2014). Many also believe that the Kremlin's fear that the Kyiv's Euromaidan might ignite similar processes in Russia and by destabilising and disintegrating Ukraine, Putin and his cabal planned to demonstrate that democratic revolutions result in chaos and the collapse of statehood.

In this light, it was by no means a coincidence that already in 1993, Yury Skokov, then Secretary of the Russian Security Council, told Oleg Bay, then Deputy Head of the Ukrainian Embassy in Moscow, that if any 'difficulties' in the Russo-Ukrainian relations occurred, they would begin in 'Donbass will start, Novorossiya will support, Transnistria will complete' (Portnikov, 2017). Put differently, well ahead of the Putin-era members of the top echelon of the Russian government considered destabilization of the Southeastern provinces of Ukraine and their factual separation from the country as an instrument of pressing upon Kyiv and returning it into Moscow's domain.[1]

War plans and preparations in 2004–2014

It is indeed difficult to find out when exactly Russia's ruling clique started to plan a war on Ukraine in a practical manner. Yet, it seems that Pavel Felgenhauer, a leading Russian independent military expert, was correct in saying that the preparation for this began just after the first Maidan in 2004. Since then, he pointed out, the Black Sea Fleet year by year reinforced its bases and facilities located in Crimea, which was evidence of preparing for annexation of the Peninsula (quoted in Tammsaar, 2015). However, since almost all combat-capable Russian military units were employed in the war in Chechnya, military aggression against Ukraine was hardly possible until 2007, when appeasement in Chechnya made Russian armed forces available for operations in Ukraine. It is also telling that Putin speaking at the North Atlantic Treaty Organisation (NATO) Summit in Bucharest in April 2008, for the first time openly threatened to dismember Ukraine by force along ethnic lines and to annex its lands populated by Russians. Aspirations to integrate with NATO, he claimed, could threaten the Ukrainian territorial integrity (Allenova, Heda, and Novikov, 2008). Almost immediately Russian media published the plan of war against Ukraine named Operation 'Mechanical Orange' (Dzhadan, 2008). It included three scenarios of the Russian invasion of Ukraine from then seizure of the Crimean Peninsula up to occupation of the entire Left Bank Ukraine and Kyiv.[2] It presumed massive use of land forces and aviation and even 'demonstration of nuclear explosions in the stratosphere above the southern part of the Pripyat marshes' to suppress Ukrainians' will to defend themselves. However, until 2012–2013, Russia had no practical ability of waging a 'large war' with Ukraine. The war in Chechnya and then not very successful experience of aggression against Georgia showed that the Russian army was in critical condition. In these circumstances, Moscow focused on economic and political pressure upon Ukraine and creating networks of agents of influence within the military and security services command, the political and business communities and the mass media.

In practical terms, the preparations for armed aggression against Ukraine started in autumn 2008. Within the framework of the 2008–2012 military reform, a large grouping of the armed forces was formed in the Southern Military District bordering with a few Ukrainian provinces. By the end of 2012, Moscow deployed there nine Motor Rifle brigades, two Special Forces (Spetsnaz) units and one reconnaissance brigade, an Airborne Assault (Mountain) Division and an Airborne Assault Brigade. In 2012, there were more than 400 tanks, about 1,000 artillery pieces, more than 2,000 armoured fighting vehicles, and a powerful air force consisting of 90 fighters, 100 theatre bombers, 80 attack aircraft and 170 attack helicopters (Ryadovoy Ru, 2012). Russian sources assured that these troops were intended for suppressing riots and local guerilla groups in the Northern Caucasus, as well as for operations against Georgia. However, since the combat might of this grouping apparently exceeded what was needed for these tasks, its most feasible mission was the occupation of the wide belt of Ukrainian lands stretching from Donetsk to Odessa oblasts by massive assault operations. Also, regular land forces, with the exception of the mountain infantry and Spetsnaz units, were hardly suitable for fighting paramilitary groups in mountainous terrain and urban guerillas in cities. This task is carried out by Russian Interior troops stationed in the Northern Caucasus. Two reinforced Motor Rifle brigades (about 10,000 men) deployed in South Ossetia and Abkhazia are more than enough for a new invasion of Georgia. Fully manned units of the 102nd Russian military base in Armenia will be quite able to strongly support Armenian troops, if a new war over Nagorno-Karabakh happens (Kavkazsky uzel, 2015).

Although, since the end of the past decade, the Kremlin has formed military units designed for a large-scale 'traditional' war with Ukraine and developed plans of such wars, its actions in Ukraine in 2014 and later were performed in accordance with a hybrid war template. There were a few reasons for that. By the end of 2013, Russian military and security services developed the concept, strategy and plans of hybrid warfare against Ukraine. Most probably, the Kremlin concluded that by mobilization of local populations and mercenaries from Russia and flinging them against the Kyiv government, Moscow would be able to attain its goals in Ukraine at much less cost than by a 'traditional' one. And by presenting its invasion of Ukraine as an uprising of the local population, the Kremlin hoped to disguise its aggression as a civil war and, thus, avoid an aggravation of relations with the West.

Russia's hybrid war concept

It seems that initially the hybrid war theory was developed in the 1960s by a prominent Russian émigré military thinker, Evgeny Messner whose monograph *A Worldwide Mutiny-war* became a desk book for officers of the Russian General Staff in the 2000s. Messner wrote that 'making war by guerrillas, subversives, terrorists, wreckers, saboteurs and propagandists will acquire an enormous scope in future'. Irregulars, he added, 'becomes powerful' since the successes of regular troops 'strengthen the activities of irregular forces and increase their numerical strength' (Messner, 2005). This theory was confirmed, at least partly, by some conflicts in the second half of the twentieth century, including the Vietnam War and the guerila warfare in Nicaragua.

At the beginning of this decade, the Russian military command developed its own concept of a hybrid war. It was initially outlined by the Chief of the Russian General Staff Colonel-General Valery Gerasimov in early 2013:

> The use of non-military methods to achieve political and strategic objectives has in some cases proved to be far more effective than the use of force [...] These [methods] include special operations and usage of internal opposition to create a zone of permanent hostilities throughout the enemy state, as well as the impact of information pressure, forms and methods of which are constantly being improved.
>
> *(Gerasimov, 2013)*

A year later, Colonel-General Vladimir Zarudnitzky, then the Head of the Main Operational Directorate of the Russian General Staff, revealed a more detailed scenario of hybrid intervention. At first, a 'hybrid agressor' kindles national, religious, social or territorial contradictions and controversies in a country that is its victim. Then such contradictions evolve into an open confrontation between the opposition and the government, which escalates into a civil war if a ruling regime is trying to retain power. Also, a country launching hybrid aggression uses its military potential for 'open pressure' with the view to

> prevent the use of the security forces (of a victim country – YuF) to restore law and order. Then, with the deployment of opposition hostilities against government forces, foreign countries begin to give the rebels military and economic aid. Later, a coalition of countries participating in the overthrow of the lawful government can start a military operation to assist opposition in the seizure of power. [...] Squads of mercenaries and band-formations purposefully use civilians as 'human shields', which results in large losses among the civilian population not involved in armed hostilities.
>
> *(Zarudnitzky, 2014)*

Finally, the current Russian military doctrine approved by President Putin in late December 2014, includes a set of distinctive facets of contemporary armed conflict elements typical of hybrid wars: the creation of zones of permanent armed hostilities on the territories of opposing states; participation of irregular armed formations and private military companies in military operations; the usage of non-direct and asymmetric means of action; and the use of political forces and social movements financed and controlled from outside (Rossiiskaya gazeta, 2014).

Plan 'A' and plan 'B'

Historically, Moscow expected to achieve its objectives towards Ukraine by controlling the Ukrainian ruling elite. In particular, right up to February 2014, Putin and his lieutenants placed their hopes in the 'Yanukovych administration that in late 2013 became fully dependent on Russia due to its refusal to sign an association agreement with the European Union. The Kremlin then believed that the 'Yanukovych regime would be able to survive the mass demonstrations against the government called Euromaidan and control the country until the presidential election in 2015. One may call this strategy 'plan A'.

At the same time, Russia was also preparing for the implementation of 'plan B', also known as 'project Novorossiya' aimed at separating the southeastern part of Ukraine, comprising Donetsk, Luhansk, Zaporizh'ya, Odessa, Mykolaiv, Kharkiv and Kherson oblasts and Crimea from the other half of the country and to turn it into Russia's protectorate. Most probably, the Kremlin planned that these regions would form a quasi-state entity, a Southeastern Ukrainian Republic, or something similar, which would be proclaimed at the Congress of deputies of the Southern and Eastern regions of Ukraine in Kharkiv on February 22, 2014 (Socor, 2014).

Russian propaganda claimed that the very idea of Novorossiya is of defensive nature. Some Moscow pundits added that among the real goals of this project, there was prevention of Ukraine's membership in NATO. Dmitry Trenin, the Head of the Carnegie Moscow Centre and a sophisticated advocate of the Putin regime, admitted in June 2014 that if 'project Novorossiya' was implemented, it would provide 'real institutional guarantees against any moves toward NATO accession' (Trenin, 2014). Yet, in effect, the Kremlin's plan 'B' was aimed at the radical strengthening of Russia's strategic position in the northwestern part of the Black Sea region. If executed, then the main Ukrainian industrial centres, including a few key military-industrial facilities, strategically important ports and transport routes would fall under Russia's control; the rest of Ukraine would turn into an economically unviable and politically unstable formation; Russian troops would appear at the border with Moldova and strategic situation in southeastern Europe would dramatically change in Russia's favour. Putting it differently, Novorossiya was seen in the Kremlin as a location of strategically important industries and a bridgehead from which its troops can threaten and attack NATO's area on its southeastern flank.

Annexation of Crimea

Both these plans were ruined. Late in the evening on February 21, 2014, 'Yanukovych in panic fled Kyiv, his regime crashed and on the next day the Congress in Kharkiv refused to discuss separatist projects. Under these circumstances, the Kremlin commanded the annexation of Crimea after which the 'Crimean scenario' was planned to be repeated in other regions of Southeastern Ukraine. In the early morning on February 23, 2014, Putin personally ordered the invasion of Crimea and putting Russian nuclear forces on a war footing (Baklanov, 2015).

The annexation was performed in four steps. At first, pro-Russian organisations in Crimea were activated, forming the so-called 'self-defence' squads and launched massive rallies in protest against the new government in Kyiv. In the next few days, pro-Russian marchers and rioters provoked clashes with pro-Ukrainian groups, yet were not able to force the then Crimean Parliament and government to declare independence from Ukraine or to address Moscow asking for unification with Russia. To turn the tide in favour of Moscow after February 24, Russian Marines stationed in Crimea and the so-called 'polite little green men', in actual fact Spetsnaz task forces without insignia airlifted and transferred to Crimea, started taking control over governmental buildings, strategic locations and key points. On February 27, Russian Spetsnaz units seized the buildings of the Crimean Parliament and the government. On the same day, regional legislators who were held at gunpoint voted for replacement of the former prime minister by Sergey Aksenov, the head of one of the pro-Russian organisations in Crimea, for the referendum on the future of the Peninsula and for dismissal of the government (Goncharova, 2015). Simultaneously, Russian troops and 'self-defence' squads established security checkpoints separating Crimea from the Ukrainian mainland.

During early March 2014, Russian troops stationed at the naval base in Sevastopol, together with troops, armour and helicopters from Russia, encircled Ukrainian units in Crimea, which did not resist the invaders – and many of them went over to the enemy side – and exercised complete control over the Crimean Peninsula. Military occupation, political pressure by the Russian security services and local 'self-defence' gangs, and an intensive propaganda campaign led to the expected result: on March 16, 2014, most of the residents of Crimea voted for joining Russia.

Many in Moscow portrayed the annexation of Crimea as the brilliant success of the hybrid war tactics and the example of excellently planned and implemented military operation. Yet, as the matter of fact, Moscow's success resulted not so much as from the potency of the Russian task forces and the intellectual capacity of the General Staff as from the dramatic situation in Ukraine just after the crash of the 'Yanukovych regime. The Ukrainian Armed Forces were incredibly weak, partly because of treachery among the top brass. Ukrainian troops deployed on the Peninsula were not prone to resist invaders, in particular because 90 per cent of their personnel were inhabitants of Crimea. A shocking propaganda campaign frightened the local population with imaginary threats emanating from the new Ukrainian authorities. And at that time, Kyiv was seeking above all the prevention of the massive invasion of the Russian Army, which would have been inevitable had the new Ukrainian government attempted to stop the annexation of Crimea by force.

Project Novorossiya and its fiasco

Simultaneously with the infiltration of the Russian Spetsnaz into Crimea all across Russia, a campaign began for recruiting mercenaries and volunteers to fight in other parts of Ukraine (Makarenko, 2014). The local branches of the FSB and the military registration and enlistment offices[3] were especially interested in hiring recently retired officers, former soldiers and non-commissioned officers who had served as airborne and Spetsnaz troops, military intelligence, specialists in military communications, former tank crew members and other varieties of men with professional military backgrounds (Kostyuchenko, 2014). This was a clear signal that Russian hybrid war plans included the formation on the territory of future Novorossiya 'quasi-armies' capable of fighting Ukrainian Armed Forces. On April 17, 2014, Putin revealed his ambitions to annex the whole southeast of Ukraine:

> What was called Novorossiya (New Russia) back in the tsarist days – Kharkov, Luhansk, Donetsk, Kherson, Nikolayev and Odessa – were not part of Ukraine back then. These territories were given to Ukraine in the 1920s by the Soviet government. [...] They were won by Potemkin and Catherine the Great in a series of well-known wars. [...] Russia lost these territories for various reasons, but the people remained.
>
> *(Putin, 2014)*

Acting on instructions from Moscow pro-Russian groups and some local bosses of the Party of Regions and the Communist Party of Ukraine in Donbas, Kharkov, Odessa and Dniepropetrovsk oblasts fomented mass disorders, arranged anti-government rallies under separatist slogans, provoked clashes with Ukrainian law-enforcement forces, attacked administrative buildings, military depots, headquarters of police and security service, and practiced 'human shields' to challenge the Ukrainian police with the dilemma either to refrain from use of force or to use weapons against civilian population. In many cases, rioting was guided by task forces of the FSB and Russian military intelligence (GRU). Core elements of violent mobs have been often grouped of the so-called 'Russian tourists', in fact petty criminals, hooligans, sports fans and members of nationalist organisations mainly from neighbouring Russian oblasts. In particular, according to Ukrainian sources, an attack on the building of the Kharkiv Regional State Administration on March 1, 2014, was committed by members of the local Oplot organisation with the assistance of about 2,000 'storm trooper tourists' from Russia (Roth, 2014).

At that point, according to Moscow's hybrid war plans, regional legislatures were to vote for no confidence in the new government in Kyiv and to appeal to Putin with a request for assistance, including by sending troops to protect the separatists and to suppress pro-Ukrainian groups. This tactic was outlined by Sergey Glaziev, an adviser to Putin and one of the main figures in planning and managing the hybrid war in Ukraine. Glaziev informed his inferiors in Odessa on March 1, 2014, that he 'was given the direct instruction from the top' to excite people in Ukraine and to get them to go in the streets 'as soon as possible'.

He declared,

> The president has signed the decree [it was not clear what particular Putin decree Glaziev had in mind, yet most probably he meant the decree of the Federation Council authorized Putin to invade Ukraine – YuF]. Hence, the operation is going on. It was reported that the military forwarded the troops already. What are they [pro-Russian rioters – YuF] sitting still?! […] Decisions of regional councils [legislatures – YuF] are very important. […] Occupy the [building of – YuF] regional council in order to allow lawmakers to come and explain them that they should come and vote. Those of them who will not come and will not vote will be traitors, Banderovites, fascists and so on with all the consequences for them.
>
> (Neimyrok, 2016)

Simultaneously, Russian troops were massing near Ukrainian borders to exert pressure upon the new Ukrainian leadership with a view to preventing the use of the Ukrainian army against the pro-Russian separatists, mutineers and rioters.

By mid-May 2014, Ukrainian authorities were able to quell separatist mutinies in the southeast and, what was most important, attempts to proclaim 'people's republics' in Kharkiv and Odessa. Yet, the key reason why the insurgency failed was the position of Ukrainian society. Despite their ethnic origins, the majority of the people living in most parts of Southeastern Ukraine did not support the very idea of separation from this country and joining Russia.

The proxy war in Donbas

Since the attempts to separate the southeastern oblasts from Ukraine failed, the Kremlin concentrated upon other goals: first, to compel Kyiv to transform a unitary state into a loose confederation of regional entities, each of which has a right of shaping foreign economic relations and foreign policy orientations; second, to deny potential membership in NATO; and third, to agree that an enclave in Donetsk and Luhansk oblasts, although formally a part of Ukraine, would be fully controlled by Moscow. The Kremlin and its followers in Ukraine called it 'federalisation' and neutrality.

Setting forth these goals was linked to developments in Donbas in some parts of which in spring 2014 pro-Russian separatists, as well as mercenaries, paramilitaries, military and security 'advisers' from Russia were able to seize power. A combination of factors has contributed to this. Donbas, especially Donetsk oblast, was the political bulwark of the Yanukovych regime. All important positions in regional legislatures and administrations, police and security apparatuses have been occupied by people belonging to the 'Yanukovych clique and, because of this, having grounds to fear the new authorities in Kyiv. Also, a large part of the local populace consisted of ethnic Russians and was highly susceptible to Moscow's propaganda that browbeat them with imaginary threats emanating from the new Ukrainian government.

The seizure of power in Donbas by local separatists and Moscow's emissaries was followed by the formation of pro-Russian administrations and political bodies pretending to represent the local population. The so-called Donetsk and Luhansk People's Republics (DPR and LPR) were proclaimed in April 2014. They allowed Moscow to substitute the previous regional administrations, which sometimes leaned towards compromises with Kyiv with ones fully controlled by Moscow. Establishment of DPR and LPR was used also to portray the Russian aggression against Ukraine as a civil war and a revolt of the Russian peoples of Eastern Ukraine against a 'fascist regime'.

However, up to mid-2015, real power in the separatist enclaves lays with a number of warlords heading armed militias practically independent of 'republican' governments. These formations were manned by some former members of Ukrainian law-enforcement agencies, activists of pro-Russian organisations, two-three dozen thousands of marginal folks and local cheaters for whom membership in militias was a cover for illegal activities; unemployed working-class and lower strata people for whom service in separatist militias was the only source of income. Militias were supported by members of the Russian security and intelligence agencies; army officers officially 'on leave', who served in the separatist gangs as trainers, advisers and planners of operations; mercenaries, including professional military folks; poorly skilled rank-and-file personnel to compensate losses in manpower; Cossacks; volunteers of far-right and far-left orientations. The key instruments of Kremlin policy in that area were FSB and GRU task forces numbering in mid-2014 according to Ukrainian sources, 1,000–2,000 officers (Kupriyanova, 2014).

Poor discipline, ineffective central command, insufficient coordination between different units and rivalry between warlords for control over economic resources reduced the combat potential of the separatists' force. By June 2014, when the Ukrainian governmental troops began an offensive against the self-proclaimed 'republics', the separatist militias were not able to resist regular troops. At the end of August 2014, separatists groups were on the brink of total defeat, and Moscow covertly sent a number of battalions of tactical groups of regular land forces into Donbas.[4] It was Russian regular troops that were responsible for the defeat of the Ukrainian army near Illovaisk and Saur Mogila in late August and early September 2014. In November 2014, it was reported that there were about 7,000 Russian troops in Ukraine, while between 40,000 and 50,000 of them massed at the country's eastern border (Harris, 2014). Finally, Russian regular troops played the decisive role in the battle near Debaltseve in February 2015. Put differently, Moscow deviated from the hybrid war template and sent to Donbas regular forces to save its local clients from defeat.

The Kremlin understood that consolidation of political circles and armed groups in the separatist enclaves under cliques fully controlled by Moscow was of crucial importance for the survival of the pro-Russian regimes there. In this light, since 2015, Moscow's efforts were focused on consolidation of different militias into an integrated armed force subordinated to a single command. Some warlords were expelled from Donbas, some others were murdered, most probably by Russian agents.

By the end of 2015, the Russian military command succeeded in consolidating and training two well-armed army corps intended to conduct offensive operations that integrated odd terrorist and separatist armed groups and formations. Ukrainian official sources summarising intelligence information revealed at the end of August 2015 that there were about 30,000 men in the terrorist/separatist forces heavily armed with armour and artillery. Russian supplies of modern armaments have turned the separatist forces into one of the best equipped forces in Central-Eastern and Eastern Europe: the pro-Russian militants had about 900 armoured vehicles, 450 tanks, nearly 370 units of artillery, and about 380 multiple rocket launchers in service with, as well as hundreds of units of other military equipment provided by the Kremlin. In addition, then there were about 9,000 Russian contract servicemen in the occupied territories of Donbas (Censor.Net, 2015).

Strategic deadlock

By mid-2015, the Russian hybrid aggression resulted in a strategic impasse in Donbas, continuing so far without any expectation for a solution. The Ukrainian army and National

Guard are unable to free the areas under the control of separatists because of the presence of Russian regular troops there and in the near vicinity in Russia's neighbouring areas. At the same time, although the very existence of the separatist-controlled territories of Donbas poses a serious economic and political problems for Kyiv, Moscow is unable to achieve its fundamental goal: to create Novorossiya. Also, Russia has not had leverage strong enough to force the Ukrainian authorities to 'federalise' the country into a lax conglomerate of semi-independent formations or to give chiefs of the DPR/LPR veto power regarding Ukraine's foreign and security policy. Due to this, since 2015 and up to now, Moscow has seen a low-intensity war in Donbas as a bleeding sore poisoning the Ukrainian state and society and hindering reforms. In this light, Moscow seeks two strategic objectives: to prevent the military defeat of the separatist enclave and to turn it into a source of permanent tensions and armed clashes in the east of the country.

Of course, Russia has enough troops to occupy the Donetsk and Luhansk oblasts, and perhaps some other areas in Eastern Ukraine, yet it would require all or almost all of Russian military forces deployed near Ukraine and the large-scale use of combat aviation. Since the separatists have neither combat aircrafts nor attack helicopters, it immediately highlights the Kremlin's lie that the Russian troops do not participate in the war in Donbas. Also, such operations will inevitably result in the mass losses of Russian servicemen and great collateral damage, especially in case of storming large cities.

There are no chances for a political solution of the Russian-Ukrainian conflict. The Kremlin declared annexed Crimea an indivisible part of Russia and flatly refuses to discuss even the theoretical possibility of returning the Peninsula to Ukraine. For the Ukrainian elites and society, the recognition of its annexation is unacceptable. Also, there is no prospect of settling the situation in Donbas. The so-called Minsk agreements providing for a ceasefire and a series of political steps aimed at restoring Ukraine's sovereignty over a secessionist enclave failed, in fact. The reason for this does not lie in the divergence of the positions of Kyiv and Moscow regarding the sequence of these steps, but in the unwillingness of the Russian leadership to resolve the situation.

> If all sides fulfilled the Minsk II provisions, a degree of peace and normalcy would return to the Donbas. And that precisely may be the problem for the Kremlin. A quiet Donbas no longer would serve as a means for Moscow to put pressure on Ukraine, in order to make it more difficult for Poroshenko [the President of Ukraine – YuF] and his government to implement needed reforms, grow the economy, and implement the Ukraine-European Union association agreement. At present, Russia does not appear prepared or willing to give up that leverage over Kyiv' wrote well-known American expert Steven Pifer.
>
> *(Pifer, 2017)*

Strategic deadlock means that Russia is not able to win the hybrid war against Ukraine. Among the causes of this failure, the fundamental one was Putin's major strategic blunder of underestimating the determination of Ukrainian society and most part of its elites to resist Russian aggression and also the resoluteness of the USA and European countries to sanction Russia to stop its invasion and prompt it to withdraw from Donbas. In addition, the ability of the Ukrainian authorities to suppress pro-Russian subversive and terrorist groups in Odessa, Kharkiv and a few other regions of Southeastern Ukraine during three or four critical months after the fall of the 'Yanukovych regime and the start of the hybrid aggression in Donbas was of critical importance for preventing the spread of the mutiny beyond the

Donbas borders. In this light, the Ukraine's experience of the resistance to Russia's intervention could be useful for preventing analogous Moscow actions against other countries – the three Baltic, above all.

However, although Russia's hybrid aggression against Ukraine, at least the first round of it, failed, it is an open question as yet whether the Kremlin has backed off from the very idea of hybrid wars in this and other neighbouring countries. The worrisome fact is that this aggression has been approved by the Russian mass mindset poisoned by anti-Ukrainian, anti-Western and militarist attitudes and great power views. This creates the preconditions for new rounds of Russia's aggression against Ukraine, either hybrid or 'traditional'.

Notes

1 This region, termed Novorossiya (New Russia), denotes a territory north of the Black Sea captured by the Russian Empire in the eighteenth century. Up to 1917, it was referred to the chain of lands stretching from Moldova at South-West along the Back Sea littoral to Donbas. Since the fall of the Russian Empire, most of these regions became part of Ukraine. In the contemporary Russian strategic discourse, this word is used to mark the area which is an object of Russian geopolitical expansion in the northern Circumpontic region.
2 Historically, Left Bank Ukraine (*Livoberezhna Ukraina*) was the name of the part of Ukraine on the East (Left) bank of the Dnieper River, comprising the modern-day Chernihiv, Poltava and Sumy oblasts, as well as the eastern parts of Kiev and Cherkasy oblasts. Today, this name often applies to the entire territory of Ukraine to the east of the Dnieper River.
3 These offices, known in Russia as Military commissariats (*Voennie komissariaty* or *Voenkomats*), are responsible for conscription and registration of reserve officers, maintaining records on military manpower, providing pre-military training and performing other military functions at the local level.
4 The Russian Battalion Tactical Group (BTG) is a battalion reinforced with assets from higher-level units, above all brigades. It includes ten armoured fighting vehicles for each of three companies plus command vehicle; the number of tanks in each case is different; at least one artillery division is allocated for each BTG.

References

Allenova, O., Heda, E., and Novikov, V. (2008) 'Blok NATO razoshelsya na blokpaketi' (The block NATO divided into blocking share holding). *Kommersant*. April 17. Accessed on May 21, 2018 at: www.kommersant.ru/doc/877224

Baklanov, A. (2015) 'Posle prisoedineniya Kryma Putin gotovilsya k yadernoy voyne' (Putin was preparing to a nuclear war after the annexation of Crimea). *Snob.ru*. March 15. Accessed on May, 15, 2018 at: http://snob.ru/selected/entry/89482

Censor.Net. (2015) 'Over 1,000 units of military equipment and 9,000 Russian Federation regular troops are in service with Russian militants – ATO deputy commander'. *Censor.Net*. April 9. Accessed on May 23, 2018 at: http://en.censor.net.ua/news/331949/over_1000_units_of_military_equipment_and_9000_russian_federation_regular_troops_are_in_service_with

Dzhadan, I. (2008) 'Operatziya "Mehanicheskii apelsin"' (Operation 'Mechanical Orange'). *Russkii zhurnal*. April 21. Accessed on May 20, 2018 at: www.russ.ru/pole/Operaciya-Mehanicheskij-apelsin

Gerasimov, V. (2013) 'Tzennost nauki v predvidenii' (The value of science is its ability to foresee). *Voenno-promishlenii kurier*. N 8. February 27. pp. 2, 20.

Goncharova, O. (2015) 'Putin's narrative on Crimea annexation takes an evolutionary leap'. *Kyiv Post*. Match 11. Accessed on May 12, 2018 at: www.kyivpost.com/content/kyiv-post-plus/putins-narrative-on-crimea-annexation-takes-an-evolutionary-leap-383183.html

Harris, S. (2014) 'Thousands of Putin's troops now in Ukraine, analysts say'. *The Daily Beast*. November 11. Accessed on May 27, 2018 at: www.thedailybeast.com/articles/2014/11/11/thousands-of-putin-s-troops-now-in-ukraine-analysts-say.html

Inozemtzev, V. (2014) 'Playing the long game with Russia. The West's Russia strategy should focus on stopping it softly, not on humiliating it'. *The American interest*. September 25. Accessed on May 18, 2018 at www.the-american-interest.com/2014/09/25/playing-the-long-game-with-russia

Kavkazsky uzel. (2015) '102-ya voennaya baza Gruppi rossiiskih voisk v Zakavkazye' (The 102nd military base if the Group of Russian troops in Transcaucasia). *Kavkazsky uzel.* April 3. Accessed on May 28, 2018 at: www.kavkaz-uzel.eu/articles/152315/

Kostyuchenko, E. (2014) 'Armiya i dobrovoltsy' (Army and volunteers). I. September 3. Accessed on May, 12, 2018 at: www.novayagazeta.ru/society/65096.html

Kupriyanova, I. (2014) 'Po sledam donbasskich separatistov: kto voyuet na storone DNR?' (Following the tracks of Donbas separatists: who fights for DPR?). *Deutsche Welle* (in Russian). July 17. Accessed on May 27, 2018 at: http://dw.de/p/1CeNK

Makarenko, V. (2014) 'Rostovskoi oblasti nachalas zapis dobrovoltsev, gotovih otpravitsya v Ukrainu' (Registration of volunteers ready to go to Ukraine started in Rostov oblast). *Novaya gazeta.* February 24. Accessed on May, 12, 2018 at: www.novayagazeta.ru/news/319251.html

Messner, E. (2005) *'Vsemirnaya myatezhvoina' (A worldwide mutiny-war).* Moscow. The Armed Force's University. Accessed on May 21, 2018 at: http://militera.lib.ru/science/0/pdf/messner_ea01.pdf

Neimyrok, D. (2016) 'Sdelat kak v Kharkove'. GPU opublikovala peregovory sovetnika Putina o besporyadkah v Ukraine' ('Do as it was in Kharkov'. GPU has published the talks of Putin's adviser about riots in Ukraine). *MediaPort.* August 23. Accessed on May 28, 2018 at: www.mediaport.ua/sdelat-kak-v-harkove-gpu-opublikovala-peregovory-sovetnika-putina-o-besporyadkah-v-ukraine

Pifer, S. (2017) *Minsk II at two years.* Brookings Institute. February 15. Accessed on May 28, 2018 at: www.brookings.edu/blog/order-from-chaos/2017/02/15/minsk-ii-at-two-years/

Portnikov, V. (2017) 'Pervoye posolstvo' (The first embassy). Interview with Oleg Bay, the former Deputy Head of the Mission in the Ukrainian Embassy in Moscow. *Radio Liberty/Radio Free Europe.* September 2. Accessed on May 23, 2018 at: www.svoboda.org/a/28708382.html

Putin, V. (2014) 'Direct line with Vladimir Putin'. President of Russia. Moscow. April 17. Accessed on May, 12, 2018 at: http://eng.kremlin.ru/transcripts/7034

Rossiiskaya gazeta (online). (2014) 'Voennaya doktrina Rossiiskoi Federatsii' (Military doctrine of the Russian Federation). Approved by the president of the Russian Federation on December 26, 2014. *Rossiiskaya gazeta* (online). December 30.

Roth, A. (2014) 'From Russia, "Tourists" stir the protests'. *The New York Times.* March 3. Accessed on May 27, 2018 at: www.nytimes.com/2014/03/04/world/europe/russias-hand-can-be-seen-in-the-protests.html

Ryadovoy.Ru. (2012) 'Yuzhnii voenii okrug (OSK 'Yug') – noveishii oblik' (The latest structure of the Southern military district (OSC 'South'). *Ryadovoy.Ru.* September 12. Accessed on May 15, 2018 at: http://archive.li/tQylU

Socor, V. (2014) 'Moscow encourages centrifugal forces in South-Eastern Ukraine'. *Eurasia Daily Monitor* Volume: 11 Issue: 36. February 25, 2014. Accessed on May 12, 2018 at: https://jamestown.org/program/moscow-encourages-centrifugal-forces-in-south-eastern-ukraine/

Trenin, D. (2014) 'Russia's goal in Ukraine remains the same: Keep NATO out'. Al Jazeera. June 2. Accessed on May 23, 2018 at: http://america.aljazeera.com/articles/2014/6/2/russiaa-s-goal-inukraineremainsthesametokeepnatoout.html

Tammsaar, R. (2015) "Zhurnal Diplomatiya': Pavel Felgengauer o zashscite perimetra Rossii' (Diplomacy magazine: Pavel Felgengauer on the defense of the Russia's perimeter). *Delfi.* March 22. Accessed on May 18, 2018 at: http://rus.delfi.ee/daily/diplomaatia/zhurnal-diplomatiya-pavel-felgengauer-o-zaschite-perimetra-rossii?id=71061427

Zarudnitzky, V. (2014) 'Voennye aspekti "tzvetnyh" revolutzii' (Military aspects of 'colored' revolutions'). Theses of the presentation at the III Moscow conference on international security. May 26. Moscow. Accessed on May 28, 2018 at: http://retrans.in.ua/?p=4571

34
RUSSIA, THE MIDDLE EAST AND THE CONFLICT IN SYRIA

Derek Averre

Introduction

Over the past few years, Russia's growing international influence has become a topic of increasing interest to scholars and the policy community alike. An important aspect of this has been Moscow's continuing support for the regime of Bashar al-Assad in its prosecution of what Western commentators portray as a merciless campaign against opposition forces in the Syrian civil war. This support has survived heated disputes at the United Nations (UN) about Assad's failure to ensure the protection of civilians and Russia's refusal to allow UN Security Council resolutions condemning Syrian excesses to be passed; the alleged use of chemical weapons (CW) by regime forces against the opposition, notably in Ghouta in August 2013 – which appeared at one stage to be about to trigger Western intervention in the conflict – and on several occasions since; and finally, Moscow's decision to intervene on the side of the regime with air strikes in September 2015, which appears to have altered decisively the balance of power in the conflict, with wider ramifications for politics and security in the Middle East.

These events have unfolded as political confrontation between Russia and the Western liberal democracies has intensified, as analysed in numerous contributions to this volume. Several questions thus arise. What are Russia's interests in the Middle East and North Africa (MENA) and to what extent is Moscow prepared to use military power to consolidate and further its position there? Will Russia henceforth support authoritarian governments when it perceives Western intervention, particularly when aimed at supporting pro-democracy movements, to be threatening 'regime stability' and when its perceived vital interests are at stake? Will Russia continue to challenge liberal governance norms that privilege human security in cases where atrocities are committed by the incumbent government? What is the relationship between Russian approaches to international order and its own domestic political governance? This chapter, first, examines Russian arguments over the Syria conflict and the wider upheaval in MENA generated by the 'Arab Spring', before going on to analyse its diplomatic engagement with the Western powers and with states in the region. It then considers the causes and consequences of Russia's intervention in Syria and the diplomatic and military tools at its disposal. Finally, it assesses the opportunities and constraints facing Moscow in its bid for a more influential regional role in MENA and the impact this is likely to have on Russia's broader foreign policy.

Derek Averre

Russian views on the Syria conflict and the wider MENA region

Russia's approach to Syria has reflected a wider set of ideas about the international system that were forming since well before the conflict started. Official and expert thinking has consistently highlighted critical challenges facing Russia: shifts in the global order, the increasing propensity towards the use of military power, a fractured West with the US struggling to sustain its global leadership, the emergence of new conflicts and security threats arising from weak governance, and the breakdown of international security mechanisms (Averre, 2008, 30–31; Stepanova, 2016, 2). In Russian eyes, the onset of the 'Arab Spring' has reinforced these trends, weakening or destroying state institutions and producing multiple cross-cutting conflicts involving powerful non-state actors, with fundamental political and social upheaval generating humanitarian crises spilling across borders and facilitating the spread of terrorism. A group of Russian experts has concluded that efforts to influence developments in MENA by external actors 'are viewed as a security challenge for the governing elites … attempts by outside forces to accelerate ongoing processes proved counterproductive' (Naumkin *et al.*, 2016, 3). It should be noted that these views bear a remarkable resemblance to some Western assessments about the challenges presented by the Middle East. A UK government report describes the declining role and influence of Western states, the weakening of state structures and dispersal of power 'in more hands than at any time in history', the rise of a younger generation and the prevalence of political patronage, religious tension and authoritarianism: 'the issues are global, the threats are global and [] the full resources of a post-Western world will be needed to turn decline and turmoil into the beginnings of sustainable peace and prosperity', including with the assistance of Russia (House of Lords, 2017, 4). One noted commentator has even argued that the Syria conflict reflects 'the incipient signs of a post-liberal polycentric world' (Tocci, 2014, 1).

The civil war in Libya – in which North Atlantic Treaty Organisation's (NATO) intervention in 2011 to protect the population from Gadaafi's forces, authorised by UN Security Council (UNSC) Resolution 1973, resulted in his overthrow and the subsequent disintegration of authority in the country – was central in determining Russia's response to the Syria conflict (Averre and Davies, 2015, 818–819). Moscow has pointed to the lack of a credible Western strategy, focusing its argument on the violence perpetrated by Islamist extremists and opposition groups linked with them, and the likely collapse of the country that would follow from regime change supported from outside. This has prompted Russia, with the support of China, to veto numerous UNSC resolutions critical of the Assad regime and to assert consistently that any military action to prevent massive violations of human rights should comply with the international legal norm of non-intervention in the internal affairs of sovereign states and be authorised by a decision of the UNSC; NATO's 1999 intervention in the Former Republic of Yugoslavia over Kosovo and the US-led coalition's 2003 campaign in Iraq have repeatedly been referenced by Moscow as examples of illegal actions by the West. This principled position has reflected a clear ambition to influence the rules of the game in terms of who decides on military intervention and what the criteria are. It has also had the instrumental aim of constraining any large-scale military action by the US and its Western allies against Assad.

In addition to engaging in a diplomatic and normative contest with the West, Russia has been faced with rapidly evolving political conflicts that have acquired inter- and intra-state dimensions. A struggle for regional supremacy between Iran and Saudi Arabia, which has spilled over into what is seen as a proxy conflict in Yemen between a Saudi-backed Arab coalition and Iran-supported Houthi rebels; the roles of Turkey, a NATO ally but increasingly intent on prioritising its own foreign and domestic policy priorities, and Israel, concerned about the threat posed by Iran and Syria through their support for Hezbollah and potentially decisive role in Lebanon; and the destructive presence of Islamic State of Iraq and Syria (ISIS) and other sectarian extremist groups – all this has created a dynamic and unpredictable set of circumstances. The ambivalent approach of the second Obama administration and the Trump administration's hostility to Iran and support for right-wing parties in Israel have given the impression that US policy in the region is both inconsistent and potentially destabilising. In Syria itself, the US has been ineffective in terms of preventing Assad from gradually gaining ascendancy over a fragmented opposition. Moscow's initial objectives – preventing regime change and limiting the power of jihadi forces – have apparently been met. However, establishing itself as an influential actor in MENA affairs presents complex challenges.

Russian diplomacy in the early stages of the Syria conflict

Initial attempts by the external powers to find a resolution of the conflict foundered on important divergences in approach between Russia and Western states. The latter supported the National Coalition of Syrian Revolutionary and Opposition Forces in their demands for Assad to step down – or be removed – before they would engage in any political process leading to transition. Moscow, with some justification, pointed to the presence of Islamist extremists within the opposition, such as the Salafist al-Qaeda affiliate Jabhat al-Nusra (which later joined other groups to become Hayat Tahrir al-Sham), as well as other forces with specific agendas driven by external patrons, and argued that Assad's removal would only exacerbate the violence. In Russian eyes, the interpretation by Western governments of the Arab Spring as primarily a struggle for democracy took little account of the ambitions of sectarian extremist groups in the wider region and the implications for Syria's sovereignty (Averre and Davies, 2015, 819–820). Moscow also had legitimate concerns over the potential emergence of a transnational militant Islamist movement linking Russia's North Caucasus with the MENA region. While critical of Assad's foot-dragging over reforms, Moscow continued to favour a political transition which would involve his Alawite administration. It pointed to the Geneva communiqué, agreed by leading external and regional powers in June 2012 and calling for full implementation of UNSC resolutions 2042 (together with the Six-Point Proposal of the Joint Special Envoy of the United Nations and the League of Arab States annexed to it) and 2043, which laid emphasis on a Syrian-led inclusive political process and stated that 'a transitional governing body ... could include members of the present government and the opposition and other groups ... formed on the basis of mutual consent' (Geneva Communiqué, 2012, 3).

As the conflict unfolded during the third Putin presidential administration, the broader implications of Russia's position on sovereignty and intervention, and its differences with the liberal human rights norms appealed to by the Western democracies, became a central issue. Foreign Minister Lavrov argued that interpreting human rights standards should rest with sovereign states and not be imposed by external states and organisations (Lavrov, 2014). Putin himself spoke out against the 'destruction of traditional values', with explicit reference to how the promotion of more progressive development models had resulted in 'regression, barbarity and extensive bloodshed' in MENA countries. They called for commonly accepted international legal norms to be observed to ensure sovereign equality among states. This refusal to accept that 'external standards of legitimacy may be applied to states ... [to] justify efforts to influence or change their political structure or support for rebellions' (Allison, 2013b, 819) has become a *leitmotif* of Russian foreign policy narratives as Moscow's relations with the West have deteriorated.

Moscow's approach came under intense scrutiny in August 2013 when an attack using CW, allegedly by Syrian government forces, killed at least several hundred people in Ghouta, including civilians (several incidents of the use of chemicals as weapons had been reported in the previous months). The US, the UK and France eventually presented evidence of chemical attacks, based on forensic tests of blood and soil samples taken out of the country, to the UN; the moral and legal taboo of the use of CW, with Syria flouting the 1925 Geneva Protocol and with the vast majority of states having signed and ratified the Chemical Weapons Convention (CWC), was being built up as a cause for military intervention. Russia, intent on denying the US and its allies any pretext for intervention, presented evidence to the UN pointing to the use of chemicals by opposition forces in previous incidents, alleging that chemical materials were secretly imported through the Turkish border into Syria and that chemical plants in Iraq were producing CW for 'terrorists' in the region. Eventually, with the UK's withdrawal after losing a parliamentary vote against military action, and France and Turkey the only major states to back a reluctant Obama over military strikes, the crisis was defused by a joint Russia-US plan for the destruction of Syria's CW stockpiles and facilities, with Syria at the same time joining the CWC. Moscow's massive diplomatic campaign to broker a political settlement appeared at the time to be something of a triumph, since UNSC Resolution 2118 underpinning the agreement did not contain the threat of an immediate military response; the resolution stated that it is up to the Organisation for the Prohibition of Chemical Weapons (OPCW) to decide if evidence about future CW use should be submitted to the UNSC so that action could be taken under a further resolution. The UN would thus be the sole legitimate authority to decide on military action; in Lavrov's words, this would prevent any politicised approach by the Western governments in an attempt to 'call the shots' in the Middle East (Lavrov, 2013; Averre and Davies, 2015, 821). As we shall see below, however, the CW issue resurfaced later.

The failure of the UN-backed Geneva II Peace Conference in January to February 2014 to bring the government and opposition groups together for negotiations over a political transition (Akgün and Tiryaki, 2017, 13) was compounded by political tensions between Russia and the Western powers, which compromised the campaign against terrorist groups in Syria and Iraq. Moscow's repeated vetoing of UNSC draft resolutions, which might have constrained the Assad regime's military excesses, hindered the opposition gains and complicated humanitarian efforts. Numerous commentators concluded that Putin had recognised sooner than Obama the limits of the major powers' influence over the warring parties; nevertheless, at this stage Russia's engagement in Syria owed more to adroit improvisation and the realisation of specific aims than to a discernible longer-term strategy (see Stepanova, 2016, 1). As Assad's forces were making little headway against the opposition, it appeared that Russia's regional diplomacy to preventing the collapse of Syria was running the risk of failure.

The causes and consequences of Russia's intervention in Syria

Five years into the conflict, there were few signs that differences over the fate of Assad were being overcome, with the National Coalition and the National Coordination Committee for Democratic Change, as well as some armed groups, still demanding his departure before negotiations could begin on a transition. The external powers continued to emphasise that a political solution was needed, but none appeared imminent. The most authoritative report on the conflict noted that 'its horrors are pervasive and ever-present' and that it had become a complex 'multisided proxy war steered from abroad by an intricate network of alliances', with 'an increasing number of belligerents'; UNSC resolutions were largely disregarded, humanitarian atrocities continued to be perpetrated by government troops (particular attention was paid to attacks on medical facilities by Assad forces) and opposition groups, and ISIS had carved out a sizeable territory in Iraq and Syria (International Commission of Inquiry, 2016, 1, 5, 7, 10–11). Even after the fall of ISIS in Raqqa to Kurdish and Sunni Arab forces, a leading newspaper stated that 'blunt military power and geopolitical opportunism governs these events in the Middle East. Diplomacy has all but been abandoned … states and non-state entities alike vie for influence and conquest. Sectarian and ethnic differences fuel a dangerous dynamic' (*The Guardian*, 2017).

It was against this background that Russia stepped up its involvement through the deployment of an air force group in Latakia. The Iranian Quds Force Commander Qassem Soleimani reportedly visited Moscow, following high-level meetings earlier, to discuss a joint intervention, though Moscow officially denied this. A bilateral Russian-Syrian agreement authorising the intervention was signed in August, following which Russian aircraft began reinforcing the troops in Syria, and the following month a joint Russian-Iranian-Iraqi-Syrian intelligence coordination centre was established in Baghdad. Russian air strikes began on 30 September and shortly afterwards Iranian ground forces launched an offensive near Aleppo using Russian air cover (Lund, 2016). In November, Putin visited Tehran and met Supreme Leader Ayatollah Khamenei; reports suggest that mutual praise for their respective positions on the Syria issue was accompanied by rhetorical condemnation of US policy. The offensive finally took the key town of Aleppo over a year later, in December 2016.

Russia's intervention, which Moscow claimed was legitimate since it came at the invitation of the Syrian authorities, contributed materially to the renewal of efforts towards a political settlement. Meetings in October and November 2015, co-sponsored by the US and Russia, led to the establishment of the International Syria Support Group (ISSG) involving the UN (through its Special Envoy for Syria Staffan de Mistura), the League of Arab States, the EU and leading regional states (Blockmans, 2016). This paved the way for the UNSC to adopt Resolution 2254 in December 2015 to create a road map for a political transition, based on the 2012 Geneva Communiqué and the Vienna Statements of November 2014 (International Commission of Inquiry, 2016, 3–4). Resolution 2254 (backed up by 2258 and 2268) also called on warring parties to allow humanitarian access and demanded a cessation of attacks against civilians. The ISSG has become central to negotiations, setting up a Ceasefire Task Force (co-chaired by the US and Russia) and an ISSG Humanitarian Task Force (chaired by the UN).

Russia's cooperation with the US since the ISSG was established has been an uneasy, and sometimes bizarre, mix of diplomatic engagement and bitter political disputes. Long-standing criticism of the US has been reiterated. Lavrov has criticised Washington's

> attempts to interfere in the internal affairs of states and impose development models on countries and nations … mentorship, superiority and exceptionalism, as well as the pursuit of one's own interests at the expense of just and equitable cooperation … unilateral reckless solutions, born of a sense of infallibility, in the bleeding region of the Middle East and North Africa

and asserted that 'the decency and legitimacy of any member of the international community should be measured by their respect for the principles of sovereign equality of states and non-interference in the internal affairs of others'; but in the more recent period criticism has intensified, with repeated accusations that the US has spared the al-Nusra front by sponsoring opposition groups linked with it (Lavrov, 2016b) with Lavrov, suggesting that this is a ploy by the US to achieve regime change. Foreign ministry spokespersons have even suggested that Washington is defending ISIS, despite the fact that the US, while still supporting the opposition's call for Assad to step down, has prioritised the destruction of ISIS. Yet, often in the same breath, the necessity of Russia's cooperation with the US and Western powers, with 'efforts to develop a shared understanding', on coordinating counterterrorism efforts, expanding humanitarian access and strengthening the ceasefire, has been emphasised (Ministry of Foreign Affairs, 2016).

An authoritative report noted that Russia's 'unprecedented' military campaign not only reaffirmed its role as an independent power prepared to defend its own global and regional interests but also heralded a more definite strategy; indeed, the intervention signalled Russia's 'departure from the post-Cold War system' in which the Western powers had disregarded Russia's interests (Naumkin *et al.*, 2016, 28). It underlined both Russia's ability to leverage its institutional power within a global legal-normative order, in which the observance of 'procedural rules, rather than basic values' is underpinned by the UNSC, and Russia's enhanced international status (Allison, 2017, 520). Commentators have suggested that a new order in the MENA region is emerging in which the regional powers, together with Moscow, act in concert to stabilise the situation and marginalise the role of the Western actors. Russia's involvement in the conflict in Libya, and its support for National Army Commander Khalifa Haftar, reflects its ambitions.

However, the protracted and fragmented nature of the political process in Syria since the establishment of the ISSG has reflected the limits of Russia's influence in an intractable conflict influenced by shifting alliances and external considerations. Moscow has attempted to steer negotiations to its advantage through the Astana process in concert with Iran and Turkey, following the latter's reconciliation with Russia after its shooting down of a Russian fighter jet in November 2015. Turkey's criticism of the Assad regime has been overshadowed by its military efforts against ISIS in Jarabulus and, increasingly, by its aim of suppressing the influence of the Kurdish Democratic Union Party (PYD) in northern Syria. These three powers signed the Moscow Declaration on 20 December 2016, laying out steps to revitalise the political process in Syria, and a few days later the UNSC passed Resolution 2336 supporting Russia-Turkey efforts to end the violence and introduce a countrywide ceasefire. In May 2017, Russia, Iran and Turkey signed a Memorandum on the creation of de-escalation areas in Syria and on other agreements reached within the framework of the Astana format. Further joint efforts were aimed at advancing a political settlement, by implementing the recommendations of the Congress of the Syrian National Dialogue in Sochi in January 2018 to form a constitutional committee comprising Syrian government representatives and a broadly based opposition delegation to draft constitutional reform proposals. Russia has also engaged in multilateral diplomacy efforts with other regional states and organisations, in particular the Saudi-convened Riyadh group and the Gulf Cooperation Council, which have run parallel to the Geneva peace talks. Progress in all formats has been slow and painful, however, with the Assad regime continuing to press home its military advantage and unwilling to relinquish power.

Cooperation between Moscow and Tehran has emerged as a central axis in the region. Although the two countries have quite different aims, their common security – a desire to limit US influence – and trade interests, with Iran bidding to join the Shanghai Cooperation Organisation and the two states building economic links in the wider

Middle East and Eurasia, have ensured close cooperation in the recent period. Nor have relations been adversely affected by Moscow's position on the Iranian nuclear issue, in which Moscow's broader nuclear non-proliferation concerns have translated into support for the Joint Comprehensive Plan of Action (JCPOA). In Syria, Iran and Hezbollah have committed ground forces and financial support to Assad; Russia's provision of air support, heavy weaponry and intelligence since its intervention, as well as diplomatic backing, has also been accompanied by closer alignment with Iraq (Trenin, 2016). But Moscow faces a number of challenges. Attempts to balance partnership with Iran with a recognition of Israel's security concerns – both in Syria and Lebanon – and to influence a wider Middle East settlement are fraught with problems. The situation is complicated by US animus towards Iran, reflected in its recent withdrawal from the JCPOA and the prospect of far-reaching sanctions, and its support for Israel, which raises the threat of a military clash (an exchange of missile strikes took place between Iran and Israel in May 2018). Also, irregular Russian forces were killed in US air strikes in eastern Syria in response to an attack in February 2018, prompting fears of an escalation between US and Russia (though it has so far been largely avoided).

Russia's interests in the Middle East

Is carving out an influential longer term role in MENA – in which the complex calculus of national, sectional and external interests becomes ever more bewildering – a high-wire act beyond Russia's capabilities? In contrast to the notion, mentioned above, of a new regional order with Moscow playing an influential role, the argument can be made that Russia's diplomatic limitations have been exposed, with no political solution in sight and regional powers locked in disputes. The notion of Syrian 'sovereignty' must be qualified; the Assad regime relies on not only Iran and Russia but also on shadow proxy forces to prop itself up. Moscow's support has not entailed the provision of combat forces on the ground but re-establishing effective governance and rebuilding the country will involve a long-term commitment and potentially require substantial financial costs, especially if, as reports suggest, Russia plans to keep forces in Syria once a political resolution to the conflict is found. Moscow's support for Assad's forces has led to an intense barrage of criticism, despite unconvincing Russian allegations of the 'politicisation' of human rights and humanitarian aid by the Western powers and international non-governmental organisations (NGOs), over the appalling human suffering experienced by the civilian population, and accusations that Moscow has been more concerned with helping to defeat the opposition rather than combating terrorism and sponsoring a political settlement. This has overshadowed its legitimate goal of maintaining Syria as a sovereign state and exacted a toll of reputational costs in the West as well as in some parts of the Middle East. The UN High Commissioner for Human Rights Zeid Ra'ad al-Hussein has likened attacks in eastern Ghouta and elsewhere to 'war crimes, and potentially crimes against humanity', though without imputing direct responsibility (UN Human Rights Office, 2016). This has been echoed by several NGOs, which refer to Assad's 'starve or surrender' tactic, restricting humanitarian and medical aid, to deal with resistance in opposition areas. Moscow's bitter diplomatic disputes with the US and its allies – involving a sustained and often vituperative information campaign in response to Western 'fabrications' of reports of atrocities (Lavrov, 2016c) – have compounded the estrangement caused by the Ukraine conflict and alleged Russian attempts to interfere in the domestic affairs of the Western states. Further incidents involving the use of CW, allegedly by government forces, in April 2017 at Khan Sheikhoun and in April 2018 near Douma, have led to punitive missile strikes by the US, again presenting a danger of escalation as

Russian troops are embedded in bases at Tartus and Hmeimim. The apparent failure of Syria to observe its commitments under the CWC, despite repeated Russian denials that Assad's forces have been proved to be responsible, has attracted renewed opprobrium.

Commentators have speculated that, since the conflict is not fundamental to Russian national security, Moscow could decide to withdraw from Syria and utilise mainly diplomatic tools to further its core interests (Lund, 2016). The perception in the Kremlin has appeared to be that the gains, in terms of curtailing US influence and demonstrating its readiness to use hard power to defend its regional security and trade interests, have strengthened Russia's legitimacy as a leading actor in regional – and even global – affairs. From this point of view, while Moscow remains pragmatic and is aware that a grand strategy is not feasible – witness the tortuous progress of peace talks – its role in Syria reflects a broader strategic approach to maximising its influence in the contemporary international environment. This entails navigating between shifting alliances and balances of power, maximising its positions within a concert, or concerts, of regional and external powers while making selective and instrumental appeals to the core norms and principles of the UN-centred international order. This is reflected in an interview with CNN, where Lavrov called for a 'business-like discussion, not another General Assembly-like debate' between Russia, the US and the major regional powers (Lavrov, 2016a); a few days earlier, he had issued veiled warnings to external forces – not least hawkish elements in the US – who advocate military strikes on positions near Russian bases in Khmeimim and Tartus: 'diplomacy has several allies in this endeavour – Russia's Aerospace Forces, Army and Navy' (Lavrov, 2016b). The subtext appears to be that transactional diplomacy will, if necessary, be backed up by military muscle. Perhaps most indicative of Russia's commitment to an ongoing role in MENA was a comment Lavrov made after a meeting with then US Secretary of State Tillerson; in response to a question about Russia's exit strategy, he declared that 'We don't have an exit strategy' (Lavrov, 2017). However, since this statement, Russia has withdrawn the bulk of its forces from Syria; noted Russian scholars have highlighted the uncertainty of the situation and argued that

> under the influence of rapidly changing events provoked by ill thought-out actions of other actors, Moscow's present military and political successes can be viewed as a result of excessive involvement with ensuing consequences ... Russia is not only distancing itself from overly friendly embraces but also developing a clear and relatively easily realizable strategy for withdrawal.
>
> *(Kuznetsov et al., 2018, 32)*

Conclusions

Three explanations have commonly been offered for Russia's role in the Syria conflict and the wider MENA region. First, that Russia is trying to re-establish its global influence using Syria as a geopolitical pawn on a kind of proxy Cold War chess board. This chapter argues that while Russian interests in some respects rival those of Western states, particularly with respect to the legitimacy of the Assad regime, Syria is a conflict with its own specific dynamic, part of a messy and unpredictable regional upheaval, which the external powers are struggling to understand and manage. Russia believes it has legitimate interests which can be defended through the careful use of political and, where necessary and on a limited scale, military instruments. But at the same time Moscow is well aware that cooperation with the US and its allies, underpinned by commonly agreed mechanisms, to limit destabilisation and imbalances of power, with the potential spillover of multiple conflicts, is necessary (Stepanova, 2016, 7–8, 11–12; Kuznetsov *et al.*, 2018, 14, 32). The central problem here is that these mechanisms have yet to be fully worked out and are often undermined by bad faith and lack of trust, partly a legacy of previous clashes and partly linked with other aspects of current relations.

The second explanation is that Moscow is motivated by defending the legitimacy of its domestic order against the Western promotion of liberal norms (see Allison, 2013a, 14, 16, 110; Allison, 2013b, 815–818); put simply, one brutal regime propping up another in a 'league of authoritarian gentlemen'. The grievous humanitarian situation can to a considerable extent be put down to the Assad regime – though it does not have a monopoly on pitiless sectarian violence – and Assad has indeed received substantial material and diplomatic support from the Putin government. But Moscow's preoccupation with sovereignty and order, stemming from the interventions in Iraq and Libya – which, in its view, led to anarchy and the collapse of law – has wider significance in the context of concerns over instability arising from a vacuum of governance. In this respect, Russian approaches to sovereignty, and its preoccupation with resisting the imposition of external norms, reflect a distinct national belief system. Its normative position should, however, be separated analytically from the values-based narratives that have increasingly challenged Western liberalism in official narratives, including in statements on Libya and Syria. Also, it is a mistake to conceptualise these shifts purely in terms of a normative contest between the Western liberal democracies, on the one hand, and Russia, on the other. As Tocci (2014, 23) notes, they suggest that 'power is diffusing globally, and that global outcomes are already being determined by the complex interplay of various forms of power' exercised by a 'much wider set of global and regional, state and non-state, actors', with attendant effects on global norms.

The third explanation focuses on Russia's insistence on the primacy of state sovereignty and sovereign equality – in its view, the fundamental legal norms which lie at the basis of international order, which enjoy the firm support of non-Western states – and its suspicions about the West's 'double standards' over humanitarian intervention and the Doctrine of Responsibility to Protect (R2P; see Averre and Davies, 2015). This idea, which underpins Moscow's emphasis on the UN as the primary authority and use of its veto power in the UNSC to counter intervention based on a Chapter VII Resolution, has explanatory power. However, states have not argued in favour of military intervention to protect Syrian civilians as the right option; even in the aftermath of the use of CW, apparently by Assad's forces, in August 2013 and in subsequent incidents, states in favour of military action argued that any forcible intervention ought to be limited to deterring the future use of CW. In short, there was little or no political will to intervene militarily in the Syria conflict to effect regime change. Yet Moscow has for several years used the spectre of regime change instrumentally to frustrate attempts through the UN to bring Assad to book while seeking UN validation for other initiatives; at the same time, the Western powers have paid scant respect for the idea of an inclusive political process to resolve the Syria conflict as called for in UNSC Resolution 2042. The loser here is the rules-based global order which appears to be unravelling: the search for a negotiated order may be undermined by increasing *realpolitik*, framing an attempt by Russia to lead a concert of powers and thereby validate its international status. Redefining the rules-based order and recovering the trust that might help to resolve Syria and other conflicts that challenge national interests is likely to take a long time and demands the kind of political will that has in recent years been largely absent.

Bibliography

Akgün, M. and Tiryaki, S. eds. (2017) *Future of Syria*. European Institute of the Mediterranean, April, at www.euromesco.net/wp-content/uploads/2017/09/201704-EuroMeSCo-Joint-Policy-Study-7.pdf (accessed 17 February 2018).

Allison, R. (2017) 'Russia and the post-2014 international legal order: revisionism and *realpolitik*'. *International Affairs*, 93:3, 519–543.

Allison, R. (2013a) *Russia, the West, and Military Intervention*. Oxford: Oxford University Press.

Allison, R. (2013b) 'Russia and Syria: explaining alignment with a regime in crisis'. *International Affairs*, 89:4, 795–823.

Averre, D. (2008) 'Russian foreign policy and the global political environment'. *Problems of Post-Communism*, 55:5, 28–39.

Averre, D. and Davies, L. (2015) 'Russia, humanitarian intervention and the Responsibility to Protect: The case of Syria'. *International Affairs*, 91:4, 813–834.

Blockmans, S. (2016) *Bleak prospects for peace in Syria*. European Neighbourhood Watch, 127, June, at www.ceps.eu/system/files/NWatch127.pdf (accessed 23 September 2016).

Geneva Communiqué (2012) *Action Group for Syria Final Communiqué*. 30 June, at www.un.org/News/dh/infocus/Syria/FinalCommuniqueActionGroupforSyria.pdf (accessed 4 May 2014).

House of Lords (2017) *The Middle East: Time for New Realism*. Select Committee on International Relations, 2nd Report of Session 2016–2017, May, at https://publications.parliament.uk/pa/ld201617/ldselect/ldintrel/159/159.pdf (accessed 10 November 2017).

International Commission of Inquiry (2016) *Report of the Independent International Commission of Inquiry on the Syrian Arab Republic*. UN Human Rights Council A/HRC/31/68, 11 February.

Kuznetsov, V, Naumkin V., and Zvyagelskaya I. (2018) *Russia in the Middle East: The Harmony of Polyphony*. Valdai Discussion Club, May, at http://valdaiclub.com/files/18375/ (accessed 31 May 2018).

Lavrov, S. (2017) *Remarks and answers to media questions following talks with US Secretary of State Rex Tillerson*. Washington DC, 10 May, at www.mid.ru/en/foreign_policy/news/-/asset_publisher/cKNonkJE02Bw/content/id/2751328 (accessed 31 May 2018).

Lavrov, S. (2016a) *Interview with CNN International*. Moscow, 12 October, at www.mid.ru/en/foreign_policy/news/-/asset_publisher/cKNonkJE02Bw/content/id/2497676 (accessed 31 May 2018).

Lavrov, S. (2016b) *Interview with Channel One's Vremya programme*. Moscow, 9 October, at www.mid.ru/en/foreign_policy/news/-/asset_publisher/cKNonkJE02Bw/content/id/2494612 (accessed 31 May 2018).

Lavrov, S. (2016c) *Interview to BBC world News Channel*. Moscow, 30 September, at www.mid.ru/en/foreign_policy/news/-/asset_publisher/cKNonkJE02Bw/content/id/2481408 (accessed 10 November 2016).

Lavrov, S. (2016d) *Remarks at the 71st session of the UN General Assembly*. New York, 23 September, at www.mid.ru/en/foreign_policy/news/-/asset_publisher/cKNonkJE02Bw/content/id/2468262 (accessed 10 November 2016).

Lavrov, S. (2014) *Speech at the 25th session of the United Nations Human Rights Council, Geneva*. 3 March, at www.mid.ru/en/foreign_policy/news/-/asset_publisher/cKNonkJE02Bw/content/id/72642 (accessed 28 May 2015).

Lavrov, S. (2013) *Interview with Channel One*. 22 September, at www.mid.ru/en/foreign_policy/news/-/asset_publisher/cKNonkJE02Bw/content/id/95878 (accessed 28 May 2015).

Lund, A. (2016) *Stand Together or Fall Apart: The Russian-Iranian Alliance in Syria*. Carnegie Middle East Center, 31 May, at http://carnegie-mec.org/diwan/63699 (accessed 23 September 2016).

Ministry of Foreign Affairs (2016) *Joint Statement of the Russian Federation and the United States on Syria*. 9 May, at www.mid.ru/en/foreign_policy/news/-/asset_publisher/cKNonkJE02Bw/content/id/2269310 (accessed 31 May 2018).

Naumkin V., Kuznetsov V., Soukhov N., and Zvyagelskaya I. (2016) *The Middle East in a Time of Troubles: Traumas of the Past and Challenges of the Future*. Valdai Discussion Club, August, at http://valdaiclub.com/files/11592/ (accessed 10 September 2017).

Stepanova, E. (2016) *Russia in the Middle East: Back to a 'Grand Strategy' – or Enforcing Munltilateralism?* IFRI Politique étrangère, 2, at www.ifri.org/sites/default/files/atoms/files/pe2_stepanova_ok.pdf (accessed 17 February 2018).

The Guardian (2017) *The Guardian view on the fall of Raqqa: as Isis loses, Iran wins*. Editorial, 22 October, at www.theguardian.com/commentisfree/2017/oct/22/the-guardian-view-on-the-fall-of-raqqa-as-isis-loses-iran-wins (accessed 29 November 2017).

Tocci, N. (2014) *On Power and Norms: Libya, Syria, and the Responsibility to Protect*. German Marshall Fund of the United States report, Transatlantic Academy paper series no 2, 25 April, at www.gmfus.org/publications/power-and-norms-libya-syria-and-responsibility-protect (accessed 29 November 2016).

Trenin, D. (2016) *Russia and Iran: Historic Mistrust and Contemporary Partnership*. Carnegie Moscow Center, 18 August, at http://carnegie.ru/2016/08/18/russia-and-iran-historic-mistrust-and-contemporary-partnership-pub-64365 (accessed 4 May 2017).

UN Human Rights Office (2016) *Urgent Debate on situation in Eastern Ghouta, 37th session of the Human Rights Council*. 2 March, at www.ohchr.org/EN/NewsEvents/Pages/DisplayNews.aspx?NewsID=22746 (accessed 31 May 2018).

UN Security Council (2012) Resolution 2042, at www.un.org/en/peacekeeping/documents/six_point_proposal.pdf (accessed 4 May 2014).

INDEX

Note: Page numbers followed by "n" denote endnotes.

Abashidze, Zurab 318
Abkhazia 21, 35, 39, 138–9, 144, 177, 262, 266, 312–17, 357–9, 377–8, 380–5
ABM Treaty 138, 229, 233, 244, 294
Adams, Rod 173
Adamsky, Dmitry 158, 164
adaptation, definition of 220
AGORA 206, 208; Internet freedom in Russia 209
Ahtisaari, Martti 370
Aksenov, Sergey 392
Alexander I, Emperor of Russia 48, 289–90
Alexander II, Emperor of Russia 290–2
Alexander III, Emperor of Russia 48, 290–2
Alexashenko, Sergey 24
Aliyev, Ilham 316
Alliance's Study of NATO Enlargement 259
Allison, Graham 186
Allison, Roy 53, 93
Al-Qaeda 197, 267, 269, 319n1
Alternative for Germany 67
ambiguity, deniability and no-lose scenarios 24–5
Andropov, Yuri 42, 113, 127, 196
Anglo-French Dardanelles expedition 291
annexation of Crimea 4, 11, 18, 21, 30, 32, 60, 62–3, 76, 78–9, 82, 94–5, 127–9, 134, 138, 207, 231, 252, 261–2, 295, 347, 392–3
anti-satellite weapons tests (ASATs) 229, 232, 235n1
APT28 (Fancy Bear) 211
APT29 (Cozy Bear) 211
Arab Spring 9, 11, 114, 250, 399–400, 401
Arbatov, Alexey 12, 48
Arbatova, N. 53

Arctic: role of outside actors 304–6; securitisation of 300–1
Arctic Commission 304
Arctic Council 300, 305–6
Arctic Economic Council 305
Armitage, Richard 186
Arms and Influence (Schelling) 135
Art, Robert 93
Asian International Infrastructure Bank (AIIB) 344, 350
al-Assad, Bashar 20, 64, 246, 267, 269, 272, 274, 399–407
Association Agreements 62, 91, 93, 251, 316, 359
asymmetrical energy interdependence 90
asymmetry, definition of 220
August War 176, 358–9, 362–3
Austro-German Dual Alliance 291
Averre, Derek 280
Avturkhanov, Umar 314

Bagirov, Taleh 318
al-Baghdadi, Abu-Bakr 251
Baker, James A., III 186
Baku-Tbilisi-Ceyhan (BTC) pipeline 186, 359
Baku-Tbilisi-Kars (BTK) railway 334, 337
Balkans: national security documents under Yeltsin 367–8; NATO enlargement, and Russia 371–2; Russia, the Kosovo War, and its aftermath 369–71; Russia and the Yugoslav wars 368–9; Russian security strategy in 366–75; Russia's scramble for influence 372–4
Balzer, Harley 172
Bank Rossiia 348
Barents Euro-Arctic Council (BEAC) 300, 305
Barents Regional Council (BRC) 300, 305

411

Index

"Basic Propositions of the Military Doctrine of the Russian Federation" 367
Bateman, Aaron 114
Battle of Borodino 47
Battle of Pereyaslav 34
Battle of Poltava 289
Baunov, Alexander 54
Bay, Oleg 389
BBC 250–2
Beijing 332–5; *see also* China
Belavezh Accords 377
Belt and Road Initiative (BRI) 295, 335, 349
Belyaninov, Andrei 31
Berezovsky, Boris 196
Berlin Wall, fall of 113
Beslan massacre 10
Beslan school hostage crises 195
'bioenergy information weapons' 220
Bittman, Ladislav 219
Blank, Stephen 110–13
Bolshevik Revolution 214
Bonaparte, Napoleon 290, 292
Bondarev, Viktor 160
Borogan, Irina 114, 164, 194
Bortnikov, Aleksandr 31
Brandt, Willy 184
Bredikhin, Anton 318
Brexit 58, 60, 93
Brezhnev, Leonid 42, 140, 184, 247
Brezhnev Doctrine 39
BRICS countries 92, 317; brief history 343–4; Contingency Reserve Arrangement (CRA) 344; GDP of 88; New Development Bank (NDB) 344; overview 342–3; Russia and 350; in Russian foreign and security policy 342–50; in Russian foreign policy, 2008–2013 344–7; in Russian foreign policy after Ukraine, 2014–2015 347–50
British Commonwealth 52
'broken lens' syndrome 19–21
Brudny, Yitzhak 113
Brzezinski, Zbigniew 186
Budyko, Mikhail 303
'Building Better Global Economic BRICS' (O'Neill) 343
building pipelines 171–3
Bush, George H. W. 368
Bush, George W. 26, 138, 245–7, 344–5
Buzan, Barry 311

Canadian Broadcasting Corporation (CBC) 250
capacity: to determine hierarchies 91–2; to determine identities 91–2
Carter, Jimmy 247
Catherine II *see* Catherine the Great
Catherine the Great 289–90

Caucasus: analysing regional security complex in 317; North Caucasus 314–15; overview 309–11; post-Soviet regional security in 313–14; Russia as the top target of Jihadists 317–18; Russian traditional foreign policy in 311–13; South Caucasus 315–17
Central Asia (CA): challenges and interconnections 321–5; overview 321; Russia and China in 335–7; Russian security strategy in 321–9; strategies for dealing with region and challenges 325–8
Central Asia-China gas pipeline (CAGP) 188
Central Asian Regional Collective Rapid Deployment Force 268
Central Bank of Russia 349
Centre for Strategic Research (CSR) 104
CFE Treaty 157
Charap, Samuel 53
Chavez, Hugo 40
Chechen Wars 126, 128, 312, 318
chekisty, as keepers of strategic culture 113–15
Chemezov, Sergey 194
Chemical Weapons Convention (CWC) 402
Cheney, Dick 186
Chernomyrdin, Viktor 188, 367, 369
Chevron 186
Chiherin, Georgi 312
China: estimated numbers of nuclear weapons in 2017 89; military might 338–9; Russia's security threatened by 338–9; share of global military expenditure 89; taking over the lead from Russia 337–8
China-Kyrgyzstan-Uzbekistan railway 336–7
Chinese Empire 288
civil society, control of 77–8
Civil War in Chechnya 197
Clark, Wesley 134
climate change: impacts on Russia's Arctic 301–2; Russian Arctic security and 299–307; securitisation of the Arctic 300–1
climate security: challenges to Russia addressing 303–4
Clinton, Bill 61, 245–6, 368
Clinton, Hillary 113–14
Coats, Daniel 232
coercive diplomacy: in action 136–8; demonstration of superior military power and limited military victory 139; historical context for emergence of 133–4; initial stage of conflict and Russian leaders 141–2; involvement of Putin in decision-making and management of 141; peculiarities 138–9; refusal of celebration of 'victory' over defeated enemy 140; resources and traditions 136–8; in Russian security strategy 133–43; theoretical perspective 135–6; 'transitional deals' and 140–1

Index

Cold War 3, 22, 32, 36–7, 39, 46, 60–1, 86, 97, 101, 109, 113, 129, 135, 170, 172, 184, 219, 227, 242, 250, 253–4, 277, 293–6, 311, 317, 338, 342, 366–7, 371, 380, 406
Collective Security Treaty Organisation (CSTO) 37, 91, 177, 210, 266, 314, 316, 356, 381
'coloured revolutions' 9; as information warfare technology 217–18; technologies 218
Committee of Soldiers' Mothers (CSM) 150
'Common European Home' 61
Common Foreign and Security Policy (CFSP) 281
'Common Spaces Agreement' 61
Commonwealth of Independent States (CIS) 30, 51, 91, 128, 142, 377; Inter-Parliamentary Assembly 220
communism 17, 92, 183, 247
Communist International (Comintern) 366
Communist Party of the Soviet Union (CPSU) 31, 125
Communist Party of Ukraine 393
'competing regionalisms' 91
complexity of power 87–92
compulsory power 88
Concept for Children's Information Security 204
'Concept of participation of the Russian Federation in BRICS' 346
'Concept of the Russian Federation's Presidency in BRICS in 2015–2016' 348
Conceptual Views on the Activities of the Armed Forces of the Russian Federation in Information Space (Conceptual Views, 2011) 215
Concert of Europe system 12
conflict: Russian leaders and 141–2; with West as key source of legitimisation 81–2; *see also specific conflicts*
Congress of Berlin 291
Congress of Russian Communities 124
Congress of Vienna 290
Conventional Forces in Europe (CFE) Treaty 35
Convention on International Information Security 209
Copenhagen School of International Relations 123, 301
Copenhagen Summit 303
Corbyn, Jeremy 58
Council for Mutual Economic Assistance (CMEA) 184–5
Council of Europe 87, 220
counter-struggle, and information warfare 216–17
counterterrorism operations 9, 266, 269, 272–3
counterterrorism policies: critical geopolitics on 271–3
counterterrorism responses (2000–2017) 267–9

counterterrorism strategies: global 266–74; regional 266–74
Covington, Stephen R. 112–13
Crimea, annexation of 4, 11, 18, 21, 30, 32, 60, 62–3, 76, 78–9, 82, 94–5, 127–9, 134, 138, 207, 231, 252, 261–2, 295, 347, 392–3
Crimean Khanate 309
Crimean War 290–1
Crimea: The Way Back Home 134, 141
Cross-Border Inter-Bank Payment System (CIPS) 349
Cutter, W. Bowman 20
Cyprus-North Cyprus dispute 357

DeBardeleben, Joan 91
decision-making: manual control and the process of 22–4; 'operational code' and strategic 17–27
dedovshchina (bullying of junior conscripts by the senior ones) 150
Deep and Comprehensive Free Trade Area (DCFTA) 91
Deep and Comprehensive Free Trade Area agreement 347
defence spending 100–4; future military expenditures 103–4; state arms procurement 102–3
defensive-reactive motivation, as strategic communication influence operation 21–2
democracy: internal 7; liberal 61, 63, 64, 68, 278, 326; Russian hybrid warfare against 66–7; sovereign 9, 62, 326; Western 11, 66–7
demonstration, of superior military power and limited military victory 139
Derzhavin, Gavrila 310
'Digital Economy' 204
disputes: inherited from the USSR 32–4; resulting from the breakup 34–6
Djukanovic, Milo 373
Doctrine on Information Security 203–8
domestic and foreign policy nexus: changes in domestic security forces 79–80; conflict with the West as key source of legitimisation 81–2; control of civil society 77–8; defining socio-political landscape through lens of security perception 75–6; insecurity of the regime 76–7; regime transformation with impact on security policy 78–9; securitisation of all policy areas and inner abroad 80–1
domestic security: forces, changes in 79–80; intelligence agencies and 195–6
Donbas: proxy war in 394–5; separatist mutiny in 388–9; West and 253
Dozhd 250, 252
Dubrovka Moscow theater 195
Dudaev, Dzhokhar 314
Dugin, Alexander 183

413

Duma Committee on Information Policy 205
Durov, Pavel 207
Dynkin, A. 53

Eagle Guardian 'defence plan' 35
Eastern Partnership 91
The Eastern Partnership (EAP) 260
Eastern Partnership Initiative 294
economic advancement 7–8
economic capabilities, comparing 88–9
economic development 98–100
economic outlook 104–5
economic tools of Rusian security strategy 169–78; building pipelines 171–3; cases of Russia's market rejection 175–6; export of nuclear technology 171–3; migration regime 173–5; 'Milk war' with Belarus 176–7; recalibration of energy tools 171–3; stabilizing oil prices 171–3; time for muscle-flexing 175–6
economy and military expenditures 97–106; defence spending 100–4; economic development 98–100; economic outlook 104–5
Eisenhower, Dwight D. 247, 252
Empress Catherine 314
'energy-informational psychological weapons' 220
energy security, and geopolitics 182–3
energy subsidies 184–5
energy trade, securitization of 185–7
Ente Nazionale Idrocarburi (ENI) 183
Erdogan, Recep Tayyip 106n2, 140, 373
Ermarth, Fritz 112
Eurasian Customs Union (ECU) 91
Eurasian Economic Community (EurAsEC) 260
Eurasian Economic Union (EEU) 91, 104, 142, 328, 356
Eurasian Economic Union (EAEU) Treaty 177
Eurasianism 326
Euro-Atlantic community 87, 93–4, 209
Euromaidan protests in Ukraine 11
Euromaidan Revolution 34
European Bank for Reconstruction and Development (EBRD) 170
European Central Bank 374
European Neighbourhood Policy (ENP) 91, 260, 294
European Security and Defence Policy (ESDP) 281
European Union (EU) 11, 36, 59, 87, 138; GDP of 88; Global Strategy 65; Neighbourhood Policy 281–2; -Russia Strategic Partnership 94
export of nuclear technology 171–3
Exxon-Mobil 245

Facebook 67, 249
Fairgrieve, James 183

Farage, Nigel 60
Federal Agency of Governmental Liaison and Information (FAPSI) 220
Federal Agency of Government Communications and Information (FAPSI) 205
Federal Security Service (FSB) 19; Putin and 194–5
Federal Treaties 50
Federation Council 100
Feklyunina, Valentina 93
Felgenhauer, Pavel 22, 113, 389
First Chechen War 49, 50, 54, 134
First Congress of Indigenous Peoples 305
First World War 366
Five Days' War 137, 140
Five Star Movement 58, 67
Foreign Intelligence Service (SVR) 19
Foreign Policy Concept 204, 367
Forsstrom, Pertti 159
Fox, Amos C. 158
France: estimated numbers of nuclear weapons in 2017 89; share of global military expenditure 89
Franco-Russian Alliance 291
Freedom Party 58
French Revolution 136, 289
Frisch, Hartvig 109
Frolov, Dmitri B. 222
Frolov, Vladimir 20
frozen conflicts 355
future military expenditures 103–4

G7 87, 252
G8 254, 346
Gaddafi, Muammar 114, 244
Gaidar, Egor 367
Galeotti, Mark 24, 92, 194
Gazprom 66, 90, 173, 187–8
Geithner, Timothy 344
Gel'man, Vladimir 113, 115
Geneva II Peace Conference 402
Geo-economics in the post-Cold War period (Luttwak) 170
geopolitics: on counterterrorism policies 271–3; and energy security 182–3; of the periphery 288–9
geopolitics of energy in Eurasia: energy subsidies 184–5; historical antecedents 183–4; politics or economics 187–9; Russian security strategy and 181–9; securitization of energy trade 185–7
geopolitics of Eurasia 288–96; geopolitics of the periphery 288–9; Russian security strategy and 288–96; security strategy of Imperial Russia 1682–1825 289–90; security strategy of Imperial Russia 1825–1917 290–2; security strategy of Muscovy 1480–1682 288–9;

security strategy of Russian Federation 1992–2018 293–6; security strategy of Soviet Union 1917–1991 292–3
George, Alexander 135
Gerasimov, Valery 154, 233, 390
Gerasimov Doctrine 21, 92, 262
Germany: Alternative for Germany and 58, 67; share of global military expenditure 89; Syrian refugee crisis and 60
glasnost' (publicity or openness) 150
Glaz'ev, Sergei 124, 393
Global Energy and Geopolitics (Russia and the World) 183
global geopolitical antagonism (*protivostoyaniya*) 222
globalisation 4, 7, 11–12, 58–60, 66, 227, 309
Global Terrorism Index 76
GLONASS-MA 231
GLONASS navigation system 80, 349
GLOSNASS 230
'gold rush mentality' 184
Golts, Alexander 75
Gorbachev, Mikhail 31, 37, 61, 125, 133, 146, 150, 193–4, 196, 255n2, 259, 293, 314
Gorchakov, Aleksandr 291
Gorenburg, Dmitry 148
GPV-2020 101
GPV-2027 104
Grachev, Pavel 146
Grand Duchy of Muscovy 288
Grande Armee 290
Gray, Colin S. 110, 158–9
greater Black Sea region: Abkhazia and South Ossetia 357–9; enhancing and countering influence 355–7; instrumentalising frozen conflicts of 355–63; Nagorno-Karabakh 361–3; Transnistria 359–61
Great Northern War 289
Great Patriotic War 47
Great Power identity 47–8
Great Power status: global context 52–4; implications for security in twenty-first century 11–13; internal context 50; military modernisation behind gaining 48–9; post-Soviet space context 51–2; Russian use of military to maintain 49–52; and security 3–13; and sovereign statehood (*gosudarstvennost'*) 8–9
Greece: Civil War 366; Cyprus-North Cyprus dispute and 357; Russian interest in 373–4
Griboedov, Aleksandr 310
Griffin, Michael 176
Gronchi, Giovanni 184
gross domestic product (GDP): annual growth rate, 1996–2014 247; decline in 79; defence budget's share of 100–2; effects of sanctions on 99–100

Group of 20 (G20) 102, 246, 344, 346, 348
GUAM (Georgia, Ukraine, Azerbaijan and Moldova) 260
Gudkov, Lev 30
guerilla warfare in Nicaragua 390
Gulf Cooperation Council 404
Gusinsky, Vladimir 196

Haushofer, Karl 182
Hayat Tahrir al-Sham 401
Heikka, Henrikki 112
Heller, Regina 52
Helsinki Process 277
Hezbollah 269, 271, 401, 405
hierarchies, capacity to determine 91–2
Howe, James 157
Howlett, Darryl 110–11
Human Right Watch 310
Hungary 65–6
Hussein, Saddam 40, 259
al-Hussein, Zeid Ra'ad 405
'hybrid' aggression against Ukraine 388–97

identities, capacity to determine 91–2
Illarionov, Andrei 171, 303
Imperial Russia 47; ethnic tensions in 55; Great Power legacy of 51; security strategy of 289–90, 290–2
'imperial subaltern syndrome' 21
India: estimated numbers of nuclear weapons in 2017 89; SCO membership of 274n1; share of global military expenditure 89
infighting: bureaucratic 23; factional 200; intelligence agencies 197–8
information and communication technology (ICT) policy 204–9, 211
'information-genetic weapons' 220
information-psychological warfare: colour revolution as information warfare technology 217–18; conceptualisation of 215–20; as form of counter-struggle 216–17; overview 214–15; reflexive control at the time of war and peace 218–20; strategic context of 220–3; towards Russian model of 222–3
information security and warfare: bureaucratic framework for 204–6; overview 203–4; in practice 206–10; Russia and 210–11
information warfare: as a form of counter-struggle 216–17; Russia and 210–11; and security in Russia 203–4
information warfare technology: colour revolution as 217–18
'information weapon' 220
INF Treaty 154, 157, 254
Inozemtsev, Vladislav 20
insecurity, of the regime 76–7

Index

Institute for Information Security Issues (IISI), Moscow State University 204
institutional arrangements 90–1
institutional power 88
intelligence agencies: and domestic security 195–6; infighting 197–8; information about 193–4; North Caucasus 196–7; Putin, the KGB, and the FSB 194–5; Putin and 192–200; skewed analysis, risky operations 198–9
intercontinental ballistic missile (ICBM) 149, 156–7, 160–1
Intergovernmental Agreement of the SCO Member States on Cooperation in the Information Space (Agreement, 2009) 215
Intermediate Nuclear Forces (INF) Treaty *see* INF Treaty
internal democracy 7; *see also* democracy
International Criminal Court 3
International Monetary Fund (IMF) 7, 59, 170, 344
international non-governmental organisations (NGOs) 405
International Relations of the Russian Academy of Sciences (IMEMO) 215, 217
International Security Assistance Force (ISAF) 261
International Syria Support Group (ISSG) 403
Internet Research Agency 210
Iranian Revolutionary Guards 269
Iron Curtain, fall of 314
Ishchenko, Rostislav 21
Islam 53, 323, 384
Islamic Jihad Union 323
Islamic Movement of Eastern Turkestan 323
Islamic Movement of Uzbekistan 323
Islamic State of Iraq and Levant (ISIL) 53, 251
Islamic State of Iraq and Syria (ISIS) 53, 197, 268, 315, 401
Israel: estimated numbers of nuclear weapons in 2017 89; right-wing parties in 401
ISSG Humanitarian Task Force 403
Ivanov, Igor 87
Ivanov, Sergei 31, 127, 155
Ivan the Terrible 310

Jabhat al-Nusra 401
Jackson, Michael 134
Japan: Greater East Asia Co-Prosperity Sphere and 292; share of global military expenditure 89
Japanese Empire 292
Jensen, Kristian 20
Jihadists: Russia as top target of 317–18; Russia-European Union cooperation and 274
Johnson, Lyndon B. 247, 252
Joint Comprehensive Plan of Action (JCPOA) 405
Juncker, Jean-Claude 65, 294

Kaczynski, Jaroslaw 65
Kadyrov, Akhmad 134, 139
Kadyrov, Ramzan 76, 80, 197, 315
Karaganov, Sergey 51
Kari, Martti 116
Kavkaz, Vilayat 315
Kazakhstan-China oil pipeline 188
Kedrov, Ilya 160
Kegley, Charles 135
Kemal Ataturk, Mustafa 313
Khamenei, Ayatollah 403
Khodorkovsky, Mikhail 98, 186, 196, 251
Khrushchev, Nikita 34, 113
King, Charles 310
Kipp, Jacob 161–2
Kirov, Sergei 312
Kiselev, Dmitri 251
Kissinger, Henry 164, 186
Kjellen, Rudolph 182
Kochnev, Dmitrii 31
Komitet Gosudarstvennoi Bezopasnosti (KGB) 23, 111; archives of 193; FSB and 114, 194–5; Putin and 194–5; as totalitarian secret police systems 114
Kondrashev, Andrey 134
Korber Foundation 64
Kosovo Liberation Army 369
Kosovo War, and its aftermath 369–71
Kosygin, Alexei 184
Kovacs, Bela 66
Kozyrev, Andrei 51, 294
Kratochvil, Petr 280
Kravchuk, Leonid 34
Kremlin grand strategy 115
Kroenig, Matthew 161–2
Kruchkov, Vladimir 196
Krutskikh, Andrei 204
Kuchma, Leonid 34
Kudrin, Aleksei 36
Kuhrt, Natasha 116
Kurdish Democratic Union Party (PYD) 404
Kurz, Sebastian 58
Kyoto Protocol 302, 303
Kyrgyz colour revolution of 2005 324

Lange, Oskar 112
Lantis, Jeffrey 110–11
Lavrov, Sergey 26, 35, 47, 177, 318, 326, 343, 374
Law on Security of March 1992 125
League for a Safe Internet 205
League of Arab States 403
Lebed, Alexander 47, 124–7
Lebedev, Aleksandr 5
Lefebvre, V. A. 219
'legal successor state': perquisites of 37–9; Russia as 37–9
Lehman Brothers 345

Index

Leites, Nathan 17, 110
Lenin, Vladimir 110–11, 163, 178n2, 183, 292, 312
Le Pen, Marine 58
Lermontov, Mikhail 310
Levada Centre 32
LGBT rights 246
liberal democracy 61, 63, 64, 68, 278, 326; *see also* democracy
liberal democratic order, challenges to 65–7; divided Europe 65–6; Donald Trump 66; Poland and Hungary 65–6; Russian hybrid warfare against democracy 66–7
liberal world order: challenges to liberal democratic order 65–7; erosion of 58–60; future prospects and conclusions 68; NATO-Russian relationship and strained European security environment 63–5; Russian challenge to 58–68; Russian-Western affairs and narratives 60–3
List, Friedrich 182
Litvinenko, Alexander 194
Lo, Bobo 52, 94
Lukashenko, Alexander 94, 177
Luttwak, Edward 170

McFaul, Donald L. 247
Mackinder, Halford 182, 288
Maduro, Nicolas 40
Magnitsky, Sergei 246
Magnitsky Act 246
Maidan Revolution 115, 242, 260
Main Intelligence Directorate (GRU) 19, 113, 115, 145, 164, 193, 197, 199, 393, 395
Makarov, Nikolai 147
Malaysian Airliner MH17 25
Mannheim, Karl 74, 109, 113
Manoilo, Andrei V. 216, 218, 222
manual control, and process of decision-making 22–4
Mao Zedong 33
'Maritime Multifunctional System Status-6' 157
Marx, Karl 170
Marxist ideology 163
'mass-media weapons' 220
Mattei, Enrico 183
Mediterranean refugee crisis 66
Medvedev, Dmitry 8, 76, 91, 114–15, 119, 121–2, 126–8, 147, 177, 195, 230, 243–5, 302, 345–6, 359, 371, 374n1, 380–1, 384–5
Messner, Evgeny 390
Miasnikian, Alexander 312
Middle East: China's access to resources and markets in 240–1; ISIS and 272, 323–4; Islamic radicalisation in 317; Russia's interests in 405–6; subversive activities in 271; transnational terrorism in 267

Middle East and North Africa (MENA) 399; Russian views on 400–1
migration 59; globalisation and 59–60; global mass 59; illegal 173, 327; labour 34, 173–4; legal 324; poor social conditions and 324
military: capabilities, comparing 89–90; use of, to maintain Great Power status 49–52; *see also specific entries*
Military Doctrine 204, 208, 229, 261, 300
military expenditures: future 103–4; as share of GDP in comparison with selected countries 101; during Soviet times 97
Military-Industrial Commission (*Voenno-promychlennaia komissiia*, VPK) 230
military might: as basis for Russian Great Power identity 46–55; Chinese 338–9; Soviet Union's 46
military modernisation: behind gaining Great Power status 48–9; intervention in Syria and 53; military victories and 54; urgency of 49
'Milk war' with Belarus 176–7
Miller, Alexei 189
Miller, Alexey 188
Milošević, Slobodan 367, 369
mimicry, defined 220
Ming Dynasty 288
Minsk Agreements 281, 283, 396
Mironov, Ivan 196
Mitrokhin, Vasili 193
modernisation, of weapons and equipment 147–9; *see also* military modernisation
Mogherini, Federica 65
Monaghan, Andrew 93
Mongol Empire 288
Monroe Doctrine 326
Morozov, Vyacheslav 21
Moscow 332–5; *see also* Russia; Soviet Union
Moscow Stock Exchange 346
Mueller, Robert 194
multilateralism 52, 54–5, 58, 65–6, 68
multiple independently targetable reentry vehicles (MIRVs) 161
Munich Security Conference 62, 261, 345
Muscovite Rus 288
Muslim Unity Group 318
Mutatis mutandis 115

Nagorno-Karabakh 361–3
Nagorno-Karabakh Autonomous Oblast 312
Nagorno-Karabakh conflict 312, 315, 317
Napoleonic wars 48
Narinamov, Nariman 312
Naryshkin, Sergei 31
National Coalition of Syrian Revolutionary and Opposition Forces 401
national energy companies (NECs) 171–2
nationalism: state-centric 9; xenophobic 9

Index

national security documents, of Yeltsin period 367–8
National Security Strategy 82, 101, 115–16, 181, 204, 208, 221, 271–2, 300
National System for Filtrating Internet Traffic (NaSFIT) 205
National System of Political Economy (List) 182
National Welfare Fund 79
NATO enlargement 257–63; and Balkans 371–2; current state of research 258; dormant security dilemma (1991–2004) 259–60; from dormant security dilemma to offensive spiral in NATO-Russia relations 258–63; imperialist security dilemma 259–61; NATO-Russia relations and 258; offensive spiral (2007–today) 261–2; overview 257–8
NATO-Russia Council 281
NATO-Russia Founding Act 63, 259
NATO-Russia relations: current state of research 258; dormant security dilemma 259–60; from dormant security dilemma to offensive spiral in 258–63; imperialist security dilemma (2004–2007) 259–61; offensive spiral (2007–today) 261–2; and strained European security environment 63–5
Navalny, Alexei 249
Nazarbayev, Nursultan 94, 328
Nazi Germany 197, 292, 366
Nazi-Soviet Non-Aggression Pact 292
Nemtsov, Boris 81
New Look *(Noviy Oblik)* programme 145
Newly Independent States (NIS) countries 51
New START Treaty 156–7, 161, 244
Nicholas I, Emperor of Russia 290
Nicholas II, Emperor of Russia 290–2
Nikonov, Vyacheslav 343
non-governmental organisations (NGOs) 77, 93, 249, 304
North Atlantic Treaty Organisation (NATO) 5; entry of several Balkan states in 353; entry of the Baltic countries into 35; Georgian membership in 345, 353, 382–3; Greece entry in 366; Hungary and 65–6; Poland and 65–6; Russian-Western relations and 62–3; Russia's disaffection with 37, 63–5, 369–74; Slovenia and 374n2; Turkey entry in 366; *see also specific entries*
North Atlantic Treaty Organisation (NATO)-Russia Founding Act 87
North Caucasus 81, 196–7, 314–15
Northern Dimension Environmental Partnership (NDEP) 300
Northern Distribution Network (NDN) 244
Northern League 58, 67
Northern Sea Route (NSR) 301, 306

North Korea: estimated numbers of nuclear weapons in 2017 89; nuclear programme of 21; Russian cooperation on denuclearisation of 254
Novaya Gazeta 77
Novikov, Vladimir 220
nuclear program 156–7
nuclear strategy 154–65; nuclear program 156–7; overview 154–6
nuclear technology, export of 171–3
Nye, Joseph S. 170

Obama, Barack 63, 66, 140, 143n1, 242–6, 250–3, 345, 348, 401–2
Obedinonnye Strategicheskoe Komandovanie (OSKs) 147
Ochrana 79
oil prices, stabilizing 171–3
Oleg Deripaska 100
O'Neill, Jim 343
On Guerrilla Warfare (Lenin) 214
Onishchenko, Gennady 175–7
'On Security of Critical Information Infrastructure of the Russian Federation' 207
'On the Necessity of the Preventative Occupation of the Baltic Region' 22
'operational code': strategic culture and 27; and strategic decision-making 17–27
The Operational Code of the Politburo (Leites) 17
Operation 'Mechanical Orange' 389
Orange Revolution 112, 138, 215, 245
Orban, Viktor 58, 66
Ordzhonikidze, Sergo 312
Organisation for the Prohibition of Chemical Weapons (OPCW) 402
Organization for Security and Cooperation in Europe (OSCE) 35, 138, 263, 281, 360, 367
Organization for Security and Co-operation (OSCE) Minsk group 316
Organization of the Petroleum Exporting Countries (OPEC) 172, 178n7
Orthodox Church 62
Orthodoxy 388
Ostpolitik 184
Ottoman Empire 291, 309, 311
outer space: 2014 and beyond 231–4; evolution of outer space strategy 2000–2008 229–30; halting modernisation and growing ambitions following Russia-Georgia conflict 230–1; moving to the offensive 231–4; securitisation and militarisation of 229–30; securitisation of 228–9; threats and opportunities 228–9
Outer Space Treaty (OST) 233

Pakistan: estimated numbers of nuclear weapons in 2017 89; SCO membership of 274n1
Paris Agreement 302
Partial Test Ban 233

Index

Partnership for Peace (PfP) 259
Party of Islamic Liberation 323
'Patriotic Education of the Citizens of the Russian Federation 2016–2020' 208
Patrushev, Nikolai 19, 31, 113, 126, 195
Paul I 289–90
Pavlovsky, Gleb 21, 24
peace: Moscow as natural guarantor of 51; reflexive control at the time of 218–20
Peace of Nystad 289
Perle, Richard 186
Permanent Joint Council (PJC) 259
Permanent Structured Cooperation (PESCO) 278
Peter I *see* Peter the Great
Peter the Great 48, 289, 292, 293, 310
Petrenko, Anatolii I. 222
pipelines, building 171–3
Poland 65–6
Polar Silk Road 306
'post-industrial society' 7
post-Soviet regional security, in Caucasus 313–14
power: acting on all fronts 92–4; capacity to determine identities and hierarchies 91–2; comparing economic capabilities 88–9; comparing military capabilities 89–90; complexity of 87–92; control over resources and asymmetrical energy interdependence 90; institutional arrangements 90–1; Russia's counter-hegemonic offensive 92–4; Russia's foreign policy in context of 86–95; Russia's security strategy in context of 86–95
'Prevention of an Arms Race in Outer Space' (PAROS) 233
Primakov, Evgenii 114, 294
Primakov Institute of World Economy 215
Pringle, Robert W. 113
productive power 88
pro-globalist movements 59
Project Novorossiya 393–4
Provisional Council of the Chechen Republic 314
proxy war: in Donbas 394–5; in Eastern Ukraine 242, 252
'psychotropic information weapons' 220
Pushkin, Aleksandr 310
Pussy Riot singers 251
Putin, Vladimir 31; ambiguity, deniability and no-lose scenarios 24–5; 'broken lens' syndrome and threat assessments informing decisions 19–21; defensive-reactive motivation as a strategic communication influence operation 21–2; FSB and 194–5; intelligence agencies and 192–200; the KGB and 194–5; manual control and the process of decision-making 22–4; 'operational code' and strategic decision-making 17–27; personal involvement in decision-making and management of coercive diplomacy 141; US as Russia's strategic benchmark 25–6
Pynnoniemi, Katri 116

radical Islam 50, 53, 273
radical Islamists 315
radical Islamist terrorism 87
Rain TV 77
Rastorguyev, Sergey 216
Reagan, Ronald 247, 252
Red Arctic of 1932–1964 300
Red Army 48, 163, 247, 366, 377
reflexive control, at the time of war and peace 218–20
regime: insecurity of 76–7; transformation with impact on security policy 78–9
regional and global counterterrorism strategies 266–74; counterterrorism responses 267–9; critical geopolitics on Russia's counterterrorism policies 271–3; explaining 270–1
Regional Anti-Terrorism Structure (RATS) of SCO 268
Renz, Bettina 47, 93, 152
research: on post-Soviet Russian strategic culture 111–13; on Soviet strategic culture 111–13
resources: control over 90; Russia's coercive diplomacy in action and 136–8
Rice, Condoleezza 186
Richards, Charles 228
Rogozin, Dmitry 304
Roscosmos 232
Rose Revolution 214, 358, 377
Rosgvardia, National Guard of presidential loyalists 115
Roskomnadzor (The Federal Service for Supervision of Communications, Information Technology and Mass Media) 205, 208
RosKomSvoboda 206
Roskosmos (The Federal Space Agency) 230
Rosneft 100, 173, 245
Rossiya v global'noy politike 94
Royal Dutch Shell 183
Royal United Services Institute, London 146
RuNet 207–8, 209, 211
Rusal 100
Russia: Balkans and 371–2; and BRICS since 2015 350; and China in Central Asia 335–7; China takes over the lead from 337–8; and climate change negotiations 302–3; counter-hegemonic offensive 92–4; counter-intelligence state 113–15; economic advancement 7–8; estimated numbers of nuclear weapons in 2017 89; foreign policy in context of power 86–95; Homeland Hybrid

Index

Strategic Offense 112; immigration to 324; and information warfare 210–11; Intended Nationally Determined Contribution (INDC) 302–3; interests in the Middle East 405–6; Kosovo War, and its aftermath 369–71; National Security Strategy of 2015 82, 101, 115–16, 181, 204, 208, 221, 271–2, 300; Northern Distribution Network (NDN) and 244; outer space strategy 2000–2008 229–30; perquisites of the 'legal successor state' 37–9; post–Cold War pursuit of security through status 9–11; securitisation of outer space 228–9; Security Council Secretary—the 1990s 124–6; Security Council Secretary—the twenty-first century 126–8; security threatened by China 338–9; share of global military expenditure 89; as target of security threats 123–4; as top target of Jihadists 317–18; weapons supplies to the Third World 39–40; and the Yugoslav wars 368–9; *see also* Russian Federation

Russia Arctic Strategy 300

Russia-China oil pipeline (Skovorodino-Daqing) 188

Russia-China Treaty 233

Russia-European Union (EU) relations: mapping the field 278–81; overview 277–8; security challenges in 277–84; security issues in 278–81

Russia-Georgia conflict *see* Russia-Georgia War

Russia-Georgia War 281, 316, 377–85; combat performance 381–2; Georgian conflict with its breakaway republics and Russia 377; halting modernisation and growing ambitions following 230–1; international law and war 383–5; longer-term political history of 377; run-up to the war 377–9; Russia's strategic war objectives 382–3; who started the war 383–5

Russian Academy of Sciences 343

Russian Arctic security: impacts of climate change on 299–307

Russian Association of Indigenous Peoples of the North (RAIPON) 305–6

Russian Central Bank 24

Russian-Chinese security cooperation 332–40; China taking over lead from Russia 337–8; cooperation and challenges 332–5; Moscow and Beijing 332–5; overview 332; Russia and China in Central Asia 335–7; Russia's security threatened by China 338–9; SCO 337–8

Russian Civil War 292

Russian diplomacy: in early stages of the Syria conflict 401–2; 'finlandisation' model of 142

Russian Empire 48, 289, 290, 312

Russian Federal Migration Service 324

Russian Federation: Foreign Policy Concept of 274n5, 321; Great Power identity and 47–8; sanctions against 66; security strategy of the 293–6; status as a leading world power 231; *see also* Russia

The Russian Federation System. Sources of Russian Strategic Behavior (Pavlovsky) 24

Russian foreign policy: BRICS in 342–50; in Caucasus 311–13

Russian Great Power identity: military might as basis for 46–55

Russian hybrid warfare against democracy 66–7

Russian leadership, and conflict 141–2

Russian military capabilities: modernisation of weapons and equipment 147–9; rebuilding of 144–52; staffing 149–51; structure and organisation 145–7

Russian Parliament 32, 38, 119, 124

Russian security policy: BRICS in 342–50; conceptions of global and regional alignments 39; disputes inherited from the USSR 32–4; disputes resulting from the breakup 34–6; domestic determinants of 247–52; legacy of personnel and worldviews 31–2; other key aspects 36–7; Russian weapons supplies to Third World 39–40; Soviet geographic legacy 32–7; Soviet legacy in 30–42; staying the course of neo-containment, selective engagement 252–4; 'too much' school 243–5; 'too weak' school 245–7; towards the United States 242–54; weighing the Soviet legacy 41–2

Russian security politics: importance of status for understanding 4–6

Russian security strategy: in the Balkans 366–75; coercive diplomacy in 133–43; constant ambition but changing 86–7; in context of power 86–95; defining socio-political landscape through lens of security perception 75–6; and geopolitics of energy in Eurasia 181–9; geopolitics of Eurasia and 288–96

Russian strategic culture 109–17; chekisty as keepers of 113–15; doctrines and strategies expressing threat perception 116; ends *vs.* means 115; Kremlin grand strategy today 115; research on soviet and post-soviet 111–13; strategic cultural studies 110–11

Russian Tax Service 100

Russian threat perception: doctrines expressing 116; strategies expressing 116

Russian-Western affairs and narratives 60–3

Russia Today 251

Russo-Turkish War: in 1711 289; 1768–1774 289; 1787–1792 289; in 1853 290

Rutskoi, Aleksandr 125

Index

Saakashvili, Mikheil 175
Sakwa, Richard 87
Salafism 311
Salafist al-Qaeda 401
sanctions: effects on Russia's GDP 99–100; EU, against Russia 42n8; U.S. economic 8, 106, 172, 210, 252, 254; Western 79–80, 94, 132, 137, 142, 172, 189, 305–6, 322
Sargsyan, Serzh 316
Sarkozy, Nicolas 381
Saudi Arabia: as OPEC member-state 172; share of global military expenditure 89; struggle for regional supremacy between Iran and 400
Schelling, Thomas 135, 137, 164
Schneider, Mark 156–7
Schulte, Paul 161
Scowcroft, Brent 186
sea-launched ballistic missiles (SLBMs) 156
Sechin, Igor 31, 194
Second Anglo-Chinese War 291
Second Chechen War 49, 50, 54–5, 81, 173
Second World War 145, 150, 366
securitisation: of all policy areas and the inner abroad 80–1; of the Arctic 300–1; of energy trade 185–7
security: decision-making 119–29; and great-power status 3–13; twenty-first-century Russia's understanding of, as status 6–8
Security Council 119–29; apparatus of 128; duties of 122–3; membership of 121; policy areas 123; role of 120–3; Russia as target of security threats 123–4; secretaries of 124–8; Security Council Secretary—the 1990s 124–6; Security Council Secretary—the twenty-first century 126–8; significance of 128–9; tasks of 122
security strategy: of Muscovy 288–9; of the Russian Federation 293–6
security strategy, of Imperial Russia 289–90, 290–2; Alexander I (1801–1825) 289–90; Alexander II (1855–1881) 290–2; Alexander III (1881–1894) 290–2; Catherine II (1762–1796) 289; Nicholas I (1825–1855) 290; Nicholas II (1894–1917) 290–2; Paul I (1796–1801) 289–90; Peter I and after (1682–1762) 289
security strategy of Soviet Union 292–3; Soviet Union and the Cold War 293; Soviet Union and World War II 292
security threats, Russia as target of 123–4
Selva, Paul 156
September 11, 2001 terrorist attacks 10, 344
Serdyukov, Anatoly 38, 97, 102, 144–5, 147
Shanghai Cooperation Organisation (SCO) 37, 92, 94, 210, 217, 267, 337–8, 356, 381, 404
Shchelin, Pavel 115
Shinzo Abe 33

al-Shishani, Abu Omar 318
Shlykov, Vitalii 145
Shoigu, Sergei 38, 102, 145, 147
Siluanov, Anton 99
Sino-American-Japanese Anti-Soviet Triple Alignment 293
Skokov, Yurii 124, 126, 389
Skripal, Sergei 199
small and medium enterprises (SMEs) 100
Smeshkov, Yuri 35
Snap 208
Snowden, Edward 250
Snyder, Jack 109
Sobchak, Anatoli 194
Sochi Olympics 251
'social mobility' 87
Sokolsky, Richard 169
Soldatov, Andrei 114, 164, 194, 221
Soleimani, Qassem 403
Solovtsov, Nikolai 160
'somatotropic-psychoinformation weapons' 220
SORM (System for Operative Investigative Activities) 205
Soufan Group 315, 318
South Caucasus 143n2, 240, 270, 310–11, 313, 315–17
South Caucasus Gas Pipeline (SCP) 187
South Korea: share of global military expenditure 89; U.S. deployment of an anti-missile system in 333
South Ossetia 357–9
sovereign democracy 9, 62, 326; *see also* democracy
'sovereign globalisation' strategy 7
sovereign statehood *(gosudarstvennost')*: great-power status *(derzhavnost')* and 8–9
Soviet Communist Party 33, 199
Soviet-Finnish War 292
Soviet geographic legacy 32–7; disputes inherited from the USSR 32–4; disputes resulting from the breakup 34–6; other key aspects 36–7
Soviet Great Fatherland War 110, 197
Soviet legacy: in Russian security policy 30–42; weighing 41–2
Soviet Marxist-Leninist ideology 41
Soviet Politburo 17, 119, 125
Soviet Union: and the Cold War 1947–1989 293; disputes inherited from 32–4; security strategy of 292–3; and World War II (1917–1945) 292; *see also* Russia
Sputnik 210
Stabilisation Force in Bosnia and Herzegovina (SFOR) 259, 369–70
stabilizing oil prices 171–3
staffing 149–51
Stalin, Joseph 312, 366

Standard Oil 183
Stanovaya, Tatyana 18
START agreements 89
State Armament Programme for 2011–2010 (SAP 2020) 149
state arms procurement 102–3
state-centric nationalism 9
State Rearmament Programme for 2018–2027 (SAP 2027) 149
State System for Detecting, Preventing and Eliminating Consequences of Computer Attacks (GosSOPKA) 207
status: importance of, for understanding Russian security politics 4–6; Russia's post-Cold War pursuit of security through 9–11; twenty-first-century Russia's understanding of security as 6–8
Steinmeier, Frank-Walter 18
Stolypin Club 104
St. Petersburg International Economic Forum 346
strategic communication influence operation: defensive-reactive motivation as 21–2
strategic cultural studies 110–11
strategic culture: chekisty as keepers of 113–15; Kremlin grand strategy today 115; Soviet and post-Soviet Russian 111–13; strategic cultural studies 110–11
strategic decision-making, and 'operational code' 17–27
Strategy for the Development of the Information Society 204
Stronski, Paul 169
structural power 88
Sun-Tzu 214
Sununu, John 186
Surkov, Vladislav 94
Swedish Empire 289
SWIFT system 349
Syrian Civil War 53, 269
Syrian conflict: causes of Russia's intervention in Syria 402–5; consequences of Russia's intervention in Syria 402–5; MENA region and 400–1; overview 399; Russian diplomacy in early stages of 401–2; Russian views on 400–1; Russia's interests in Middle East 405–6; *see also* Syrian War
Syrian War 93, 142; *see also* Syrian conflict
System for Operative Investigative Activities (SORM) 196

Tajik Civil War 323–7
Taliban 268–9
Tatar Khans 310
T-bills (GKO) 97
T-bonds (OFZ) 97
Telegram 208–9

Temporary Commission for Protection of State Sovereignty and Prevention of Interference in Russia's Internal Affairs 205
Temporary Commission on Information Politics 205
Ten-Day War 368
Third World 40; Russian weapons supplies to 39–40
Thomas, Tim 219
threat assessments informing decisions 19–21
Tichy, Lukas 280
Tito, Josip Broz 366
Tolstoy, Leo 310
Torbakov, Igor 75
Trans-Anatolian Natural Gas Pipeline (TANAP) 187
'transcendence' 60–1
'transitional deals': as inherently valued 140–1; as optimal for keeping a favourable status quo 140–1
Transnistria 359–61
transparency and confidence-building measures (TCBMs) 227, 233–4
Transparency International (TI) 103
Trans-Siberian railway 334
Treaty of Brest-Litovsk 292
Treaty of London 291
Treaty of Paris 290, 291
Trenin, Dmitry 81, 155, 391
Trump, Donald 58, 66; approach towards EU 65; approach towards NATO 65; election of 58–60, 66, 198, 232; Russian autocracy and 246; Russia's membership in the G8 and 254; Wilsonian liberal international order and 66
Tsar Alexander I 290
Tsarist Russia 240, 309–10, 312, 313, 317
Tsar Ivan IV 288
Tsipras, Alexis 58
Tsypkin, Mikhail 51
Turchynov, Oleksandr 251
Twain, Mark 114
Twitter 249

Ukraine: annexation of Crimea 4, 11, 18, 21, 30, 32, 60, 62–3, 76, 78–9, 82, 94–5, 127–9, 134, 138, 207, 231, 252, 261–2, 295, 347, 392–3; 'hybrid' aggression against 388–97; plan 'A' and plan 'B' 391–2; Project Novorossiya and its fiasco 393–4; proxy war in Donbas 394–5; in Russia's 'grand strategy' 388–9; Russia's hybrid war concept 390–1; strategic deadlock 395–7; war plans and preparations in 2004–2014 389–90
Ukraine-EU Association Agreement 251
Ulyukaev, Aleksei 196

Index

United Kingdom: estimated numbers of nuclear weapons in 2017 89; share of global military expenditure 89
United Nation Framework Convention on Climate Change (UNFCCC) 302, 306
United Nations (UN) 59, 209; Group of Governmental Experts (GGE) 234; Security Council 9, 30, 37, 90
United Nations General Assembly (UNGA) 343, 348
United Rocket and Space Corporation 232
United States: estimated numbers of nuclear weapons in 2017 89; GDP of 88; Greater East Asia Co-Prosperity Sphere and 292; Northern Distribution Network (NDN) and 244; 'radically' individualist values of 4; Russian security policy towards 242–54; as Russia's strategic benchmark 25–6; share of global military expenditure 89; war against Serbia 37–8
United States Agency for International Development (USAID) 250
UN Protection Force (UNPROFOR) 368
UN R2P (Responsibility to Protect) 383
UN Security Council Resolution 1244 370
UN Security Council (UNSC) Resolution 1973 400
Urengoi-Pomary-Uzhgorod pipeline 184
USA-Azerbaijan Chamber of Commerce 186
Usackas, Vygaudas 19
U.S. Defense Intelligence Agency 155
U.S. Global positioning system (GPS) 349
U.S. Library of Congress 193
USS *McFaul* 246
USSR *see* Soviet Union

Vasiliev, Victor 234
Vassilev, Alexander 193
Vietnam War 390
'virtual information-psychological weapons' 220
VKontakte 208, 249
Vladislavlev, Alexander 51
Volkov, Denis 48
Vyakhirev, Rem 188

Wagner Group 199
Walesa, Lech 247
Waller, J. Michael 114
The Wall Street Journal 372
war, reflexive control at the time of 218–20

War of the Second Coalition 289
Warsaw Pact 36, 39, 185, 259, 366–7
weapons and equipment, modernisation of 147–9
Weltanschauung 31
Western democracies 11, 66–7, 68; *see also* democracy
Western hegemony 11, 61, 86, 92
Western human rights 3
Western liberal democratic values 59–60
WikiLeaks 35, 67
Wirtz, James J. 112
World Bank 7, 170, 174; Doing Business Index 78
World Economic Forum 169
World Trade Organization (WTO) 59, 244, 302, 378
World War I 47, 136
World War II 33, 47, 48, 133, 193, 247, 291–2
A Worldwide Mutiny-war 390

xenophobic nationalism 9
Xi Jinping 335

Yandex 80, 208
Yanukovych, Viktor 34, 184–5, 260, 347, 363
Yarovaia, Irina 208
Yarovaia Package 205, 208
Yasin, Yevgeny 176
Yatsenyuk, Arseniy 251
Yeltsin, Boris 10, 33, 61, 86; Federal Treaties and 50; Japanese investments in Russia and 33; national security documents under 367–8; pro-Western approach to international relations 61; rapprochement with Europe and 133; rapprochement with the USA and 138–9; resigned in 195; Soviet collapse and 322; standoff between parliament and 243–4; Ukraine's gas debt and 188
Yergin, Daniel 186
Yugoslav wars, and Russia 368–9
Yukos 98, 186
Yushchenko, Viktor 34, 245

Zapad 2017 exercise 20, 155–6, 161, 262–3
Zarudnitzky, Vladimir 391
Zolotov, Viktor 31, 79
Zuma, Jacob 343
Zygar, Mikhail 127
Zyuganov, Gennady 17, 125